TADATOSHI FUJIMAKI

Being a man with a rather plain personality, I've never had much of the color pink in my life. I think that's why I actually get really excited when coloring in Momoi's hair.

—2011

Tadatoshi Fujimaki was born on June 9, 1982, in Tokyo. He made his debut in 2007 in *Akamaru Jump* with *Kuroko's Basketball*, which was later serialized in *Weekly Shonen Jump*. *Kuroko's Basketball* quickly gained popularity and became an anime in Japan in 2012.

Kuroko's BASKETBALL

11 & 12

SHONEN JUMP Manga Edition
BY TADATOSHI FUJIMAKI

Translation/Caleb Cook
Touch-Up Art & Lettering/Mark McMurray
Design/Sam Elzway
Editor/John Bae

KUROKO NO BASUKE © 2008 by Tadatoshi Fujimaki
All rights reserved.
First published in Japan in 2008 by SHUEISHA Inc., Tokyo.
English translation rights arranged by SHUEISHA Inc.

The stories, characters and incidents mentioned in this
publication are entirely fictional.

Printed in the U.S.A.

Published by VIZ Media, LLC
P.O. Box 77010
San Francisco, CA 94107

10 9 8 7 6 5 4 3 2 1
First printing, June 2017

SHONEN JUMP MANGA

Kuroko's BASKETBALL

11

THE SEIRIN HIGH BASKETBALL CLUB!!

TADATOSHI FUJIMAKI

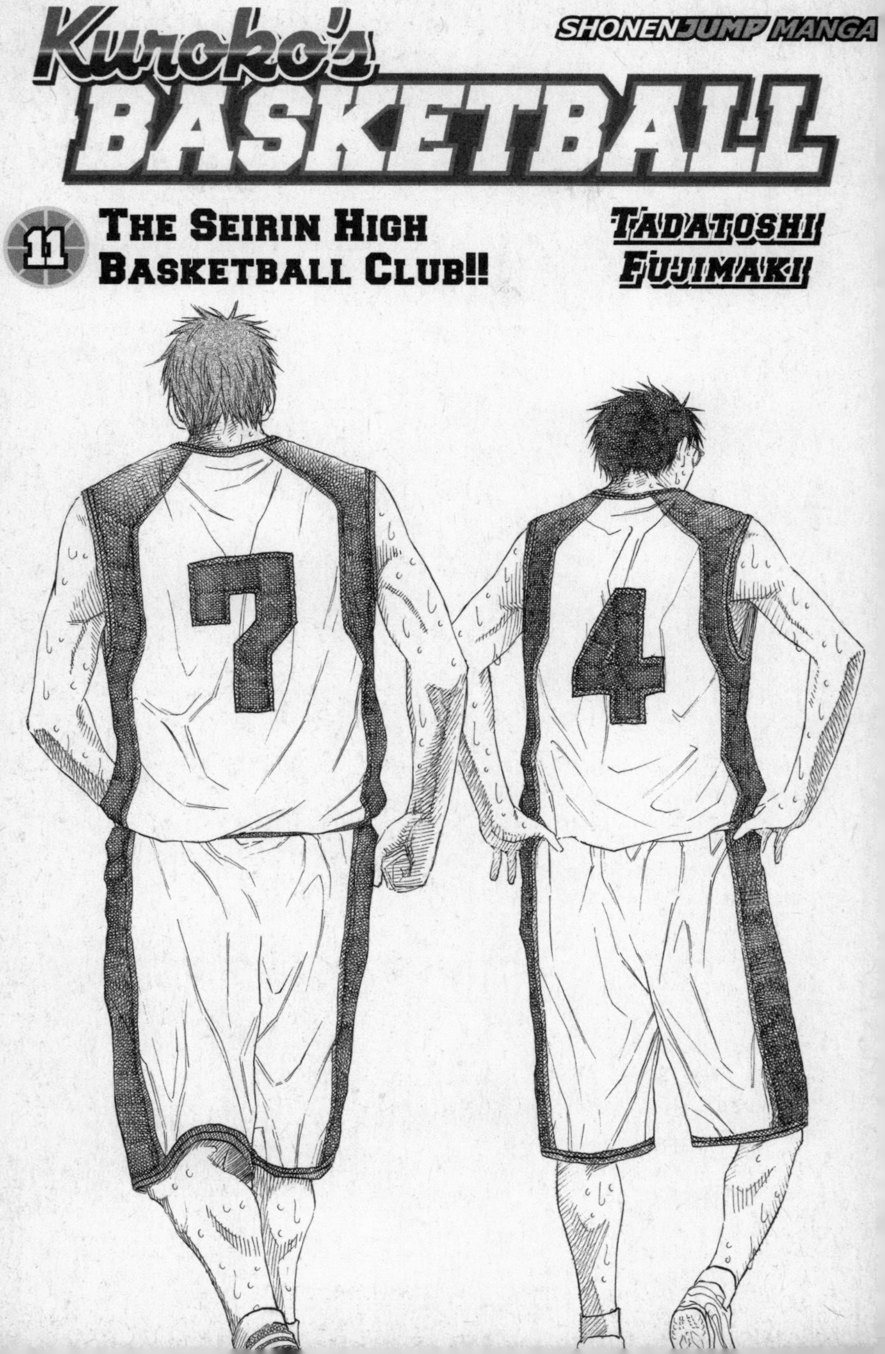
7
4

CHARACTERS

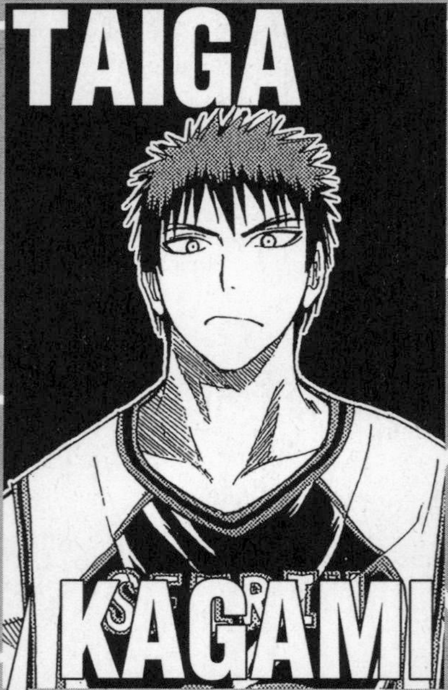
TAIGA
KAGAMI

A first-year on Seirin High's basketball team. Though he's rough around the edges, he's a gifted player with a lot of potential. His goal is to beat the Miracle Generation.

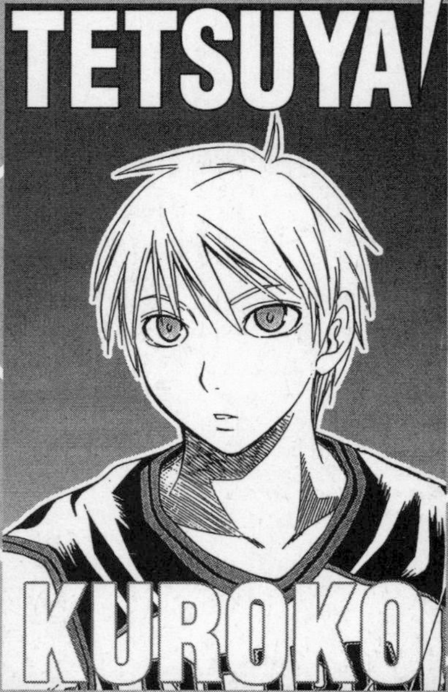
TETSUYA
KUROKO

A first-year on Seirin High's basketball team. Gifted with a natural lack of presence, he utilizes misdirection on the court to make nearly invisible passes.

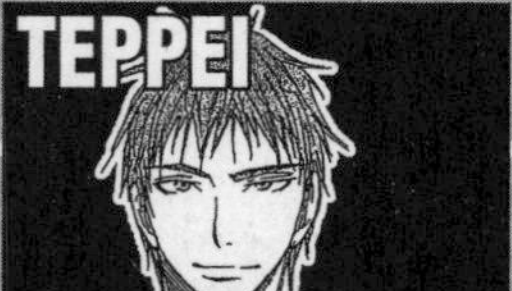
TEPPEI
KIYOSHI

A second-year on Seirin High's basketball team and the club's founder. He was hospitalized but returned shortly after Inter-High.

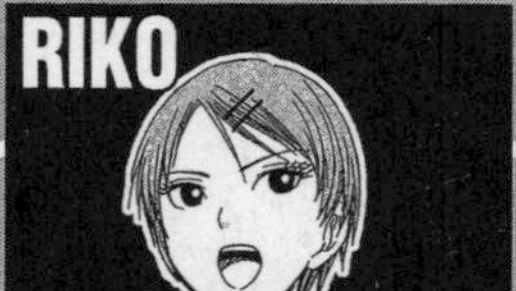
RIKO
AIDA

A second-year and coach of the Seirin High basketball team.

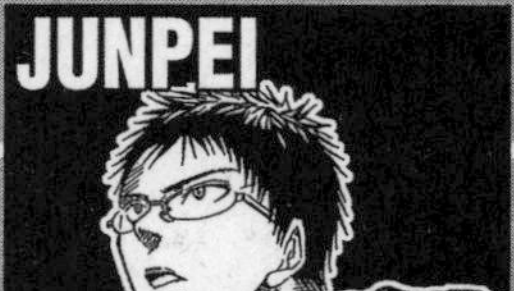
JUNPEI
HYUGA

A second-year on Seirin High's basketball team. As captain, he led his team to the Finals League last year despite only playing first-year players.

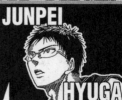

KUROKO'S BASKETBALL

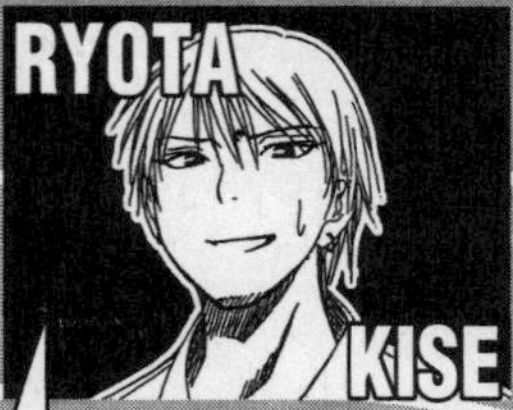
RYOTA
KISE

One of the Miracle Generation. Any basketball move he sees, he can mimic in an instant.

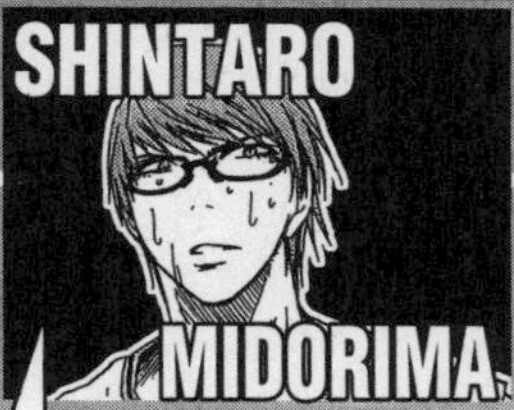
SHINTARO
MIDORIMA

A first-year at Shutoku High, he's the top shooter of the Miracle Generation.

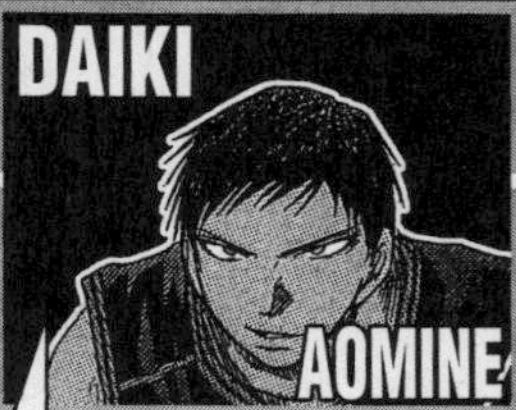
DAIKI
AOMINE

The ace of the Miracle Generation and Kuroko's former friend, he's now a first-year at To-oh Academy.

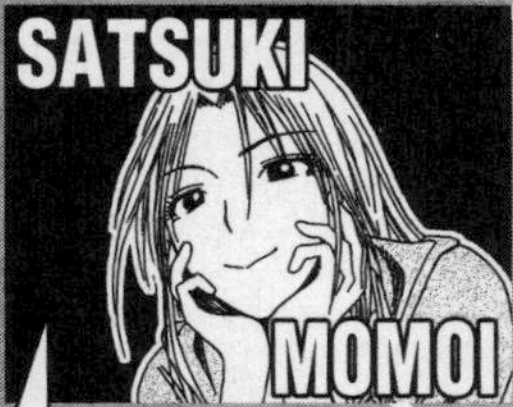
SATSUKI
MOMOI

A first-year member of To-Oh Academy's basketball club, she was the team manager for the Miracle Generation. Is she really Kuroko's girlfriend?!

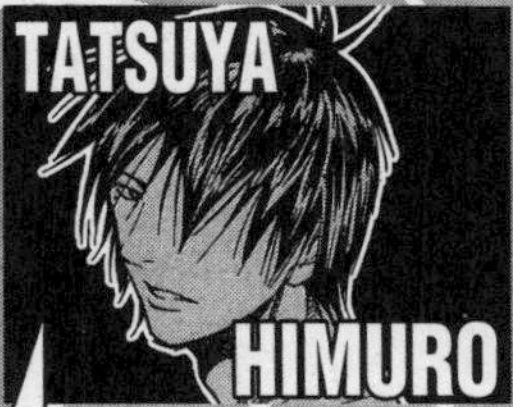
TATSUYA
HIMURO

A brother figure to Kagami. He introduced Kagami to basketball in America. He's now on Yosen High's basketball team, and he reunites with Kagami at a street tournament.

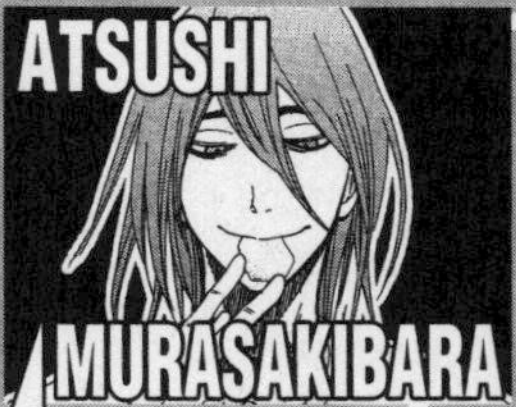
ATSUSHI
MURASAKIBARA

One of the Miracle Generation. A first-year on Yosen High's basketball team. He plays center, but he doesn't actually enjoy basketball all that much.

Teiko Middle School is an elite championship school whose basketball team once fielded five prodigies collectively known as "the Miracle Generation." But supporting those five was a phantom sixth man—Tetsuya Kuroko. Now Kuroko's a first-year high school student with zero presence who joins Seirin High's basketball club. Though his physical abilities and stats are well below average, Kuroko thrives on the court by making passes his opponents can't detect!

The Winter Cup qualifiers are shaking out to be quite the challenge for Seirin's basketball team. They're currently locked in an epic struggle with Shutoku and its star player Midorima. Shutoku is looking to avenge an earlier defeat and seems to have the game in hand...until Kuroko unleashes his new move to shrink the gap! And now, with the final seconds of the game ticking down, Seirin has possession of the ball with a chance to win...

STORY THUS FAR

TABLE OF CONTENTS

90TH QUARTER: NOW....THE UNVEILING!!

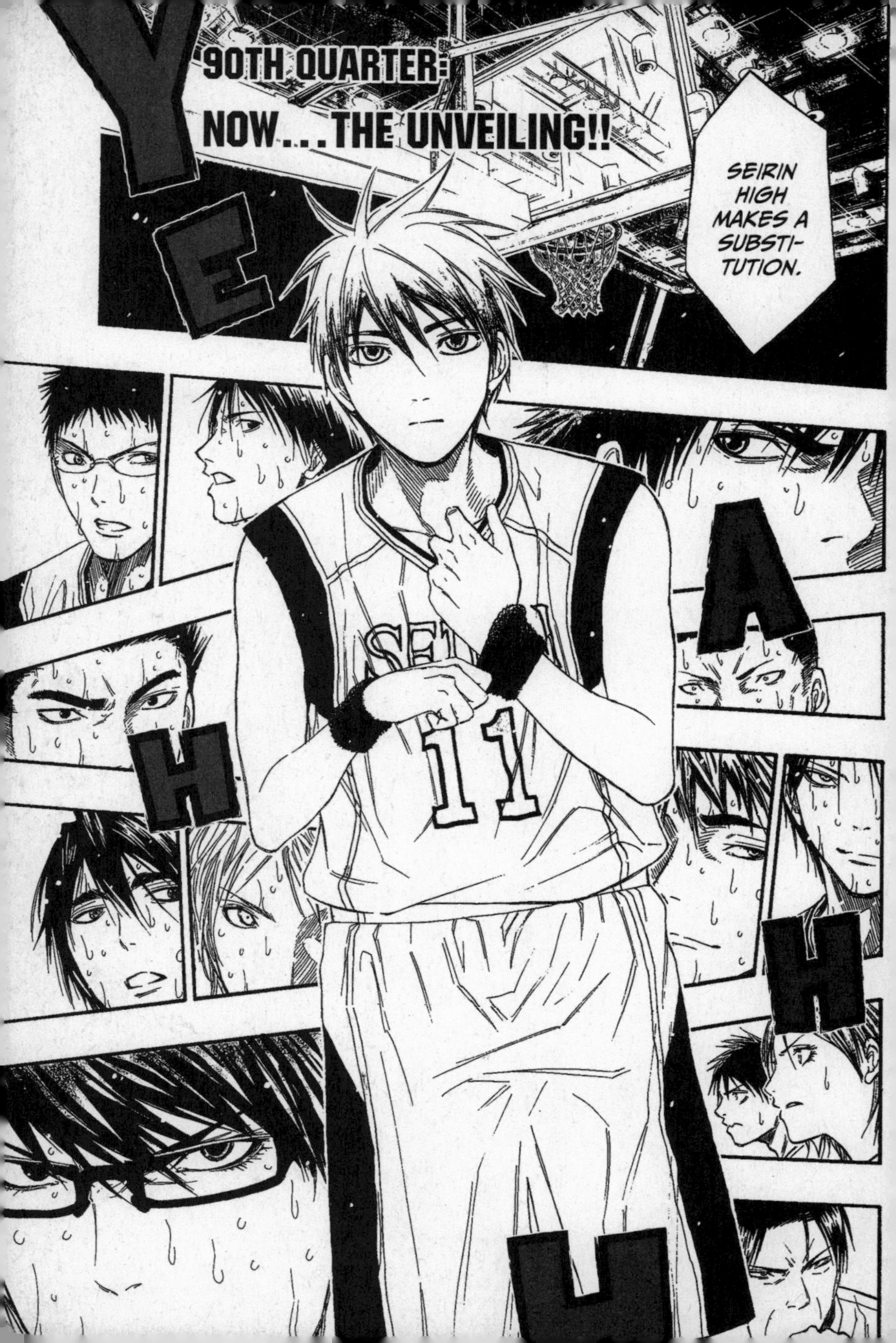
SEIRIN HIGH MAKES A SUBSTITUTION.
Y
E
A
H
H
U

Kuroko's
BASKETBALL

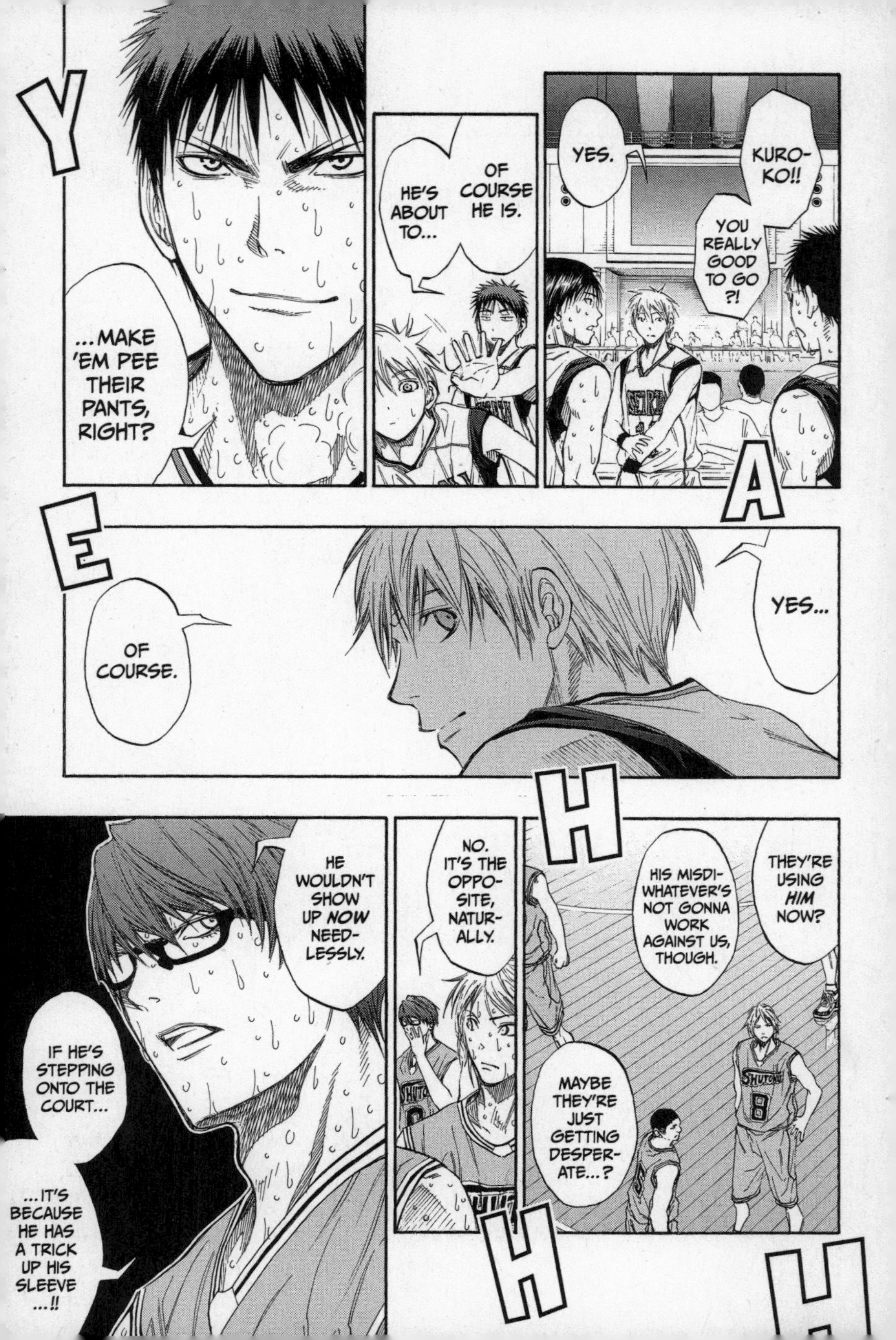
KURO-KO!!
YOU REALLY GOOD TO GO?!
YES.
OF COURSE HE IS.
HE'S ABOUT TO...
...MAKE 'EM PEE THEIR PANTS, RIGHT?
Y
A
YES...
OF COURSE.
E
H
THEY'RE USING *HIM* NOW?
HIS MISDI-WHATEVER'S NOT GONNA WORK AGAINST US, THOUGH.
MAYBE THEY'RE JUST GETTING DESPERATE...?
NO. IT'S THE OPPO-SITE, NATUR-ALLY.
HE WOULDN'T SHOW UP *NOW* NEED-LESSLY.
IF HE'S STEPPING ONTO THE COURT...
...IT'S BECAUSE HE HAS A TRICK UP HIS SLEEVE...!!
H
H

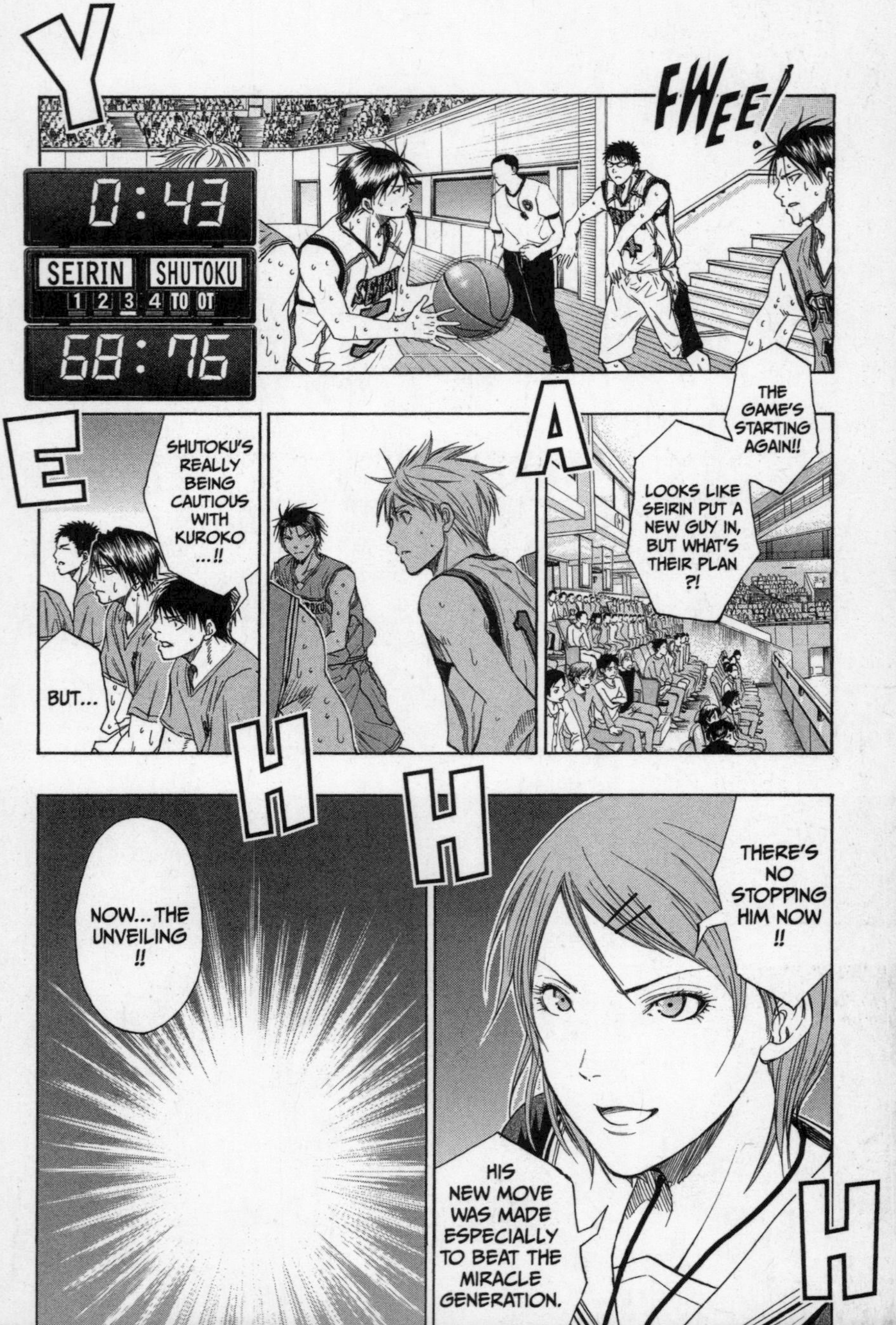
YEAHHH
FWEE!
0:43
SEIRIN
SHUTOKU
1 2 3 4 TO OT
68:76
THE GAME'S STARTING AGAIN!!
LOOKS LIKE SEIRIN PUT A NEW GUY IN, BUT WHAT'S THEIR PLAN?!
SHUTOKU'S REALLY BEING CAUTIOUS WITH KUROKO...!!
BUT...
THERE'S NO STOPPING HIM NOW!!
HIS NEW MOVE WAS MADE ESPECIALLY TO BEAT THE MIRACLE GENERATION.
NOW... THE UNVEILING!!

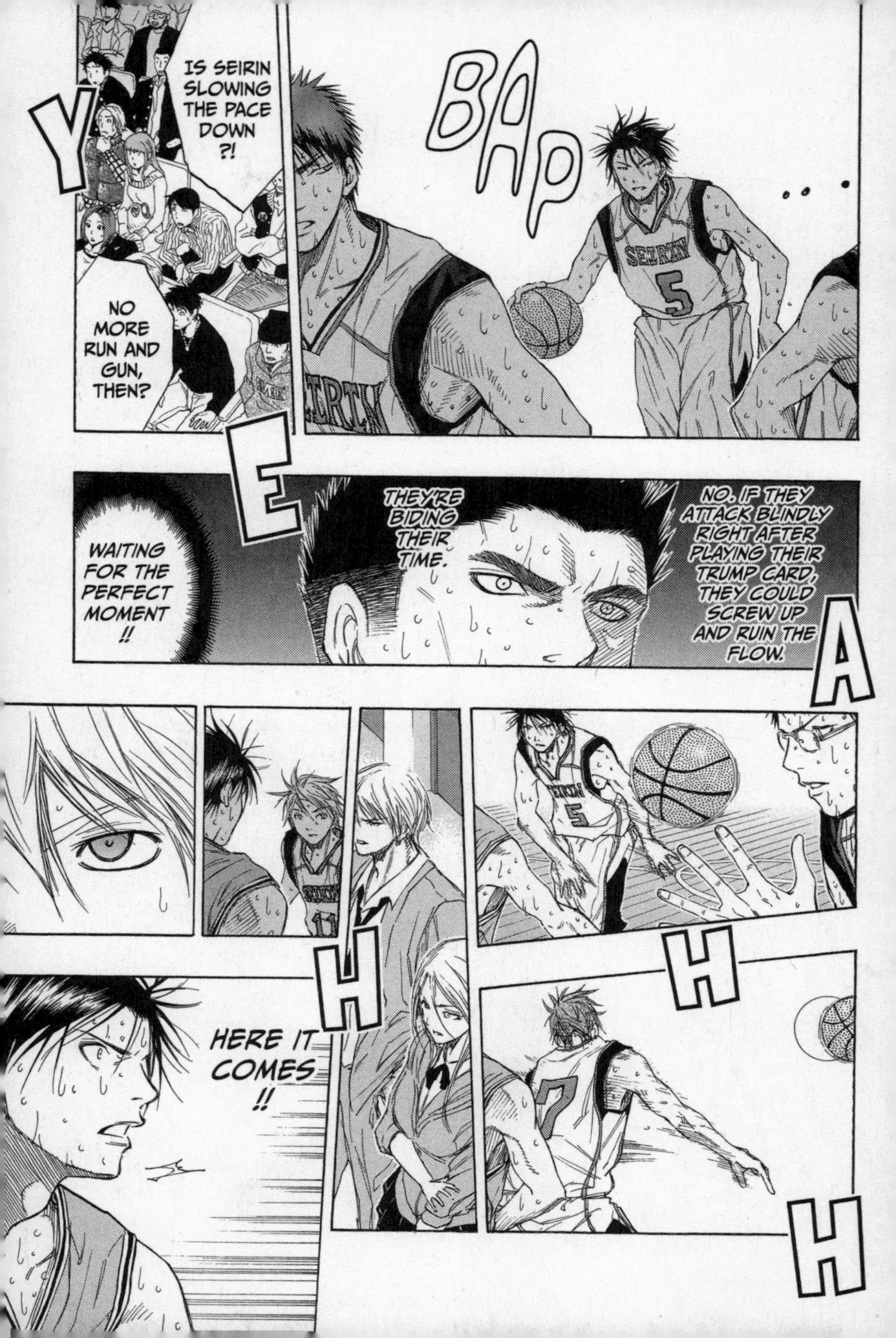
BAP
. . .
IS SEIRIN SLOWING THE PACE DOWN ?!
NO MORE RUN AND GUN, THEN?
YEAHHH
NO. IF THEY ATTACK BLINDLY RIGHT AFTER PLAYING THEIR TRUMP CARD, THEY COULD SCREW UP AND RUIN THE FLOW.
THEY'RE BIDING THEIR TIME.
WAITING FOR THE PERFECT MOMENT !!
HERE IT COMES !!

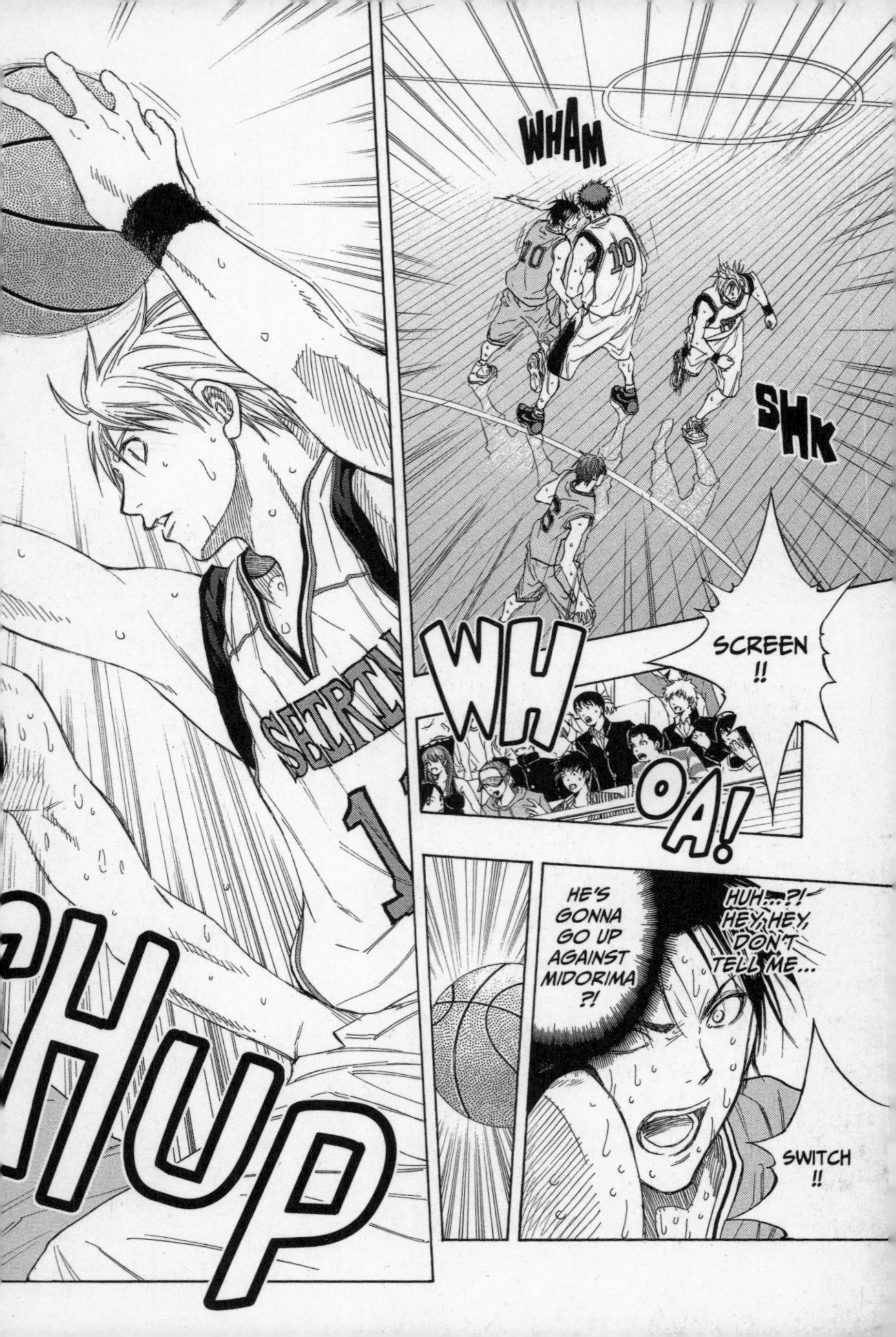
WHAM
SHK
SCREEN !!
WHOA!
HUH...?! HEY, HEY, DON'T TELL ME...
HE'S GONNA GO UP AGAINST MIDORIMA ?!
SWITCH !!
HUP

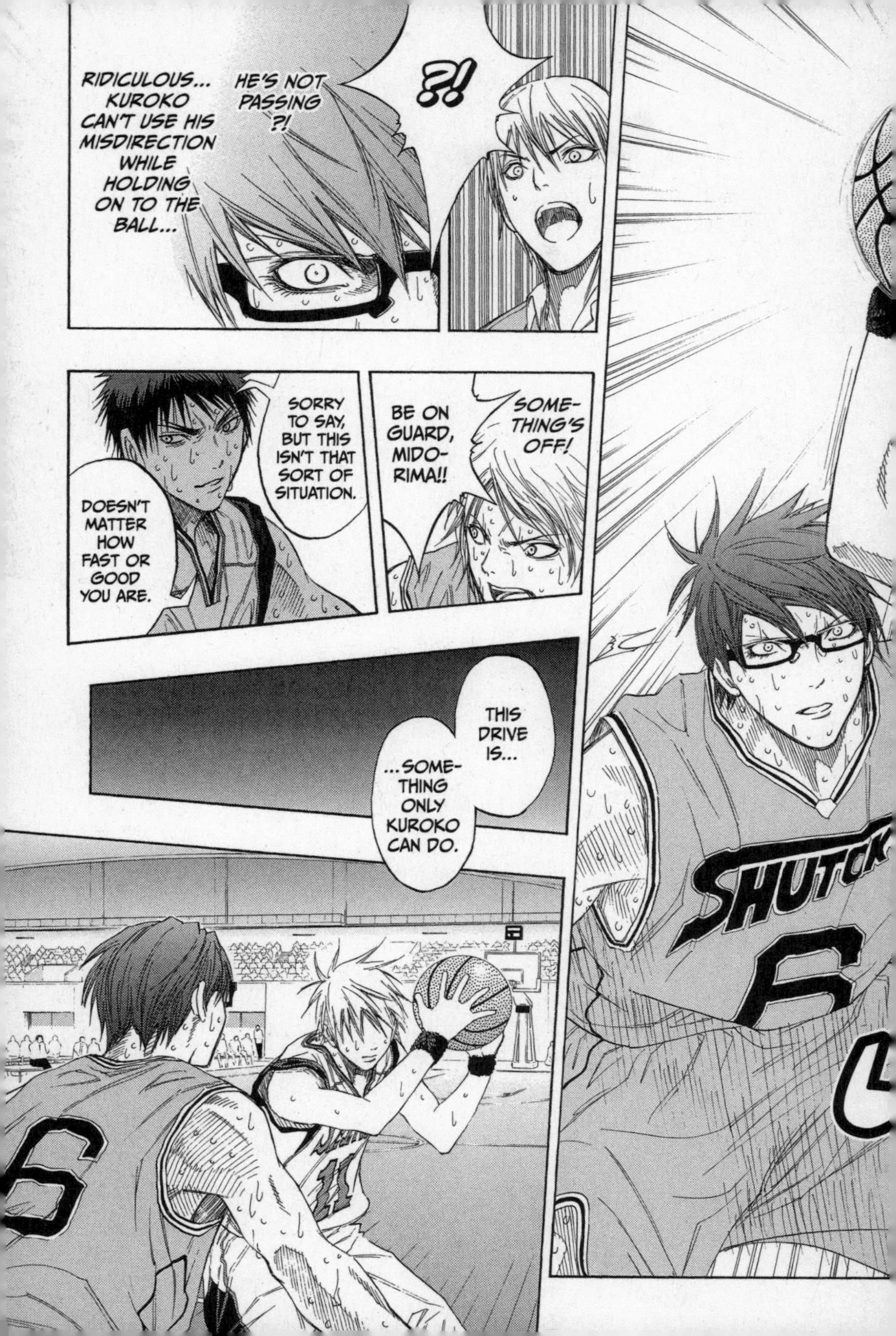
?!
HE'S NOT PASSING ?!
RIDICULOUS... KUROKO CAN'T USE HIS MISDIRECTION WHILE HOLDING ON TO THE BALL...
SOME-THING'S OFF!
BE ON GUARD, MIDO-RIMA!!
SORRY TO SAY, BUT THIS ISN'T THAT SORT OF SITUATION.
DOESN'T MATTER HOW FAST OR GOOD YOU ARE.
THIS DRIVE IS...
...SOME-THING ONLY KUROKO CAN DO.

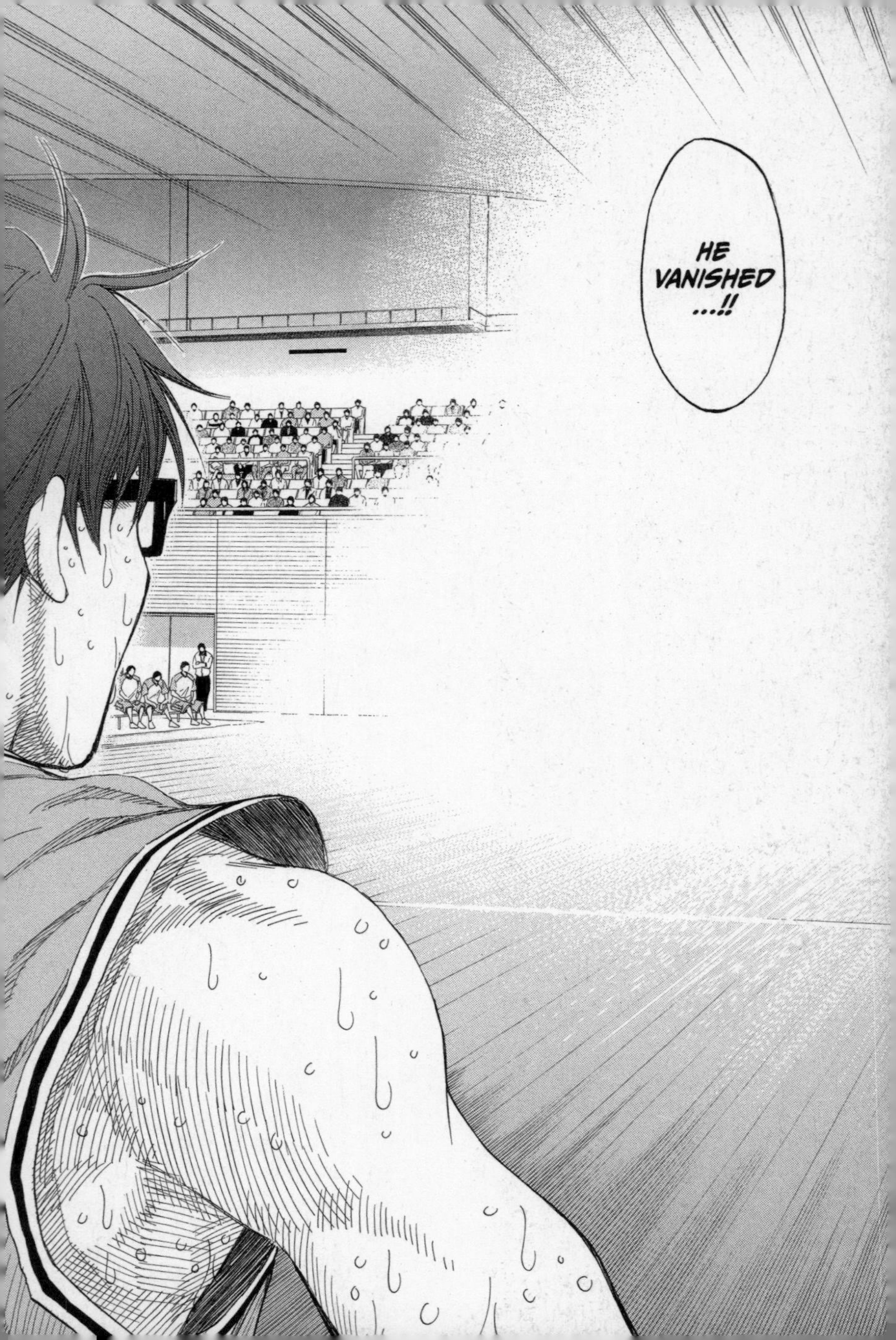
HE VANISHED ...!!

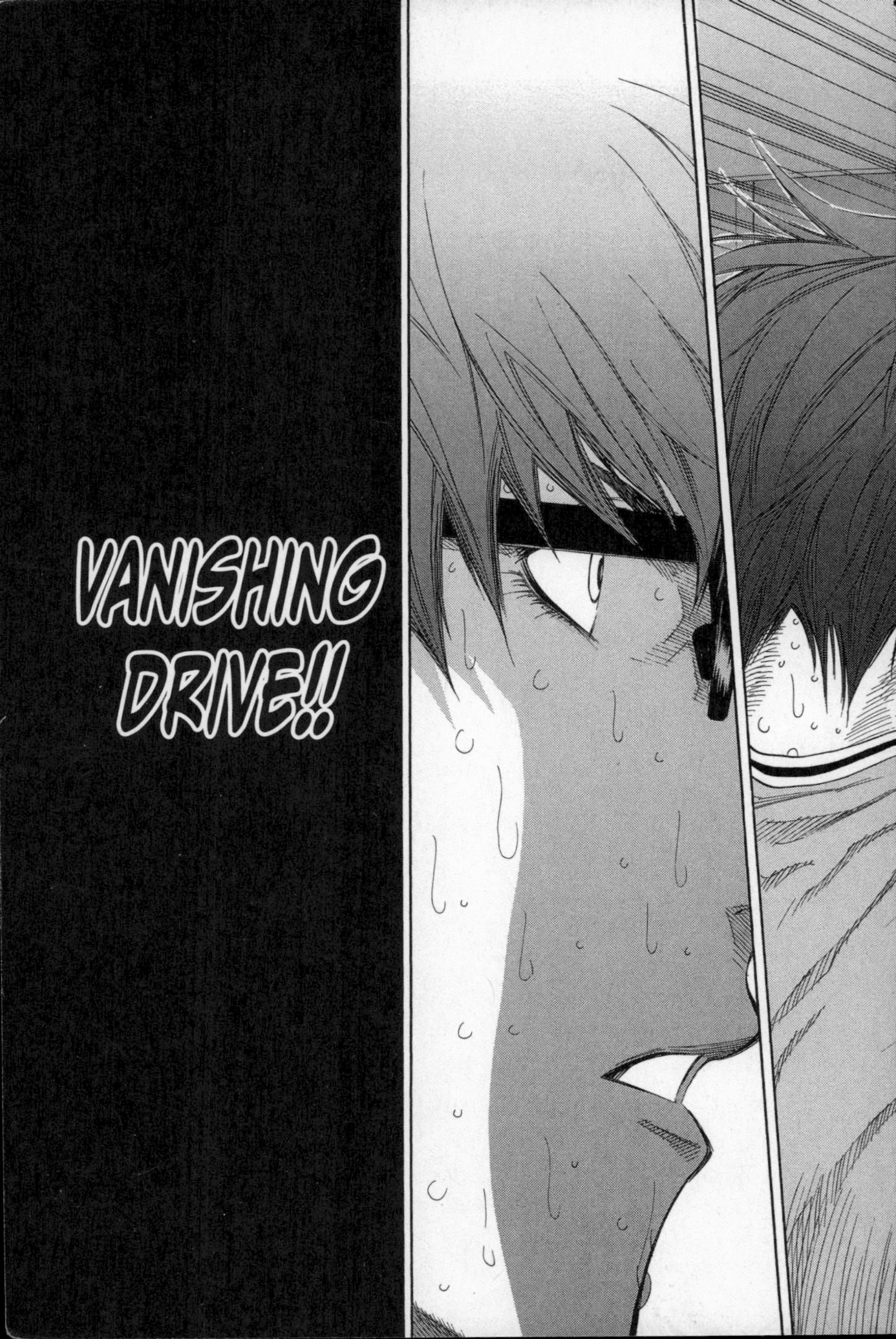
VANISHING DRIVE!!

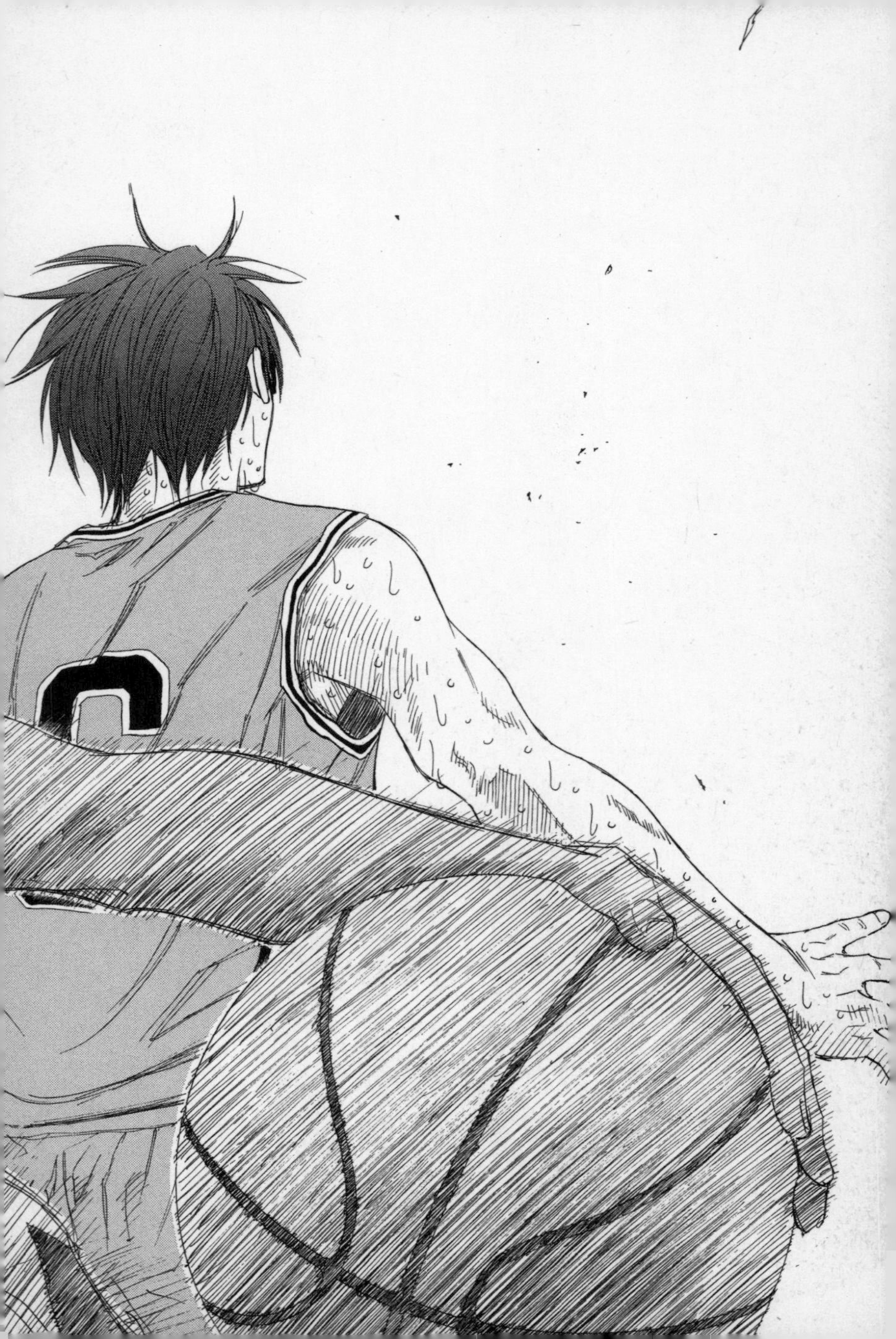

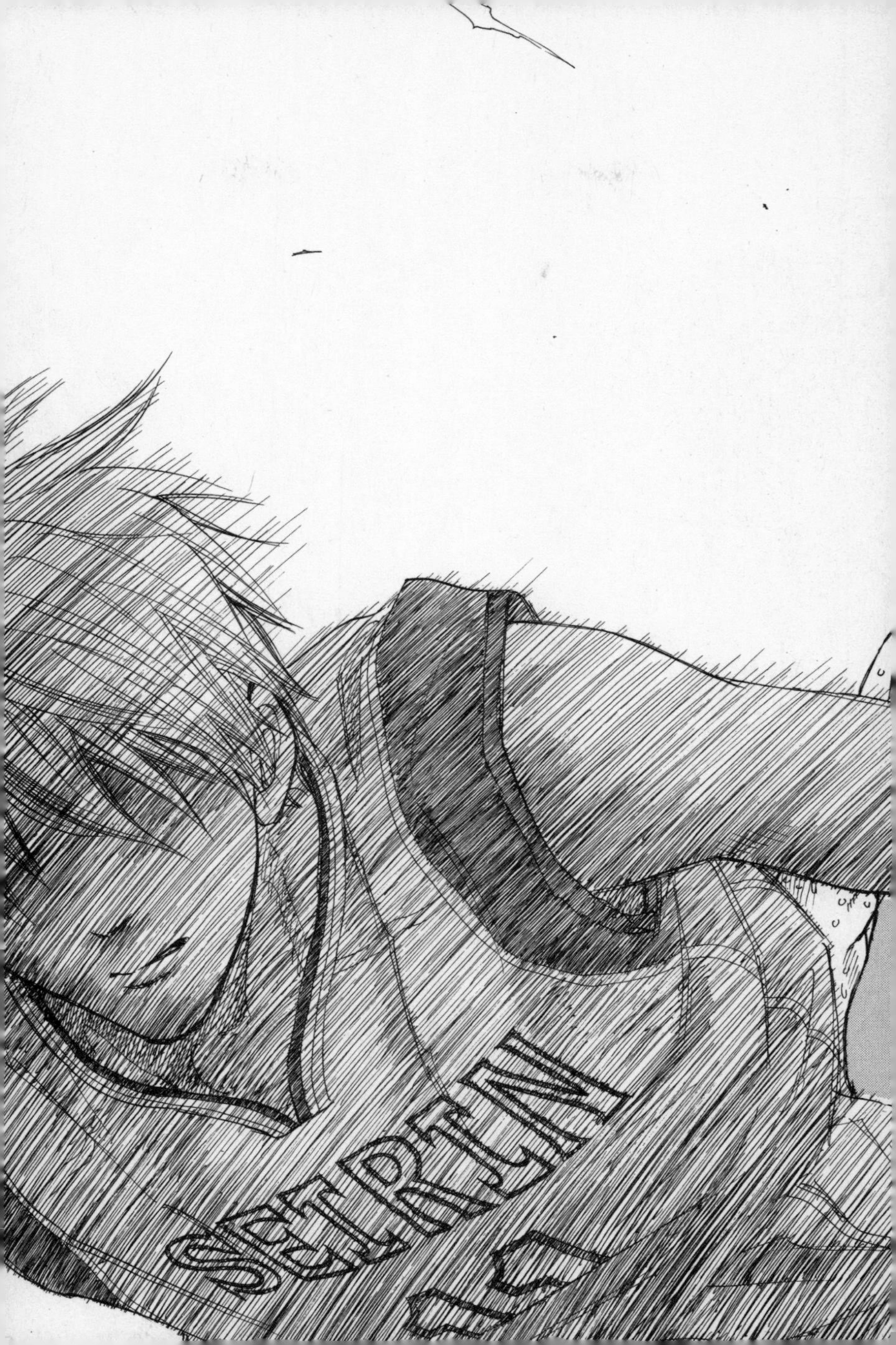
SEIRIN

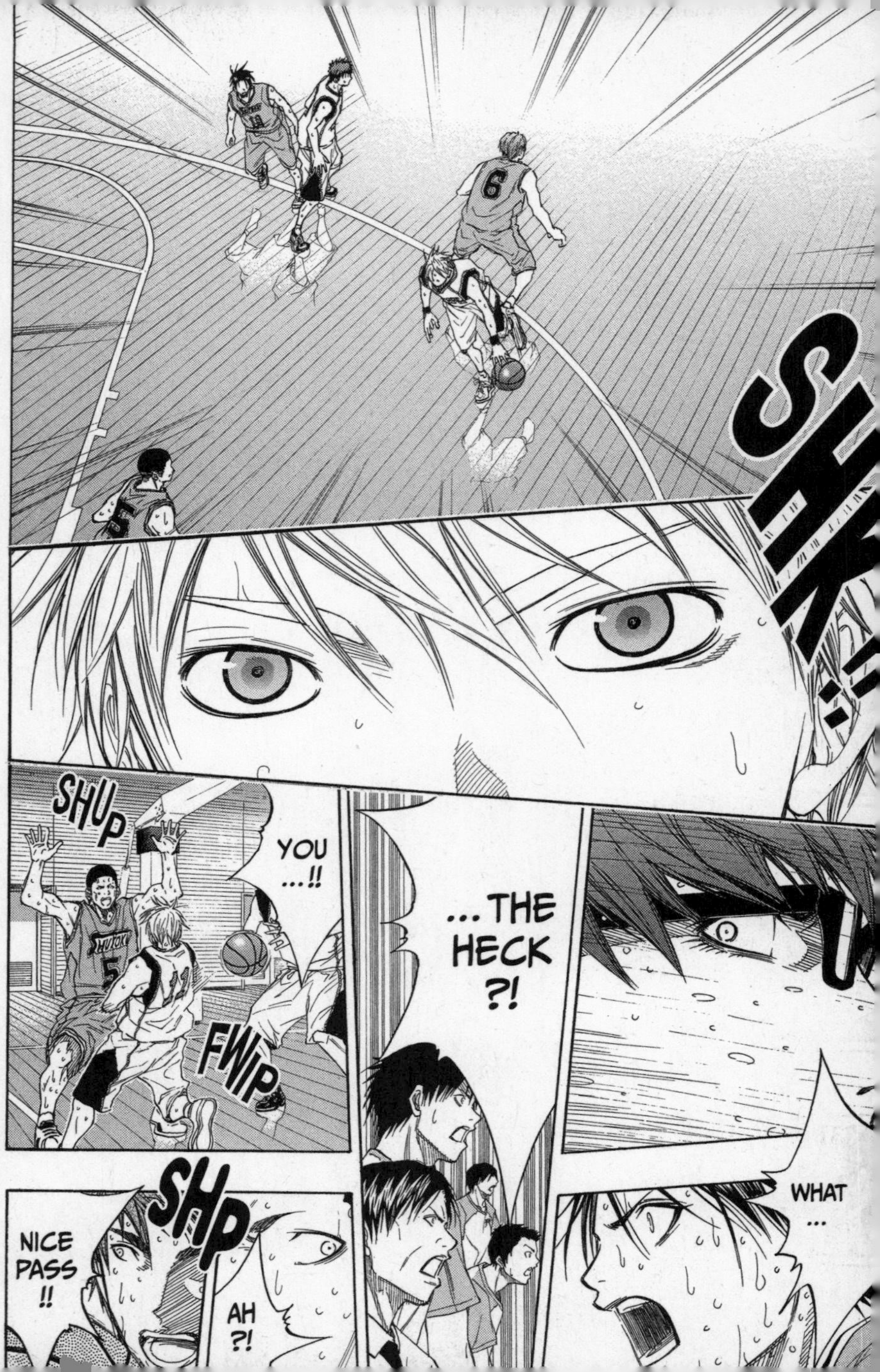
SHK!!
... THE HECK ?!
YOU ...!!
SHUP
FWIP
WHAT ...
SHP
NICE PASS !!
AH ?!

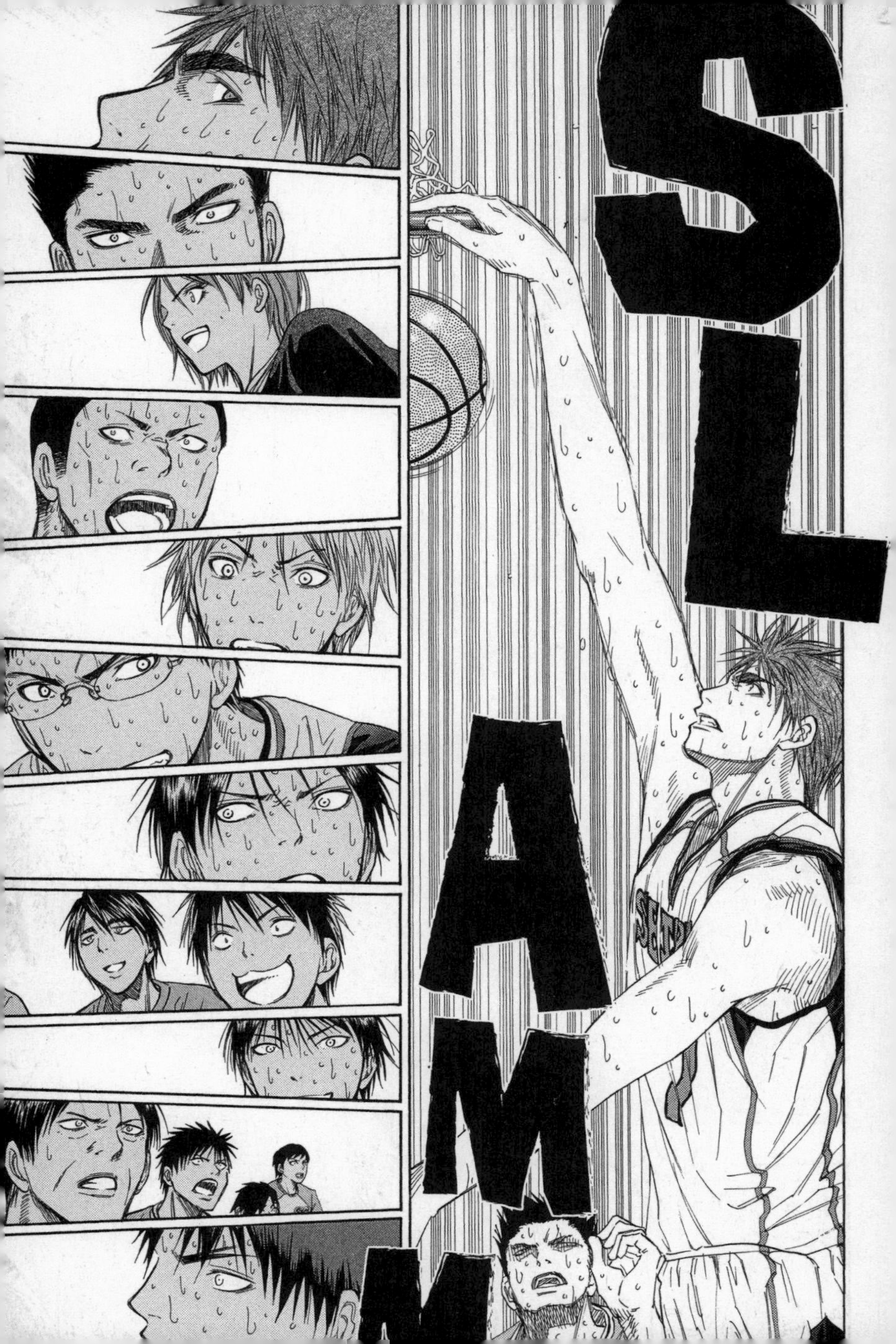
SLAMM

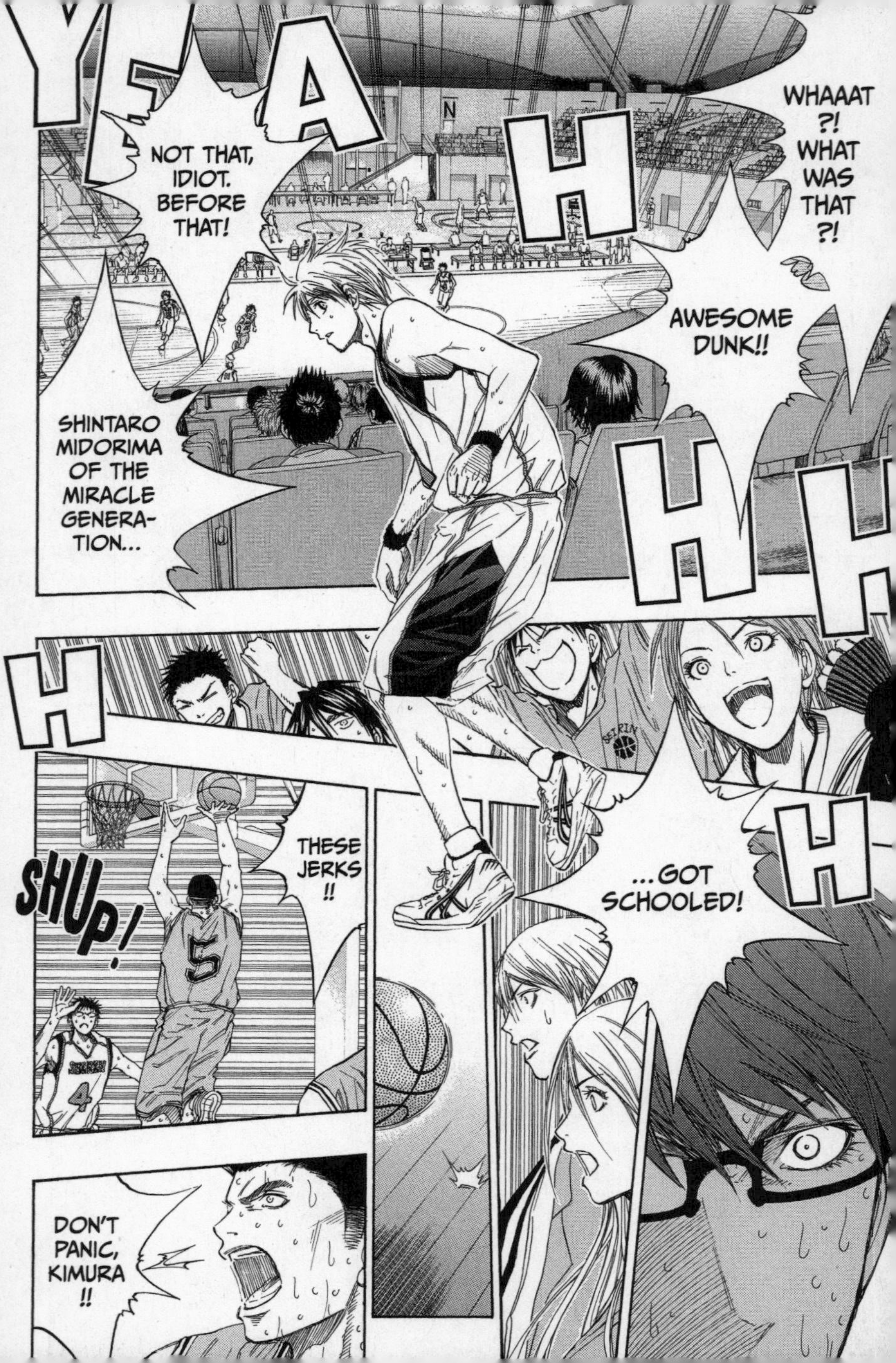
YEAHHHHH
WHAAAT?! WHAT WAS THAT?!
AWESOME DUNK!!
NOT THAT, IDIOT. BEFORE THAT!
SHINTARO MIDORIMA OF THE MIRACLE GENERATION...
...GOT SCHOOLED!
THESE JERKS!!
SHUP!
DON'T PANIC, KIMURA!!

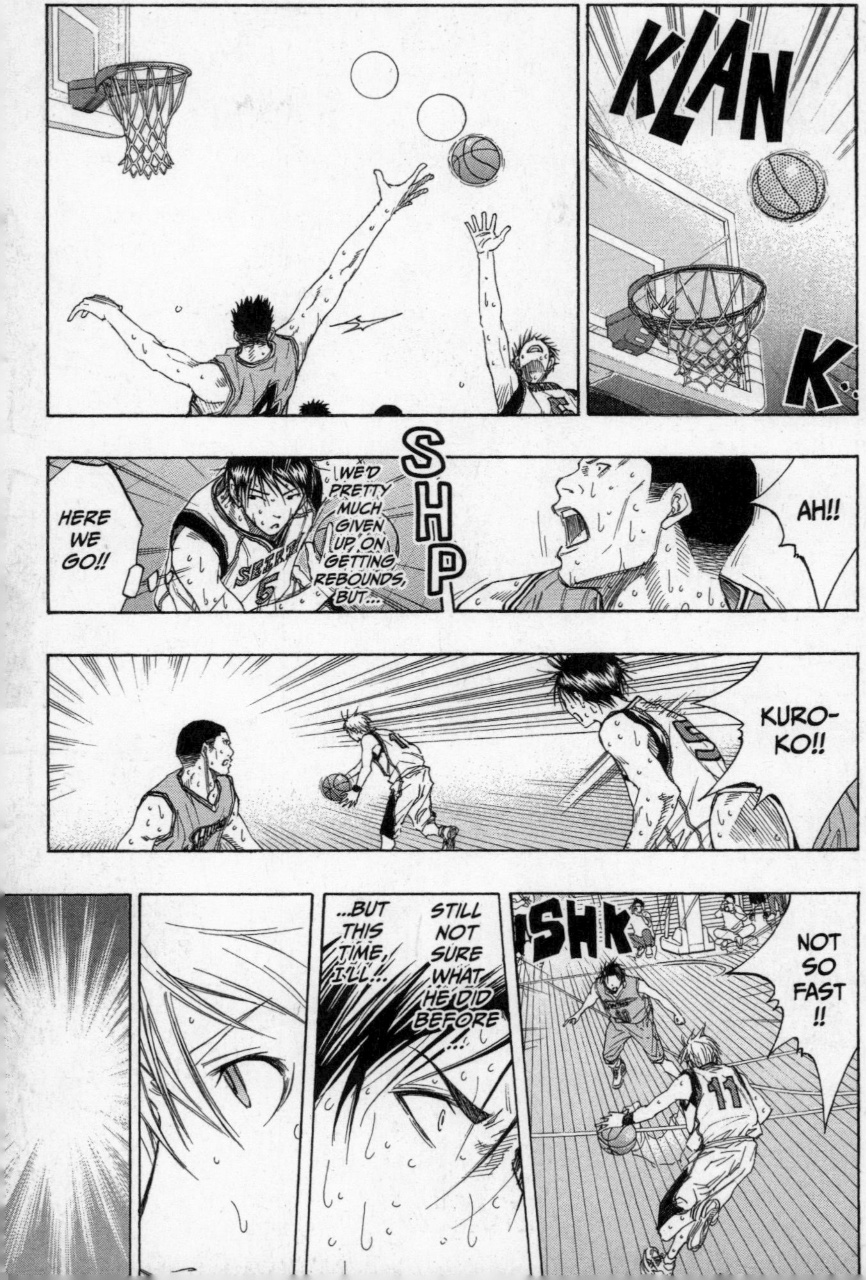
KLAN
K...
AH!!
SHP
WE'D PRETTY MUCH GIVEN UP ON GETTING REBOUNDS, BUT...
HERE WE GO!!
KURO-KO!!
NOT SO FAST!!
SHK
STILL NOT SURE WHAT HE DID BEFORE...!!
...BUT THIS TIME, I'LL...!!

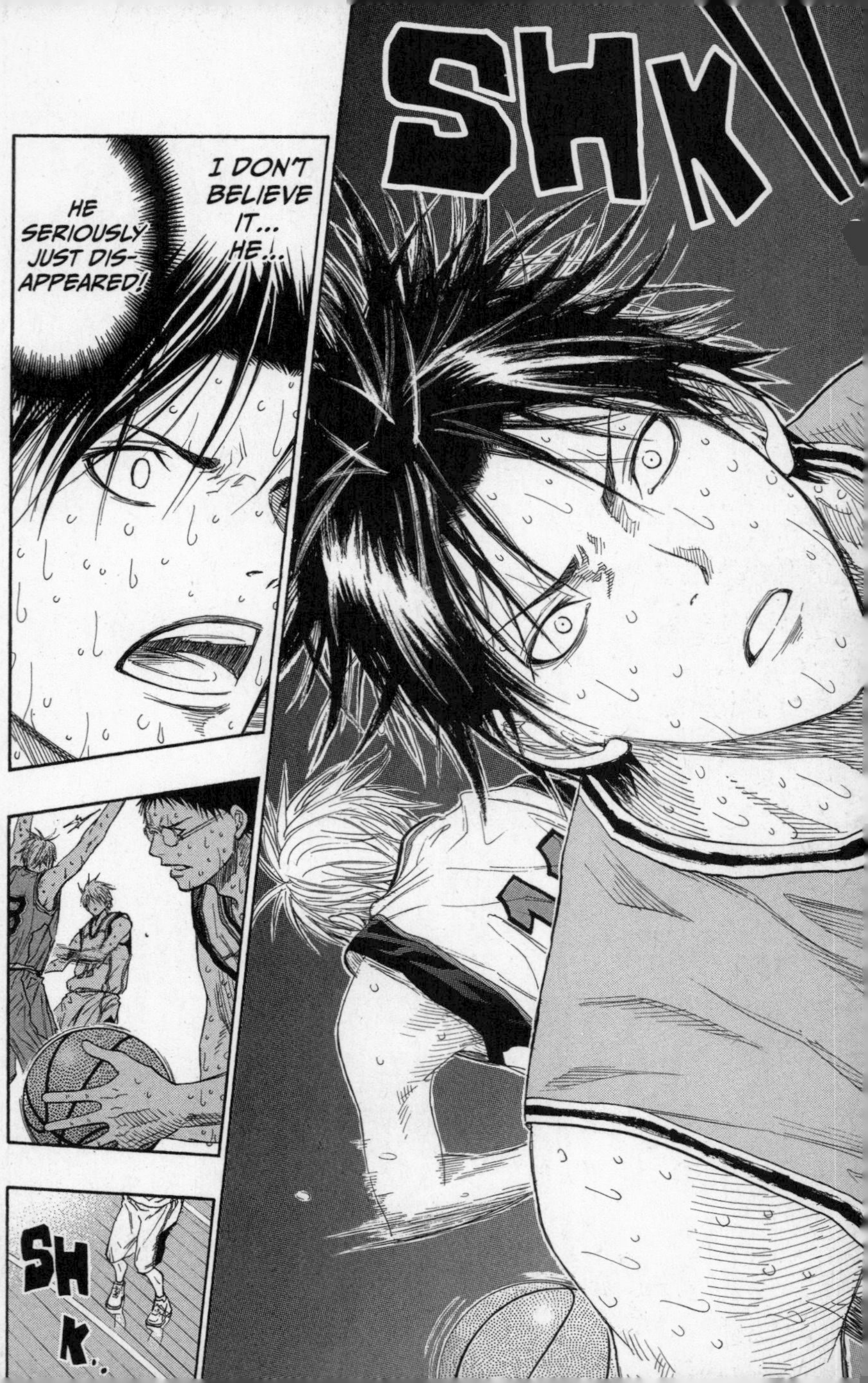
SHK
I DON'T BELIEVE IT... HE...
HE SERIOUSLY JUST DIS-APPEARED!
SH K..

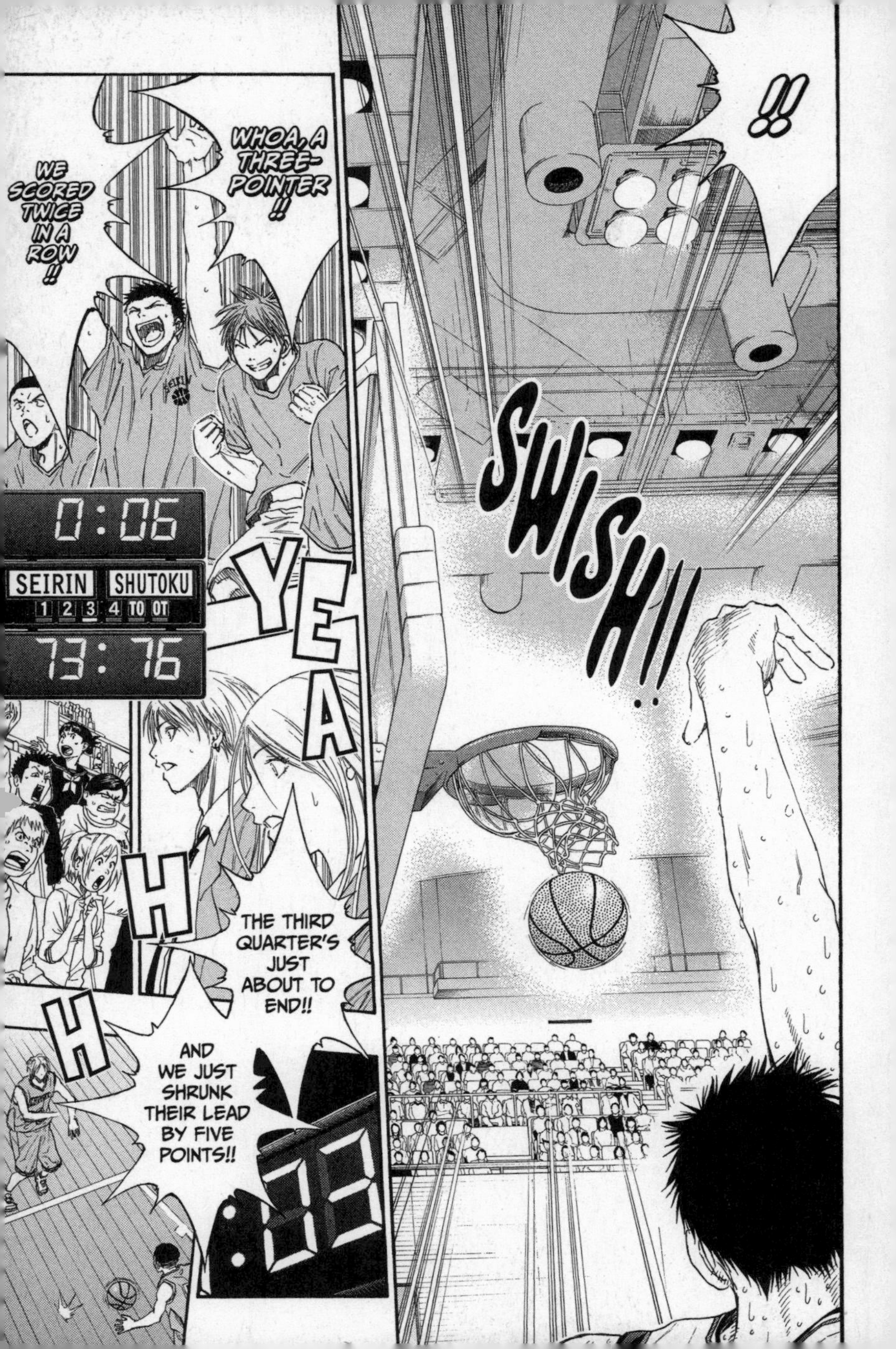
!!
SWISH!!
WHOA, A THREE-POINTER!!
WE SCORED TWICE IN A ROW!!
0:06
SEIRIN
SHUTOKU
1 2 3 4 TO OT
73 : 76
YEAHHH
THE THIRD QUARTER'S JUST ABOUT TO END!!
AND WE JUST SHRUNK THEIR LEAD BY FIVE POINTS!!

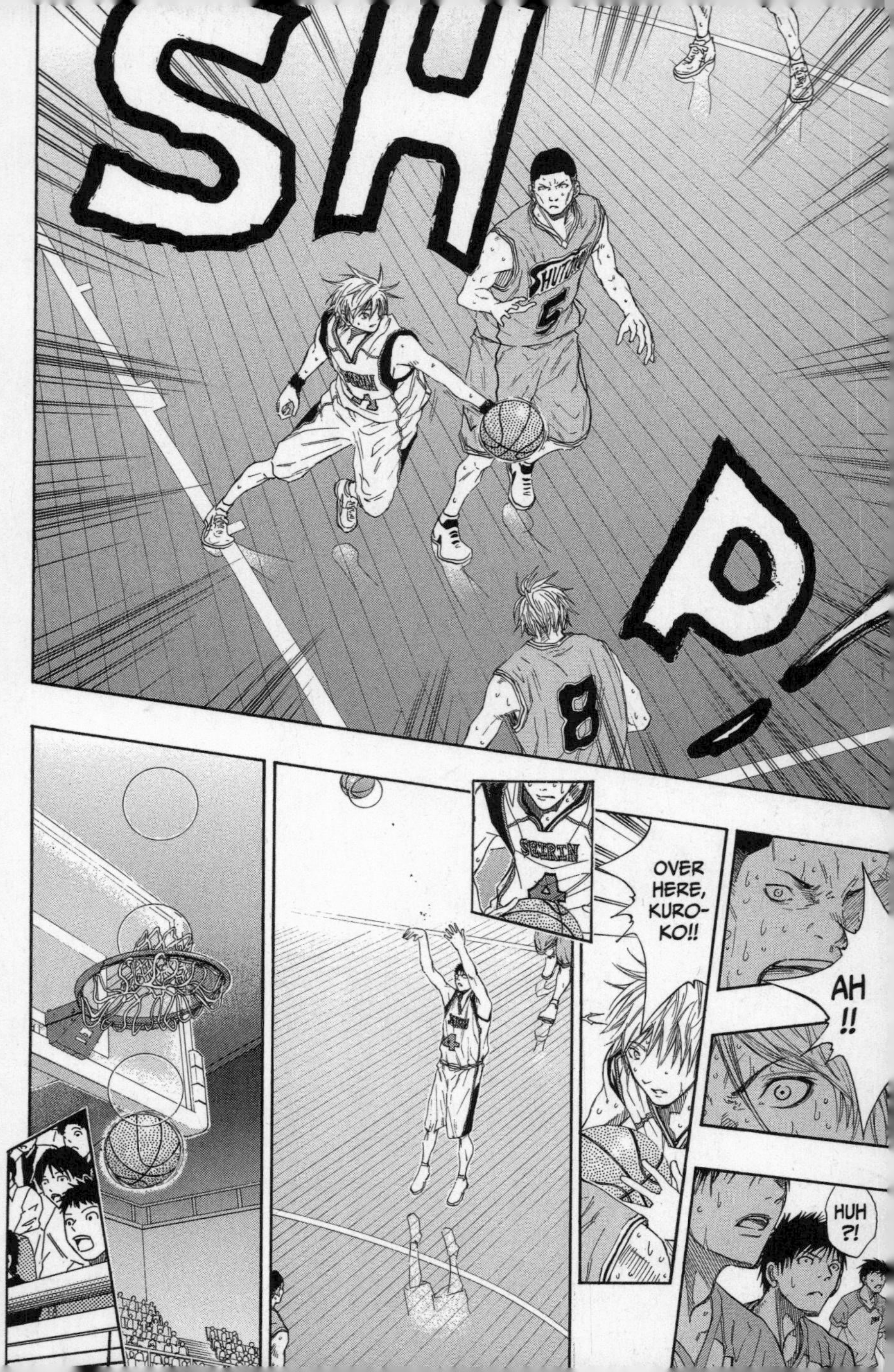
SHP!
AH !!
HUH ?!
OVER HERE, KURO-KO!!

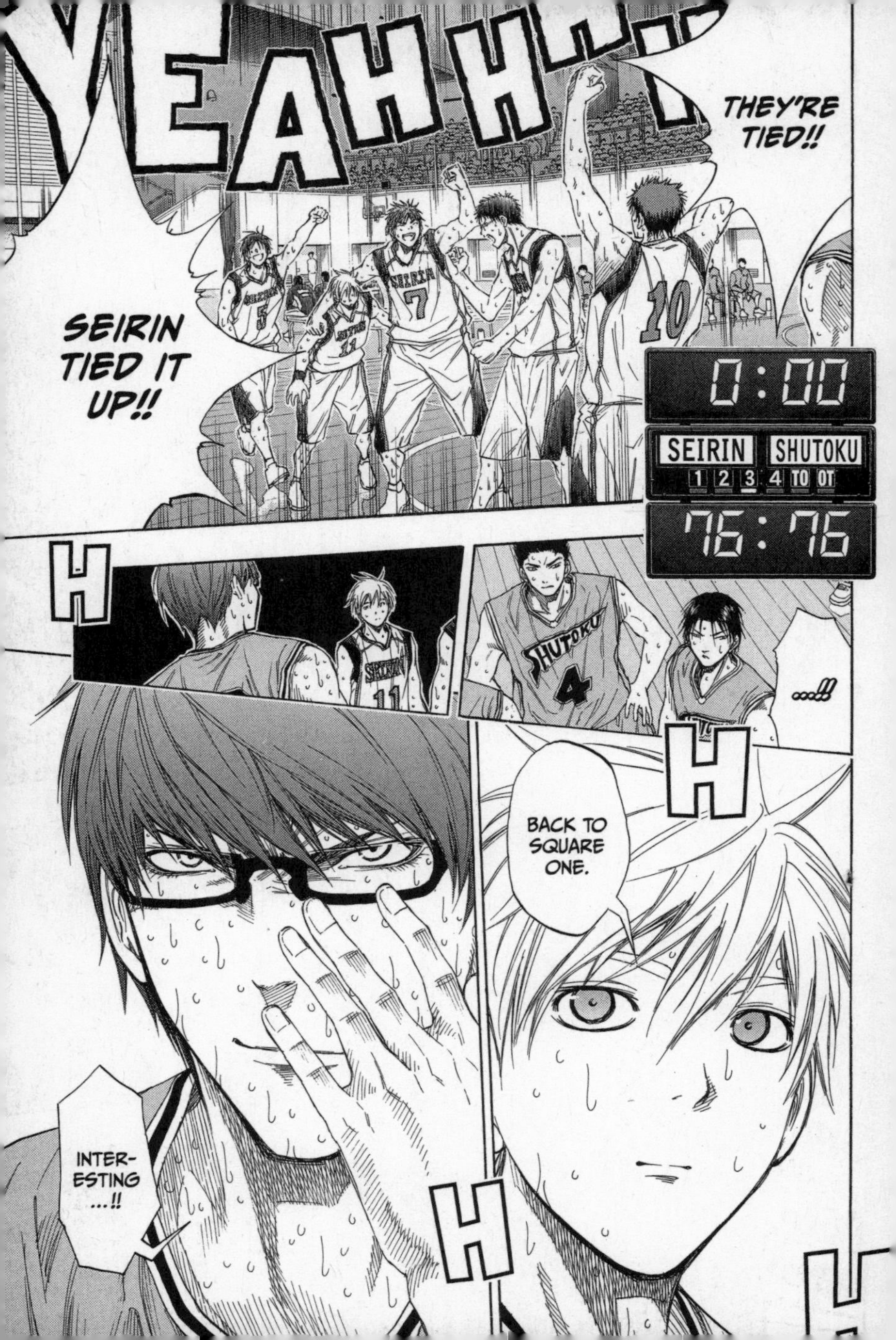
YEAHH
THEY'RE TIED!!
SEIRIN TIED IT UP!!
0:00
SEIRIN SHUTOKU
1 2 3 4 TO OT
76:76
H
...!!
H
H
BACK TO SQUARE ONE.
H
INTER-ESTING ...!!
H

KUROKO'S BASKETBALL BLOOPERS

TAKE 1

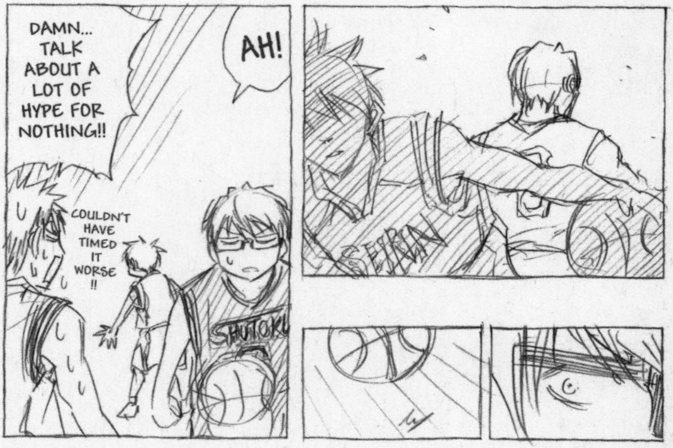
SEIRIN
AH!
DAMN... TALK ABOUT A LOT OF HYPE FOR NOTHING!!
COULDN'T HAVE TIMED IT WORSE!!
SHUTOKU

91ST QUARTER: SURPASSED MY LIMIT

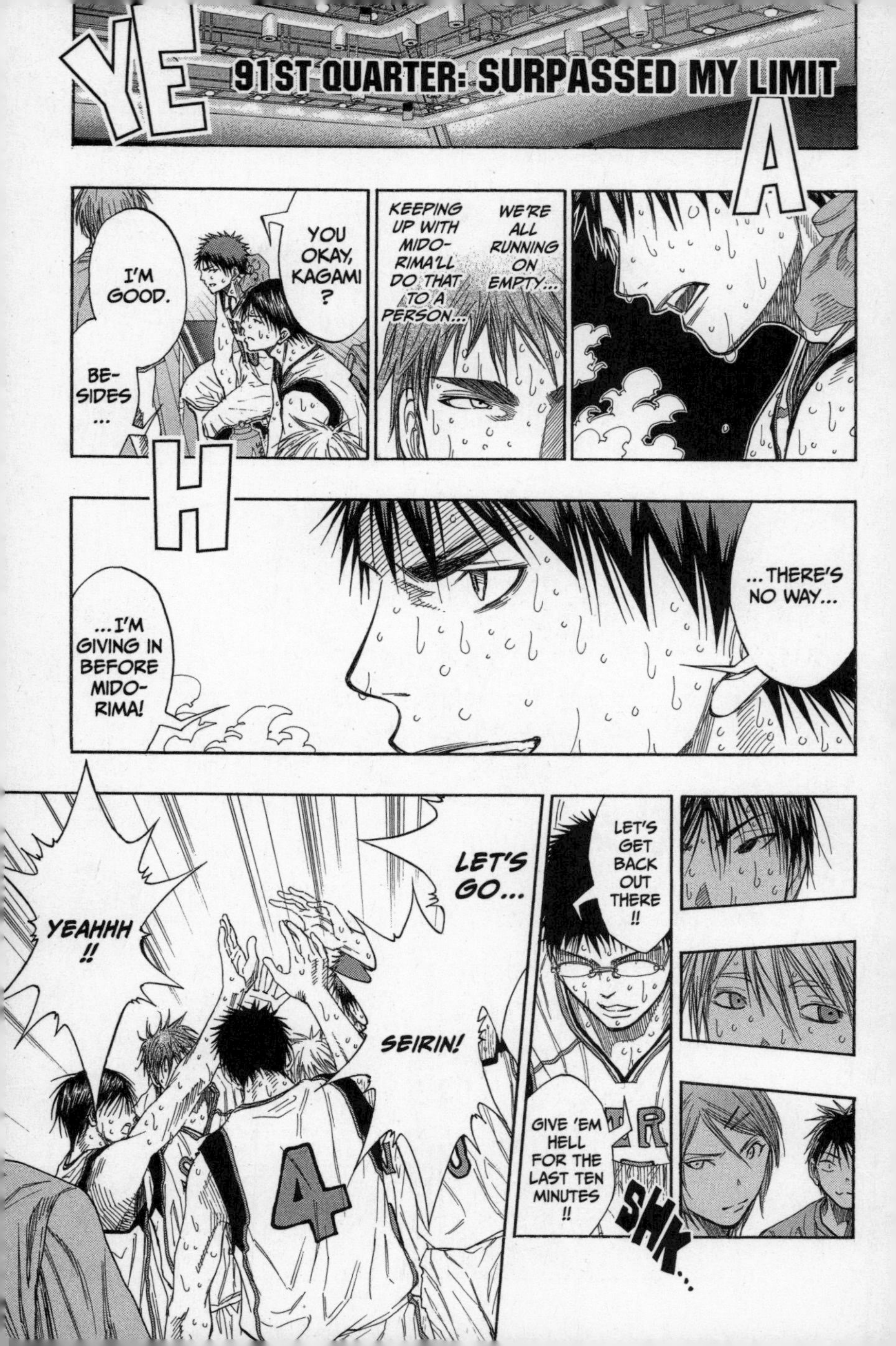
YEAH
WE'RE ALL RUNNING ON EMPTY...
KEEPING UP WITH MIDO-RIMA'LL DO THAT TO A PERSON...
YOU OKAY, KAGAMI?
I'M GOOD.
BE-SIDES...
...THERE'S NO WAY...
...I'M GIVING IN BEFORE MIDO-RIMA!
LET'S GET BACK OUT THERE!!
GIVE 'EM HELL FOR THE LAST TEN MINUTES!!
SHK...
LET'S GO...
SEIRIN!
YEAHHH!!

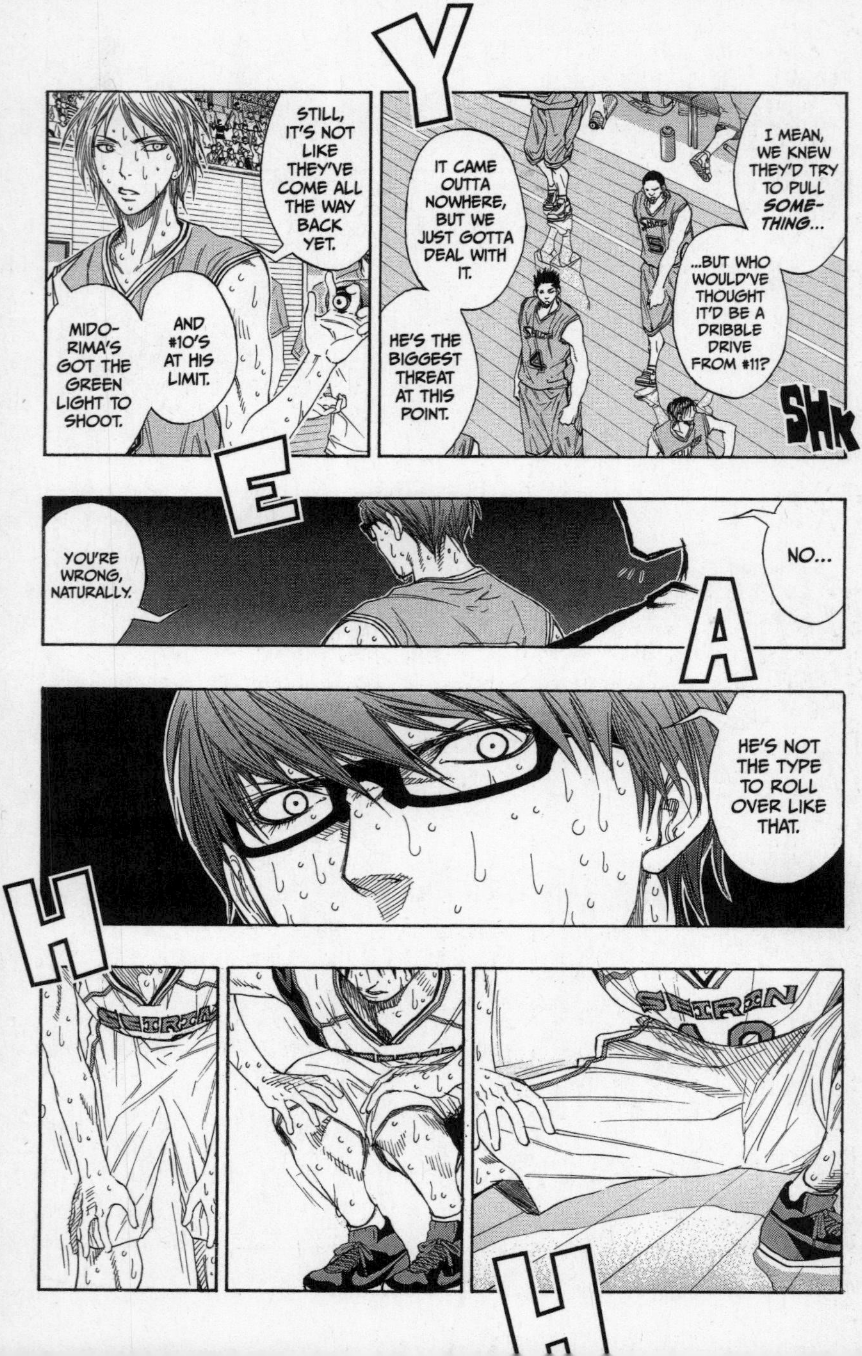
YEAHH
I MEAN, WE KNEW THEY'D TRY TO PULL SOMETHING...
...BUT WHO WOULD'VE THOUGHT IT'D BE A DRIBBLE DRIVE FROM #11?
SHK
IT CAME OUTTA NOWHERE, BUT WE JUST GOTTA DEAL WITH IT.
HE'S THE BIGGEST THREAT AT THIS POINT.
STILL, IT'S NOT LIKE THEY'VE COME ALL THE WAY BACK YET.
AND #10'S AT HIS LIMIT.
MIDO-RIMA'S GOT THE GREEN LIGHT TO SHOOT.
NO...
YOU'RE WRONG, NATURALLY.
HE'S NOT THE TYPE TO ROLL OVER LIKE THAT.

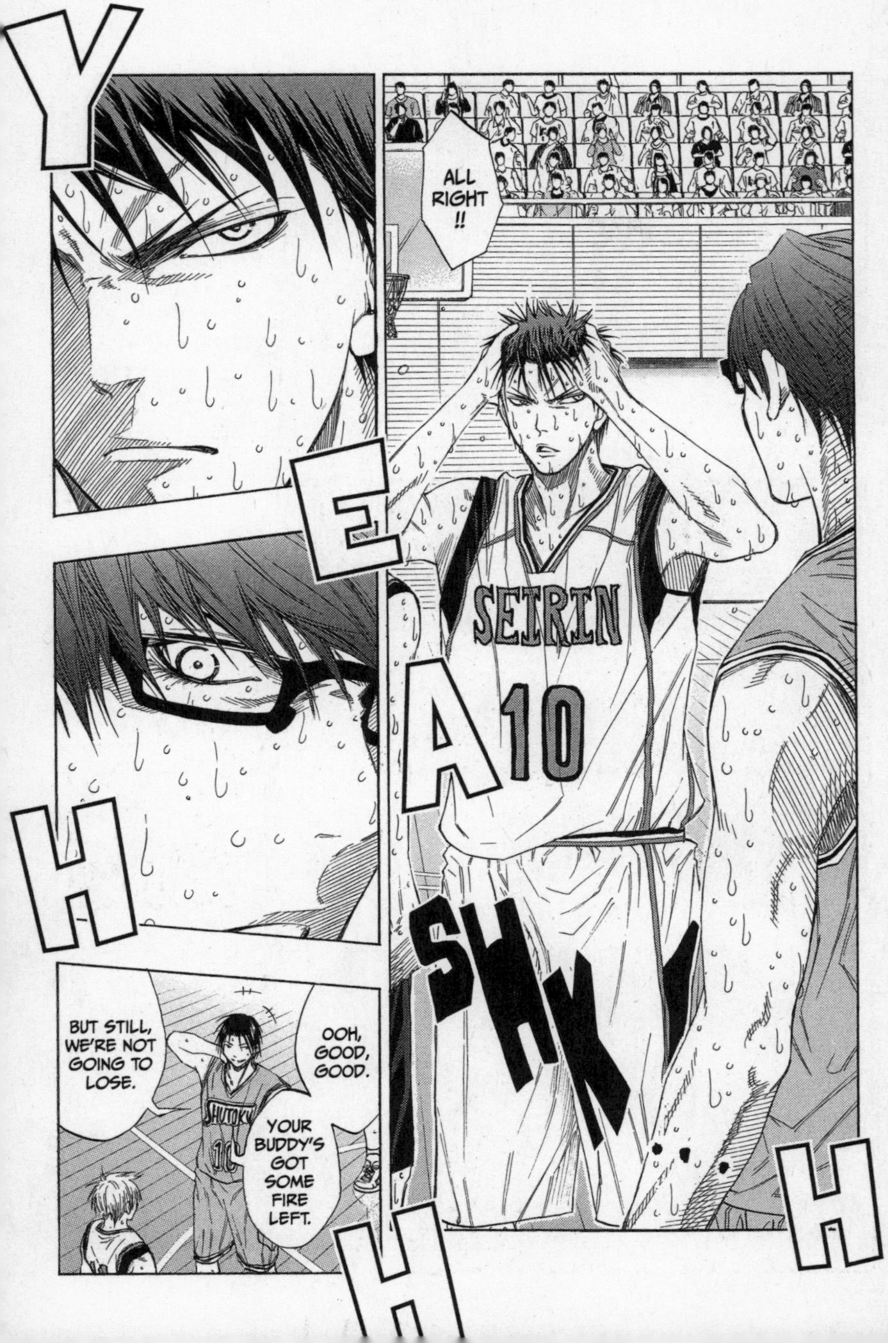
YEAHHH
ALL RIGHT !!
SHK
OOH, GOOD, GOOD.
YOUR BUDDY'S GOT SOME FIRE LEFT.
BUT STILL, WE'RE NOT GOING TO LOSE.

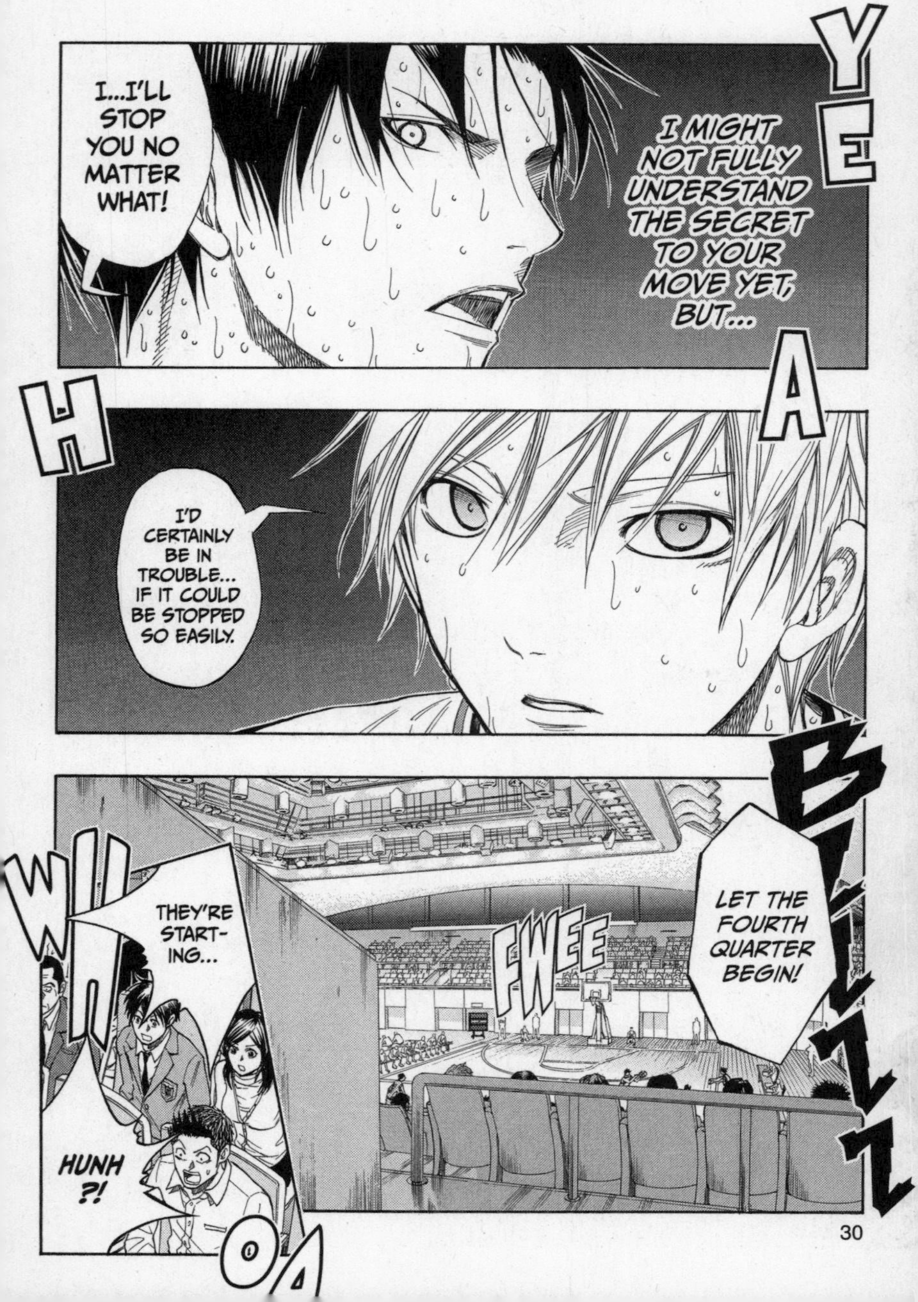
I MIGHT NOT FULLY UNDERSTAND THE SECRET TO YOUR MOVE YET, BUT...
I...I'LL STOP YOU NO MATTER WHAT!
YEAH
I'D CERTAINLY BE IN TROUBLE... IF IT COULD BE STOPPED SO EASILY.
LET THE FOURTH QUARTER BEGIN!
FWEE
THEY'RE START-ING...
HUNH ?!

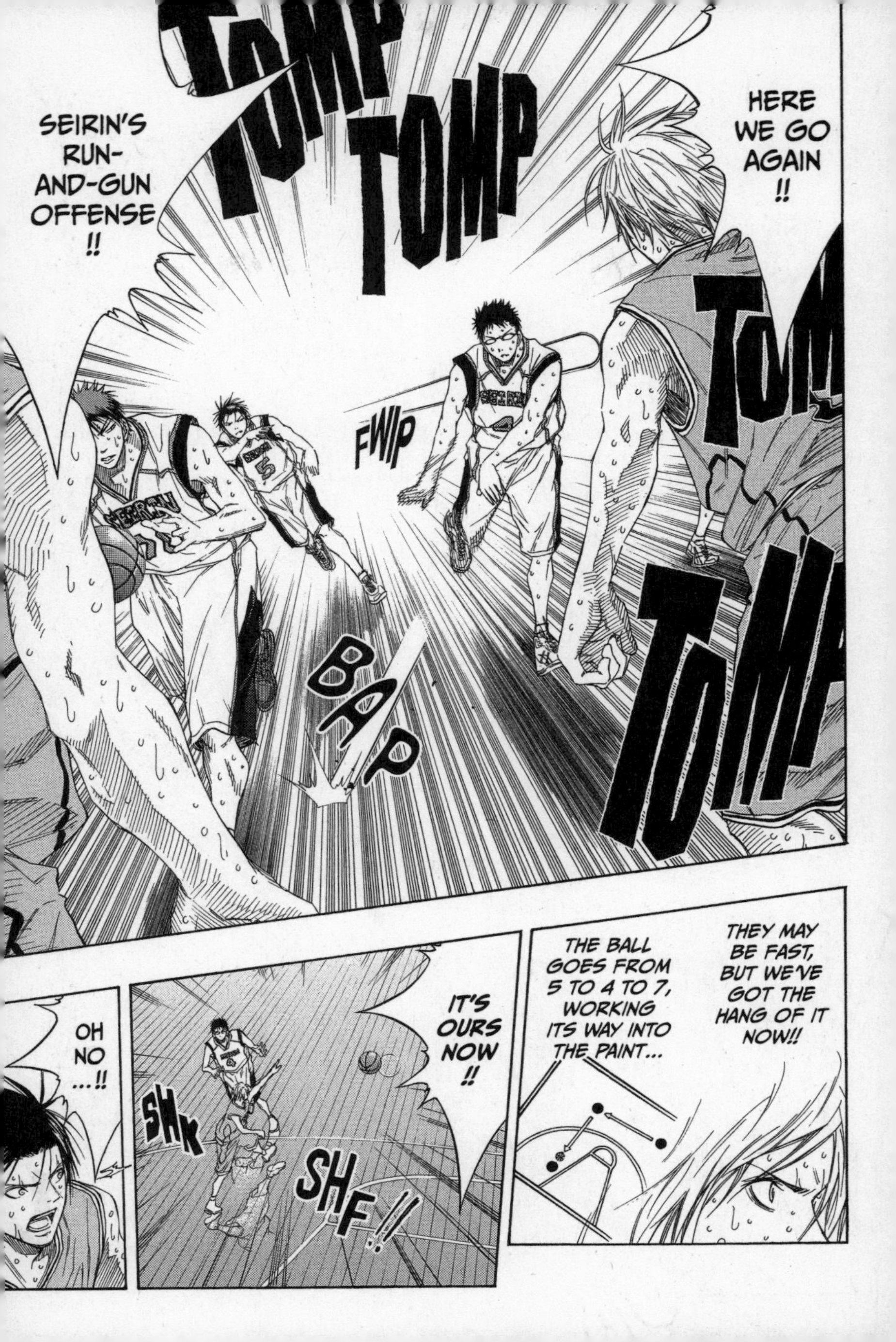
HERE WE GO AGAIN !!
TOMP
TOMP
TOMP
TOMP
SEIRIN'S RUN-AND-GUN OFFENSE !!
FWIP
BAP
THEY MAY BE FAST, BUT WE'VE GOT THE HANG OF IT NOW!!
THE BALL GOES FROM 5 TO 4 TO 7, WORKING ITS WAY INTO THE PAINT...
IT'S OURS NOW !!
SHK
SHF !!
OH NO ...!!

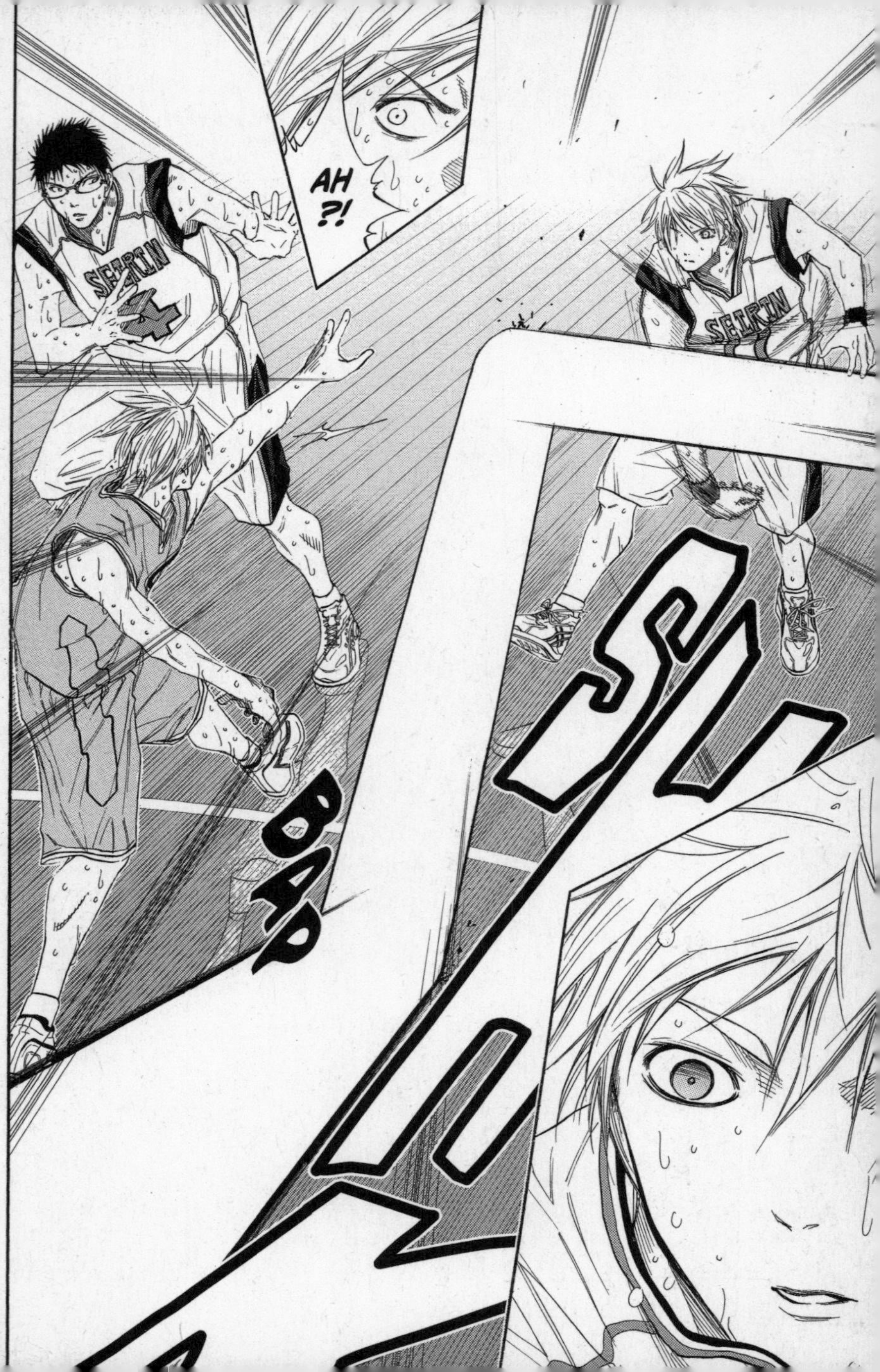
AH ?!
BAP
SEIRIN
SEIRIN

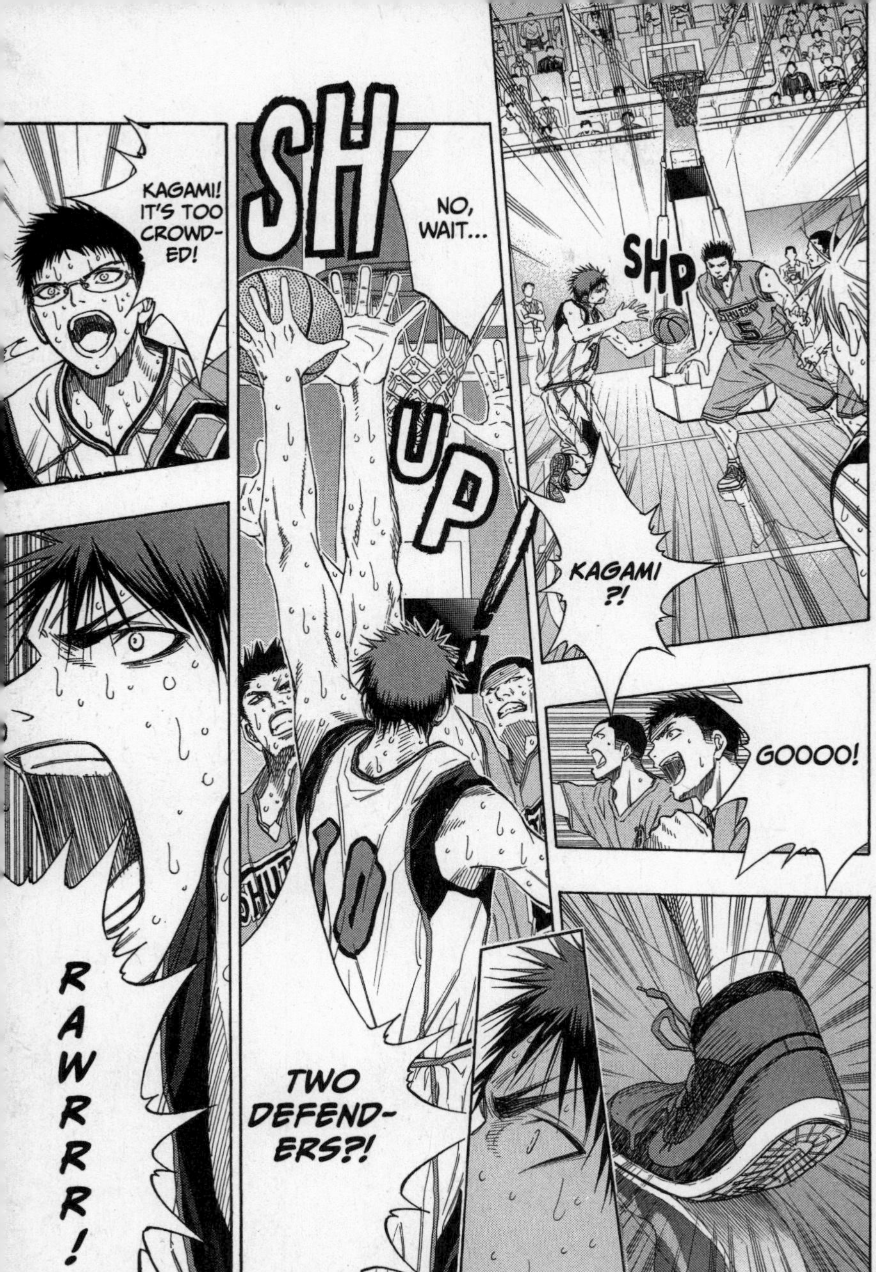
SHP
KAGAMI ?!
GOOOO!
SHUP!
NO, WAIT...
TWO DEFENDERS?!
KAGAMI! IT'S TOO CROWDED!
RAWRRRR!

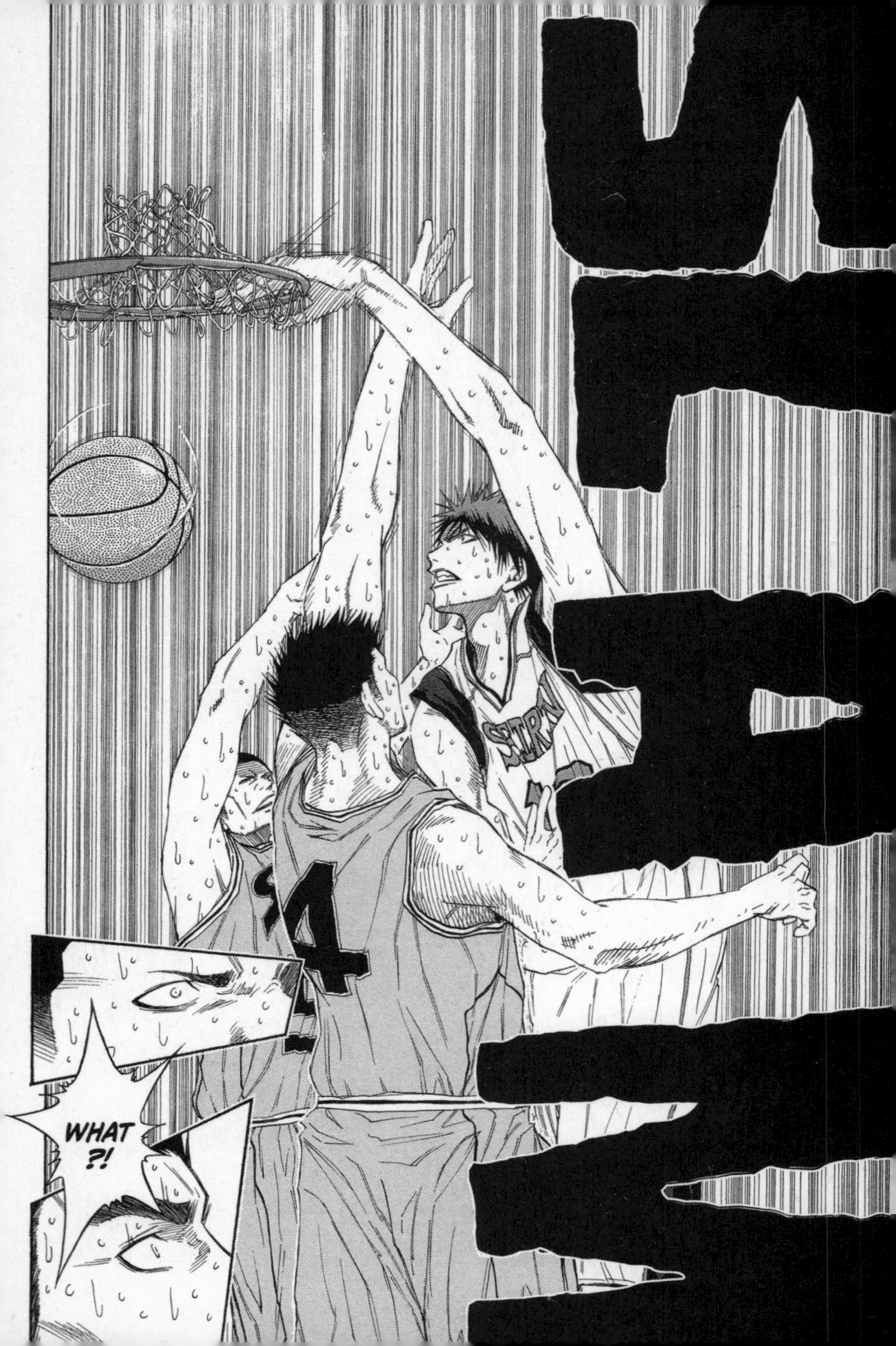
WHAT ?!

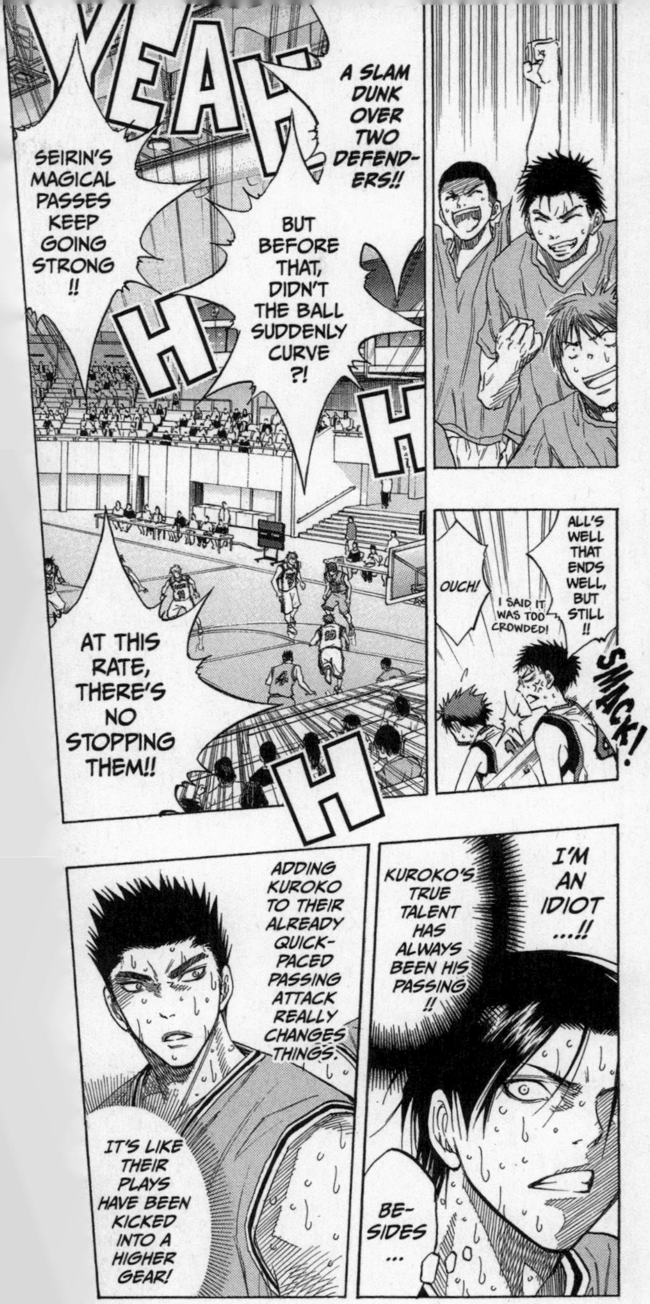
YEAHHHHH
A SLAM DUNK OVER TWO DEFENDERS!!
BUT BEFORE THAT, DIDN'T THE BALL SUDDENLY CURVE?!
SEIRIN'S MAGICAL PASSES KEEP GOING STRONG!!
AT THIS RATE, THERE'S NO STOPPING THEM!!
ALL'S WELL THAT ENDS WELL, BUT STILL!!
SMACK!
I SAID IT WAS TOO CROWDED!
OUCH!
I'M AN IDIOT...!!
KUROKO'S TRUE TALENT HAS ALWAYS BEEN HIS PASSING!!
BE-SIDES...
ADDING KUROKO TO THEIR ALREADY QUICK-PACED PASSING ATTACK REALLY CHANGES THINGS.
IT'S LIKE THEIR PLAYS HAVE BEEN KICKED INTO A HIGHER GEAR!

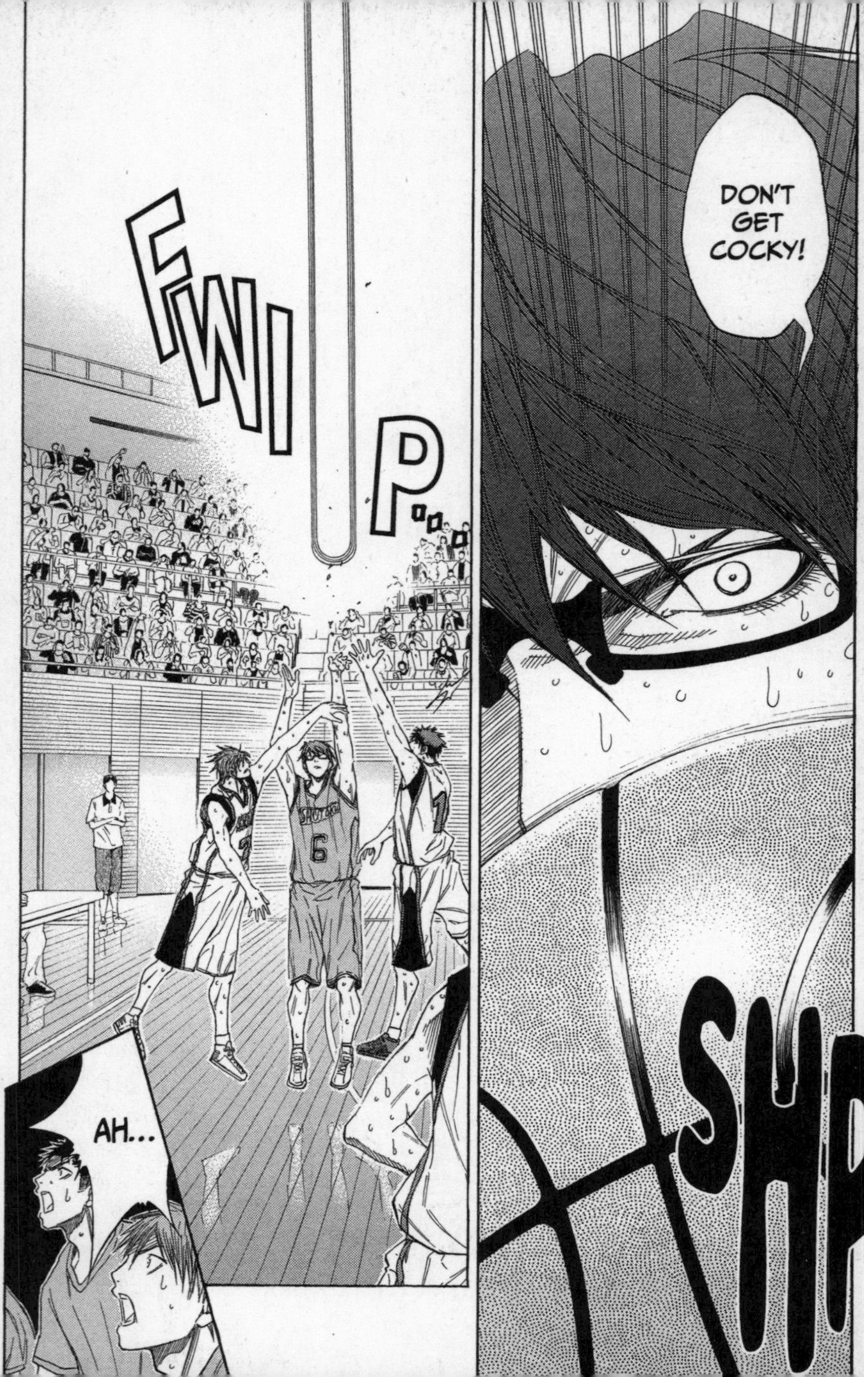
DON'T GET COCKY!
SHP
FWIP
P...
AH...

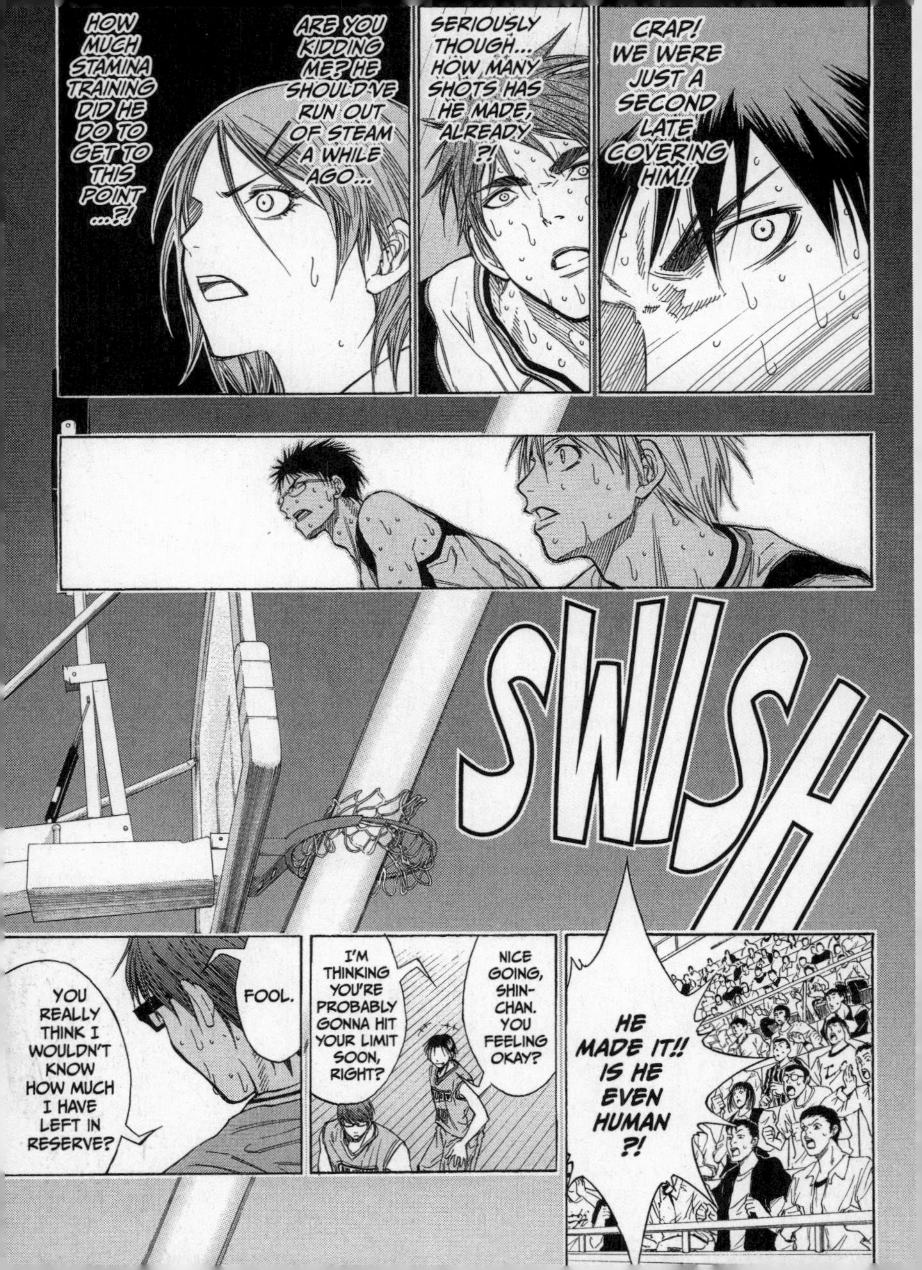
CRAP! WE WERE JUST A SECOND LATE COVERING HIM!!
SERIOUSLY THOUGH... HOW MANY SHOTS HAS HE MADE, ALREADY ?!
ARE YOU KIDDING ME? HE SHOULD'VE RUN OUT OF STEAM A WHILE AGO...
HOW MUCH STAMINA TRAINING DID HE DO TO GET TO THIS POINT ...?!
SWISH
HE MADE IT!! IS HE EVEN HUMAN ?!
NICE GOING, SHIN-CHAN. YOU FEELING OKAY?
I'M THINKING YOU'RE PROBABLY GONNA HIT YOUR LIMIT SOON, RIGHT?
FOOL.
YOU REALLY THINK I WOULDN'T KNOW HOW MUCH I HAVE LEFT IN RESERVE?

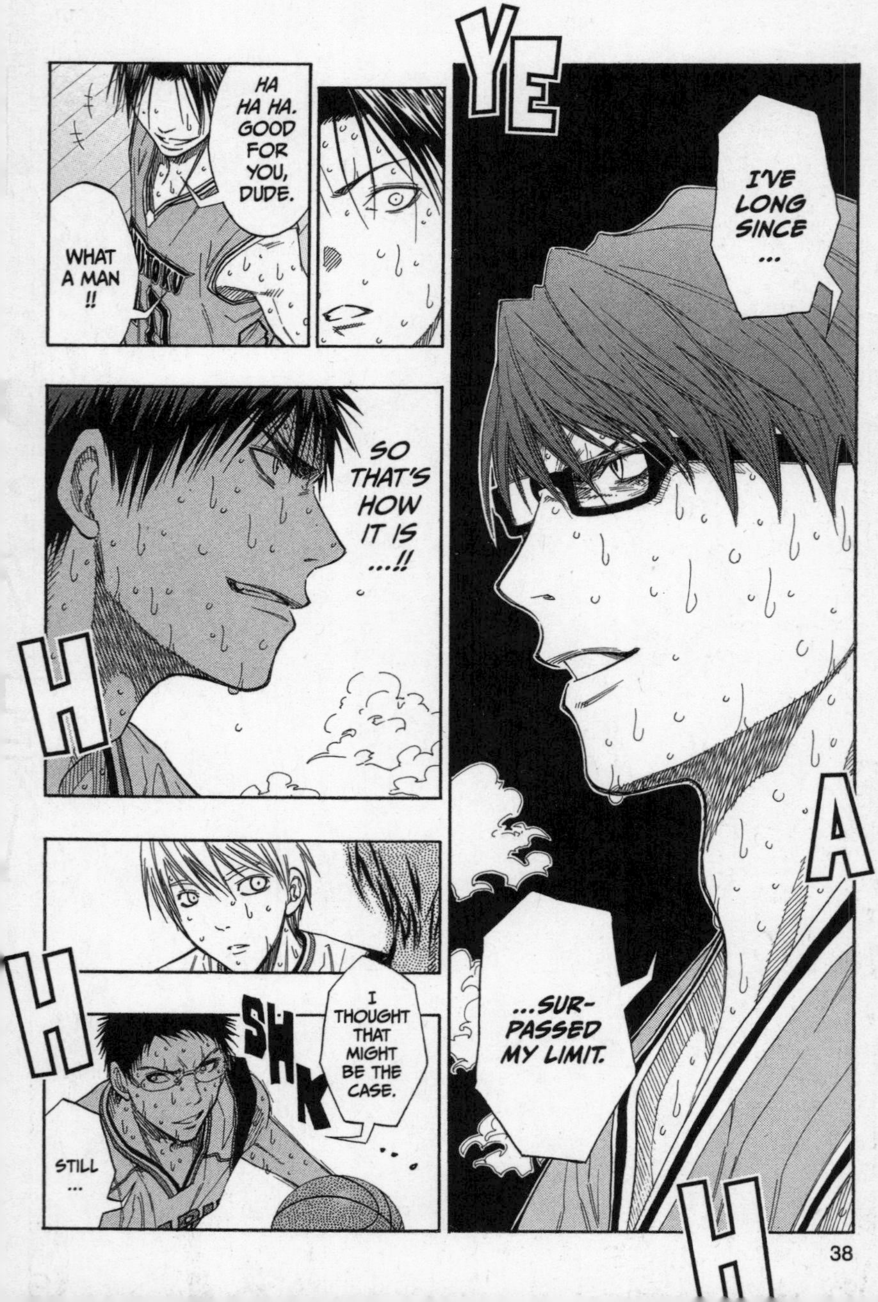

YE
I'VE LONG SINCE ...
A
...SUR-PASSED MY LIMIT.
H
HA HA HA. GOOD FOR YOU, DUDE.
WHAT A MAN !!
SO THAT'S HOW IT IS ...!!
H
H
I THOUGHT THAT MIGHT BE THE CASE.
SHK
STILL ...

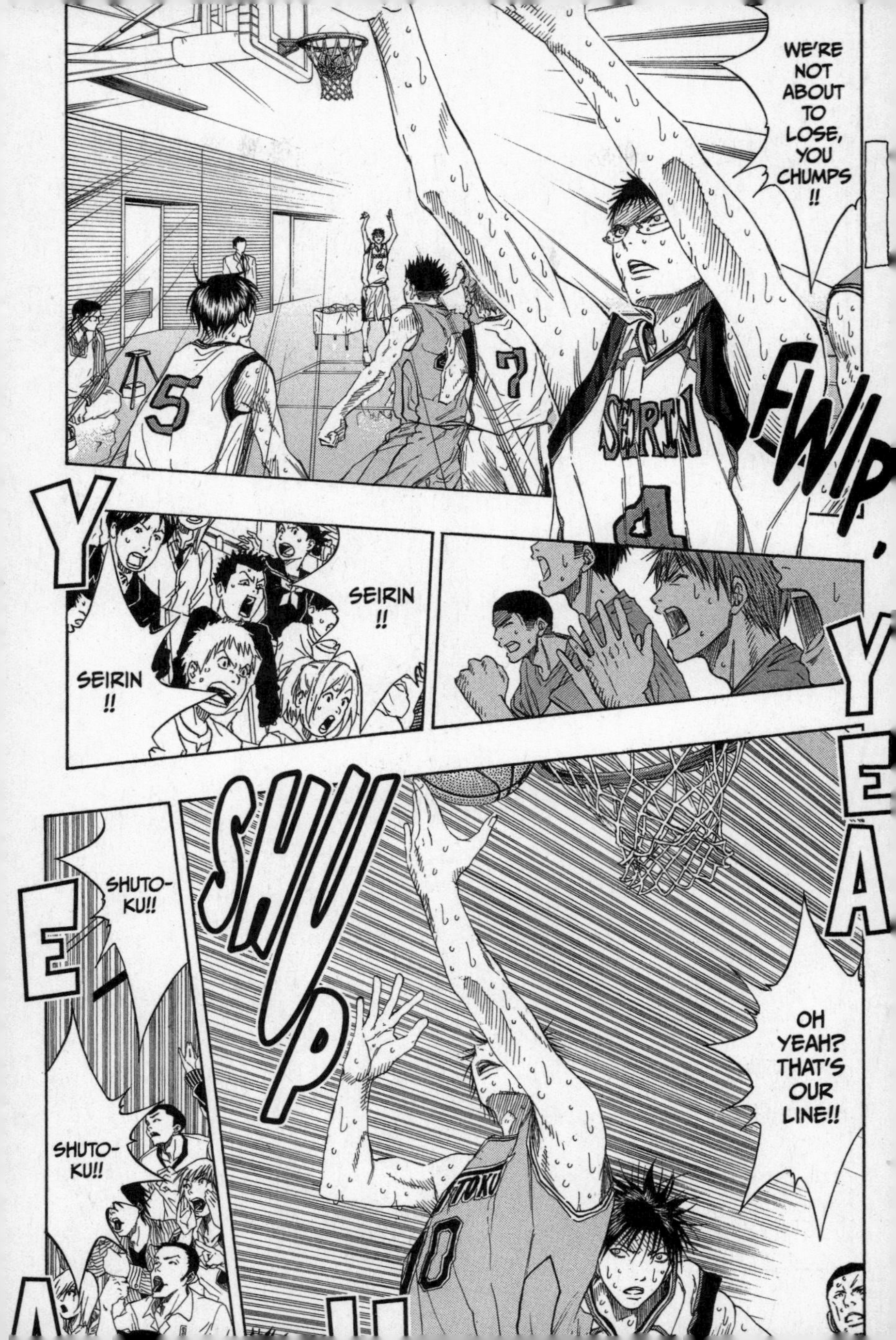
WE'RE NOT ABOUT TO LOSE, YOU CHUMPS!!
FWIP
YEA
SEIRIN!!
SEIRIN!!
Y
OH YEAH? THAT'S OUR LINE!!
SHUP
SHUTO-KU!!
E
SHUTO-KU!!

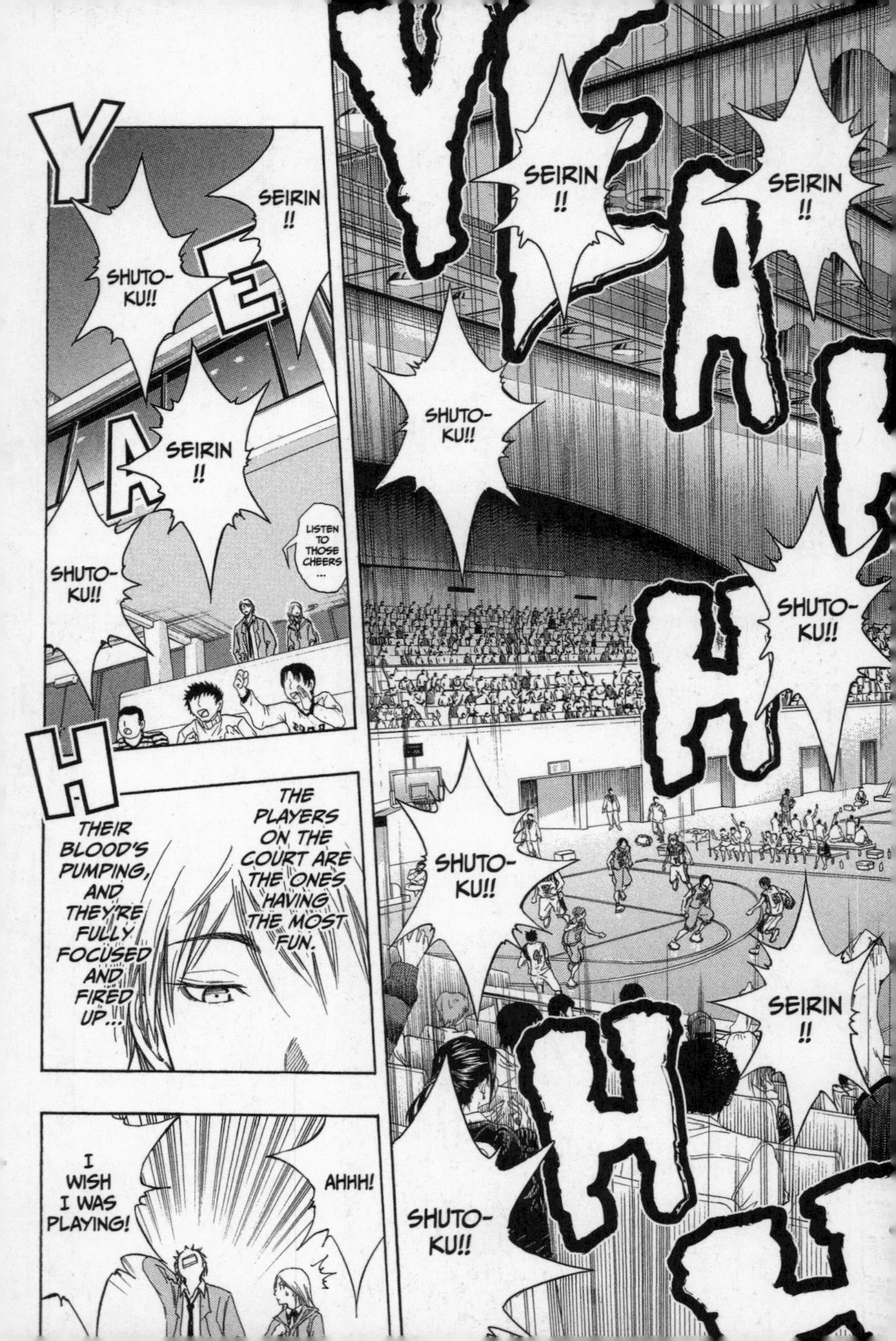
SEIRIN !!
SEIRIN !!
SHUTO-KU!!
SHUTO-KU!!
SHUTO-KU!!
SEIRIN !!
SHUTO-KU!!
SEIRIN !!
SHUTO-KU!!
SEIRIN !!
LISTEN TO THOSE CHEERS ...
SHUTO-KU!!
THE PLAYERS ON THE COURT ARE THE ONES HAVING THE MOST FUN.
THEIR BLOOD'S PUMPING, AND THEY'RE FULLY FOCUSED AND FIRED UP...
AHHH!
I WISH I WAS PLAYING!

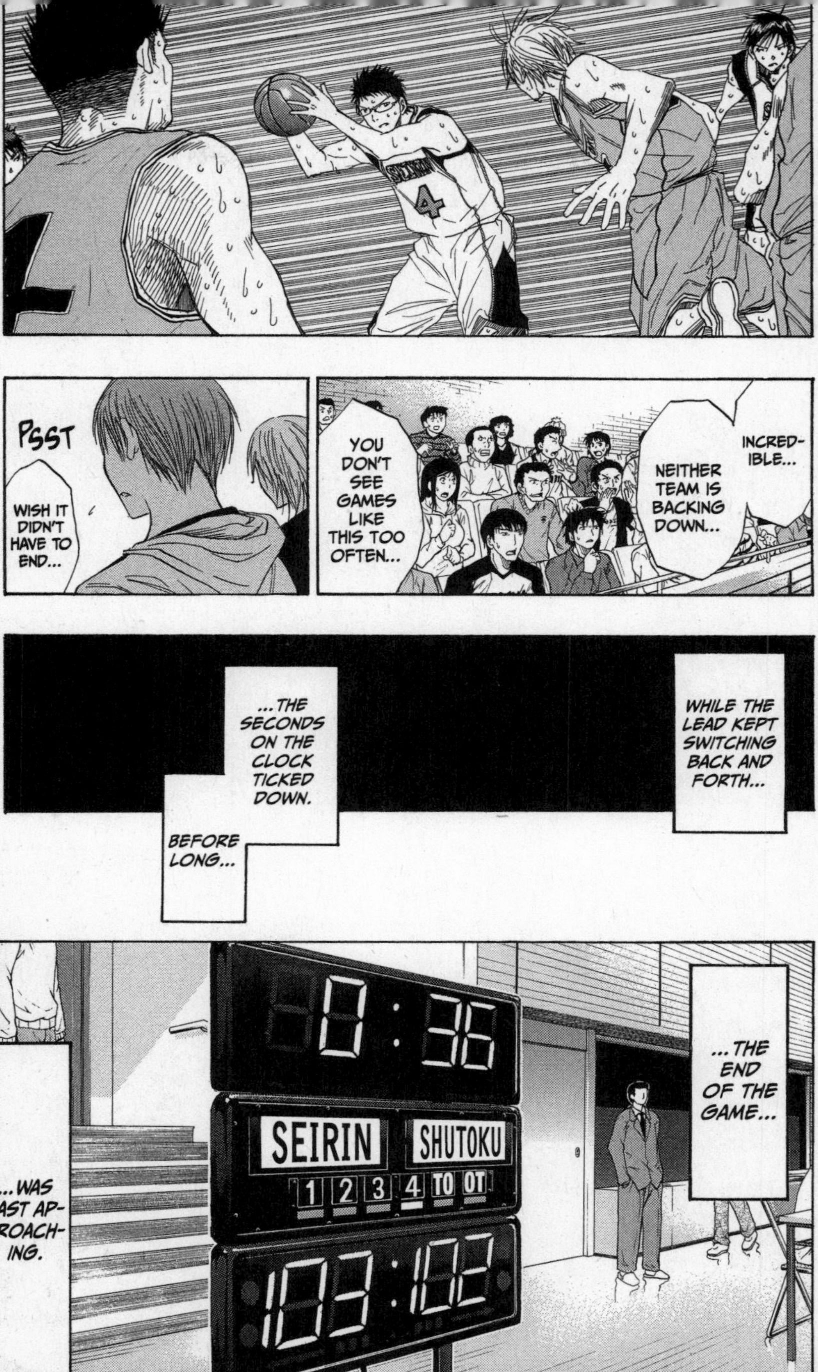
INCRED-IBLE...
NEITHER TEAM IS BACKING DOWN...
YOU DON'T SEE GAMES LIKE THIS TOO OFTEN...
PSST
WISH IT DIDN'T HAVE TO END...
WHILE THE LEAD KEPT SWITCHING BACK AND FORTH...
...THE SECONDS ON THE CLOCK TICKED DOWN.
BEFORE LONG...
...THE END OF THE GAME...
SEIRIN
SHUTOKU
1 2 3 4 TO OT
...WAS FAST AP-PROACH-ING.

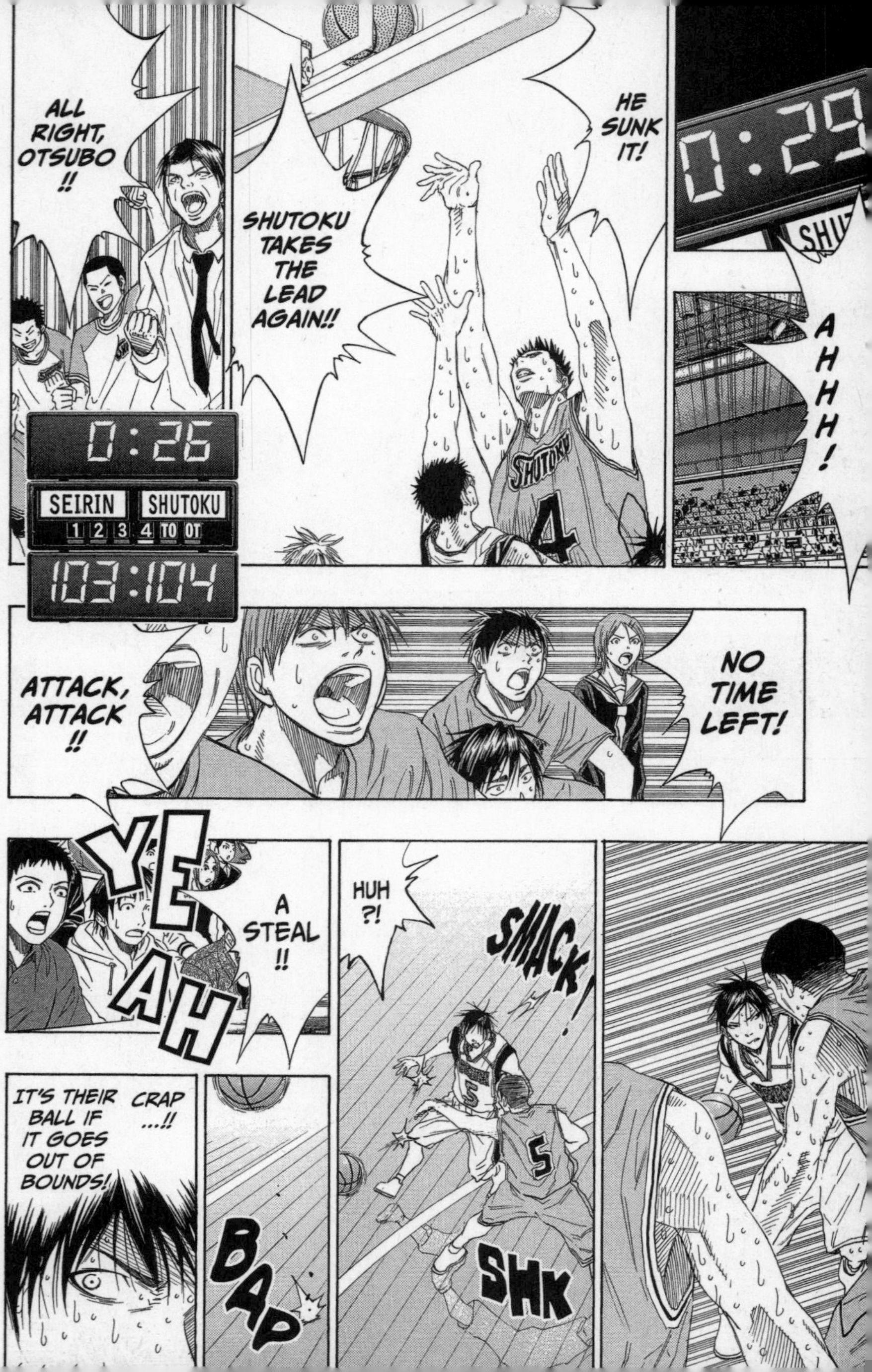
0:29
SHU
AHHHH!
HE SUNK IT!
SHUTOKU TAKES THE LEAD AGAIN!!
ALL RIGHT, OTSUBO!!
0:26
SEIRIN SHUTOKU
1 2 3 4 TO OT
103:104
NO TIME LEFT!
ATTACK, ATTACK!!
SMACK!
HUH?!
A STEAL!!
YEAH
SHK
BAP
CRAP...!!
IT'S THEIR BALL IF IT GOES OUT OF BOUNDS!

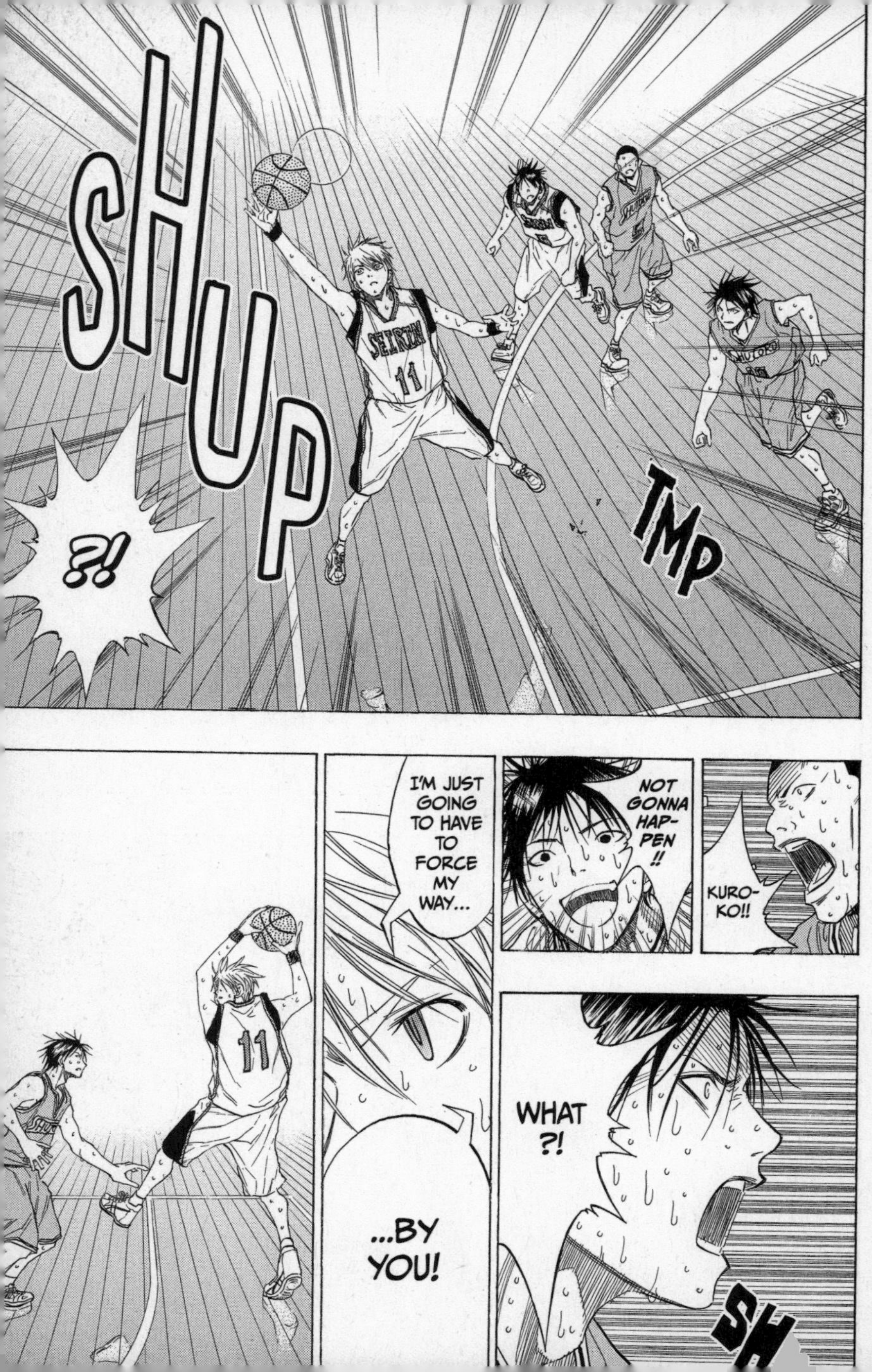
SHUP
TMP
?!
KURO-KO!!
NOT GONNA HAP-PEN!!
WHAT?!
SH
I'M JUST GOING TO HAVE TO FORCE MY WAY...
...BY YOU!

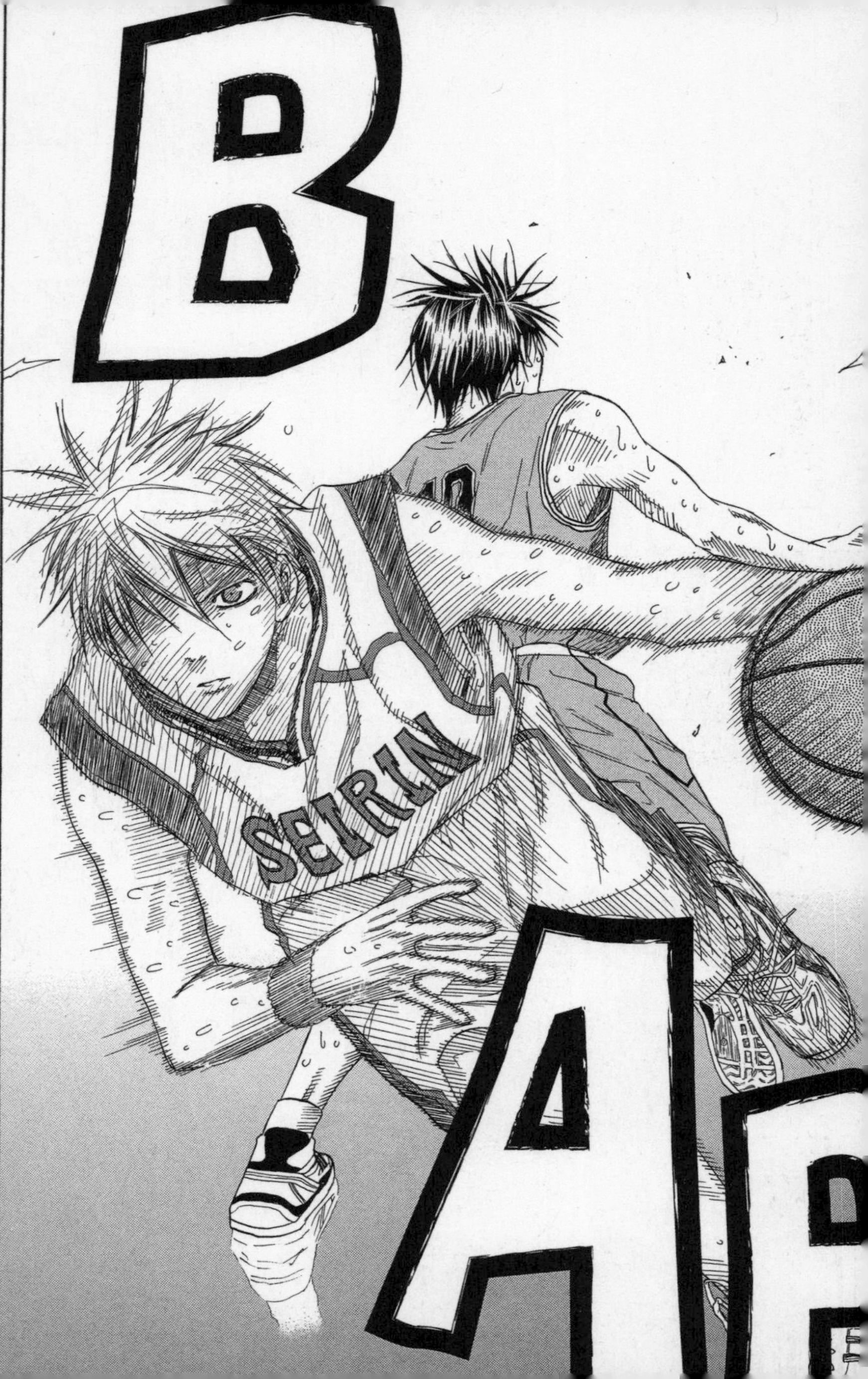
B
A
SEIRIN

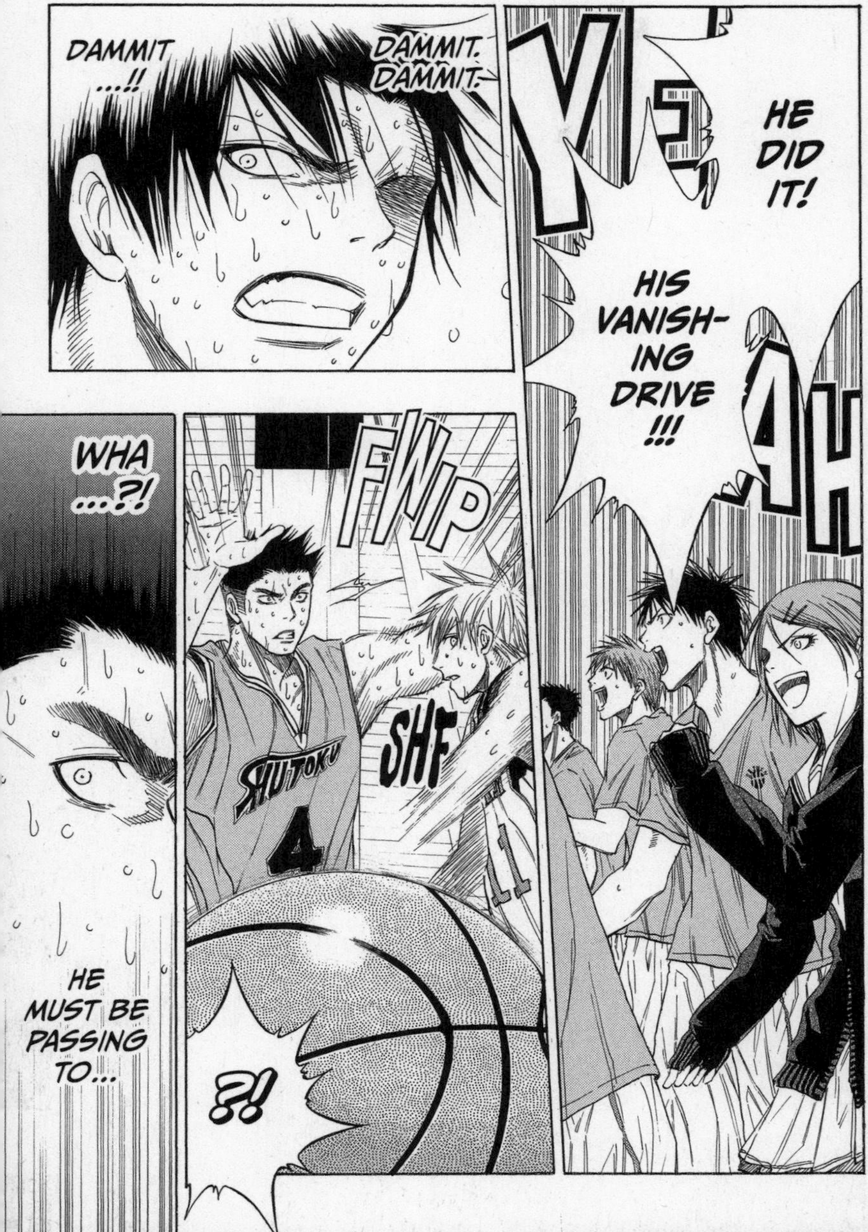
HE DID IT!
HIS VANISH-ING DRIVE !!!
AH
DAMMIT. DAMMIT.
DAMMIT ...!!
FWIP
SHF
?!
WHA ...?!
HE MUST BE PASSING TO...

KUROKO'S BASKETBALL BLOOPERS

TAKE 8

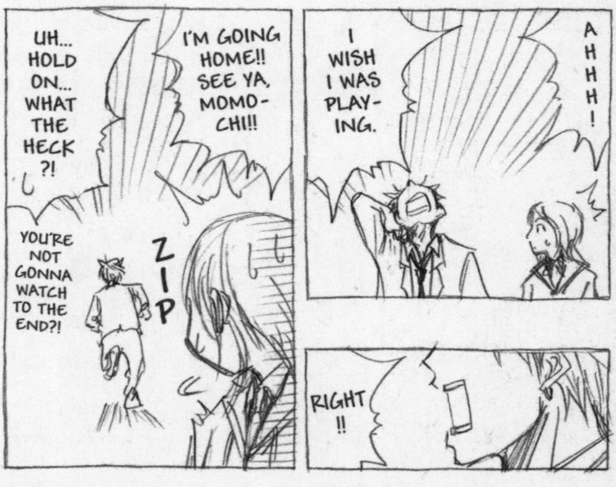
I WISH I WAS PLAY-ING.
AHHH!
RIGHT !!
I'M GOING HOME!! SEE YA, MOMO-CHI!!
UH... HOLD ON... WHAT THE HECK ?!
ZIP
YOU'RE NOT GONNA WATCH TO THE END?!

92ND QUARTER: TIME'S UP

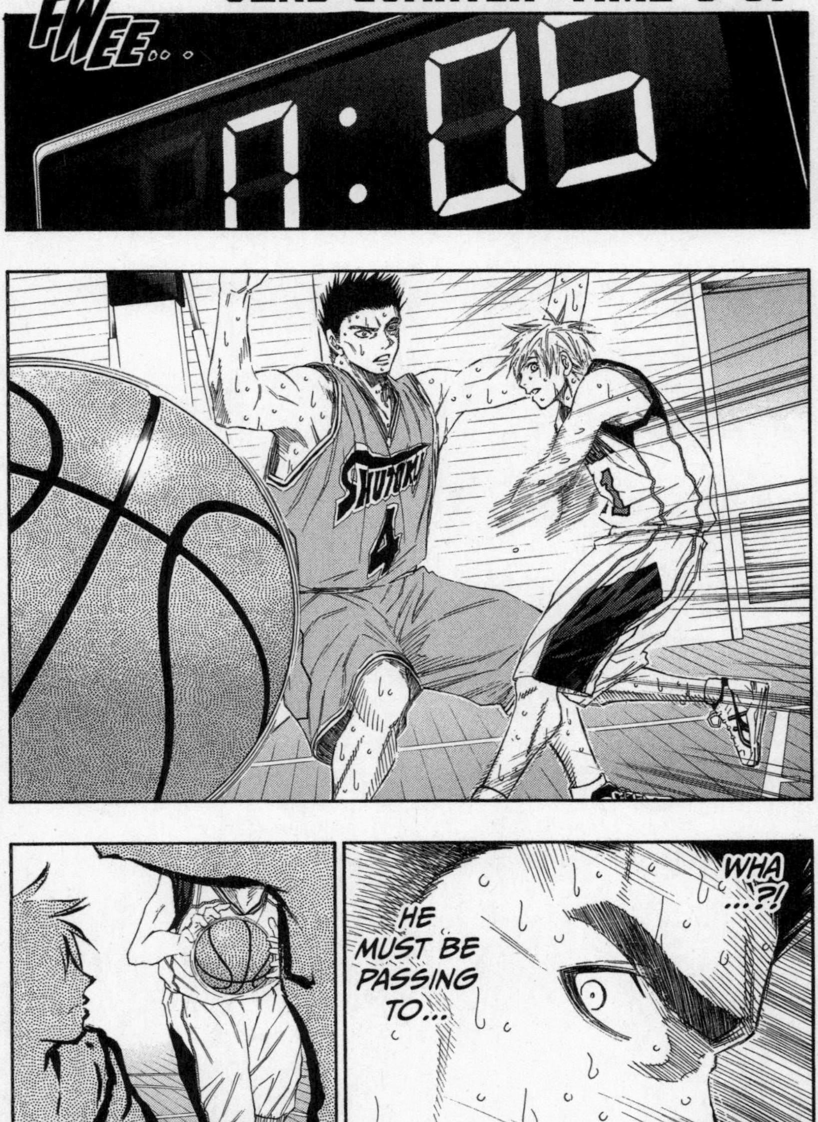
FWEE...
WHA...?!
HE MUST BE PASSING TO...

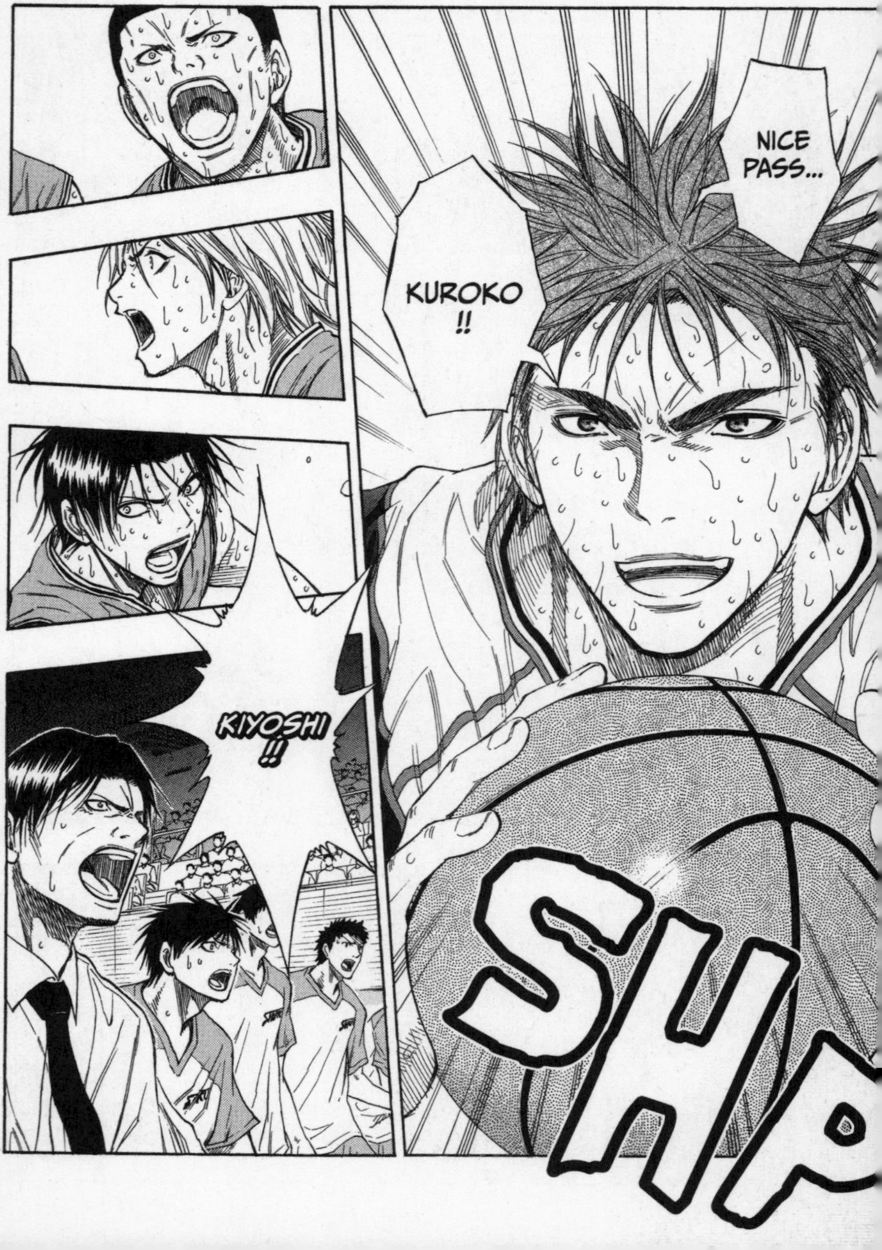
NICE PASS...
KUROKO !!
SHIP
KIYOSHI !!

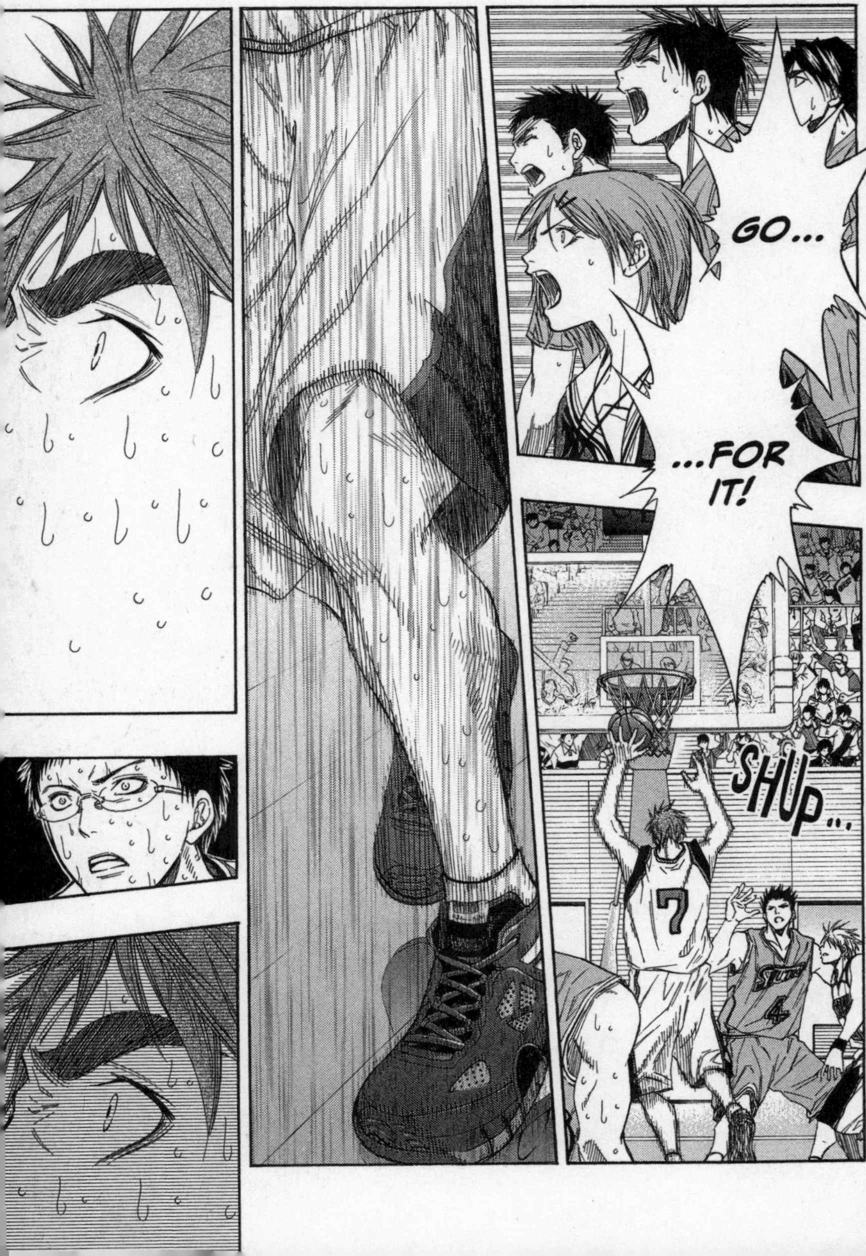
GO...
...FOR IT!
SHUP...

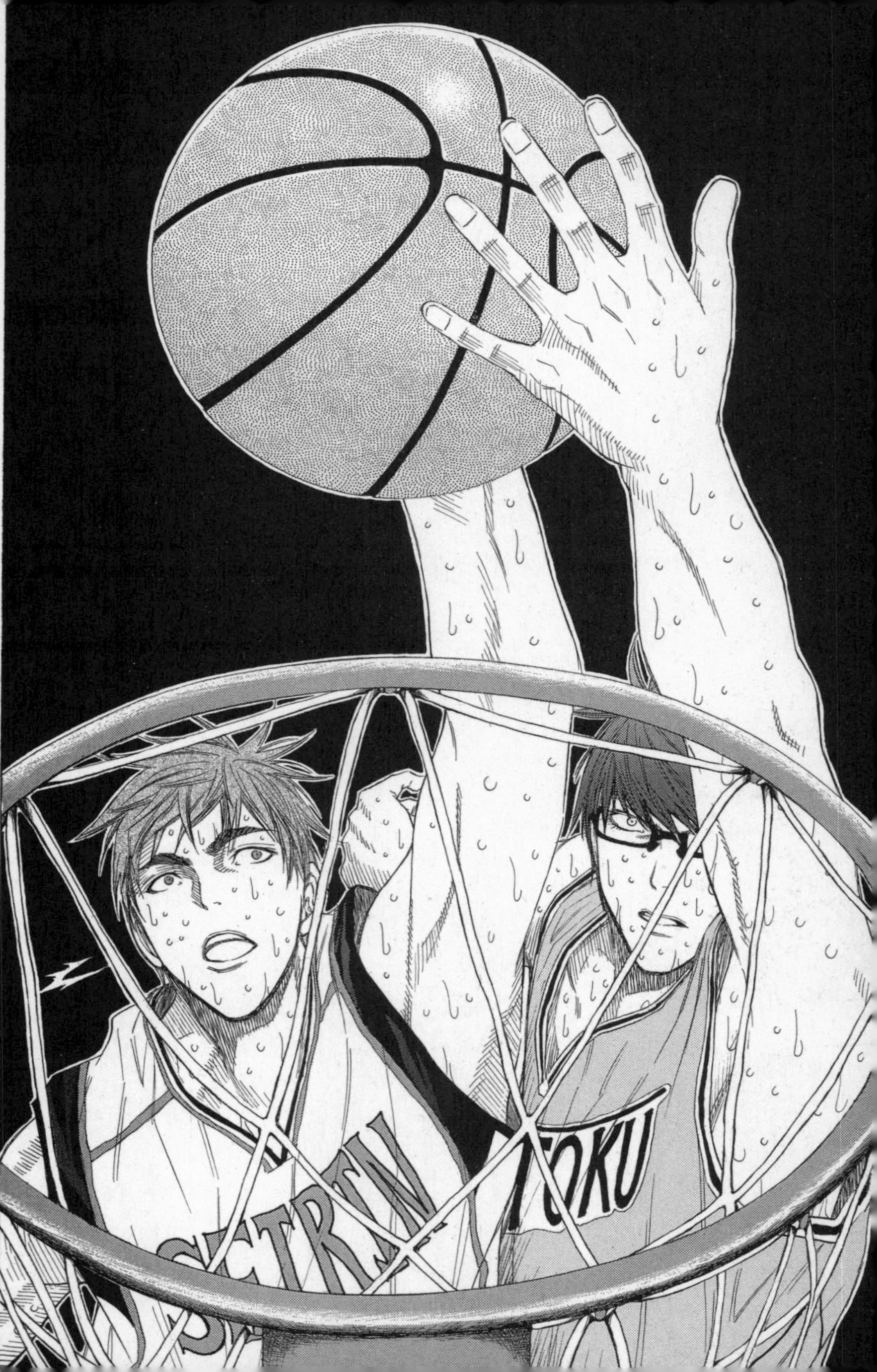

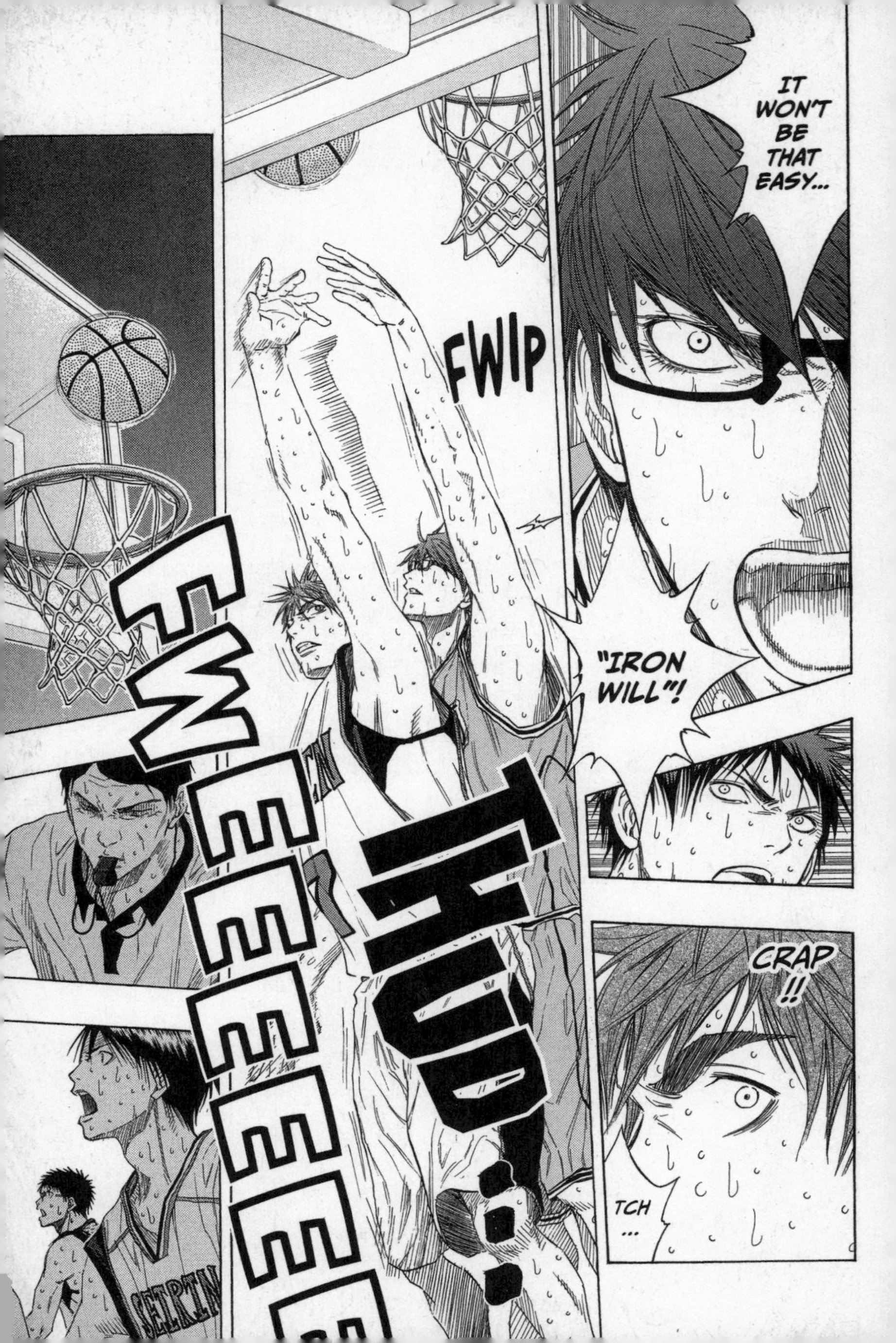
IT WON'T BE THAT EASY...
"IRON WILL"!
CRAP!!
TCH...
FWIP
THUD
FWEEEEEEE

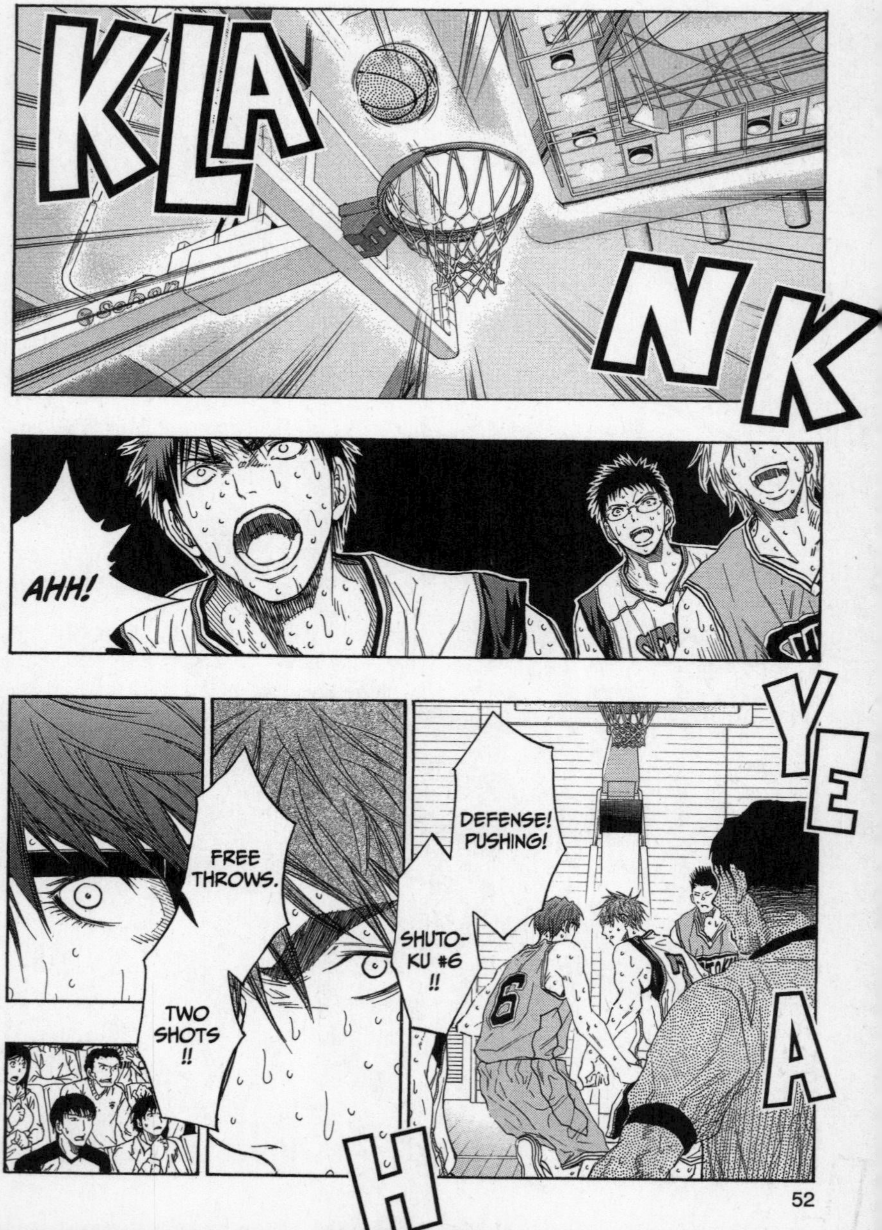
KLANK
AHH!
YEAH
DEFENSE! PUSHING!
SHUTO-KU #6 !!
FREE THROWS.
TWO SHOTS !!

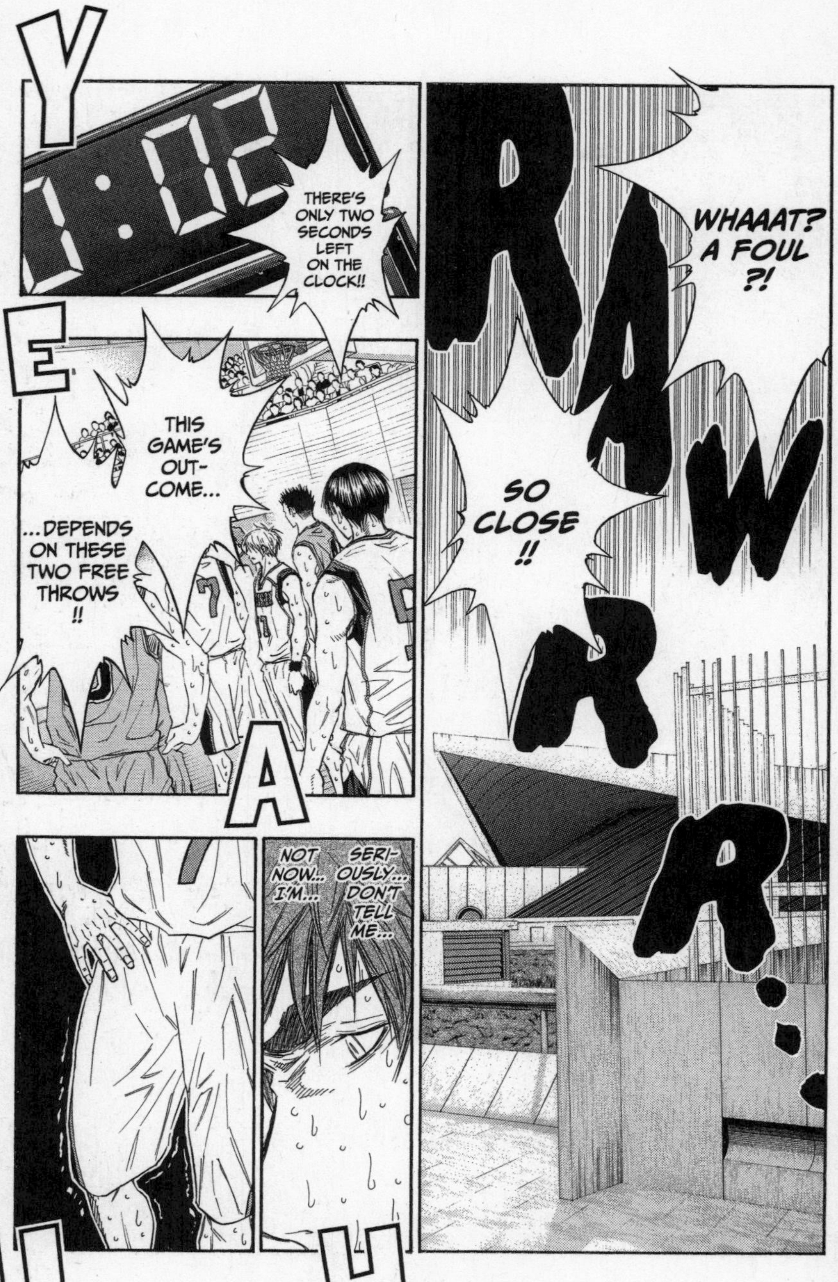
RAAWRRR
WHAAAT? A FOUL ?!
SO CLOSE !!
YEAHH
1:02
THERE'S ONLY TWO SECONDS LEFT ON THE CLOCK!!
THIS GAME'S OUT-COME...
...DEPENDS ON THESE TWO FREE THROWS !!
SERI-OUSLY... DON'T TELL ME...
NOT NOW... I'M...

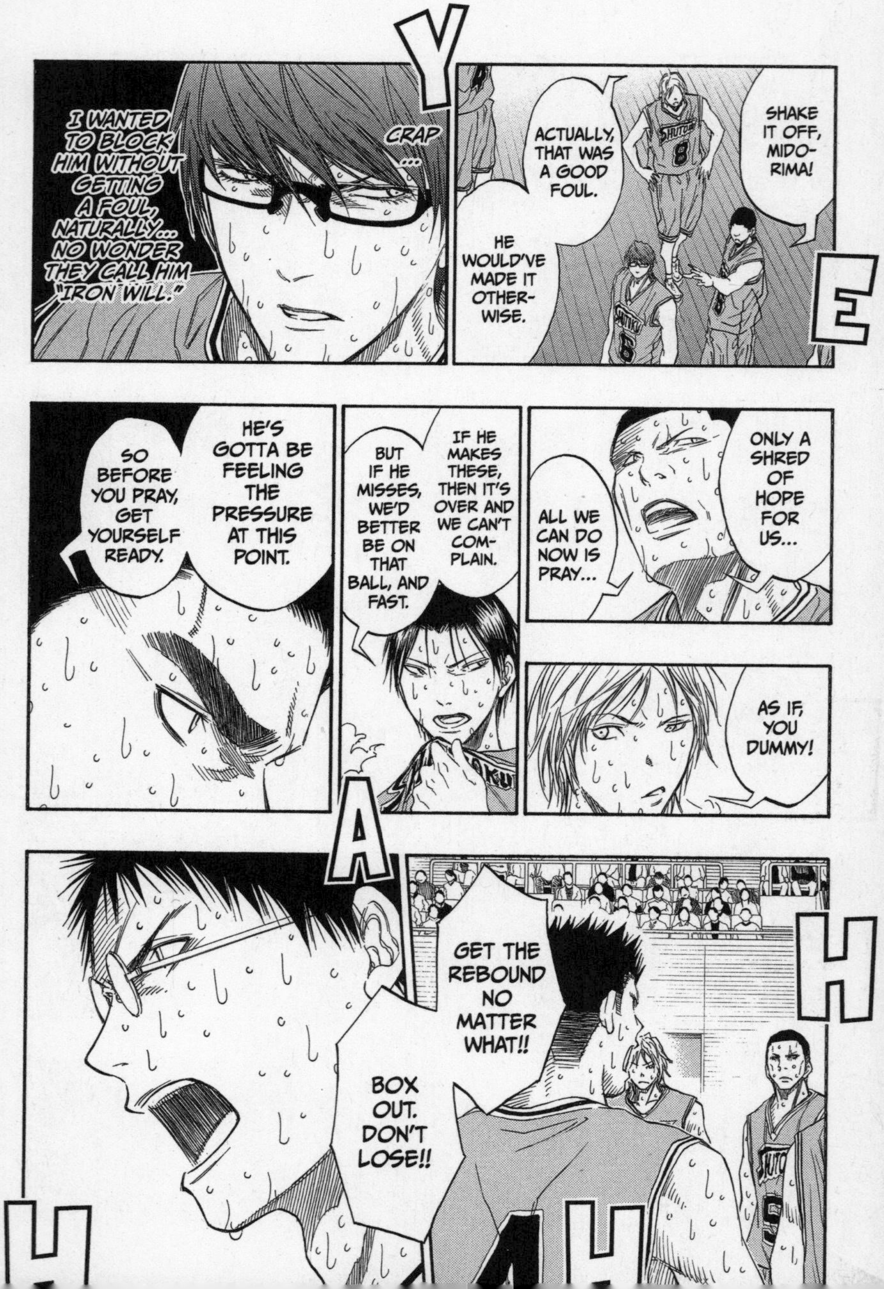
SHAKE IT OFF, MIDORIMA!
ACTUALLY, THAT WAS A GOOD FOUL.
HE WOULD'VE MADE IT OTHERWISE.
CRAP...
I WANTED TO BLOCK HIM WITHOUT GETTING A FOUL, NATURALLY... NO WONDER THEY CALL HIM "IRON WILL."
ONLY A SHRED OF HOPE FOR US...
ALL WE CAN DO NOW IS PRAY...
AS IF, YOU DUMMY!
IF HE MAKES THESE, THEN IT'S OVER AND WE CAN'T COMPLAIN.
BUT IF HE MISSES, WE'D BETTER BE ON THAT BALL, AND FAST.
HE'S GOTTA BE FEELING THE PRESSURE AT THIS POINT.
SO BEFORE YOU PRAY, GET YOURSELF READY.
GET THE REBOUND NO MATTER WHAT!!
BOX OUT. DON'T LOSE!!

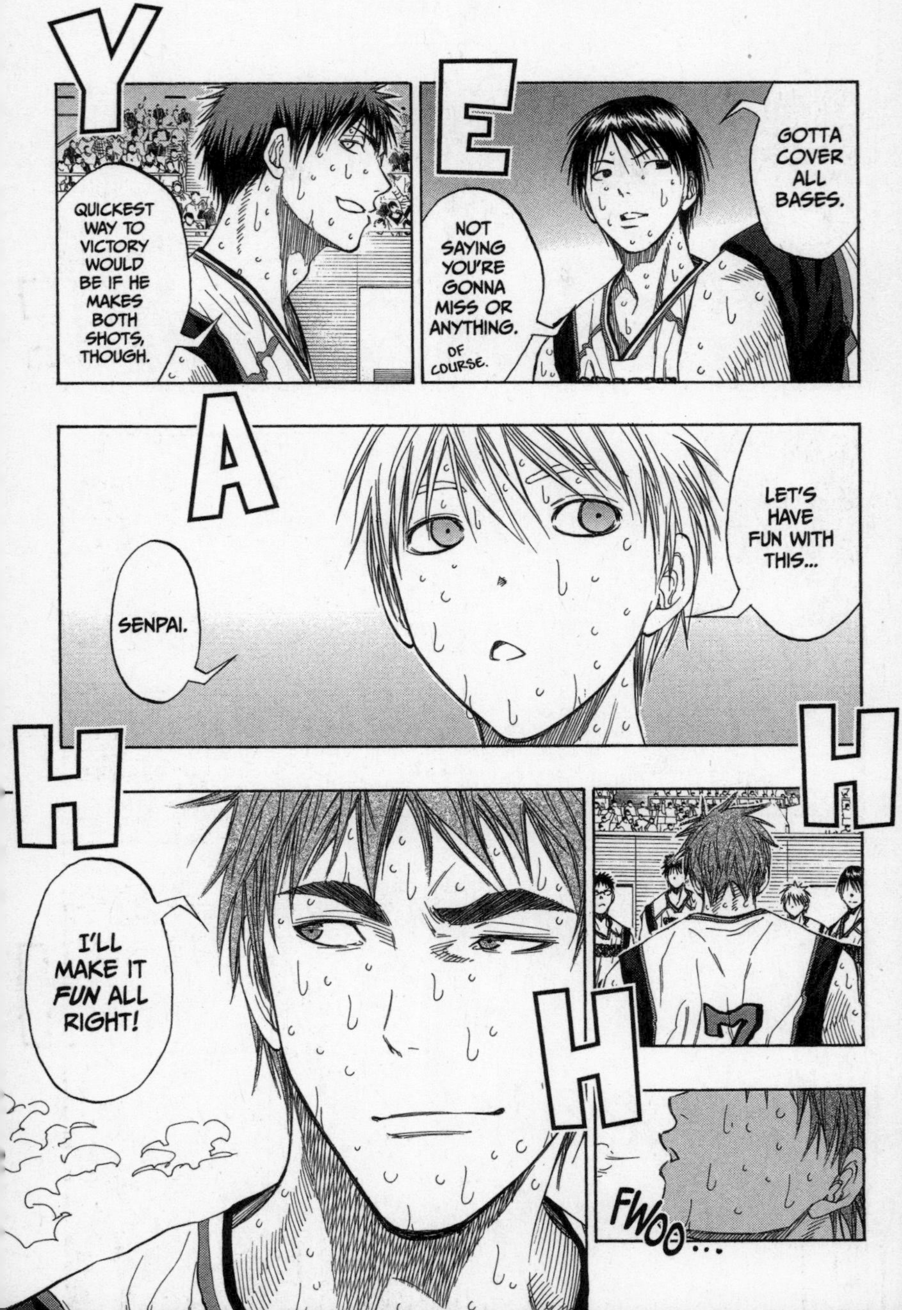

YEAHHH
GOTTA COVER ALL BASES.
NOT SAYING YOU'RE GONNA MISS OR ANYTHING.
OF COURSE.
QUICKEST WAY TO VICTORY WOULD BE IF HE MAKES BOTH SHOTS, THOUGH.
LET'S HAVE FUN WITH THIS...
SENPAI.
I'LL MAKE IT *FUN* ALL RIGHT!
FWOO...

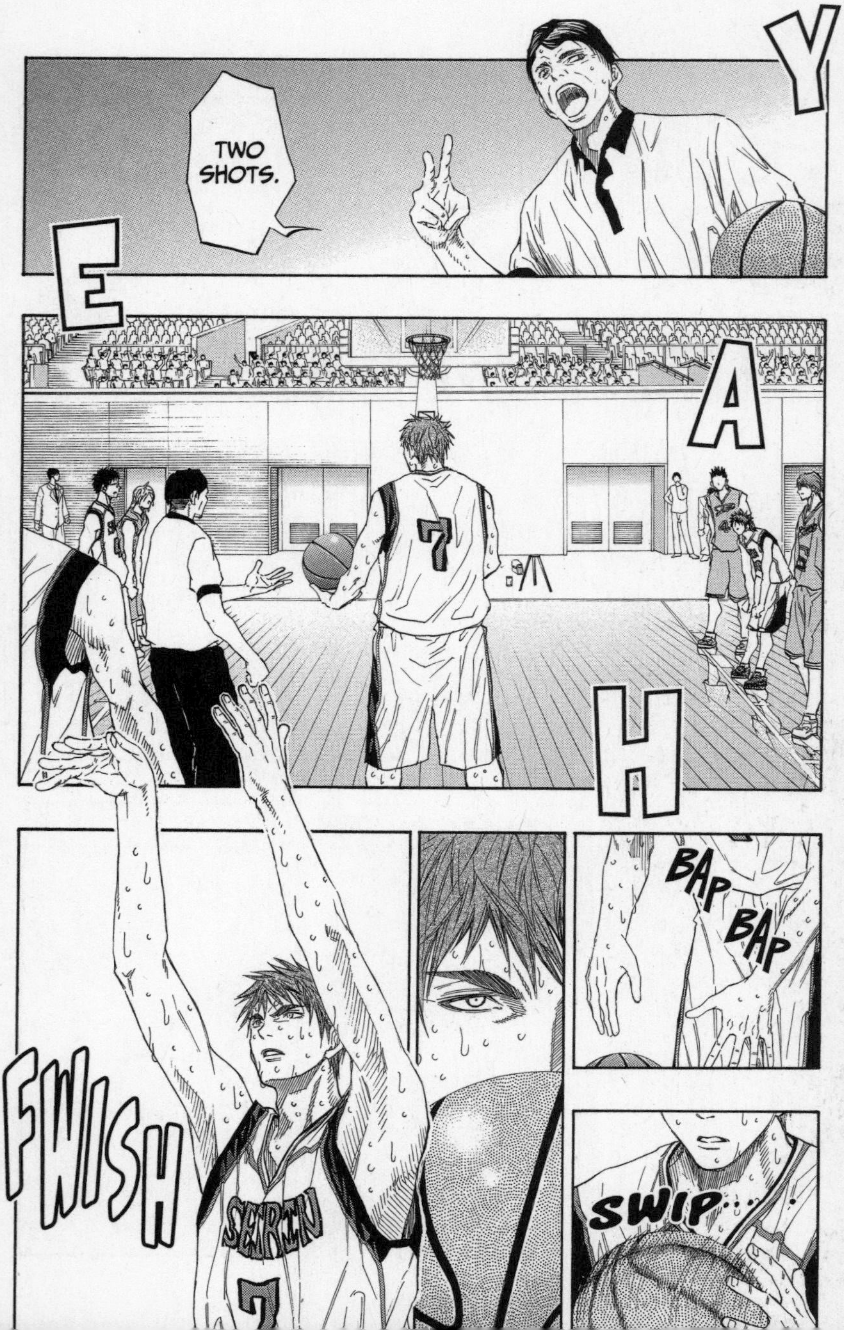

TWO SHOTS.
YEAH
BAP
BAP
SWIP...
FWISH

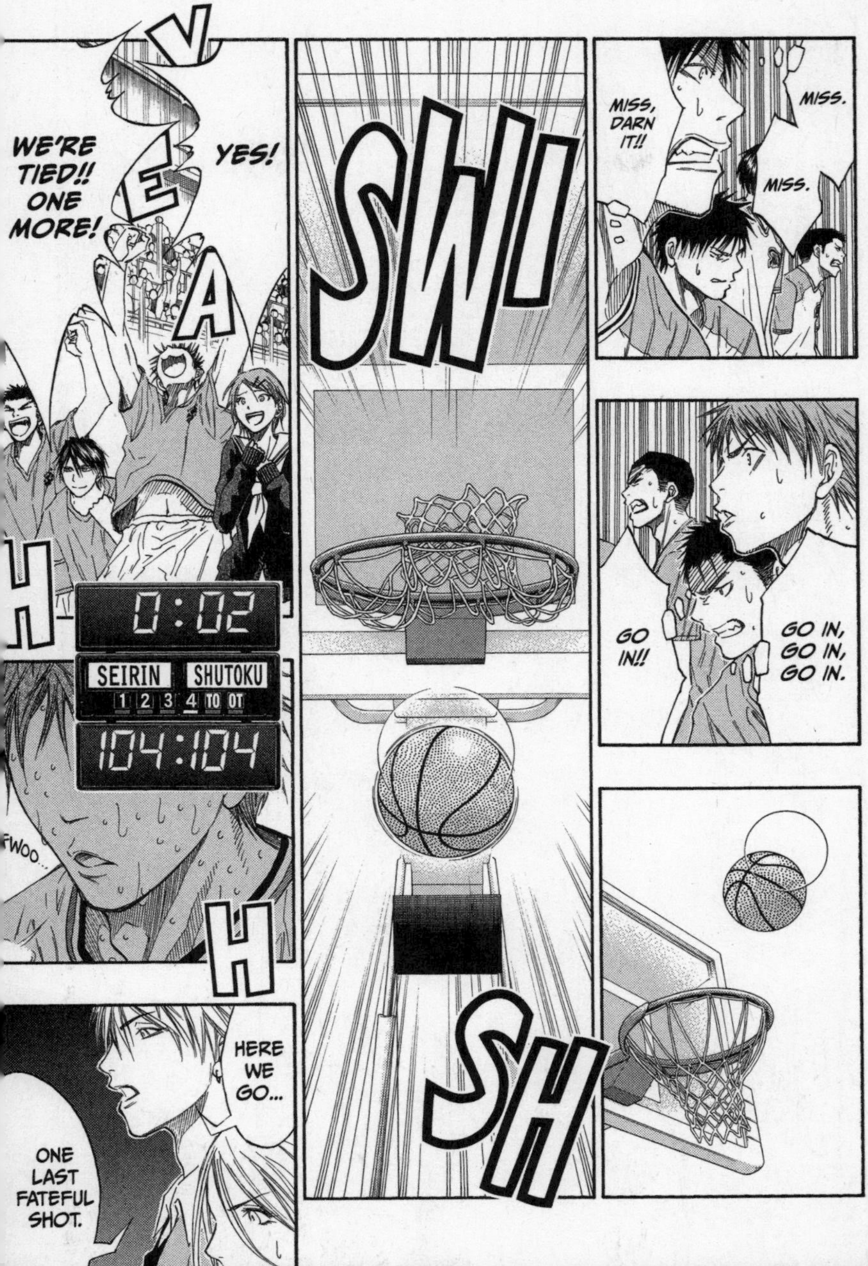
MISS.
MISS, DARN IT!!
MISS.
GO IN, GO IN, GO IN.
GO IN!!
SWI
SH
YES!
WE'RE TIED!! ONE MORE!
V
E
A
H
0:02
SEIRIN
SHUTOKU
1 2 3 4 TO OT
104:104
FWOO...
H
HERE WE GO...
ONE LAST FATEFUL SHOT.

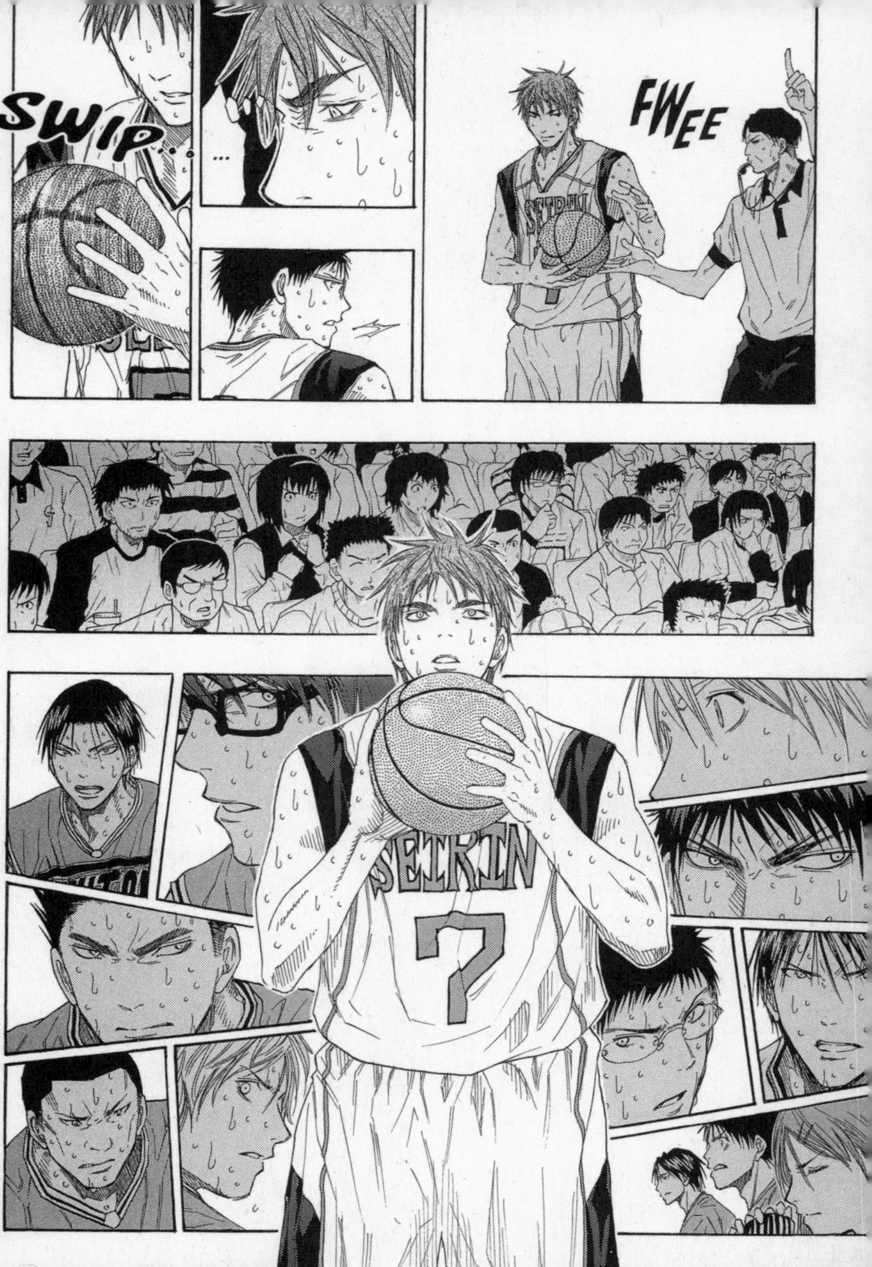
FWEE
...
SWIP...

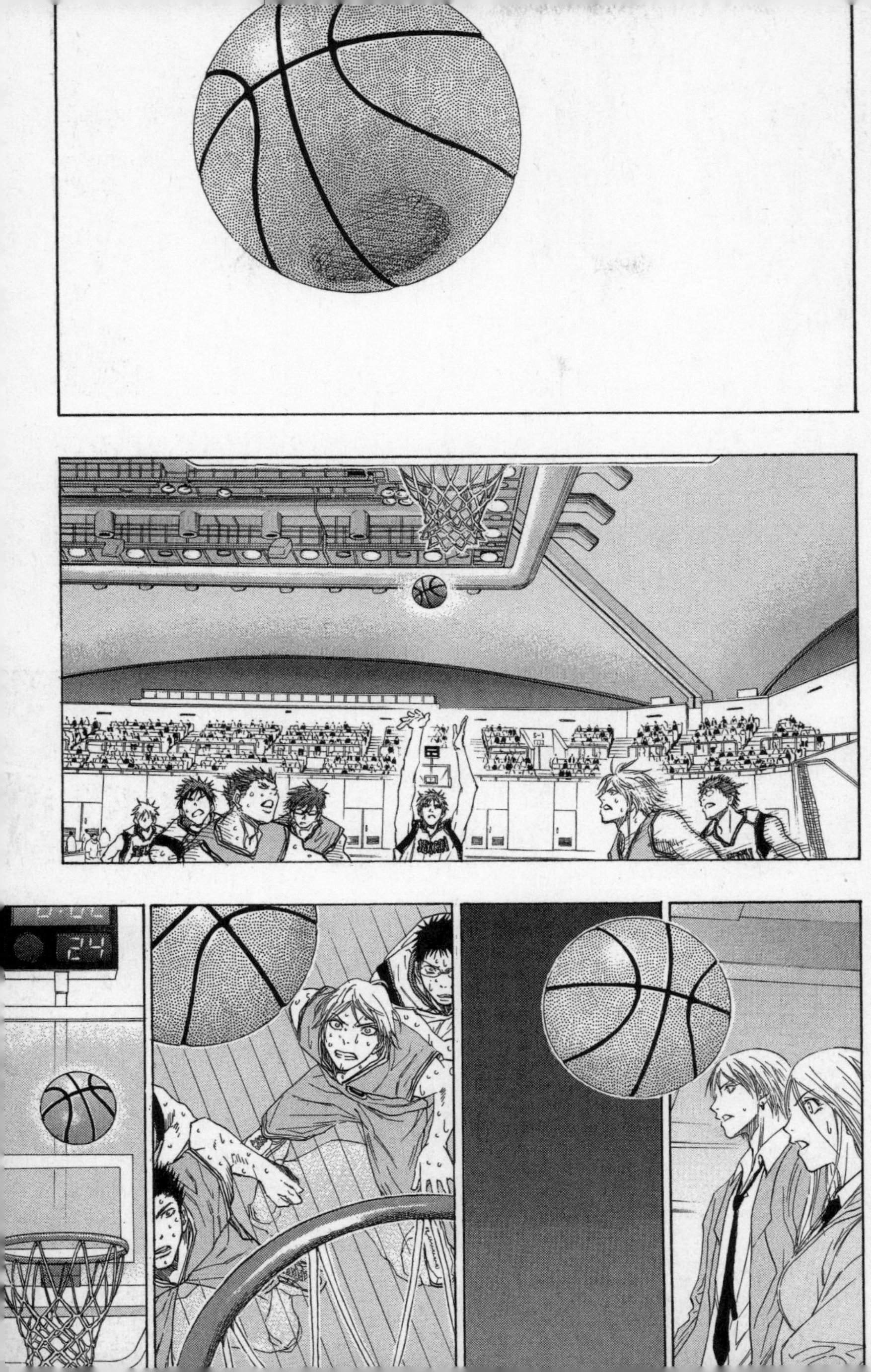
24

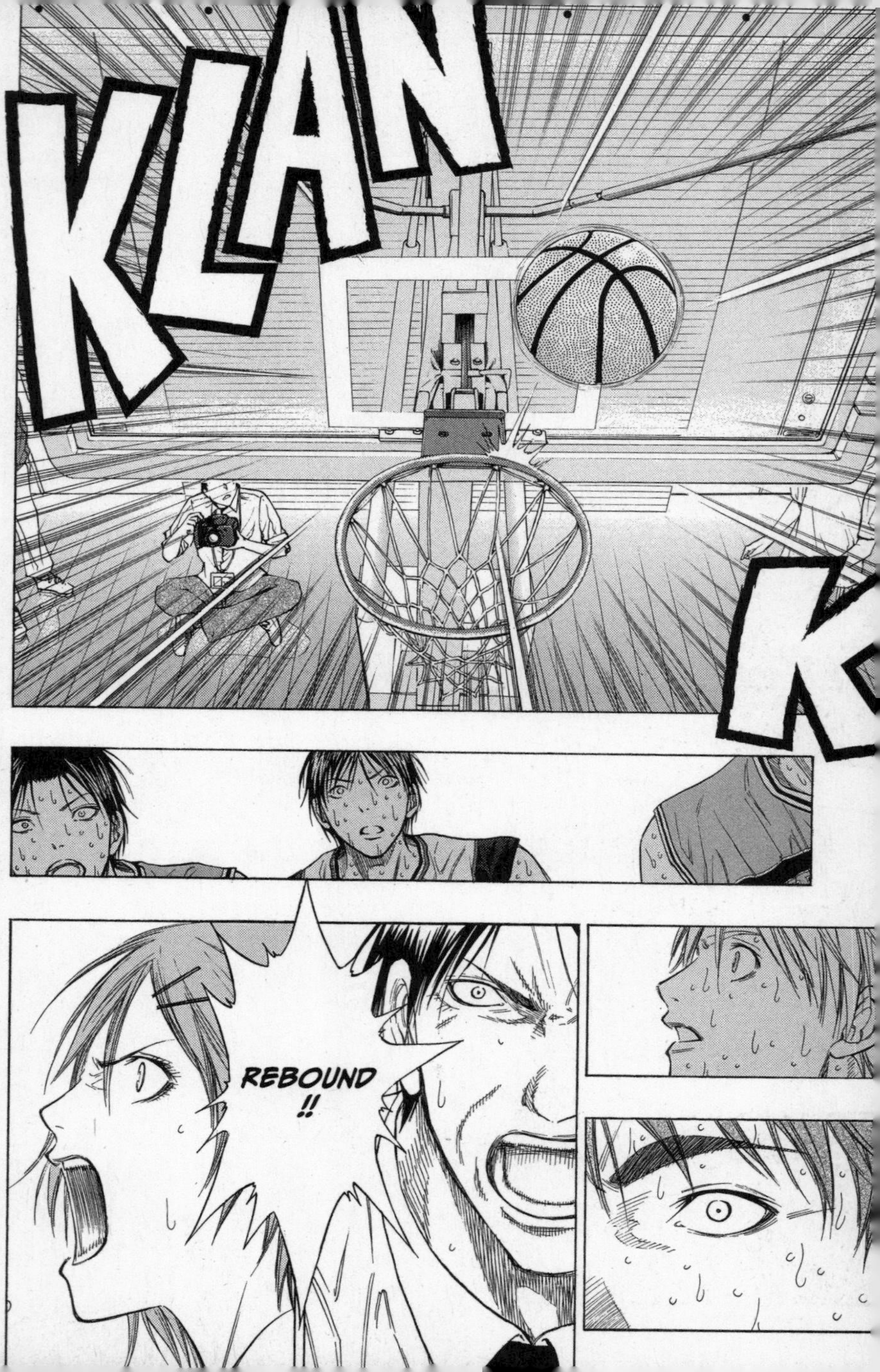
KLAN
K
REBOUND !!

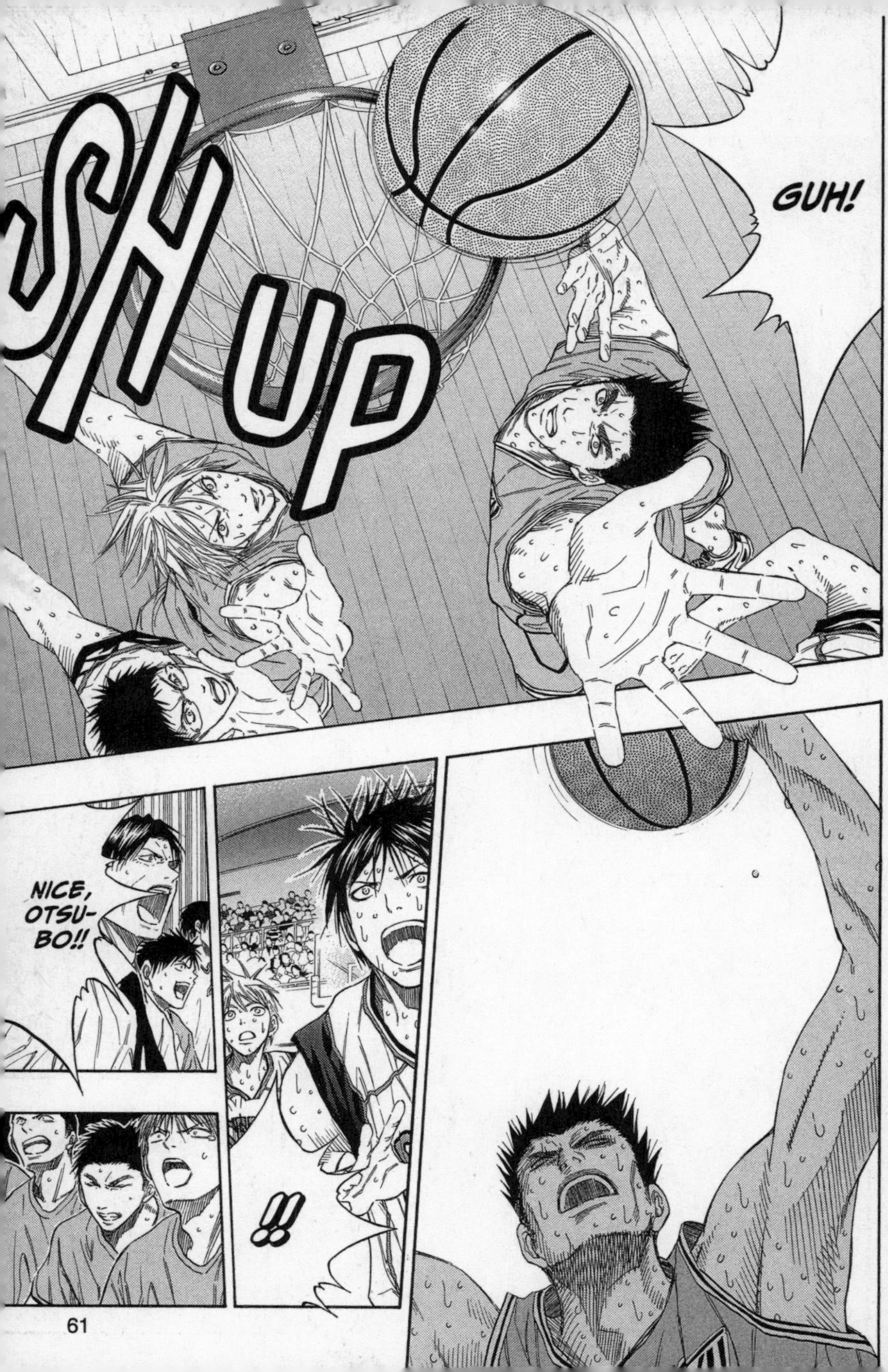
SHUP
GUH!
!!
NICE, OTSU-BO!!

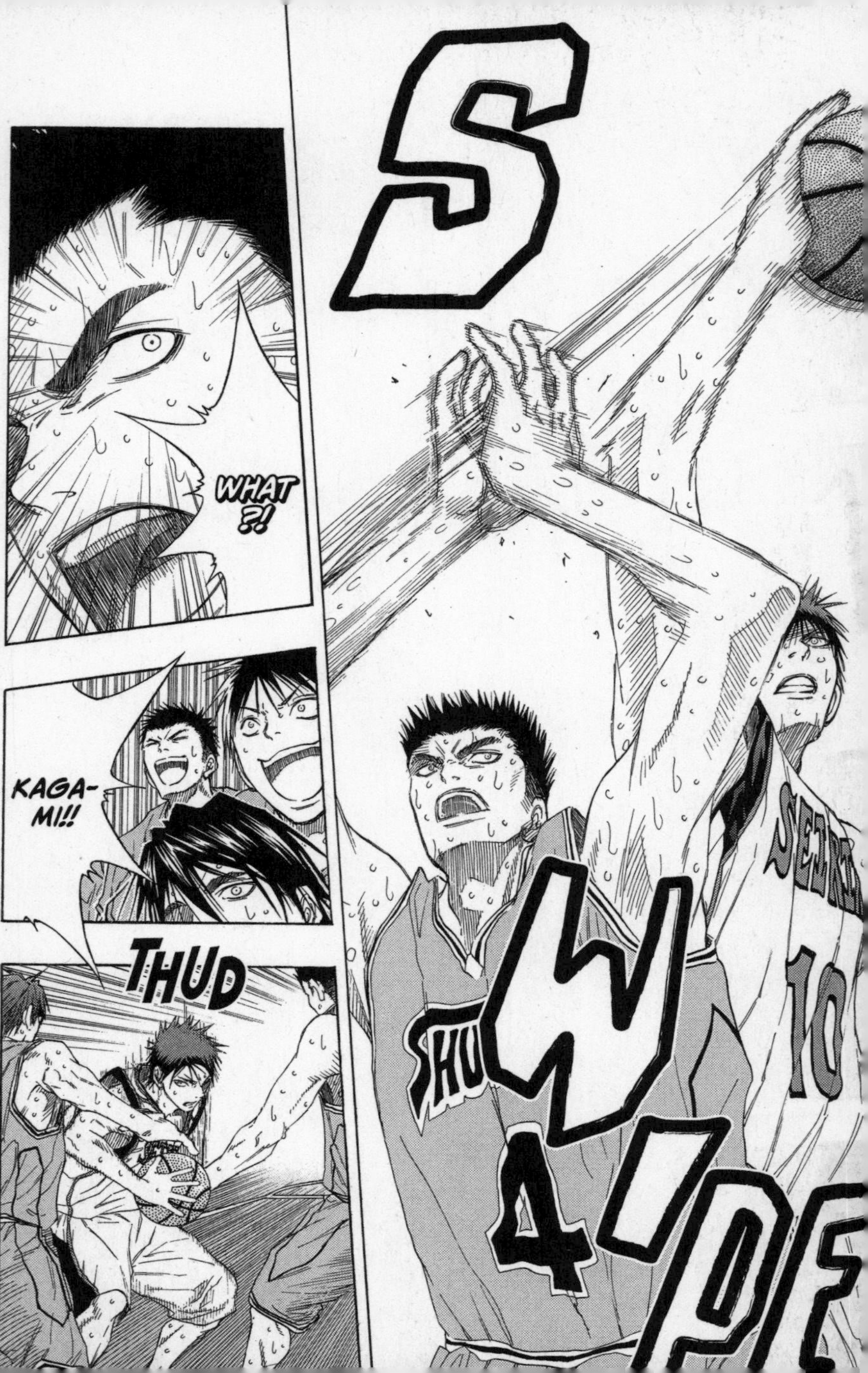
WHAT ?!
KAGA-
MI!!
THUD

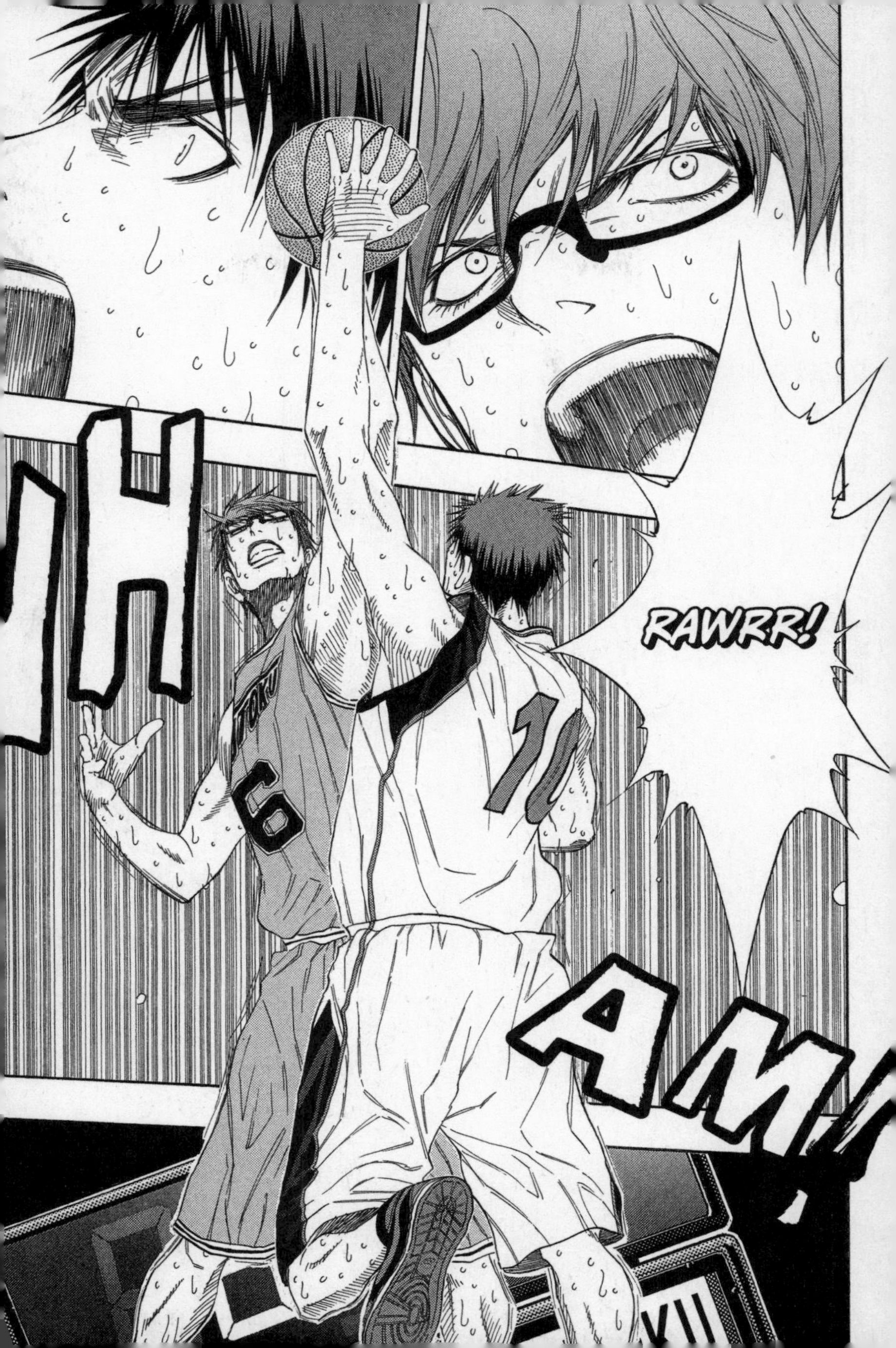
RAWRR!
WH
AM!

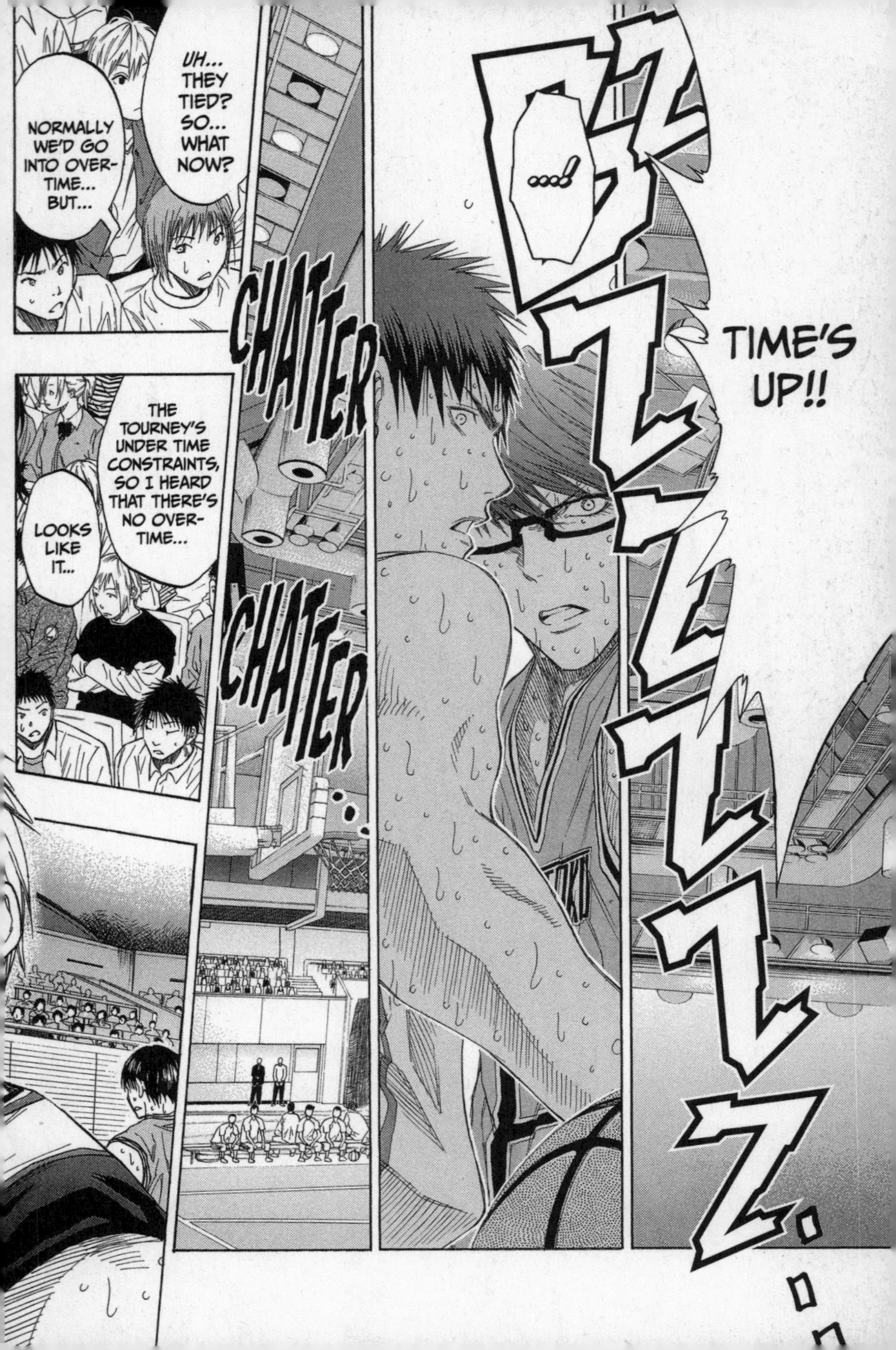
...!
TIME'S UP!!
CHATTER
CHATTER
UH... THEY TIED? SO... WHAT NOW?
NORMALLY WE'D GO INTO OVER-TIME... BUT...
THE TOURNEY'S UNDER TIME CONSTRAINTS, SO I HEARD THAT THERE'S NO OVER-TIME...
LOOKS LIKE IT...

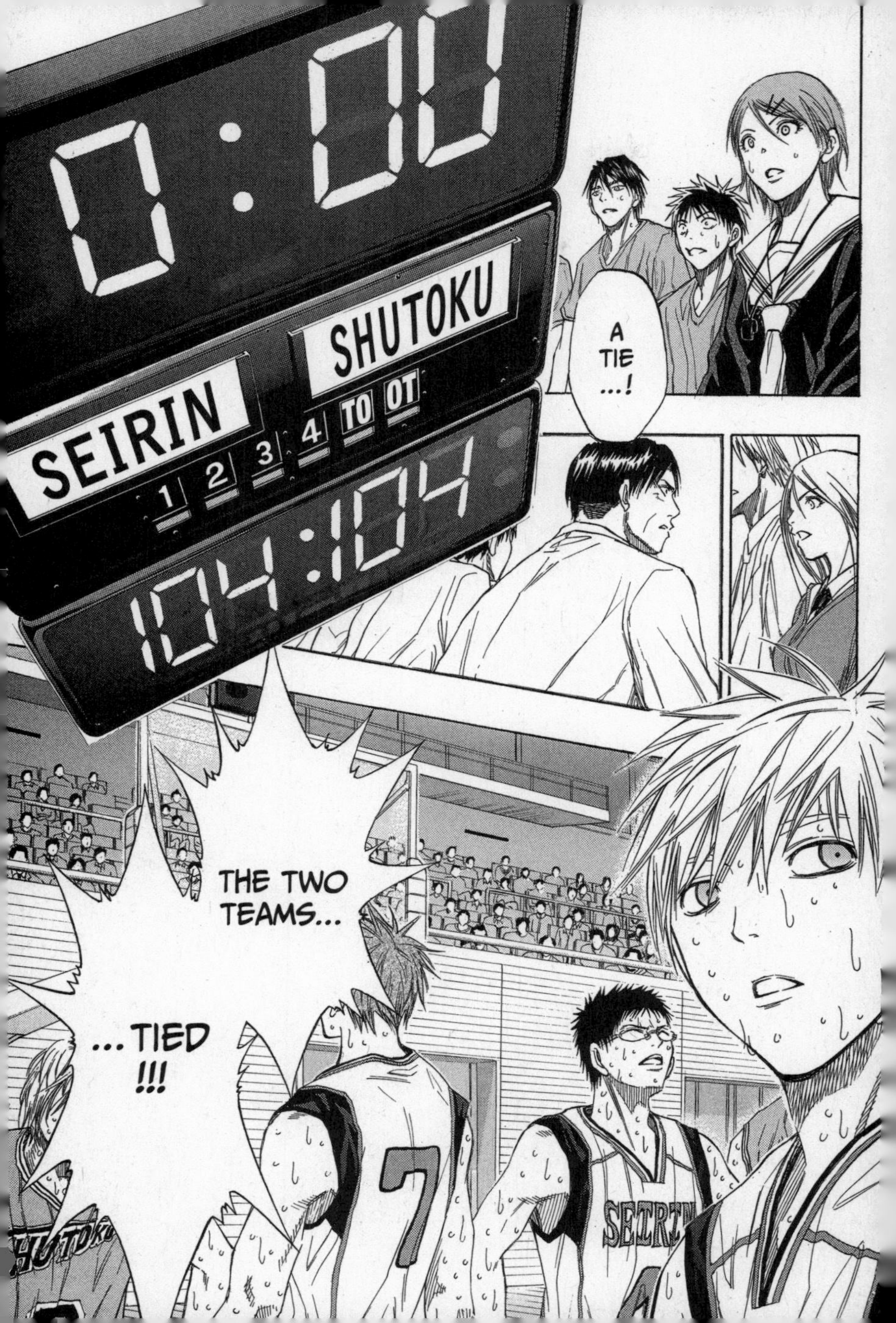
A TIE ...!
0:00
SHUTOKU
SEIRIN
1 2 3 4 TO OT
104:104
THE TWO TEAMS...
...TIED !!!
SEIRIN
7
SHUTOKU

KUROKO'S BASKETBALL BLOOPERS TAKE 5

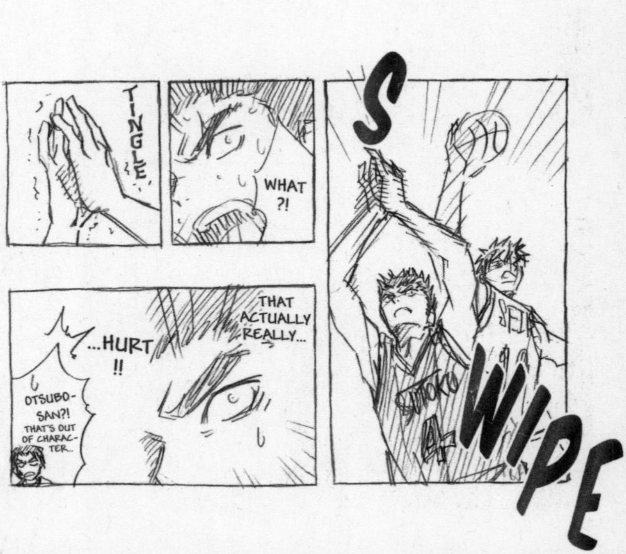
S
WIPE
WHAT ?!
TINGLE
THAT ACTUALLY REALLY...
...HURT !!
OTSUBO-SAN?! THAT'S OUT OF CHARACTER...

93RD QUARTER: EXACTLY WHAT I'M HOPING

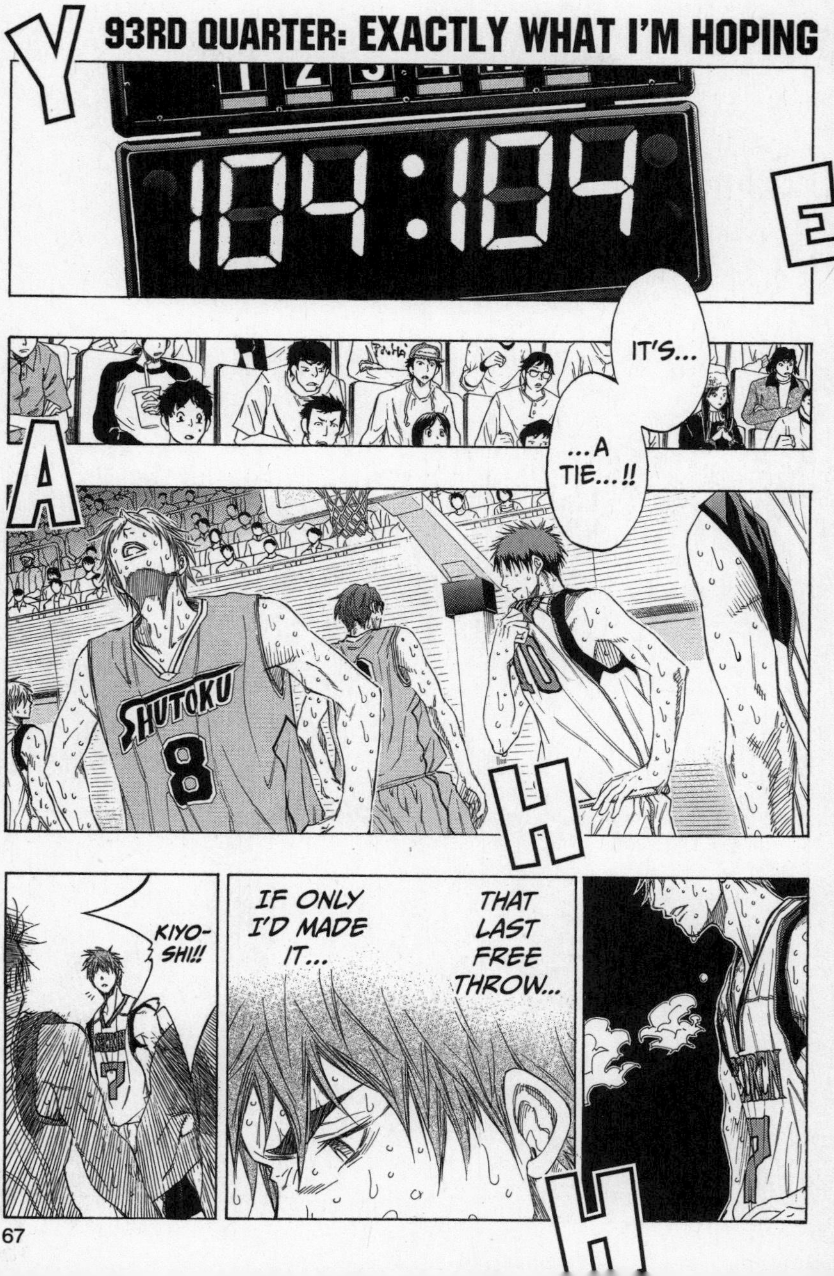
104:104
YEAHH
IT'S...
...A TIE...!!
THAT LAST FREE THROW...
IF ONLY I'D MADE IT...
KIYO-SHI!!

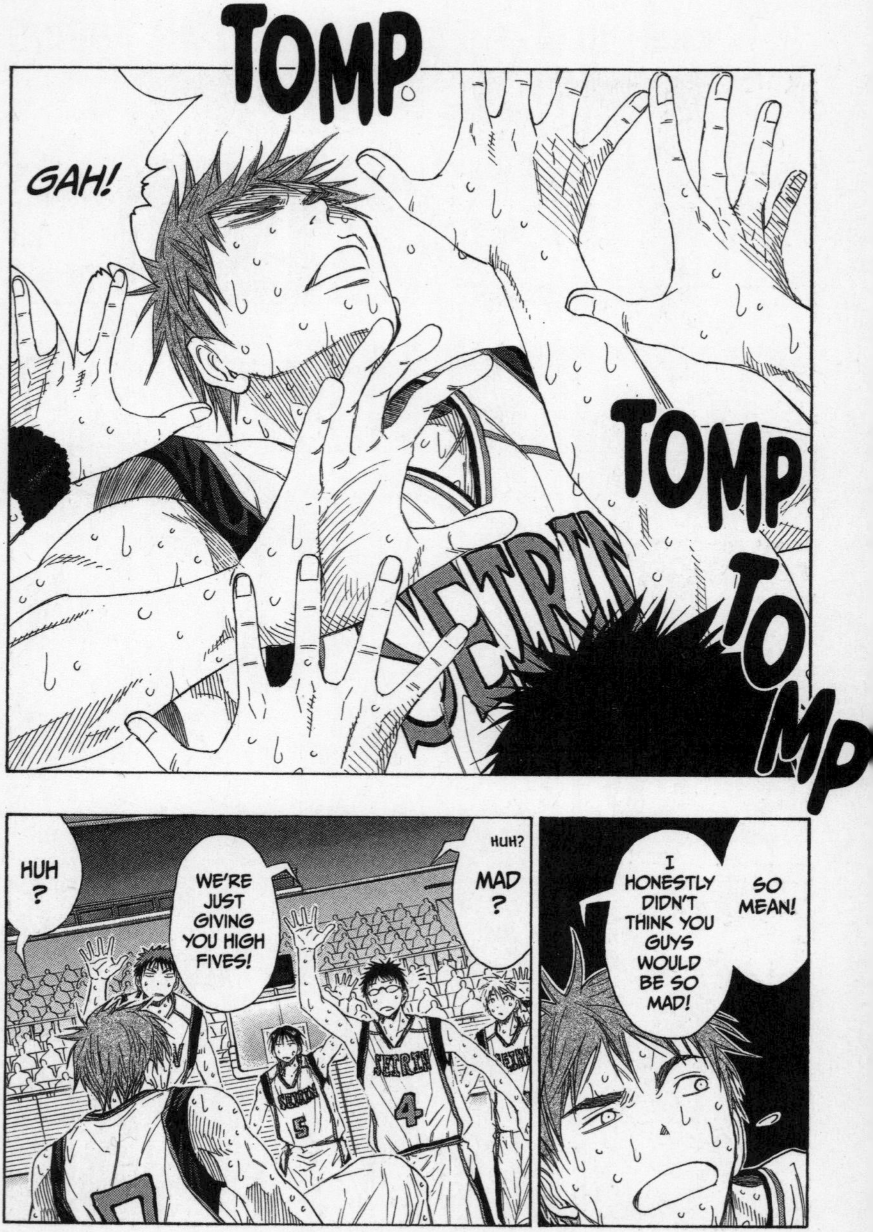
TOMP
GAH!
TOMP
TOMP
SO MEAN!
I HONESTLY DIDN'T THINK YOU GUYS WOULD BE SO MAD!
HUH?
MAD?
WE'RE JUST GIVING YOU HIGH FIVES!
HUH?

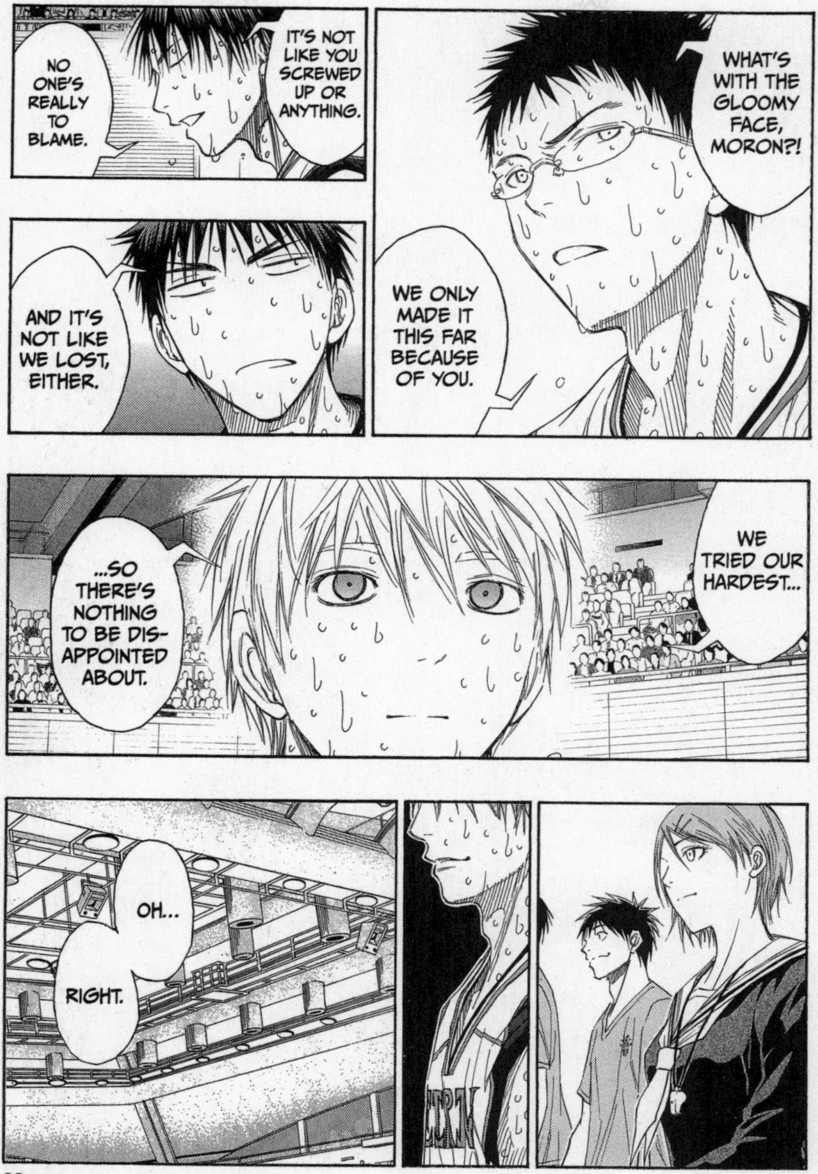
WHAT'S WITH THE GLOOMY FACE, MORON?!
WE ONLY MADE IT THIS FAR BECAUSE OF YOU.
IT'S NOT LIKE YOU SCREWED UP OR ANYTHING.
NO ONE'S REALLY TO BLAME.
AND IT'S NOT LIKE WE LOST, EITHER.
WE TRIED OUR HARDEST...
...SO THERE'S NOTHING TO BE DIS-APPOINTED ABOUT.
OH...
RIGHT.

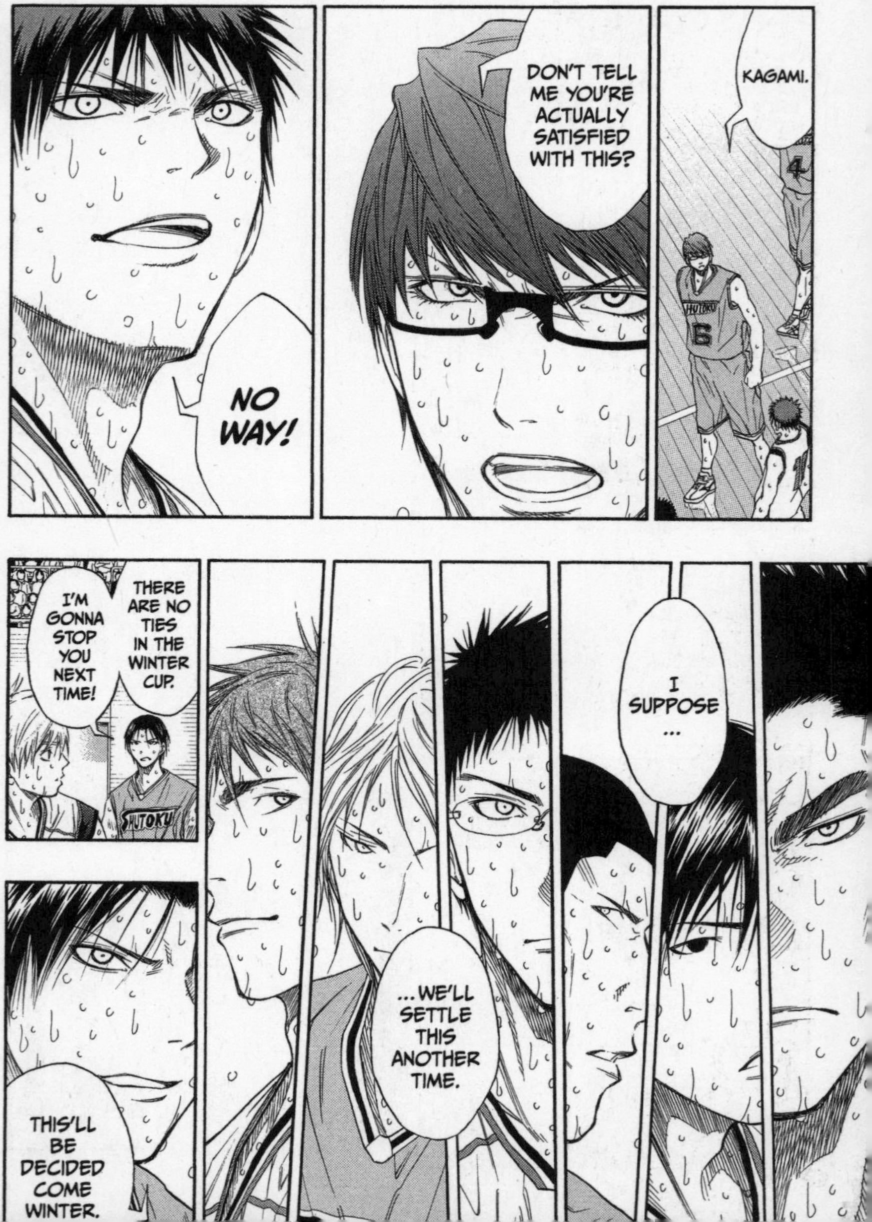
KAGAMI.
DON'T TELL ME YOU'RE ACTUALLY SATISFIED WITH THIS?
NO WAY!
I SUPPOSE...
...WE'LL SETTLE THIS ANOTHER TIME.
THERE ARE NO TIES IN THE WINTER CUP.
I'M GONNA STOP YOU NEXT TIME!
THIS'LL BE DECIDED COME WINTER.

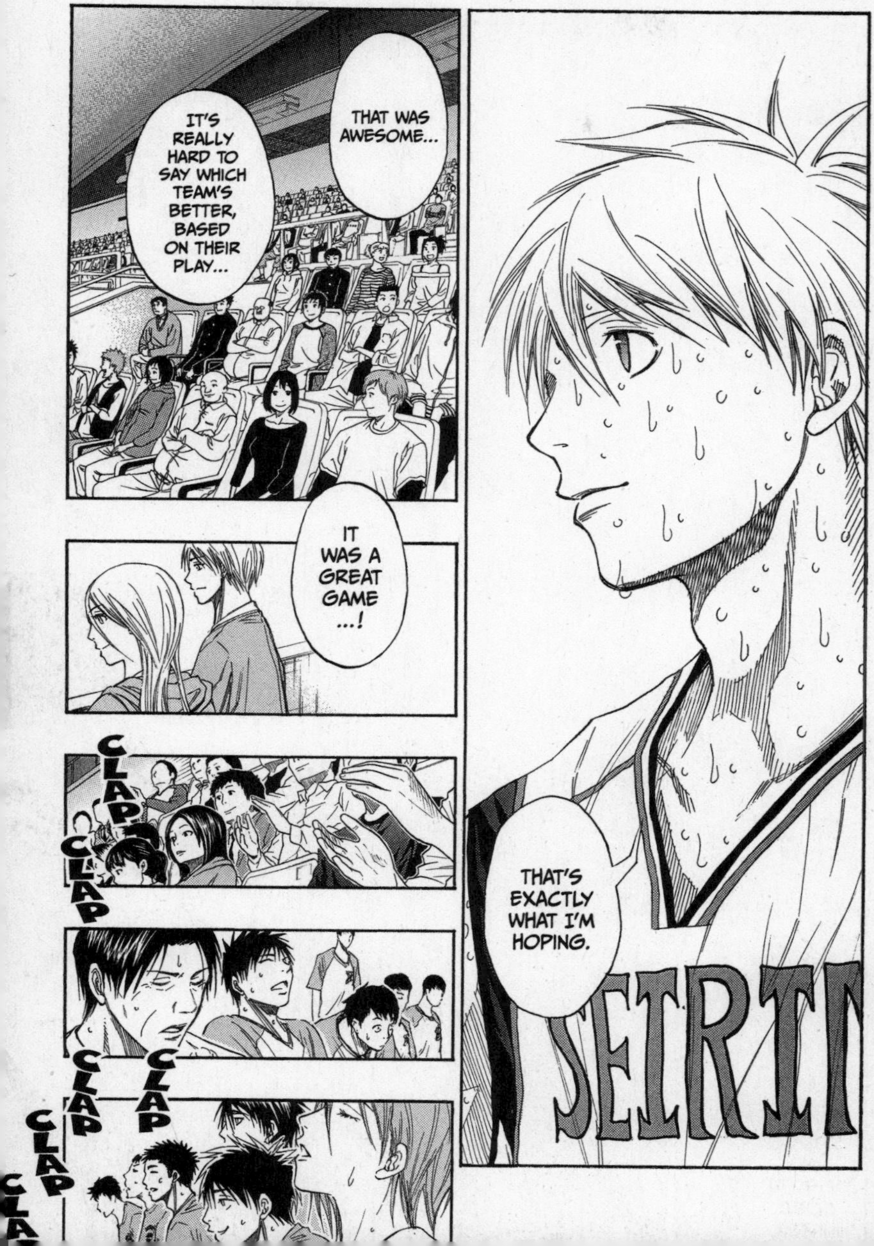
THAT'S EXACTLY WHAT I'M HOPING.
THAT WAS AWESOME...
IT'S REALLY HARD TO SAY WHICH TEAM'S BETTER, BASED ON THEIR PLAY...
IT WAS A GREAT GAME ...!
CLAP CLAP CLAP
CLAP CLAP
CLAP

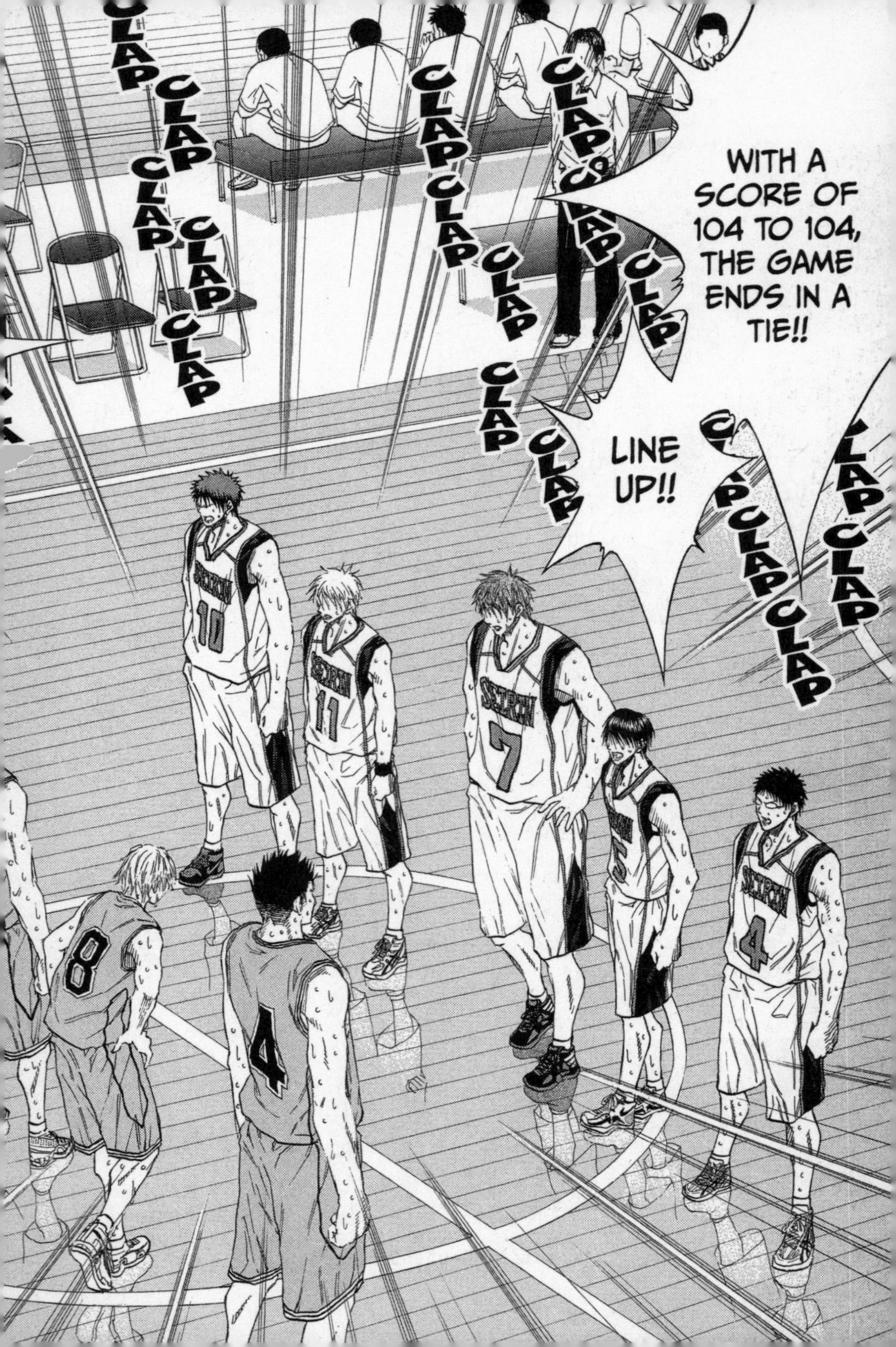
WITH A SCORE OF 104 TO 104, THE GAME ENDS IN A TIE!!
CLAP CLAP CLAP CLAP
LINE UP!!
CLAP CLAP CLAP CLAP CLAP
CLAP CLAP CLAP CLAP
CLAP CLAP CLAP CLAP CLAP CLAP CLAP

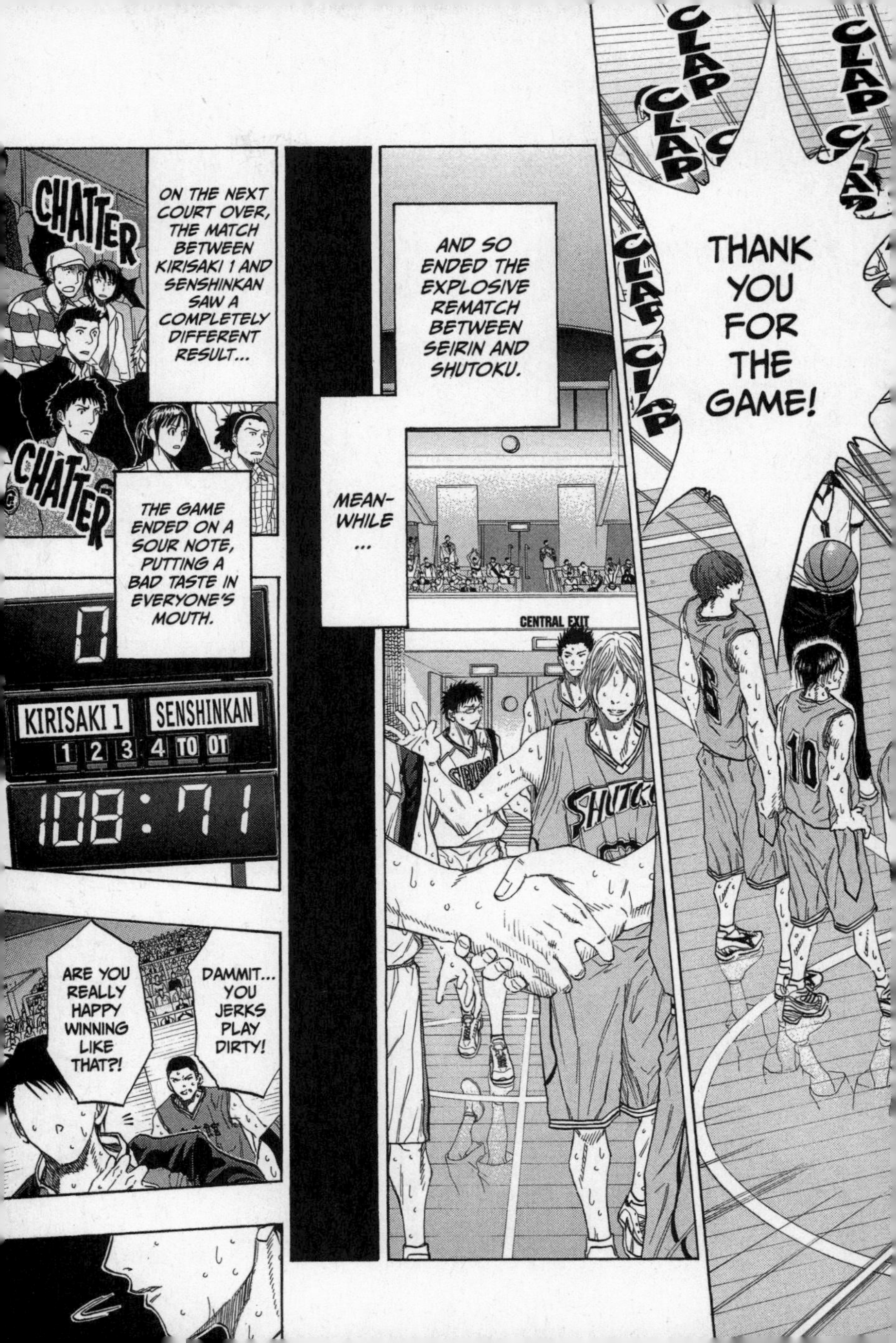
CLAP CLAP
CLAP CLAP
CLAP CLAP
THANK YOU FOR THE GAME!
AND SO ENDED THE EXPLOSIVE REMATCH BETWEEN SEIRIN AND SHUTOKU.
MEAN-WHILE ...
CENTRAL EXIT
SHUTOKU
ON THE NEXT COURT OVER, THE MATCH BETWEEN KIRISAKI 1 AND SENSHINKAN SAW A COMPLETELY DIFFERENT RESULT...
CHATTER
CHATTER
THE GAME ENDED ON A SOUR NOTE, PUTTING A BAD TASTE IN EVERYONE'S MOUTH.
0
KIRISAKI 1
SENSHINKAN
1 2 3 4 TO OT
108 : 71
DAMMIT... YOU JERKS PLAY DIRTY!
ARE YOU REALLY HAPPY WINNING LIKE THAT?!

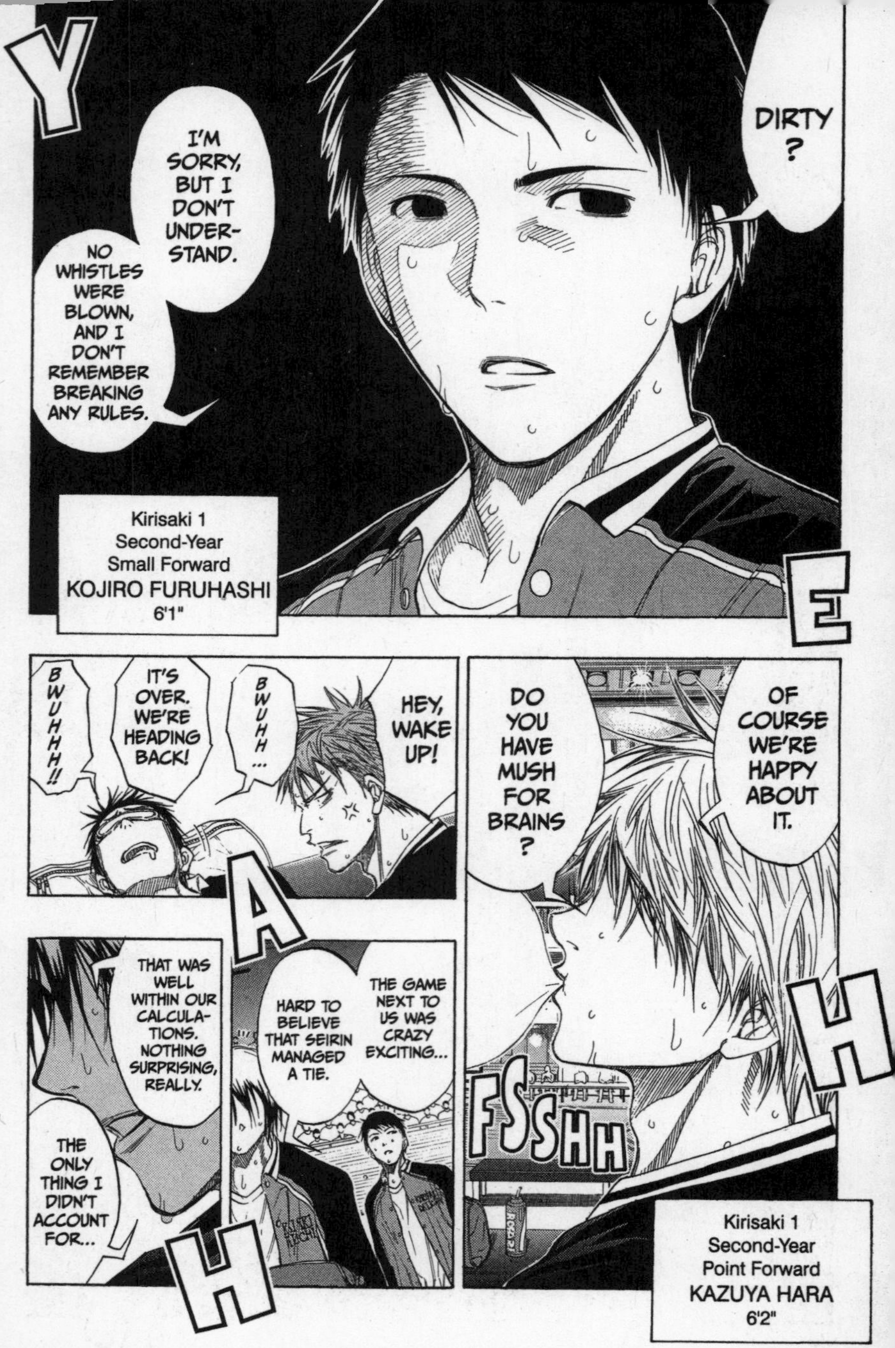
DIRTY?
I'M SORRY, BUT I DON'T UNDERSTAND.
NO WHISTLES WERE BLOWN, AND I DON'T REMEMBER BREAKING ANY RULES.
Kirisaki 1 Second-Year Small Forward KOJIRO FURUHASHI 6'1"
Y
E
OF COURSE WE'RE HAPPY ABOUT IT.
DO YOU HAVE MUSH FOR BRAINS?
FSSHH
Kirisaki 1 Second-Year Point Forward KAZUYA HARA 6'2"
H
HEY, WAKE UP!
BWUHH...
IT'S OVER. WE'RE HEADING BACK!
BWUHHH!!
A
THE GAME NEXT TO US WAS CRAZY EXCITING...
HARD TO BELIEVE THAT SEIRIN MANAGED A TIE.
THAT WAS WELL WITHIN OUR CALCULATIONS. NOTHING SURPRISING, REALLY.
THE ONLY THING I DIDN'T ACCOUNT FOR...
H

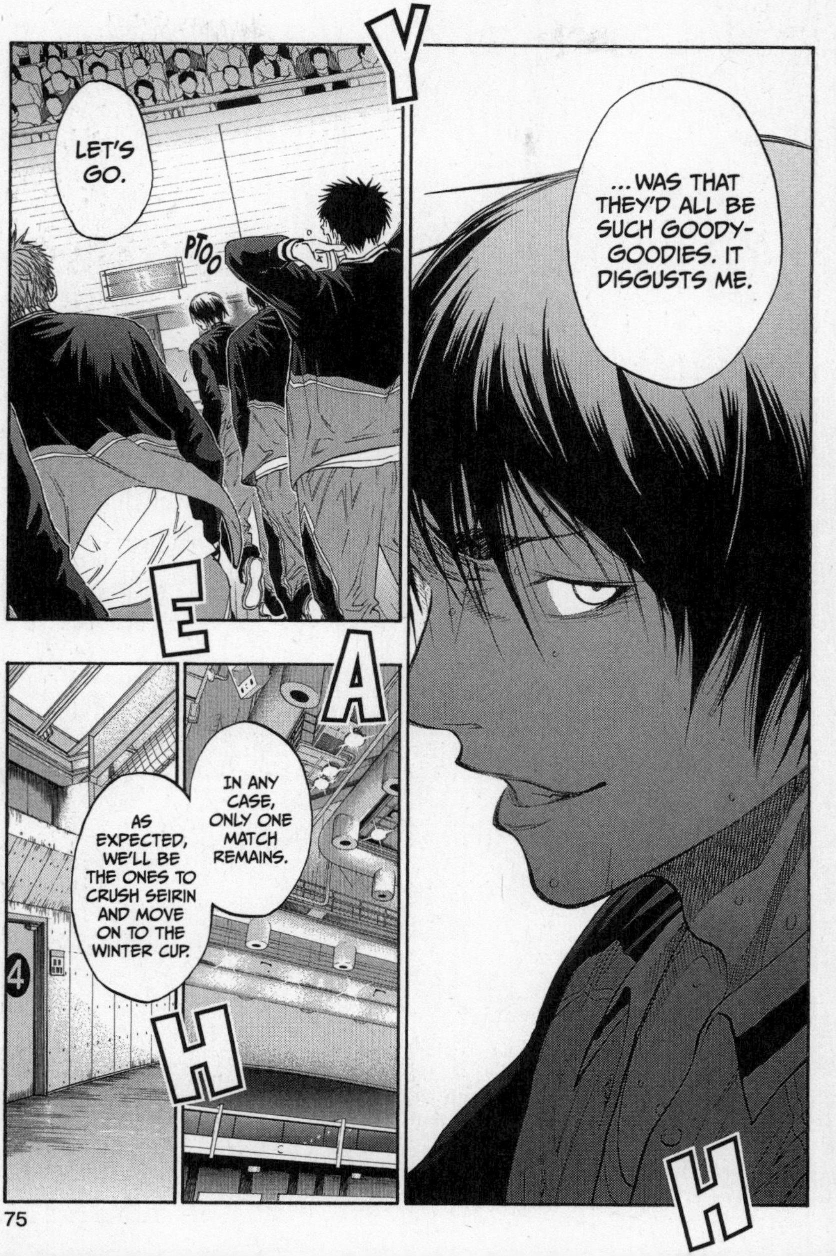
...WAS THAT THEY'D ALL BE SUCH GOODY-GOODIES. IT DISGUSTS ME.
YEAHH
LET'S GO.
PTOO
IN ANY CASE, ONLY ONE MATCH REMAINS.
AS EXPECTED, WE'LL BE THE ONES TO CRUSH SEIRIN AND MOVE ON TO THE WINTER CUP.

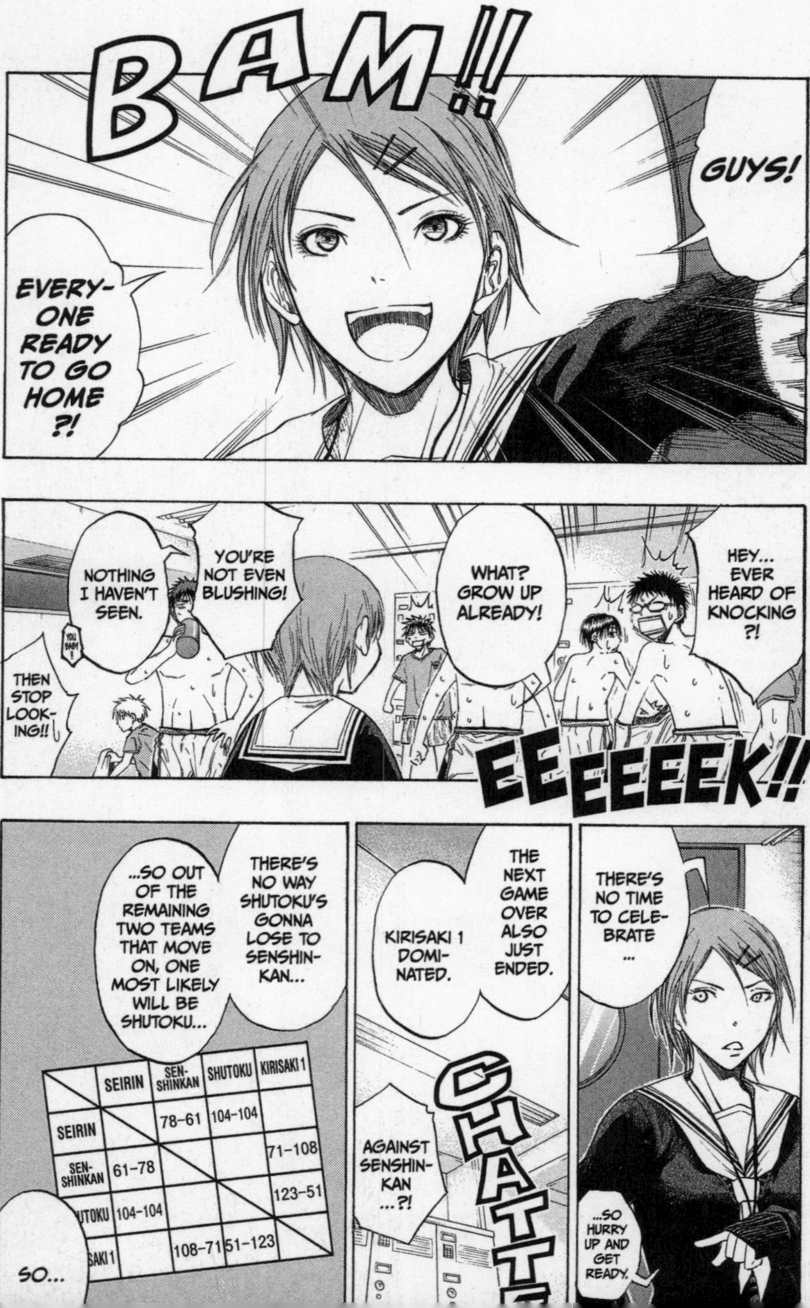
BAM!!
GUYS!
EVERY-ONE READY TO GO HOME?!
HEY... EVER HEARD OF KNOCKING?!
WHAT? GROW UP ALREADY!
YOU'RE NOT EVEN BLUSHING!
NOTHING I HAVEN'T SEEN.
YOU BABY!!
THEN STOP LOOKING!!
EEEEEEK!!
THERE'S NO TIME TO CELE-BRATE ...
...SO HURRY UP AND GET READY.
THE NEXT GAME OVER ALSO JUST ENDED.
KIRISAKI 1 DOMI-NATED.
AGAINST SENSHIN-KAN ...?!
CHATT
THERE'S NO WAY SHUTOKU'S GONNA LOSE TO SENSHIN-KAN...
...SO OUT OF THE REMAINING TWO TEAMS THAT MOVE ON, ONE MOST LIKELY WILL BE SHUTOKU...

	SEIRIN	SEN-SHINKAN	SHUTOKU	KIRISAKI 1
SEIRIN		78–61	104–104	
SEN-SHINKAN	61–78			71–108
UTOKU	104–104			123–51
SAKI 1		108–71	51–123	

SO...

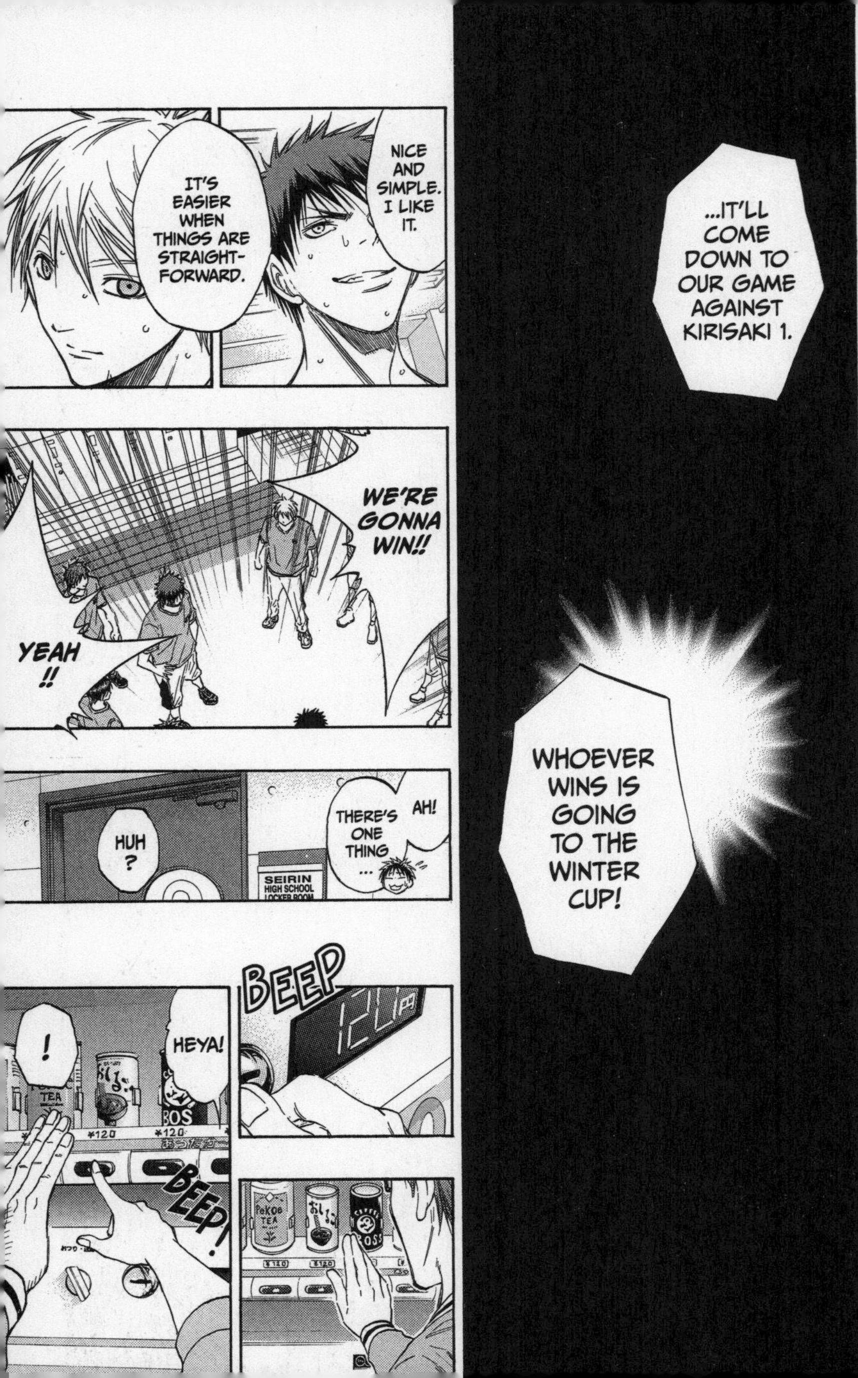
...IT'LL COME DOWN TO OUR GAME AGAINST KIRISAKI 1.
WHOEVER WINS IS GOING TO THE WINTER CUP!
NICE AND SIMPLE. I LIKE IT.
IT'S EASIER WHEN THINGS ARE STRAIGHTFORWARD.
WE'RE GONNA WIN!!
YEAH!!
AH!
THERE'S ONE THING...
SEIRIN HIGH SCHOOL LOCKER ROOM
HUH?
BEEP
120
HEYA!
!
¥120
¥120
BEEP!
Pekoe TEA
BOSS

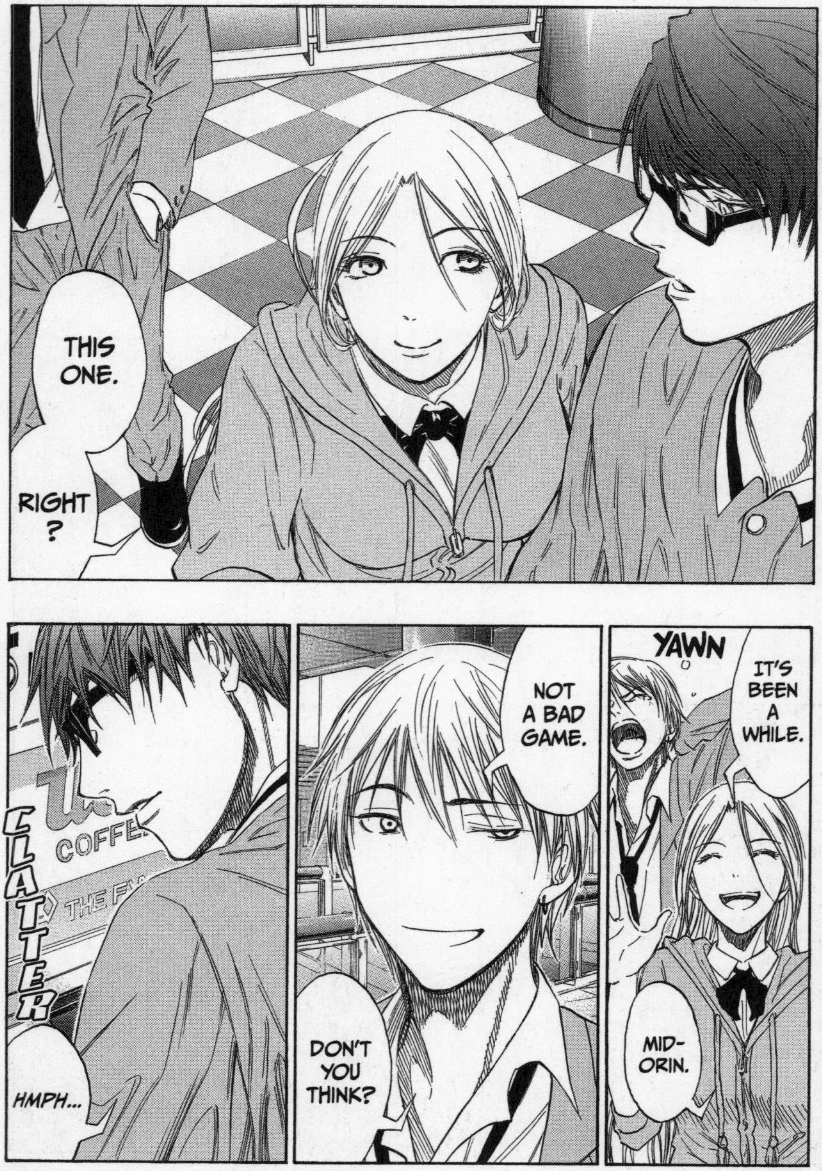
THIS ONE.
RIGHT ?
YAWN
IT'S BEEN A WHILE.
MID-ORIN.
NOT A BAD GAME.
DON'T YOU THINK?
CLATTER
HMPH...

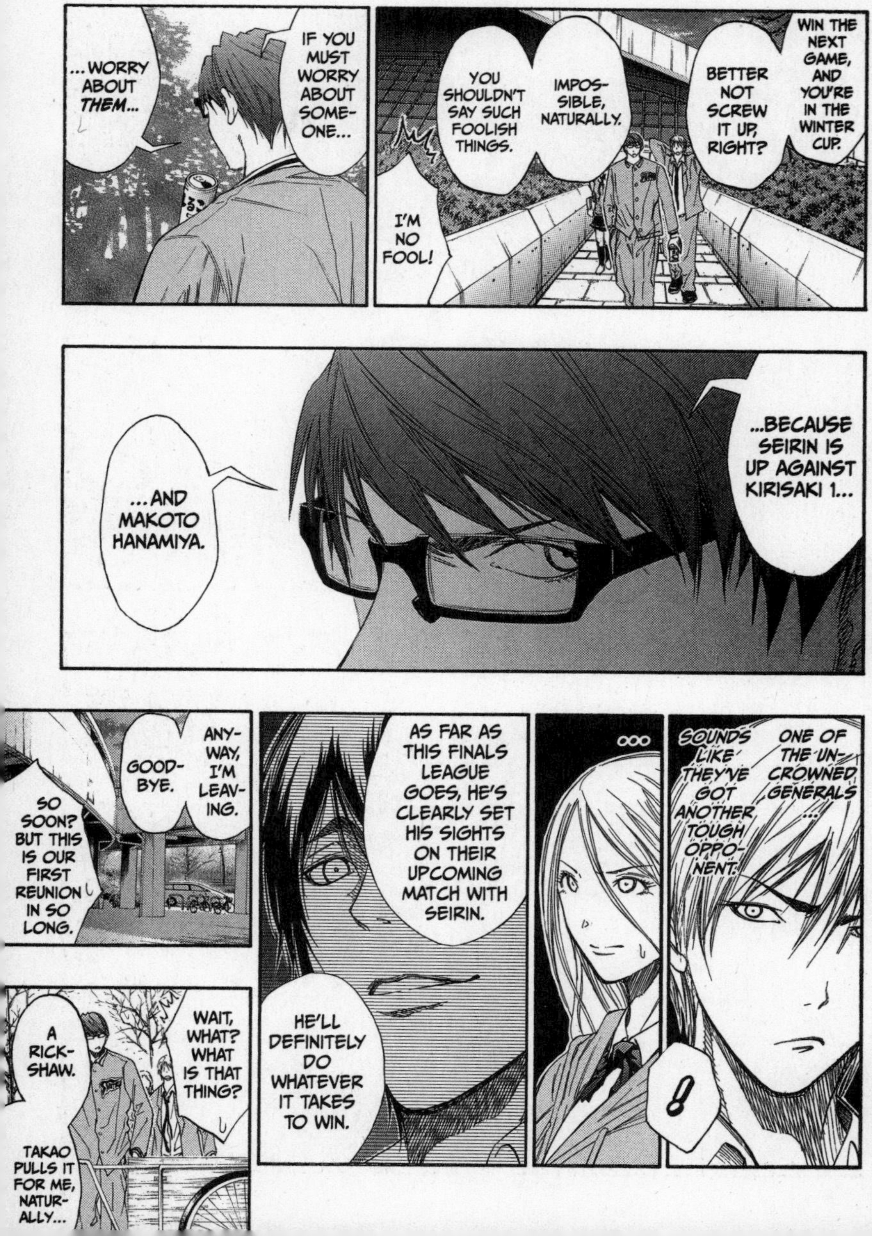
WIN THE NEXT GAME, AND YOU'RE IN THE WINTER CUP.
BETTER NOT SCREW IT UP, RIGHT?
IMPOS-SIBLE, NATURALLY.
YOU SHOULDN'T SAY SUCH FOOLISH THINGS.
I'M NO FOOL!
IF YOU MUST WORRY ABOUT SOME-ONE...
...WORRY ABOUT *THEM*...
...BECAUSE SEIRIN IS UP AGAINST KIRISAKI 1...
...AND MAKOTO HANAMIYA.
ONE OF THE UN-CROWNED GENERALS...
SOUNDS LIKE THEY'VE GOT ANOTHER TOUGH OPPO-NENT.
!
...
AS FAR AS THIS FINALS LEAGUE GOES, HE'S CLEARLY SET HIS SIGHTS ON THEIR UPCOMING MATCH WITH SEIRIN.
HE'LL DEFINITELY DO WHATEVER IT TAKES TO WIN.
ANY-WAY, I'M LEAV-ING.
GOOD-BYE.
SO SOON? BUT THIS IS OUR FIRST REUNION IN SO LONG.
WAIT, WHAT? WHAT IS THAT THING?
A RICK-SHAW.
TAKAO PULLS IT FOR ME, NATUR-ALLY...

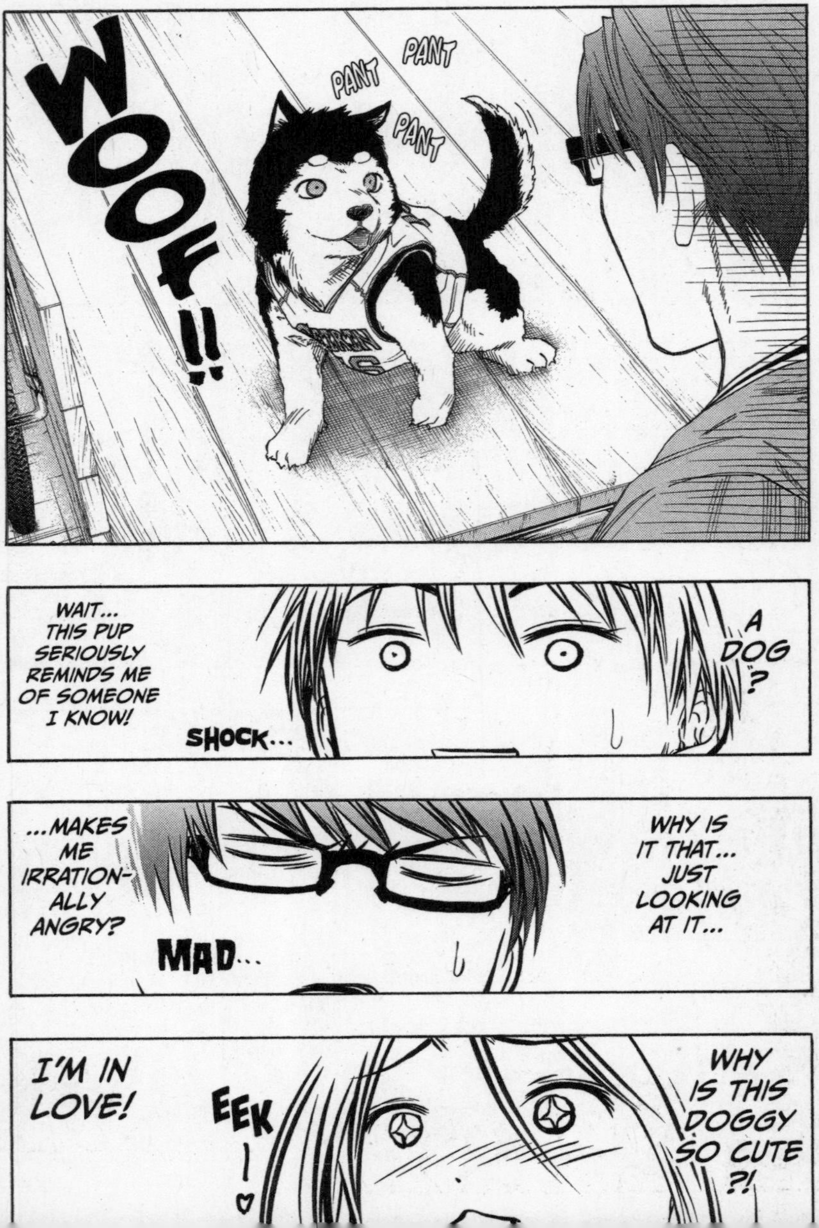
WOOF!!
PANT
PANT
PANT
A DOG?
SHOCK...
WAIT... THIS PUP SERIOUSLY REMINDS ME OF SOMEONE I KNOW!
WHY IS IT THAT... JUST LOOKING AT IT...
MAD...
...MAKES ME IRRATION-ALLY ANGRY?
WHY IS THIS DOGGY SO CUTE?!
EEK
I'M IN LOVE!

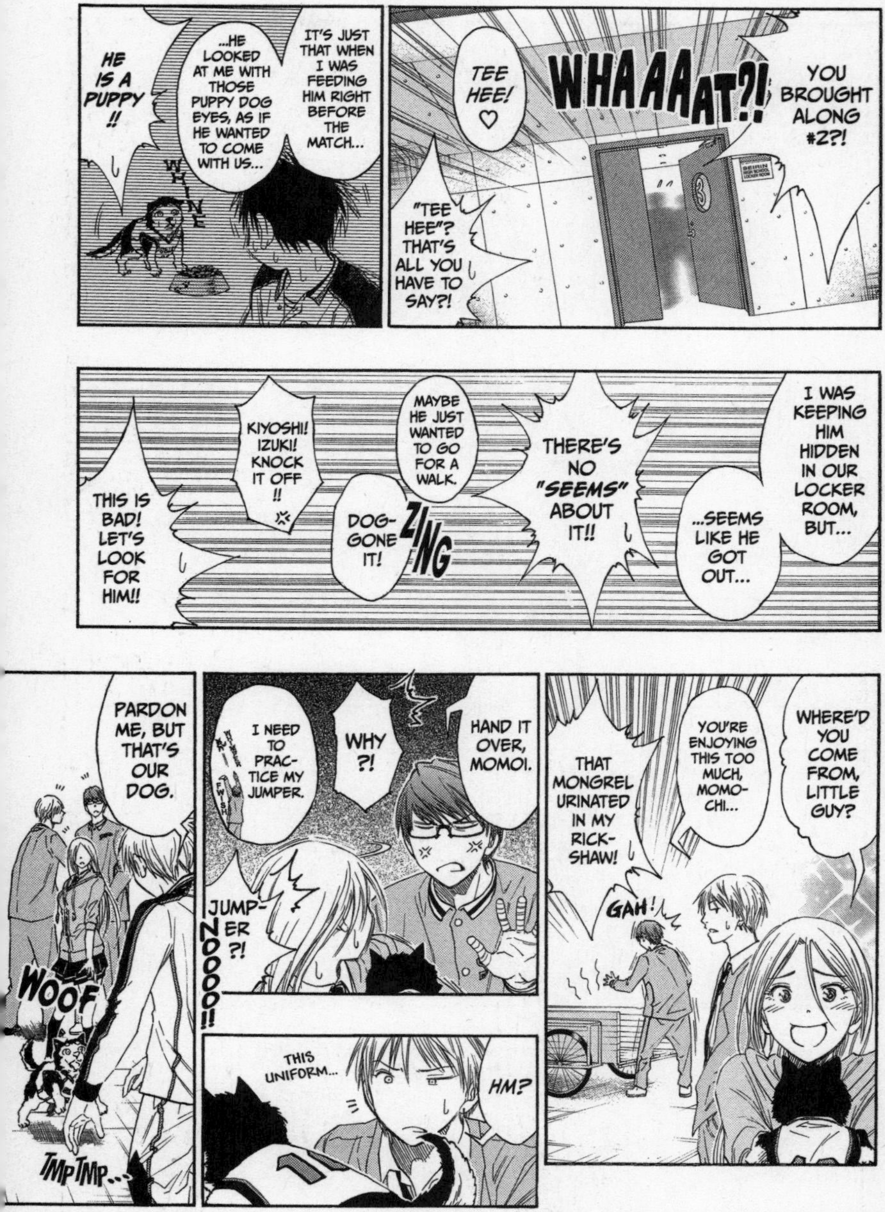
YOU BROUGHT ALONG #2?!
WHAAAAAT?!
TEE HEE! ♡
"TEE HEE"? THAT'S ALL YOU HAVE TO SAY?!
IT'S JUST THAT WHEN I WAS FEEDING HIM RIGHT BEFORE THE MATCH...
...HE LOOKED AT ME WITH THOSE PUPPY DOG EYES, AS IF HE WANTED TO COME WITH US...
WHINE
HE IS A PUPPY!!
I WAS KEEPING HIM HIDDEN IN OUR LOCKER ROOM, BUT...
...SEEMS LIKE HE GOT OUT...
THERE'S NO "SEEMS" ABOUT IT!!
MAYBE HE JUST WANTED TO GO FOR A WALK.
DOG-GONE IT!
ZING
KIYOSHI! IZUKI! KNOCK IT OFF!!
THIS IS BAD! LET'S LOOK FOR HIM!!
WHERE'D YOU COME FROM, LITTLE GUY?
YOU'RE ENJOYING THIS TOO MUCH, MOMO-CHI...
THAT MONGREL URINATED IN MY RICK-SHAW!
GAH!
HAND IT OVER, MOMOI.
WHY?!
I NEED TO PRAC-TICE MY JUMPER.
FWISH
JUMP-ER?!
NOOOOO!!
HM?
THIS UNIFORM...
PARDON ME, BUT THAT'S OUR DOG.
WOOF
TMP TMP...

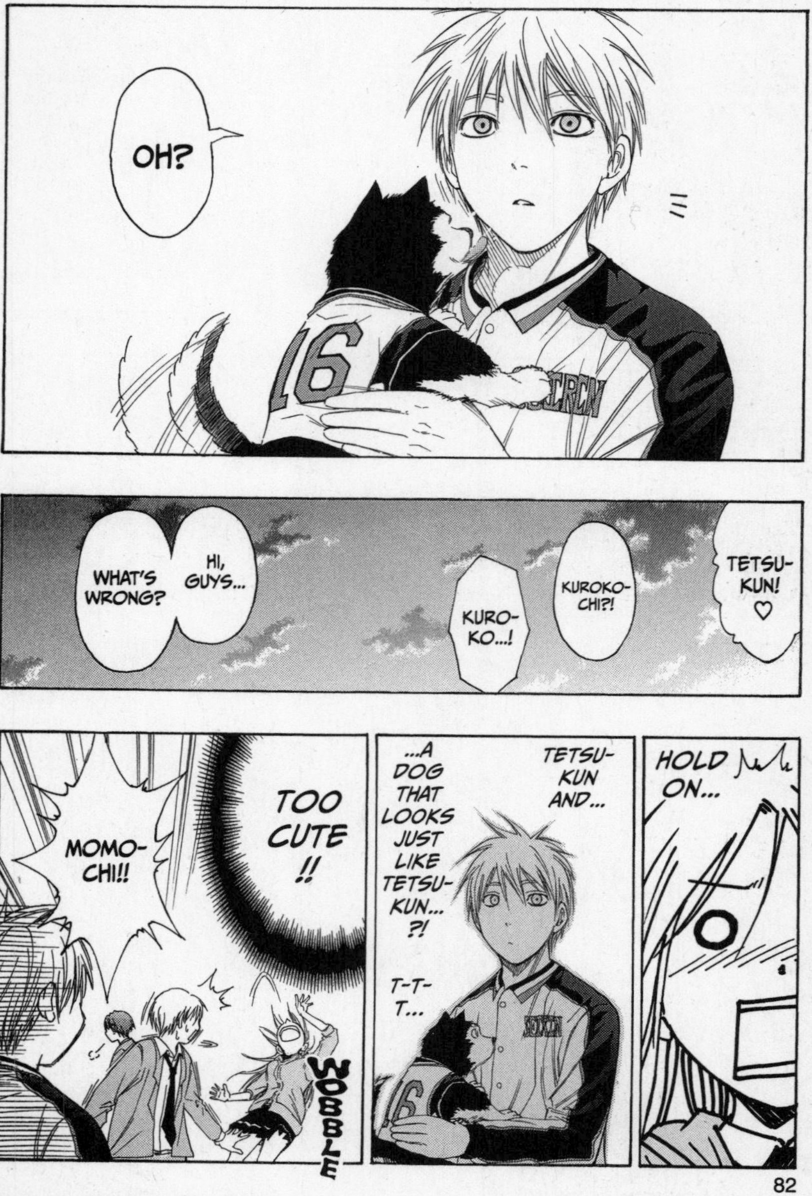
OH?
TETSU-KUN! ♡
KUROKO-CHI?!
KURO-KO...!
HI, GUYS...
WHAT'S WRONG?
HOLD ON...
TETSU-KUN AND...
...A DOG THAT LOOKS JUST LIKE TETSU-KUN...?!
T-T-T...
TOO CUTE!!
MOMO-CHI!!
WOBBLE

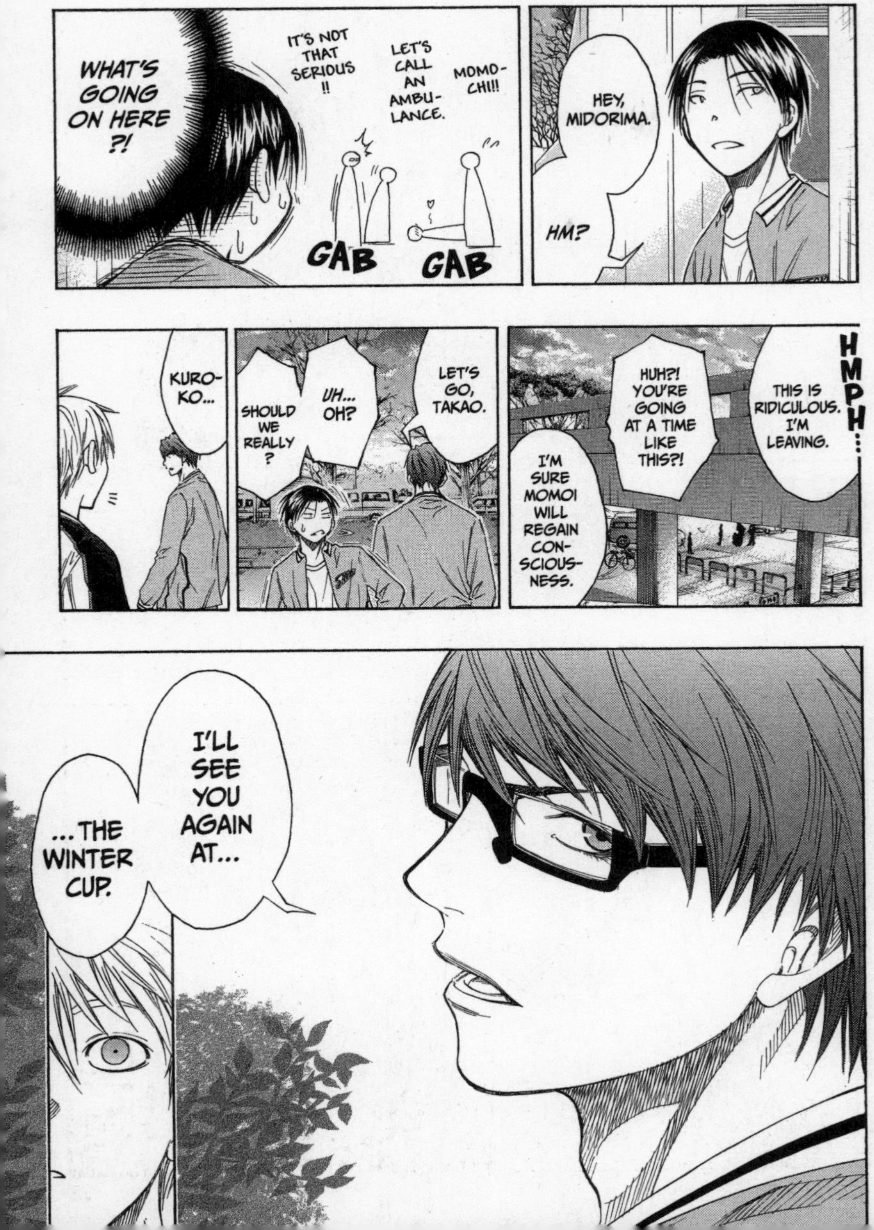
HEY, MIDORIMA.
HM?
MOMO-CHI!!
LET'S CALL AN AMBULANCE.
IT'S NOT THAT SERIOUS!!
WHAT'S GOING ON HERE?!
GAB
GAB
HMPH...
THIS IS RIDICULOUS. I'M LEAVING.
HUH?! YOU'RE GOING AT A TIME LIKE THIS?!
I'M SURE MOMOI WILL REGAIN CONSCIOUSNESS.
LET'S GO, TAKAO.
UH... OH?
SHOULD WE REALLY?
KURO-KO...
I'LL SEE YOU AGAIN AT...
...THE WINTER CUP.

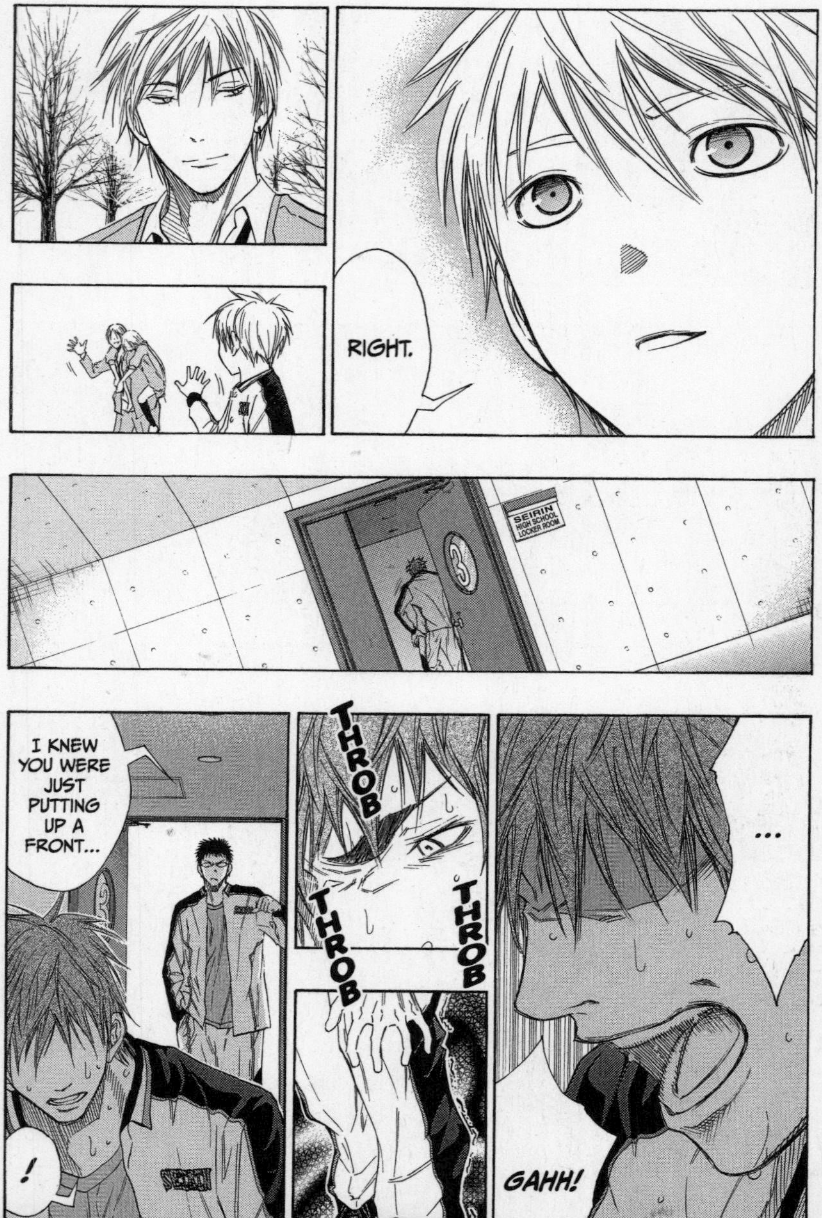
RIGHT.
SEIRIN HIGH SCHOOL LOCKER ROOM
...
GAHH!
THROB
THROB
THROB
I KNEW YOU WERE JUST PUTTING UP A FRONT...
!

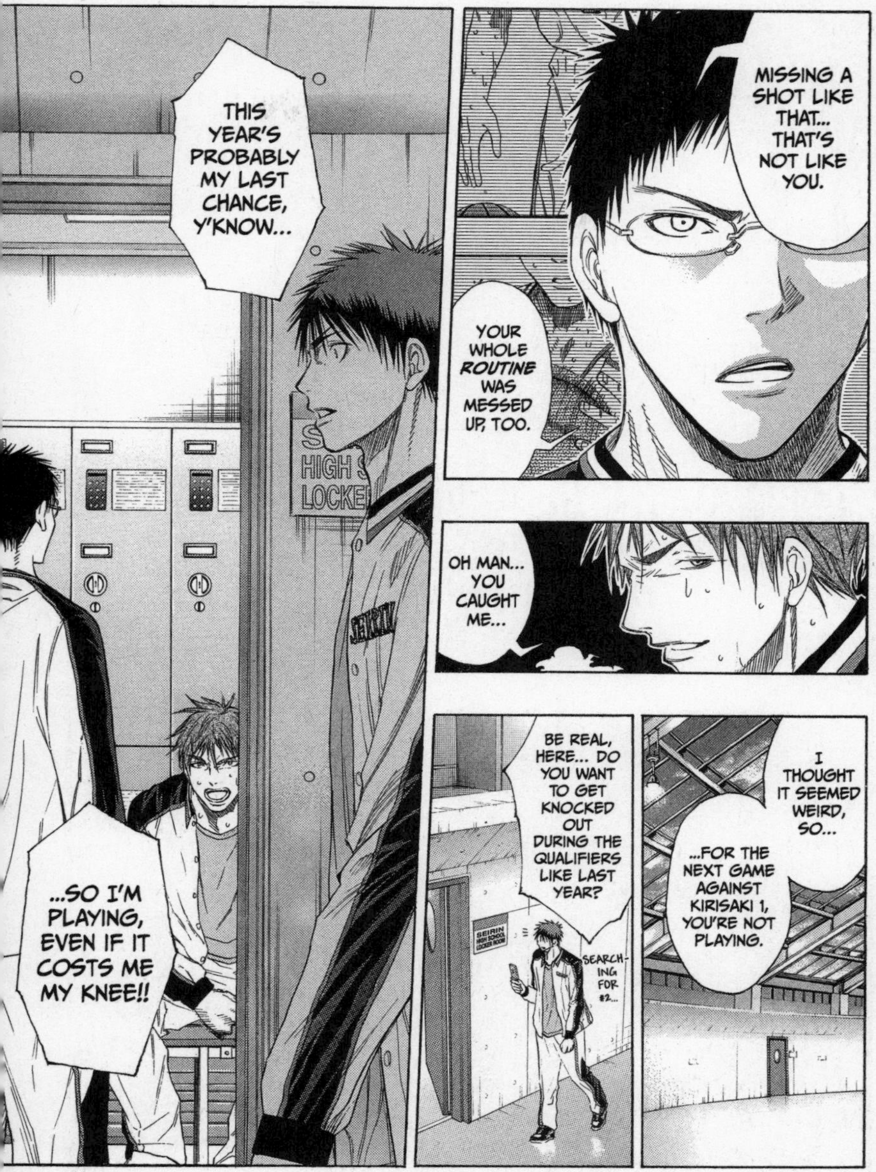
MISSING A SHOT LIKE THAT... THAT'S NOT LIKE YOU.
YOUR WHOLE *ROUTINE* WAS MESSED UP, TOO.
OH MAN... YOU CAUGHT ME...
I THOUGHT IT SEEMED WEIRD, SO...
...FOR THE NEXT GAME AGAINST KIRISAKI 1, YOU'RE NOT PLAYING.
BE REAL, HERE... DO YOU WANT TO GET KNOCKED OUT DURING THE QUALIFIERS LIKE LAST YEAR?
SEARCHING FOR #2...
THIS YEAR'S PROBABLY MY LAST CHANCE, Y'KNOW...
...SO I'M PLAYING, EVEN IF IT COSTS ME MY KNEE!!

KUROKO'S BASKETBALL BLOOPERS
TAKE 2

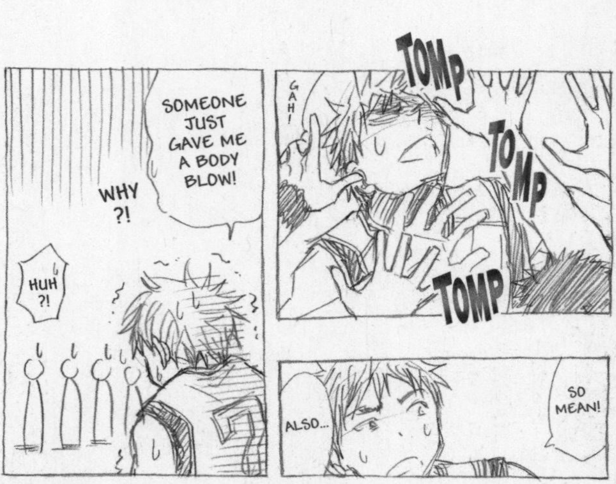
TOMP
GAH!
TOMP
TOMP
SO MEAN!
ALSO...
SOMEONE JUST GAVE ME A BODY BLOW!
WHY ?!
HUH ?!

94TH QUARTER: TIME TO TIDY UP!

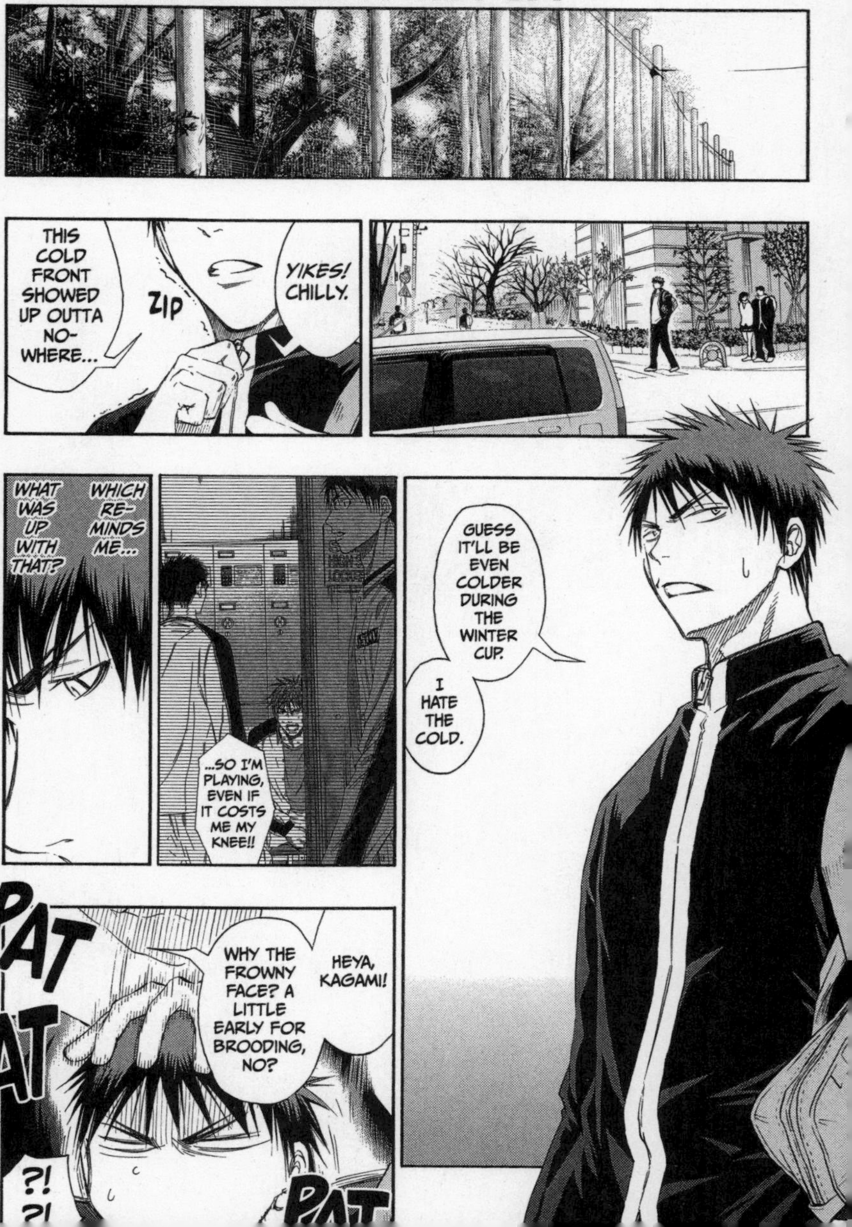
YIKES! CHILLY.
ZIP
THIS COLD FRONT SHOWED UP OUTTA NO-WHERE...
GUESS IT'LL BE EVEN COLDER DURING THE WINTER CUP.
I HATE THE COLD.
...SO I'M PLAYING, EVEN IF IT COSTS ME MY KNEE!!
WHICH RE-MINDS ME...
WHAT WAS UP WITH THAT?
HEYA, KAGAMI!
WHY THE FROWNY FACE? A LITTLE EARLY FOR BROODING, NO?
PAT
PAT
?!
?!
PAT

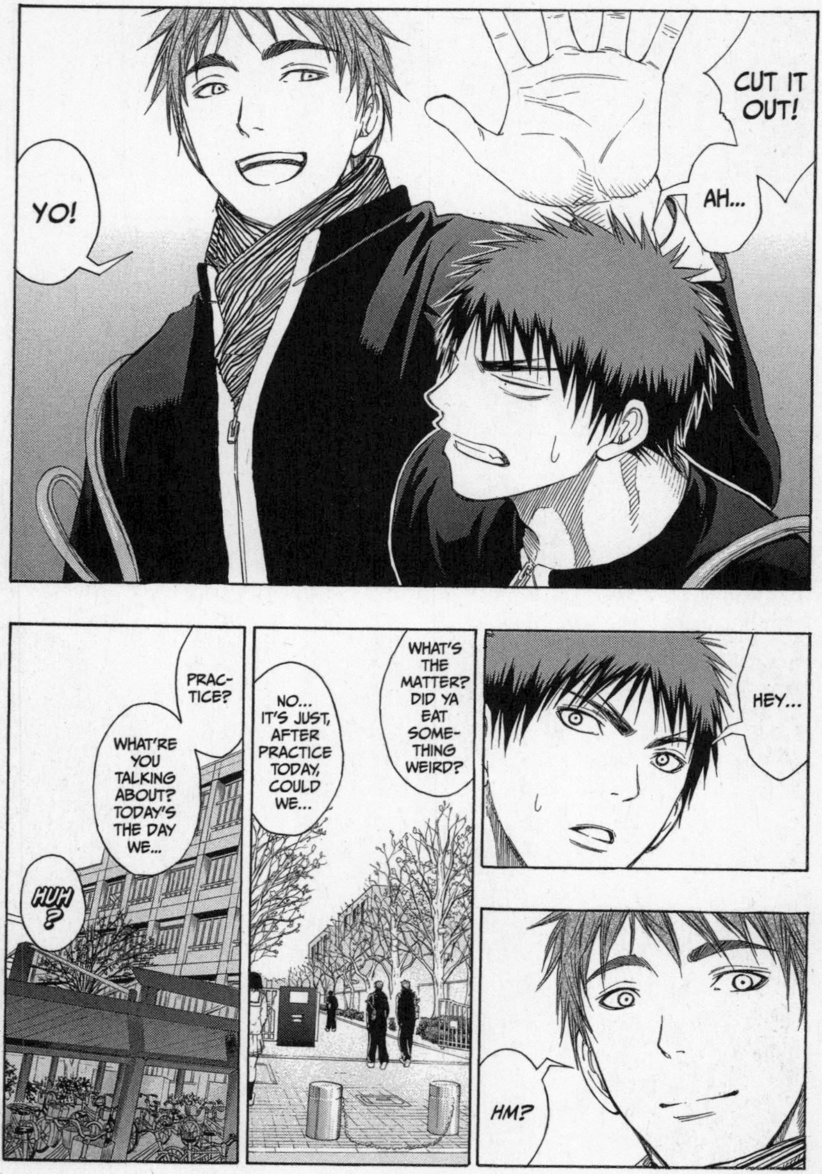
CUT IT OUT!
AH...
YO!
HEY...
HM?
WHAT'S THE MATTER? DID YA EAT SOME-THING WEIRD?
NO... IT'S JUST, AFTER PRACTICE TODAY, COULD WE...
PRAC-TICE?
WHAT'RE YOU TALKING ABOUT? TODAY'S THE DAY WE...
HUH?

94TH QUARTER: TIME TO TIDY UP!

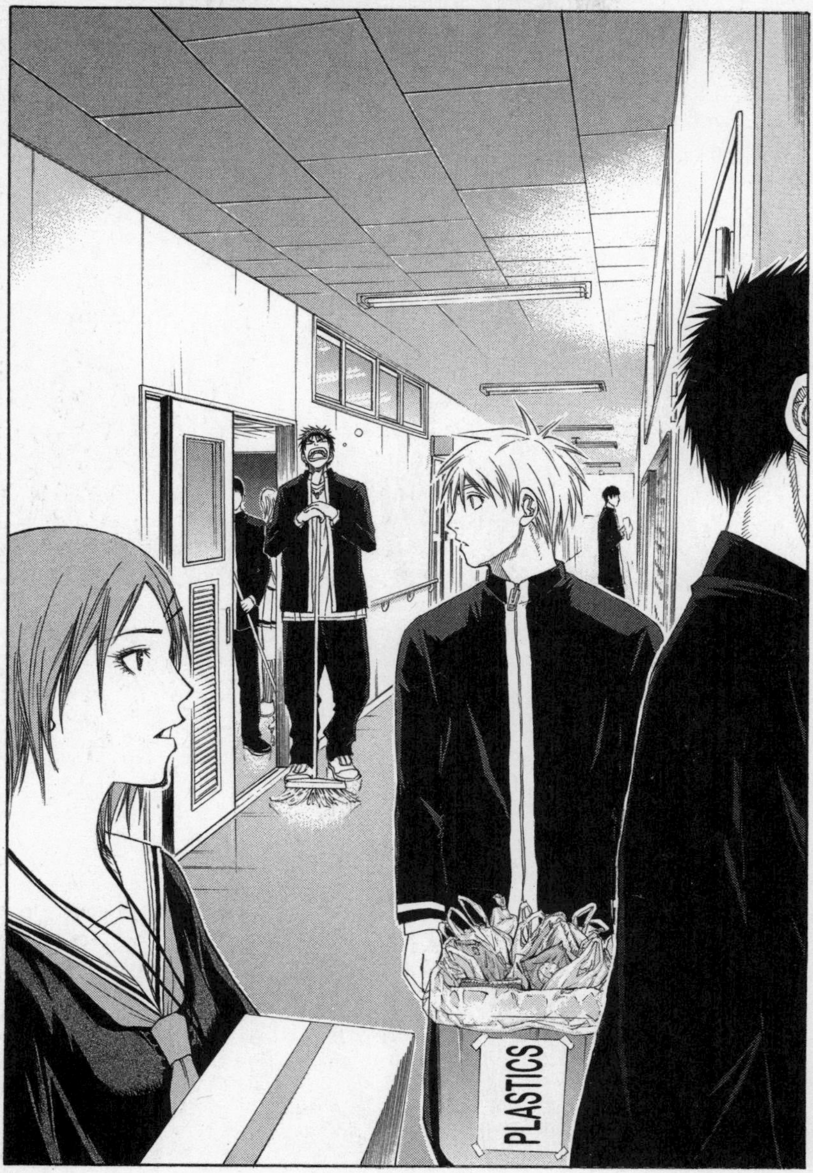
PLASTICS

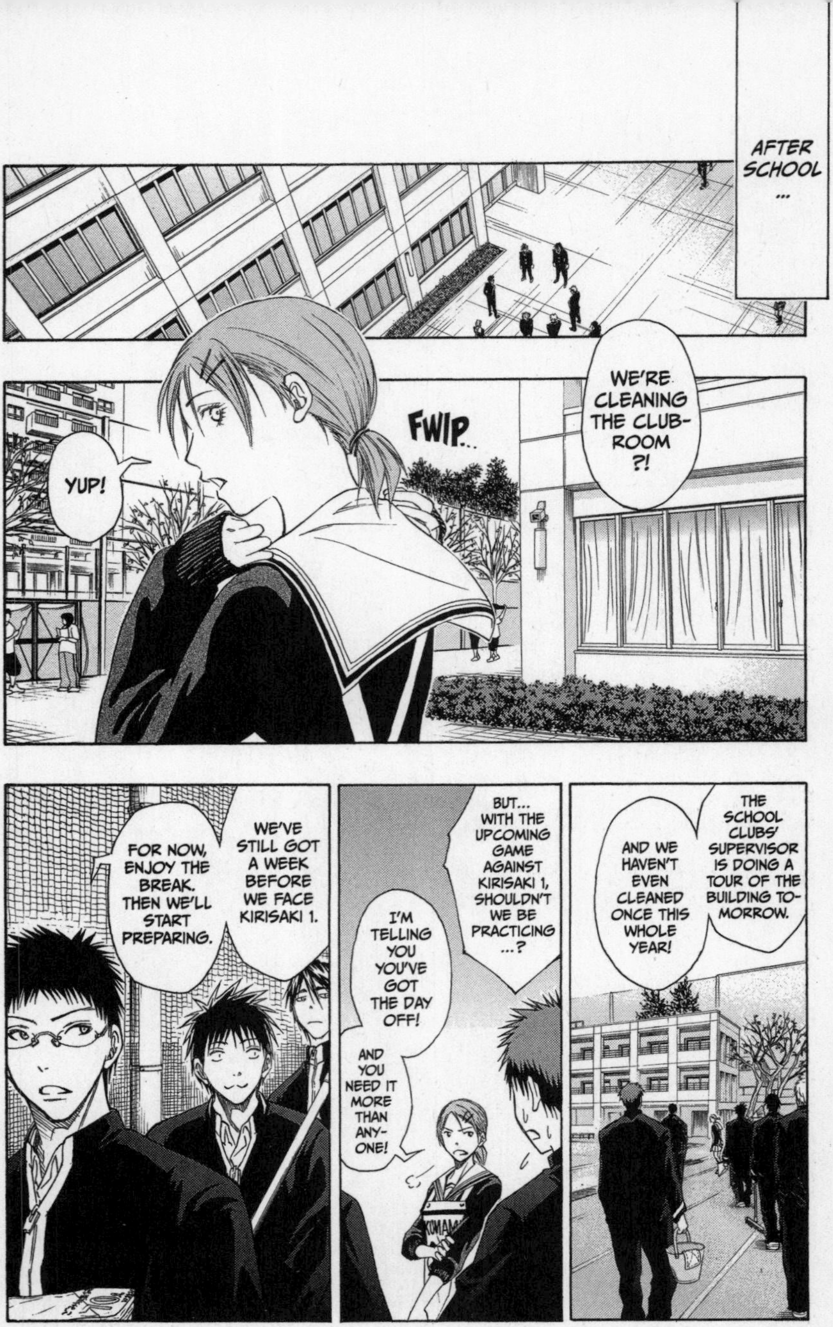
AFTER SCHOOL ...
WE'RE CLEANING THE CLUB-ROOM ?!
FWIP...
YUP!
THE SCHOOL CLUBS' SUPERVISOR IS DOING A TOUR OF THE BUILDING TO-MORROW.
AND WE HAVEN'T EVEN CLEANED ONCE THIS WHOLE YEAR!
BUT... WITH THE UPCOMING GAME AGAINST KIRISAKI 1, SHOULDN'T WE BE PRACTICING ...?
I'M TELLING YOU YOU'VE GOT THE DAY OFF!
AND YOU NEED IT MORE THAN ANY-ONE!
WE'VE STILL GOT A WEEK BEFORE WE FACE KIRISAKI 1.
FOR NOW, ENJOY THE BREAK. THEN WE'LL START PREPARING.

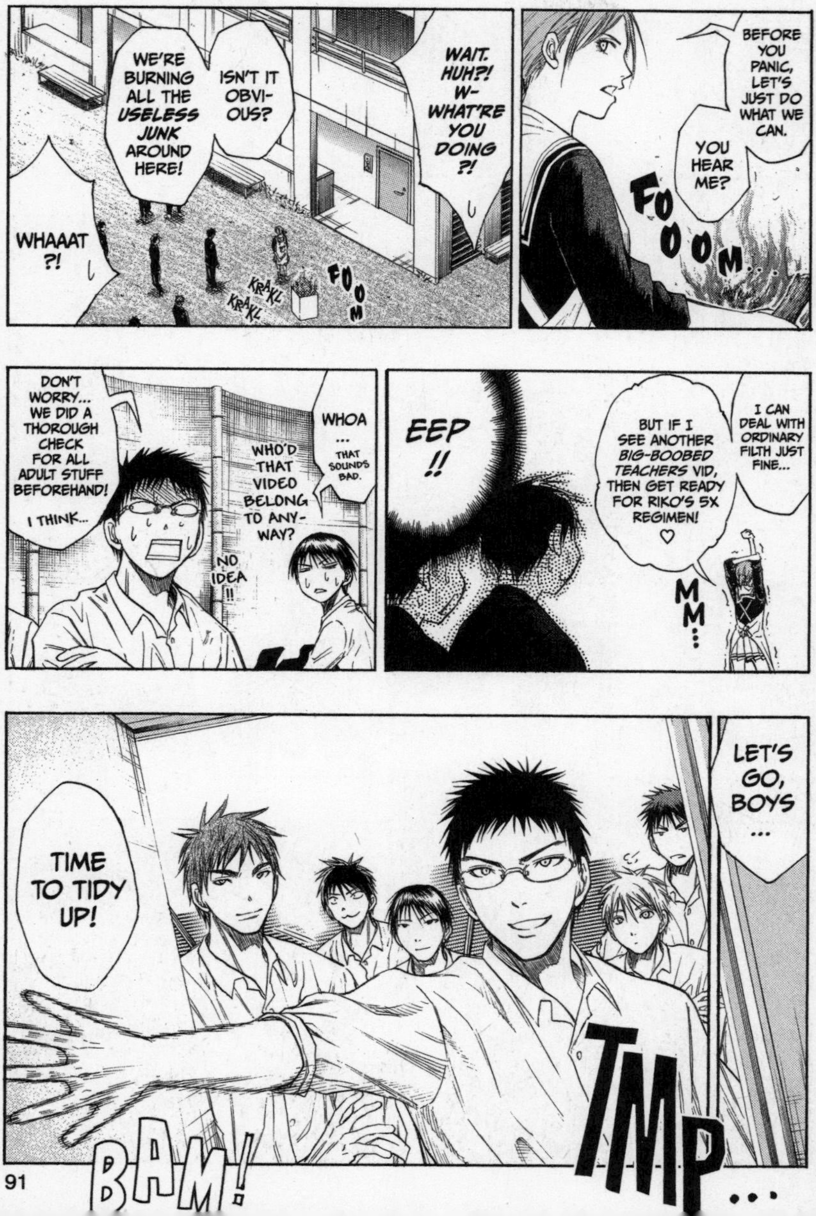
BEFORE YOU PANIC, LET'S JUST DO WHAT WE CAN.
YOU HEAR ME?
FOOOM...
WAIT. HUH?! W-WHAT'RE YOU DOING?!
ISN'T IT OBVIOUS?
WE'RE BURNING ALL THE USELESS JUNK AROUND HERE!
FOOOM
KRAKL KRAKL
WHAAAT?!
I CAN DEAL WITH ORDINARY FILTH JUST FINE...
BUT IF I SEE ANOTHER BIG-BOOBED TEACHERS VID, THEN GET READY FOR RIKO'S 5X REGIMEN! ♡
MM...
EEP!!
WHOA...
THAT SOUNDS BAD.
WHO'D THAT VIDEO BELONG TO ANY-WAY?
NO IDEA!!
DON'T WORRY... WE DID A THOROUGH CHECK FOR ALL ADULT STUFF BEFOREHAND!
I THINK...
LET'S GO, BOYS...
TMP...
TIME TO TIDY UP!
BAM!

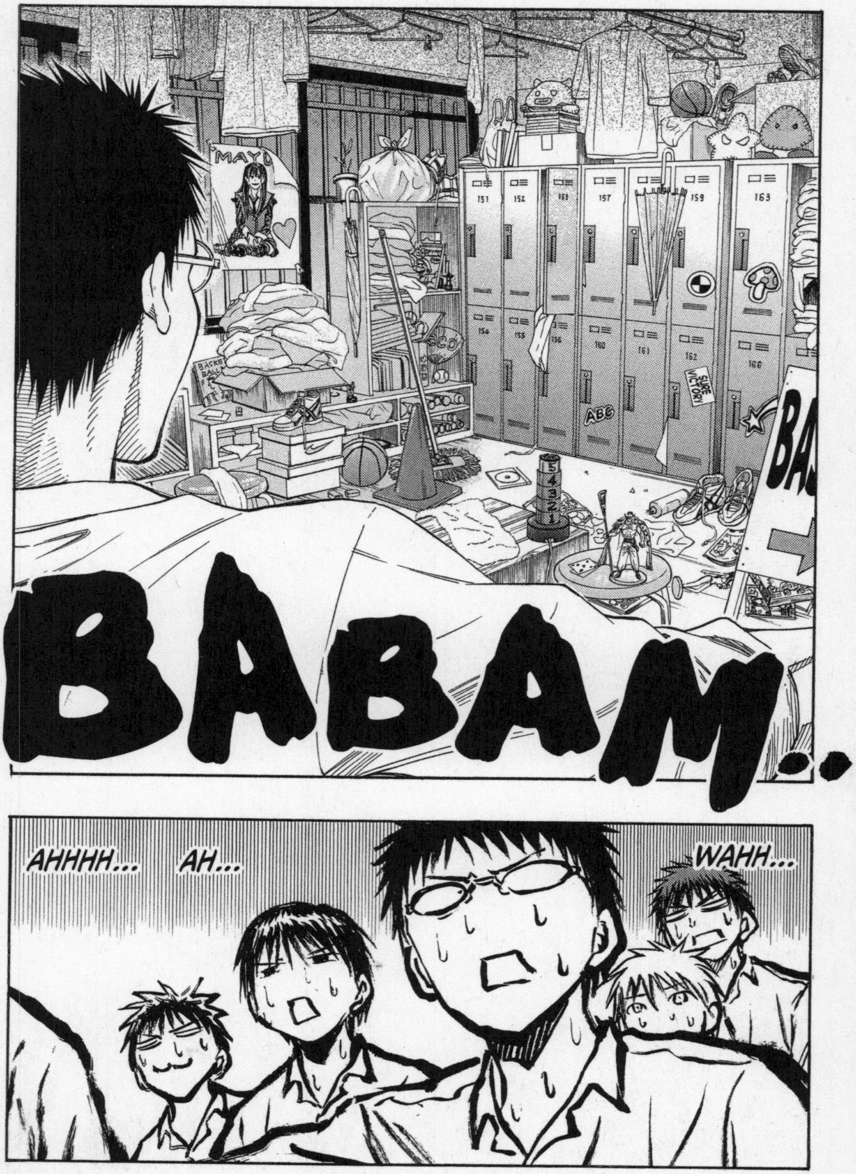
MAYU
SURE VICTORY!
ABC
BABAM..
WAHH...
AH...
AHHHH...

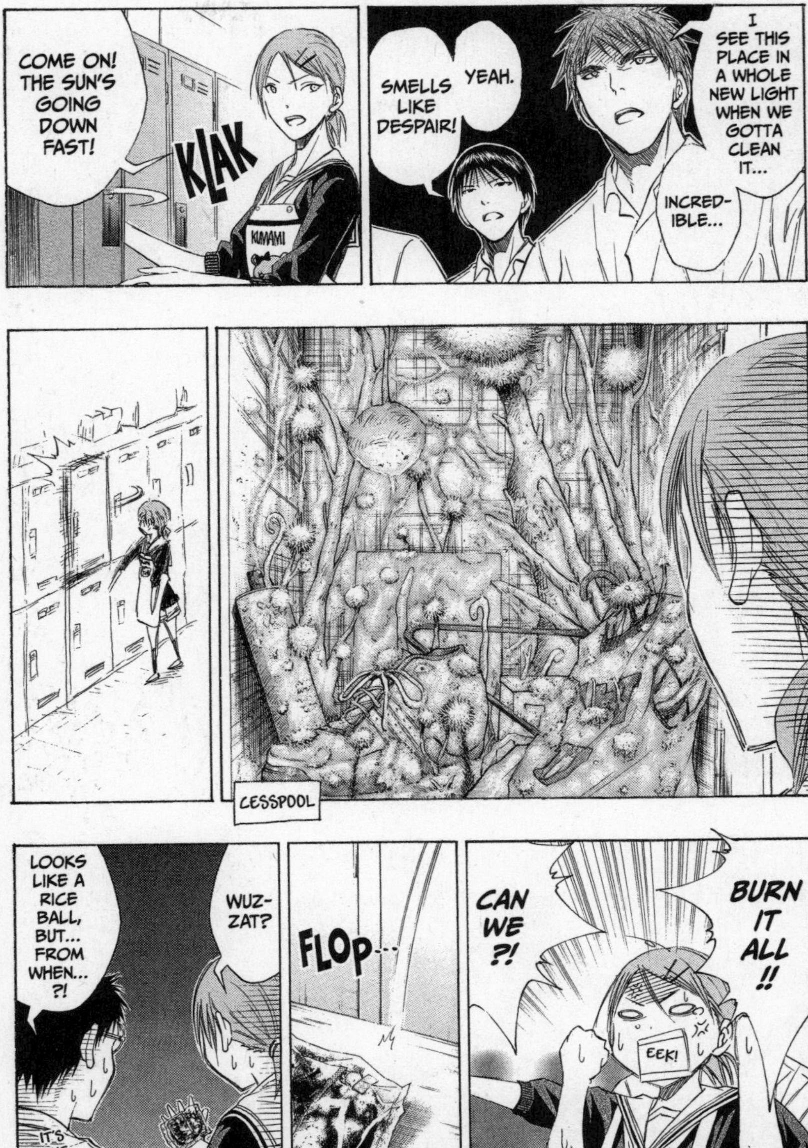
I SEE THIS PLACE IN A WHOLE NEW LIGHT WHEN WE GOTTA CLEAN IT...
INCREDIBLE...
YEAH.
SMELLS LIKE DESPAIR!
COME ON! THE SUN'S GOING DOWN FAST!
KLAK
KUMAMI
CESSPOOL
BURN IT ALL!!
CAN WE ?!
EEK!
WUZ-ZAT?
FLOP...
LOOKS LIKE A RICE BALL, BUT... FROM WHEN... ?!
IT'S LIQUE-FIED ...?!

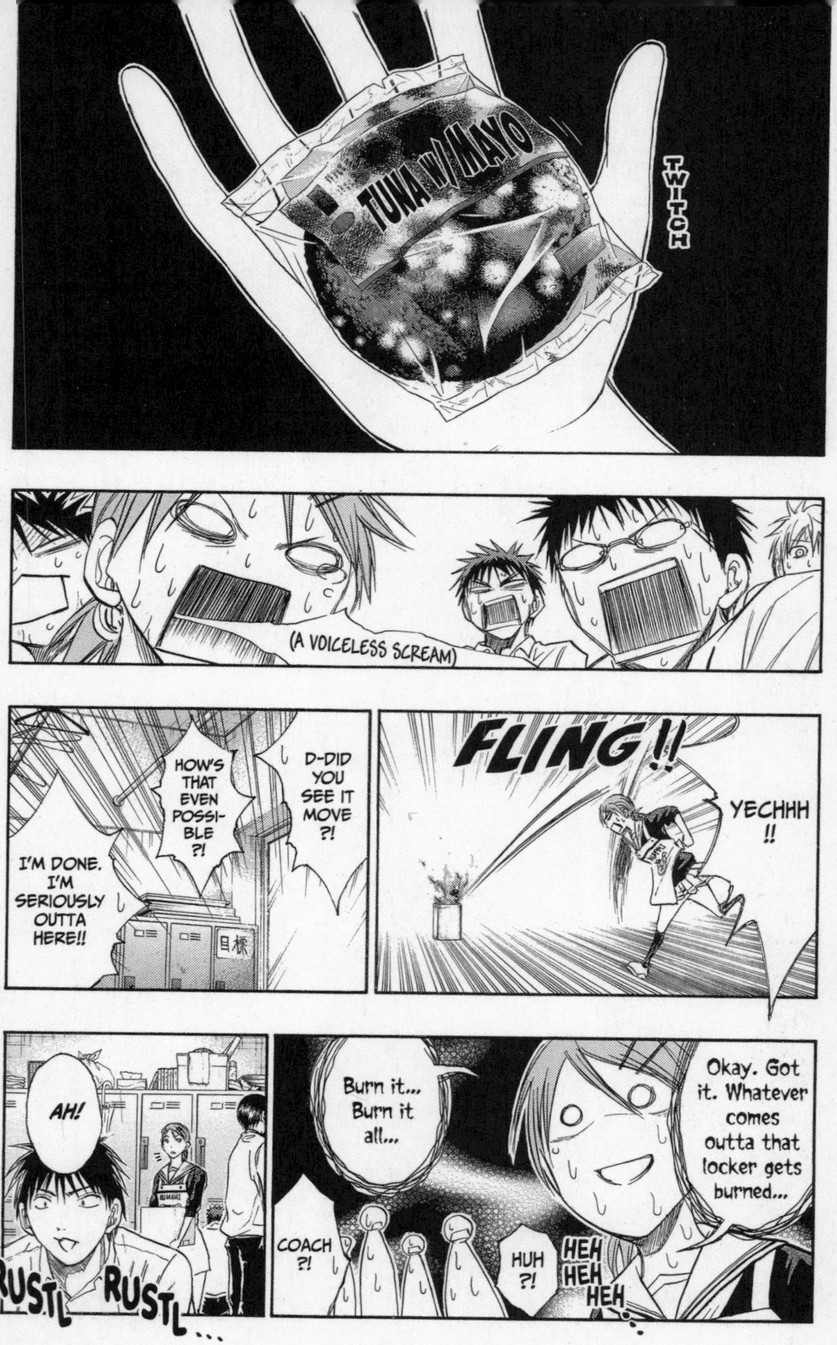
TUNA w/ MAYO
TWITCH
(A VOICELESS SCREAM)
FLING!!
YECHHH!!
D-DID YOU SEE IT MOVE?!
HOW'S THAT EVEN POSSIBLE?!
I'M DONE. I'M SERIOUSLY OUTTA HERE!!
目標
Okay. Got it. Whatever comes outta that locker gets burned...
HEH HEH HEH...
Burn it... Burn it all...
HUH?!
COACH?!
AH!
RUSTL RUSTL...

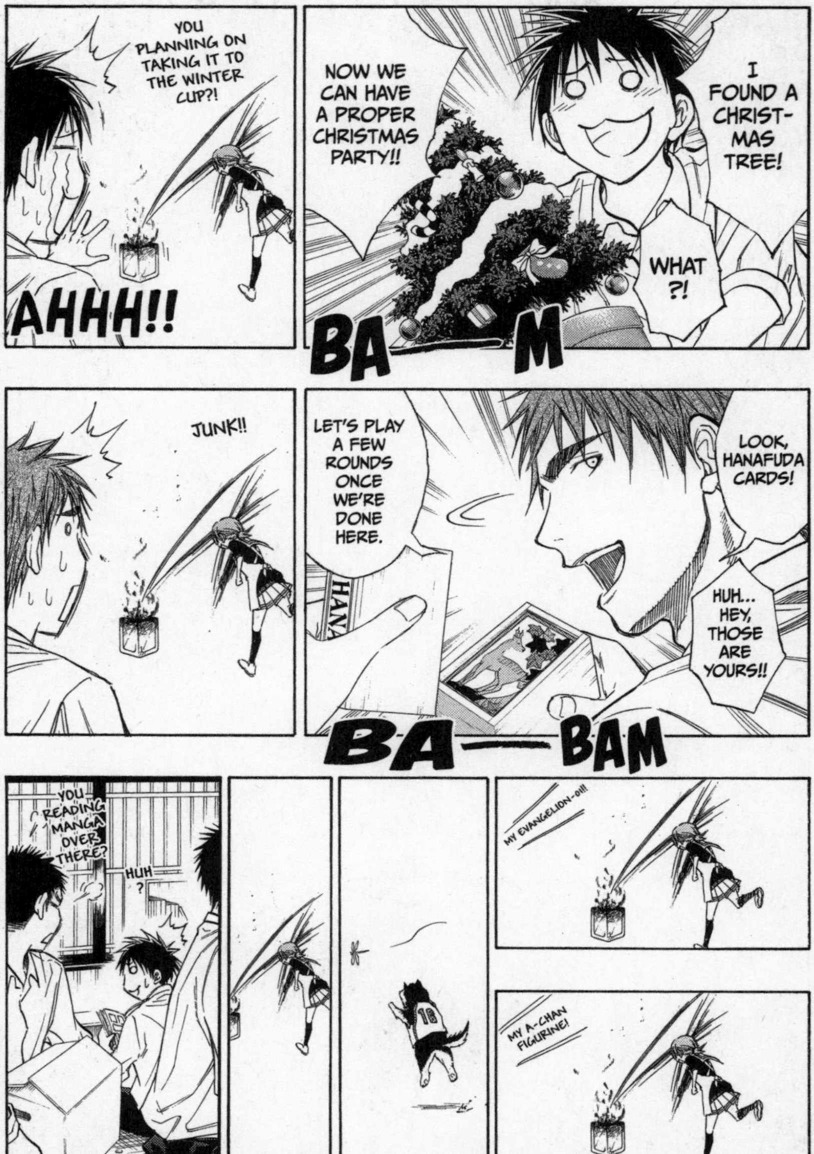
I FOUND A CHRIST-MAS TREE!
NOW WE CAN HAVE A PROPER CHRISTMAS PARTY!!
WHAT?!
BA—M
YOU PLANNING ON TAKING IT TO THE WINTER CUP?!
AHHH!!
LOOK, HANAFUDA CARDS!
LET'S PLAY A FEW ROUNDS ONCE WE'RE DONE HERE.
HUH... HEY, THOSE ARE YOURS!!
BA—BAM
JUNK!!
MY EVANGELION-01!!
MY A-CHAN FIGURINE!
YOU READING MANGA OVER THERE?
HUH?

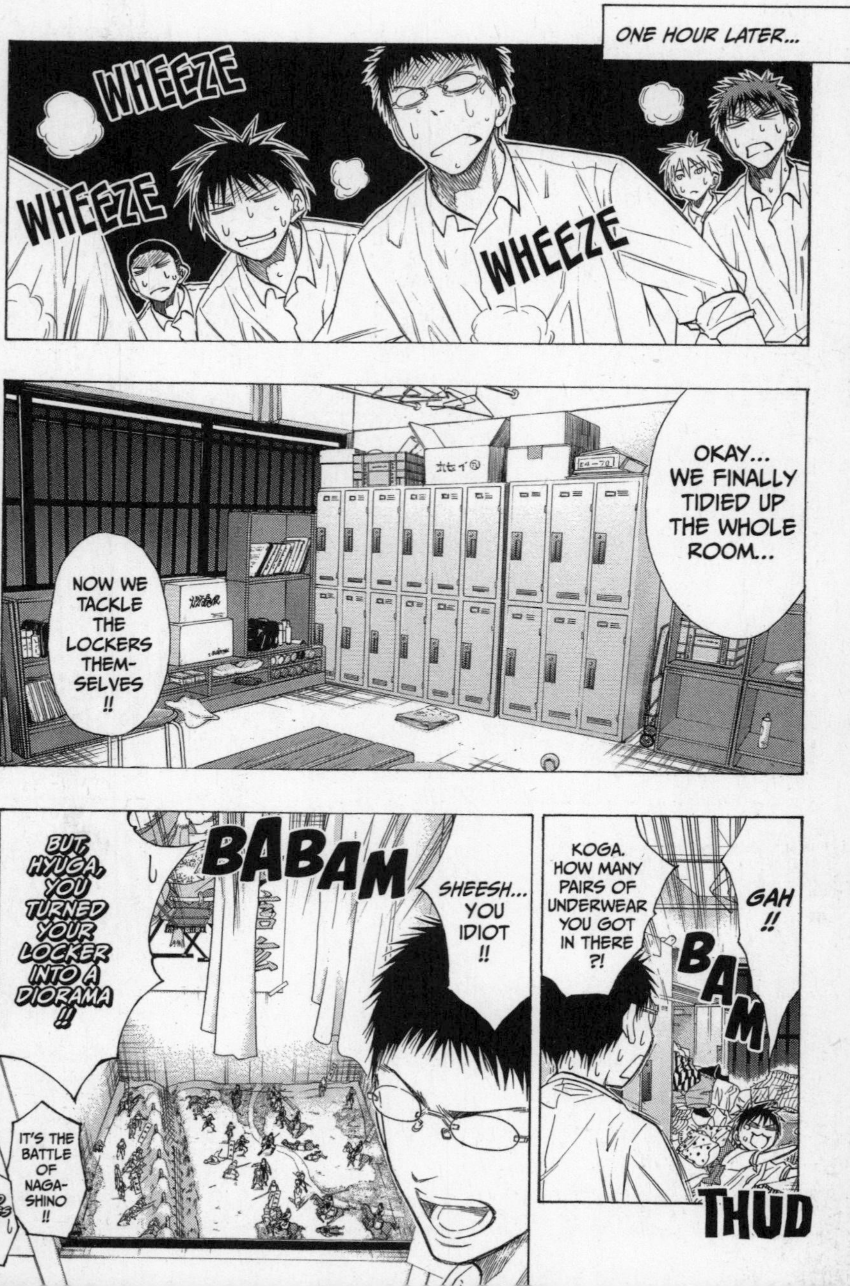
ONE HOUR LATER...
WHEEZE
WHEEZE
WHEEZE
OKAY... WE FINALLY TIDIED UP THE WHOLE ROOM...
NOW WE TACKLE THE LOCKERS THEM-SELVES !!
KOGA. HOW MANY PAIRS OF UNDERWEAR YOU GOT IN THERE ?!
GAH !!
BAM
THUD
SHEESH... YOU IDIOT !!
BABAM
BUT, HYUGA, YOU TURNED YOUR LOCKER INTO A DIORAMA !!
IT'S THE BATTLE OF NAGA-SHINO !!
WHO CARES !!

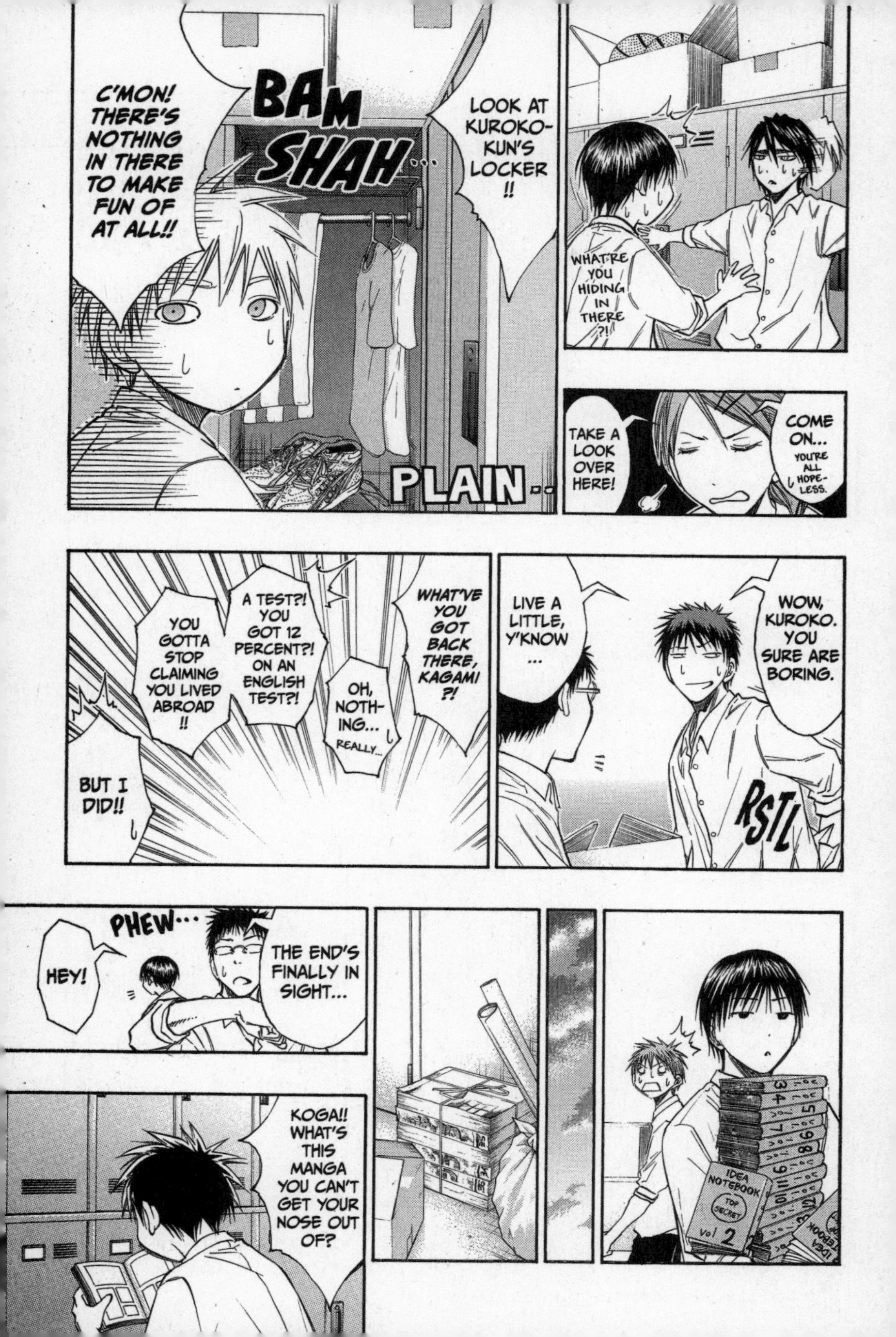
WHAT'RE YOU HIDING IN THERE?!
COME ON... YOU'RE ALL HOPELESS.
TAKE A LOOK OVER HERE!
LOOK AT KUROKO-KUN'S LOCKER!!
BAM SHAH...
C'MON! THERE'S NOTHING IN THERE TO MAKE FUN OF AT ALL!!
PLAIN..
WOW, KUROKO. YOU SURE ARE BORING.
RSTL
LIVE A LITTLE, Y'KNOW...
WHAT'VE YOU GOT BACK THERE, KAGAMI?!
OH, NOTHING... REALLY...
A TEST?! YOU GOT 12 PERCENT?! ON AN ENGLISH TEST?!
YOU GOTTA STOP CLAIMING YOU LIVED ABROAD!!
BUT I DID!!
IDEA NOTEBOOK
TOP SECRET
vol 2
PHEW...
THE END'S FINALLY IN SIGHT...
HEY!
KOGA!! WHAT'S THIS MANGA YOU CAN'T GET YOUR NOSE OUT OF?

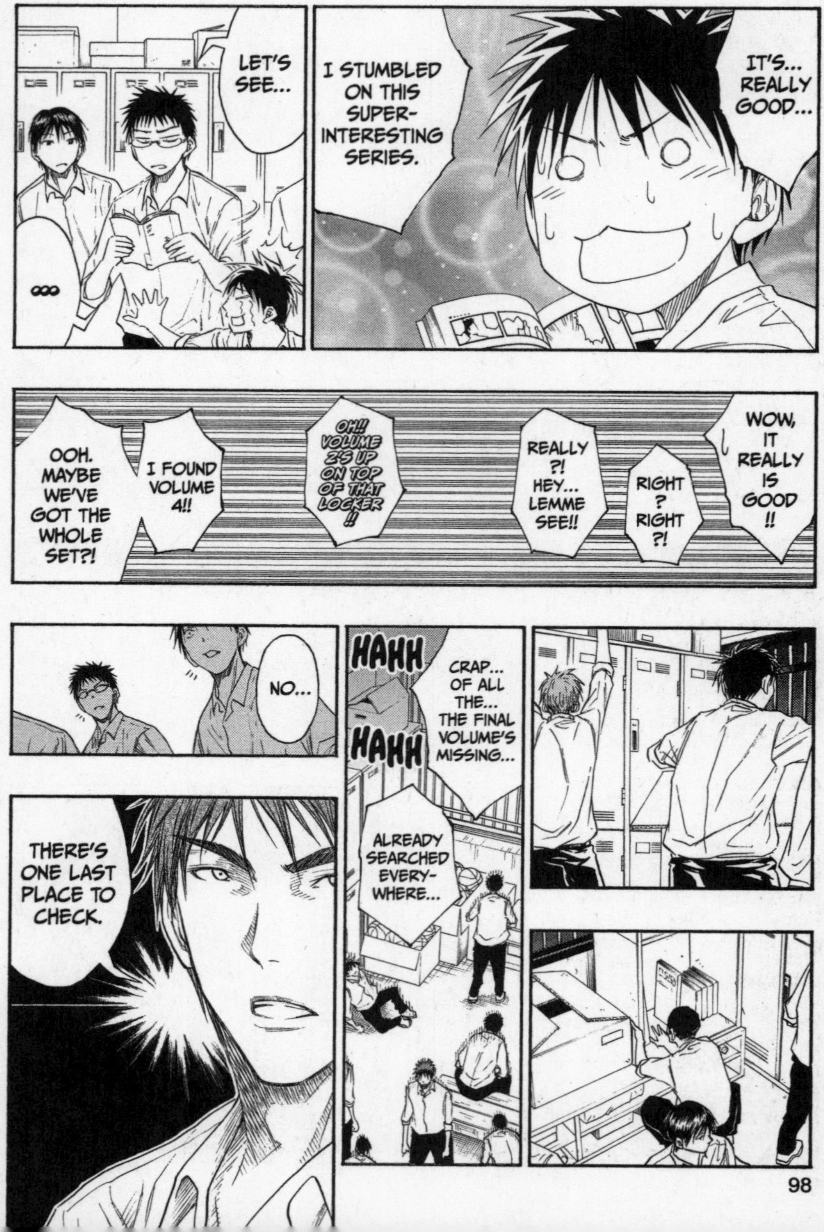
IT'S... REALLY GOOD...
I STUMBLED ON THIS SUPER-INTERESTING SERIES.
LET'S SEE...
...
WOW, IT REALLY IS GOOD!!
RIGHT? RIGHT?!
REALLY?! HEY... LEMME SEE!!
OH!! VOLUME 2'S UP ON TOP OF THAT LOCKER!!
I FOUND VOLUME 4!!
OOH. MAYBE WE'VE GOT THE WHOLE SET?!
HAHH
CRAP... OF ALL THE... THE FINAL VOLUME'S MISSING...
HAHH
ALREADY SEARCHED EVERY-WHERE...
NO...
THERE'S ONE LAST PLACE TO CHECK.

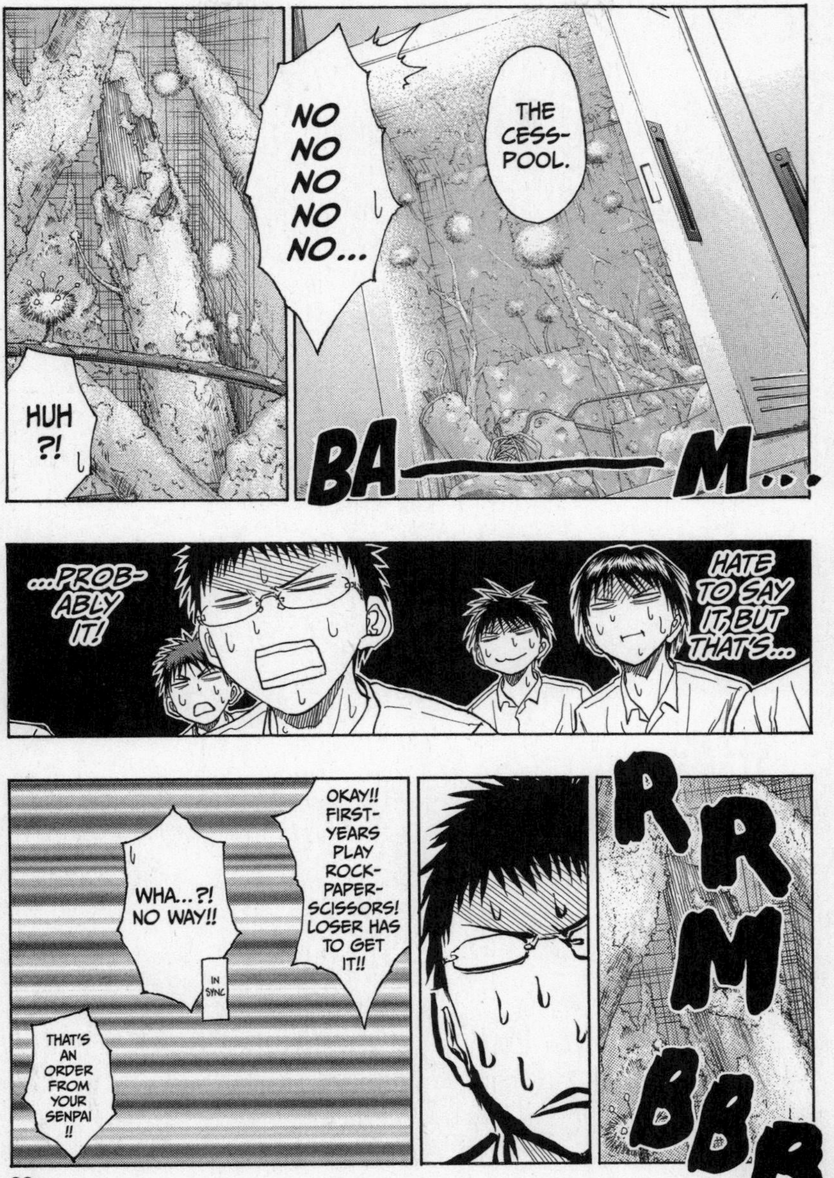
THE CESS-POOL.
NO NO NO NO NO...
BA——M...
HUH ?!
HATE TO SAY IT, BUT THAT'S...
...PROB-ABLY IT!
RRRMBBB
OKAY!! FIRST-YEARS PLAY ROCK-PAPER-SCISSORS! LOSER HAS TO GET IT!!
WHA...?! NO WAY!!
IN SYNC
THAT'S AN ORDER FROM YOUR SENPAI!!

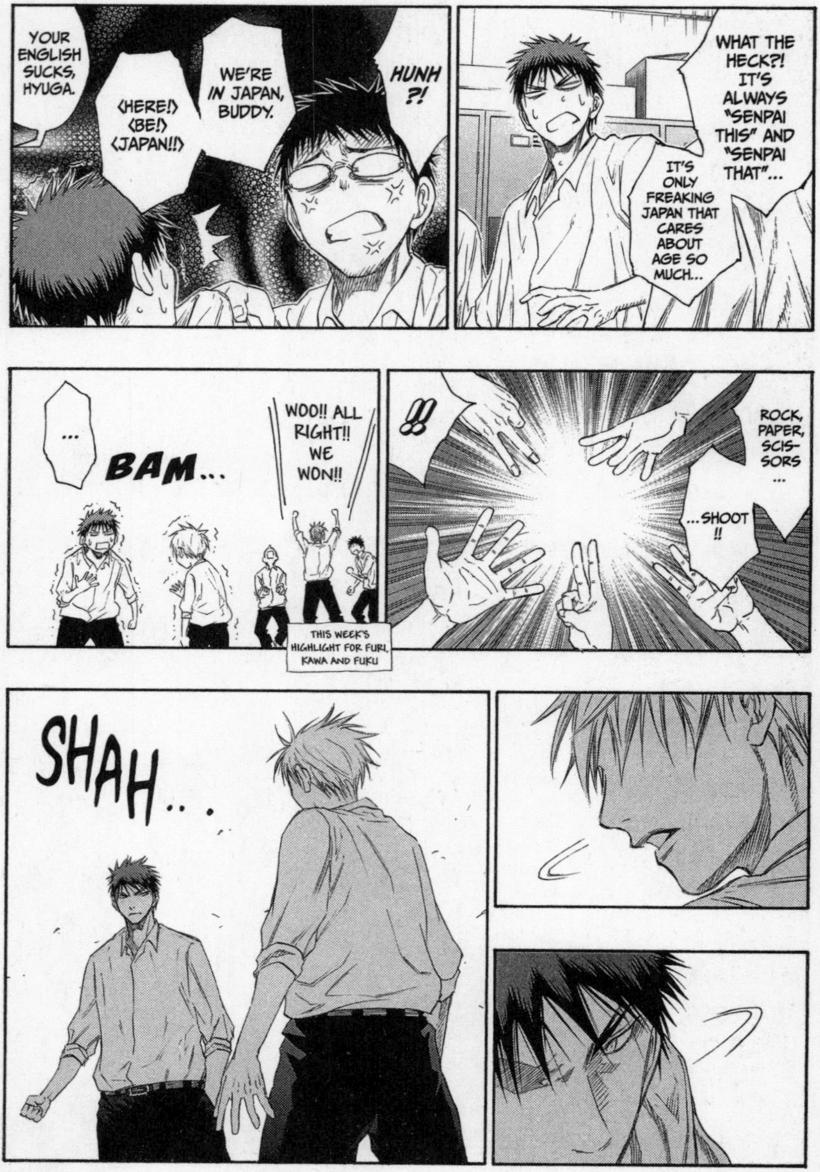
WHAT THE HECK?! IT'S ALWAYS "SENPAI THIS" AND "SENPAI THAT"...
IT'S ONLY FREAKING JAPAN THAT CARES ABOUT AGE SO MUCH...
HUNH ?!
WE'RE IN JAPAN, BUDDY.
<HERE!> <BE!> <JAPAN!!>
YOUR ENGLISH SUCKS, HYUGA.
ROCK, PAPER, SCISSORS ...
...SHOOT !!
!!
WOO!! ALL RIGHT!! WE WON!!
BAM...
...
THIS WEEK'S HIGHLIGHT FOR FURI, KAWA AND FUKU
SHAH...

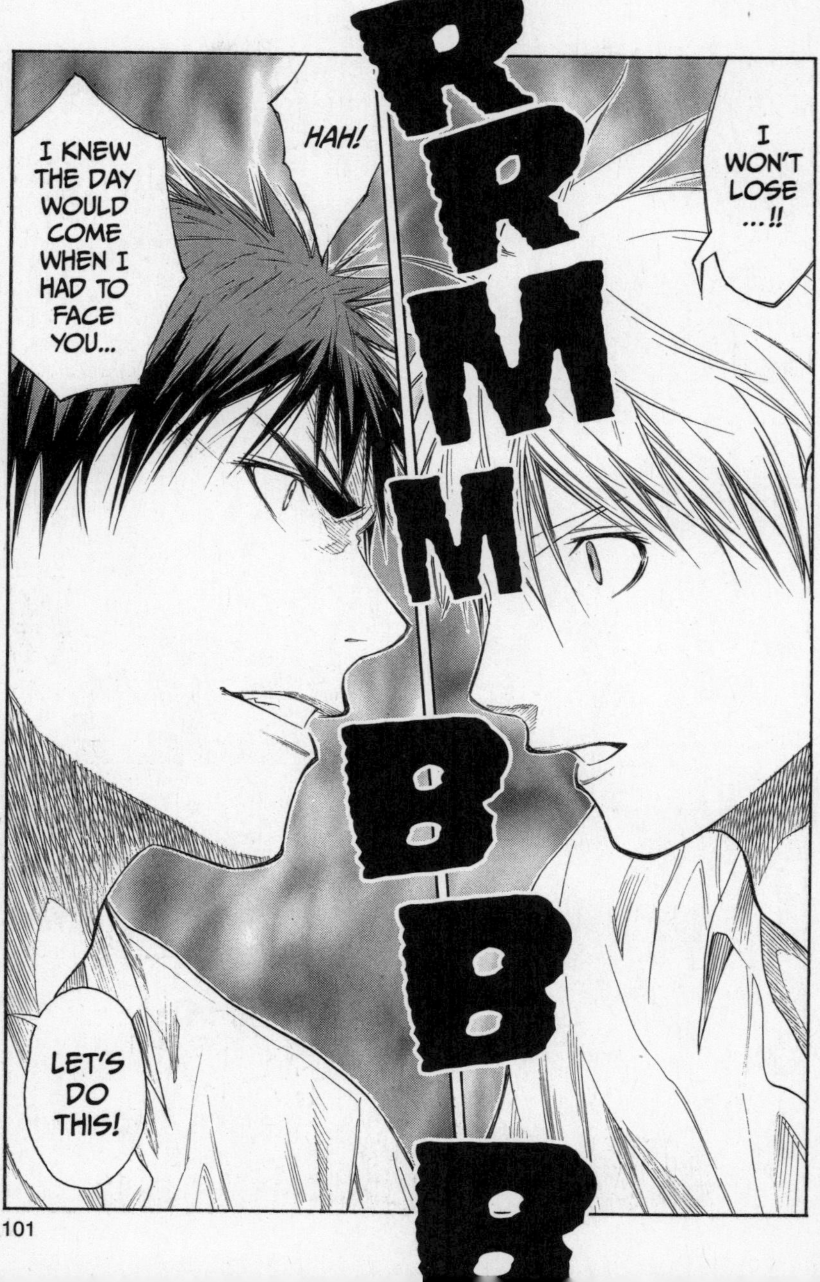

I WON'T LOSE ...!!
HAH!
RRMMBBB
I KNEW THE DAY WOULD COME WHEN I HAD TO FACE YOU...
LET'S DO THIS!

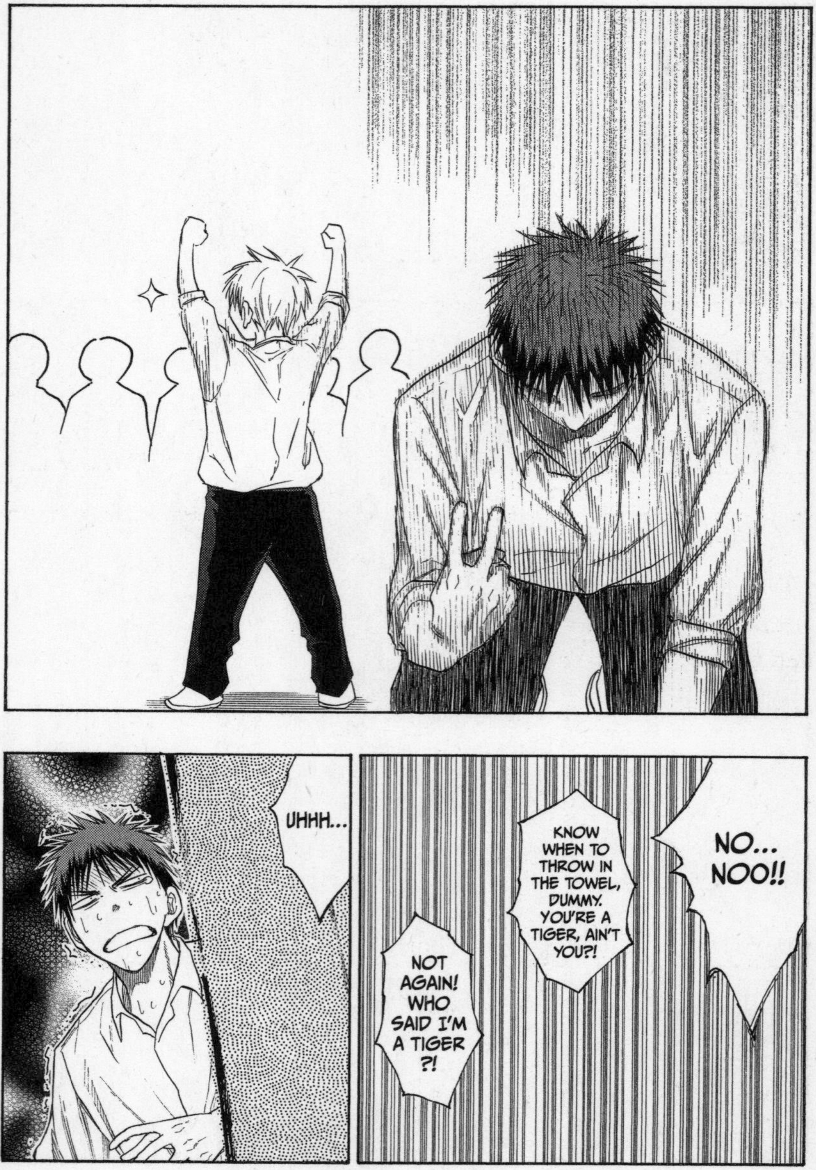
NO... NOO!!
KNOW WHEN TO THROW IN THE TOWEL, DUMMY. YOU'RE A TIGER, AIN'T YOU?!
NOT AGAIN! WHO SAID I'M A TIGER ?!
UHHH...

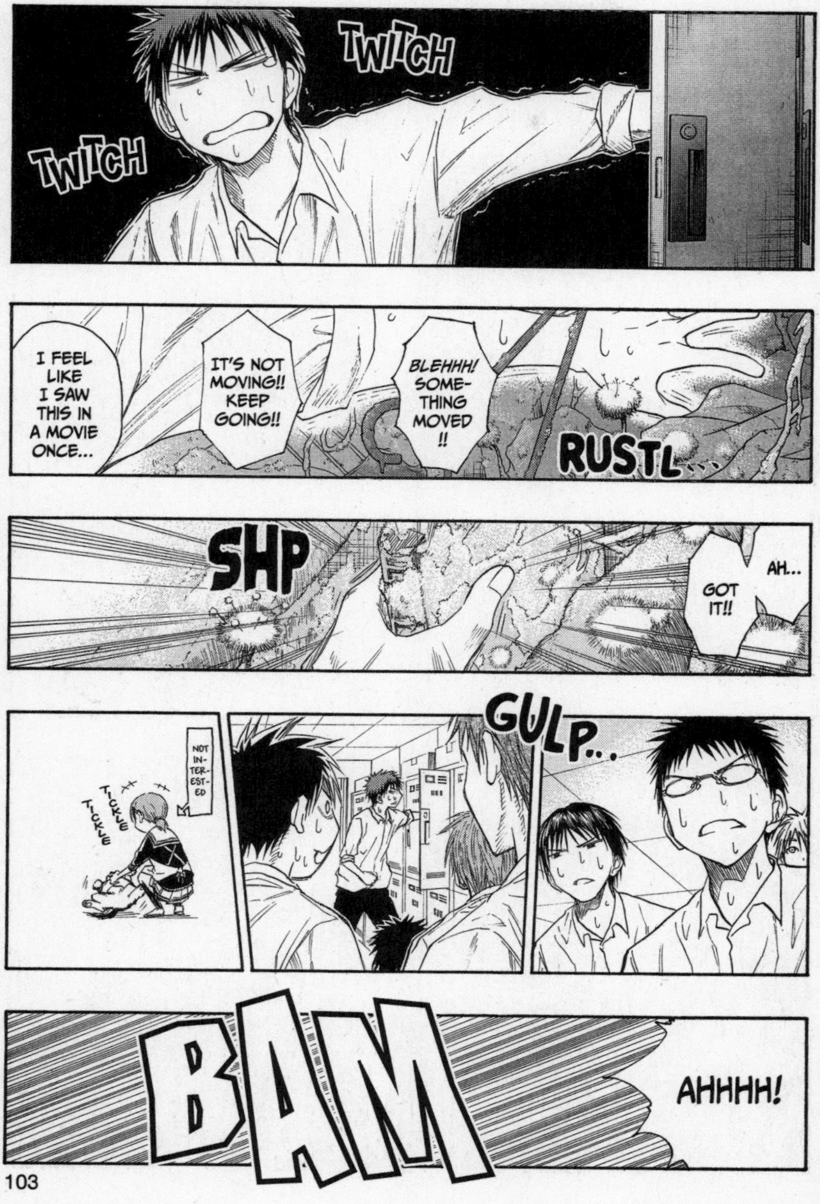

TWITCH
TWITCH
RUSTL...
BLEHHH! SOMETHING MOVED !!
IT'S NOT MOVING!! KEEP GOING!!
I FEEL LIKE I SAW THIS IN A MOVIE ONCE...
AH...
GOT IT!!
SHP
GULP...
NOT INTERESTED
TICKLE TICKLE
AHHHH!
BAM

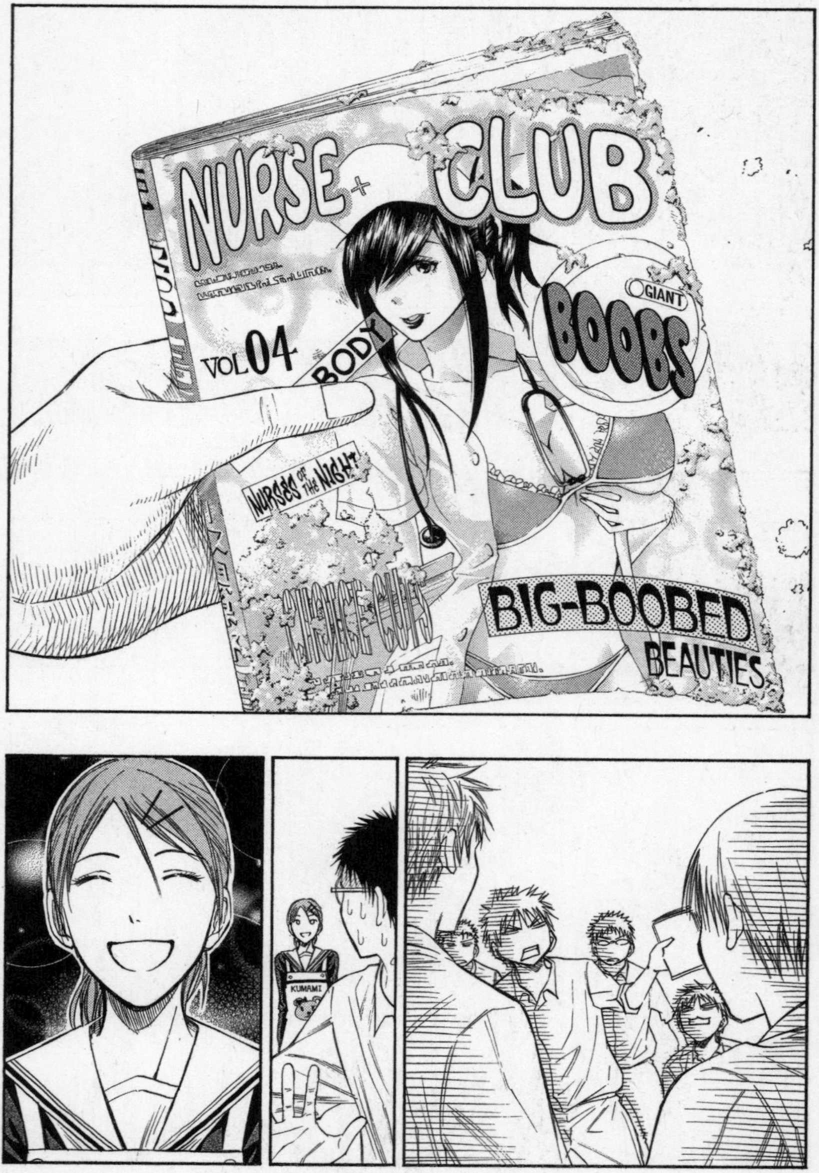
NURSE + CLUB
VOL 04
BODY
GIANT
BOOBS
NURSES OF THE NIGHT
BIG-BOOBED
BEAUTIES
KUMAMI

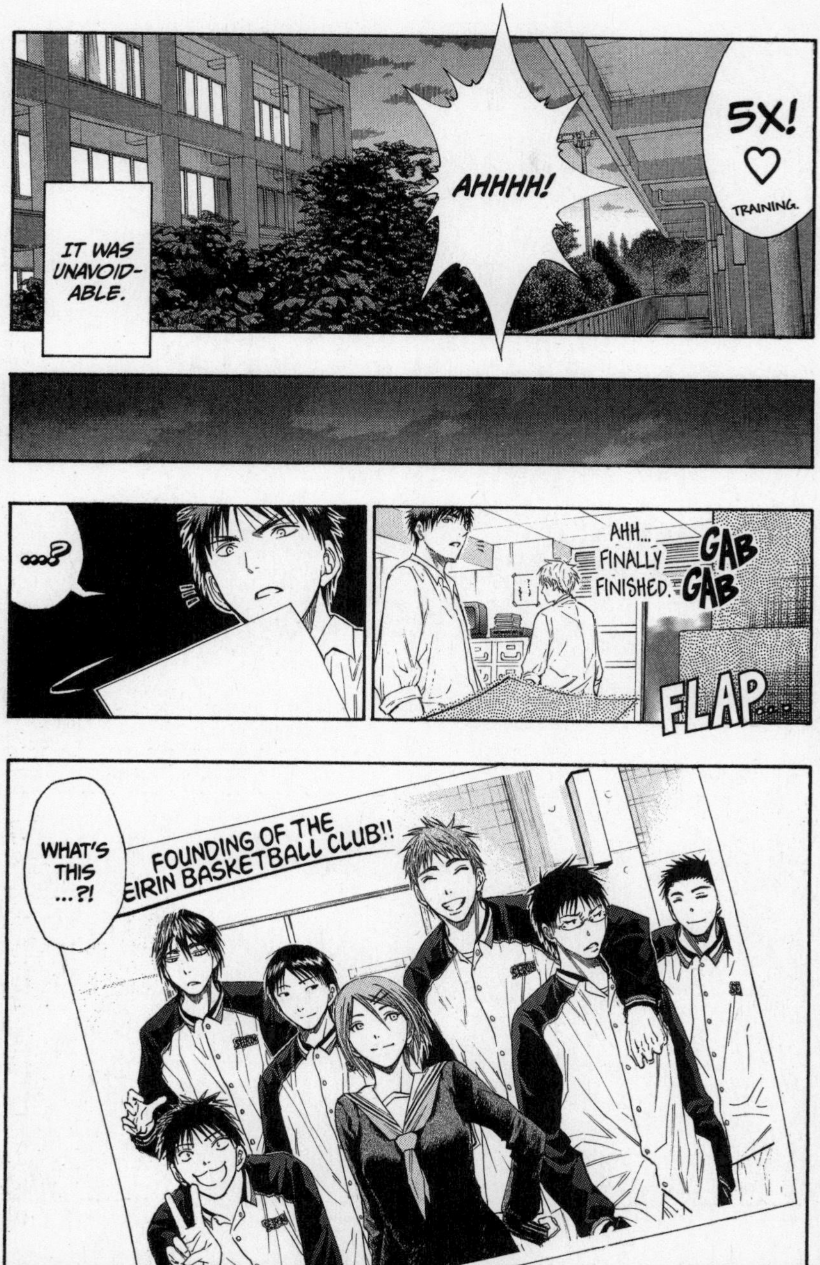
5X! ♡ TRAINING.
AHHHH!
IT WAS UNAVOID-ABLE.
AHH... FINALLY FINISHED.
GAB GAB
FLAP...
...?
FOUNDING OF THE EIRIN BASKETBALL CLUB!!
WHAT'S THIS ...?!

KUROKO'S BASKETBALL BLOOPERS

TAKE 3

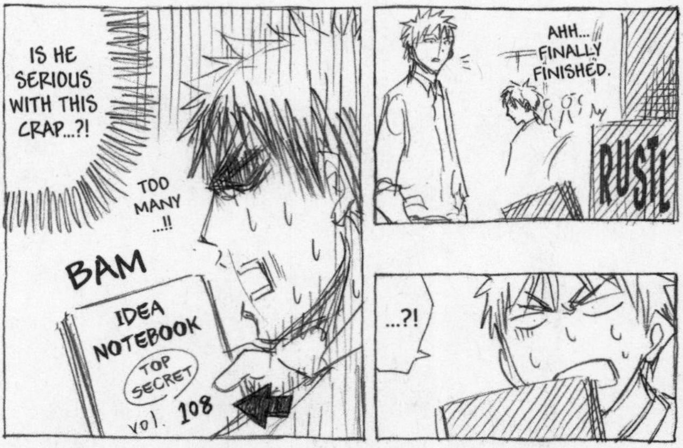
AHH... FINALLY FINISHED.
RUSTL
...?!
IS HE SERIOUS WITH THIS CRAP...?!
TOO MANY ...!!
BAM
IDEA NOTEBOOK
TOP SECRET
vol. 108

95TH QUARTER: LET'S START IT OURSELVES

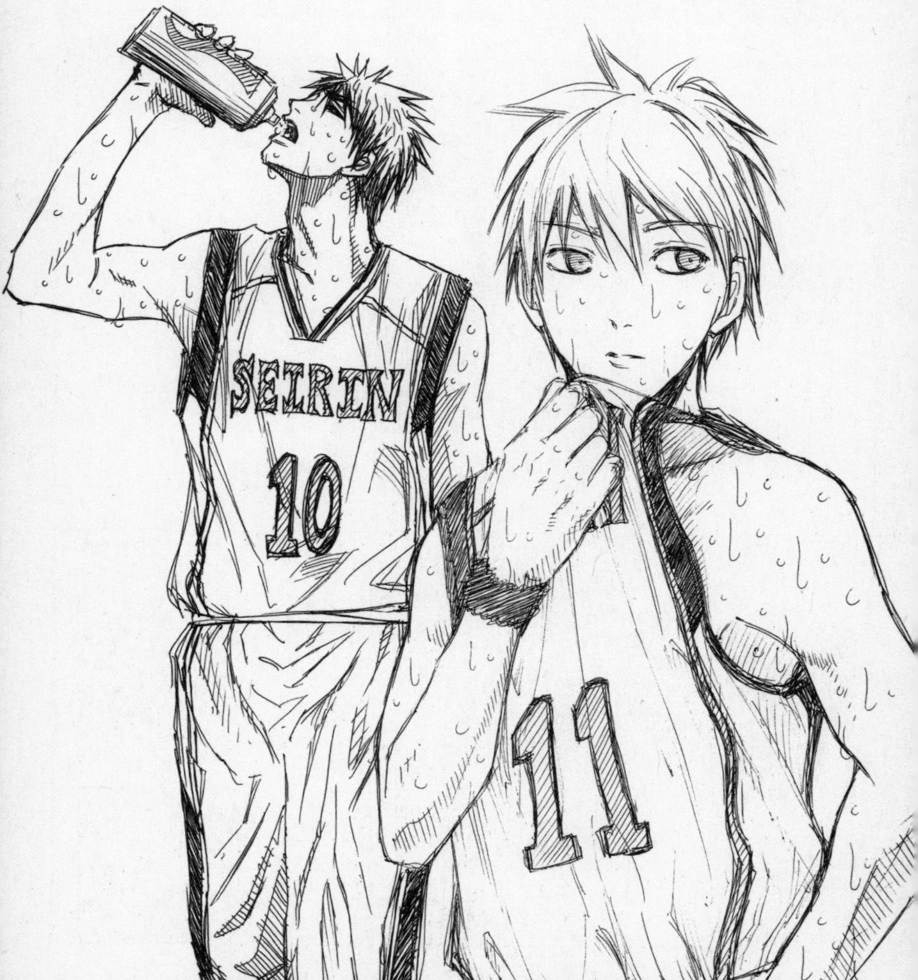
SEIRIN
10
11

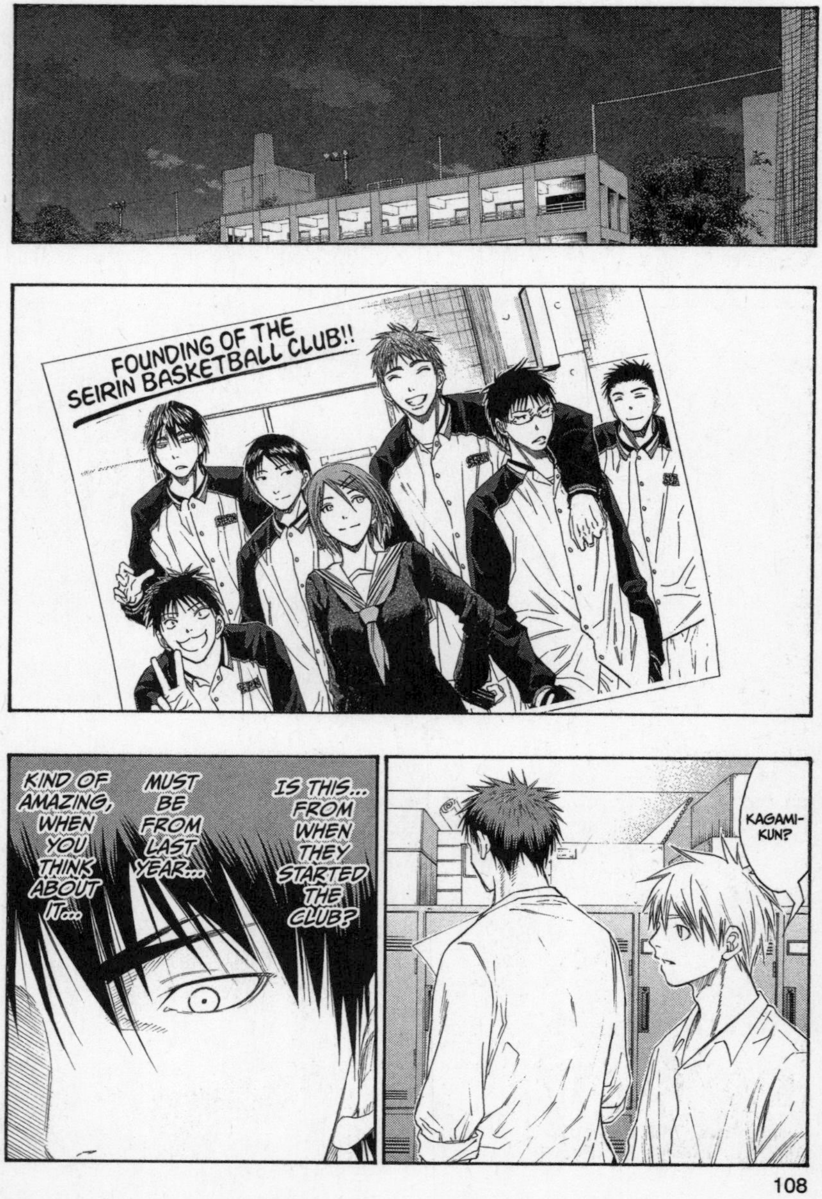
FOUNDING OF THE SEIRIN BASKETBALL CLUB!!
KAGAMI-KUN?
IS THIS... FROM WHEN THEY STARTED THE CLUB?
MUST BE FROM LAST YEAR...
KIND OF AMAZING, WHEN YOU THINK ABOUT IT...

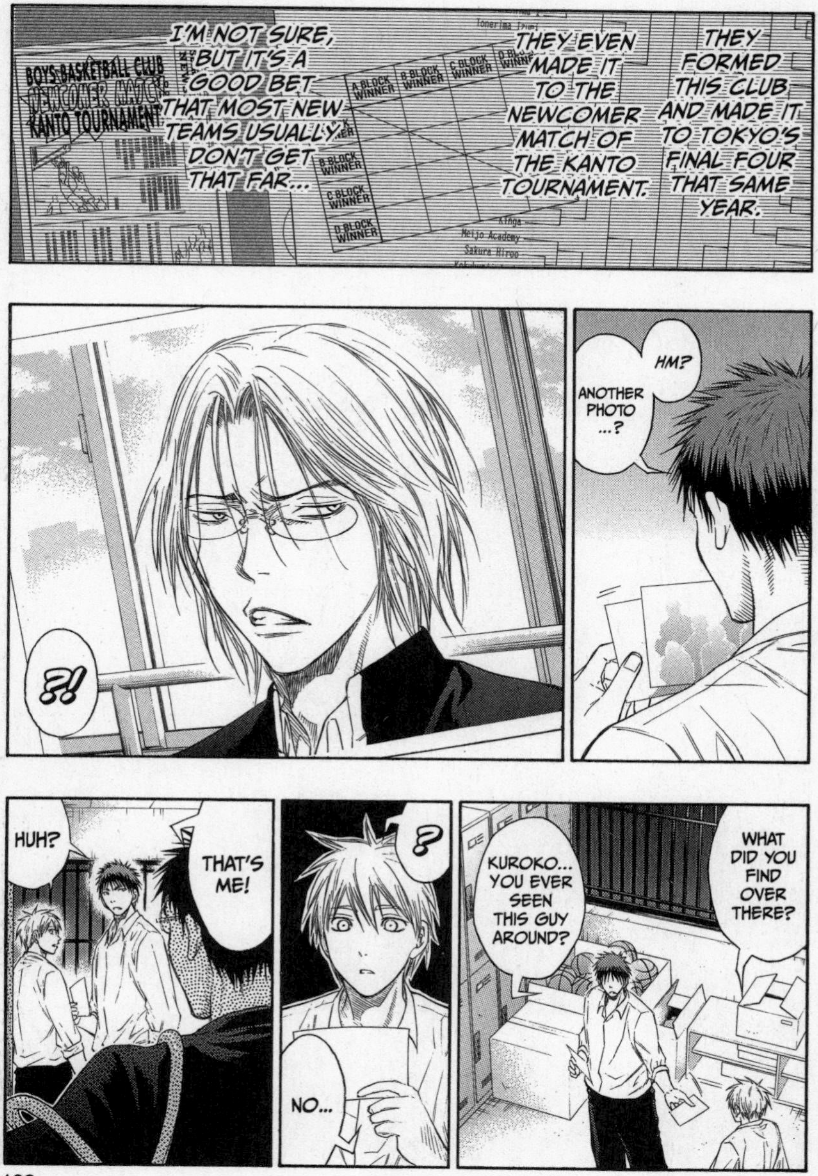
THEY FORMED THIS CLUB AND MADE IT TO TOKYO'S FINAL FOUR THAT SAME YEAR.
THEY EVEN MADE IT TO THE NEWCOMER MATCH OF THE KANTO TOURNAMENT.
I'M NOT SURE, BUT IT'S A GOOD BET THAT MOST NEW TEAMS USUALLY DON'T GET THAT FAR...
BOYS BASKETBALL CLUB
NEWCOMER MATCH
KANTO TOURNAMENT
A BLOCK WINNER
B BLOCK WINNER
C BLOCK WINNER
B BLOCK WINNER
C BLOCK WINNER
D BLOCK WINNER
Tonerima Izumi
Kinga
Meijo Academy
Sakura Hiroo
HM?
ANOTHER PHOTO ...?
?!
WHAT DID YOU FIND OVER THERE?
KUROKO... YOU EVER SEEN THIS GUY AROUND?
?
NO...
THAT'S ME!
HUH?

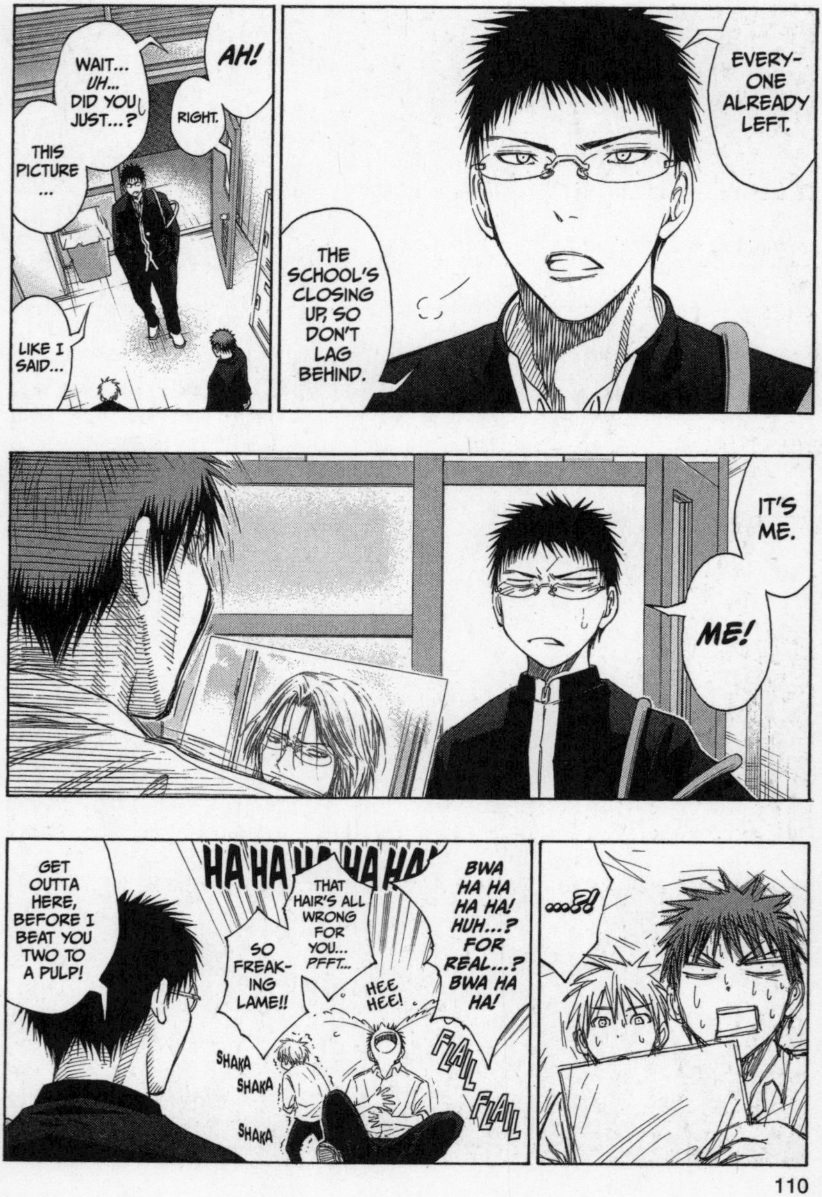
EVERY-ONE ALREADY LEFT.
THE SCHOOL'S CLOSING UP, SO DON'T LAG BEHIND.
AH!
RIGHT.
WAIT... UH... DID YOU JUST...?
THIS PICTURE ...
LIKE I SAID...
IT'S ME.
ME!
...?!
BWA HA HA HA HA! HUH...? FOR REAL...? BWA HA HA HA!
HA HA HA HA HA
FLAIL
FLAIL
THAT HAIR'S ALL WRONG FOR YOU... PFFT...
HEE HEE!
SO FREAKING LAME!!
SHAKA
SHAKA
SHAKA
GET OUTTA HERE, BEFORE I BEAT YOU TWO TO A PULP!

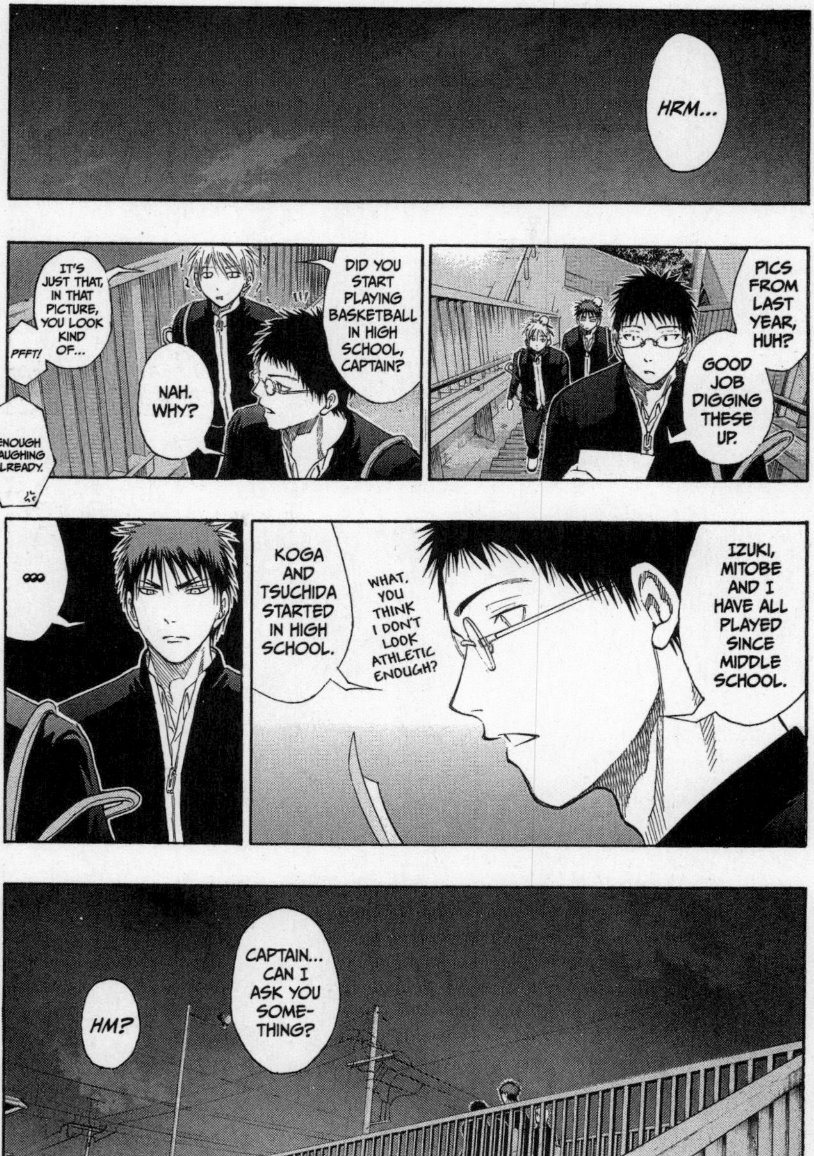
HRM...
PICS FROM LAST YEAR, HUH?
GOOD JOB DIGGING THESE UP.
DID YOU START PLAYING BASKETBALL IN HIGH SCHOOL, CAPTAIN?
NAH. WHY?
IT'S JUST THAT, IN THAT PICTURE, YOU LOOK KIND OF...
PFFT!
ENOUGH LAUGHING ALREADY.
IZUKI, MITOBE AND I HAVE ALL PLAYED SINCE MIDDLE SCHOOL.
KOGA AND TSUCHIDA STARTED IN HIGH SCHOOL.
WHAT, YOU THINK I DON'T LOOK ATHLETIC ENOUGH?
...
CAPTAIN... CAN I ASK YOU SOMETHING?
HM?

WHA—?

WHEN KIYOSHI SENPAI SAID THIS YEAR'S HIS *LAST* CHANCE...

WHAT'D HE MEAN?

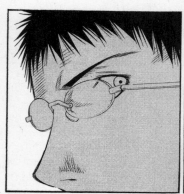

YOU OVER-HEARD ...?

GUESS I SHOULD TELL YOU.

...

RIGHT.

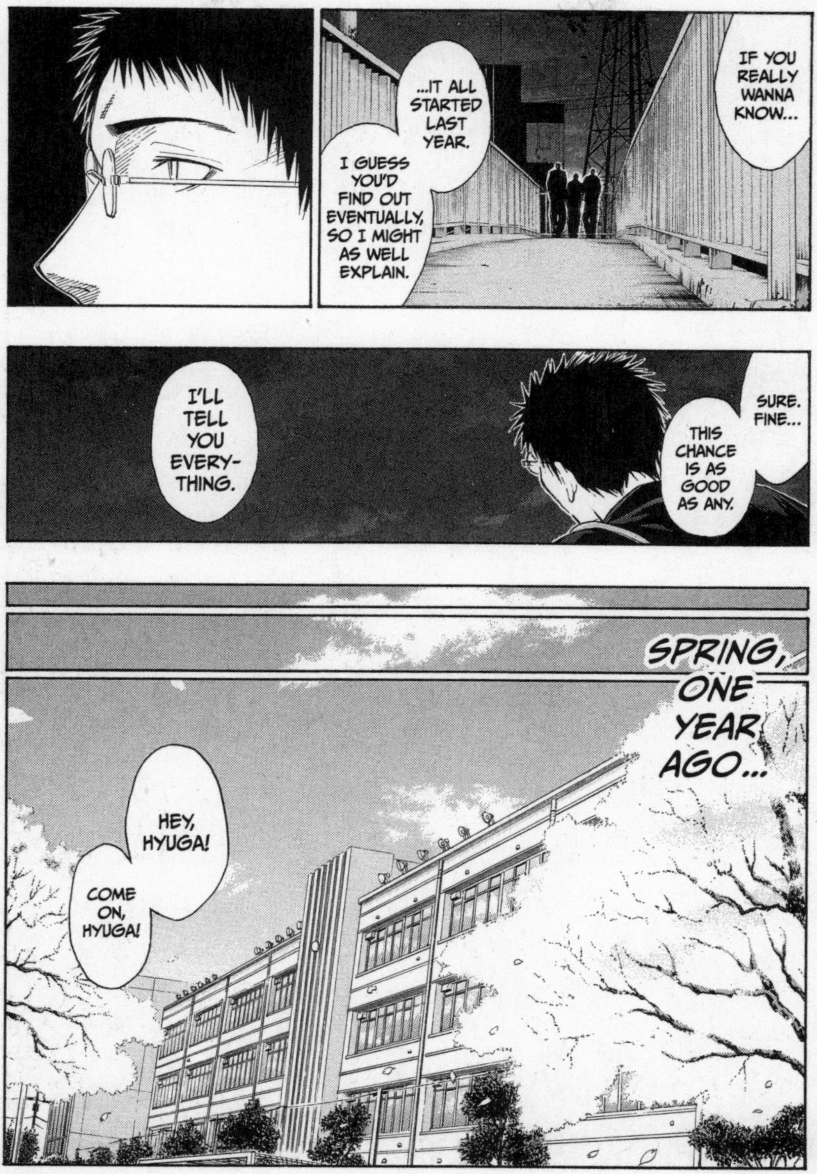
IF YOU REALLY WANNA KNOW...
...IT ALL STARTED LAST YEAR.
I GUESS YOU'D FIND OUT EVENTUALLY, SO I MIGHT AS WELL EXPLAIN.
SURE. FINE...
THIS CHANCE IS AS GOOD AS ANY.
I'LL TELL YOU EVERYTHING.
SPRING, ONE YEAR AGO...
HEY, HYUGA!
COME ON, HYUGA!

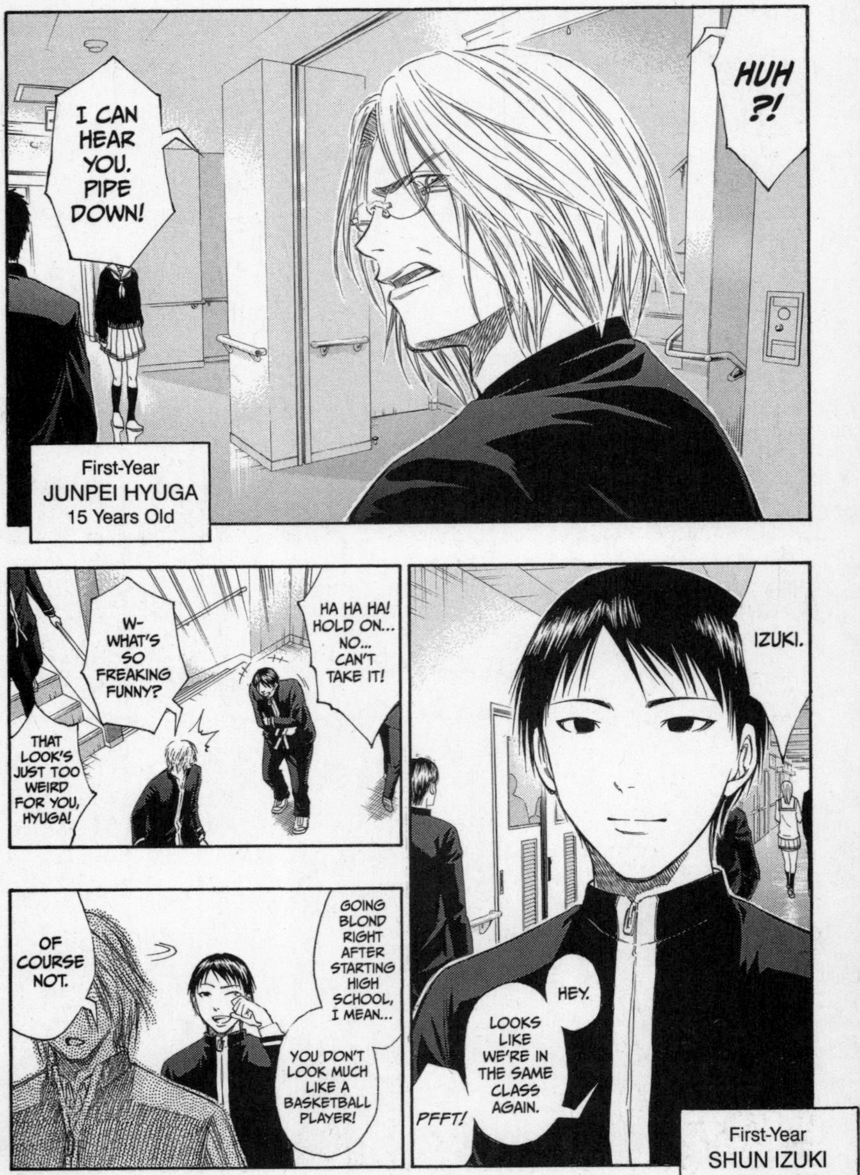
HUH ?!
I CAN HEAR YOU. PIPE DOWN!
First-Year JUNPEI HYUGA 15 Years Old
IZUKI.
HEY.
LOOKS LIKE WE'RE IN THE SAME CLASS AGAIN.
PFFT!
First-Year SHUN IZUKI 15 Years Old
HA HA HA! HOLD ON... NO... CAN'T TAKE IT!
W-WHAT'S SO FREAKING FUNNY?
THAT LOOK'S JUST TOO WEIRD FOR YOU, HYUGA!
GOING BLOND RIGHT AFTER STARTING HIGH SCHOOL, I MEAN...
YOU DON'T LOOK MUCH LIKE A BASKETBALL PLAYER!
OF COURSE NOT.

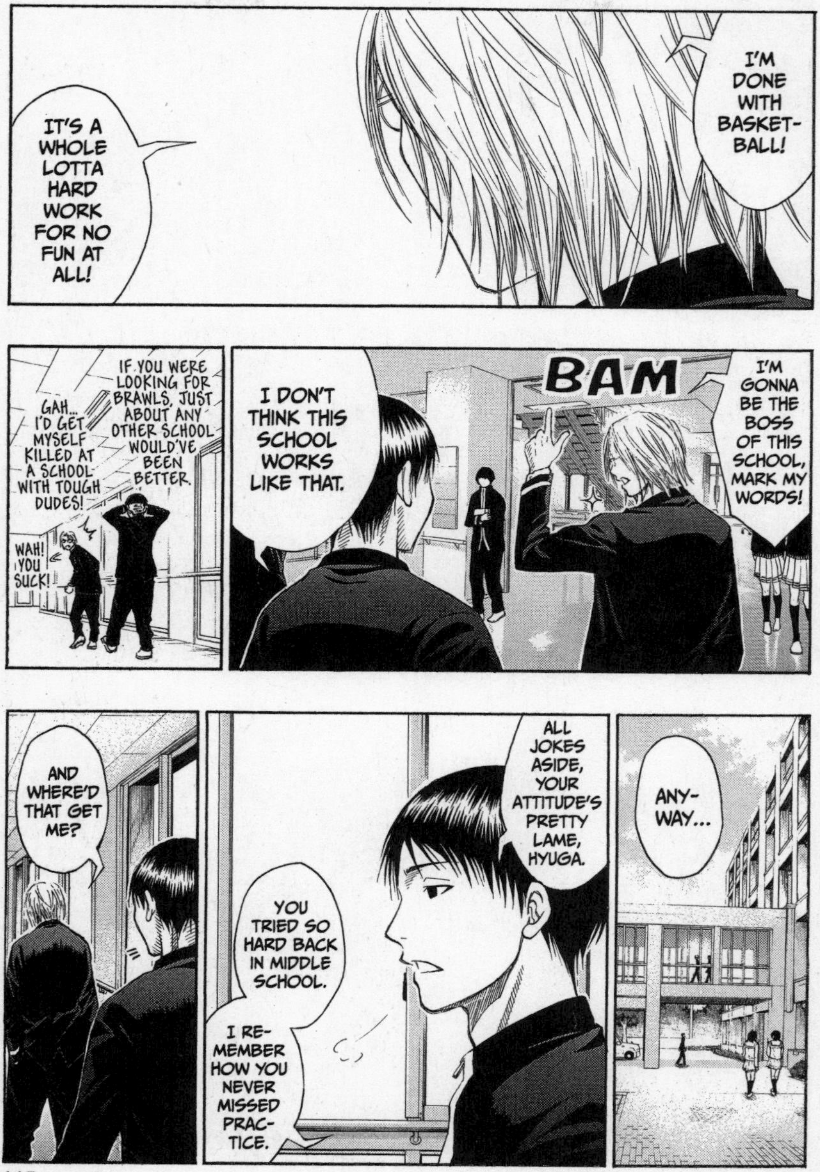
I'M DONE WITH BASKET-BALL!
IT'S A WHOLE LOTTA HARD WORK FOR NO FUN AT ALL!
BAM
I'M GONNA BE THE BOSS OF THIS SCHOOL, MARK MY WORDS!
I DON'T THINK THIS SCHOOL WORKS LIKE THAT.
IF YOU WERE LOOKING FOR BRAWLS, JUST ABOUT ANY OTHER SCHOOL WOULD'VE BEEN BETTER.
GAH... I'D GET MYSELF KILLED AT A SCHOOL WITH TOUGH DUDES!
WAH! YOU SUCK!
ANY-WAY...
ALL JOKES ASIDE, YOUR ATTITUDE'S PRETTY LAME, HYUGA.
YOU TRIED SO HARD BACK IN MIDDLE SCHOOL.
I RE-MEMBER HOW YOU NEVER MISSED PRAC-TICE.
AND WHERE'D THAT GET ME?

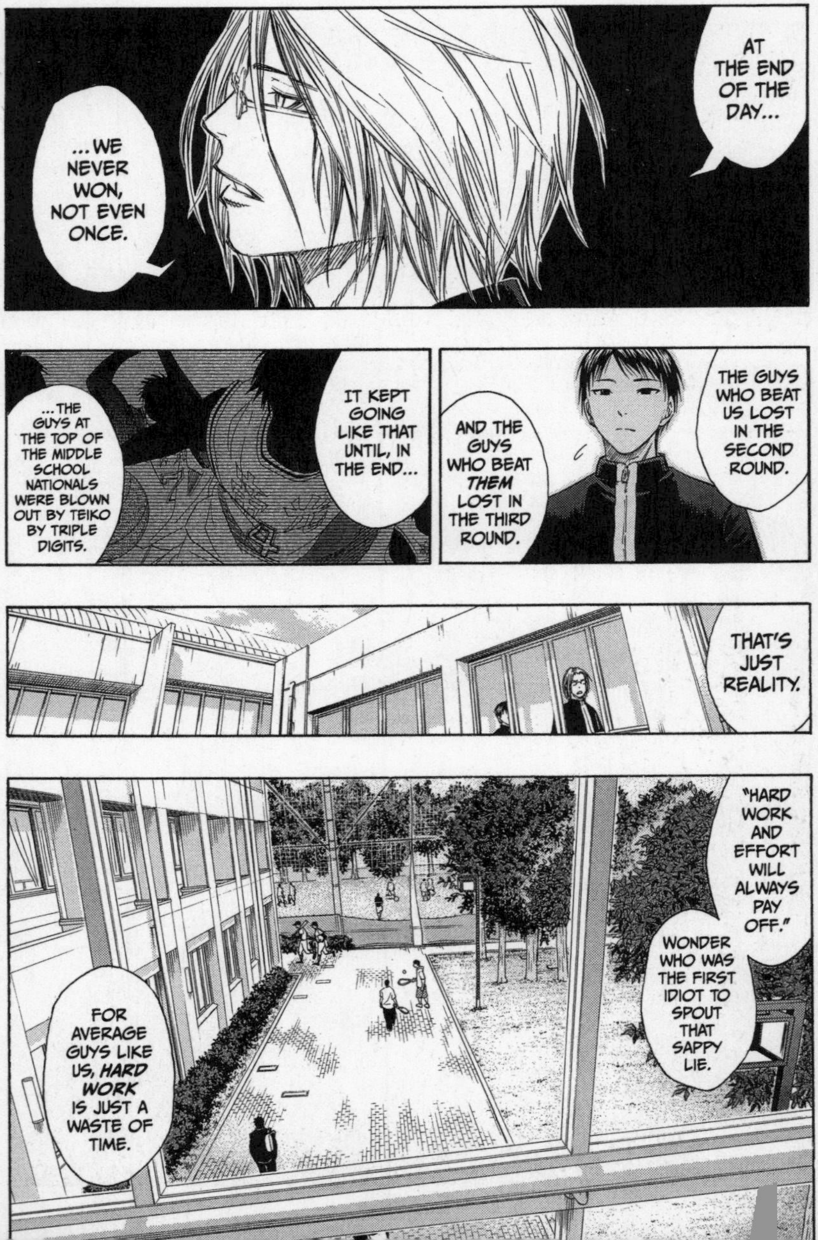
AT THE END OF THE DAY...
...WE NEVER WON, NOT EVEN ONCE.
THE GUYS WHO BEAT US LOST IN THE SECOND ROUND.
AND THE GUYS WHO BEAT *THEM* LOST IN THE THIRD ROUND.
IT KEPT GOING LIKE THAT UNTIL, IN THE END...
...THE GUYS AT THE TOP OF THE MIDDLE SCHOOL NATIONALS WERE BLOWN OUT BY TEIKO BY TRIPLE DIGITS.
THAT'S JUST REALITY.
"HARD WORK AND EFFORT WILL ALWAYS PAY OFF."
WONDER WHO WAS THE FIRST IDIOT TO SPOUT THAT SAPPY LIE.
FOR AVERAGE GUYS LIKE US, *HARD WORK* IS JUST A WASTE OF TIME.

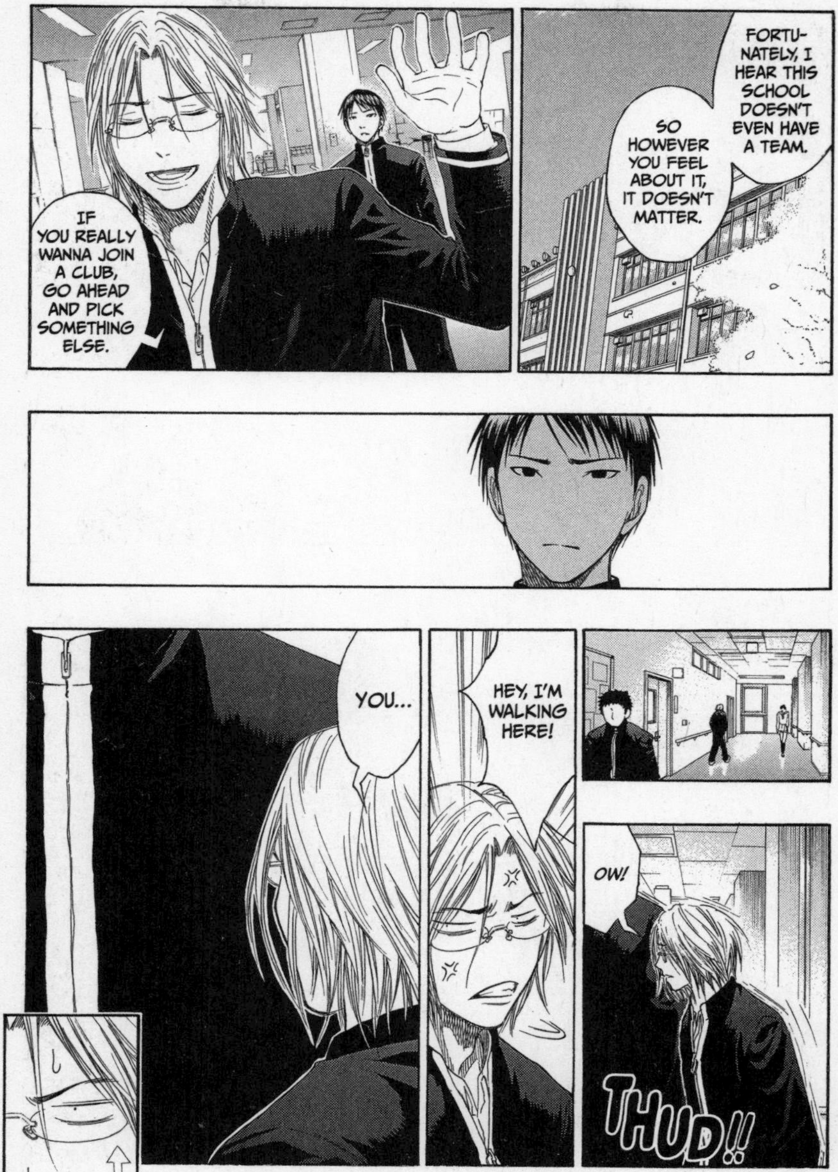
FORTU-NATELY, I HEAR THIS SCHOOL DOESN'T EVEN HAVE A TEAM.
SO HOWEVER YOU FEEL ABOUT IT, IT DOESN'T MATTER.
IF YOU REALLY WANNA JOIN A CLUB, GO AHEAD AND PICK SOMETHING ELSE.
OW!
THUD!!
HEY, I'M WALKING HERE!
YOU...

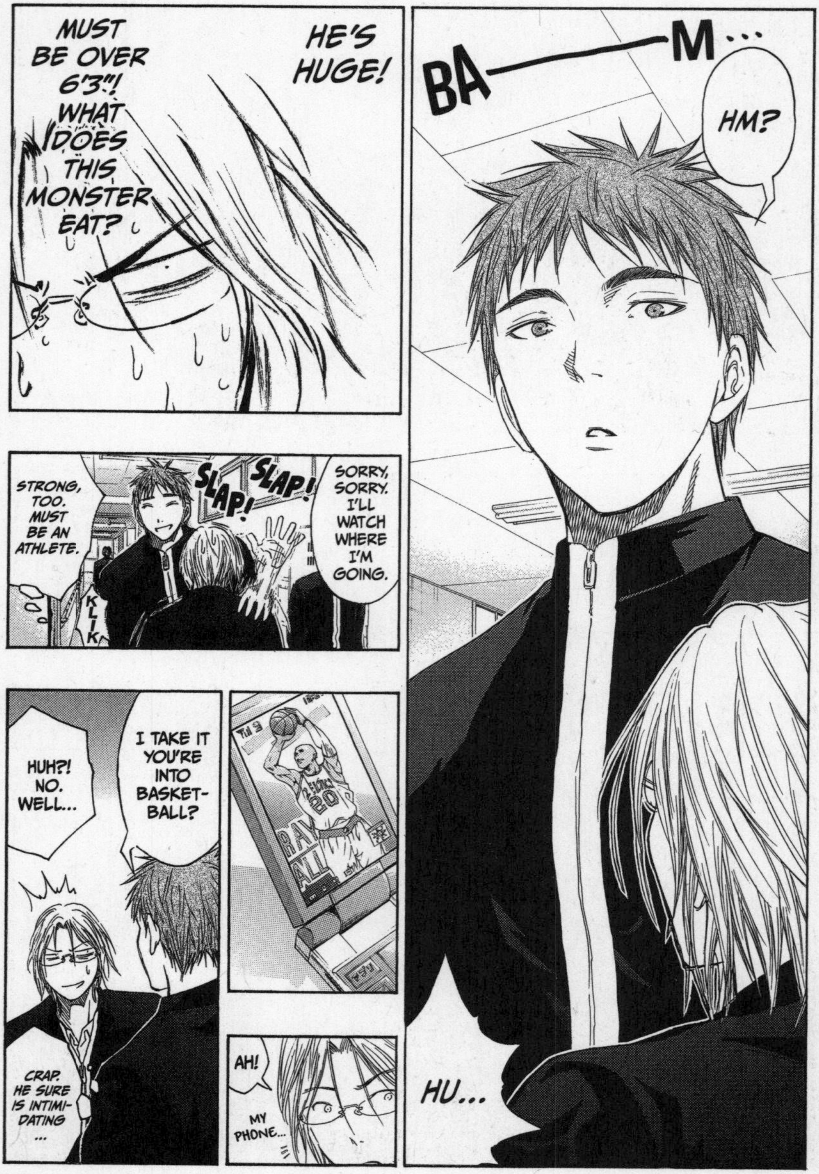
BA———M...
HM?
HU...
HE'S HUGE!
MUST BE OVER 6'3"! WHAT DOES THIS MONSTER EAT?
SLAP! SLAP!
SORRY, SORRY. I'LL WATCH WHERE I'M GOING.
STRONG, TOO. MUST BE AN ATHLETE.
KLIK
AH!
MY PHONE...
I TAKE IT YOU'RE INTO BASKET-BALL?
HUH?! NO. WELL...
CRAP. HE SURE IS INTIMI-DATING ...

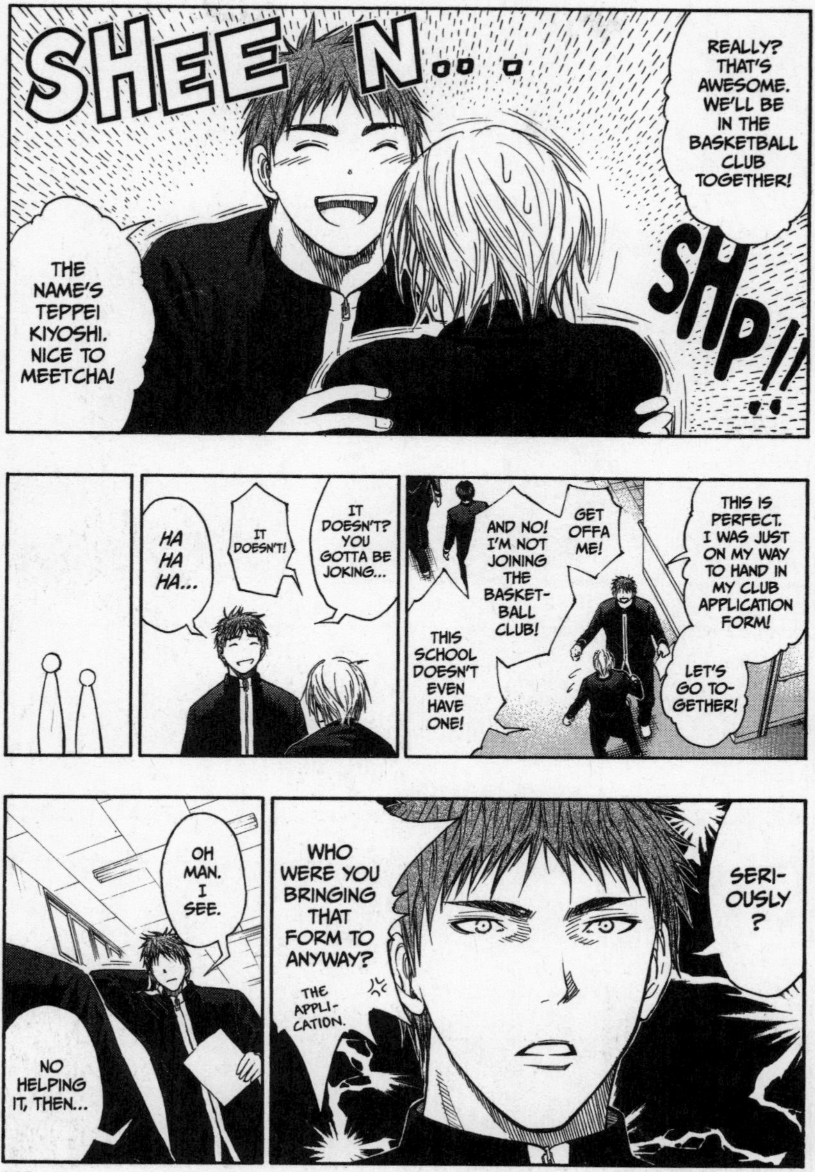
REALLY? THAT'S AWESOME. WE'LL BE IN THE BASKETBALL CLUB TOGETHER!
SHP!!
SHEE...N...
THE NAME'S TEPPEI KIYOSHI. NICE TO MEETCHA!
THIS IS PERFECT. I WAS JUST ON MY WAY TO HAND IN MY CLUB APPLICATION FORM!
LET'S GO TO-GETHER!
GET OFFA ME!
AND NO! I'M NOT JOINING THE BASKET-BALL CLUB!
THIS SCHOOL DOESN'T EVEN HAVE ONE!
IT DOESN'T? YOU GOTTA BE JOKING...
IT DOESN'T!
HA HA HA...
SERI-OUSLY?
WHO WERE YOU BRINGING THAT FORM TO ANYWAY?
THE APPLI-CATION.
OH MAN. I SEE.
NO HELPING IT, THEN...

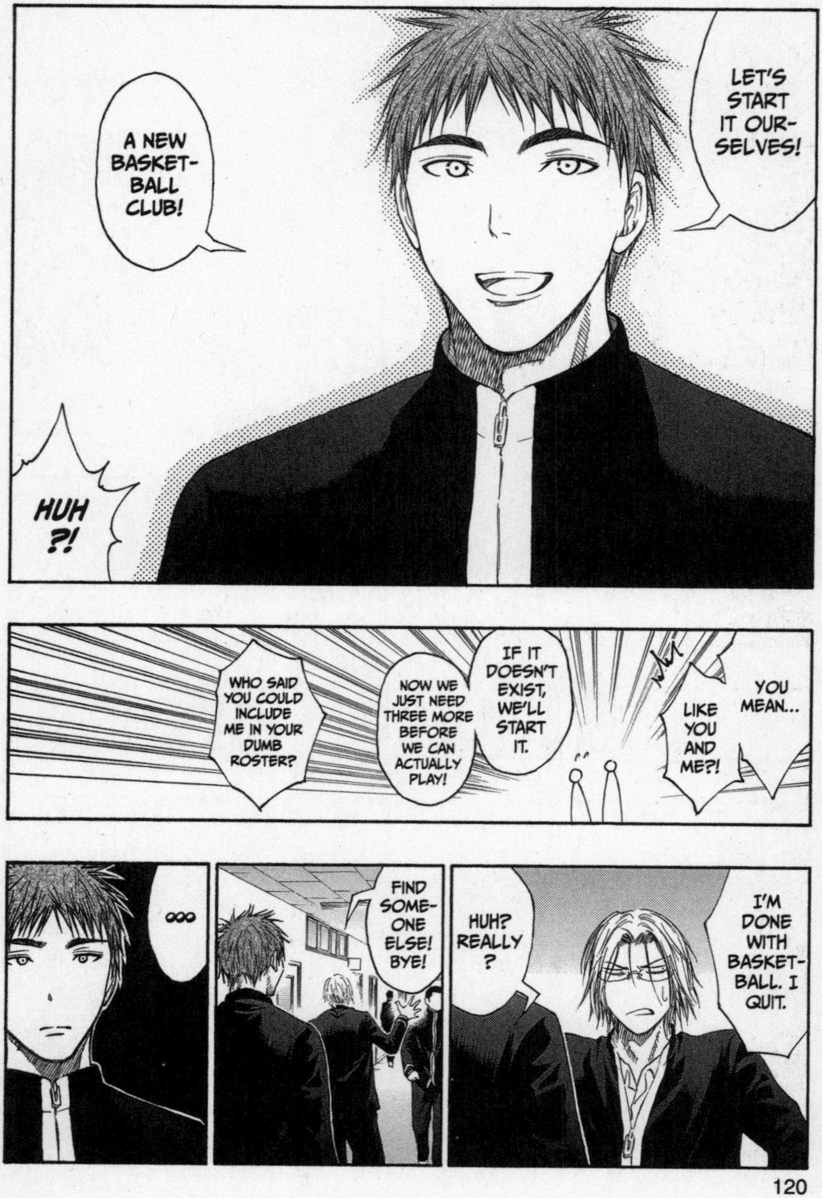
LET'S START IT OUR-SELVES!
A NEW BASKET-BALL CLUB!
HUH ?!
YOU MEAN...
LIKE YOU AND ME?!
IF IT DOESN'T EXIST, WE'LL START IT.
NOW WE JUST NEED THREE MORE BEFORE WE CAN ACTUALLY PLAY!
WHO SAID YOU COULD INCLUDE ME IN YOUR DUMB ROSTER?
I'M DONE WITH BASKET-BALL. I QUIT.
HUH? REALLY ?
FIND SOME-ONE ELSE! BYE!
...

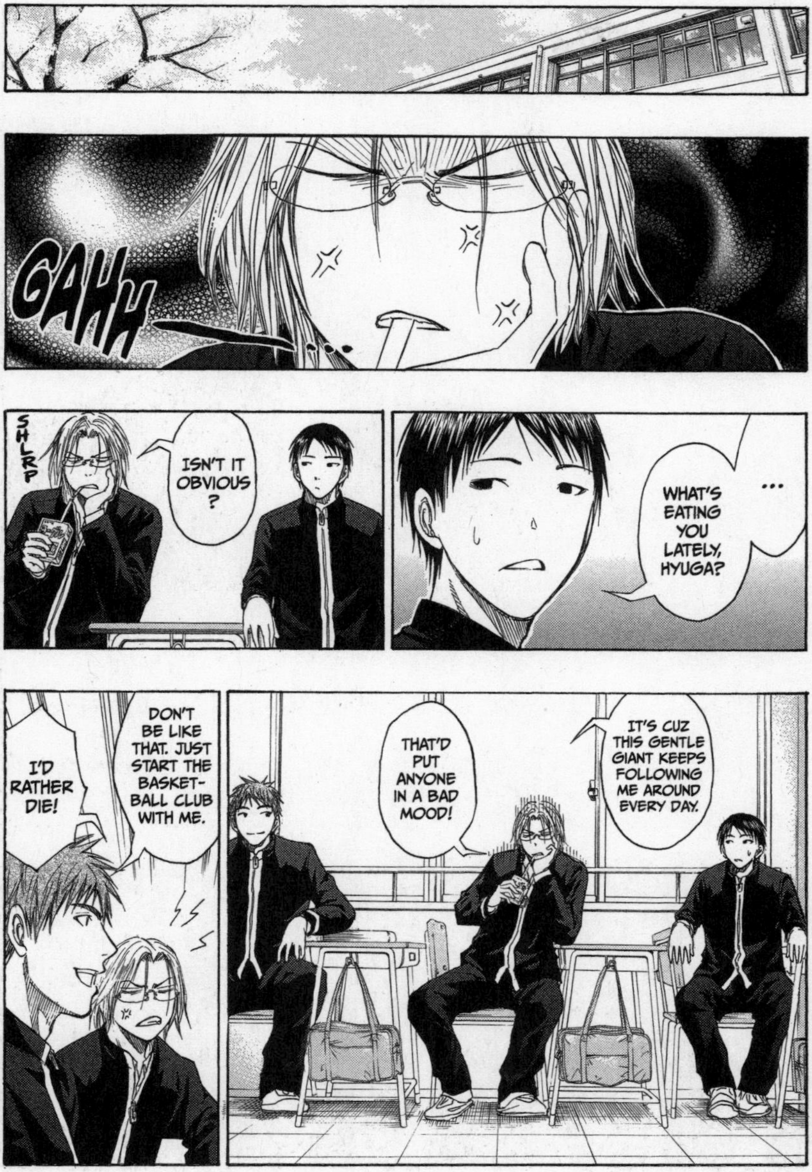
GAHH
...
WHAT'S EATING YOU LATELY, HYUGA?
SHLRP
ISN'T IT OBVIOUS?
IT'S CUZ THIS GENTLE GIANT KEEPS FOLLOWING ME AROUND EVERY DAY.
THAT'D PUT ANYONE IN A BAD MOOD!
DON'T BE LIKE THAT. JUST START THE BASKET-BALL CLUB WITH ME.
I'D RATHER DIE!

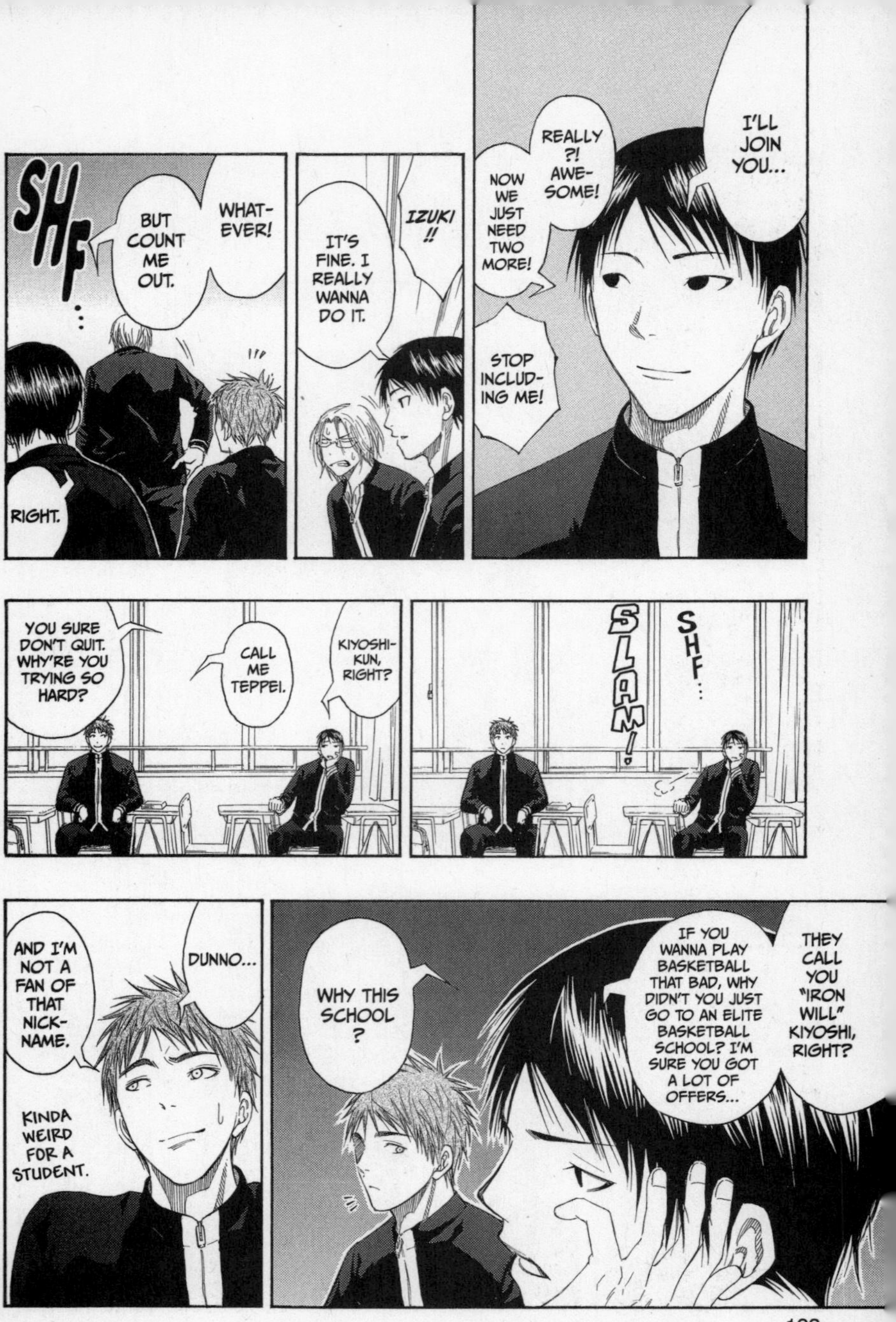
I'LL JOIN YOU...
REALLY ?! AWE-SOME!
NOW WE JUST NEED TWO MORE!
STOP INCLUDING ME!
IZUKI !!
IT'S FINE. I REALLY WANNA DO IT.
WHAT-EVER!
BUT COUNT ME OUT.
SHF...
RIGHT.
SLAM!
SHF...
KIYOSHI-KUN, RIGHT?
CALL ME TEPPEI.
YOU SURE DON'T QUIT. WHY'RE YOU TRYING SO HARD?
THEY CALL YOU "IRON WILL" KIYOSHI, RIGHT?
IF YOU WANNA PLAY BASKETBALL THAT BAD, WHY DIDN'T YOU JUST GO TO AN ELITE BASKETBALL SCHOOL? I'M SURE YOU GOT A LOT OF OFFERS...
WHY THIS SCHOOL ?
DUNNO...
AND I'M NOT A FAN OF THAT NICK-NAME.
KINDA WEIRD FOR A STUDENT.

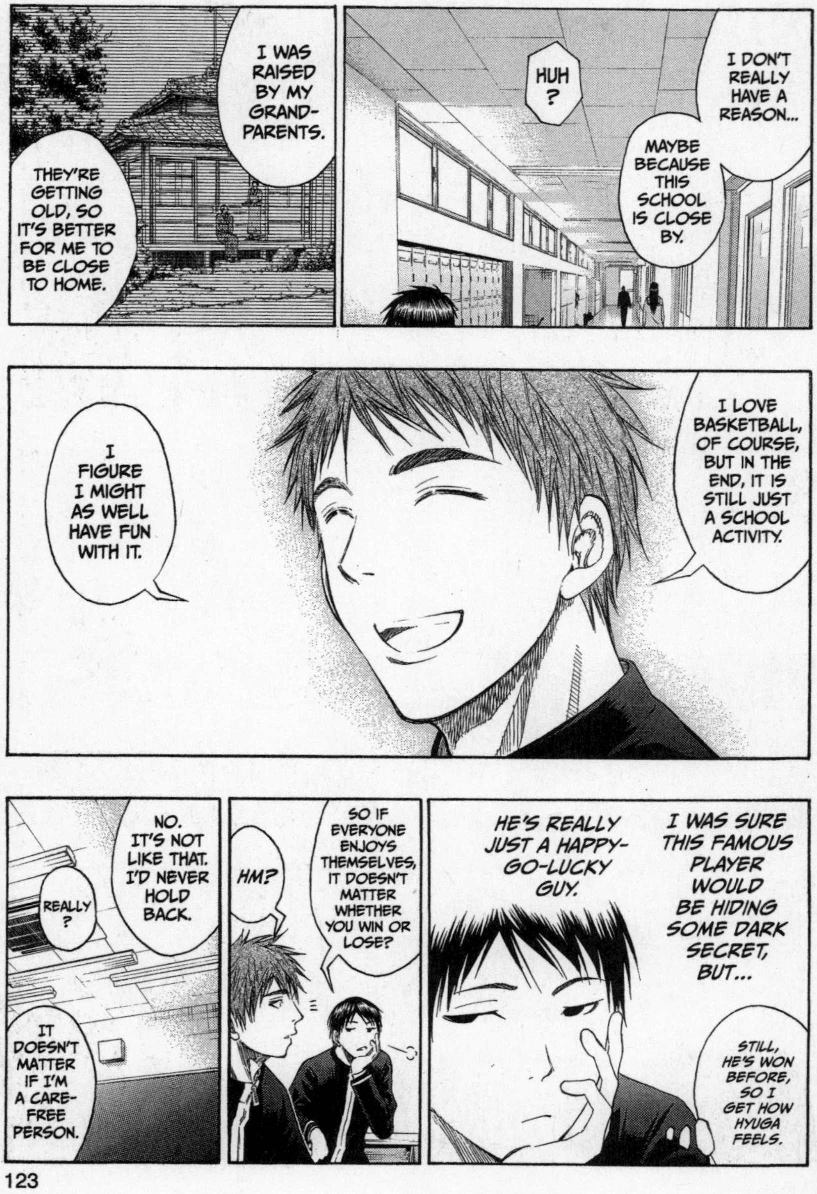
I DON'T REALLY HAVE A REASON...
HUH?
MAYBE BECAUSE THIS SCHOOL IS CLOSE BY.
I WAS RAISED BY MY GRAND-PARENTS.
THEY'RE GETTING OLD, SO IT'S BETTER FOR ME TO BE CLOSE TO HOME.
I LOVE BASKETBALL, OF COURSE, BUT IN THE END, IT IS STILL JUST A SCHOOL ACTIVITY.
I FIGURE I MIGHT AS WELL HAVE FUN WITH IT.
I WAS SURE THIS FAMOUS PLAYER WOULD BE HIDING SOME DARK SECRET, BUT...
HE'S REALLY JUST A HAPPY-GO-LUCKY GUY.
STILL, HE'S WON BEFORE, SO I GET HOW HYUGA FEELS.
SO IF EVERYONE ENJOYS THEMSELVES, IT DOESN'T MATTER WHETHER YOU WIN OR LOSE?
HM?
NO. IT'S NOT LIKE THAT. I'D NEVER HOLD BACK.
REALLY?
IT DOESN'T MATTER IF I'M A CARE-FREE PERSON.

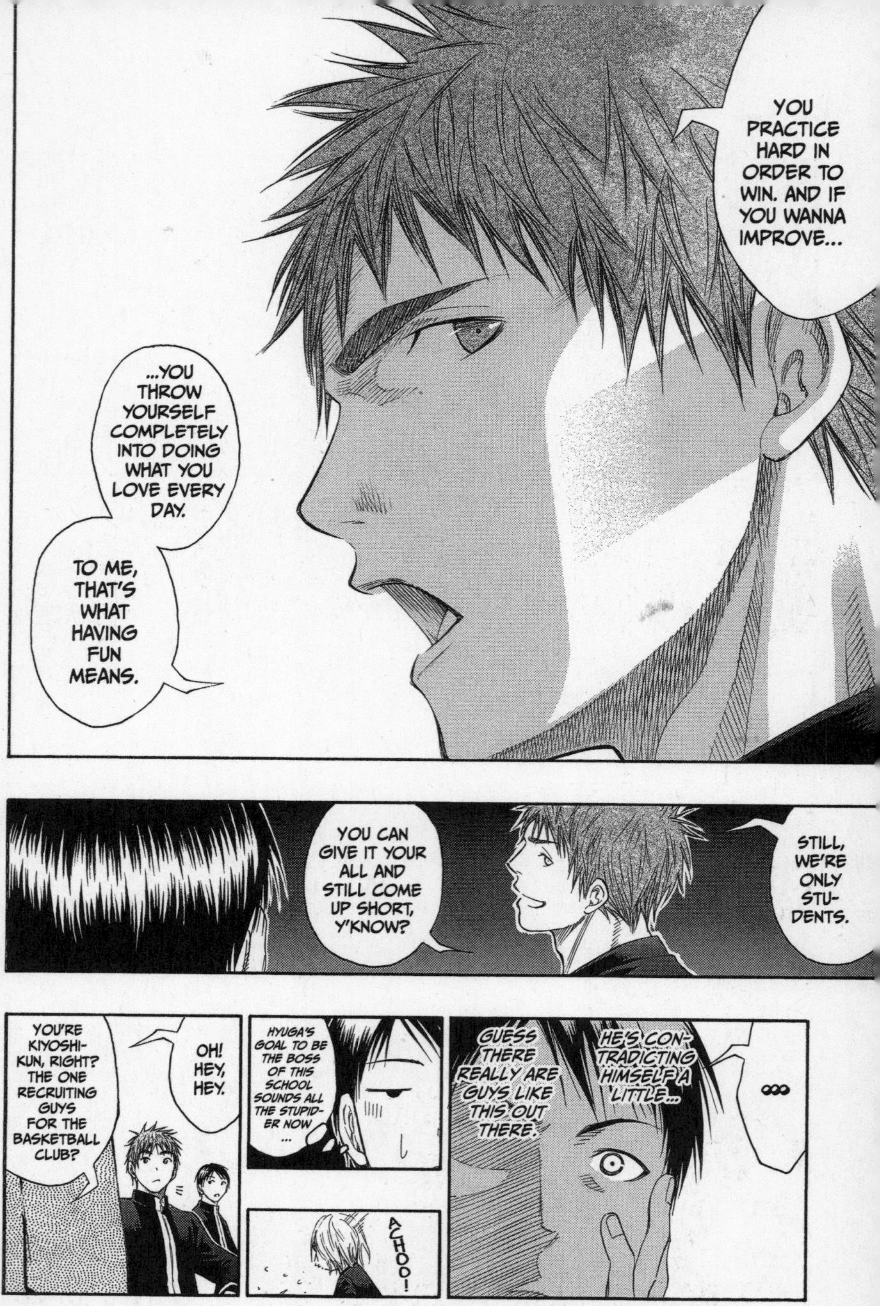
YOU PRACTICE HARD IN ORDER TO WIN. AND IF YOU WANNA IMPROVE...
...YOU THROW YOURSELF COMPLETELY INTO DOING WHAT YOU LOVE EVERY DAY.
TO ME, THAT'S WHAT HAVING FUN MEANS.
STILL, WE'RE ONLY STU-DENTS.
YOU CAN GIVE IT YOUR ALL AND STILL COME UP SHORT, Y'KNOW?
...
HE'S CON-TRADICTING HIMSELF A LITTLE...
GUESS THERE REALLY ARE GUYS LIKE THIS OUT THERE.
HYUGA'S GOAL TO BE THE BOSS OF THIS SCHOOL SOUNDS ALL THE STUPID-ER NOW ...
ACHOO!
OH! HEY, HEY.
YOU'RE KIYOSHI-KUN, RIGHT? THE ONE RECRUITING GUYS FOR THE BASKETBALL CLUB?

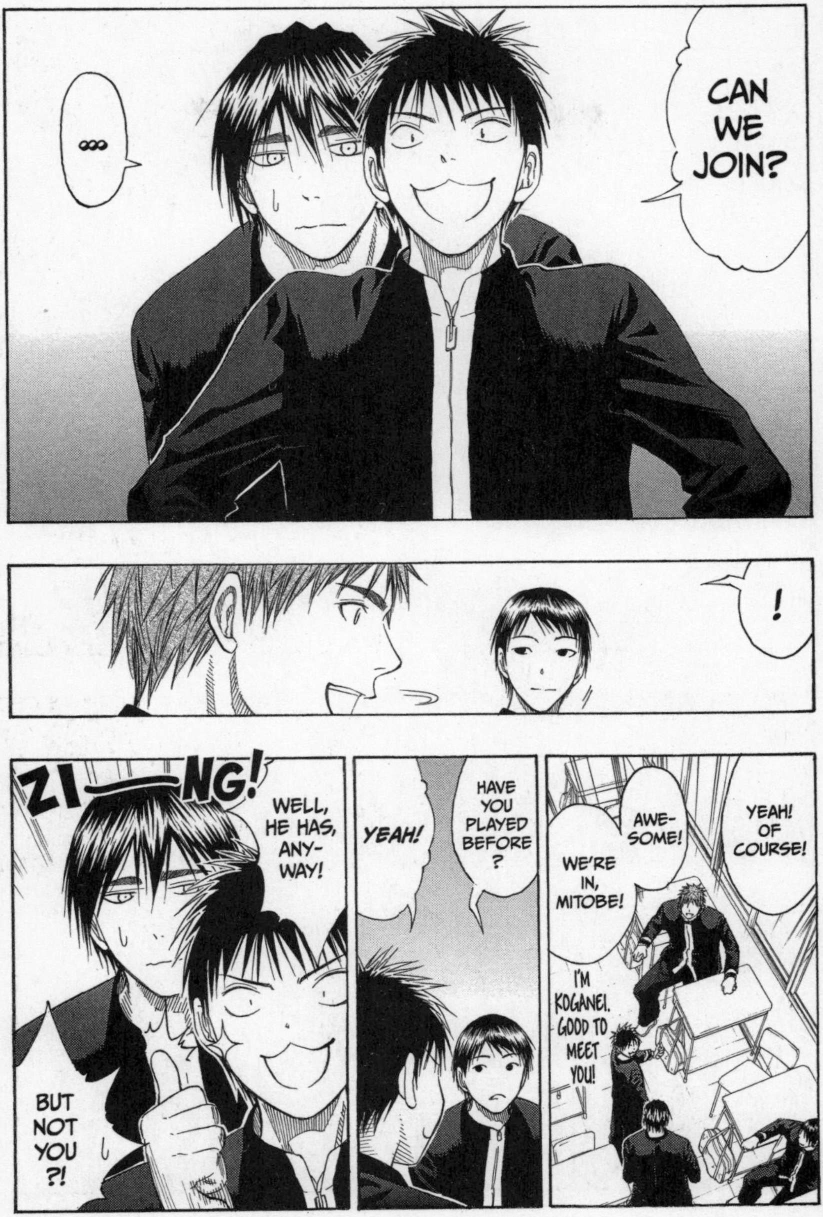
CAN WE JOIN?
...
!
YEAH! OF COURSE!
AWE-SOME!
WE'RE IN, MITOBE!
I'M KOGANEI. GOOD TO MEET YOU!
HAVE YOU PLAYED BEFORE?
YEAH!
WELL, HE HAS, ANYWAY!
ZI—NG!
BUT NOT YOU?!

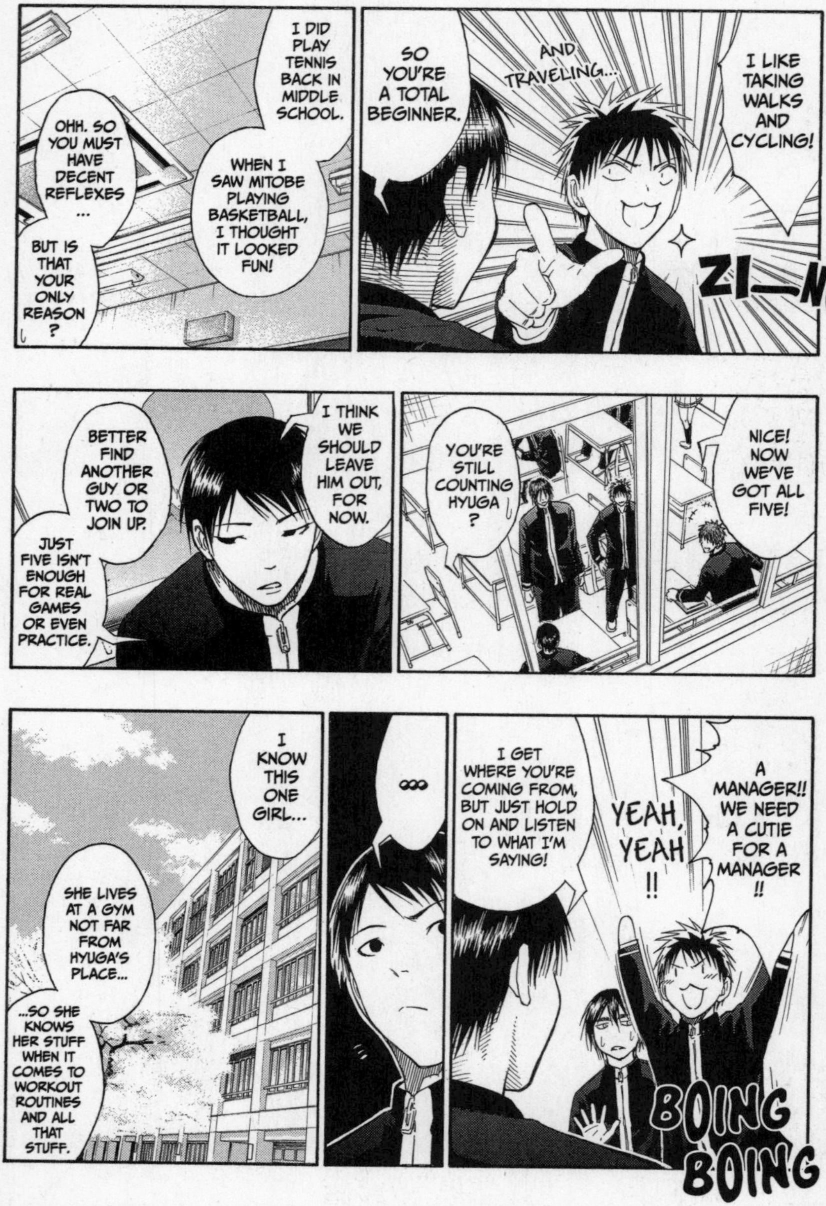
I LIKE TAKING WALKS AND CYCLING!
ZI—NG!
AND TRAVELING...
SO YOU'RE A TOTAL BEGINNER.
I DID PLAY TENNIS BACK IN MIDDLE SCHOOL.
WHEN I SAW MITOBE PLAYING BASKETBALL, I THOUGHT IT LOOKED FUN!
OHH. SO YOU MUST HAVE DECENT REFLEXES ...
BUT IS THAT YOUR ONLY REASON ?
NICE! NOW WE'VE GOT ALL FIVE!
YOU'RE STILL COUNTING HYUGA ?
I THINK WE SHOULD LEAVE HIM OUT, FOR NOW.
BETTER FIND ANOTHER GUY OR TWO TO JOIN UP.
JUST FIVE ISN'T ENOUGH FOR REAL GAMES OR EVEN PRACTICE.
A MANAGER!! WE NEED A CUTIE FOR A MANAGER !!
YEAH, YEAH !!
I GET WHERE YOU'RE COMING FROM, BUT JUST HOLD ON AND LISTEN TO WHAT I'M SAYING!
BOING BOING
...
I KNOW THIS ONE GIRL...
SHE LIVES AT A GYM NOT FAR FROM HYUGA'S PLACE...
...SO SHE KNOWS HER STUFF WHEN IT COMES TO WORKOUT ROUTINES AND ALL THAT STUFF.

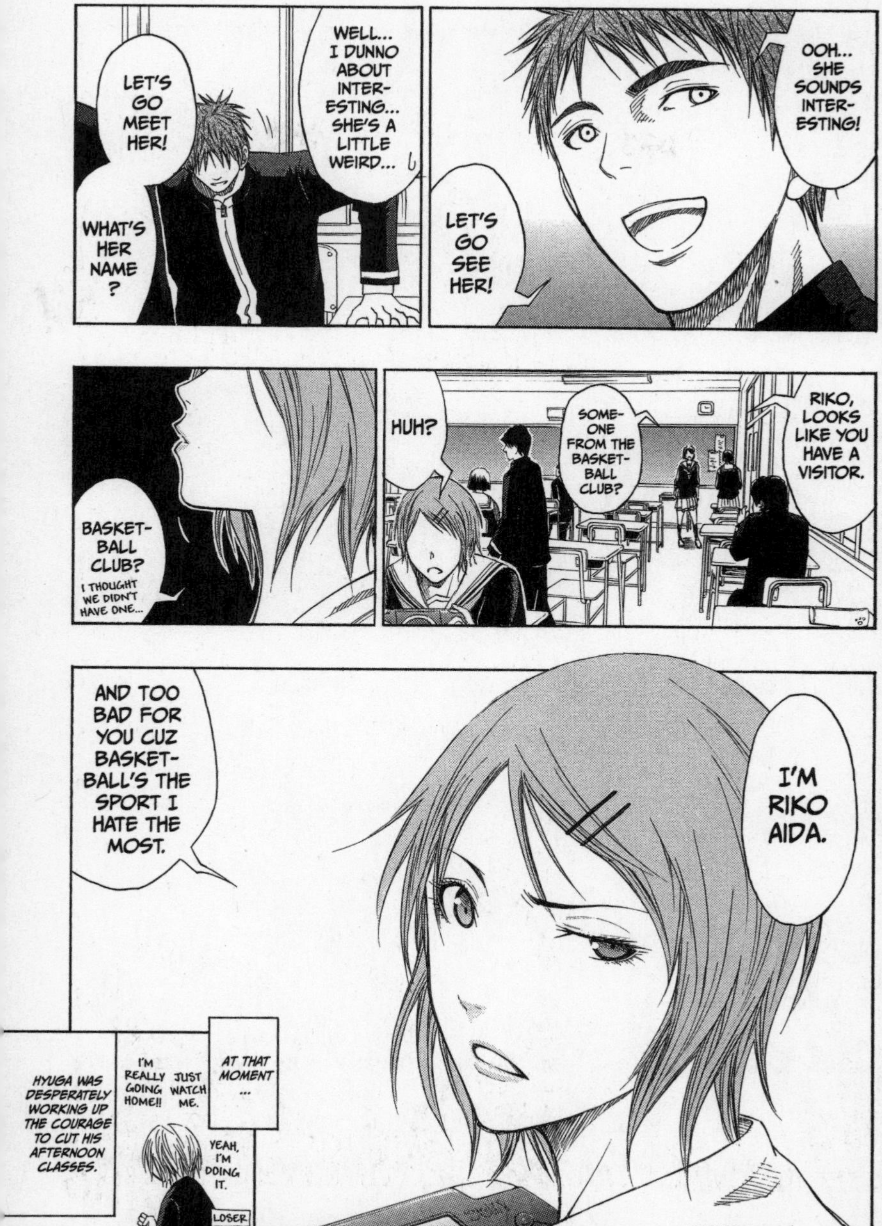
OOH... SHE SOUNDS INTER-ESTING!
LET'S GO SEE HER!
WELL... I DUNNO ABOUT INTER-ESTING... SHE'S A LITTLE WEIRD...
LET'S GO MEET HER!
WHAT'S HER NAME ?
RIKO, LOOKS LIKE YOU HAVE A VISITOR.
SOME-ONE FROM THE BASKET-BALL CLUB?
HUH?
BASKET-BALL CLUB?
I THOUGHT WE DIDN'T HAVE ONE...
I'M RIKO AIDA.
AND TOO BAD FOR YOU CUZ BASKET-BALL'S THE SPORT I HATE THE MOST.
AT THAT MOMENT ...
JUST WATCH ME.
I'M REALLY GOING HOME!!
YEAH, I'M DOING IT.
HYUGA WAS DESPERATELY WORKING UP THE COURAGE TO CUT HIS AFTERNOON CLASSES.
LOSER

Kuroko's BASKETBALL

96TH QUARTER: JUST GIVE UP

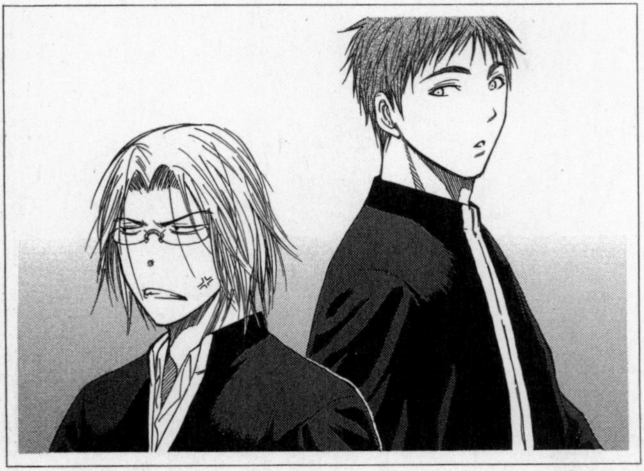

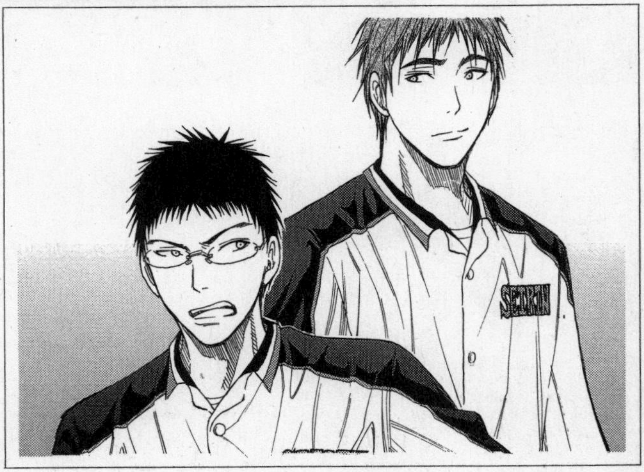
SEIRIN

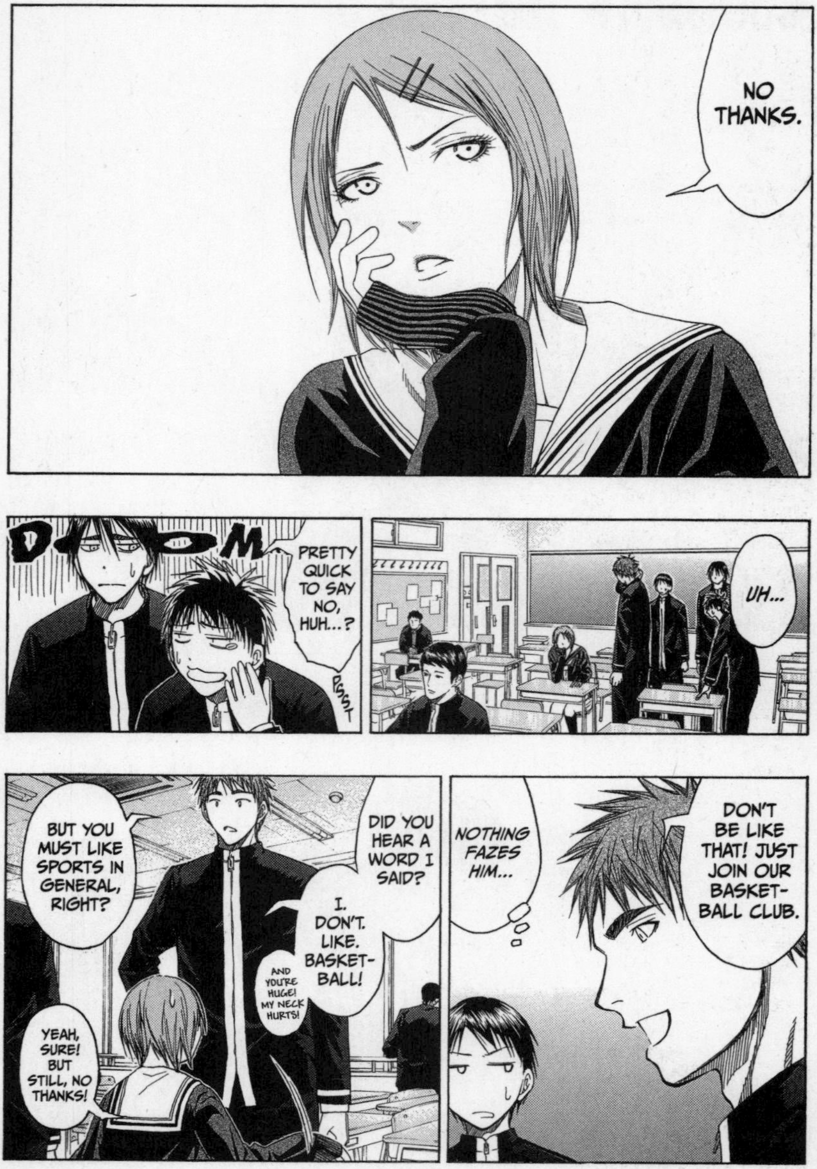
NO THANKS.
UH...
D-DOM
PRETTY QUICK TO SAY NO, HUH...?
PSST
DON'T BE LIKE THAT! JUST JOIN OUR BASKET-BALL CLUB.
NOTHING FAZES HIM...
DID YOU HEAR A WORD I SAID?
I. DON'T. LIKE. BASKET-BALL!
BUT YOU MUST LIKE SPORTS IN GENERAL, RIGHT?
AND YOU'RE HUGE! MY NECK HURTS!
YEAH, SURE! BUT STILL, NO THANKS!

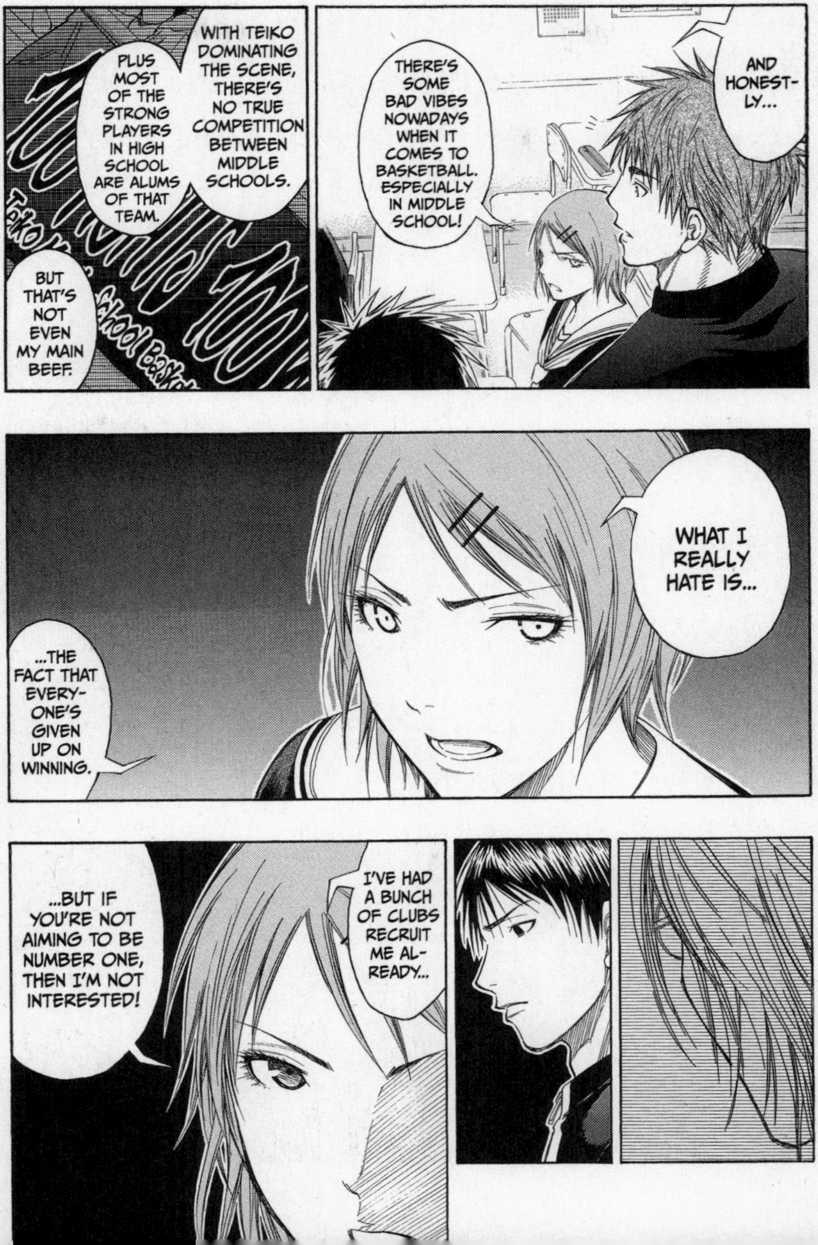
AND HONESTLY...
THERE'S SOME BAD VIBES NOWADAYS WHEN IT COMES TO BASKETBALL. ESPECIALLY IN MIDDLE SCHOOL!
WITH TEIKO DOMINATING THE SCENE, THERE'S NO TRUE COMPETITION BETWEEN MIDDLE SCHOOLS.
PLUS MOST OF THE STRONG PLAYERS IN HIGH SCHOOL ARE ALUMS OF THAT TEAM.
BUT THAT'S NOT EVEN MY MAIN BEEF.
WHAT I REALLY HATE IS...
...THE FACT THAT EVERYONE'S GIVEN UP ON WINNING.
I'VE HAD A BUNCH OF CLUBS RECRUIT ME ALREADY...
...BUT IF YOU'RE NOT AIMING TO BE NUMBER ONE, THEN I'M NOT INTERESTED!

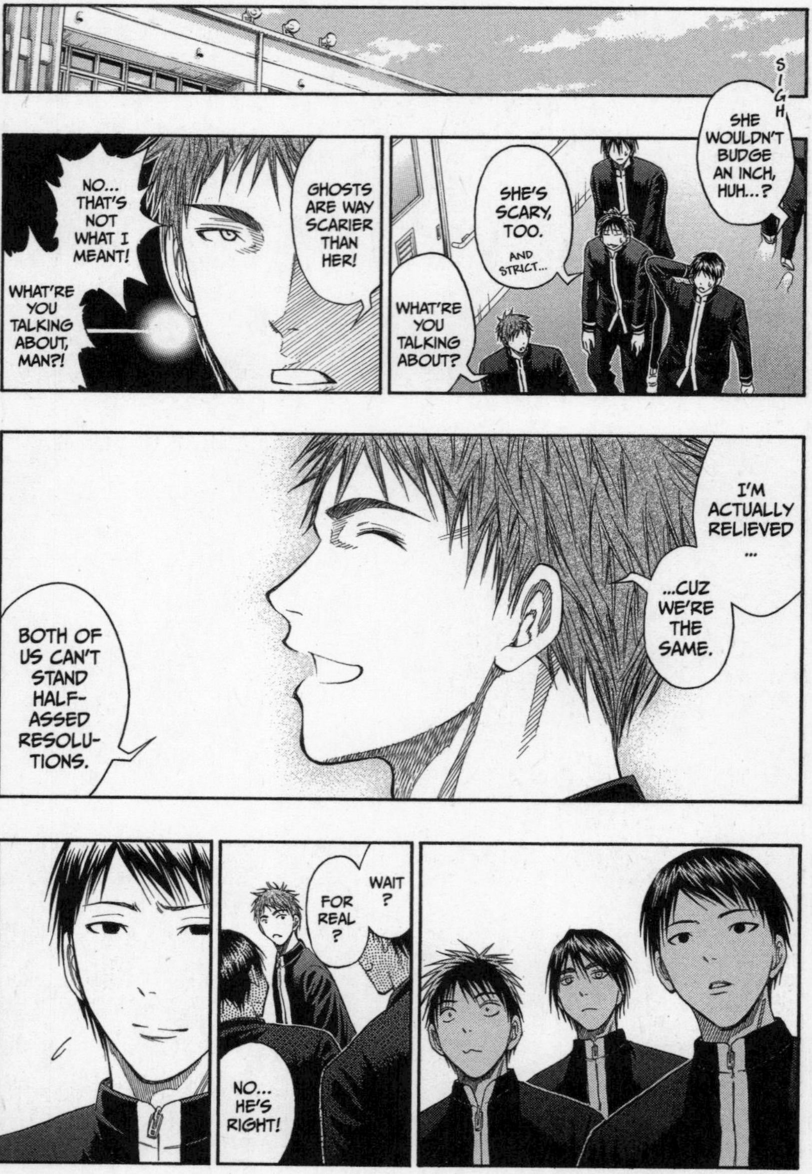
SIGH
SHE WOULDN'T BUDGE AN INCH, HUH...?
SHE'S SCARY, TOO.
AND STRICT...
WHAT'RE YOU TALKING ABOUT?
GHOSTS ARE WAY SCARIER THAN HER!
NO... THAT'S NOT WHAT I MEANT!
WHAT'RE YOU TALKING ABOUT, MAN?!
I'M ACTUALLY RELIEVED ...
...CUZ WE'RE THE SAME.
BOTH OF US CAN'T STAND HALF-ASSED RESOLU-TIONS.
WAIT?
FOR REAL?
NO... HE'S RIGHT!

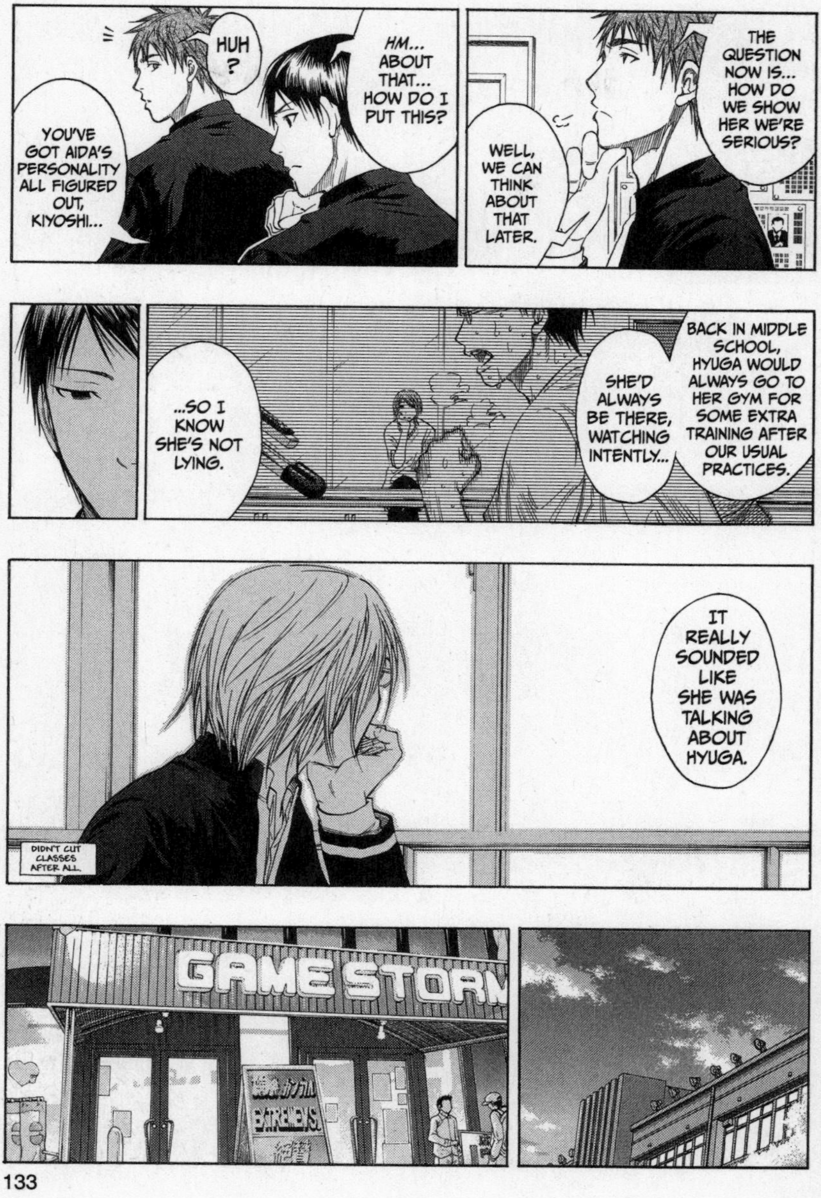
THE QUESTION NOW IS... HOW DO WE SHOW HER WE'RE SERIOUS?
WELL, WE CAN THINK ABOUT THAT LATER.
HM... ABOUT THAT... HOW DO I PUT THIS?
HUH?
YOU'VE GOT AIDA'S PERSONALITY ALL FIGURED OUT, KIYOSHI...
BACK IN MIDDLE SCHOOL, HYUGA WOULD ALWAYS GO TO HER GYM FOR SOME EXTRA TRAINING AFTER OUR USUAL PRACTICES.
SHE'D ALWAYS BE THERE, WATCHING INTENTLY...
...SO I KNOW SHE'S NOT LYING.
IT REALLY SOUNDED LIKE SHE WAS TALKING ABOUT HYUGA.
DIDN'T CUT CLASSES AFTER ALL.
GAME STORM

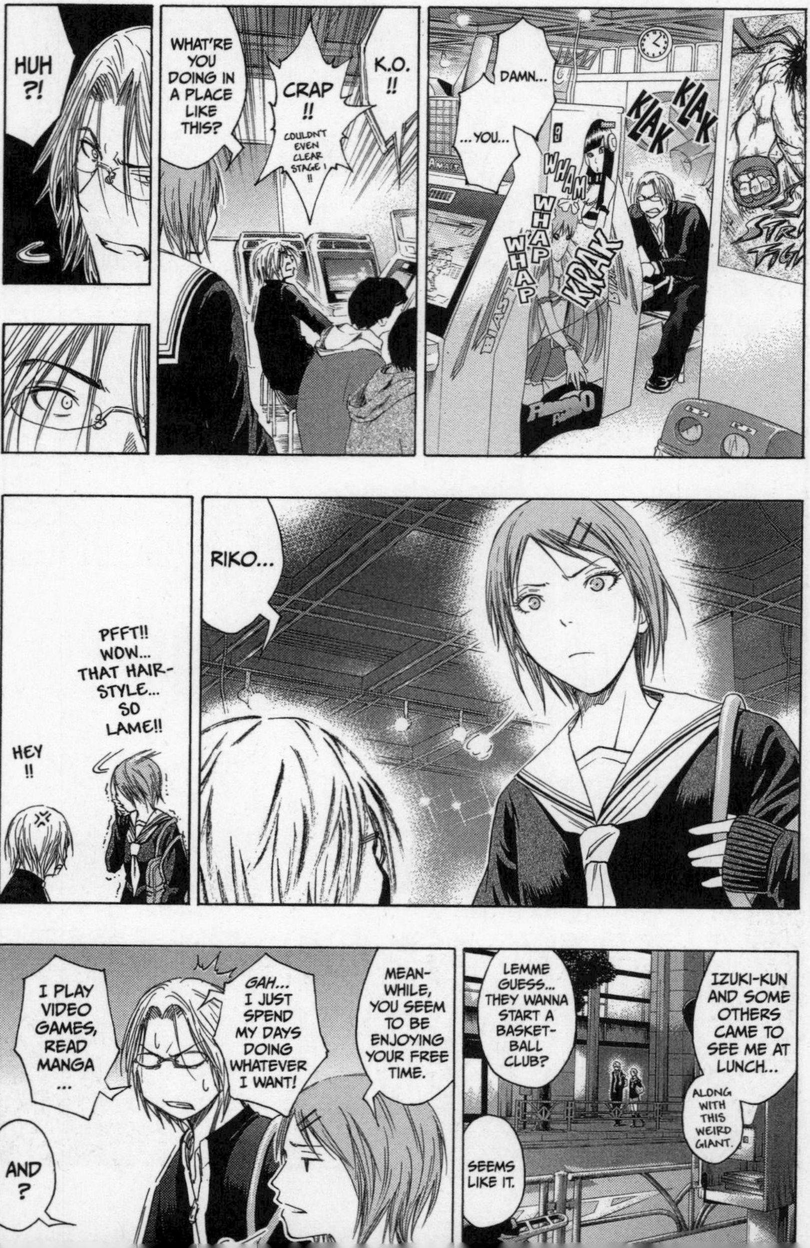
KLAK KLAK
DAMN...
...YOU...
WHAM
WHAP WHAP
KRAK
K.O. !!
CRAP !!
COULDN'T EVEN CLEAR STAGE 1 !!
WHAT'RE YOU DOING IN A PLACE LIKE THIS?
HUH ?!
RIKO...
PFFT!! WOW... THAT HAIR-STYLE... SO LAME!!
HEY !!
IZUKI-KUN AND SOME OTHERS CAME TO SEE ME AT LUNCH...
ALONG WITH THIS WEIRD GIANT.
LEMME GUESS... THEY WANNA START A BASKET-BALL CLUB?
SEEMS LIKE IT.
MEAN-WHILE, YOU SEEM TO BE ENJOYING YOUR FREE TIME.
GAH... I JUST SPEND MY DAYS DOING WHATEVER I WANT!
I PLAY VIDEO GAMES, READ MANGA ...
AND ?

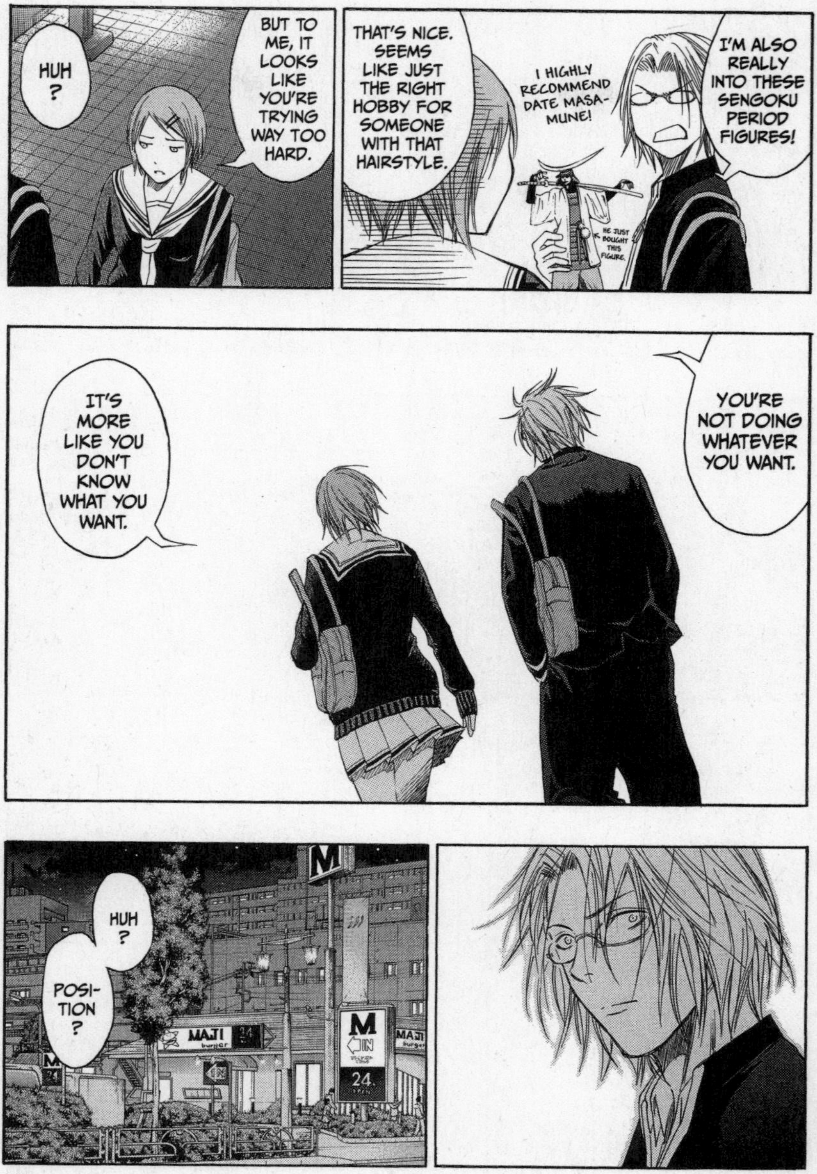
I'M ALSO REALLY INTO THESE SENGOKU PERIOD FIGURES!
I HIGHLY RECOMMEND DATE MASA-MUNE!
HE JUST BOUGHT THIS FIGURE.
THAT'S NICE. SEEMS LIKE JUST THE RIGHT HOBBY FOR SOMEONE WITH THAT HAIRSTYLE.
BUT TO ME, IT LOOKS LIKE YOU'RE TRYING WAY TOO HARD.
HUH?
YOU'RE NOT DOING WHATEVER YOU WANT.
IT'S MORE LIKE YOU DON'T KNOW WHAT YOU WANT.
HUH?
POSI-TION?
M
MAJI burger
24.

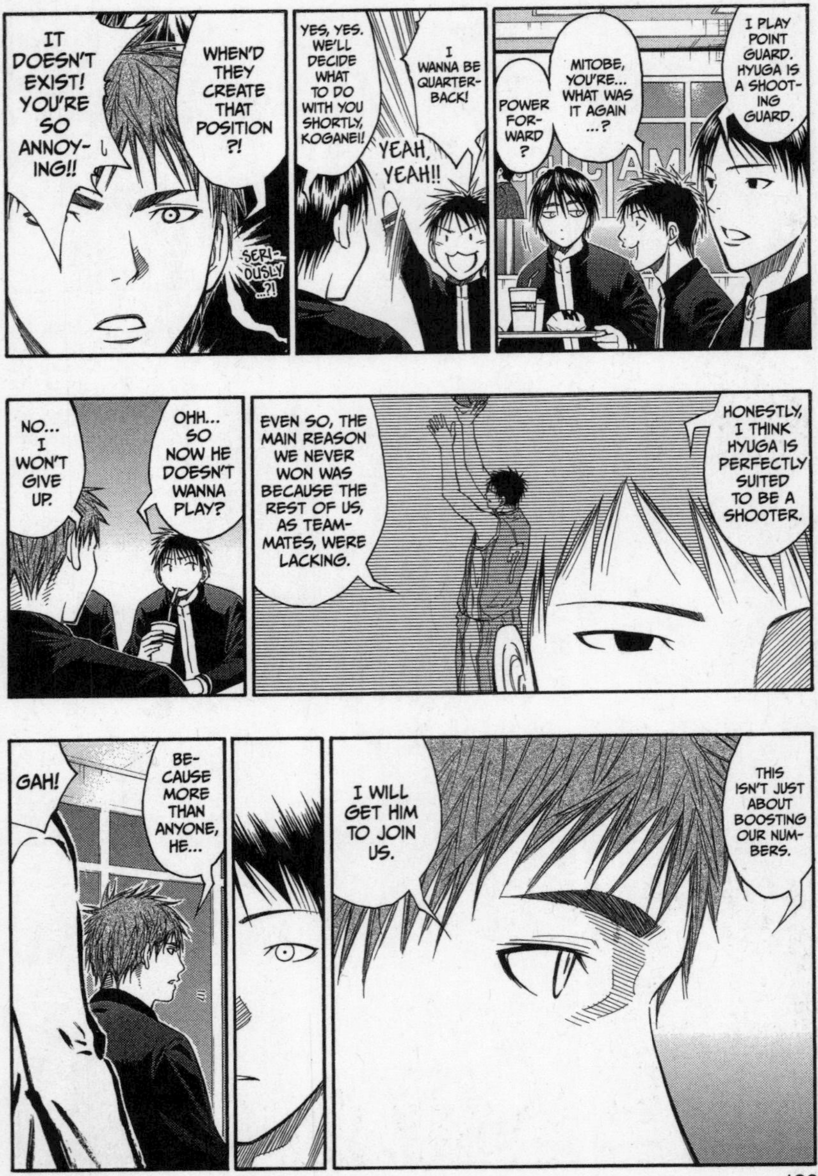
I PLAY POINT GUARD. HYUGA IS A SHOOTING GUARD.
MITOBE, YOU'RE... WHAT WAS IT AGAIN ...?
POWER FORWARD ?
I WANNA BE QUARTERBACK!
YES, YES. WE'LL DECIDE WHAT TO DO WITH YOU SHORTLY, KOGANEI!
YEAH, YEAH!!
WHEN'D THEY CREATE THAT POSITION ?!
IT DOESN'T EXIST! YOU'RE SO ANNOYING!!
SERIOUSLY ...?!
HONESTLY, I THINK HYUGA IS PERFECTLY SUITED TO BE A SHOOTER.
EVEN SO, THE MAIN REASON WE NEVER WON WAS BECAUSE THE REST OF US, AS TEAMMATES, WERE LACKING.
OHH... SO NOW HE DOESN'T WANNA PLAY?
NO... I WON'T GIVE UP.
THIS ISN'T JUST ABOUT BOOSTING OUR NUMBERS.
I WILL GET HIM TO JOIN US.
BECAUSE MORE THAN ANYONE, HE...
GAH!

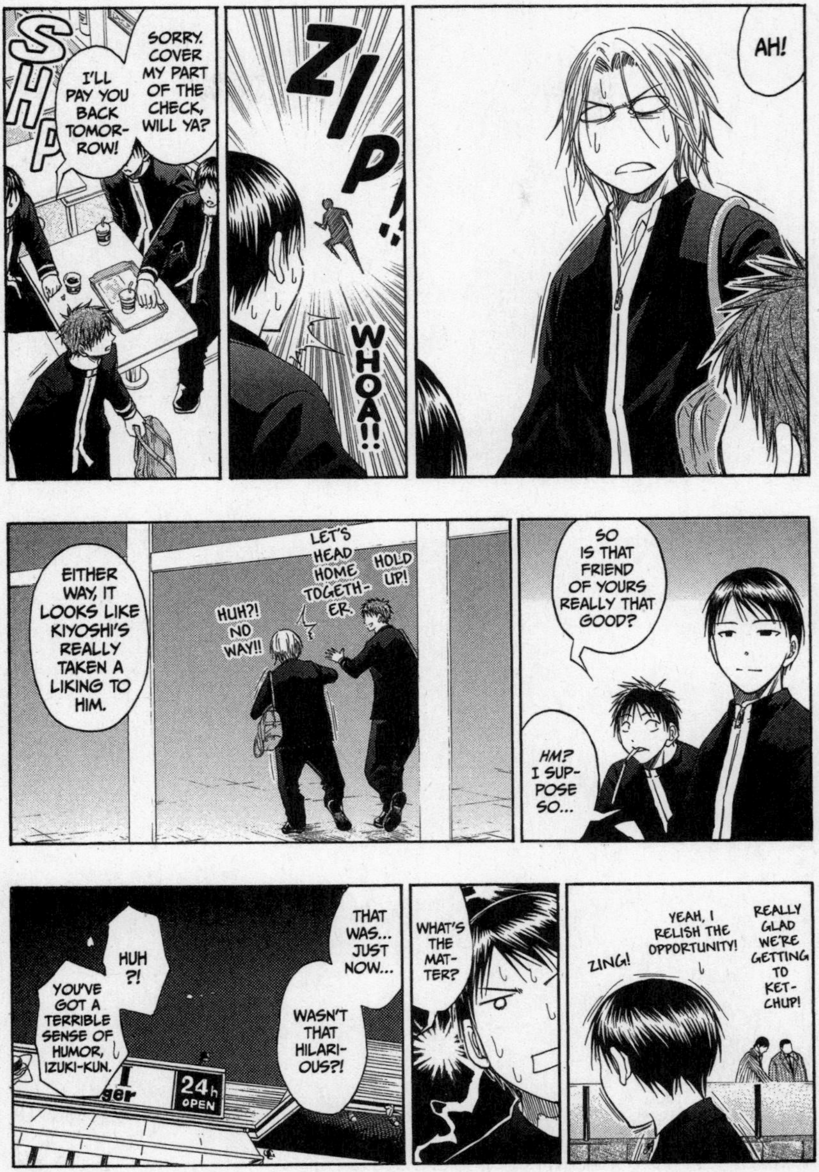
AH!
ZIP!!
WHOA!!
SHP
SORRY. COVER MY PART OF THE CHECK, WILL YA?
I'LL PAY YOU BACK TOMOR-ROW!
SO IS THAT FRIEND OF YOURS REALLY THAT GOOD?
HM? I SUP-POSE SO...
LET'S HEAD HOME TOGETH-ER.
HOLD UP!
HUH?! NO WAY!!
EITHER WAY, IT LOOKS LIKE KIYOSHI'S REALLY TAKEN A LIKING TO HIM.
REALLY GLAD WE'RE GETTING TO KET-CHUP!
YEAH, I RELISH THE OPPORTUNITY!
ZING!
WHAT'S THE MAT-TER?
THAT WAS... JUST NOW...
WASN'T THAT HILARI-OUS?!
HUH ?!
YOU'VE GOT A TERRIBLE SENSE OF HUMOR, IZUKI-KUN.
24h OPEN

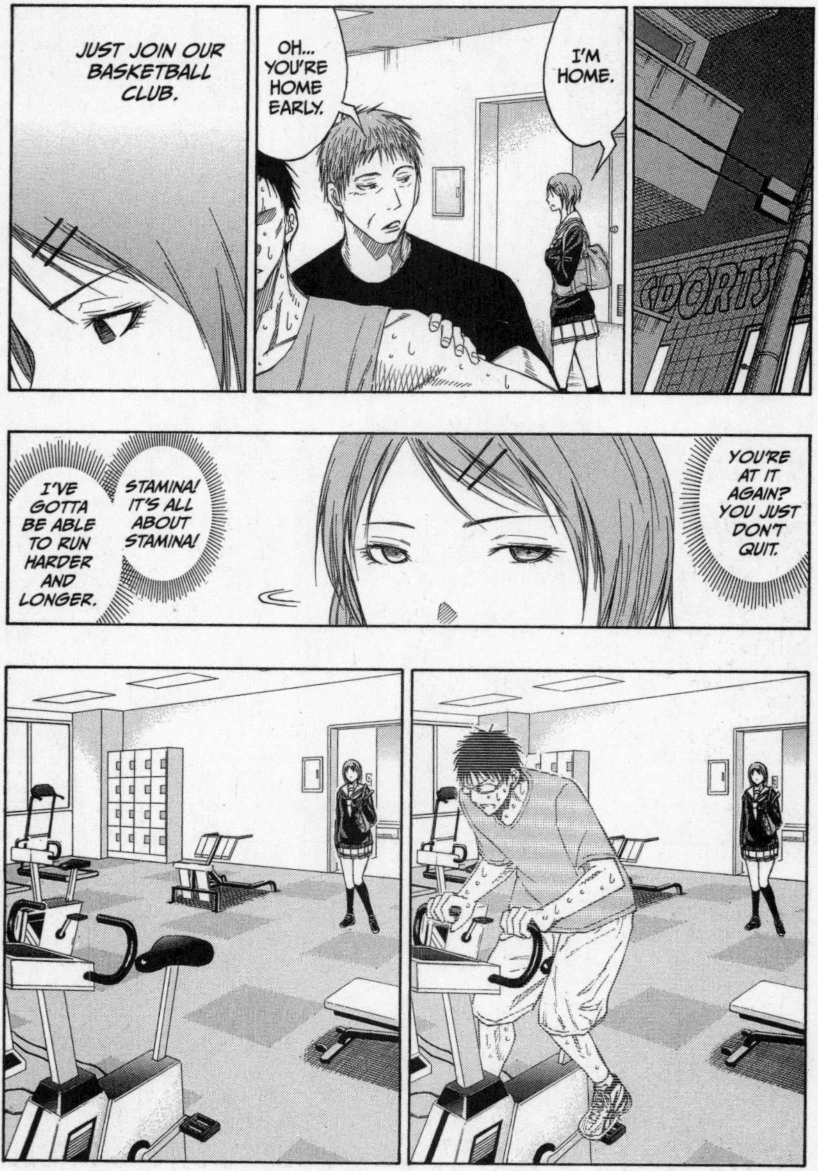
I'M HOME.
OH... YOU'RE HOME EARLY.
JUST JOIN OUR BASKETBALL CLUB.
YOU'RE AT IT AGAIN? YOU JUST DON'T QUIT.
STAMINA! IT'S ALL ABOUT STAMINA!
I'VE GOTTA BE ABLE TO RUN HARDER AND LONGER.

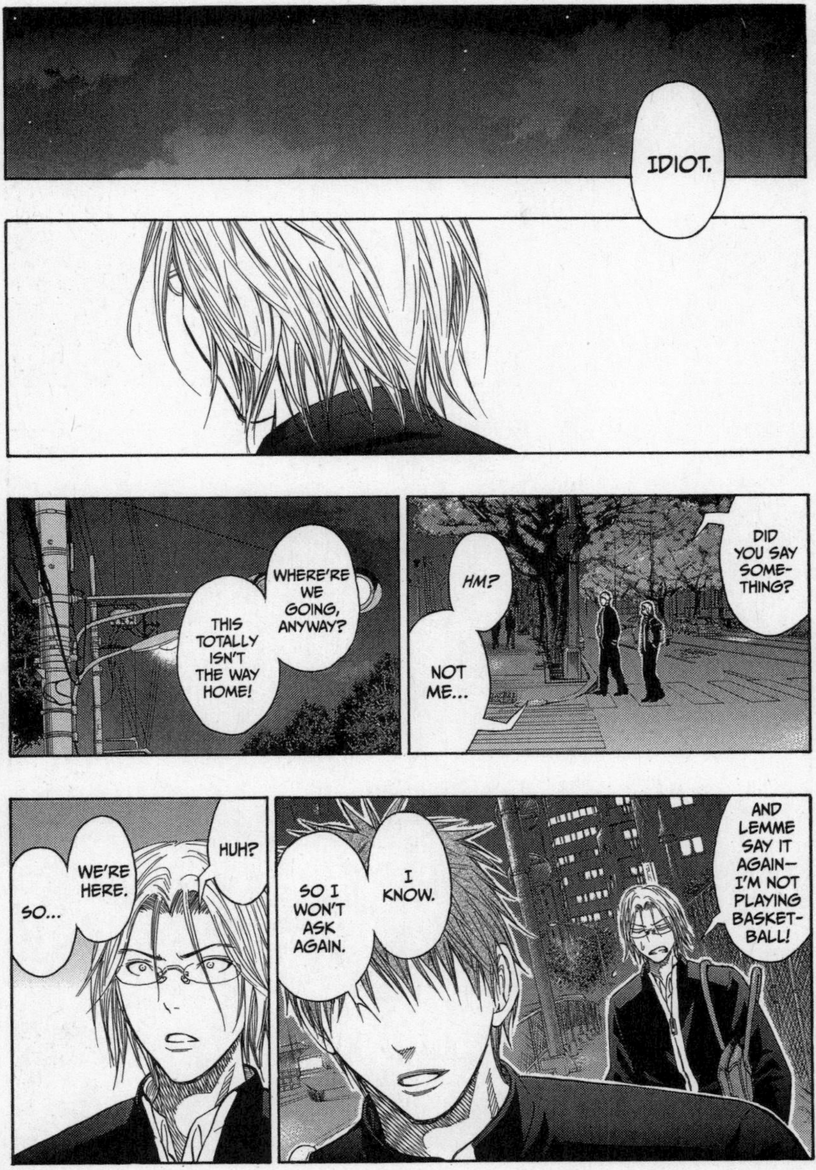
IDIOT.
DID YOU SAY SOME-THING?
HM?
NOT ME...
WHERE'RE WE GOING, ANYWAY?
THIS TOTALLY ISN'T THE WAY HOME!
AND LEMME SAY IT AGAIN— I'M NOT PLAYING BASKET-BALL!
I KNOW.
SO I WON'T ASK AGAIN.
HUH?
WE'RE HERE.
SO...

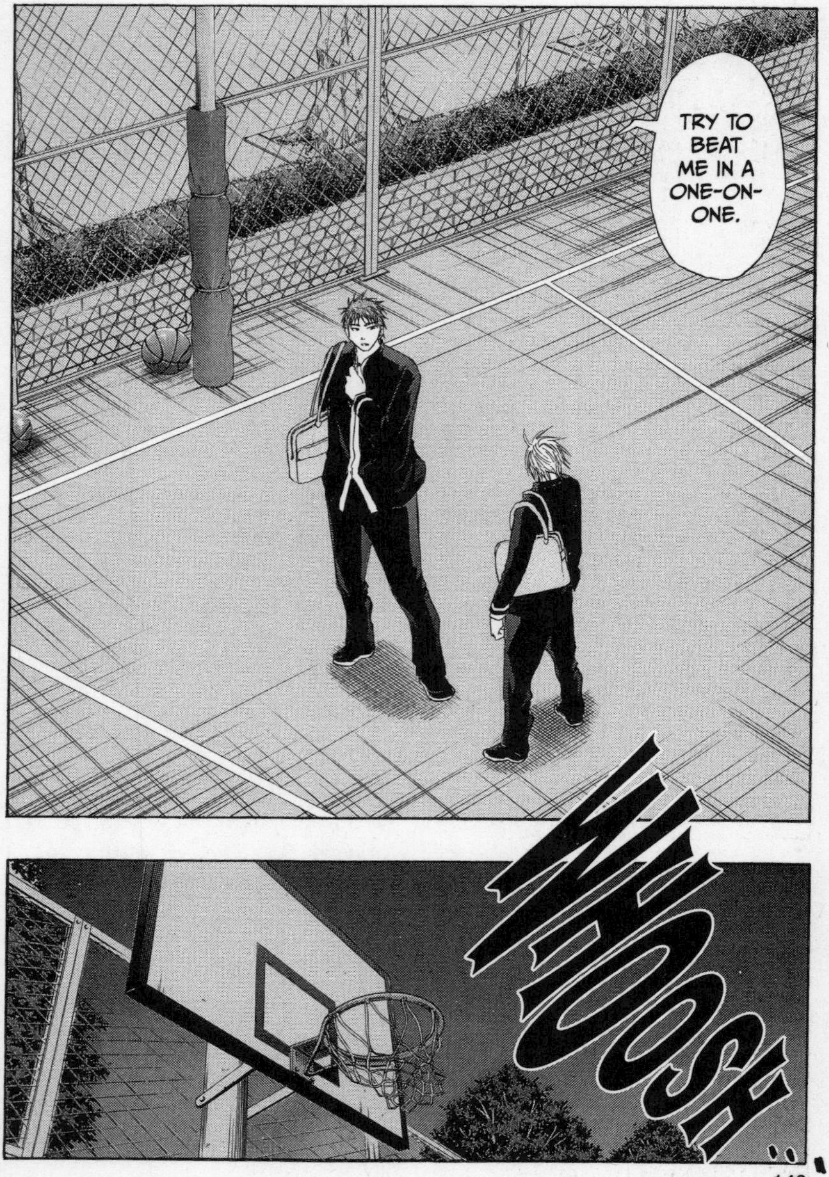
TRY TO BEAT ME IN A ONE-ON-ONE.
WHOOSH!!

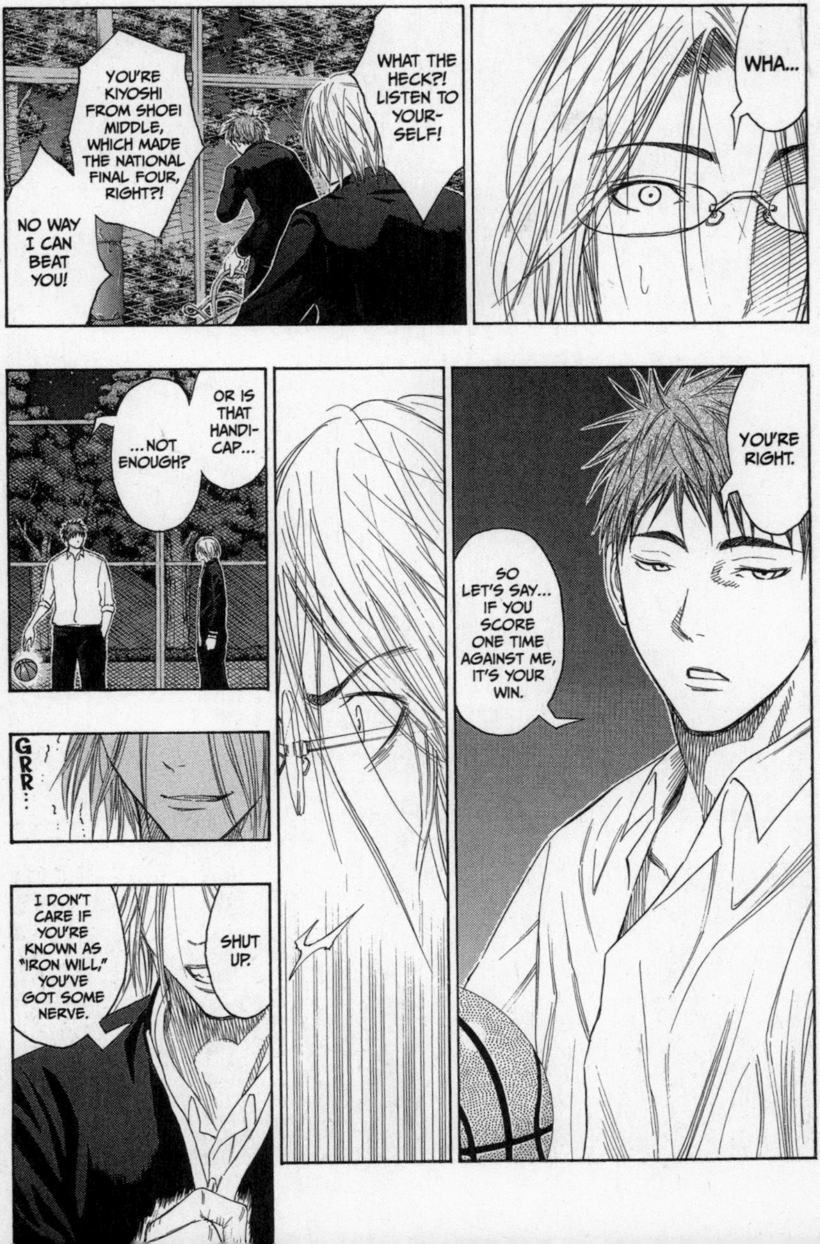
WHA...
WHAT THE HECK?! LISTEN TO YOURSELF!
YOU'RE KIYOSHI FROM SHOEI MIDDLE, WHICH MADE THE NATIONAL FINAL FOUR, RIGHT?!
NO WAY I CAN BEAT YOU!
YOU'RE RIGHT.
SO LET'S SAY... IF YOU SCORE ONE TIME AGAINST ME, IT'S YOUR WIN.
OR IS THAT HANDICAP...
...NOT ENOUGH?
GRR...
SHUT UP.
I DON'T CARE IF YOU'RE KNOWN AS "IRON WILL," YOU'VE GOT SOME NERVE.

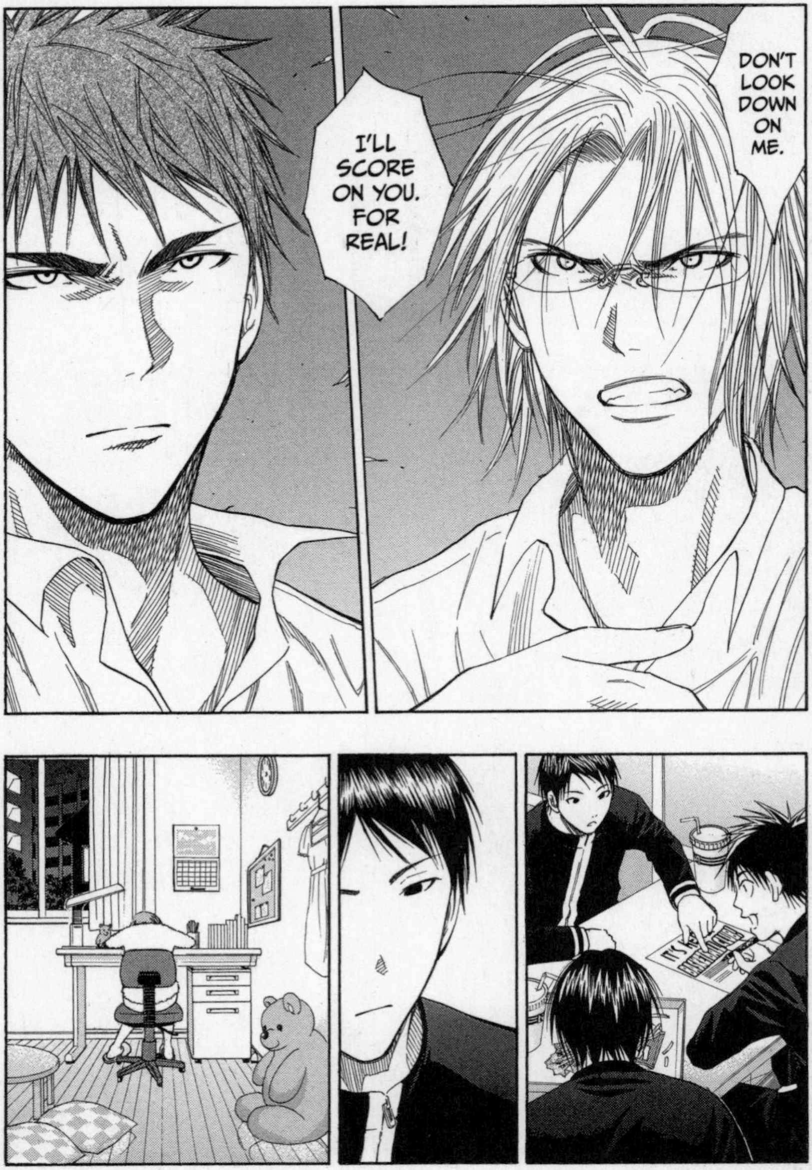
DON'T LOOK DOWN ON ME.
I'LL SCORE ON YOU. FOR REAL!

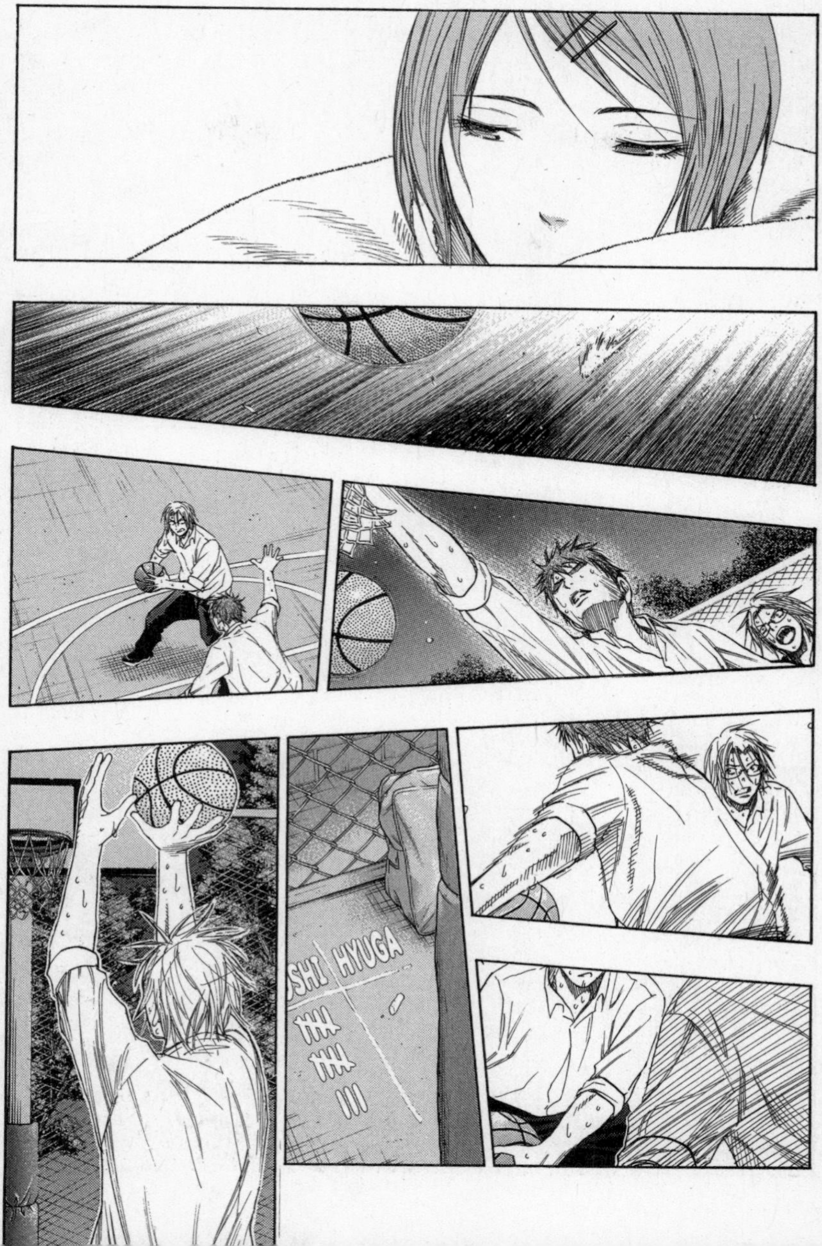
OSHI HYUGA

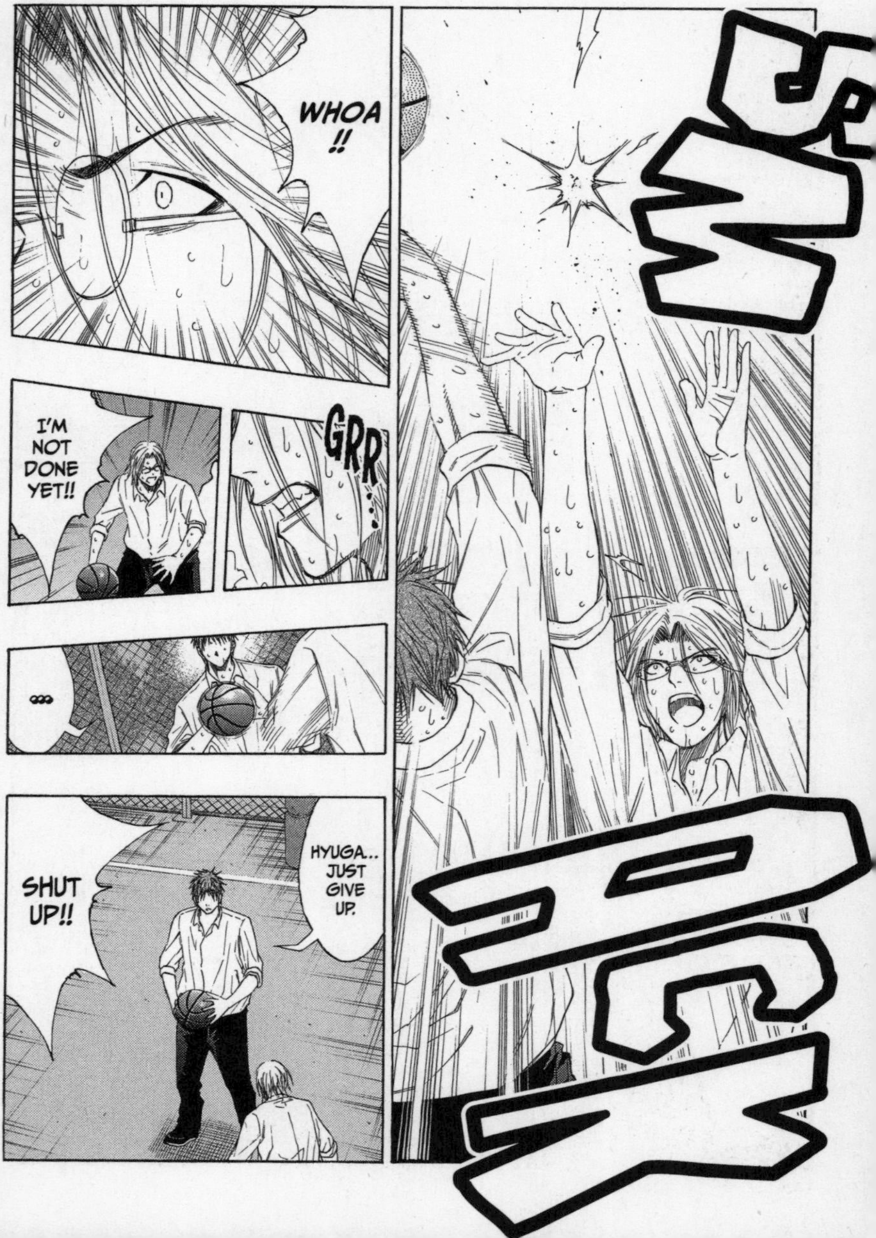
WHOA !!
GRR
I'M NOT DONE YET!!
...
HYUGA... JUST GIVE UP.
SHUT UP!!

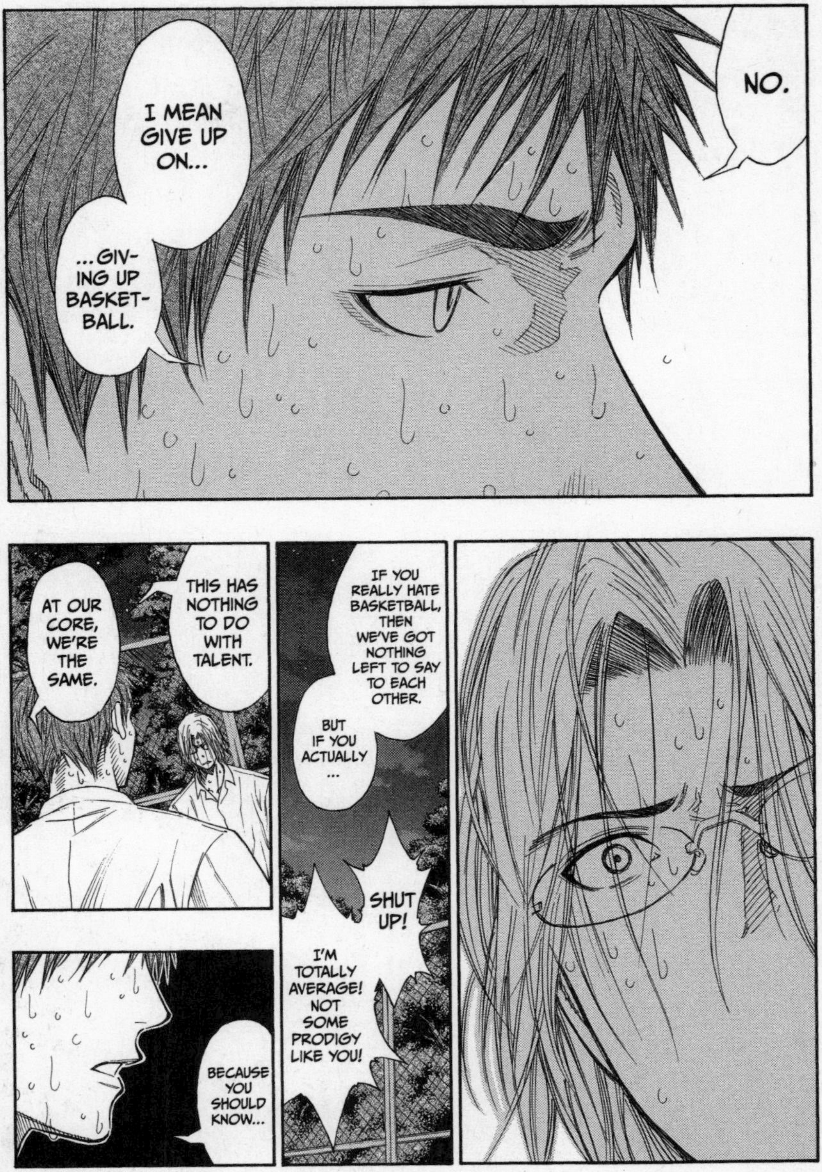
NO.
I MEAN GIVE UP ON...
...GIVING UP BASKETBALL.
IF YOU REALLY HATE BASKETBALL, THEN WE'VE GOT NOTHING LEFT TO SAY TO EACH OTHER.
BUT IF YOU ACTUALLY ...
SHUT UP!
I'M TOTALLY AVERAGE! NOT SOME PRODIGY LIKE YOU!
THIS HAS NOTHING TO DO WITH TALENT.
AT OUR CORE, WE'RE THE SAME.
BECAUSE YOU SHOULD KNOW...

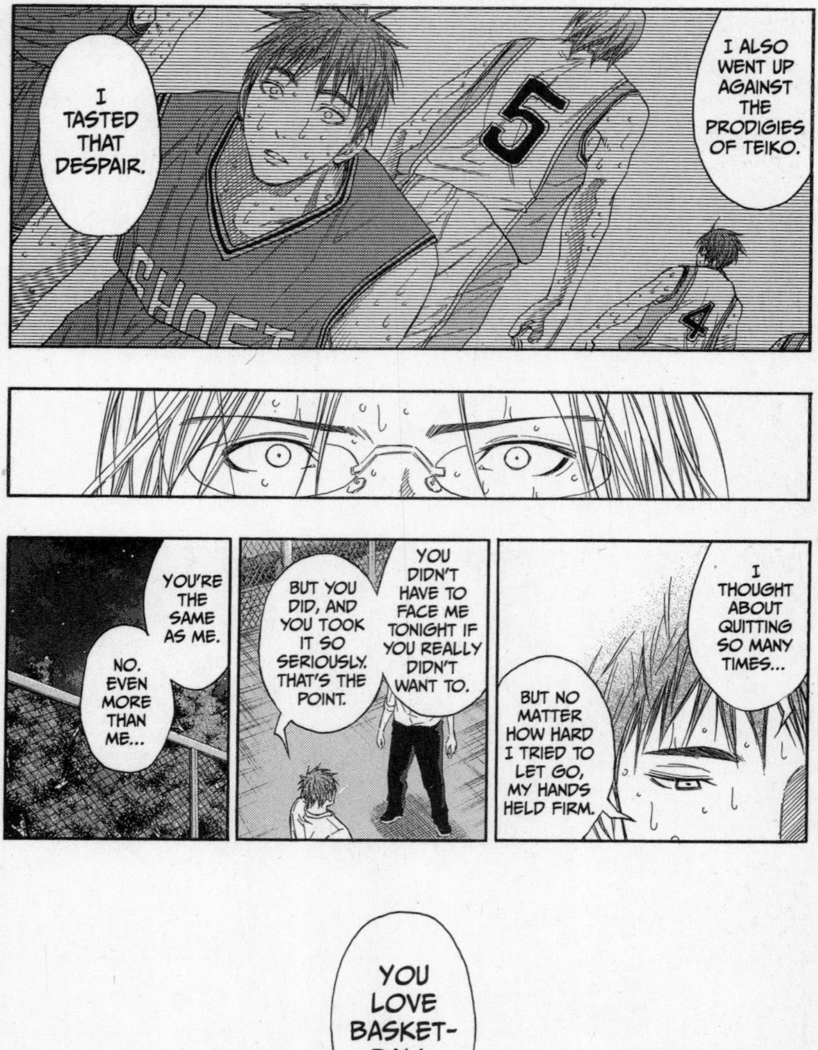
I ALSO WENT UP AGAINST THE PRODIGIES OF TEIKO.
I TASTED THAT DESPAIR.
I THOUGHT ABOUT QUITTING SO MANY TIMES...
BUT NO MATTER HOW HARD I TRIED TO LET GO, MY HANDS HELD FIRM.
YOU DIDN'T HAVE TO FACE ME TONIGHT IF YOU REALLY DIDN'T WANT TO.
BUT YOU DID, AND YOU TOOK IT SO SERIOUSLY. THAT'S THE POINT.
YOU'RE THE SAME AS ME.
NO. EVEN MORE THAN ME...
YOU LOVE BASKET-BALL.

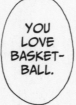

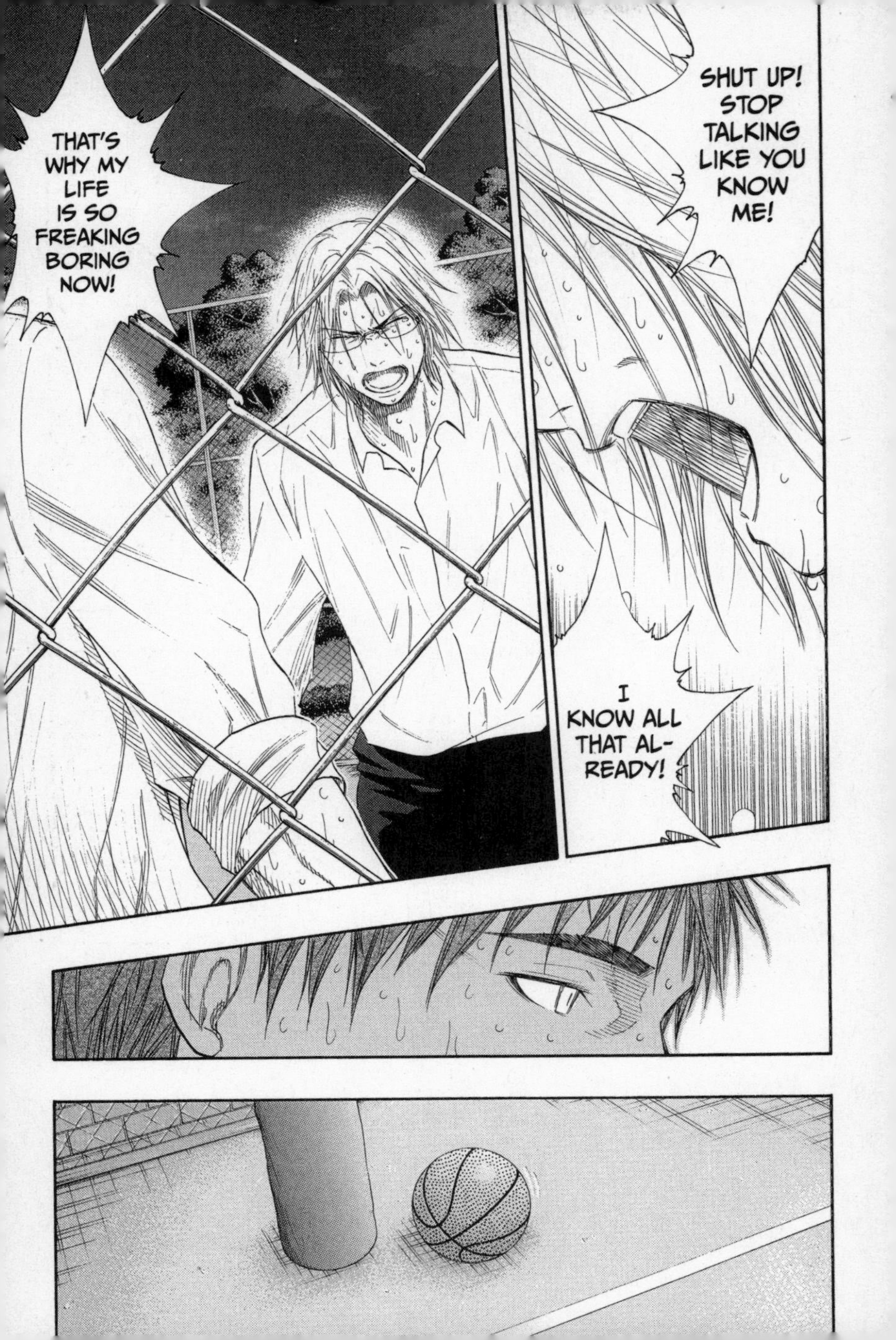
SHUT UP! STOP TALKING LIKE YOU KNOW ME!
I KNOW ALL THAT AL-READY!
THAT'S WHY MY LIFE IS SO FREAKING BORING NOW!

Kuroko's
BASKETBALL

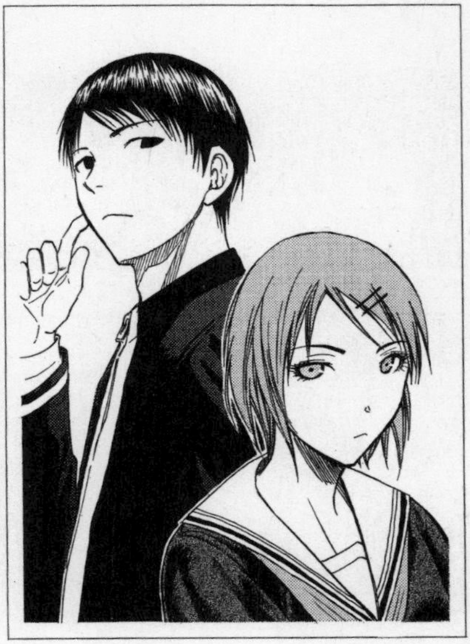

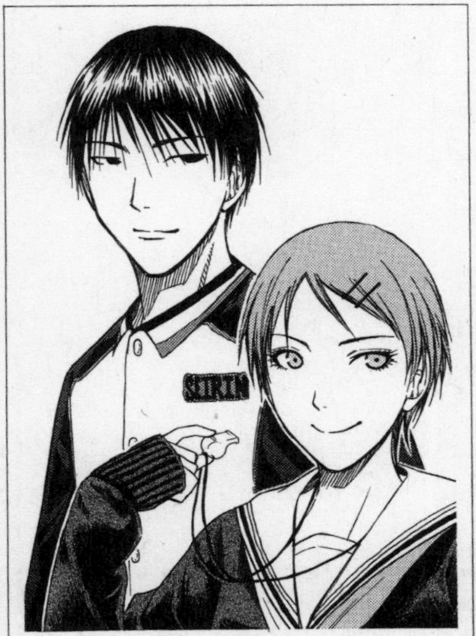
SEIRIN

97TH QUARTER: THE SEIRIN HIGH BASKETBALL CLUB!!

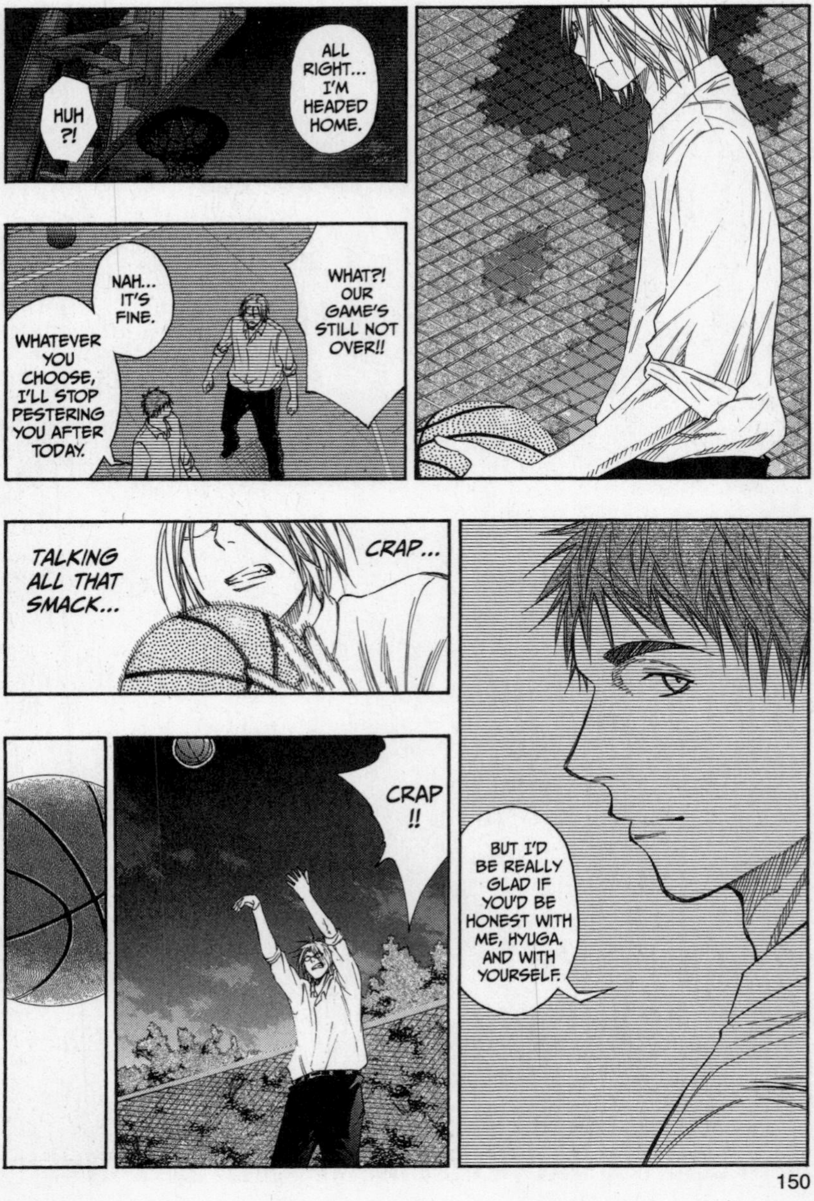
ALL RIGHT... I'M HEADED HOME.
HUH ?!
WHAT?! OUR GAME'S STILL NOT OVER!!
NAH... IT'S FINE.
WHATEVER YOU CHOOSE, I'LL STOP PESTERING YOU AFTER TODAY.
BUT I'D BE REALLY GLAD IF YOU'D BE HONEST WITH ME, HYUGA. AND WITH YOURSELF.
CRAP...
TALKING ALL THAT SMACK...
CRAP !!

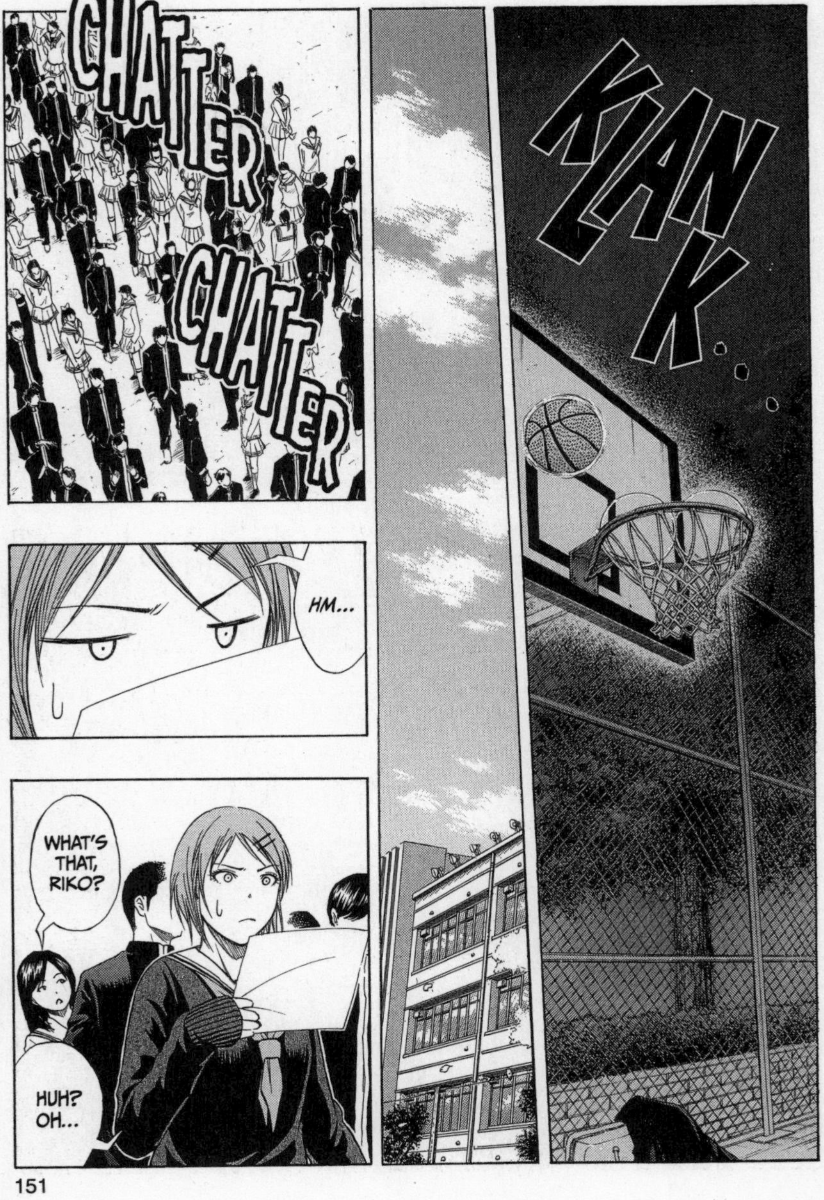
KLANK
CHATTER
CHATTER
HM...
WHAT'S THAT, RIKO?
HUH? OH...

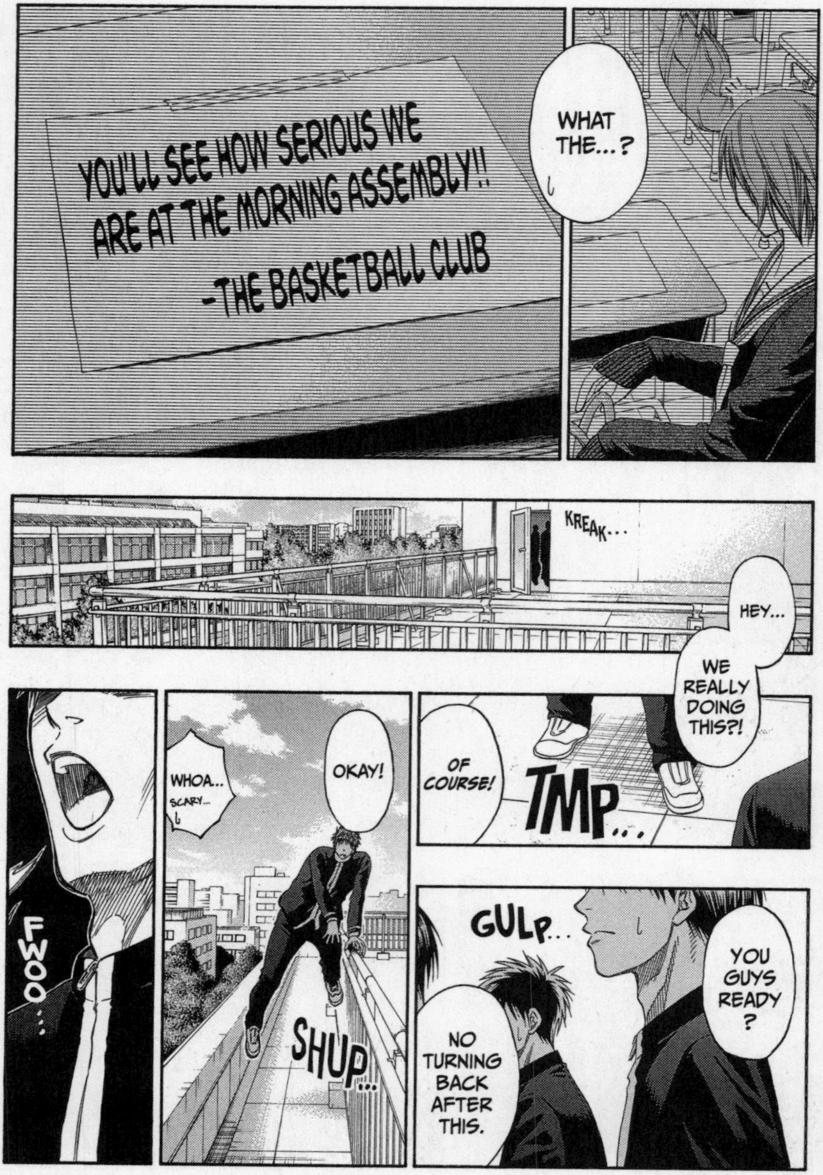
WHAT THE...?
YOU'LL SEE HOW SERIOUS WE ARE AT THE MORNING ASSEMBLY!!
-THE BASKETBALL CLUB
KREAK...
HEY...
WE REALLY DOING THIS?!
TMP...
OF COURSE!
GULP...
YOU GUYS READY?
NO TURNING BACK AFTER THIS.
OKAY!
WHOA... SCARY...
SHUP...
FWOO...

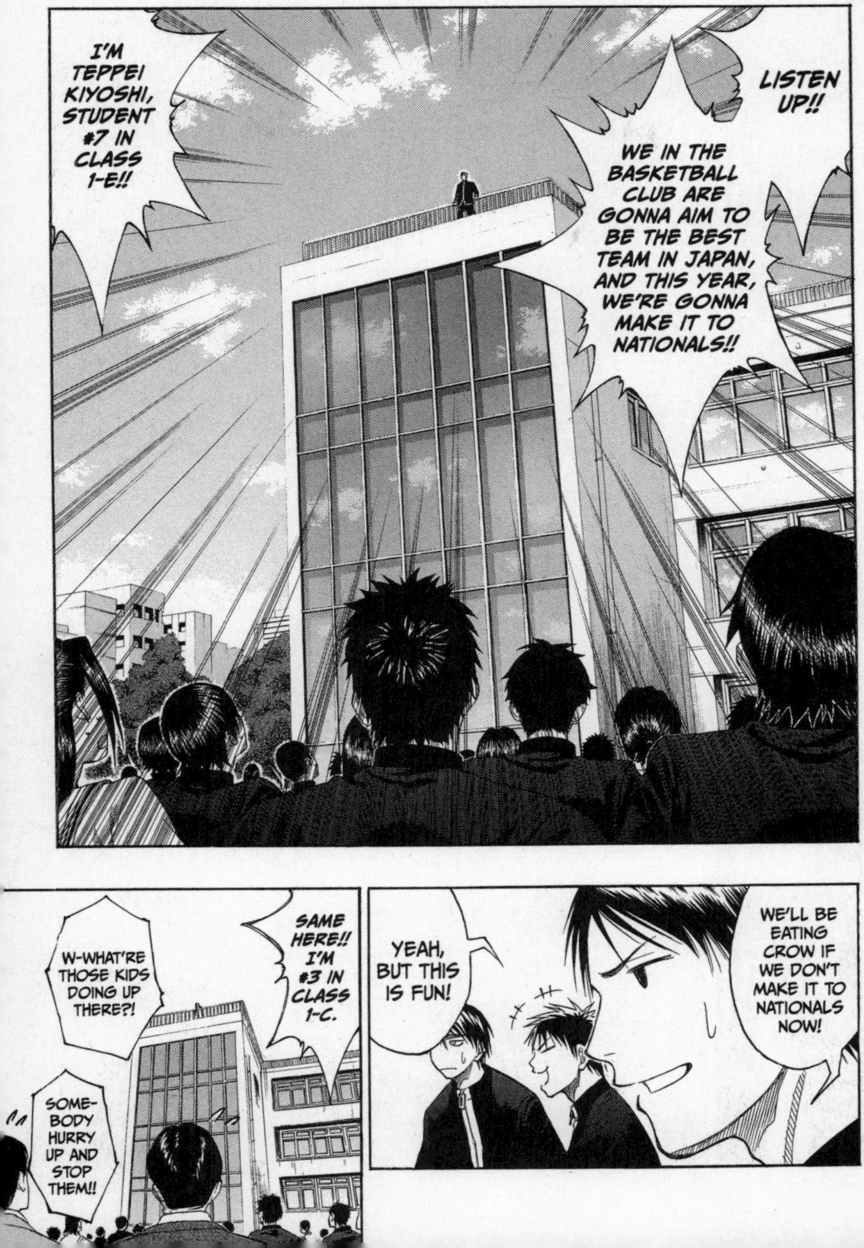
LISTEN UP!!
WE IN THE BASKETBALL CLUB ARE GONNA AIM TO BE THE BEST TEAM IN JAPAN, AND THIS YEAR, WE'RE GONNA MAKE IT TO NATIONALS!!
I'M TEPPEI KIYOSHI, STUDENT #7 IN CLASS 1-E!!
WE'LL BE EATING CROW IF WE DON'T MAKE IT TO NATIONALS NOW!
YEAH, BUT THIS IS FUN!
SAME HERE!! I'M #3 IN CLASS 1-C.
W-WHAT'RE THOSE KIDS DOING UP THERE?!
SOME-BODY HURRY UP AND STOP THEM!!

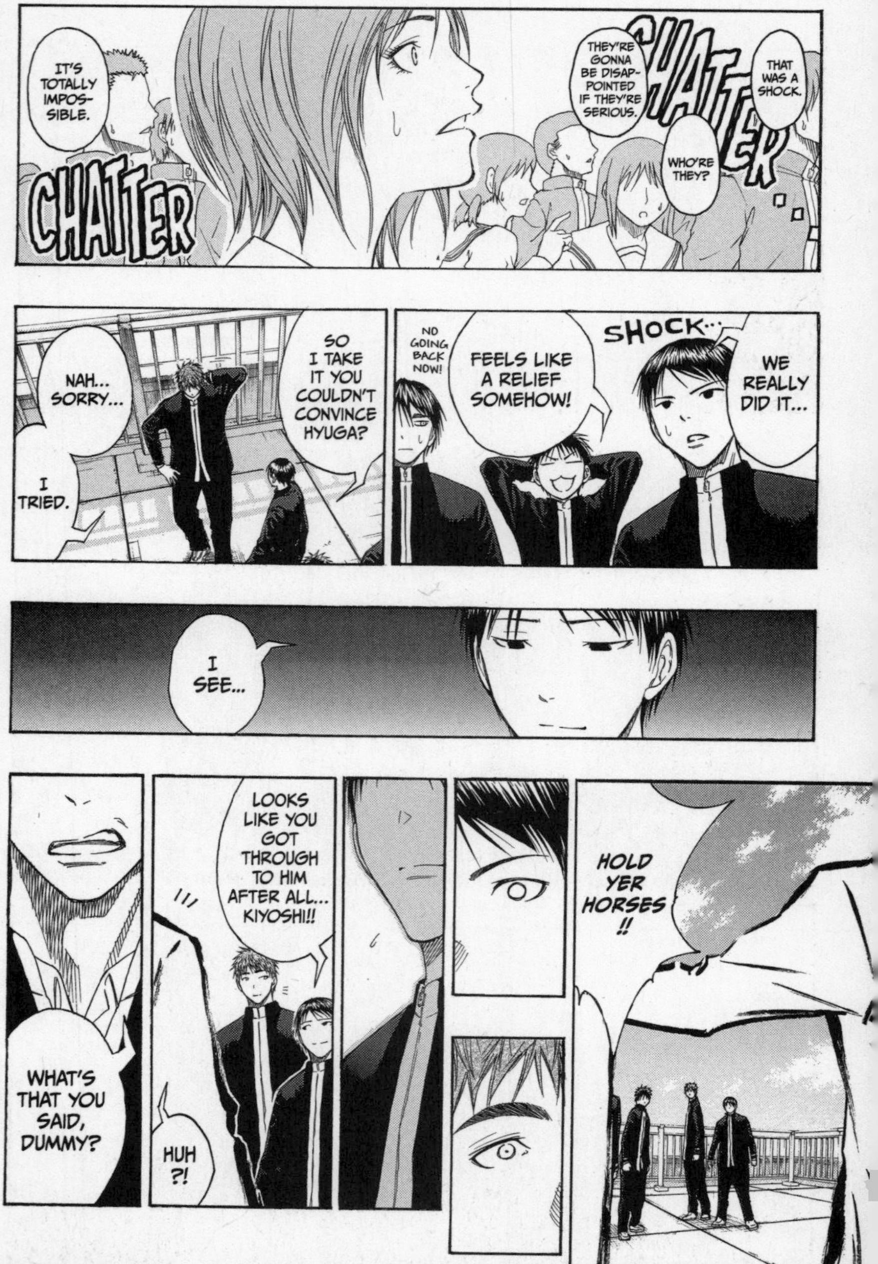

THAT WAS A SHOCK.
CHATTER
WHO'RE THEY?
THEY'RE GONNA BE DISAP-POINTED IF THEY'RE SERIOUS.
IT'S TOTALLY IMPOS-SIBLE.
CHATTER
WE REALLY DID IT...
SHOCK...
FEELS LIKE A RELIEF SOMEHOW!
NO GOING BACK NOW!
SO I TAKE IT YOU COULDN'T CONVINCE HYUGA?
NAH... SORRY...
I TRIED.
I SEE...
HOLD YER HORSES!!
LOOKS LIKE YOU GOT THROUGH TO HIM AFTER ALL... KIYOSHI!!
HUH ?!
WHAT'S THAT YOU SAID, DUMMY?

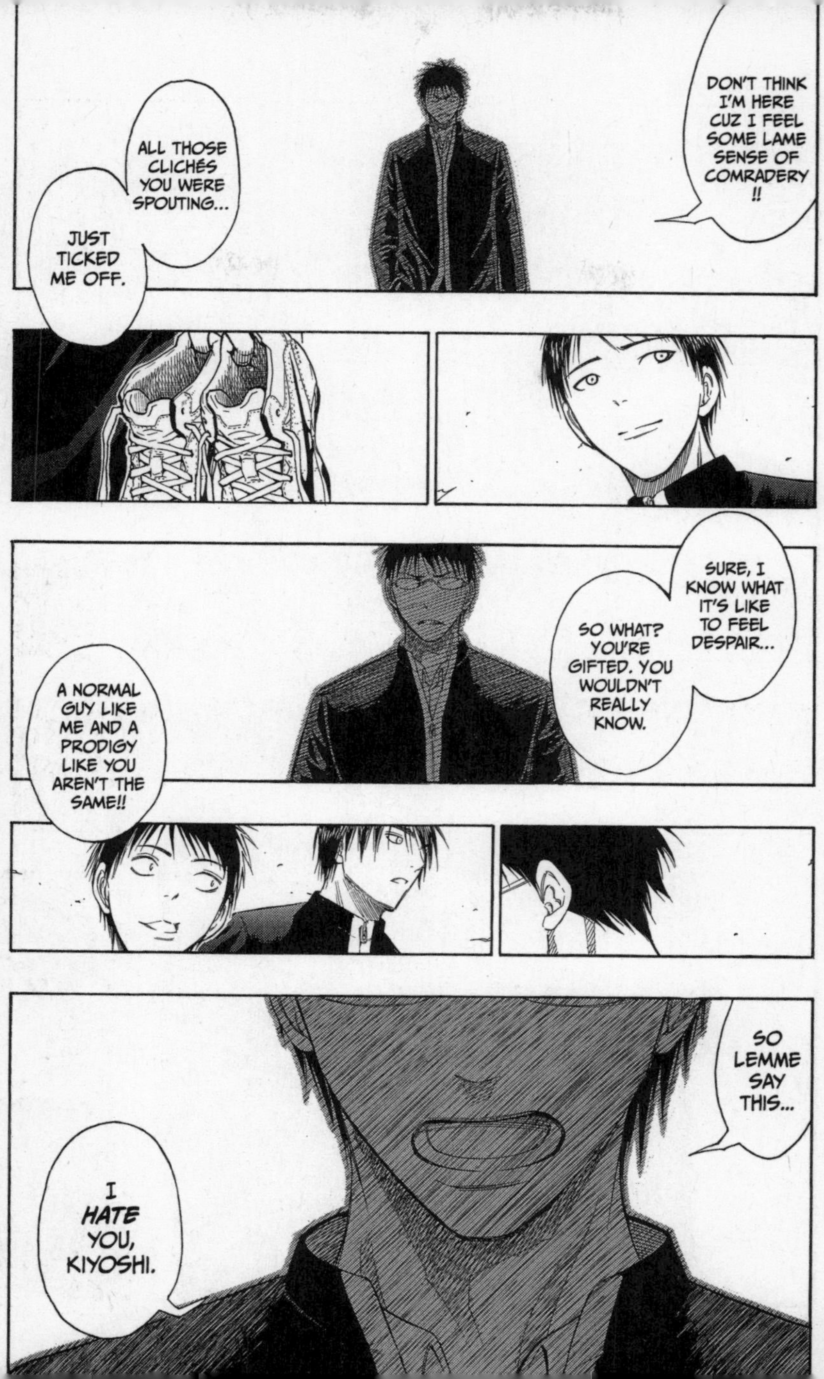
DON'T THINK I'M HERE CUZ I FEEL SOME LAME SENSE OF COMRADERY !!
ALL THOSE CLICHÉS YOU WERE SPOUTING...
JUST TICKED ME OFF.
SURE, I KNOW WHAT IT'S LIKE TO FEEL DESPAIR...
SO WHAT? YOU'RE GIFTED. YOU WOULDN'T REALLY KNOW.
A NORMAL GUY LIKE ME AND A PRODIGY LIKE YOU AREN'T THE SAME!!
SO LEMME SAY THIS...
I *HATE* YOU, KIYOSHI.

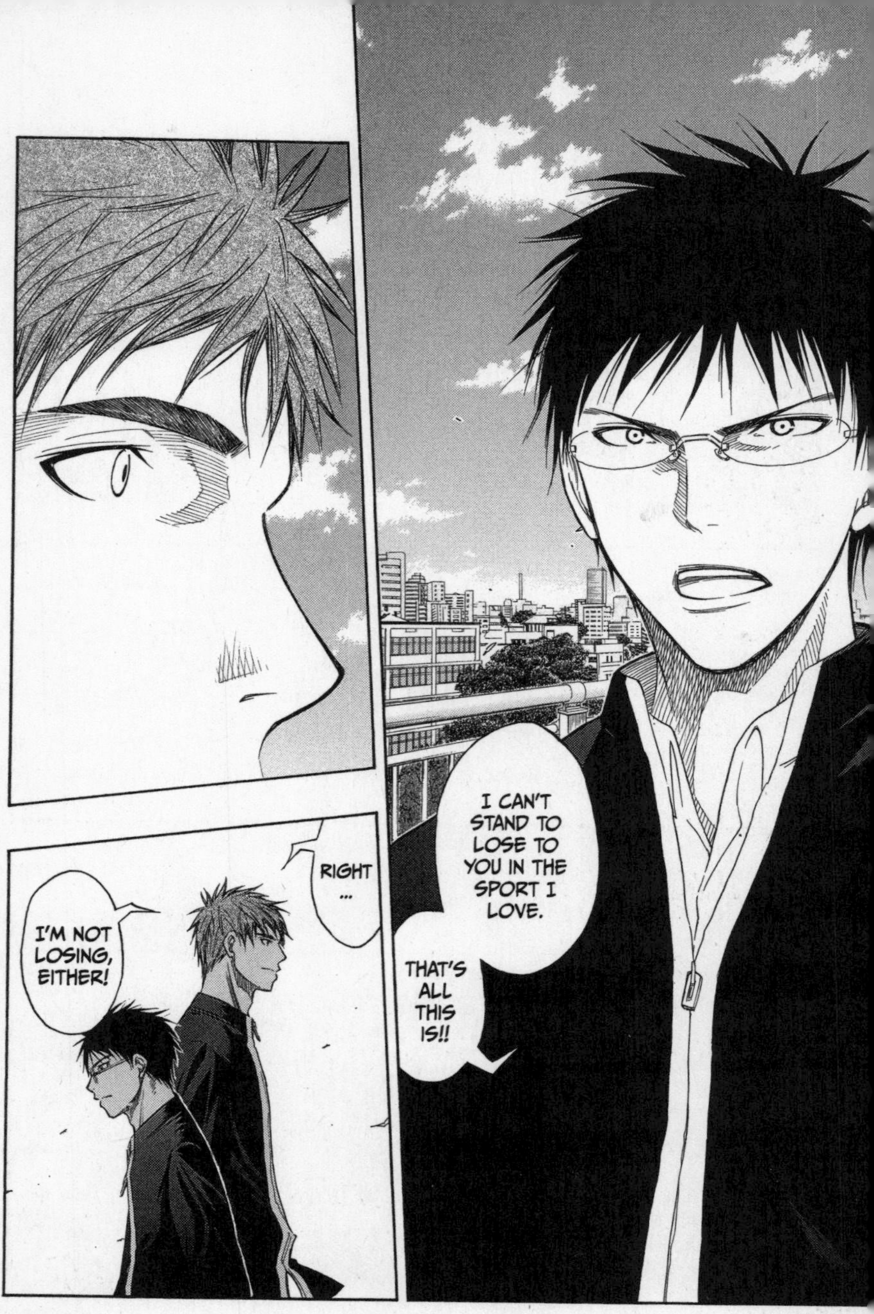
I CAN'T STAND TO LOSE TO YOU IN THE SPORT I LOVE.
THAT'S ALL THIS IS!!
RIGHT ...
I'M NOT LOSING, EITHER!

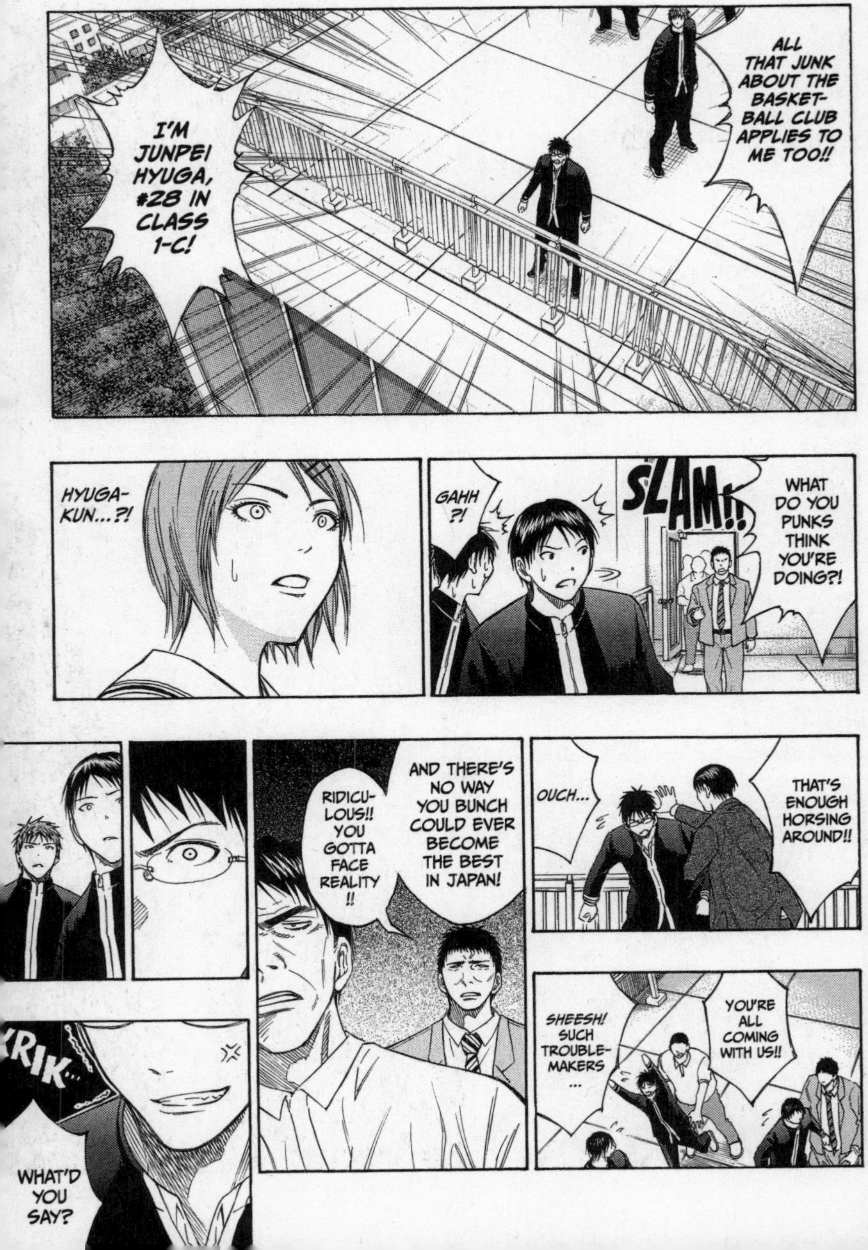
ALL THAT JUNK ABOUT THE BASKET-BALL CLUB APPLIES TO ME TOO!!
I'M JUNPEI HYUGA, #28 IN CLASS 1-C!
WHAT DO YOU PUNKS THINK YOU'RE DOING?!
SLAM!!
GAHH ?!
HYUGA-KUN...?!
THAT'S ENOUGH HORSING AROUND!!
OUCH...
YOU'RE ALL COMING WITH US!!
SHEESH! SUCH TROUBLE-MAKERS ...
AND THERE'S NO WAY YOU BUNCH COULD EVER BECOME THE BEST IN JAPAN!
RIDICU-LOUS!! YOU GOTTA FACE REALITY !!
KRIK...
WHAT'D YOU SAY?

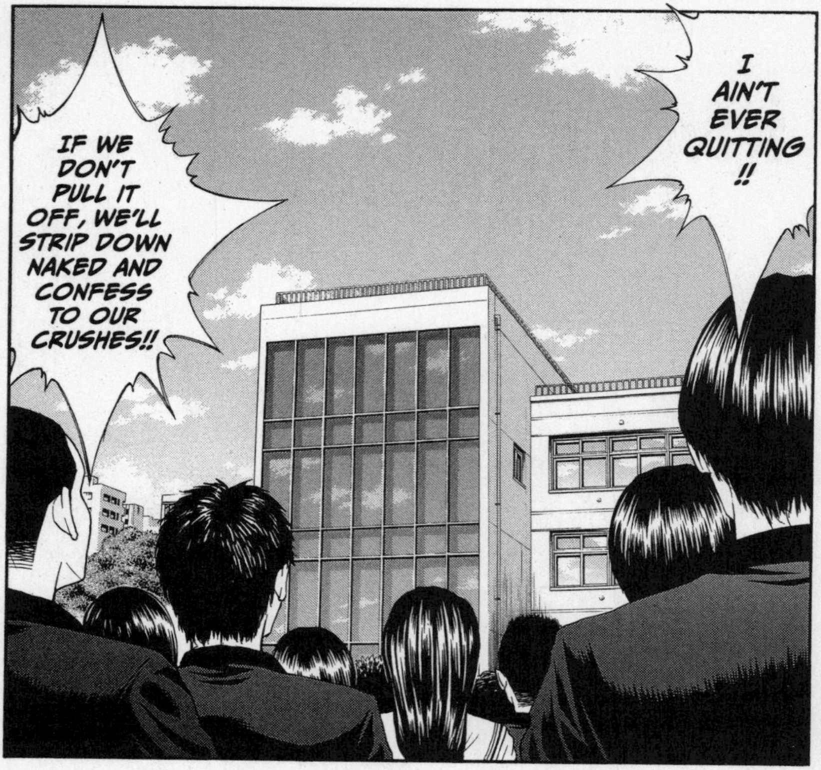
I AIN'T EVER QUITTING!!
IF WE DON'T PULL IT OFF, WE'LL STRIP DOWN NAKED AND CONFESS TO OUR CRUSHES!!

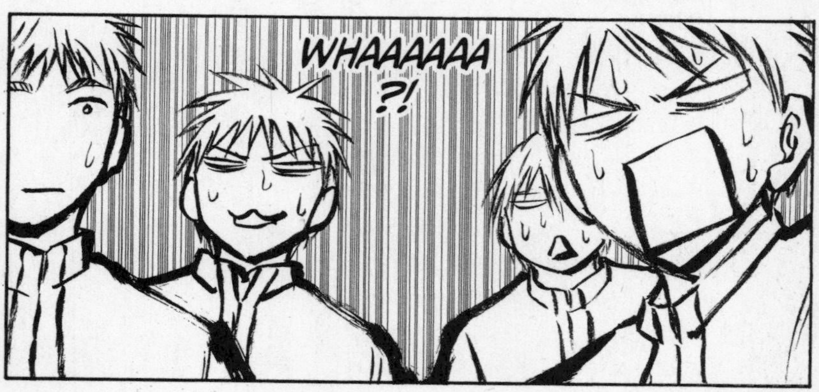
WHAAAAAA?!

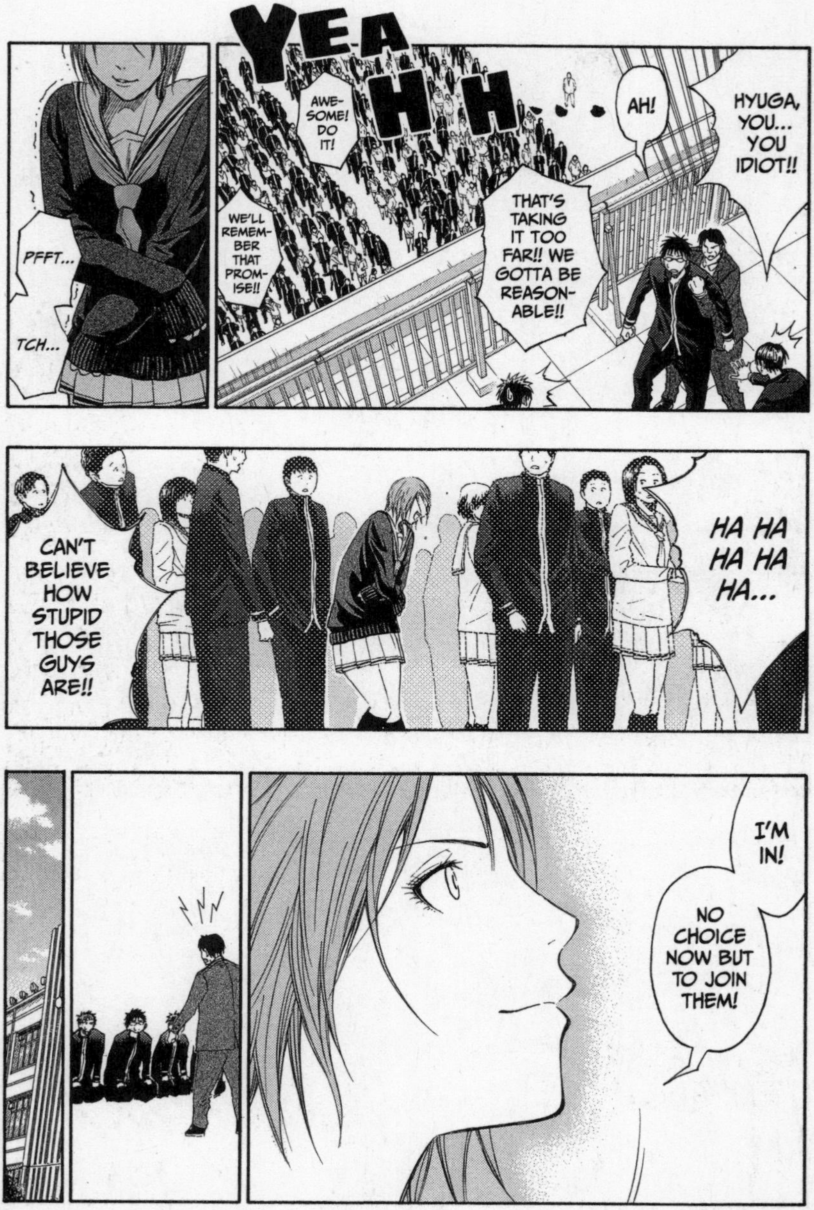
HYUGA, YOU... YOU IDIOT!!
AH!
THAT'S TAKING IT TOO FAR!! WE GOTTA BE REASONABLE!!
YEAHH
AWESOME! DO IT!
WE'LL REMEMBER THAT PROMISE!!
PFFT...
TCH...
HA HA HA HA HA...
CAN'T BELIEVE HOW STUPID THOSE GUYS ARE!!
I'M IN!
NO CHOICE NOW BUT TO JOIN THEM!

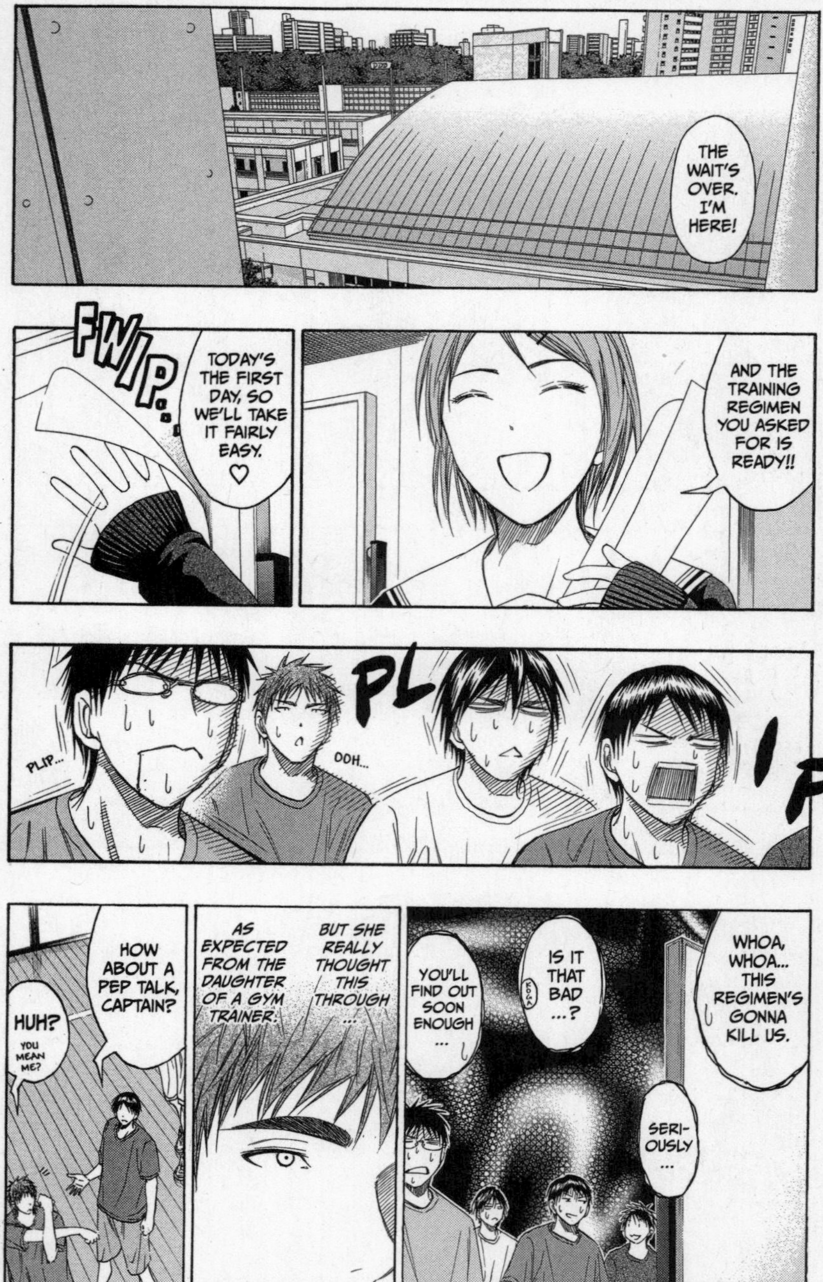
THE WAIT'S OVER. I'M HERE!
AND THE TRAINING REGIMEN YOU ASKED FOR IS READY!!
FWIP...
TODAY'S THE FIRST DAY, SO WE'LL TAKE IT FAIRLY EASY. ♡
PLIP...
PLIP...
OOH...
WHOA, WHOA... THIS REGIMEN'S GONNA KILL US.
SERIOUSLY...
IS IT THAT BAD...?
KOGA
YOU'LL FIND OUT SOON ENOUGH...
BUT SHE REALLY THOUGHT THIS THROUGH...
AS EXPECTED FROM THE DAUGHTER OF A GYM TRAINER.
HOW ABOUT A PEP TALK, CAPTAIN?
HUH?
YOU MEAN ME?

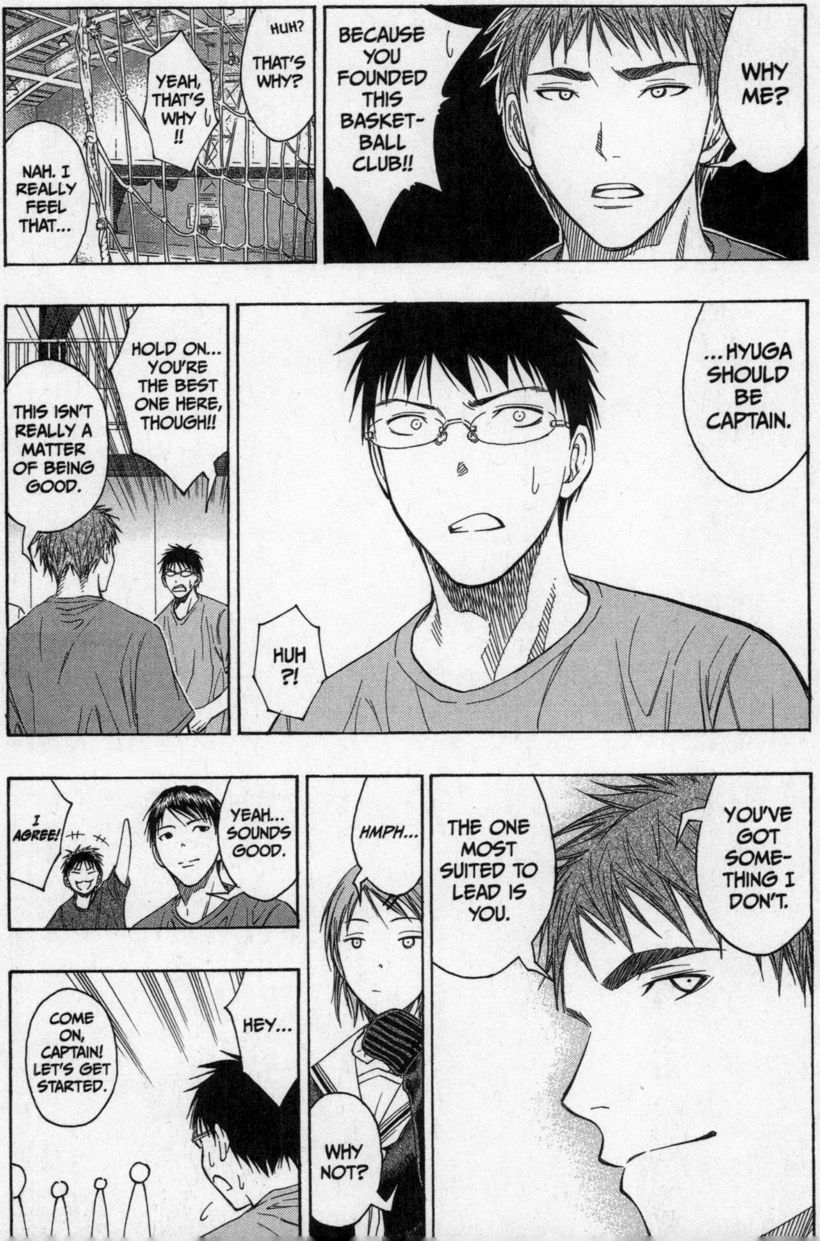
WHY ME?
BECAUSE YOU FOUNDED THIS BASKET-BALL CLUB!!
HUH? THAT'S WHY?
YEAH, THAT'S WHY!!
NAH. I REALLY FEEL THAT...
...HYUGA SHOULD BE CAPTAIN.
HUH?!
HOLD ON... YOU'RE THE BEST ONE HERE, THOUGH!!
THIS ISN'T REALLY A MATTER OF BEING GOOD.
YOU'VE GOT SOME-THING I DON'T.
THE ONE MOST SUITED TO LEAD IS YOU.
HMPH...
WHY NOT?
YEAH... SOUNDS GOOD.
I AGREE!
HEY...
COME ON, CAPTAIN! LET'S GET STARTED.

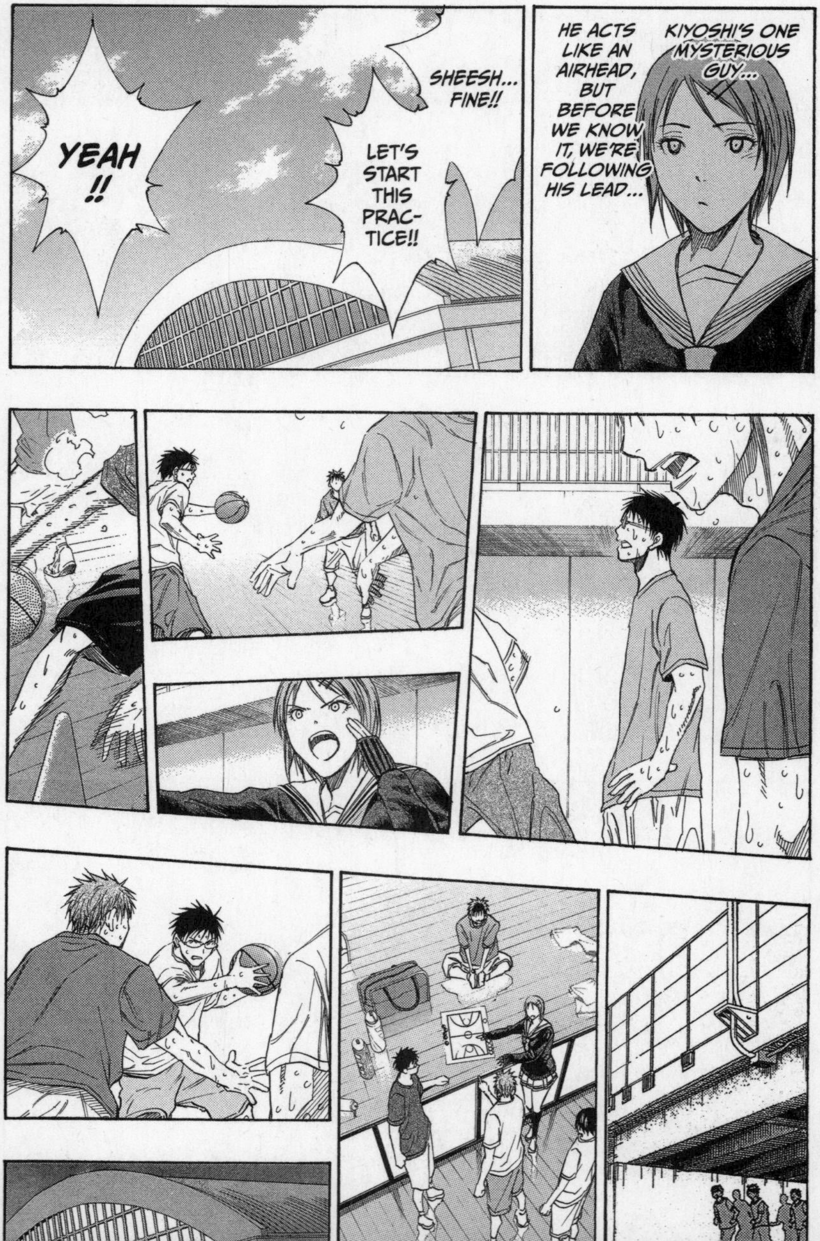
KIYOSHI'S ONE MYSTERIOUS GUY...
HE ACTS LIKE AN AIRHEAD, BUT BEFORE WE KNOW IT, WE'RE FOLLOWING HIS LEAD...
SHEESH... FINE!!
LET'S START THIS PRAC- TICE!!
YEAH !!

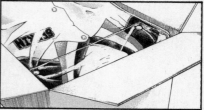

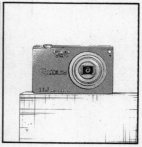

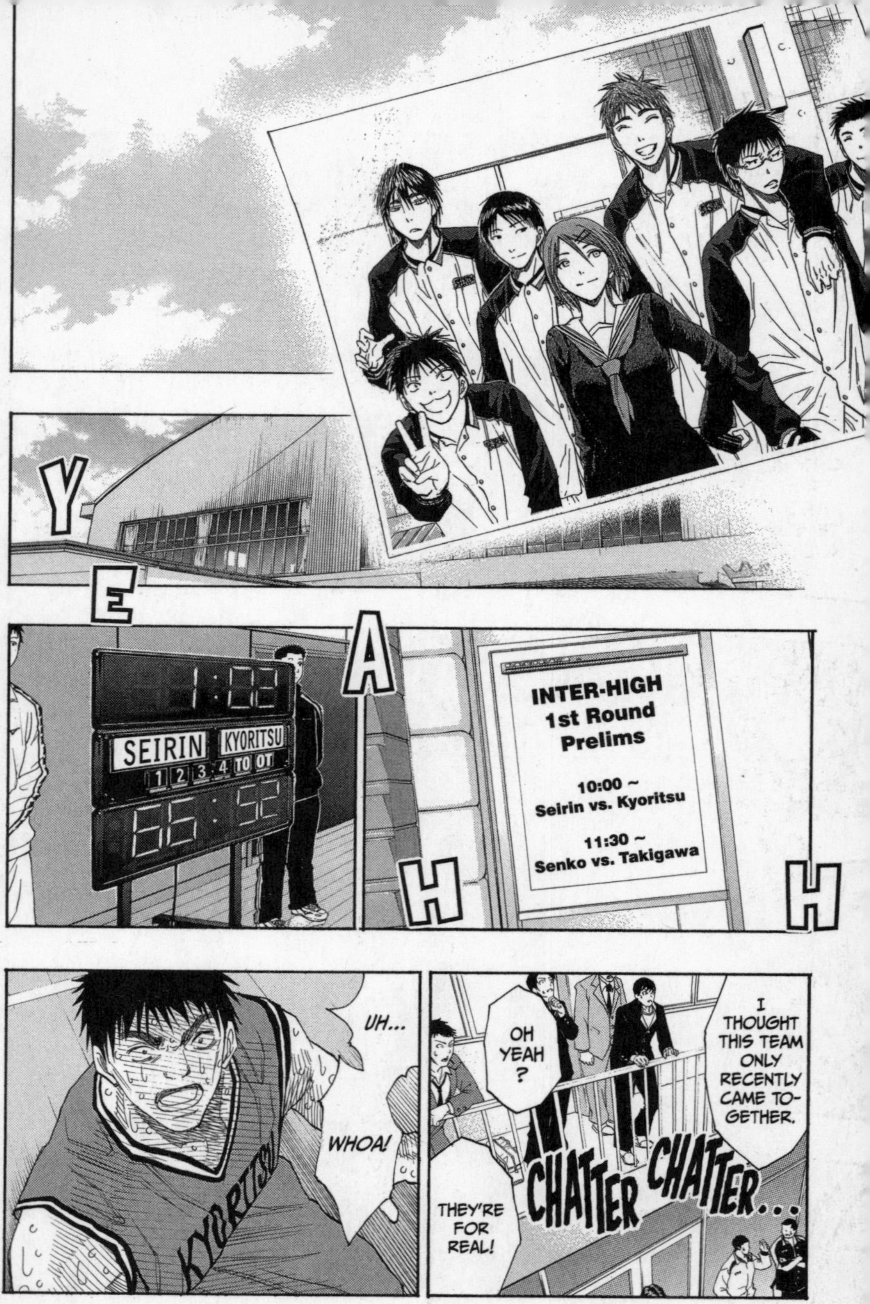
YEAHH
INTER-HIGH
1st Round
Prelims
10:00 ~
Seirin vs. Kyoritsu
11:30 ~
Senko vs. Takigawa
SEIRIN
KYORITSU
I THOUGHT THIS TEAM ONLY RECENTLY CAME TO-GETHER.
OH YEAH?
CHATTER CHATTER...
THEY'RE FOR REAL!
UH...
WHOA!
KYORITSU

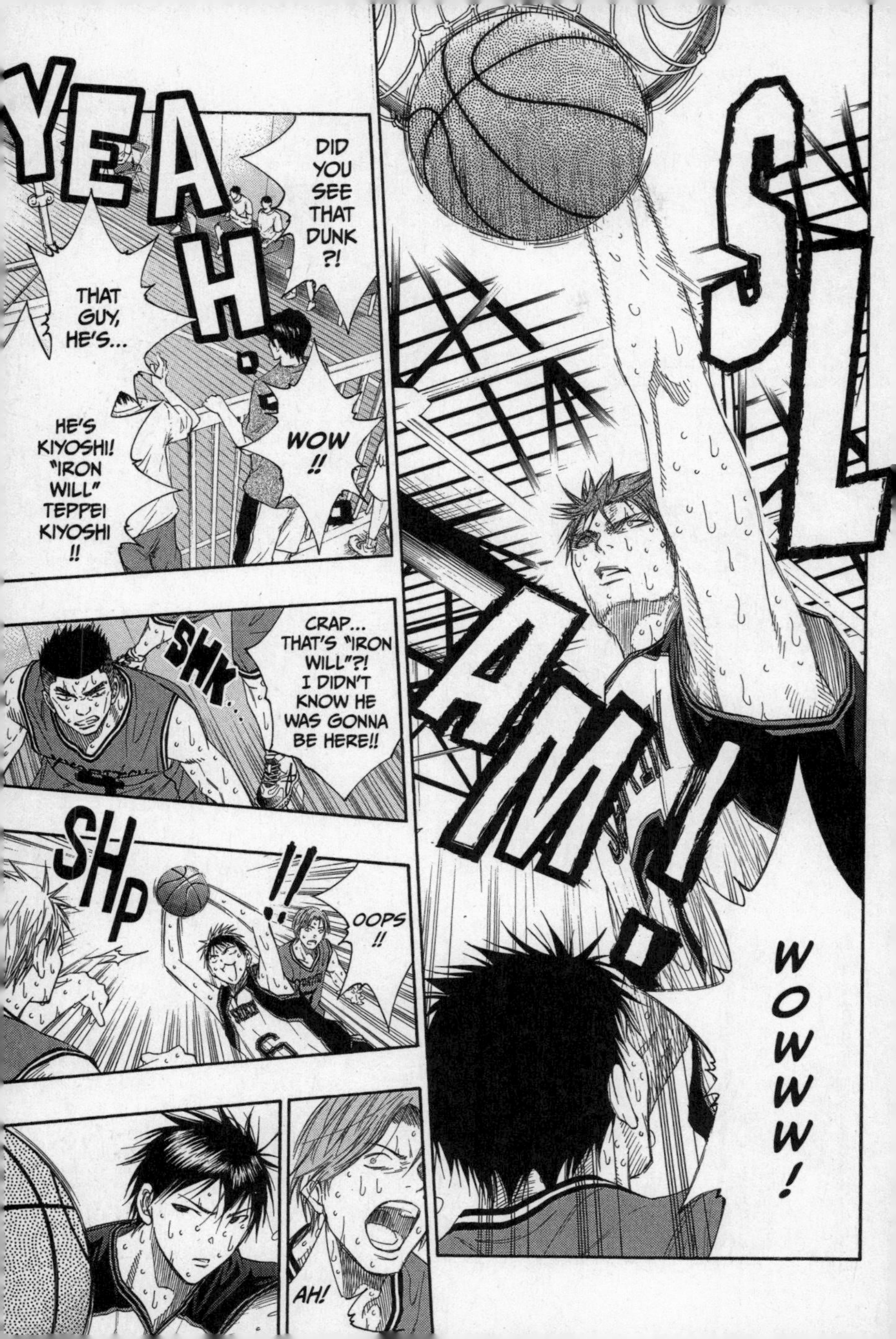
SLAM!
WOWWWW!
DID YOU SEE THAT DUNK?!
YEAH
THAT GUY, HE'S...
WOW!!
HE'S KIYOSHI! "IRON WILL" TEPPEI KIYOSHI!!
CRAP... THAT'S "IRON WILL"?! I DIDN'T KNOW HE WAS GONNA BE HERE!!
SHK...
SHP
!!
OOPS!!
AH!

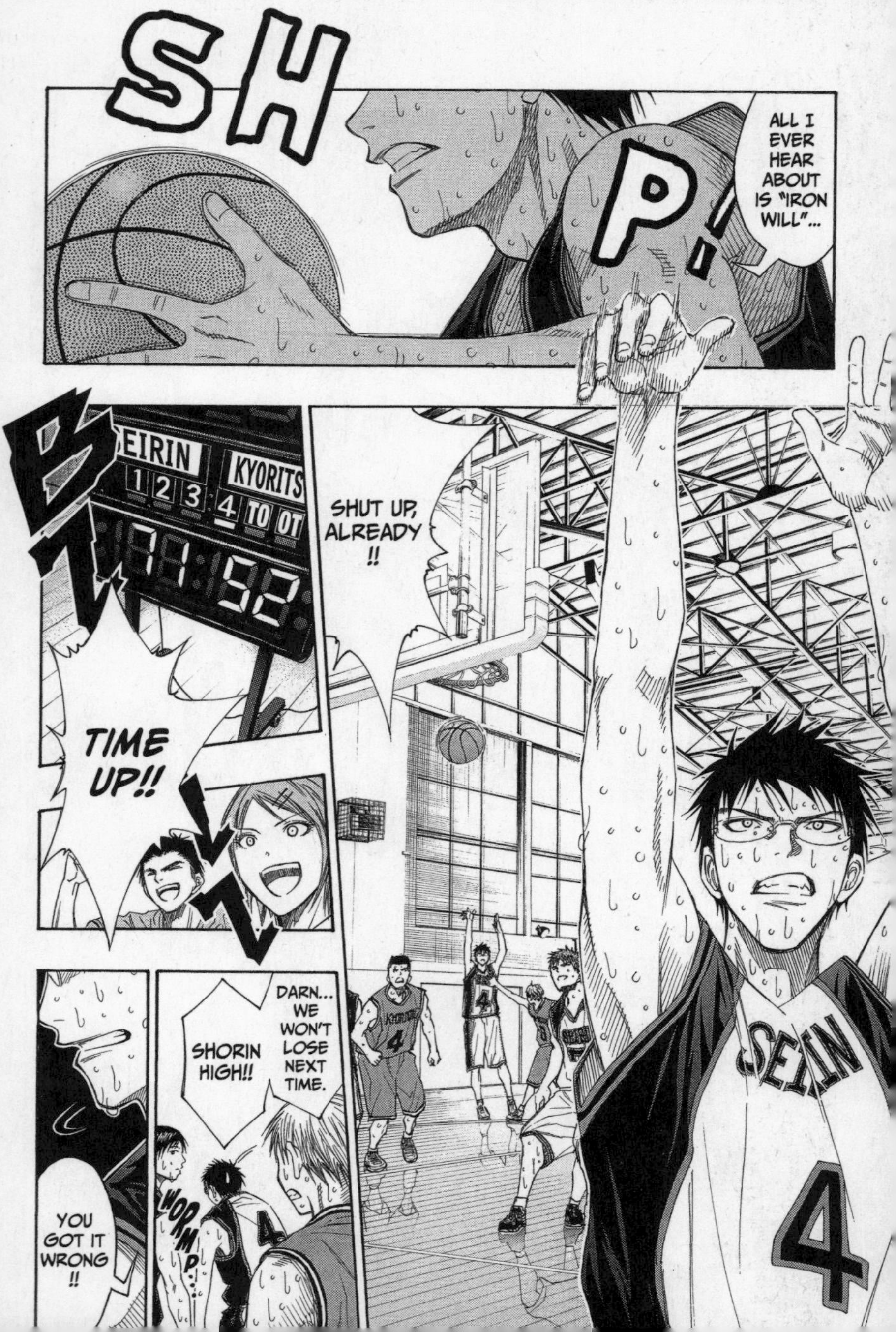
SHP!!
ALL I EVER HEAR ABOUT IS "IRON WILL"...
SHUT UP, ALREADY!!
TIME UP!!
DARN... WE WON'T LOSE NEXT TIME.
SHORIN HIGH!!
WORMP!..
YOU GOT IT WRONG!!

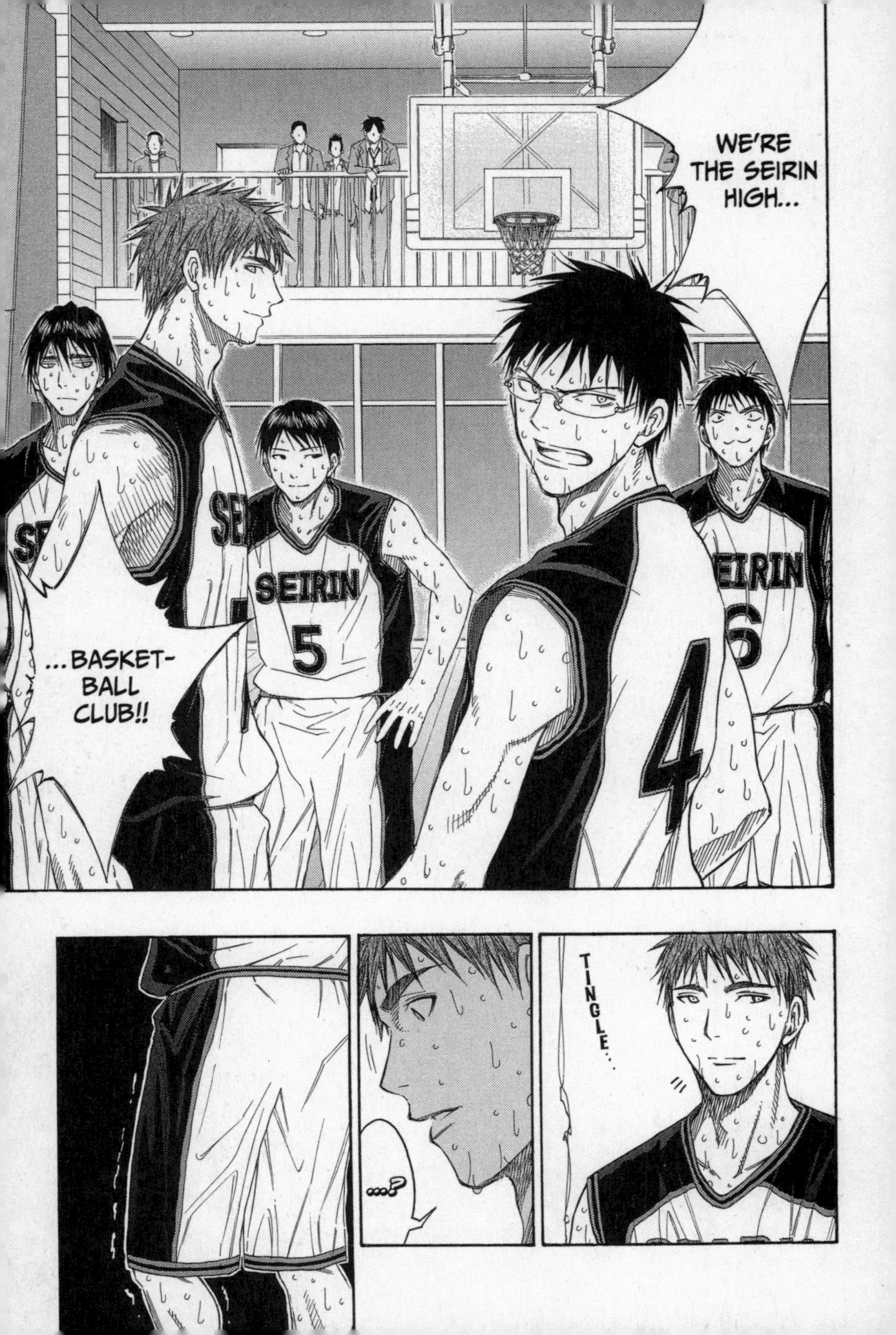
WE'RE THE SEIRIN HIGH...
...BASKETBALL CLUB!!
TINGLE...
...?

Kuroko's BASKETBALL

98TH QUARTER:
GLAD I MET YOU

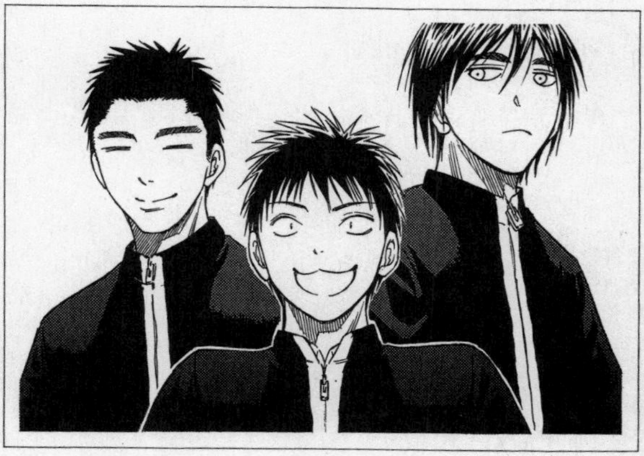

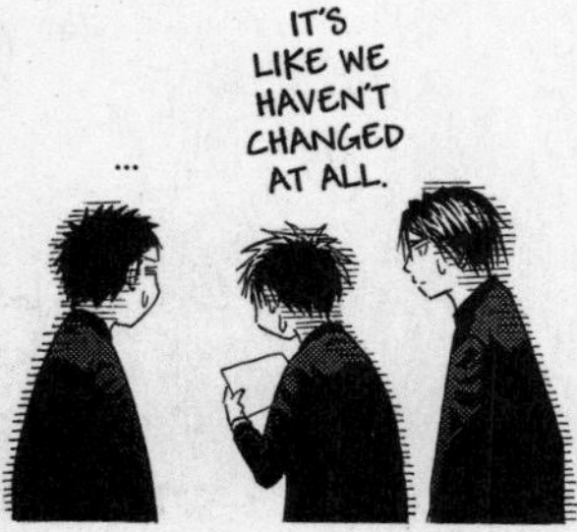
IT'S LIKE WE HAVEN'T CHANGED AT ALL.
...

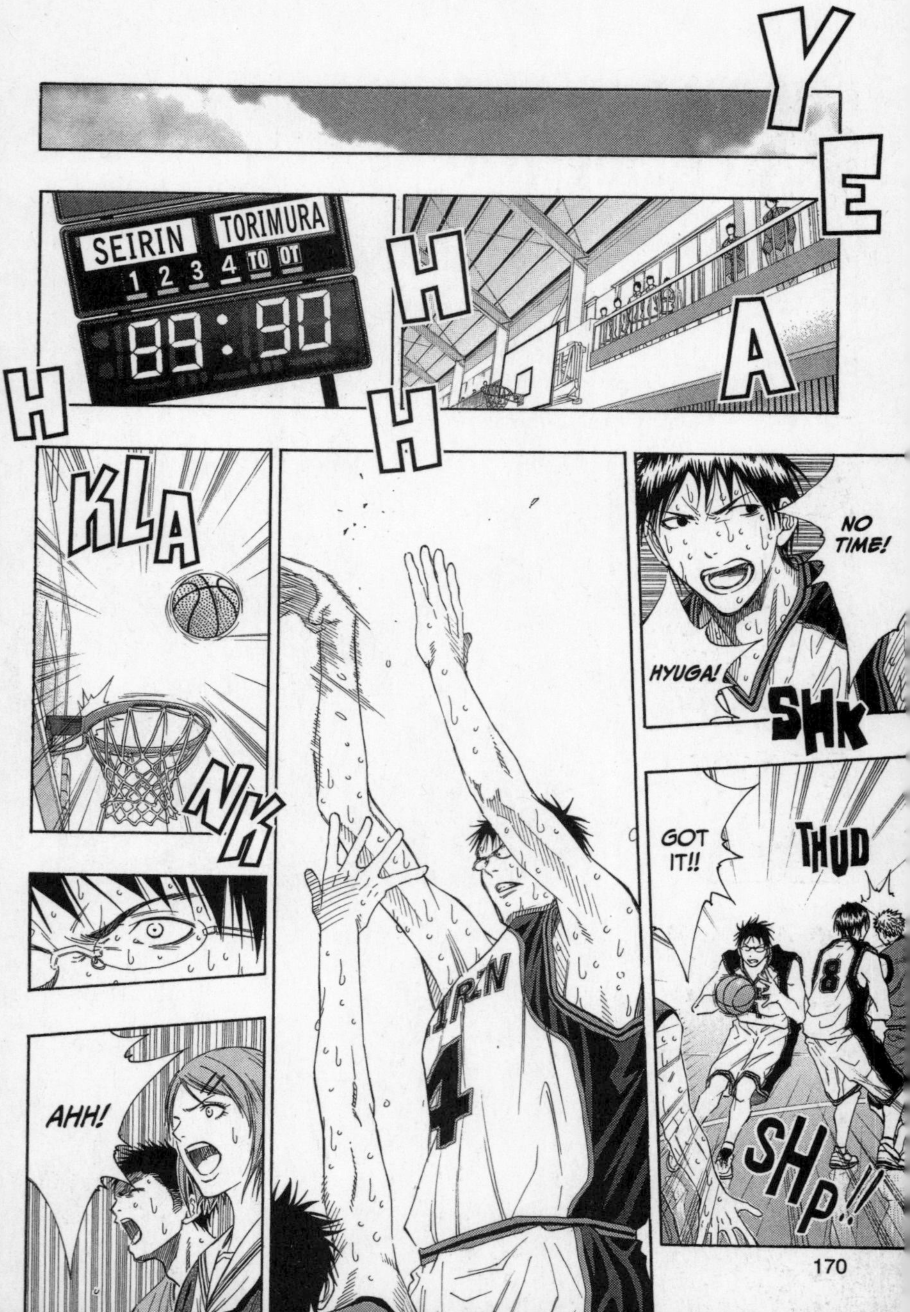
YEAHHH
TORIMURA
SEIRIN
1 2 3 4 TO OT
89 : 90
NO TIME!
HYUGA!
SHK
KLANK
GOT IT!!
THUD
SHP!!
AHH!

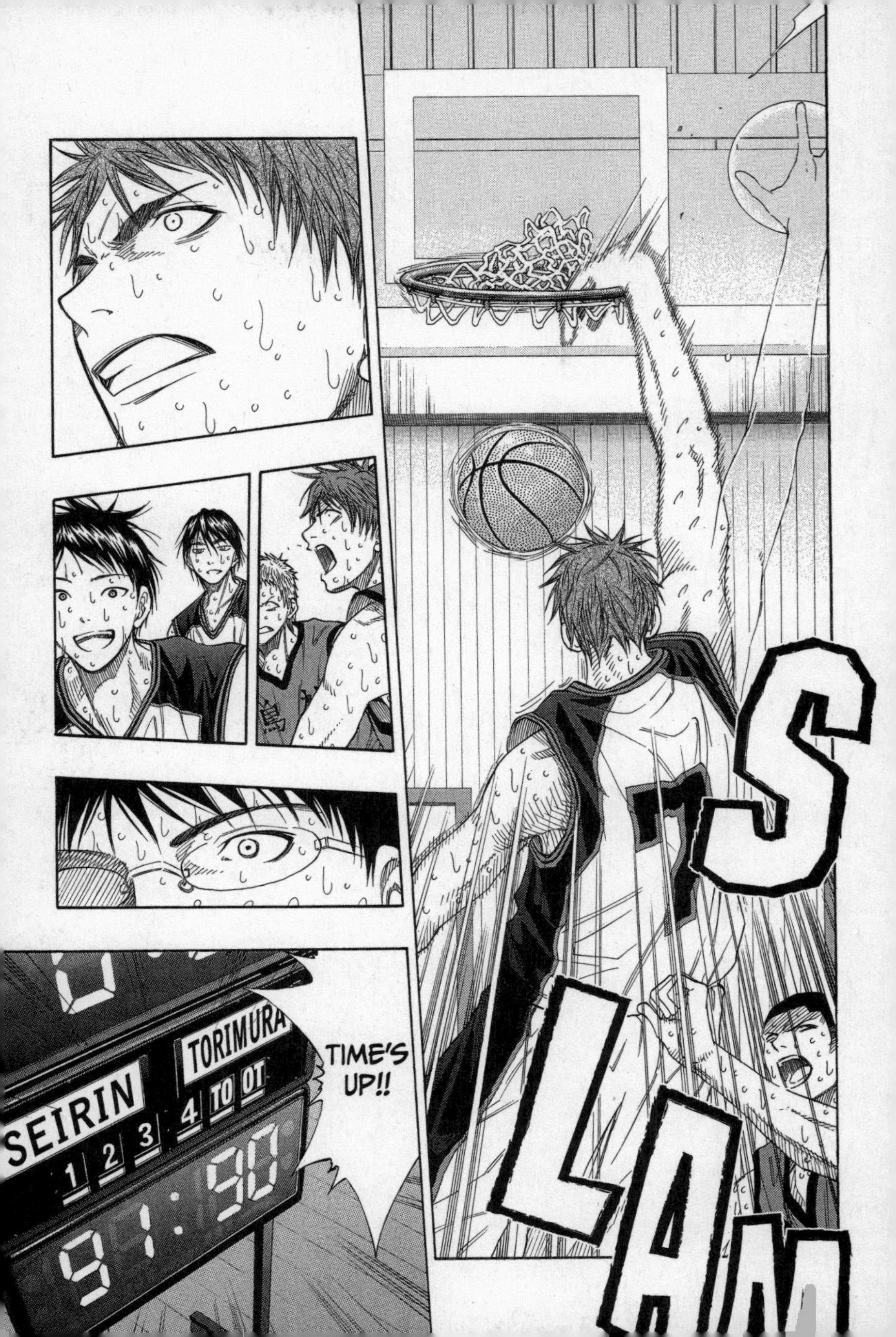
SLAM
TIME'S UP!!
TORIMURA
SEIRIN
1 2 3 4 TO OT
91 : 90

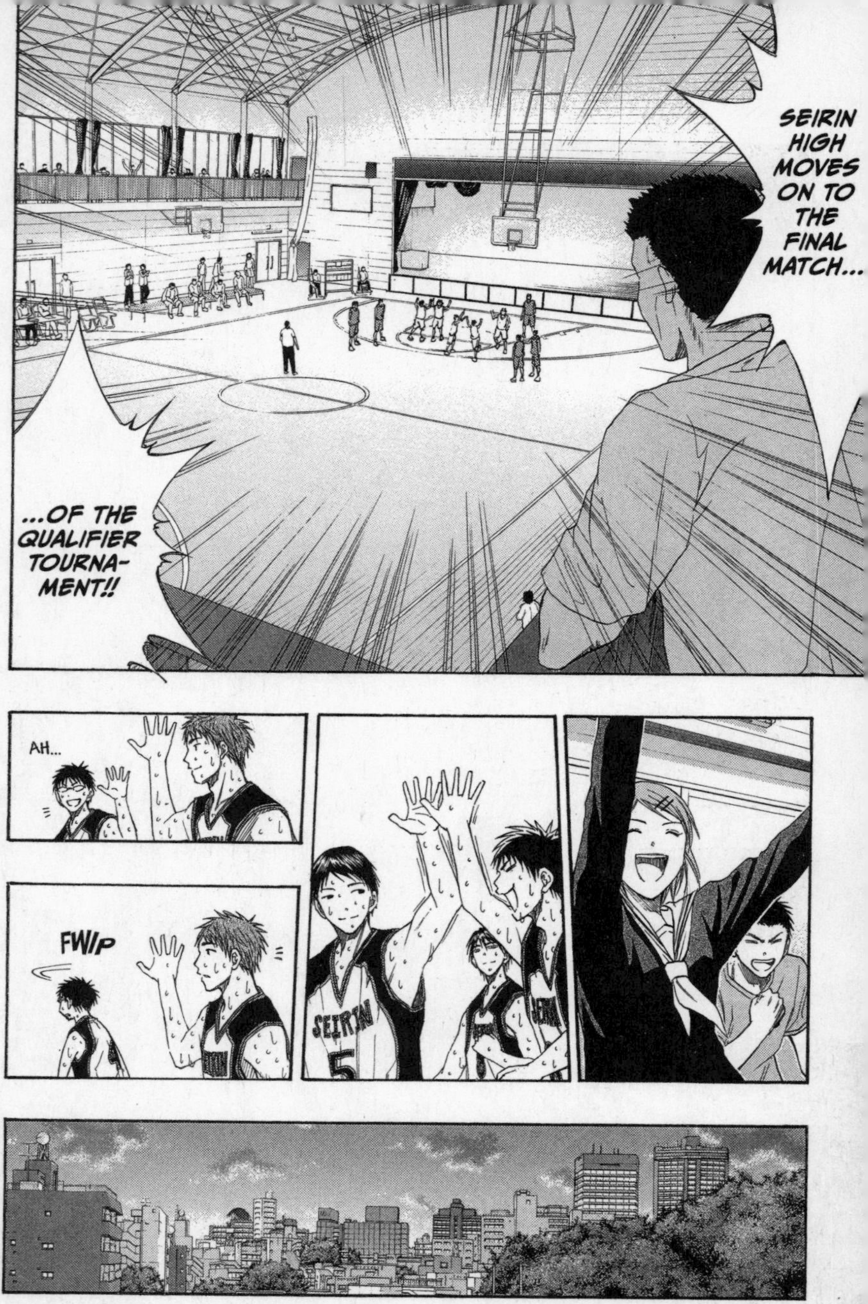
SEIRIN HIGH MOVES ON TO THE FINAL MATCH...
...OF THE QUALIFIER TOURNA-MENT!!
AH...
FWIP

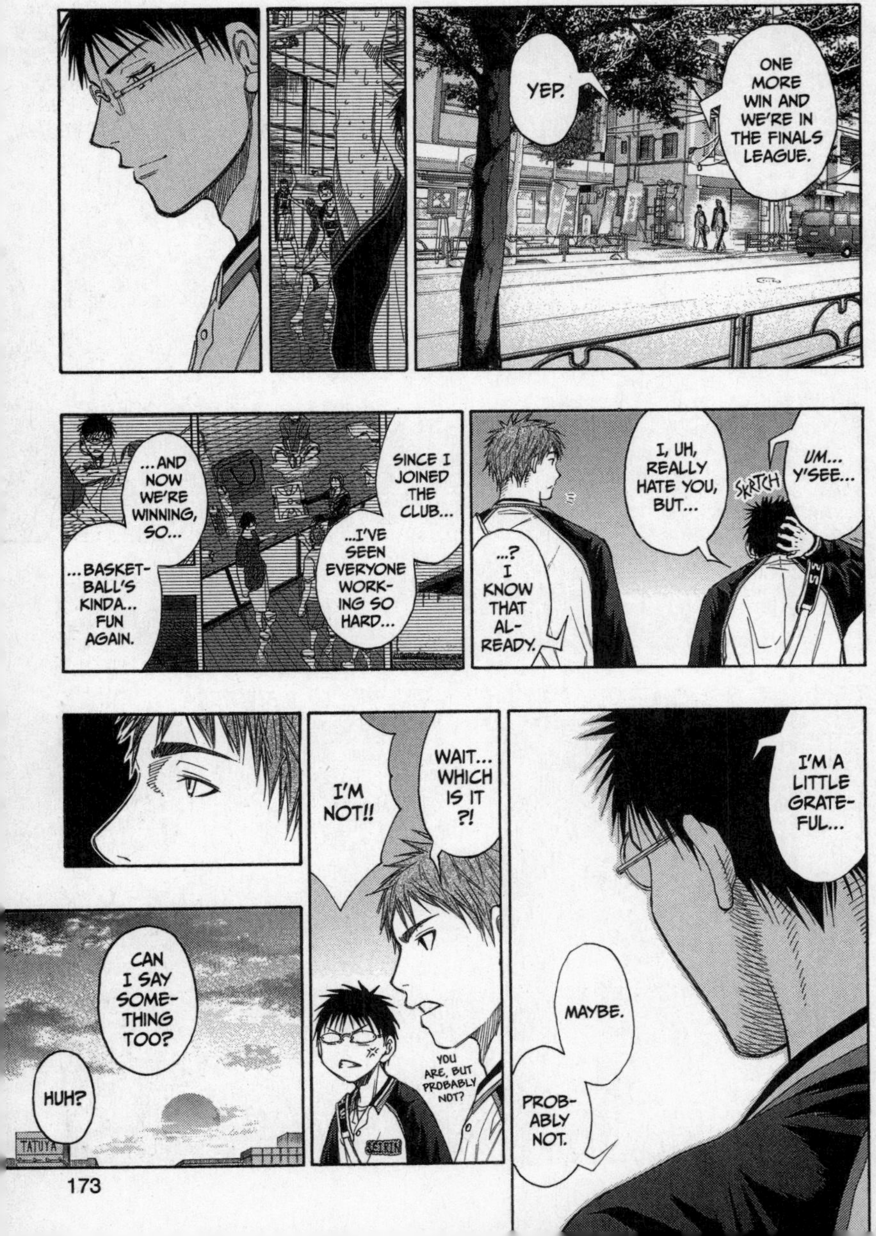
ONE MORE WIN AND WE'RE IN THE FINALS LEAGUE.
YEP.
UM... Y'SEE...
SKRTCH
I, UH, REALLY HATE YOU, BUT...
...? I KNOW THAT AL-READY.
SINCE I JOINED THE CLUB...
...I'VE SEEN EVERYONE WORK-ING SO HARD...
...AND NOW WE'RE WINNING, SO...
...BASKET-BALL'S KINDA... FUN AGAIN.
I'M A LITTLE GRATE-FUL...
MAYBE.
PROB-ABLY NOT.
WAIT... WHICH IS IT ?!
I'M NOT!!
YOU ARE, BUT PROBABLY NOT?
SEIRIN
CAN I SAY SOME-THING TOO?
HUH?
TATUYA

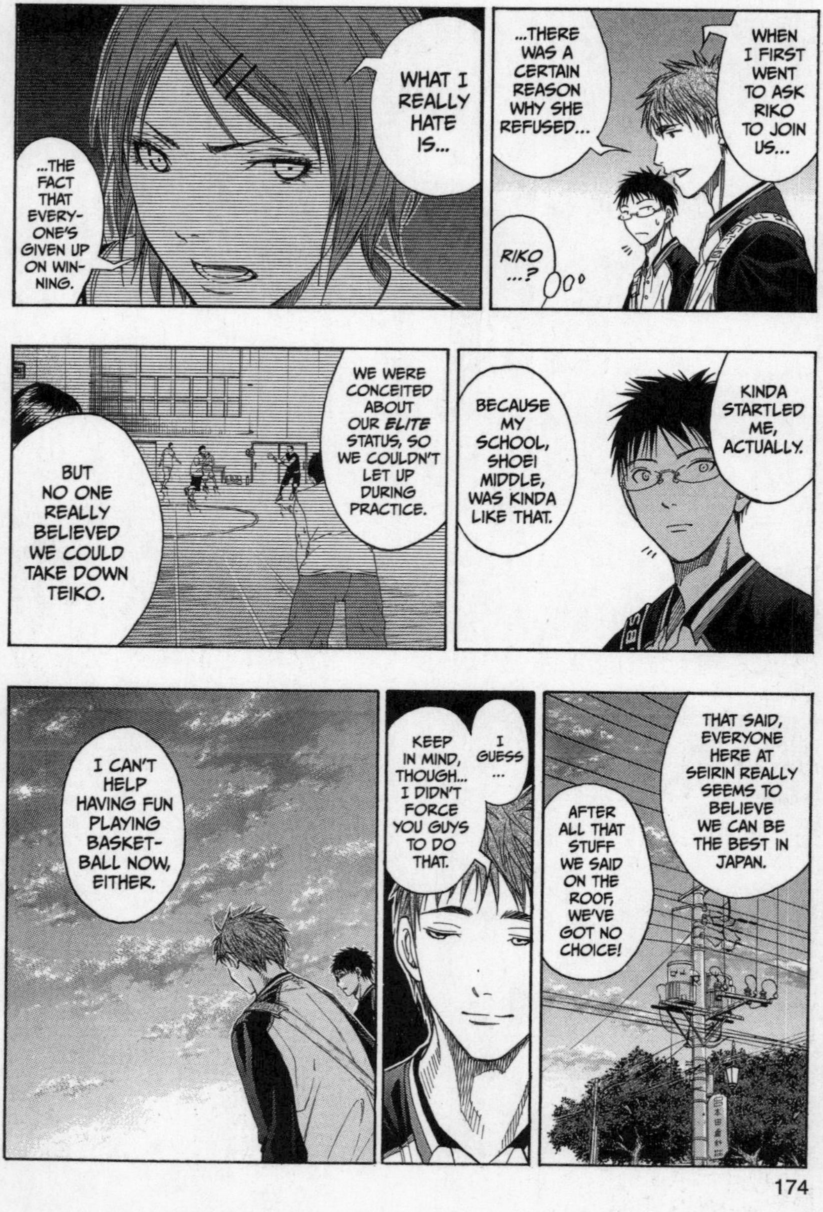
WHEN I FIRST WENT TO ASK RIKO TO JOIN US...
...THERE WAS A CERTAIN REASON WHY SHE REFUSED...
RIKO ...?
WHAT I REALLY HATE IS...
...THE FACT THAT EVERY-ONE'S GIVEN UP ON WIN-NING.
KINDA STARTLED ME, ACTUALLY.
BECAUSE MY SCHOOL, SHOEI MIDDLE, WAS KINDA LIKE THAT.
WE WERE CONCEITED ABOUT OUR *ELITE* STATUS, SO WE COULDN'T LET UP DURING PRACTICE.
BUT NO ONE REALLY BELIEVED WE COULD TAKE DOWN TEIKO.
THAT SAID, EVERYONE HERE AT SEIRIN REALLY SEEMS TO BELIEVE WE CAN BE THE BEST IN JAPAN.
AFTER ALL THAT STUFF WE SAID ON THE ROOF, WE'VE GOT NO CHOICE!
I GUESS ...
KEEP IN MIND, THOUGH... I DIDN'T FORCE YOU GUYS TO DO THAT.
I CAN'T HELP HAVING FUN PLAYING BASKET-BALL NOW, EITHER.

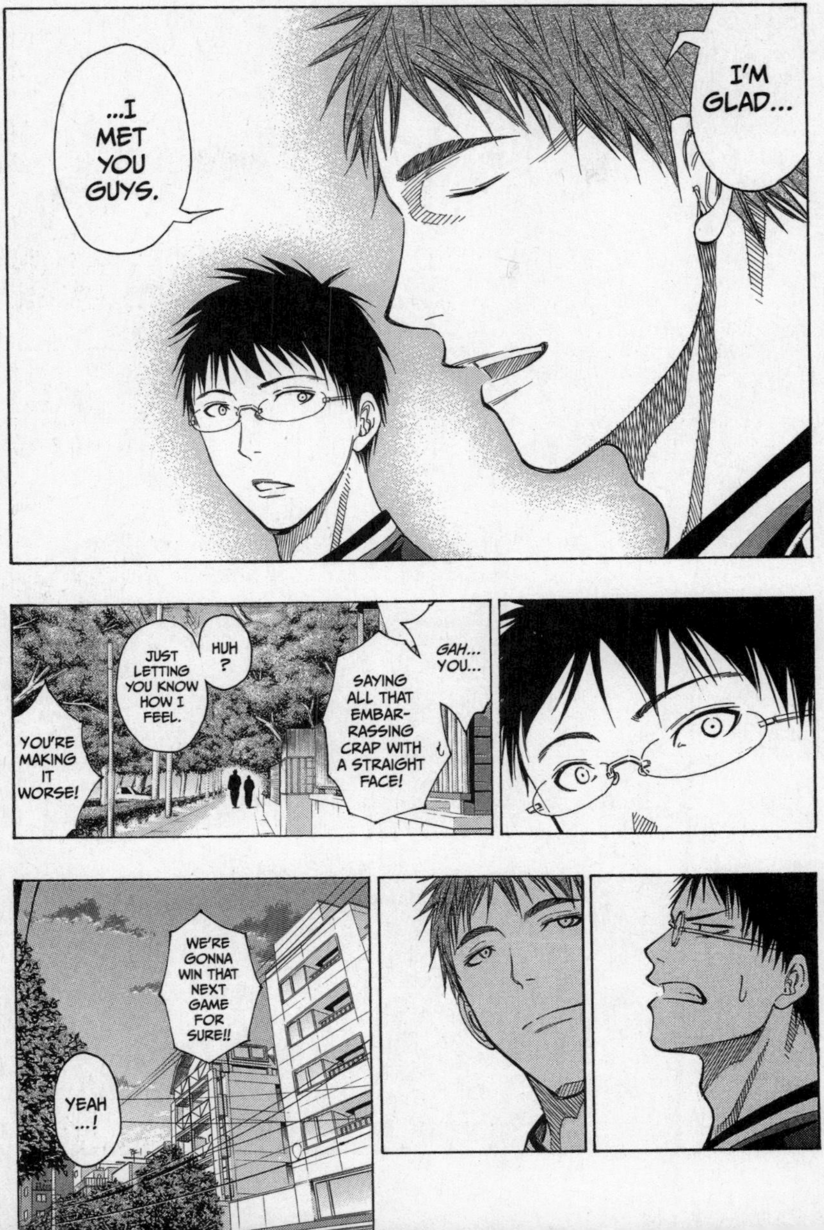
I'M GLAD...
...I MET YOU GUYS.
GAH... YOU...
SAYING ALL THAT EMBAR-RASSING CRAP WITH A STRAIGHT FACE!
HUH?
JUST LETTING YOU KNOW HOW I FEEL.
YOU'RE MAKING IT WORSE!
WE'RE GONNA WIN THAT NEXT GAME FOR SURE!!
YEAH ...!

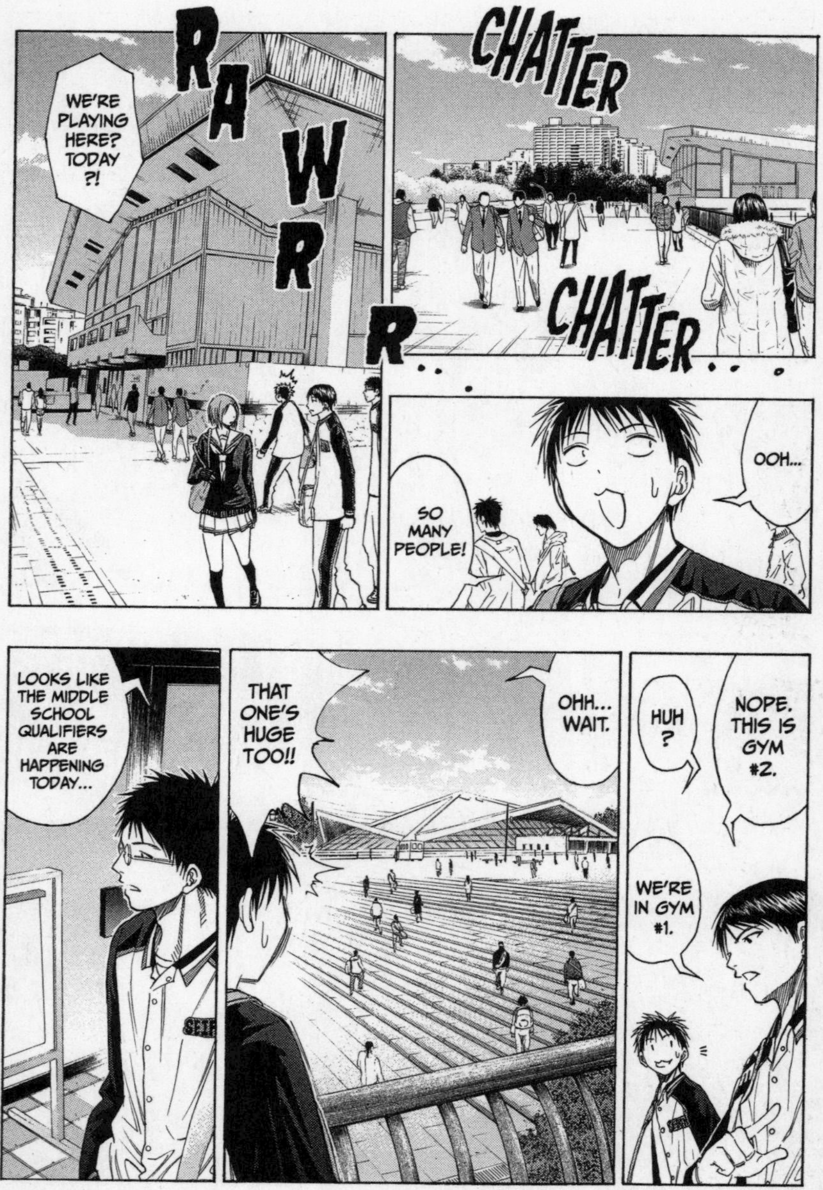
CHATTER
CHATTER...
OOH...
SO MANY PEOPLE!
RAWR
WE'RE PLAYING HERE? TODAY?!
NOPE. THIS IS GYM #2.
HUH?
WE'RE IN GYM #1.
OHH... WAIT.
THAT ONE'S HUGE TOO!!
LOOKS LIKE THE MIDDLE SCHOOL QUALIFIERS ARE HAPPENING TODAY...

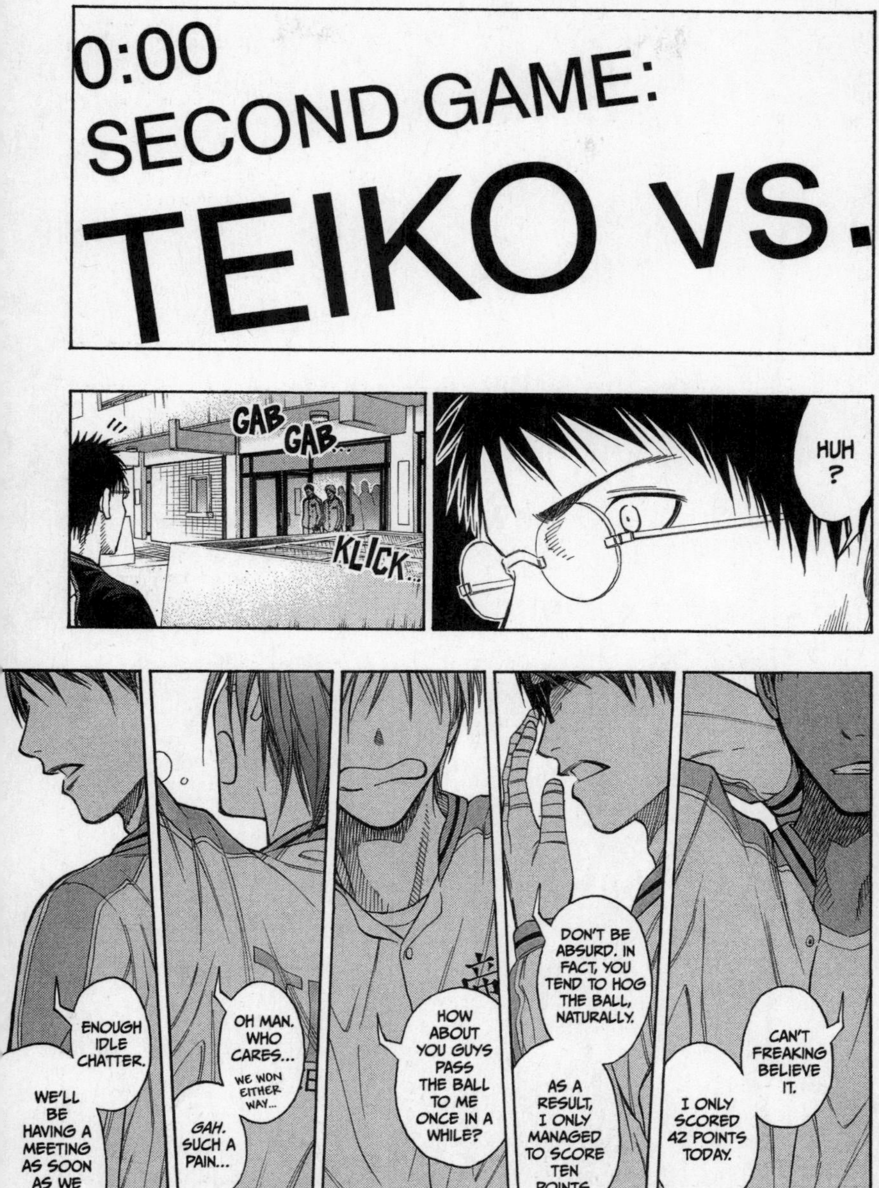
0:00
SECOND GAME:
TEIKO VS.
HUH ?
GAB
GAB...
KLICK...
CAN'T FREAKING BELIEVE IT.
I ONLY SCORED 42 POINTS TODAY.
DON'T BE ABSURD. IN FACT, YOU TEND TO HOG THE BALL, NATURALLY.
AS A RESULT, I ONLY MANAGED TO SCORE TEN POINTS.
HOW ABOUT YOU GUYS PASS THE BALL TO ME ONCE IN A WHILE?
OH MAN. WHO CARES...
WE WON EITHER WAY...
GAH. SUCH A PAIN...
ENOUGH IDLE CHATTER.
WE'LL BE HAVING A MEETING AS SOON AS WE GET BACK.

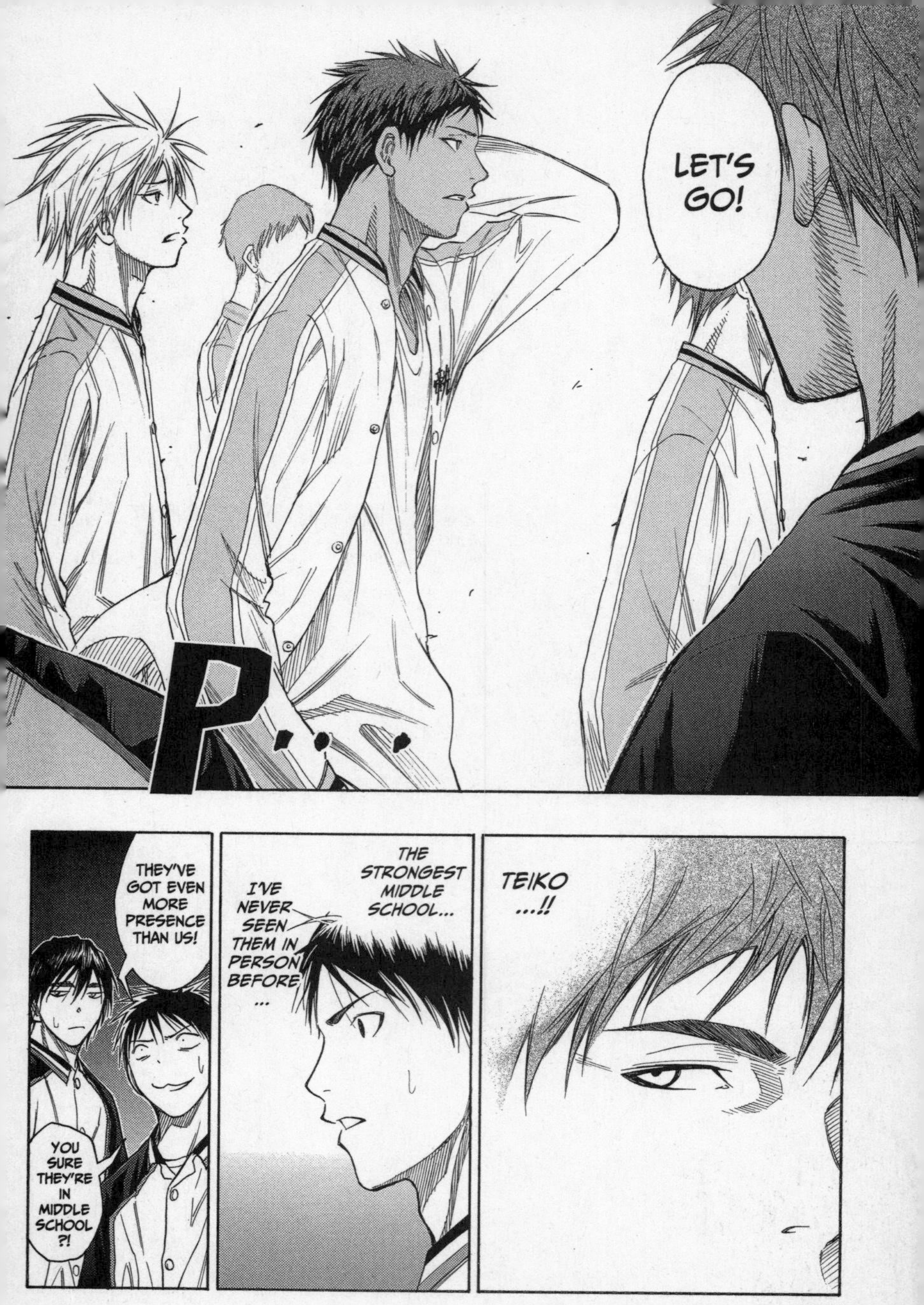
LET'S GO!
P...
TEIKO ...!!
THE STRONGEST MIDDLE SCHOOL...
I'VE NEVER SEEN THEM IN PERSON BEFORE...
THEY'VE GOT EVEN MORE PRESENCE THAN US!
YOU SURE THEY'RE IN MIDDLE SCHOOL?!

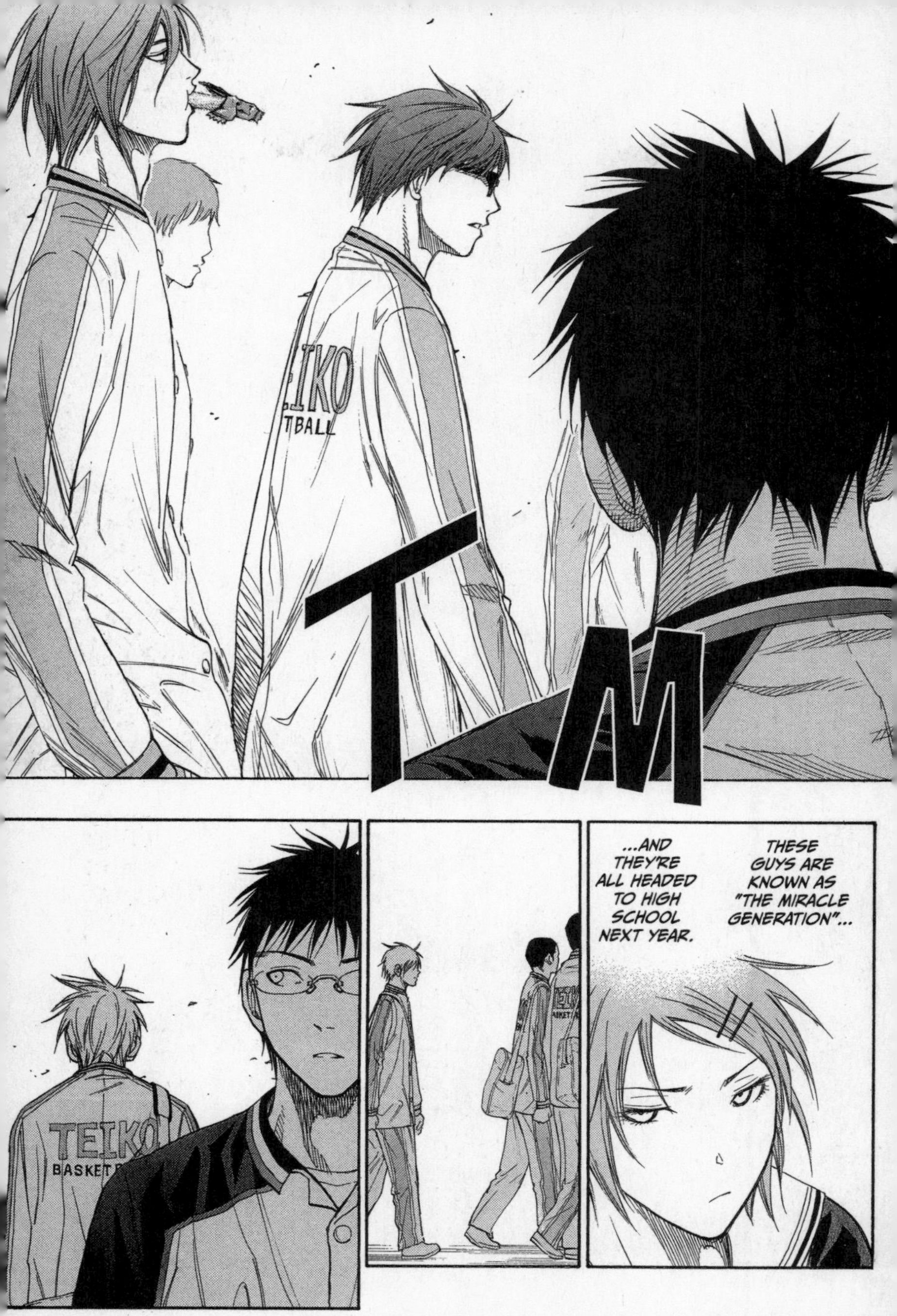
TM
THESE GUYS ARE KNOWN AS "THE MIRACLE GENERATION"...
...AND THEY'RE ALL HEADED TO HIGH SCHOOL NEXT YEAR.

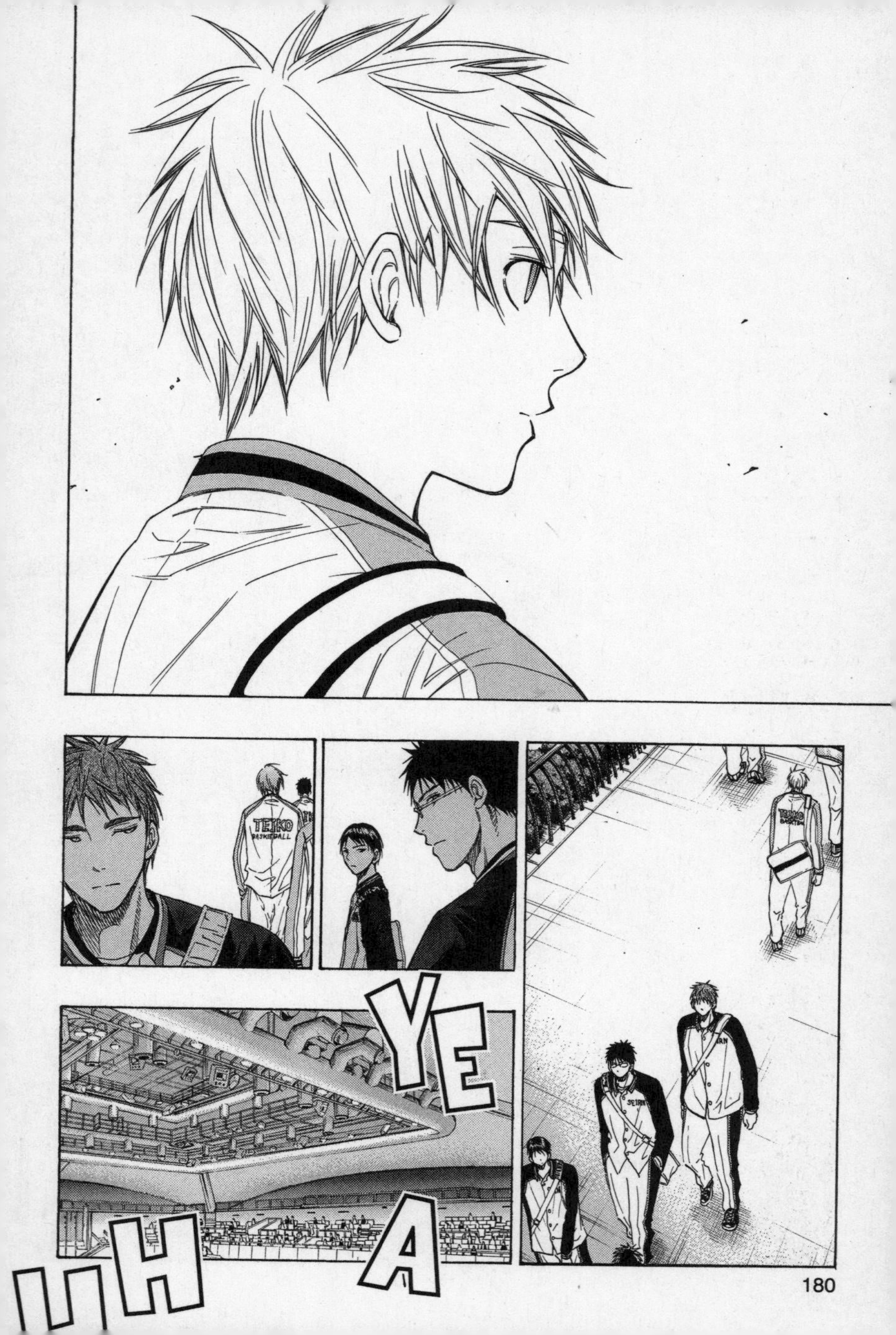
TEIKO
BASKETBALL
YE
A
H

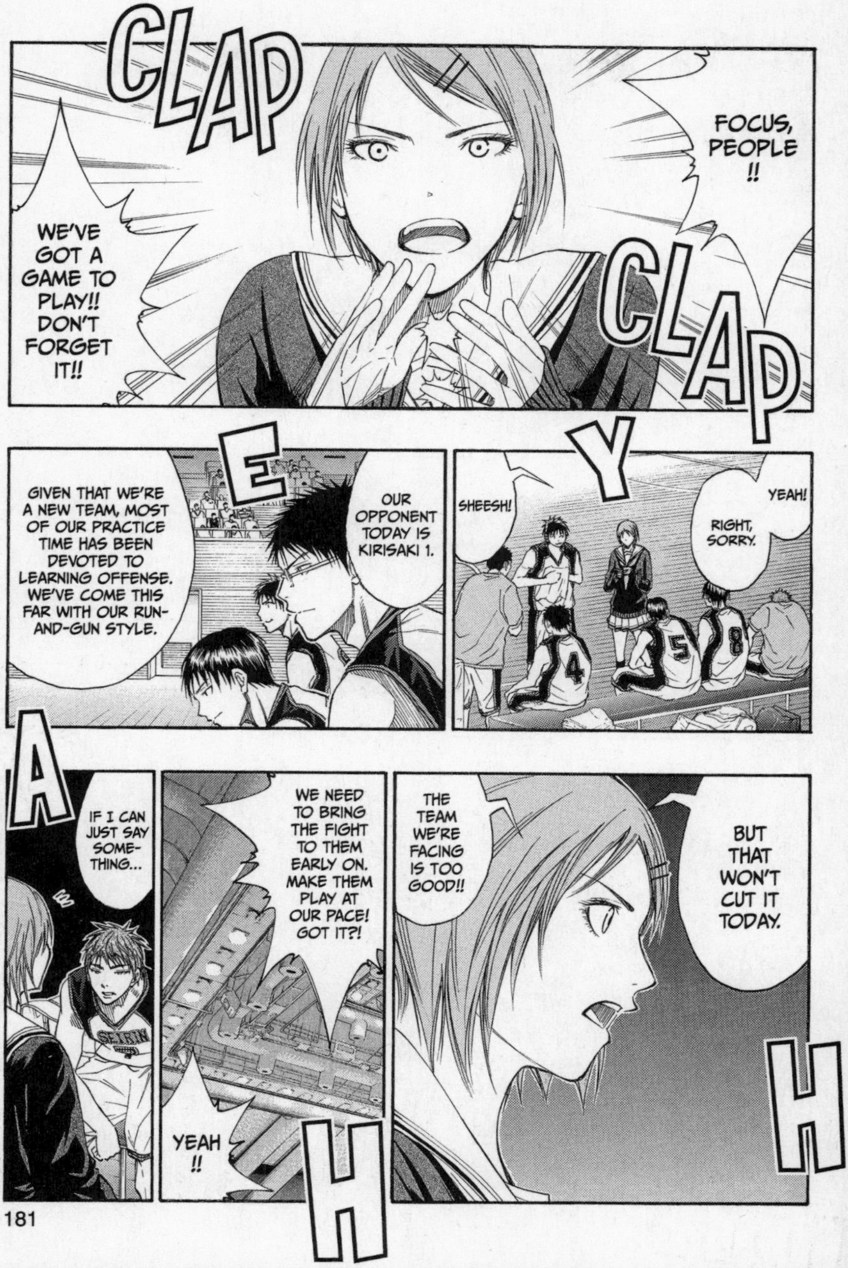
FOCUS, PEOPLE!!
CLAP
CLAP
WE'VE GOT A GAME TO PLAY!! DON'T FORGET IT!!
YEAH!
RIGHT, SORRY.
SHEESH!
Y
OUR OPPONENT TODAY IS KIRISAKI 1.
E
GIVEN THAT WE'RE A NEW TEAM, MOST OF OUR PRACTICE TIME HAS BEEN DEVOTED TO LEARNING OFFENSE. WE'VE COME THIS FAR WITH OUR RUN-AND-GUN STYLE.
A
BUT THAT WON'T CUT IT TODAY.
THE TEAM WE'RE FACING IS TOO GOOD!!
H
WE NEED TO BRING THE FIGHT TO THEM EARLY ON. MAKE THEM PLAY AT OUR PACE! GOT IT?!
YEAH!!
H
IF I CAN JUST SAY SOME-THING...
SEIRIN

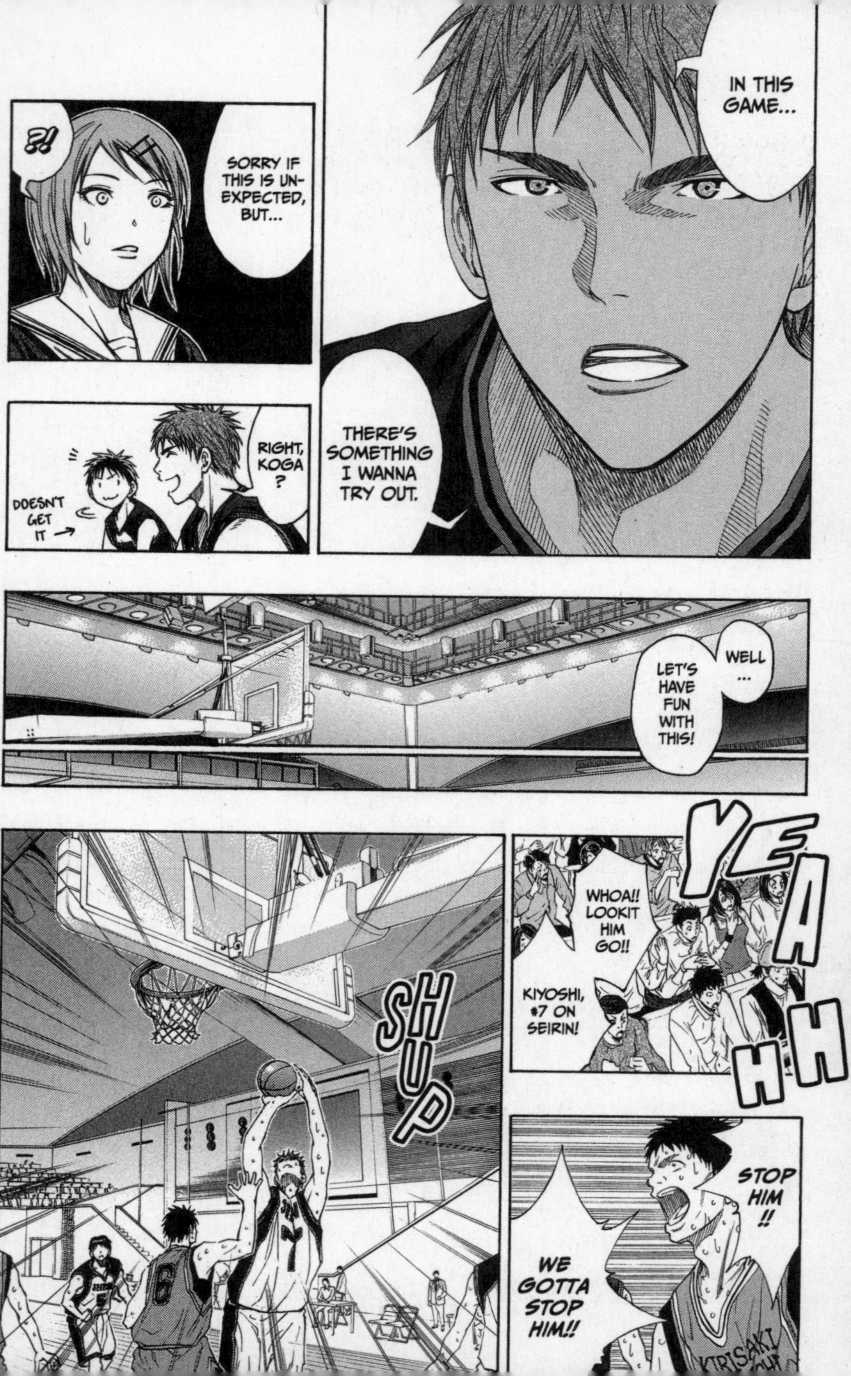
IN THIS GAME...
THERE'S SOMETHING I WANNA TRY OUT.
?!
SORRY IF THIS IS UN-EXPECTED, BUT...
RIGHT, KOGA?
DOESN'T GET IT →
WELL...
LET'S HAVE FUN WITH THIS!
YEAHHH
WHOA!! LOOKIT HIM GO!!
KIYOSHI, #7 ON SEIRIN!
STOP HIM!!
WE GOTTA STOP HIM!!
SHUP

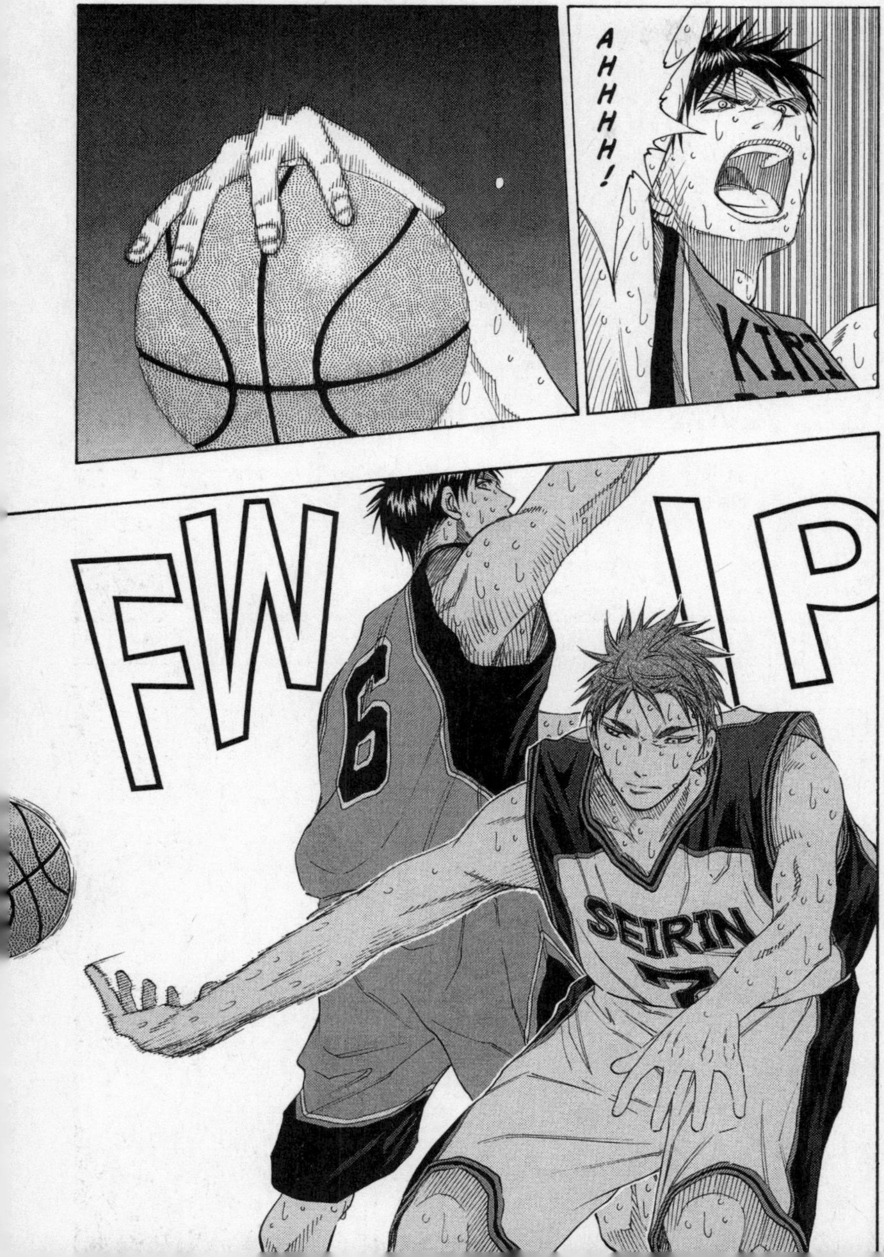
AHHHHH!
FWIP
SEIRIN

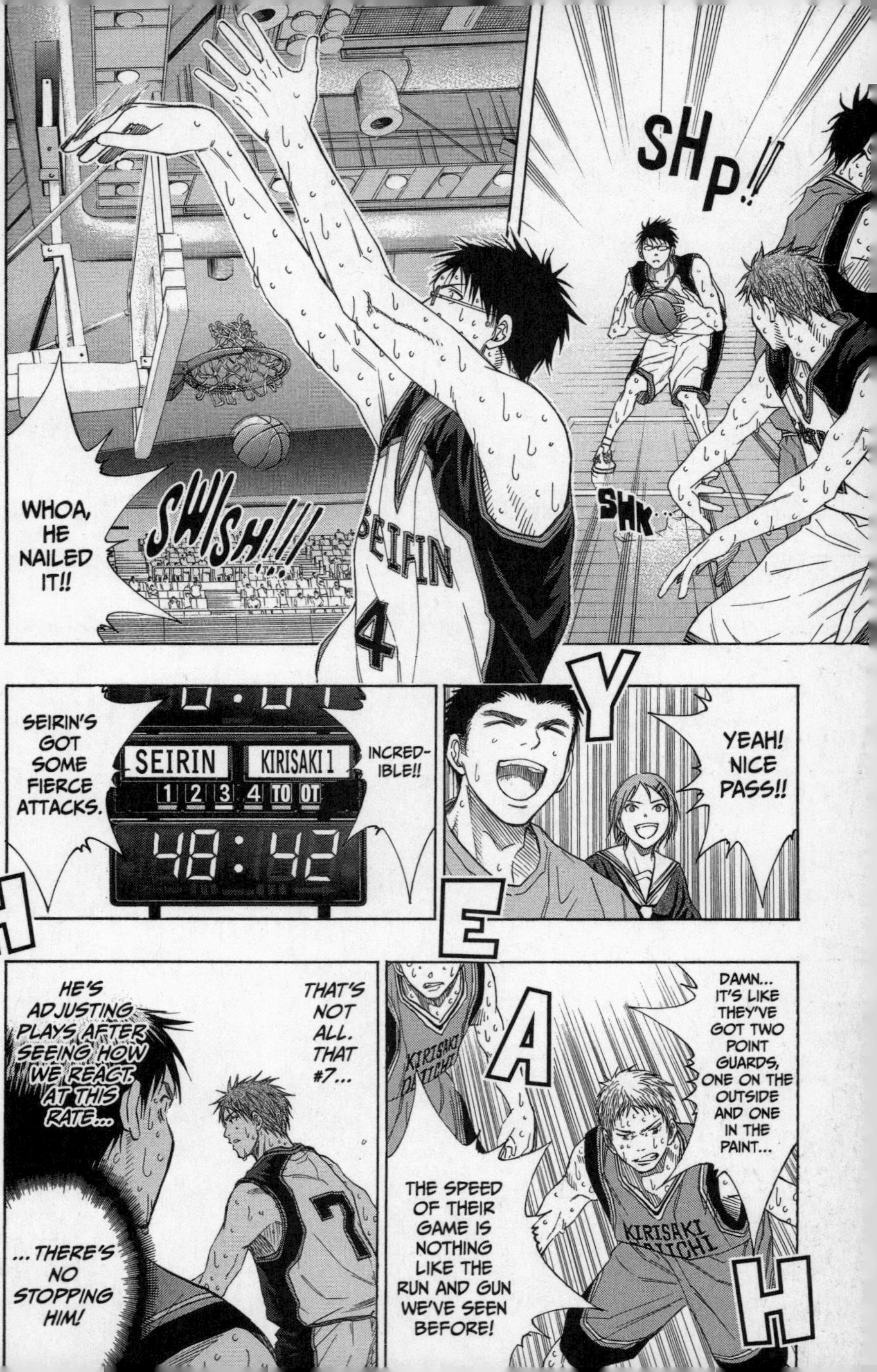
SHP!!
SHK...
SWISH!!
WHOA, HE NAILED IT!!
Y
YEAH! NICE PASS!!
INCREDIBLE!!
SEIRIN'S GOT SOME FIERCE ATTACKS.
SEIRIN
KIRISAKI 1
1 2 3 4 TO OT
48 : 42
H
E
DAMN... IT'S LIKE THEY'VE GOT TWO POINT GUARDS, ONE ON THE OUTSIDE AND ONE IN THE PAINT...
A
THE SPEED OF THEIR GAME IS NOTHING LIKE THE RUN AND GUN WE'VE SEEN BEFORE!
H
THAT'S NOT ALL. THAT #7...
HE'S ADJUSTING PLAYS AFTER SEEING HOW WE REACT. AT THIS RATE...
...THERE'S NO STOPPING HIM!

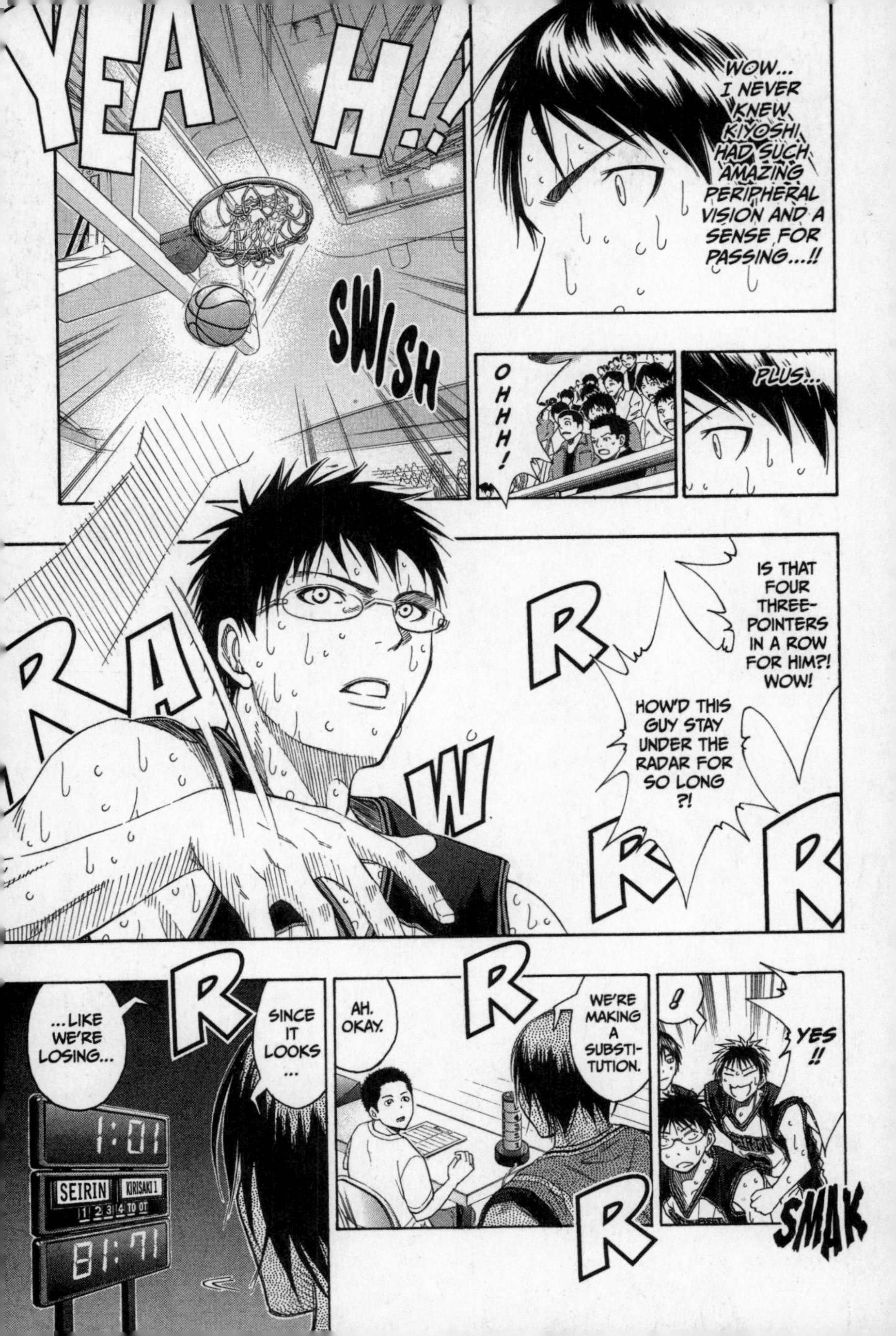
WOW... I NEVER KNEW KIYOSHI HAD SUCH AMAZING PERIPHERAL VISION AND A SENSE FOR PASSING...!!
PLUS...
OHHHH!
YEAH!!
SWISH
IS THAT FOUR THREE-POINTERS IN A ROW FOR HIM?! WOW!
HOW'D THIS GUY STAY UNDER THE RADAR FOR SO LONG?!
RAWRRRRRR
YES!!
SMAK
WE'RE MAKING A SUBSTITUTION.
AH. OKAY.
SINCE IT LOOKS...
...LIKE WE'RE LOSING...
1:01
SEIRIN
KIRISAKI 1
1 2 3 4 TO OT
81:71

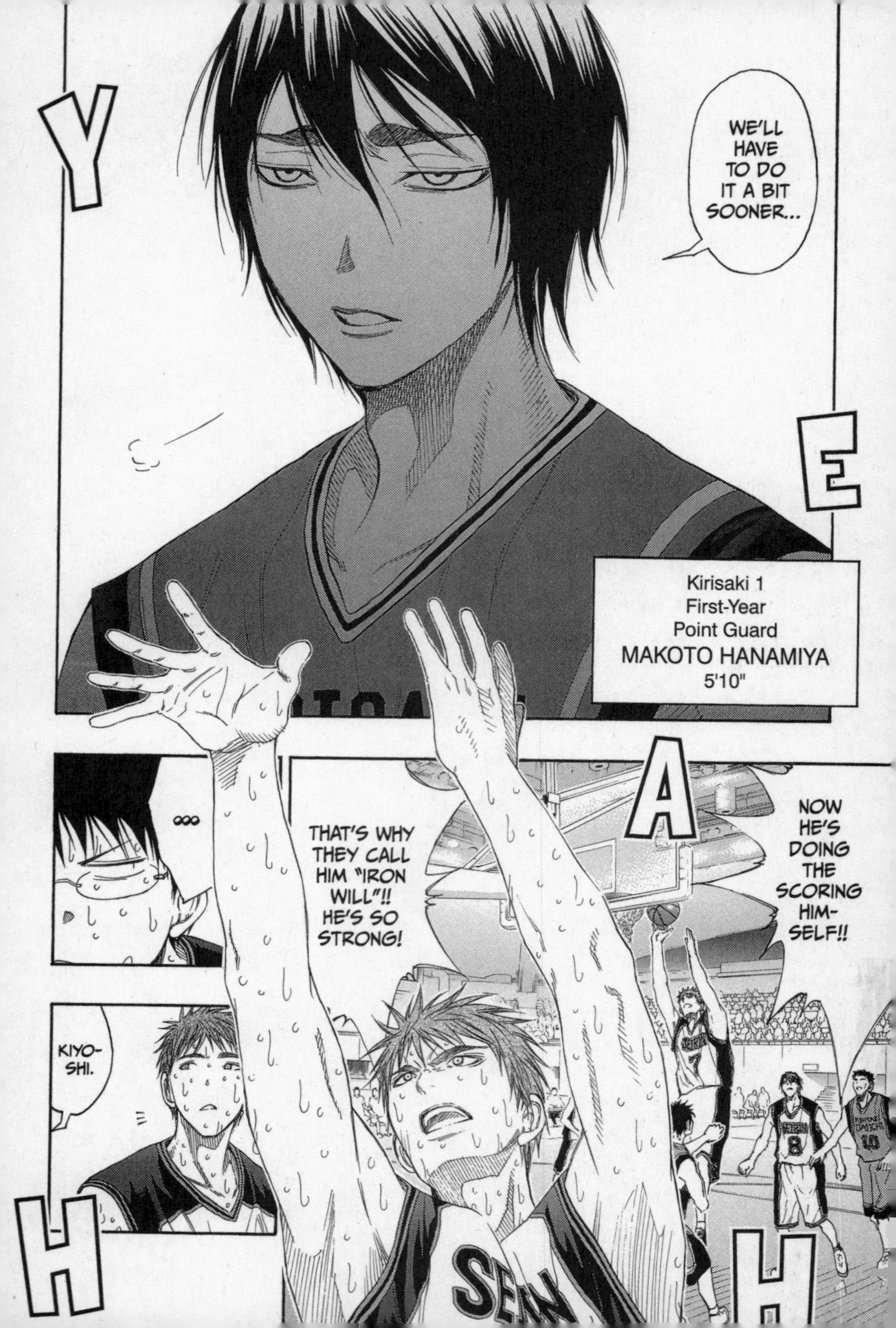
WE'LL HAVE TO DO IT A BIT SOONER...
Kirisaki 1 First-Year Point Guard MAKOTO HANAMIYA 5'10"
YEAHH
NOW HE'S DOING THE SCORING HIM-SELF!!
THAT'S WHY THEY CALL HIM "IRON WILL"!! HE'S SO STRONG!
...
KIYO-SHI.

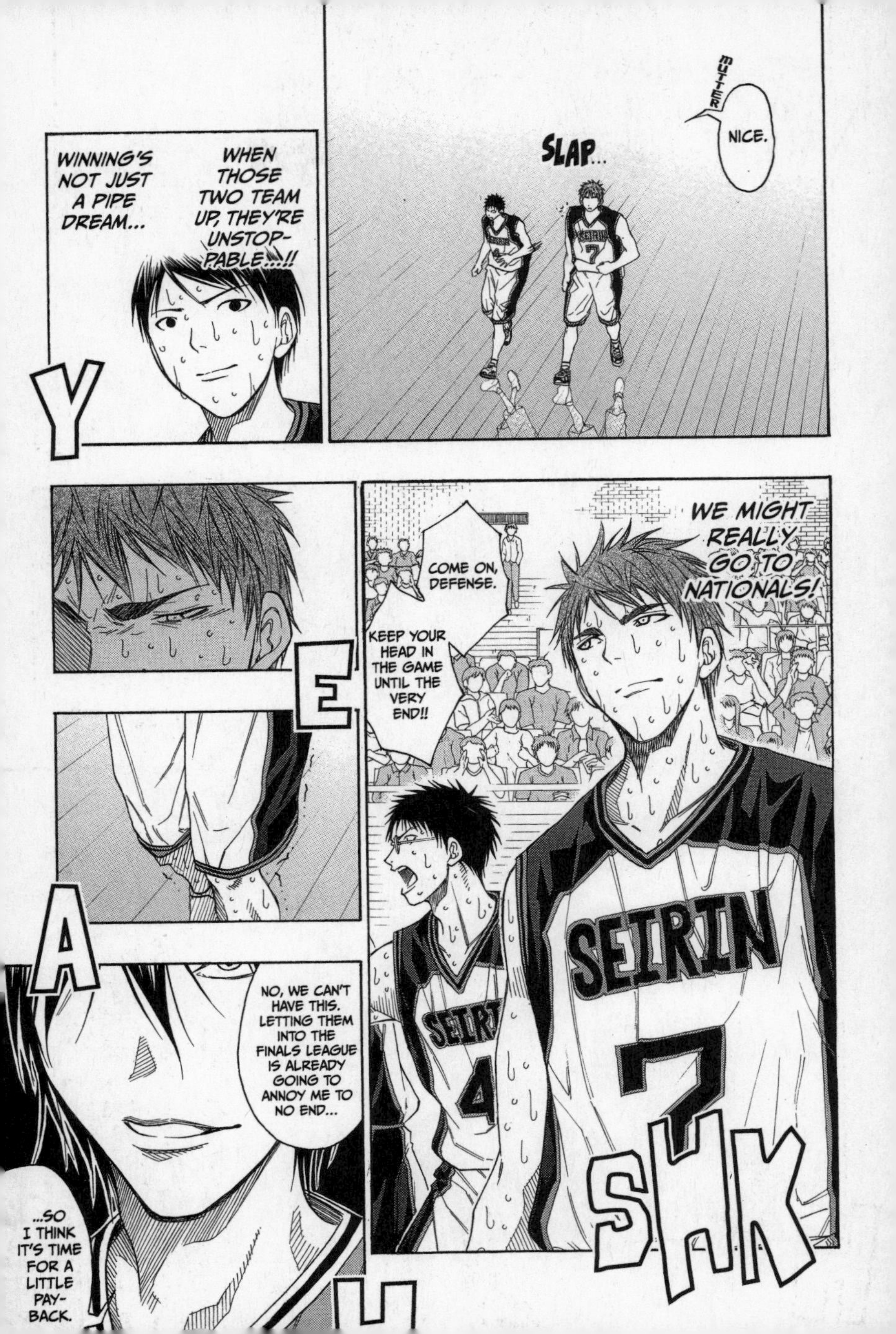
MUTTER
NICE.
SLAP...
WHEN THOSE TWO TEAM UP, THEY'RE UNSTOPPABLE...!!
WINNING'S NOT JUST A PIPE DREAM...
YEAH
WE MIGHT REALLY GO TO NATIONALS!
COME ON, DEFENSE.
KEEP YOUR HEAD IN THE GAME UNTIL THE VERY END!!
SHK
NO, WE CAN'T HAVE THIS. LETTING THEM INTO THE FINALS LEAGUE IS ALREADY GOING TO ANNOY ME TO NO END...
...SO I THINK IT'S TIME FOR A LITTLE PAYBACK.

99TH QUARTER: I'LL BE BACK SOON

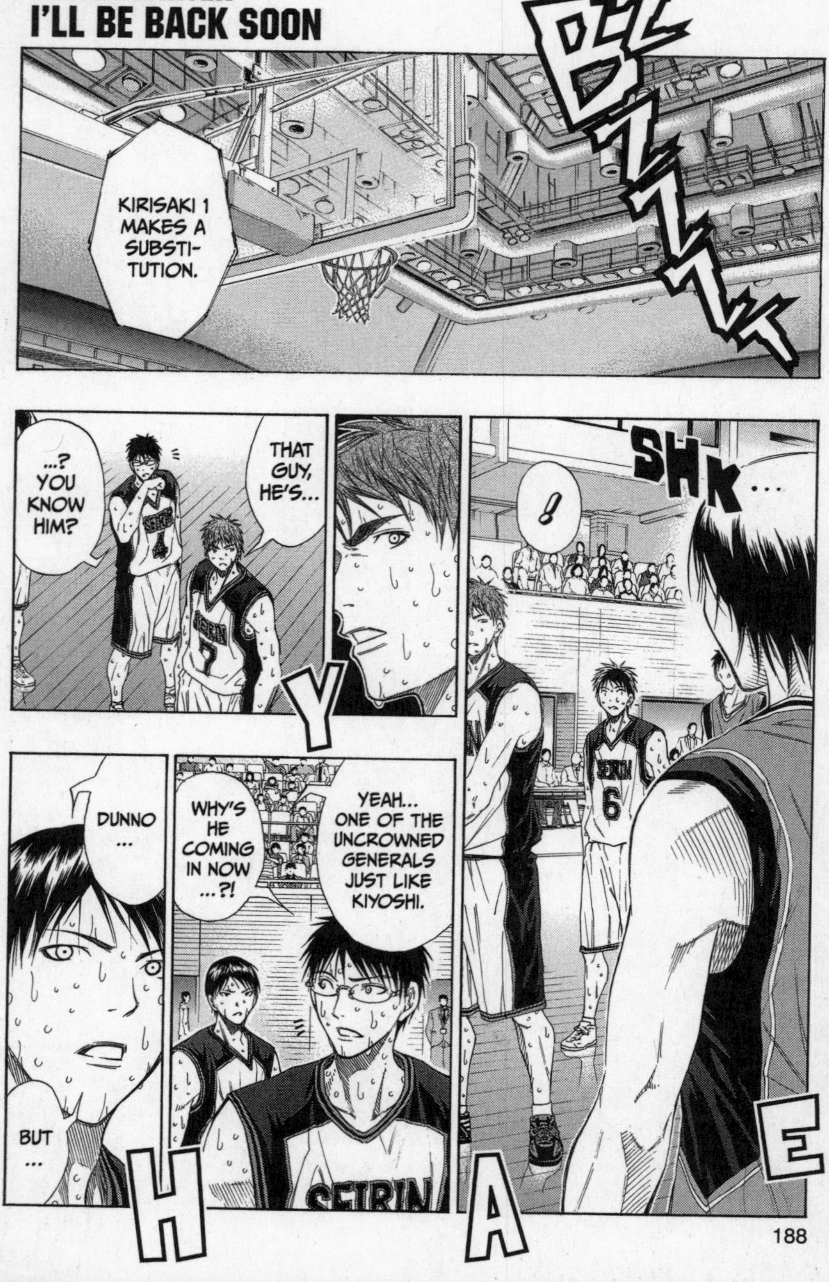
BZZZT
KIRISAKI 1 MAKES A SUBSTITUTION.
SHK...
!
THAT GUY, HE'S...
...? YOU KNOW HIM?
YEAH... ONE OF THE UNCROWNED GENERALS JUST LIKE KIYOSHI.
WHY'S HE COMING IN NOW...?!
DUNNO...
BUT...

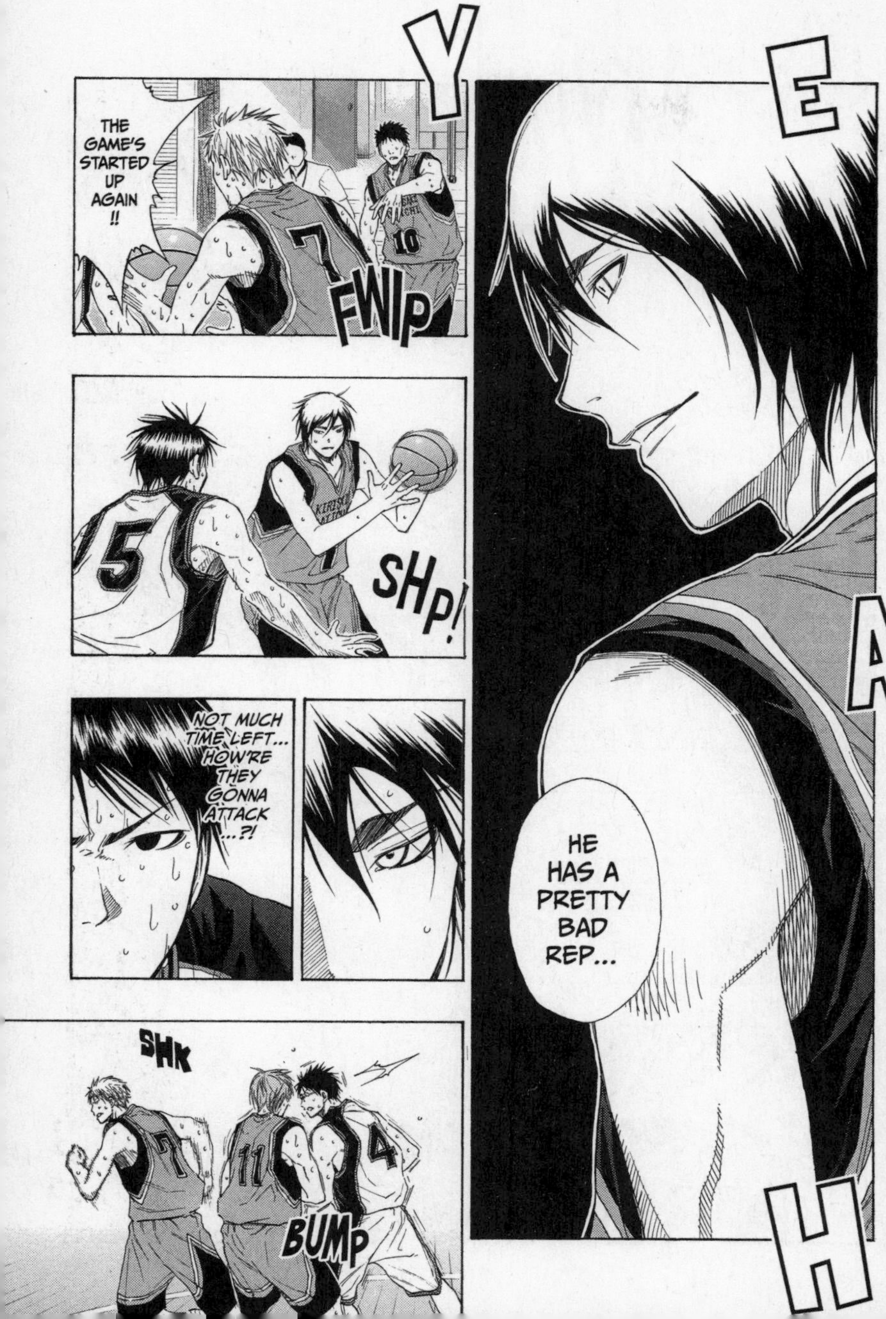
YEAH
HE HAS A PRETTY BAD REP...
THE GAME'S STARTED UP AGAIN!!
FWIP
SHP!
NOT MUCH TIME LEFT... HOW'RE THEY GONNA ATTACK...?!
SHK
BUMP

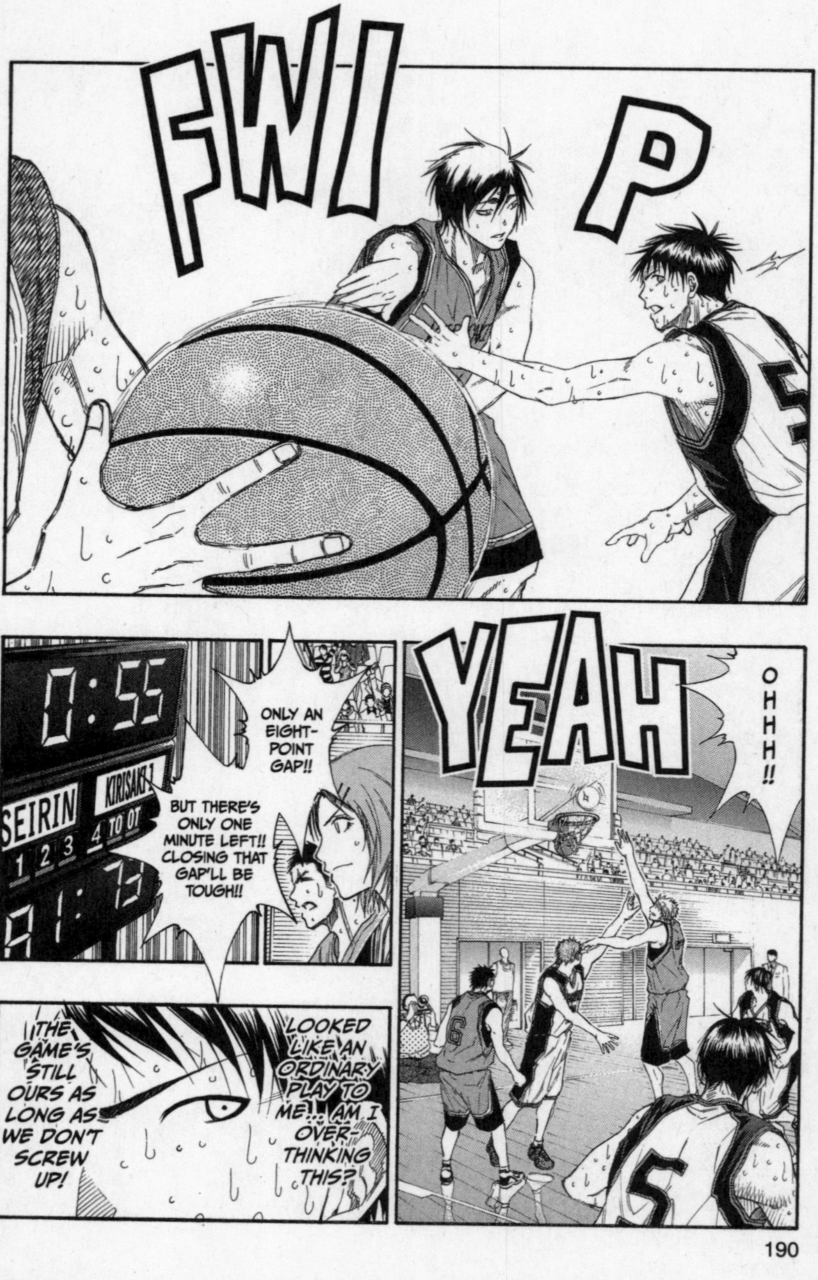
FWI P
YEAH
OHHH!!
0:55
SEIRIN
ONLY AN EIGHT-POINT GAP!!
BUT THERE'S ONLY ONE MINUTE LEFT!! CLOSING THAT GAP'LL BE TOUGH!!
LOOKED LIKE AN ORDINARY PLAY TO ME... AM I OVER-THINKING THIS?
THE GAME'S STILL OURS AS LONG AS WE DON'T SCREW UP!

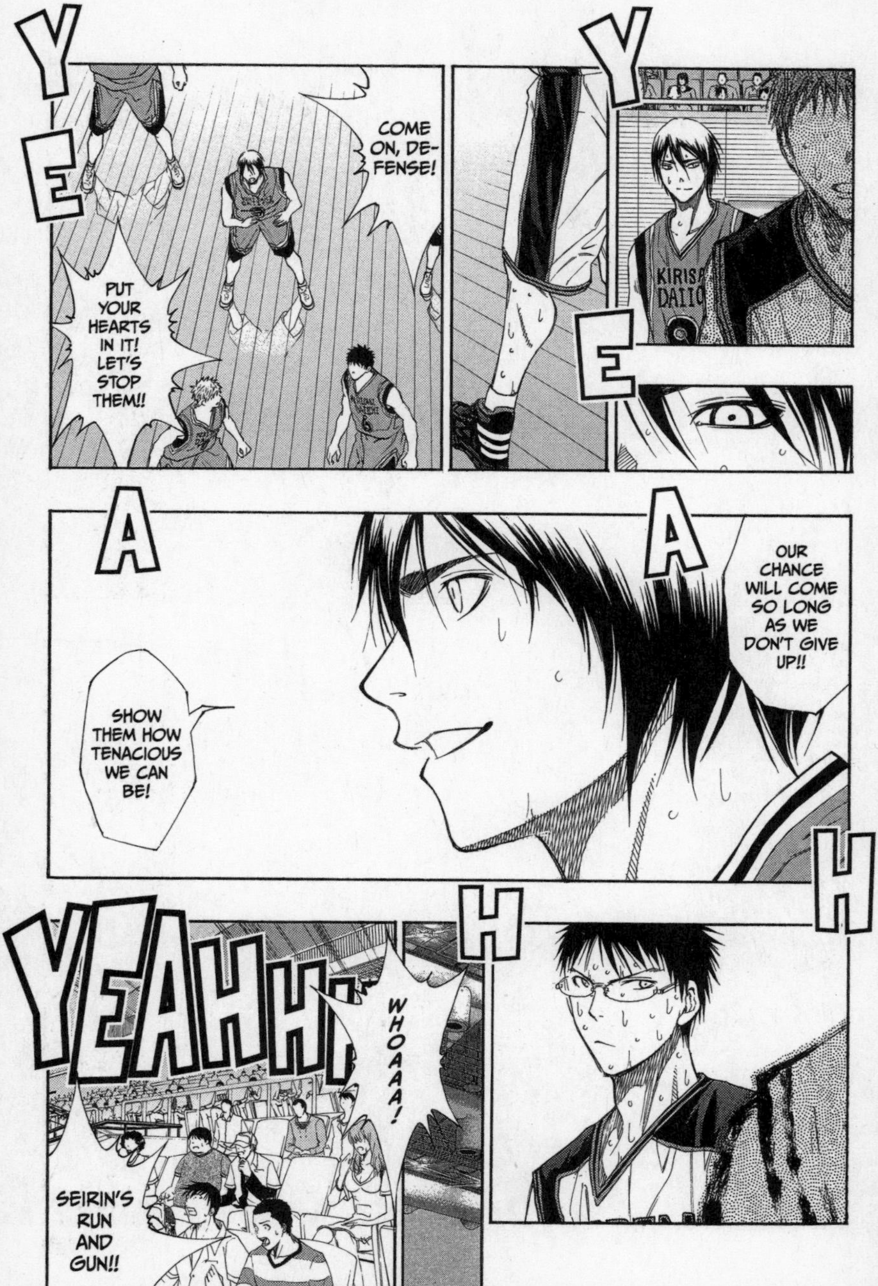
Y
E
Y
E
COME ON, DE-FENSE!
PUT YOUR HEARTS IN IT! LET'S STOP THEM!!
A
A
OUR CHANCE WILL COME SO LONG AS WE DON'T GIVE UP!!
SHOW THEM HOW TENACIOUS WE CAN BE!
H
H
YEAHH
WHOAAA!
SEIRIN'S RUN AND GUN!!

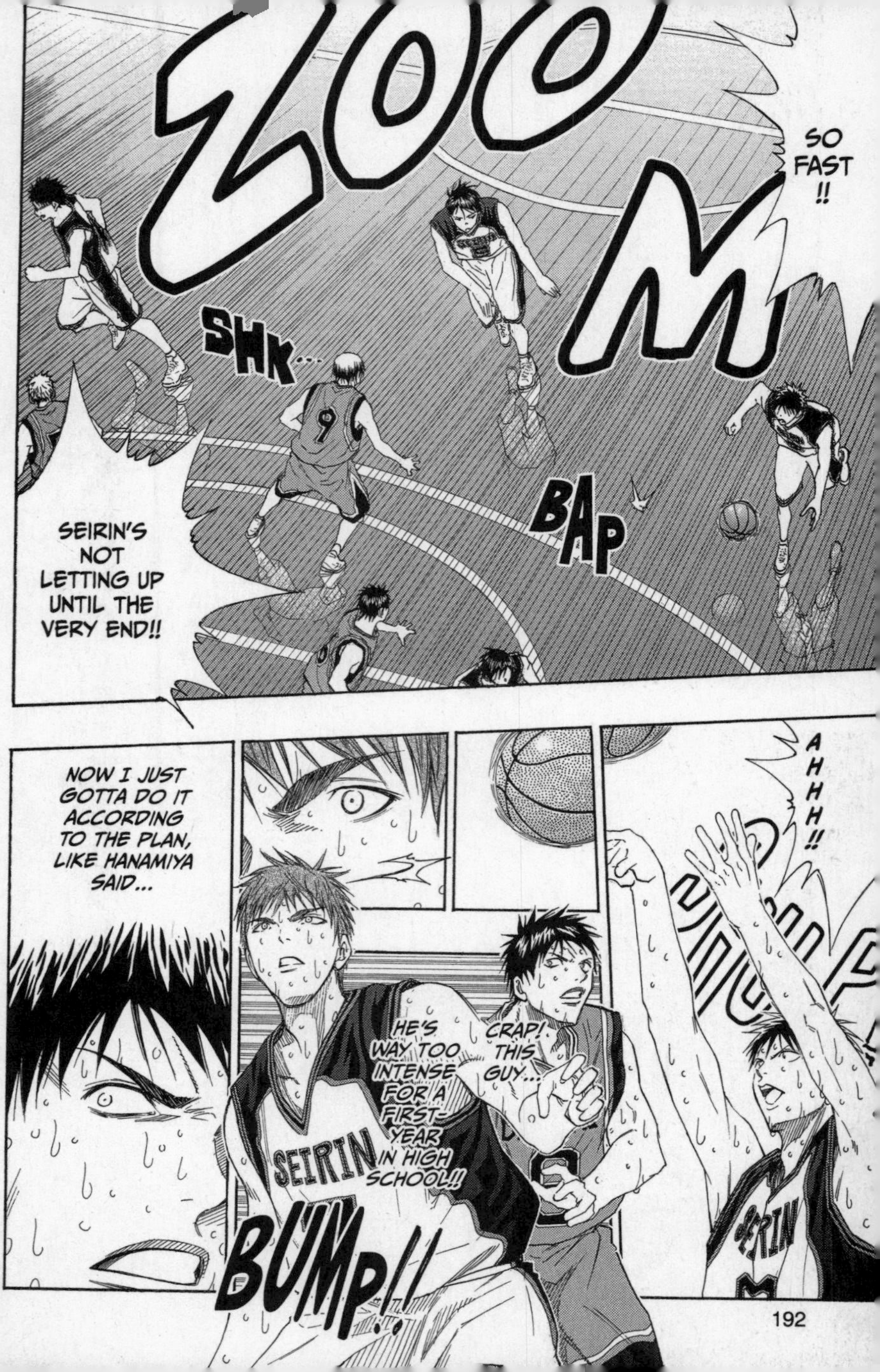
SO FAST!!
ZOOM
SHK...
BAP
SEIRIN'S NOT LETTING UP UNTIL THE VERY END!!
AHHHH!!
CRAP! THIS GUY...
HE'S WAY TOO INTENSE FOR A FIRST-YEAR IN HIGH SCHOOL!!
NOW I JUST GOTTA DO IT ACCORDING TO THE PLAN, LIKE HANAMIYA SAID...
BUMP!!

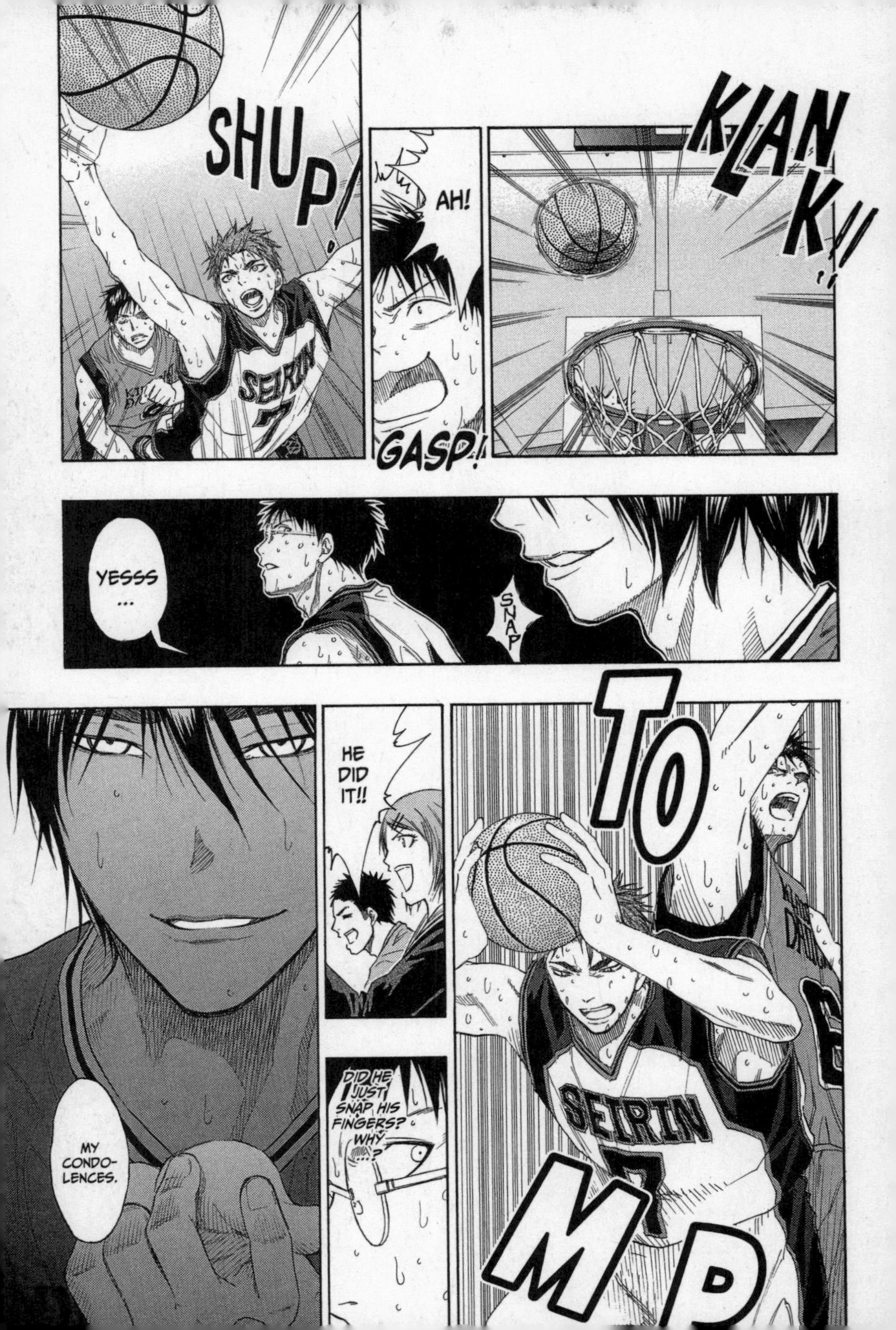
KLANK!!
AH!
GASP!
SHUP!
SNAP
YESSS ...
TOMP
HE DID IT!!
DID HE JUST SNAP HIS FINGERS? WHY...?
MY CONDOLENCES.

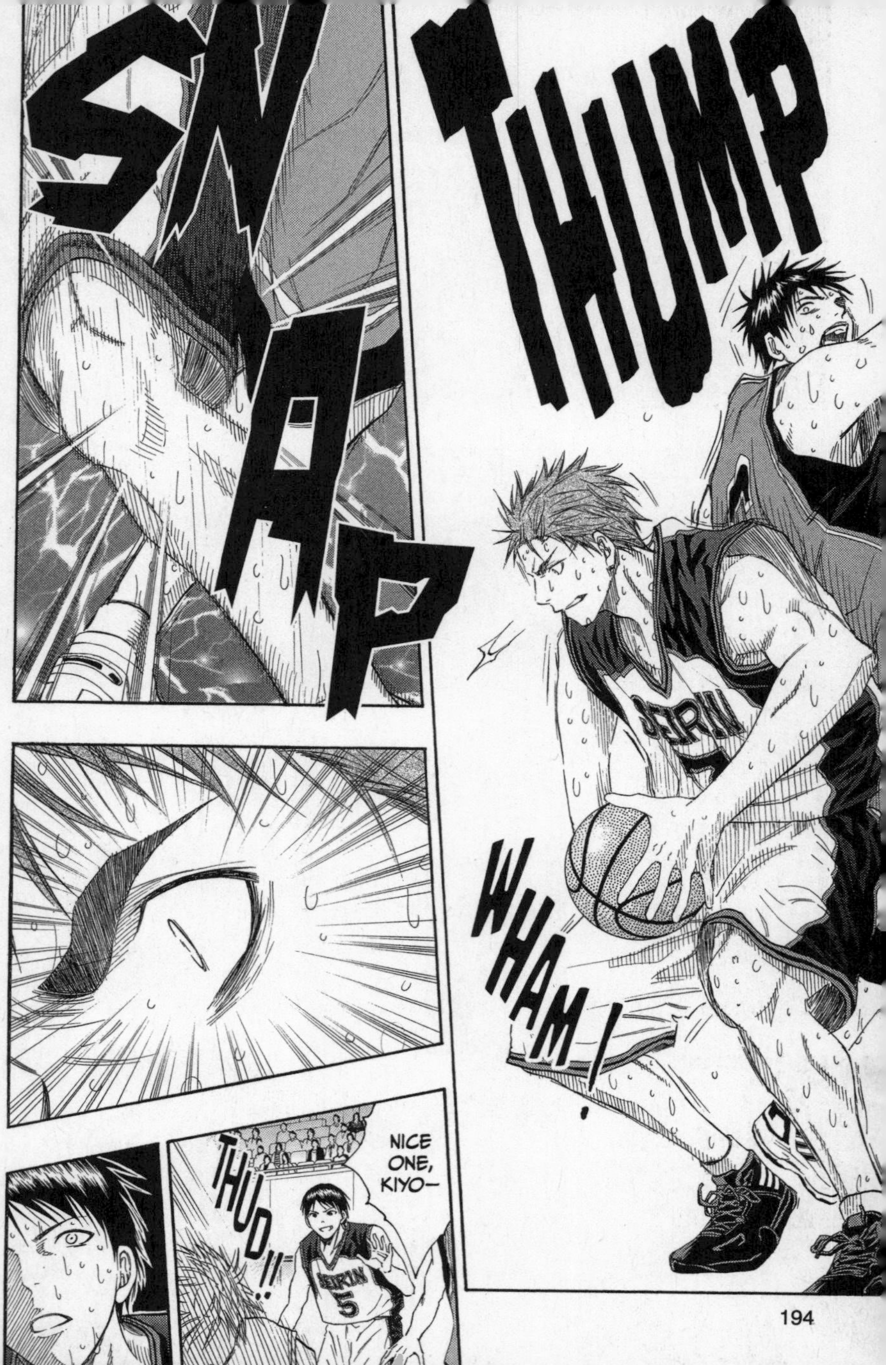
THUMP
WHAM!
SNAP
NICE ONE, KIYO—
THUD!!

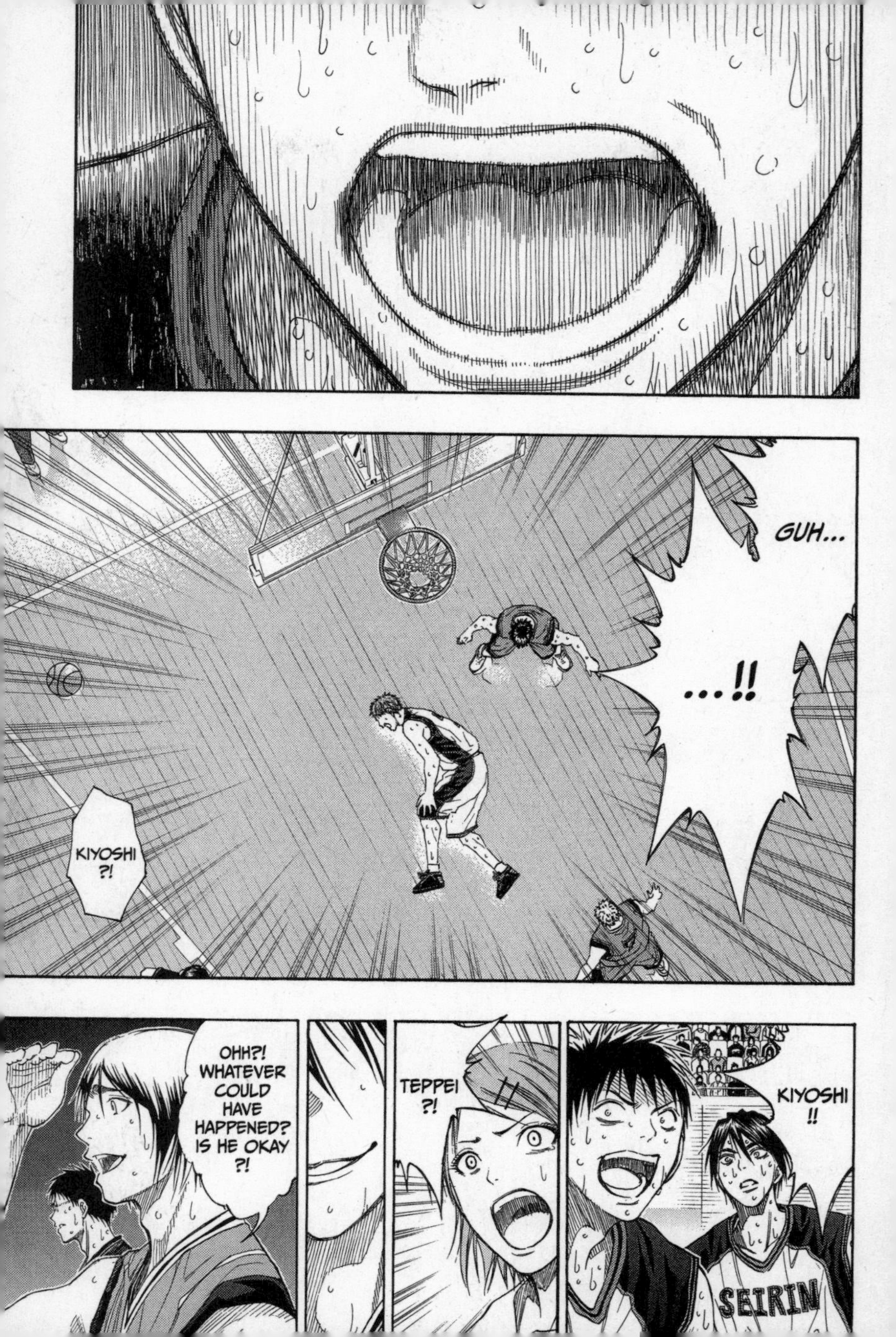
GUH...
...!!
KIYOSHI ?!
KIYOSHI !!
TEPPEI ?!
OHH?! WHATEVER COULD HAVE HAPPENED? IS HE OKAY ?!

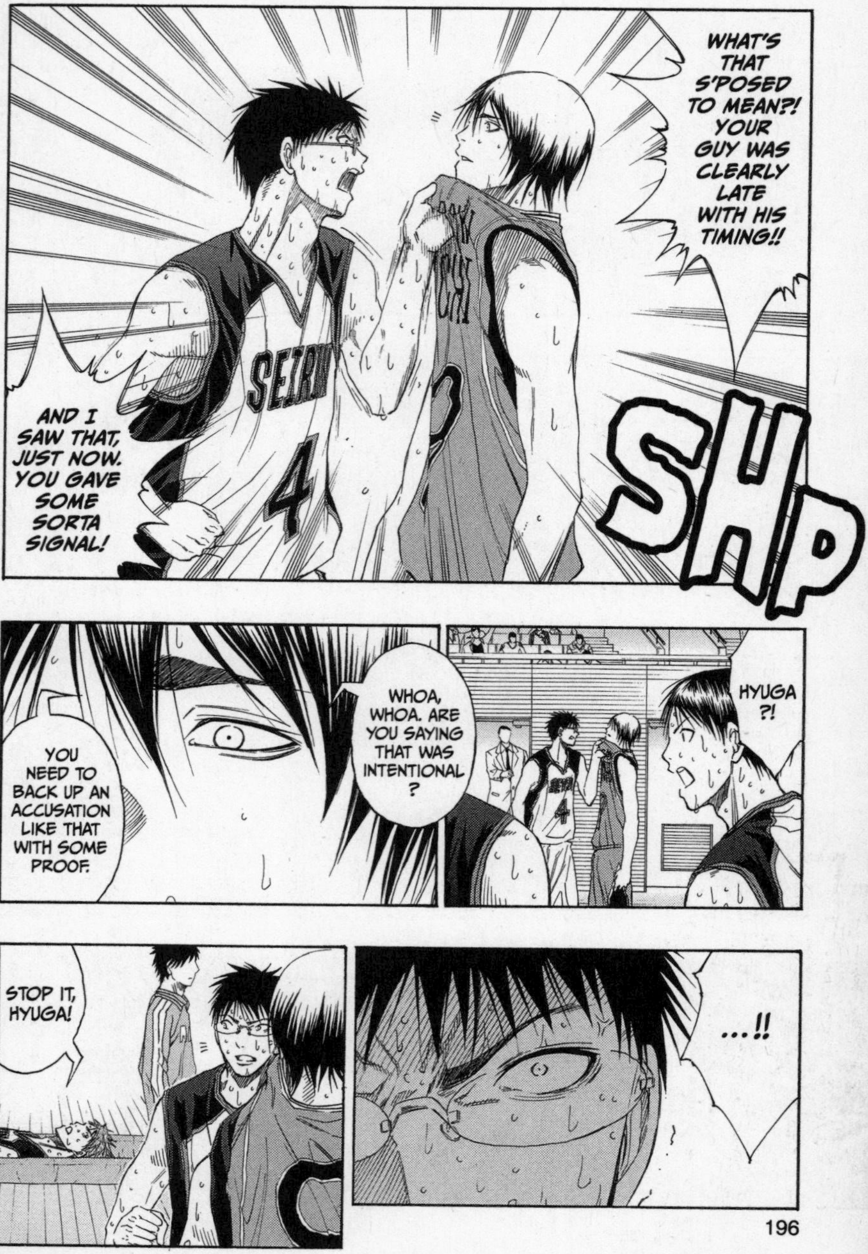
WHAT'S THAT S'POSED TO MEAN?! YOUR GUY WAS CLEARLY LATE WITH HIS TIMING!!
SHP
AND I SAW THAT, JUST NOW. YOU GAVE SOME SORTA SIGNAL!
HYUGA?!
WHOA, WHOA. ARE YOU SAYING THAT WAS INTENTIONAL?
YOU NEED TO BACK UP AN ACCUSATION LIKE THAT WITH SOME PROOF.
...!!
STOP IT, HYUGA!

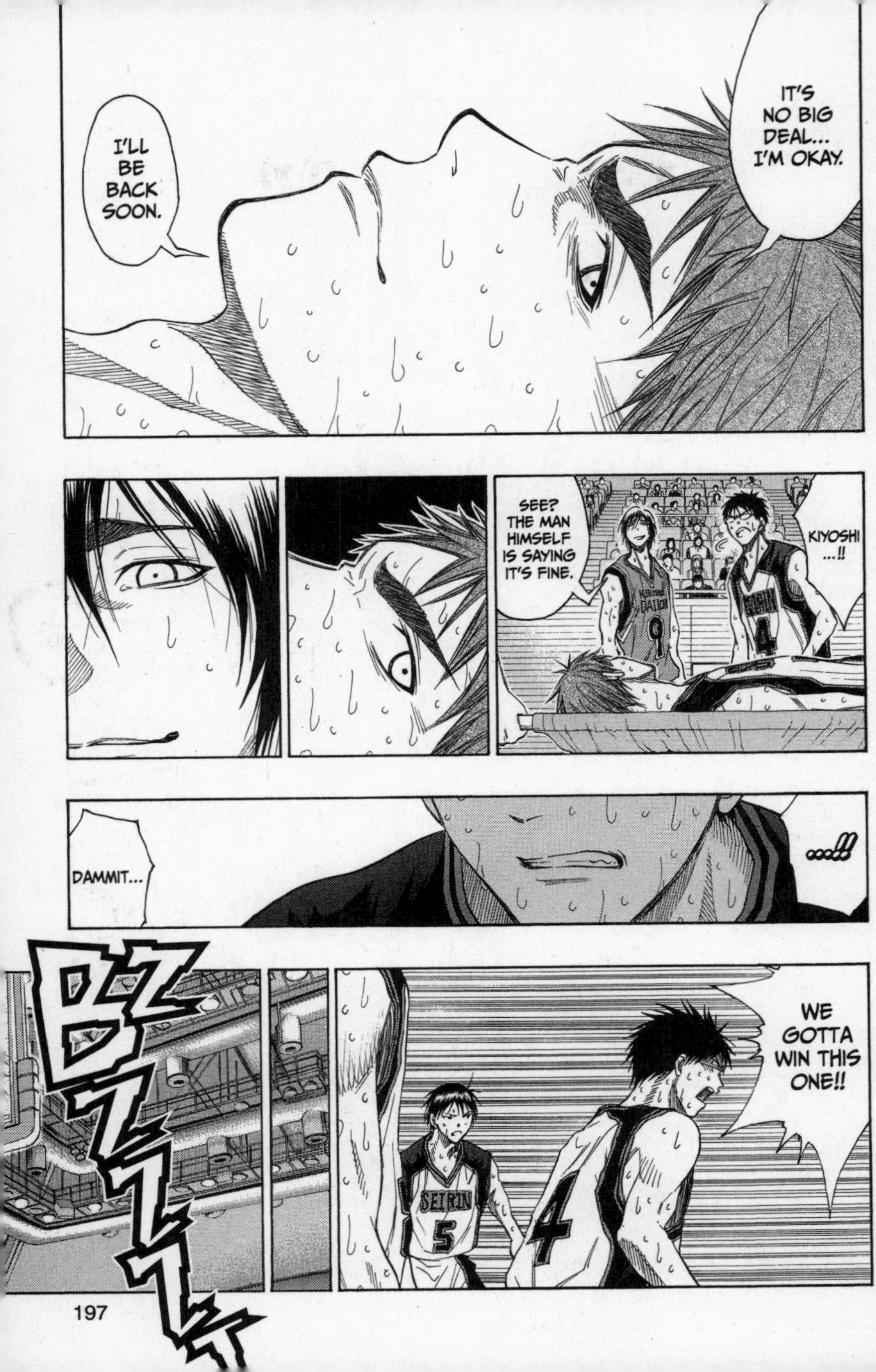
IT'S NO BIG DEAL... I'M OKAY.
I'LL BE BACK SOON.
KIYOSHI ...!!
SEE? THE MAN HIMSELF IS SAYING IT'S FINE.
...!!
DAMMIT...
WE GOTTA WIN THIS ONE!!
BZZZZ

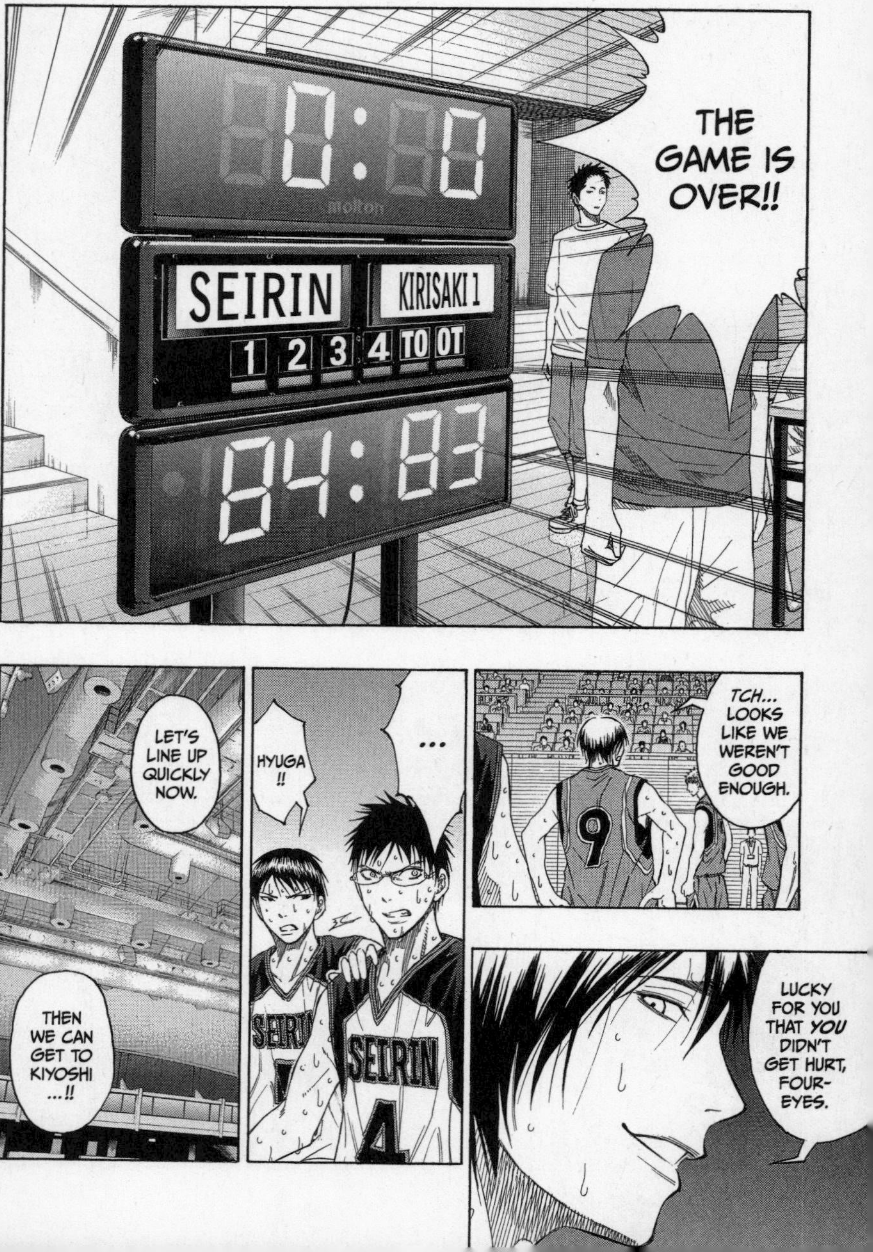
SEIRIN
KIRISAKI 1
1 2 3 4 TO OT
84:83
THE GAME IS OVER!!
TCH... LOOKS LIKE WE WEREN'T GOOD ENOUGH.
LUCKY FOR YOU THAT *YOU* DIDN'T GET HURT, FOUR-EYES.
...
HYUGA !!
SEIRIN
SEIRIN
LET'S LINE UP QUICKLY NOW.
THEN WE CAN GET TO KIYOSHI ...!!

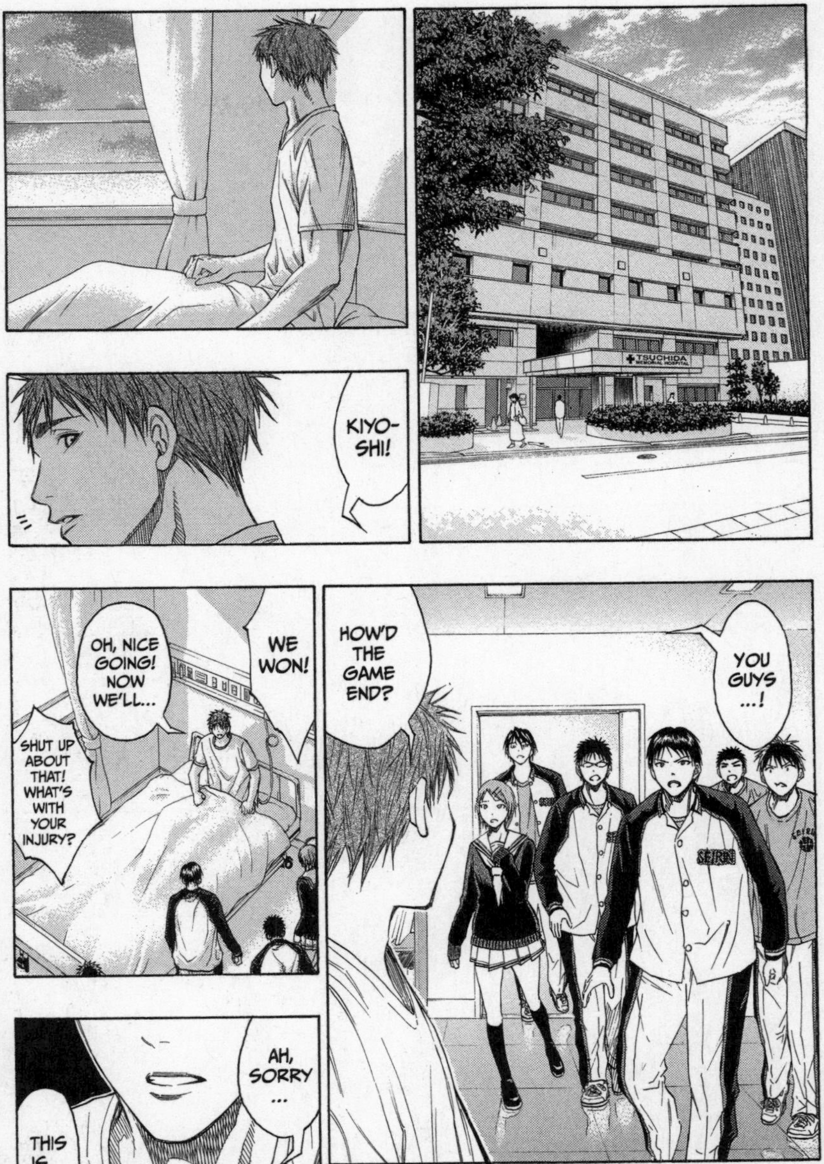
TSUCHIDA
MEMORIAL HOSPITAL
KIYO-SHI!
YOU GUYS ...!
HOW'D THE GAME END?
WE WON!
OH, NICE GOING! NOW WE'LL...
SHUT UP ABOUT THAT! WHAT'S WITH YOUR INJURY?
AH, SORRY ...
THIS IS...

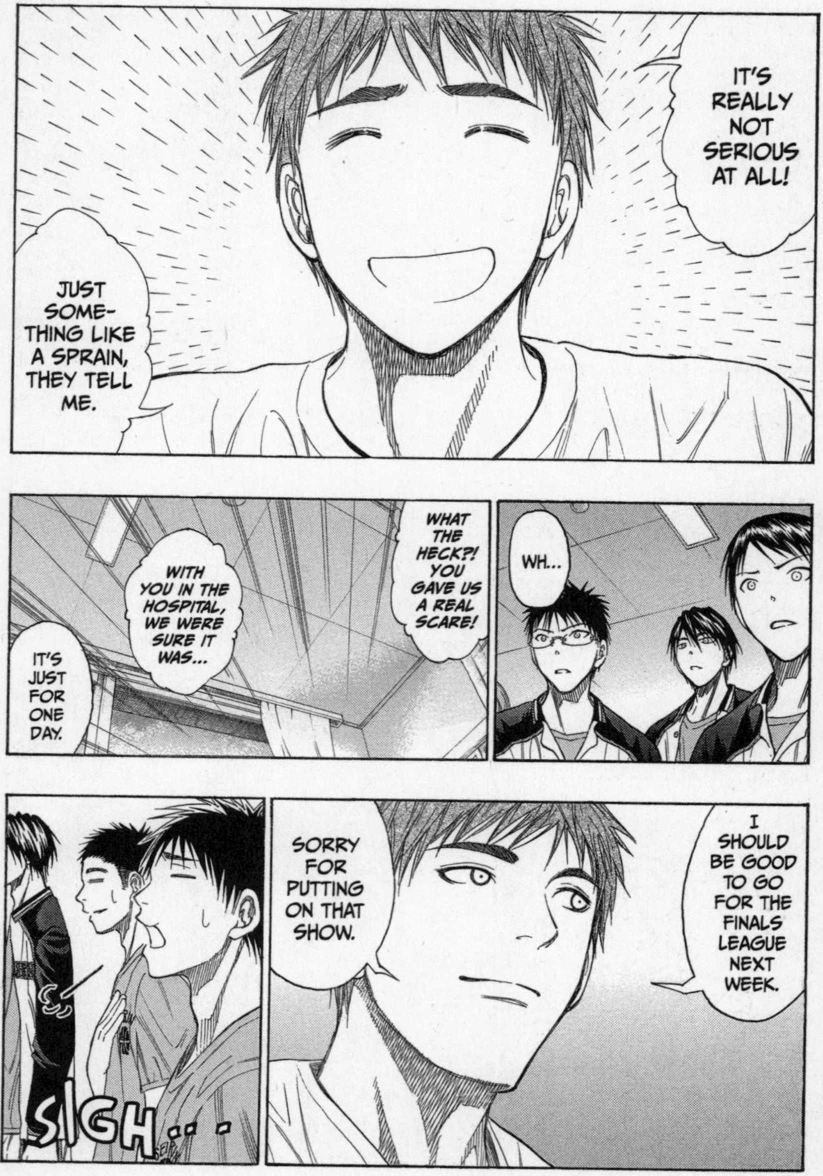
IT'S REALLY NOT SERIOUS AT ALL!
JUST SOME-THING LIKE A SPRAIN, THEY TELL ME.
WH...
WHAT THE HECK?! YOU GAVE US A REAL SCARE!
WITH YOU IN THE HOSPITAL, WE WERE SURE IT WAS...
IT'S JUST FOR ONE DAY.
I SHOULD BE GOOD TO GO FOR THE FINALS LEAGUE NEXT WEEK.
SORRY FOR PUTTING ON THAT SHOW.
SIGH...

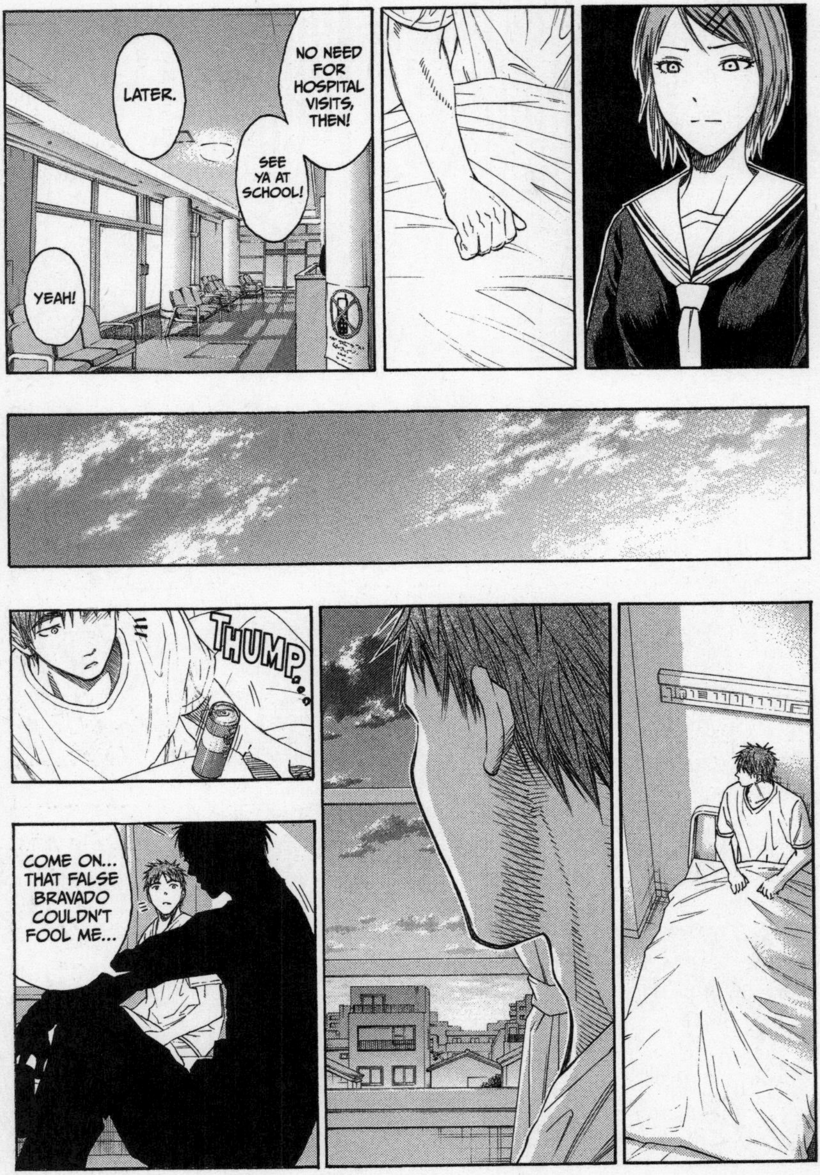
NO NEED FOR HOSPITAL VISITS, THEN!
SEE YA AT SCHOOL!
LATER.
YEAH!
THUMP
COME ON... THAT FALSE BRAVADO COULDN'T FOOL ME...

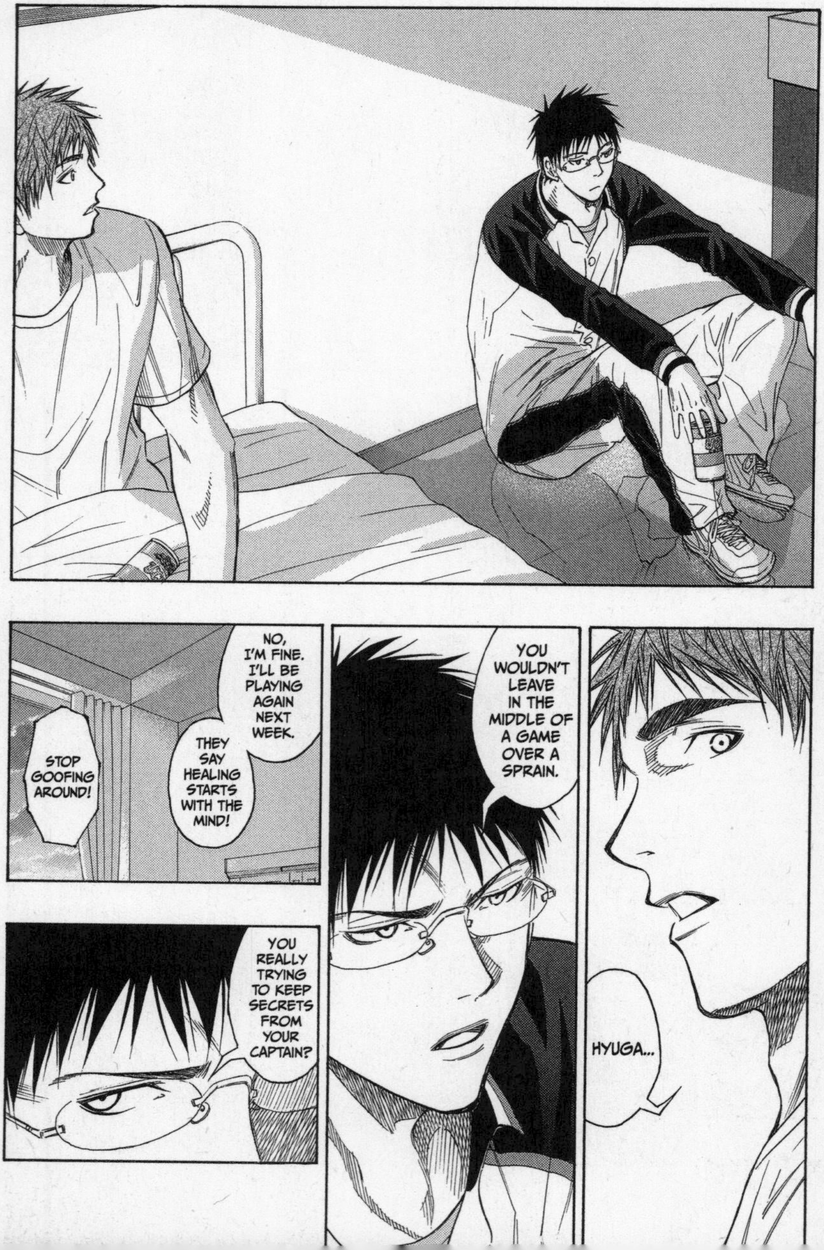
HYUGA...
YOU WOULDN'T LEAVE IN THE MIDDLE OF A GAME OVER A SPRAIN.
NO, I'M FINE. I'LL BE PLAYING AGAIN NEXT WEEK.
THEY SAY HEALING STARTS WITH THE MIND!
STOP GOOFING AROUND!
YOU REALLY TRYING TO KEEP SECRETS FROM YOUR CAPTAIN?

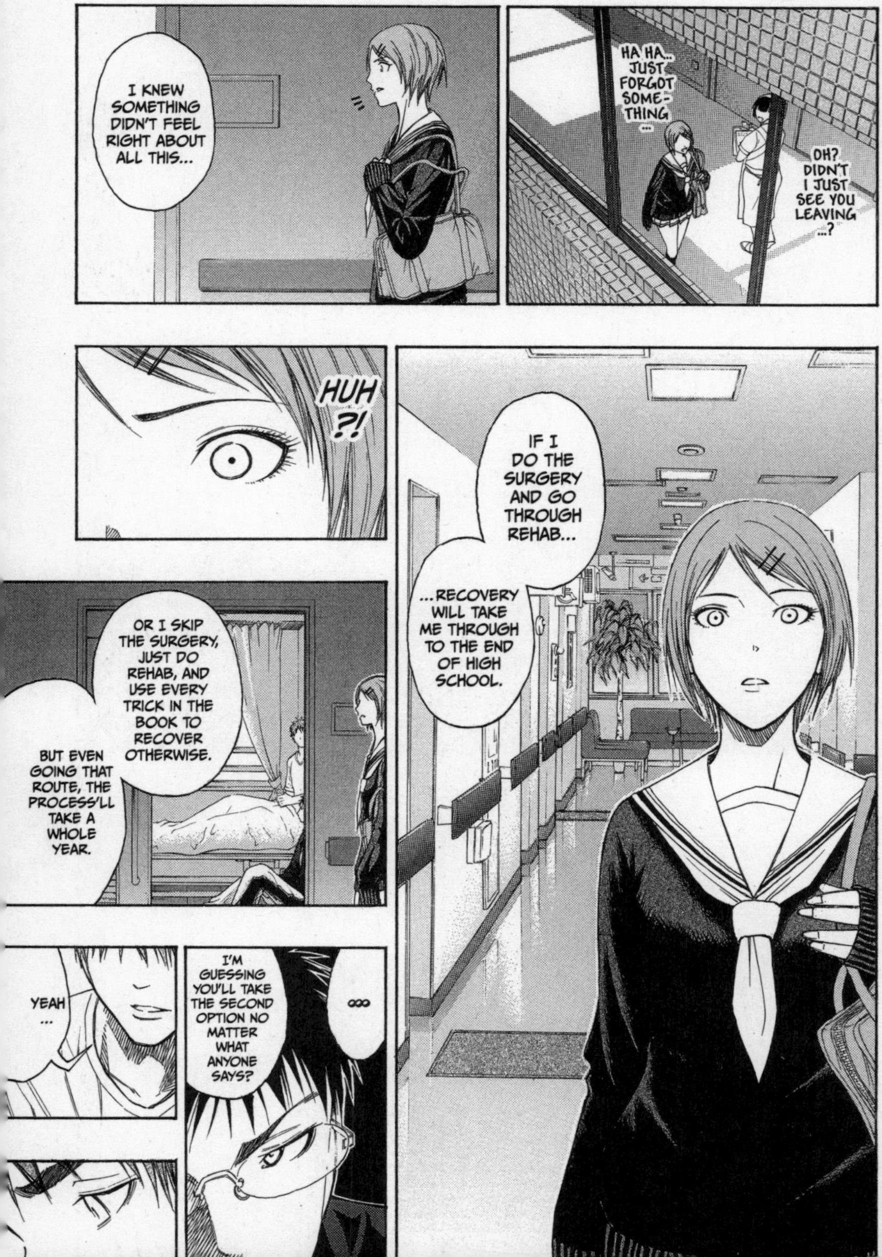
OH? DIDN'T I JUST SEE YOU LEAVING ...?
HA HA.. JUST FORGOT SOME-THING ...
I KNEW SOMETHING DIDN'T FEEL RIGHT ABOUT ALL THIS...
IF I DO THE SURGERY AND GO THROUGH REHAB...
...RECOVERY WILL TAKE ME THROUGH TO THE END OF HIGH SCHOOL.
HUH ?!
OR I SKIP THE SURGERY, JUST DO REHAB, AND USE EVERY TRICK IN THE BOOK TO RECOVER OTHERWISE.
BUT EVEN GOING THAT ROUTE, THE PROCESS'LL TAKE A WHOLE YEAR.
...
I'M GUESSING YOU'LL TAKE THE SECOND OPTION NO MATTER WHAT ANYONE SAYS?
YEAH ...

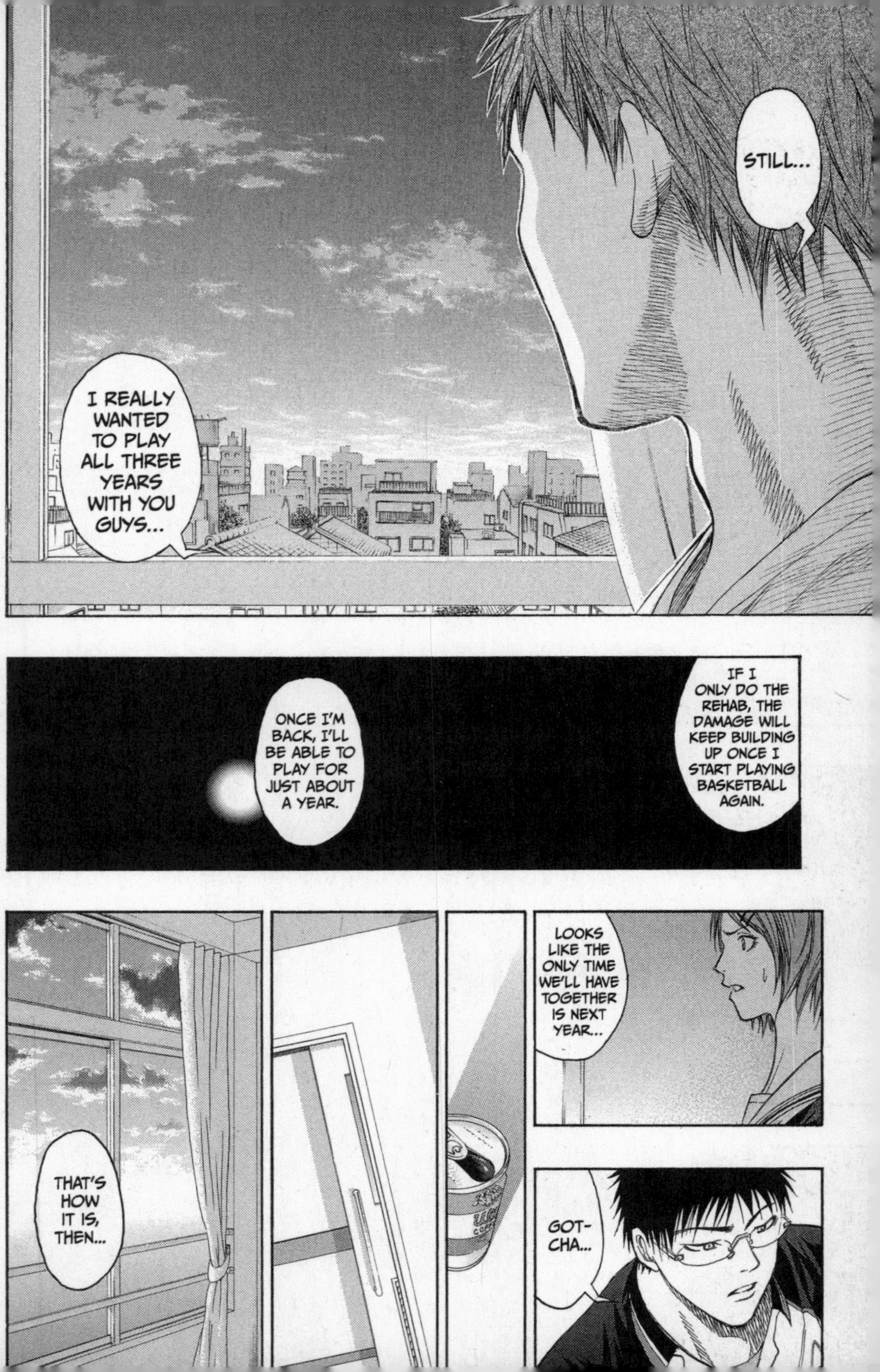
STILL...
I REALLY WANTED TO PLAY ALL THREE YEARS WITH YOU GUYS...
IF I ONLY DO THE REHAB, THE DAMAGE WILL KEEP BUILDING UP ONCE I START PLAYING BASKETBALL AGAIN.
ONCE I'M BACK, I'LL BE ABLE TO PLAY FOR JUST ABOUT A YEAR.
LOOKS LIKE THE ONLY TIME WE'LL HAVE TOGETHER IS NEXT YEAR...
GOT-CHA...
THAT'S HOW IT IS, THEN...

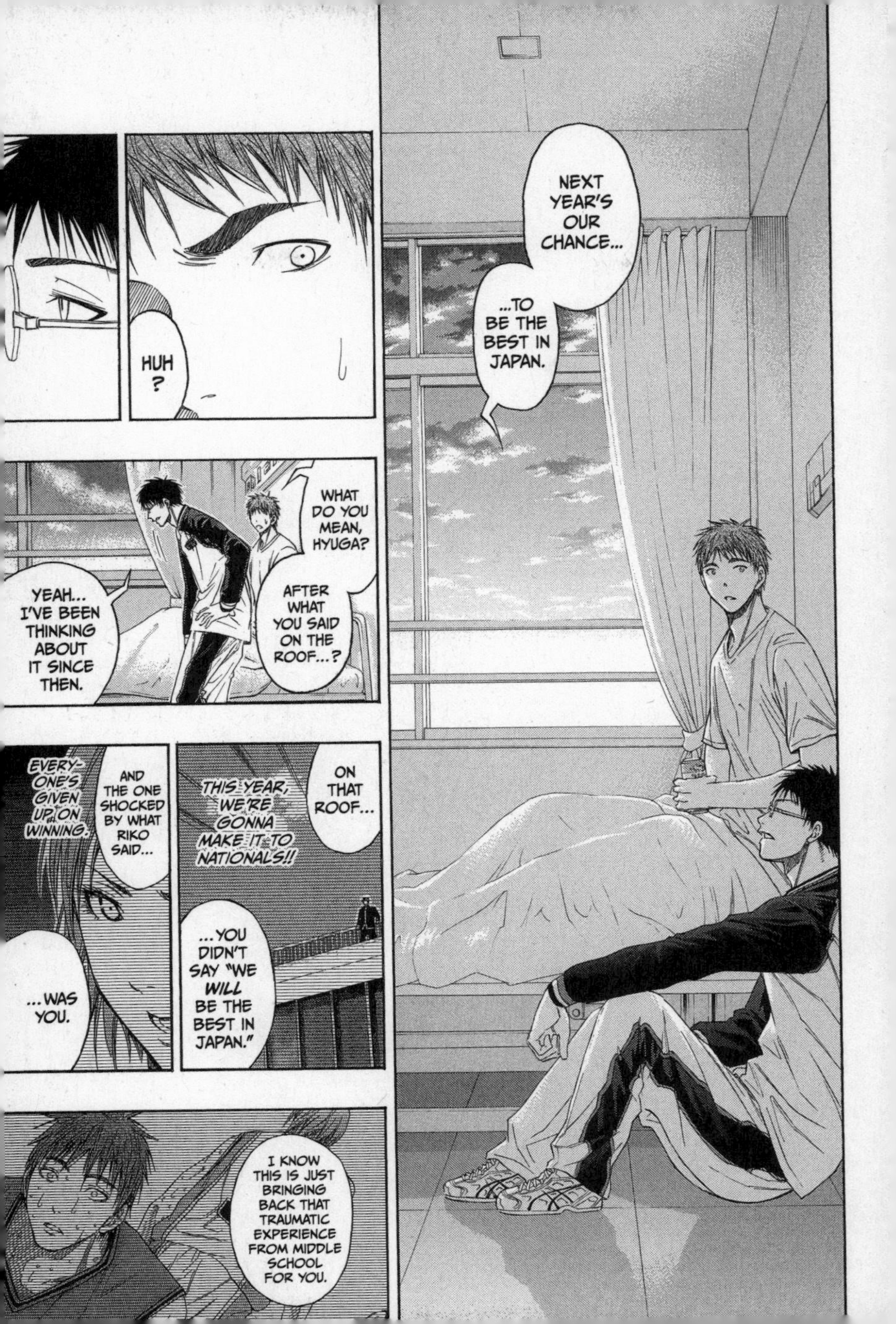
NEXT YEAR'S OUR CHANCE...
...TO BE THE BEST IN JAPAN.
HUH?
WHAT DO YOU MEAN, HYUGA?
AFTER WHAT YOU SAID ON THE ROOF...?
YEAH... I'VE BEEN THINKING ABOUT IT SINCE THEN.
ON THAT ROOF...
THIS YEAR, WE'RE GONNA MAKE IT TO NATIONALS!!
...YOU DIDN'T SAY "WE *WILL* BE THE BEST IN JAPAN."
AND THE ONE SHOCKED BY WHAT RIKO SAID...
EVERYONE'S GIVEN UP ON WINNING.
...WAS YOU.
I KNOW THIS IS JUST BRINGING BACK THAT TRAUMATIC EXPERIENCE FROM MIDDLE SCHOOL FOR YOU.

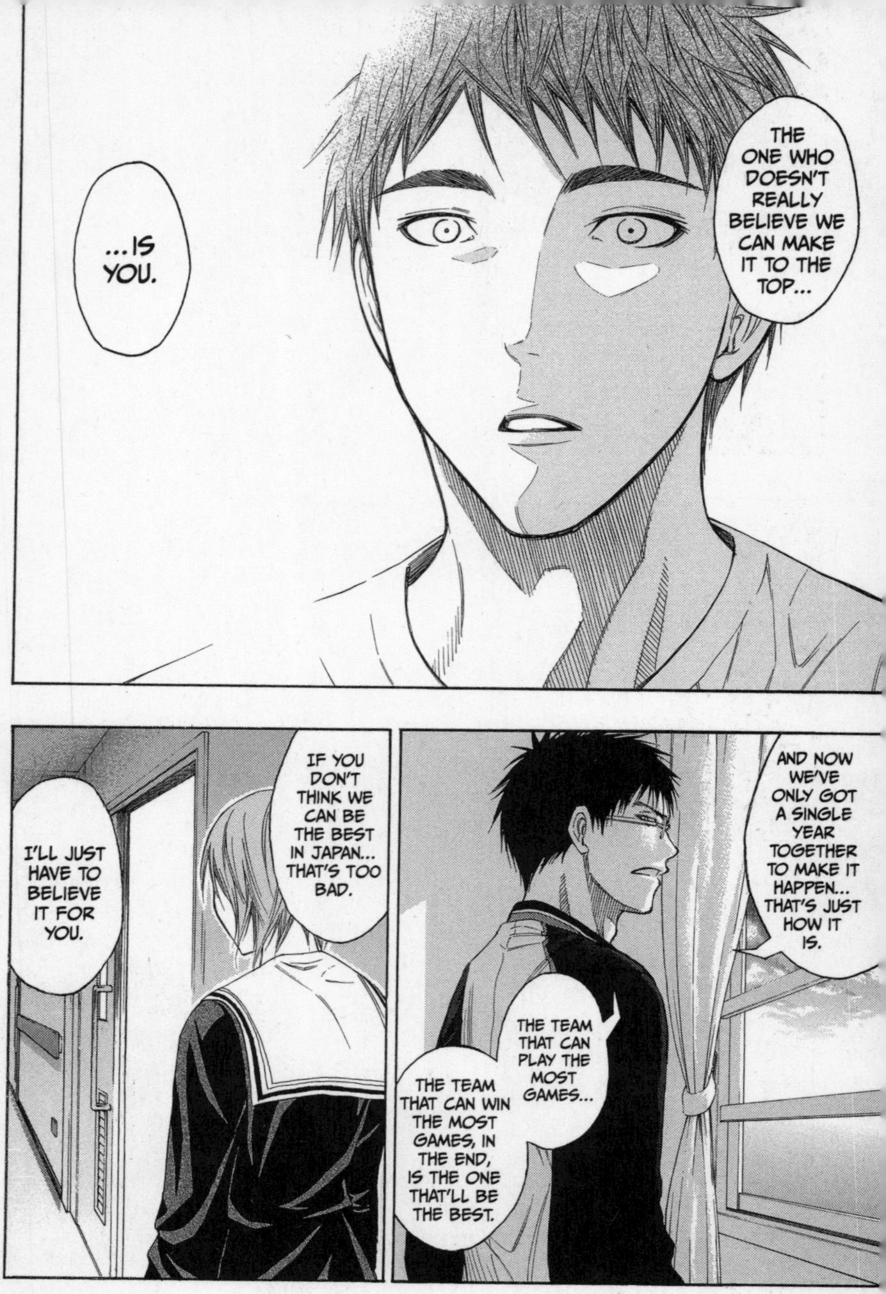
THE ONE WHO DOESN'T REALLY BELIEVE WE CAN MAKE IT TO THE TOP...
...IS YOU.
AND NOW WE'VE ONLY GOT A SINGLE YEAR TOGETHER TO MAKE IT HAPPEN... THAT'S JUST HOW IT IS.
THE TEAM THAT CAN PLAY THE MOST GAMES...
THE TEAM THAT CAN WIN THE MOST GAMES, IN THE END, IS THE ONE THAT'LL BE THE BEST.
IF YOU DON'T THINK WE CAN BE THE BEST IN JAPAN... THAT'S TOO BAD.
I'LL JUST HAVE TO BELIEVE IT FOR YOU.

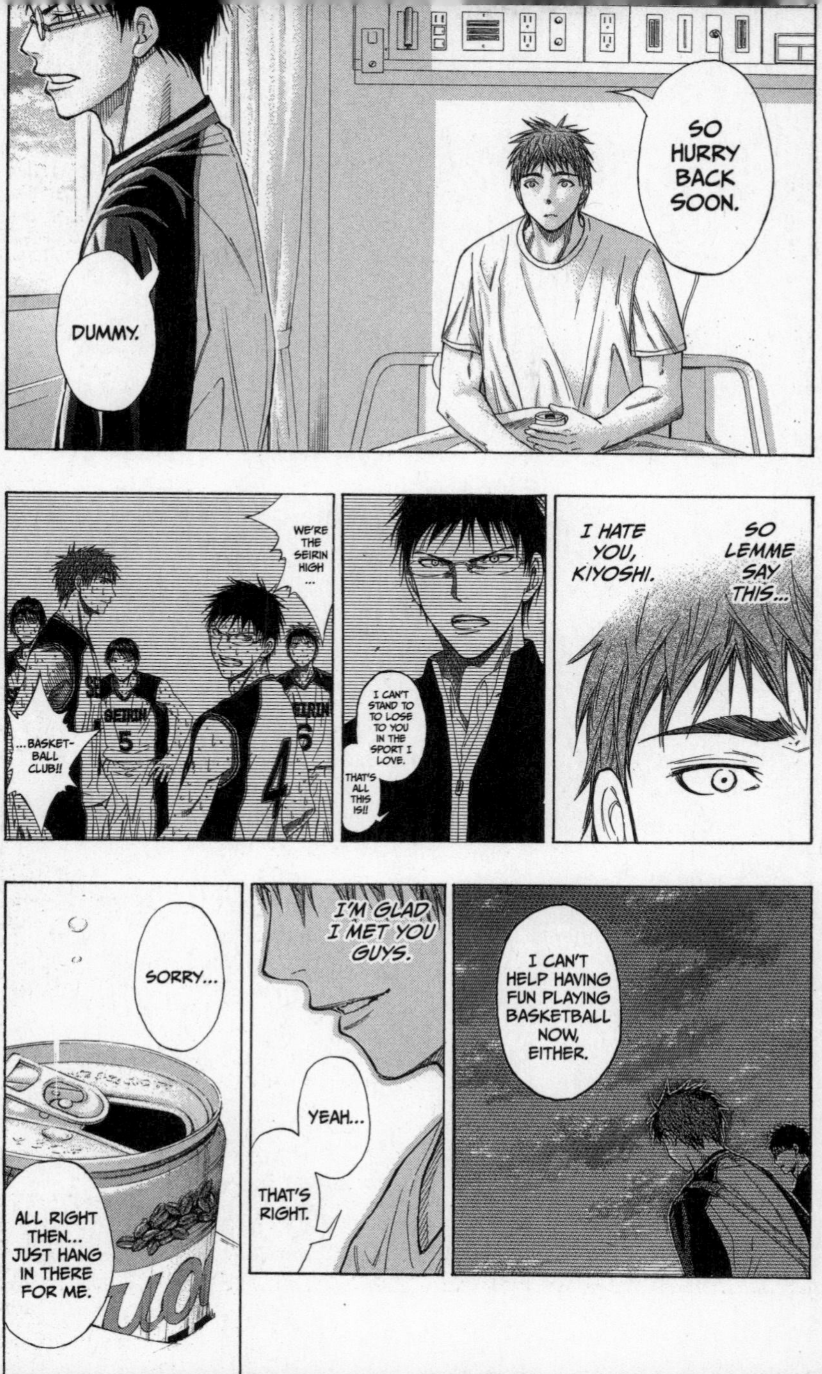
SO HURRY BACK SOON.
DUMMY.
SO LEMME SAY THIS...
I HATE YOU, KIYOSHI.
I CAN'T STAND TO TO LOSE TO YOU IN THE SPORT I LOVE.
THAT'S ALL THIS IS!!
WE'RE THE SEIRIN HIGH...
...BASKETBALL CLUB!!
I CAN'T HELP HAVING FUN PLAYING BASKETBALL NOW, EITHER.
I'M GLAD I MET YOU GUYS.
YEAH...
THAT'S RIGHT.
SORRY...
ALL RIGHT THEN... JUST HANG IN THERE FOR ME.

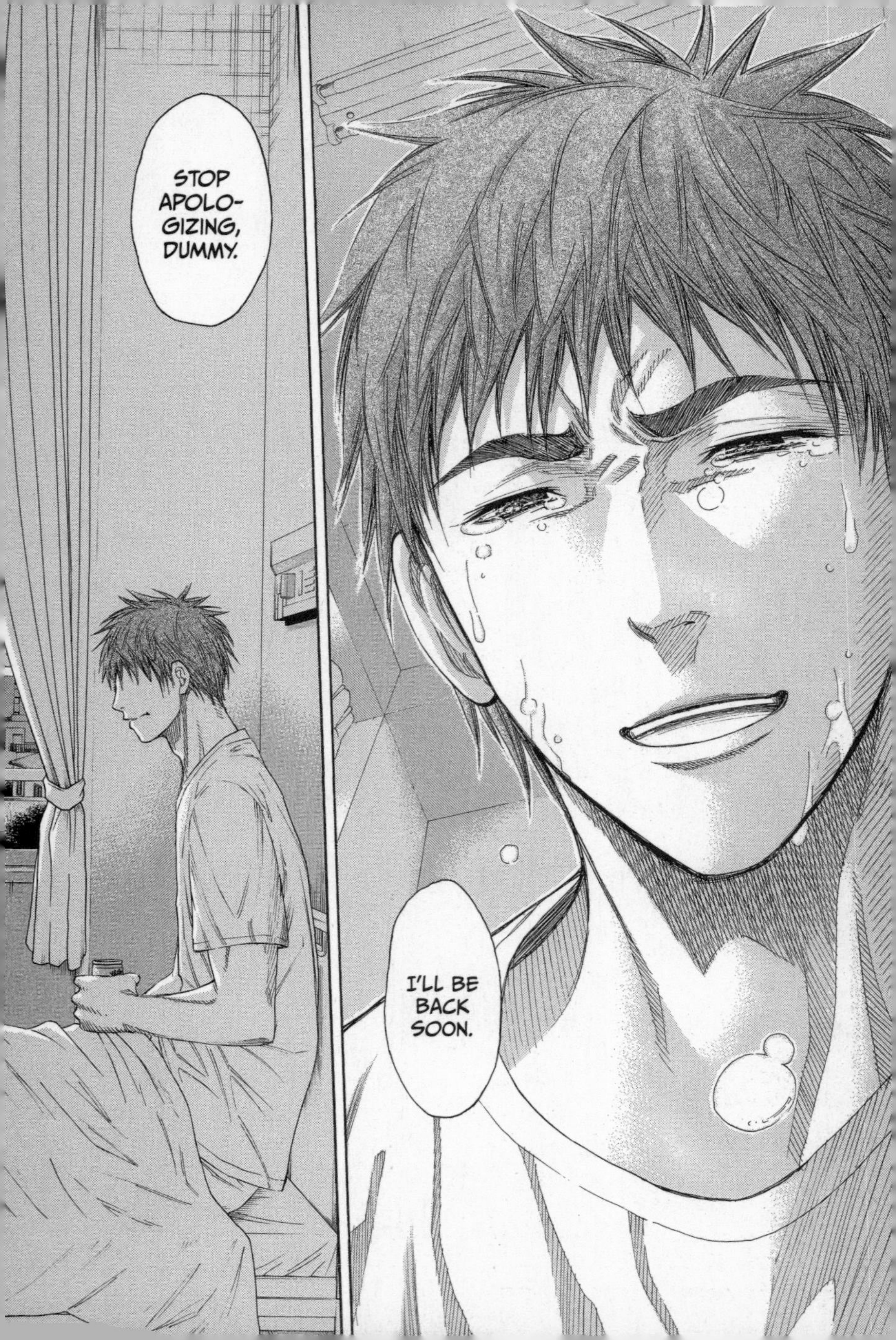
I'LL BE BACK SOON.
STOP APOLO-GIZING, DUMMY.

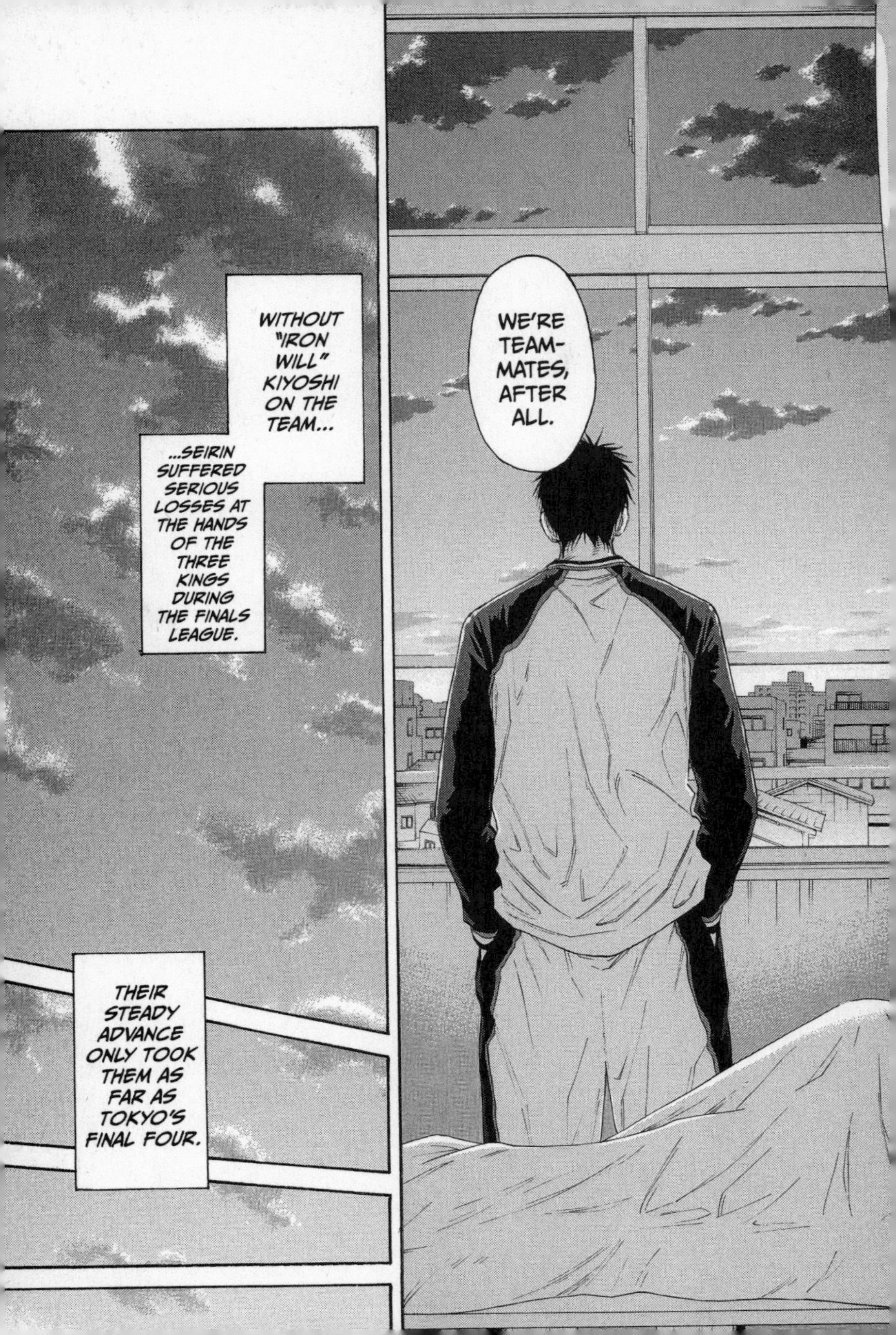
WE'RE TEAM-MATES, AFTER ALL.
WITHOUT "IRON WILL" KIYOSHI ON THE TEAM...
...SEIRIN SUFFERED SERIOUS LOSSES AT THE HANDS OF THE THREE KINGS DURING THE FINALS LEAGUE.
THEIR STEADY ADVANCE ONLY TOOK THEM AS FAR AS TOKYO'S FINAL FOUR.

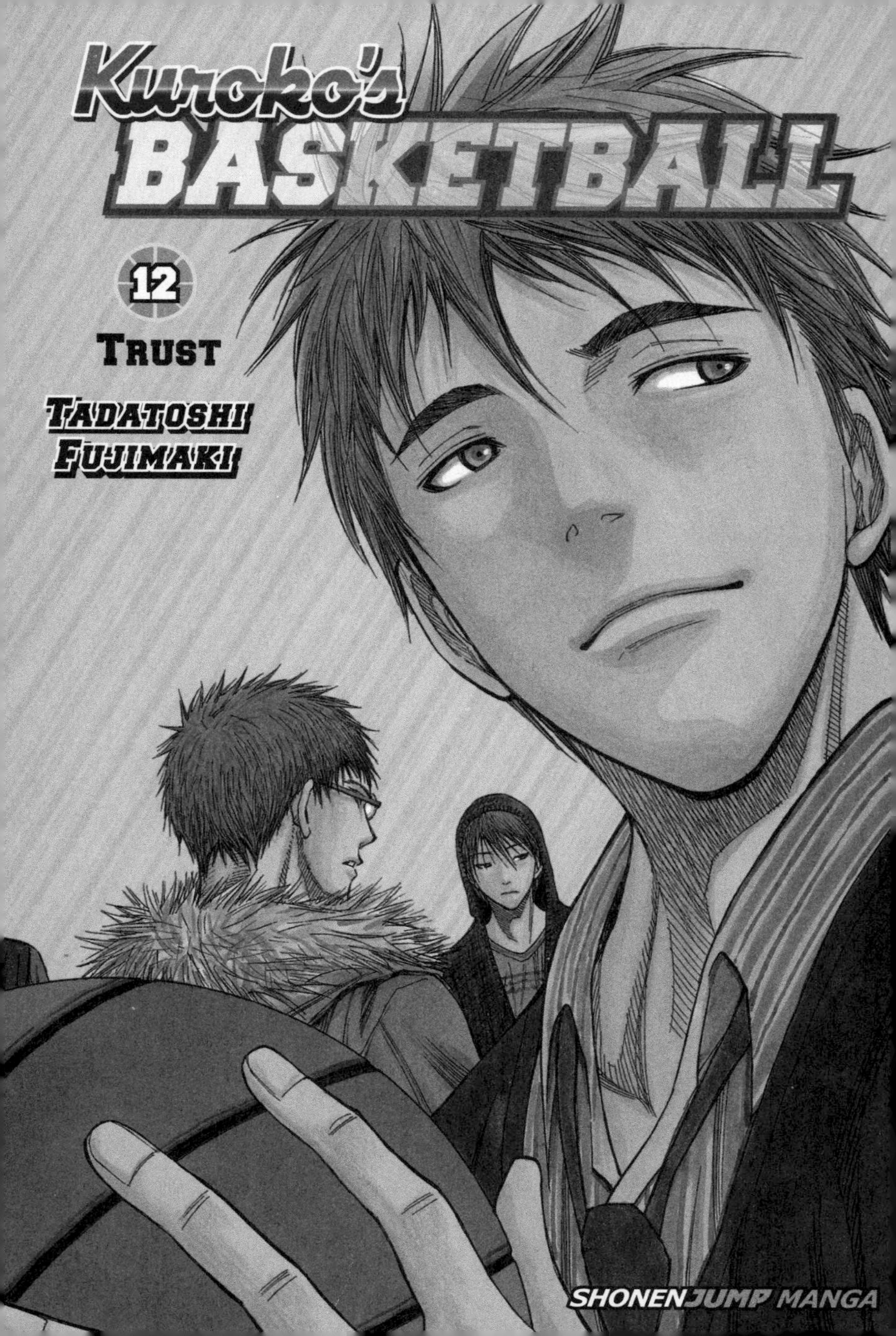
Kuroko's
BASKETBALL
12
TRUST
TADATOSHI
FUJIMAKI
SHONENJUMP MANGA

Kuroko's BASKETBALL

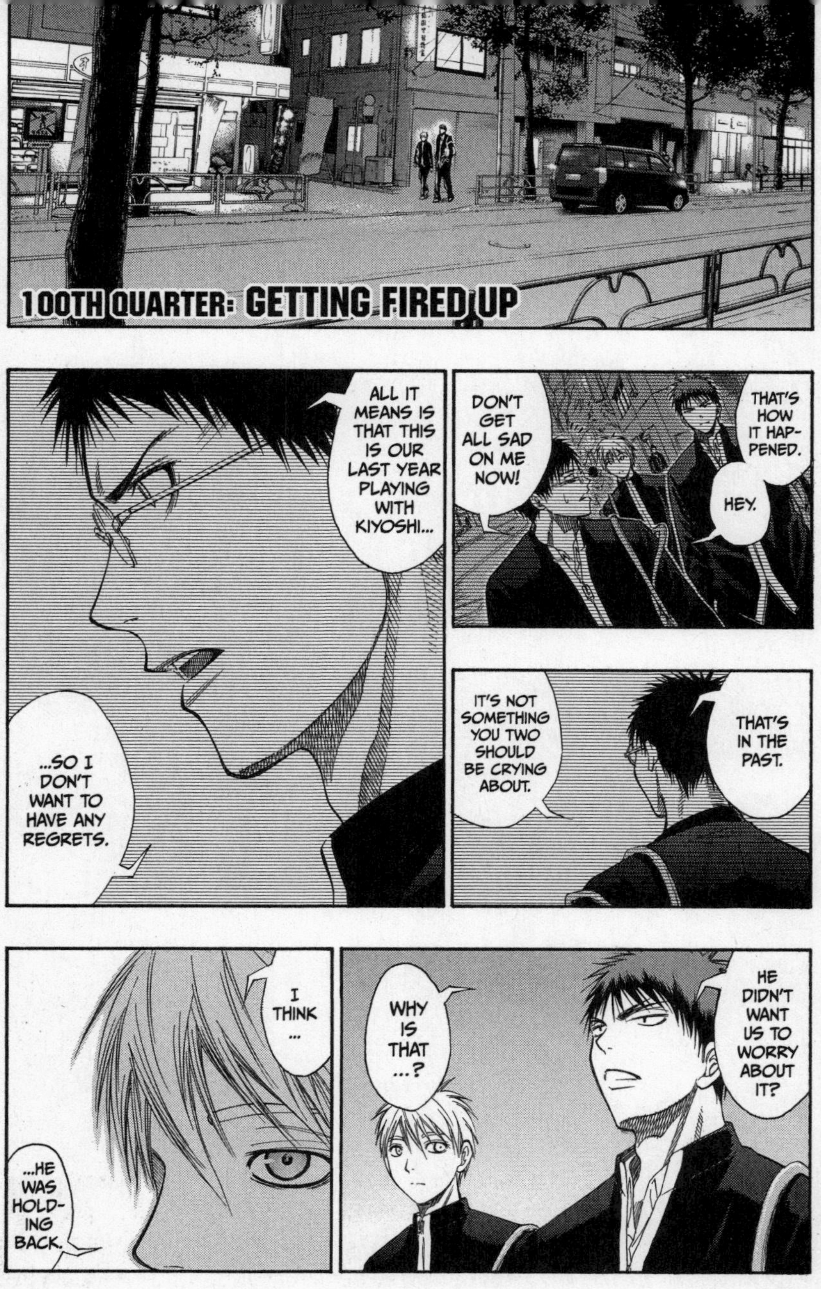
100TH QUARTER: GETTING FIRED UP
THAT'S HOW IT HAPPENED.
HEY.
DON'T GET ALL SAD ON ME NOW!
THAT'S IN THE PAST.
IT'S NOT SOMETHING YOU TWO SHOULD BE CRYING ABOUT.
ALL IT MEANS IS THAT THIS IS OUR LAST YEAR PLAYING WITH KIYOSHI...
...SO I DON'T WANT TO HAVE ANY REGRETS.
HE DIDN'T WANT US TO WORRY ABOUT IT?
WHY IS THAT...?
I THINK...
...HE WAS HOLDING BACK.

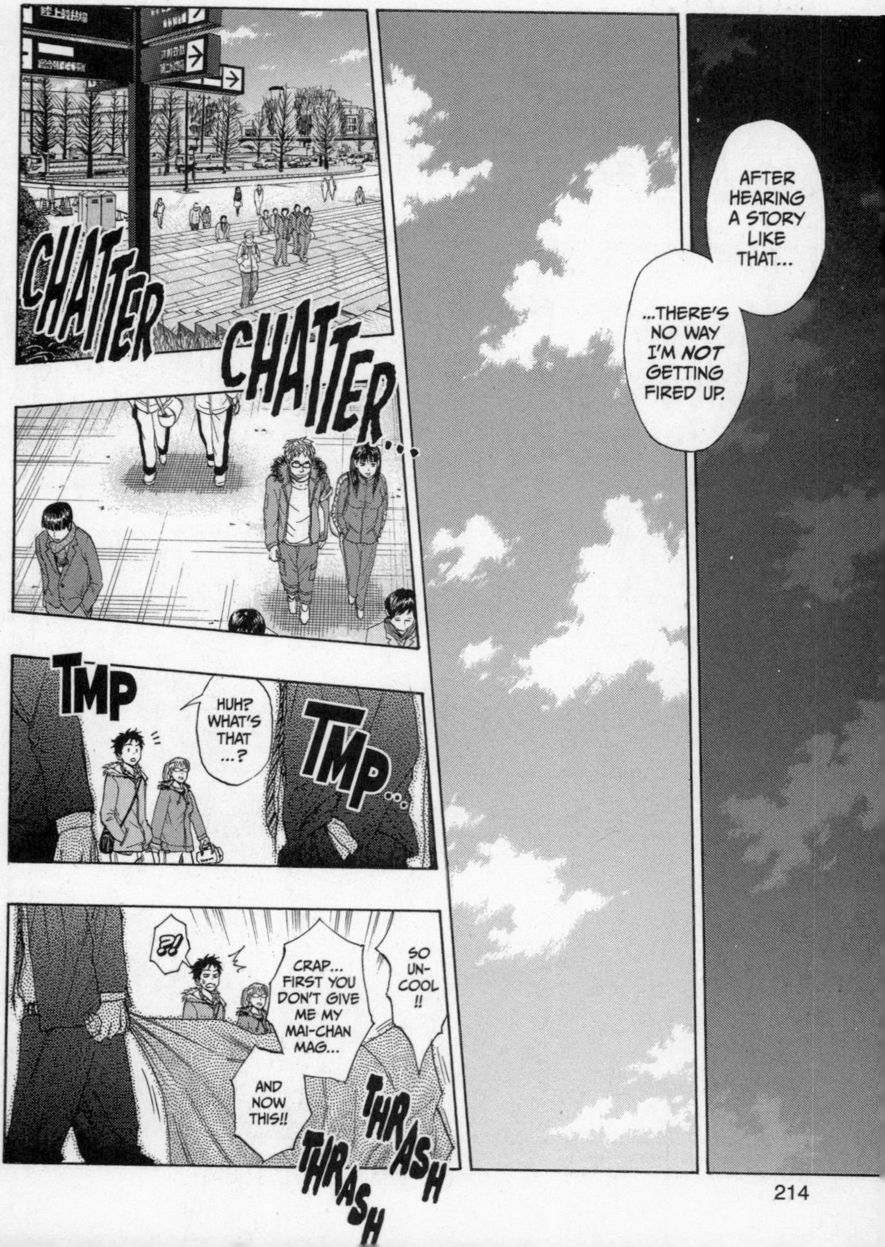
AFTER HEARING A STORY LIKE THAT...
...THERE'S NO WAY I'M *NOT* GETTING FIRED UP.
CHATTER
CHATTER
CHATTER...
TMP
HUH? WHAT'S THAT ...?
TMP...
SO UN-COOL!!
CRAP... FIRST YOU DON'T GIVE ME MY MAI-CHAN MAG...
?!
AND NOW THIS!!
THRASH
THRASH

100TH QUARTER:

GETTING FIRED UP

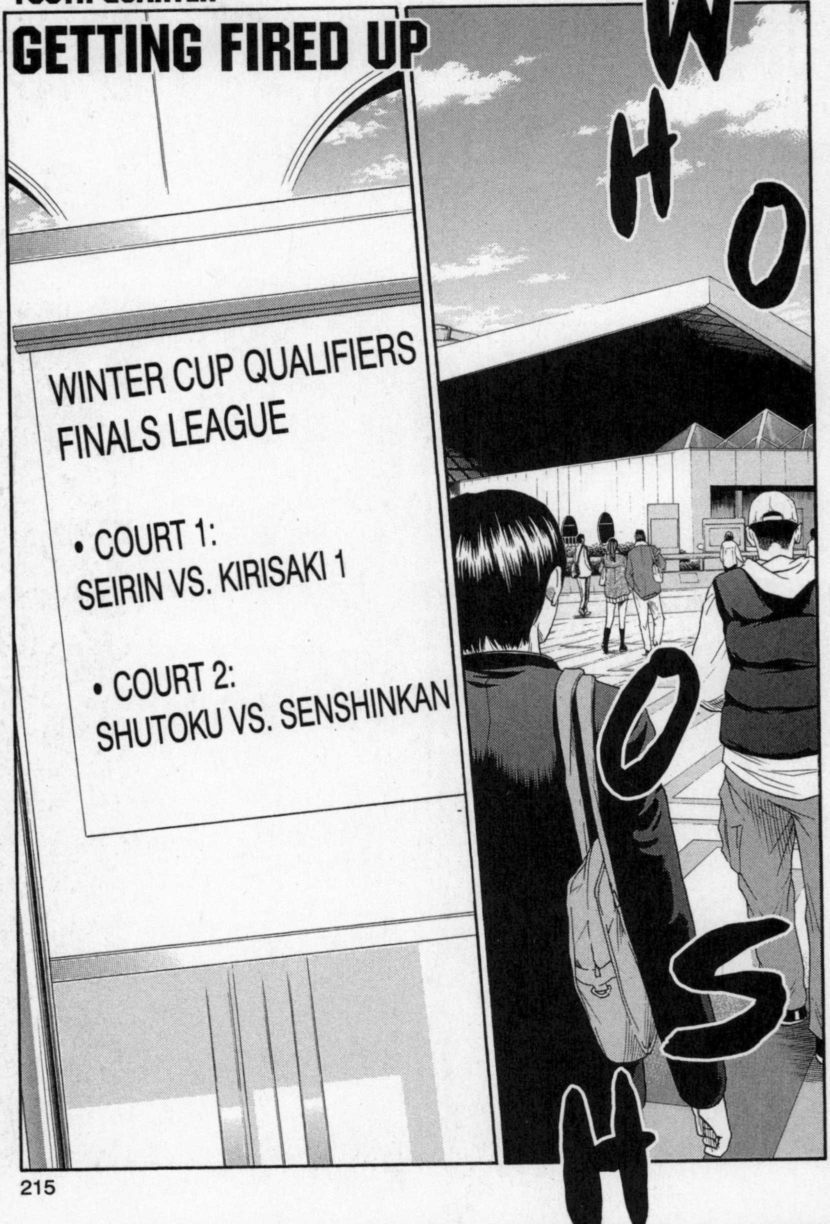
WHOOOSH
WINTER CUP QUALIFIERS
FINALS LEAGUE
• COURT 1:
SEIRIN VS. KIRISAKI 1
• COURT 2:
SHUTOKU VS. SENSHINKAN

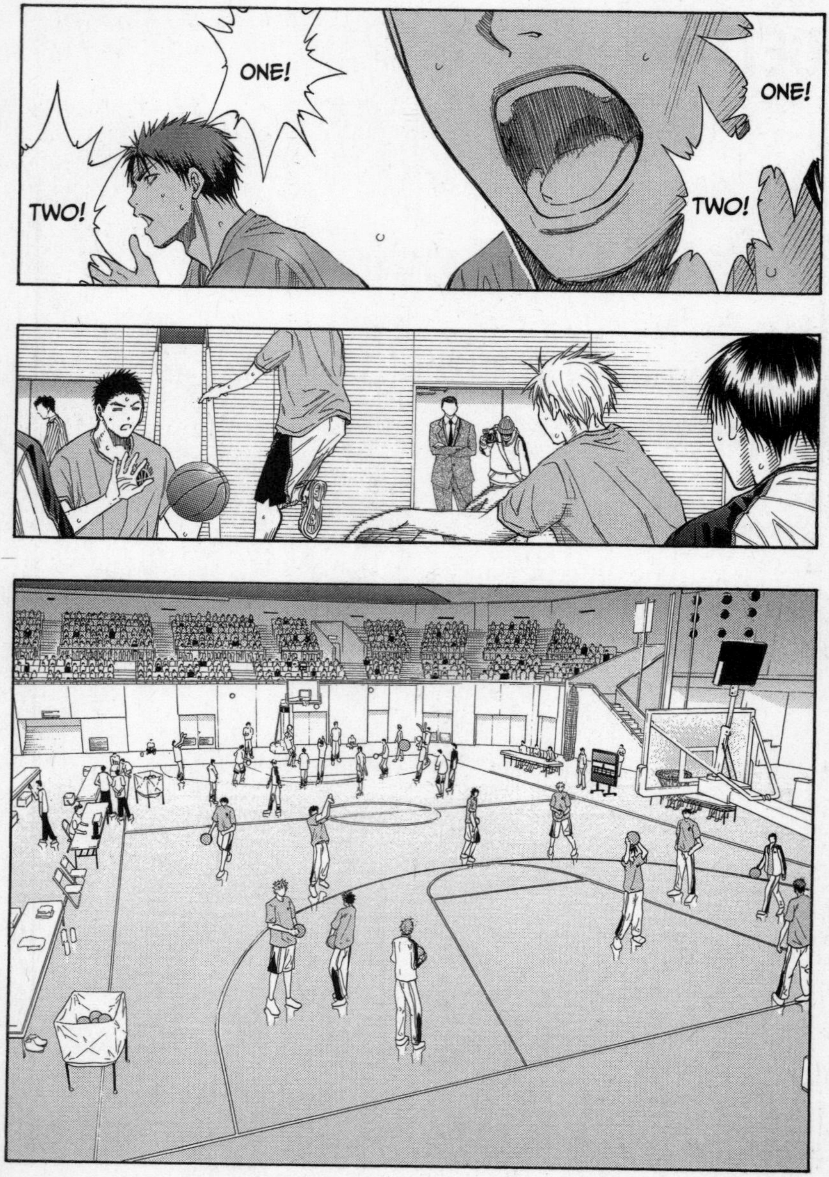
ONE!
TWO!
ONE!
TWO!

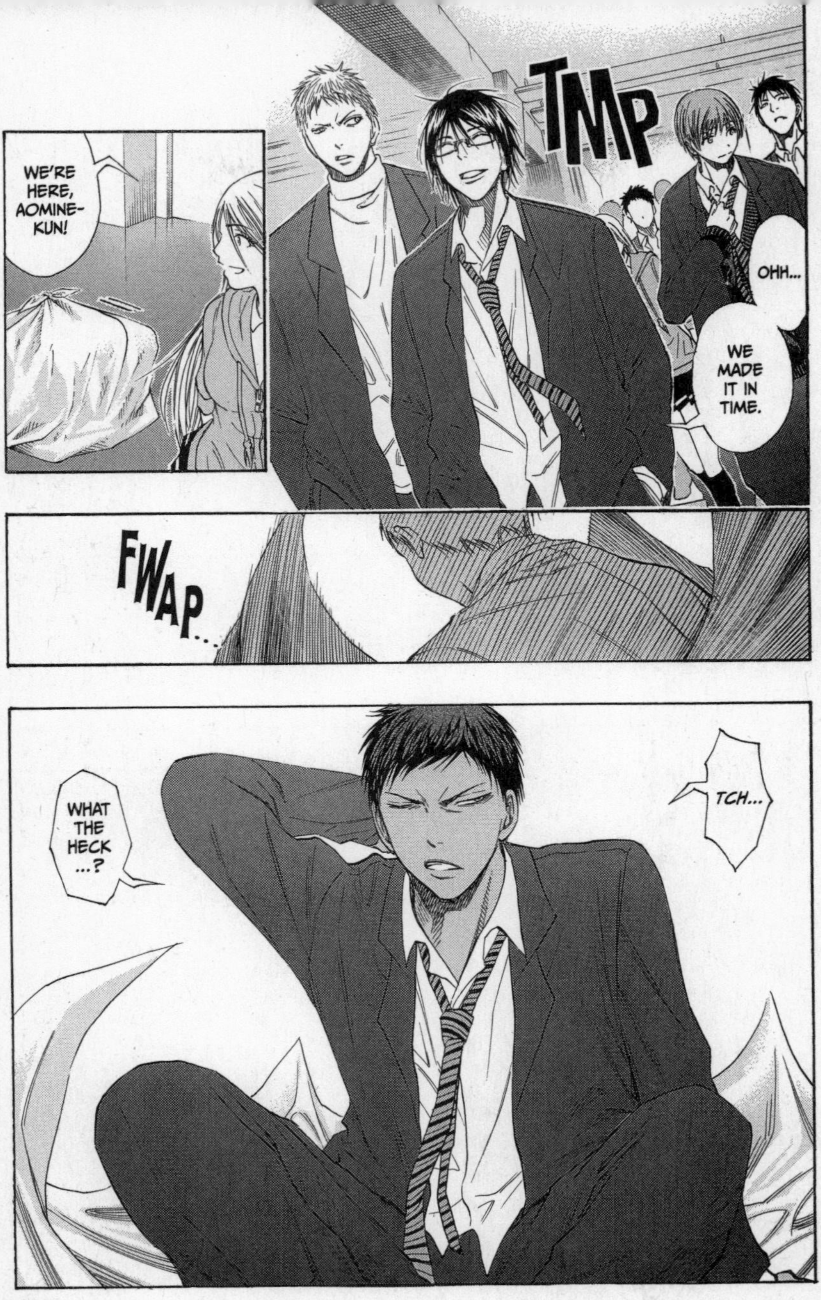
TMP
OHH...
WE MADE IT IN TIME.
WE'RE HERE, AOMINE-KUN!
FWAP...
TCH...
WHAT THE HECK ...?

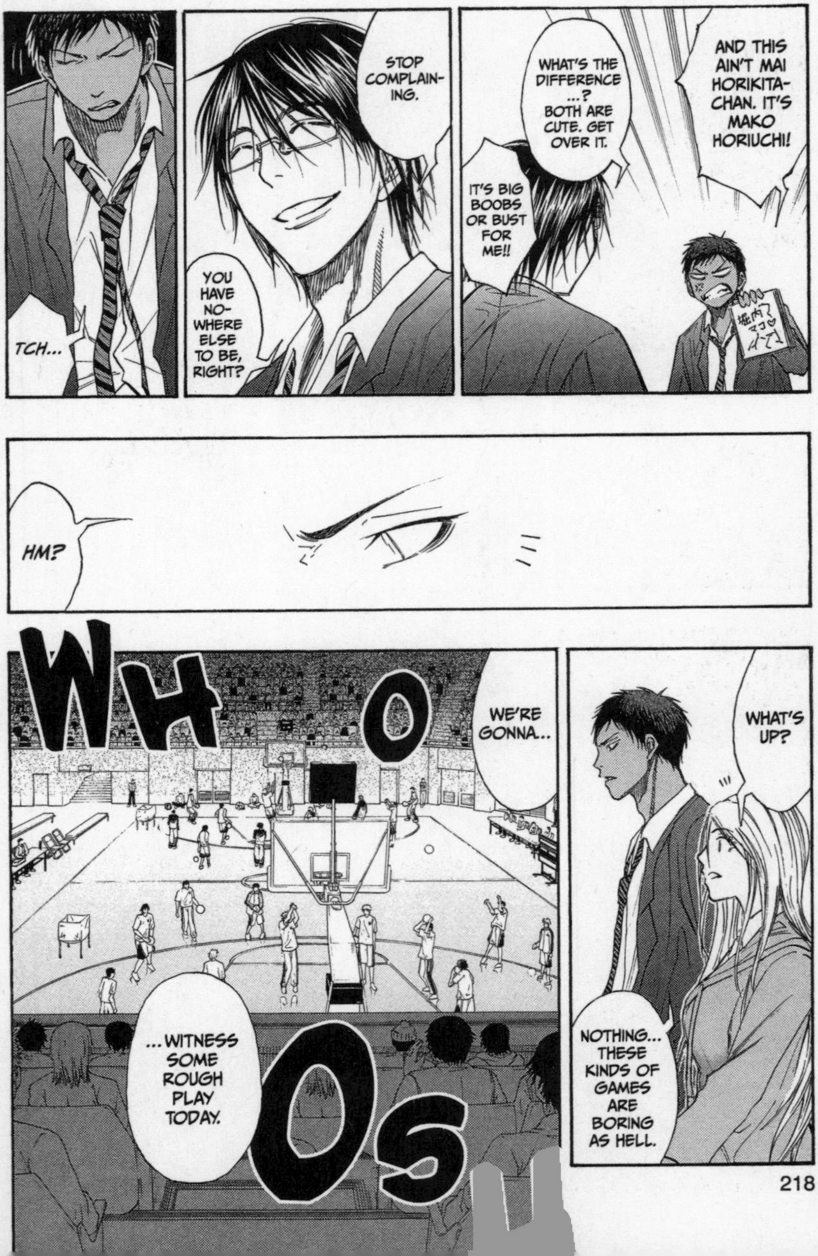
AND THIS AIN'T MAI HORIKITA-CHAN. IT'S MAKO HORIUCHI!
WHAT'S THE DIFFERENCE ...? BOTH ARE CUTE. GET OVER IT.
IT'S BIG BOOBS OR BUST FOR ME!!
STOP COMPLAINING.
YOU HAVE NOWHERE ELSE TO BE, RIGHT?
TCH...
HM?
WHAT'S UP?
NOTHING... THESE KINDS OF GAMES ARE BORING AS HELL.
WE'RE GONNA...
...WITNESS SOME ROUGH PLAY TODAY.
WHOOOSH

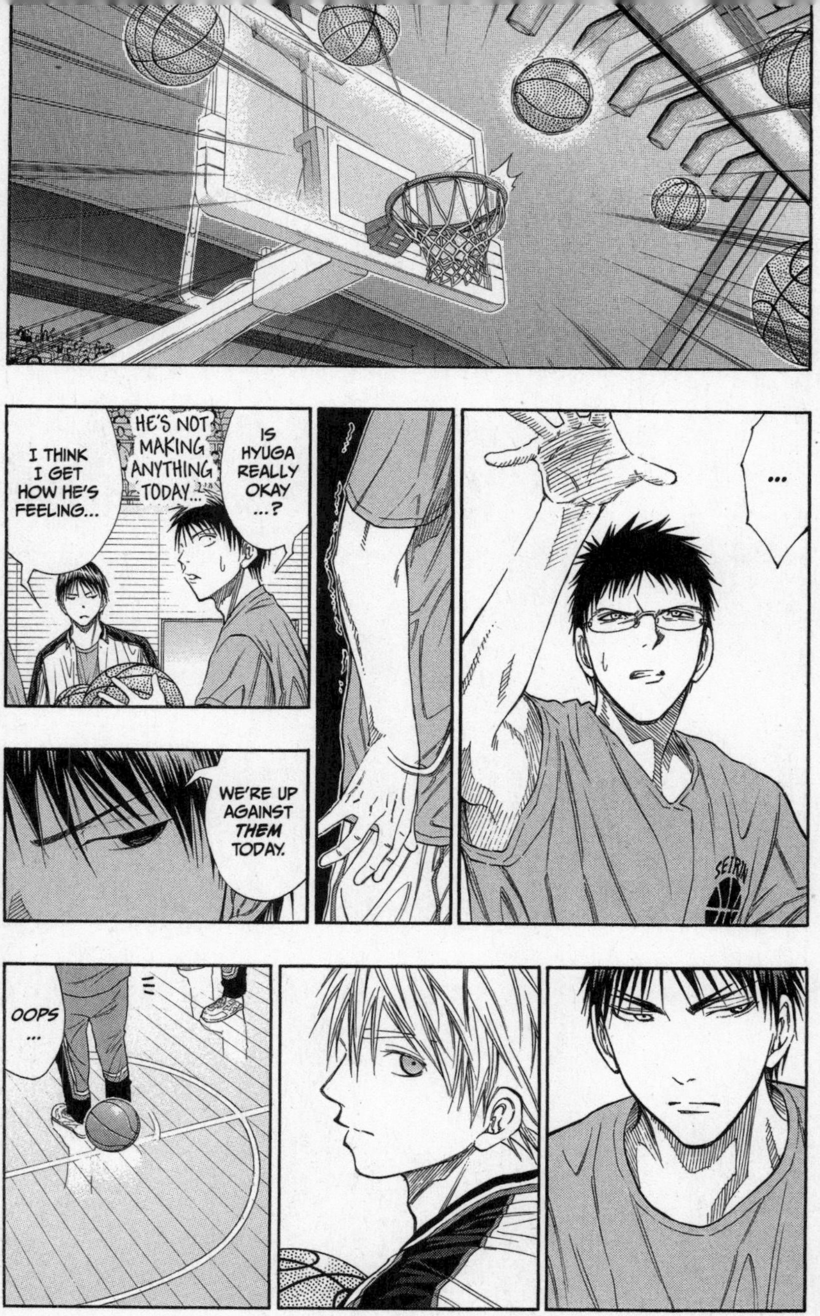
...
IS HYUGA REALLY OKAY ...?
HE'S NOT MAKING ANYTHING TODAY...
I THINK I GET HOW HE'S FEELING...
WE'RE UP AGAINST *THEM* TODAY.
OOPS ...

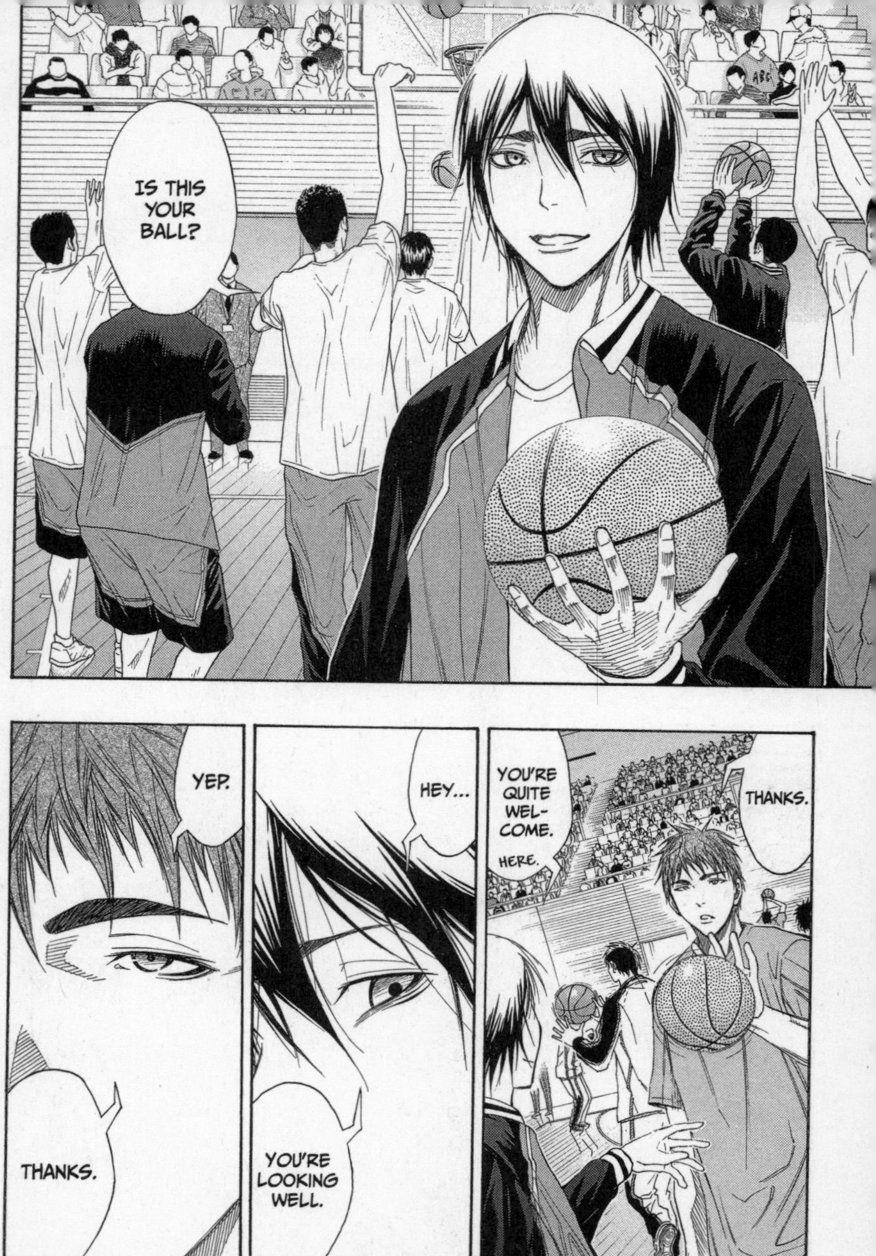

IS THIS YOUR BALL?
THANKS.
YOU'RE QUITE WEL-COME.
HERE.
HEY...
YOU'RE LOOKING WELL.
YEP.
THANKS.

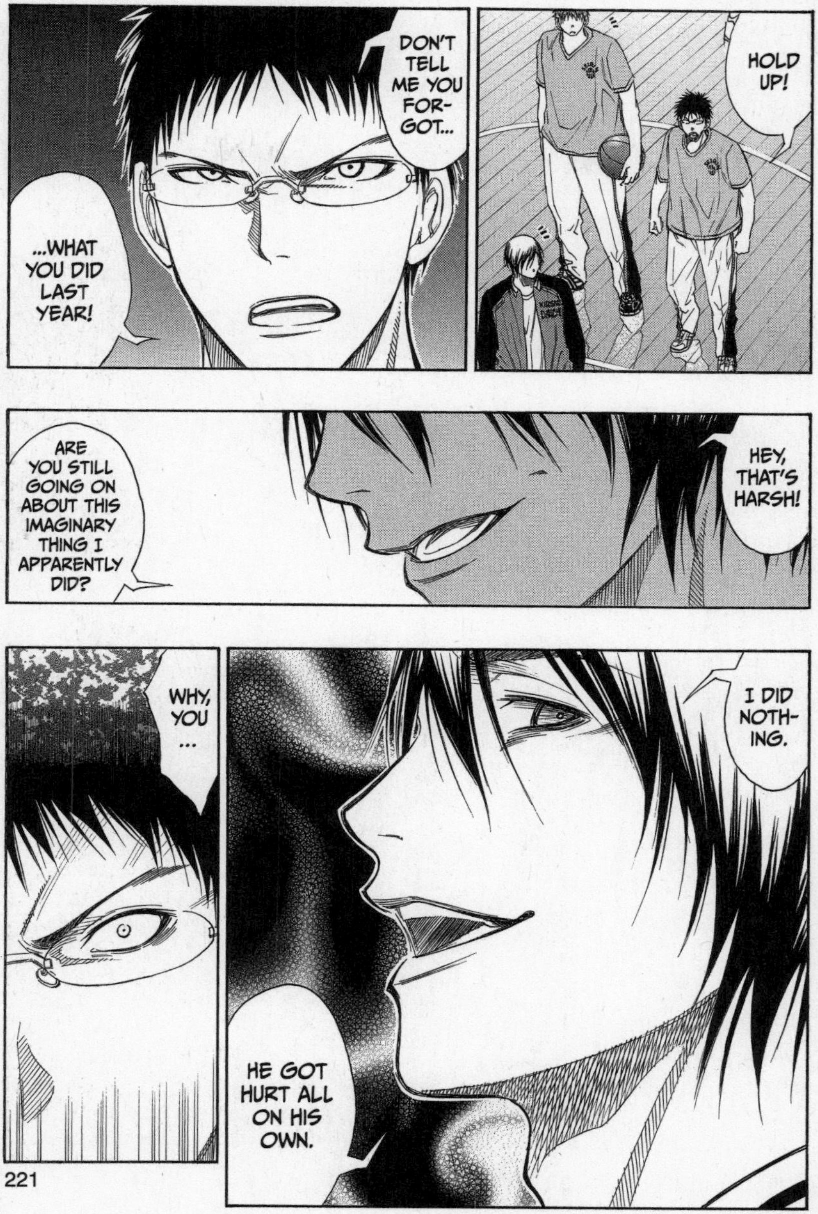
HOLD UP!
DON'T TELL ME YOU FOR-GOT...
...WHAT YOU DID LAST YEAR!
HEY, THAT'S HARSH!
ARE YOU STILL GOING ON ABOUT THIS IMAGINARY THING I APPARENTLY DID?
I DID NOTH-ING.
HE GOT HURT ALL ON HIS OWN.
WHY, YOU ...

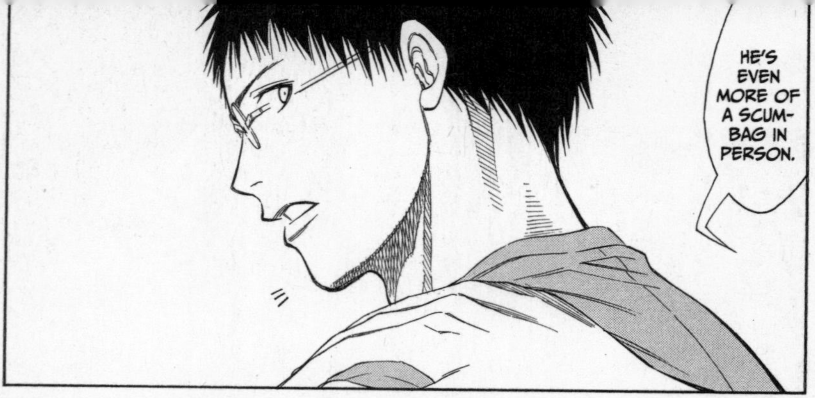
HE'S EVEN MORE OF A SCUM-BAG IN PERSON.

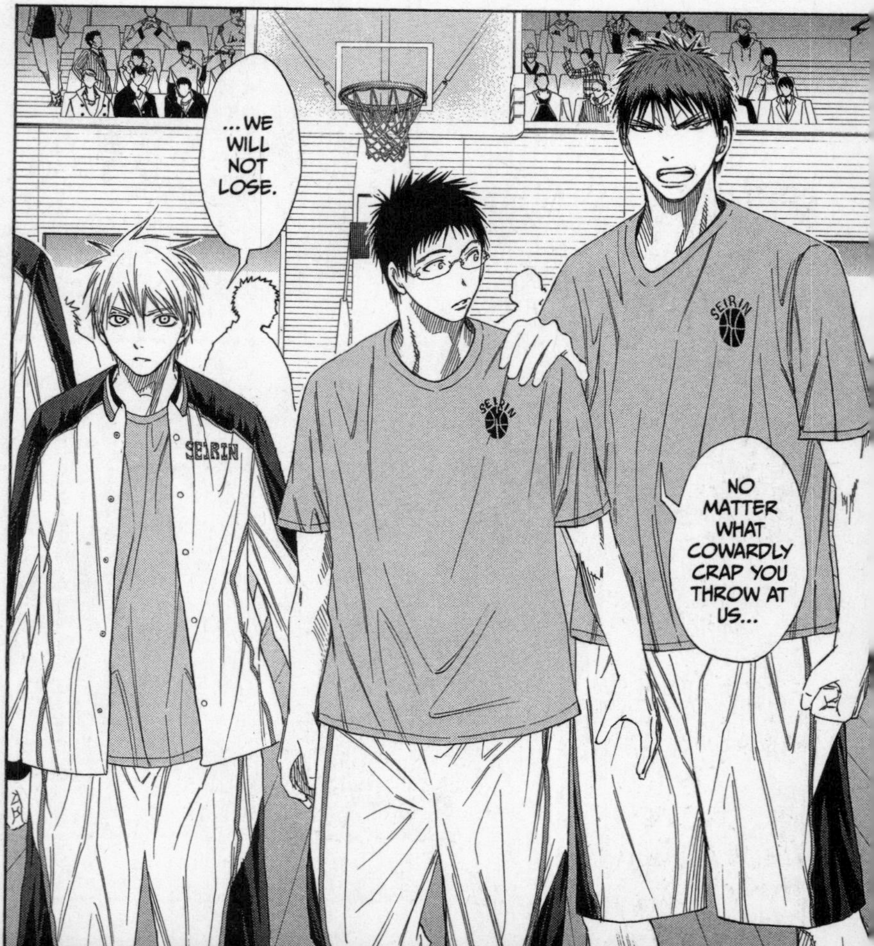
NO MATTER WHAT COWARDLY CRAP YOU THROW AT US...
...WE WILL NOT LOSE.

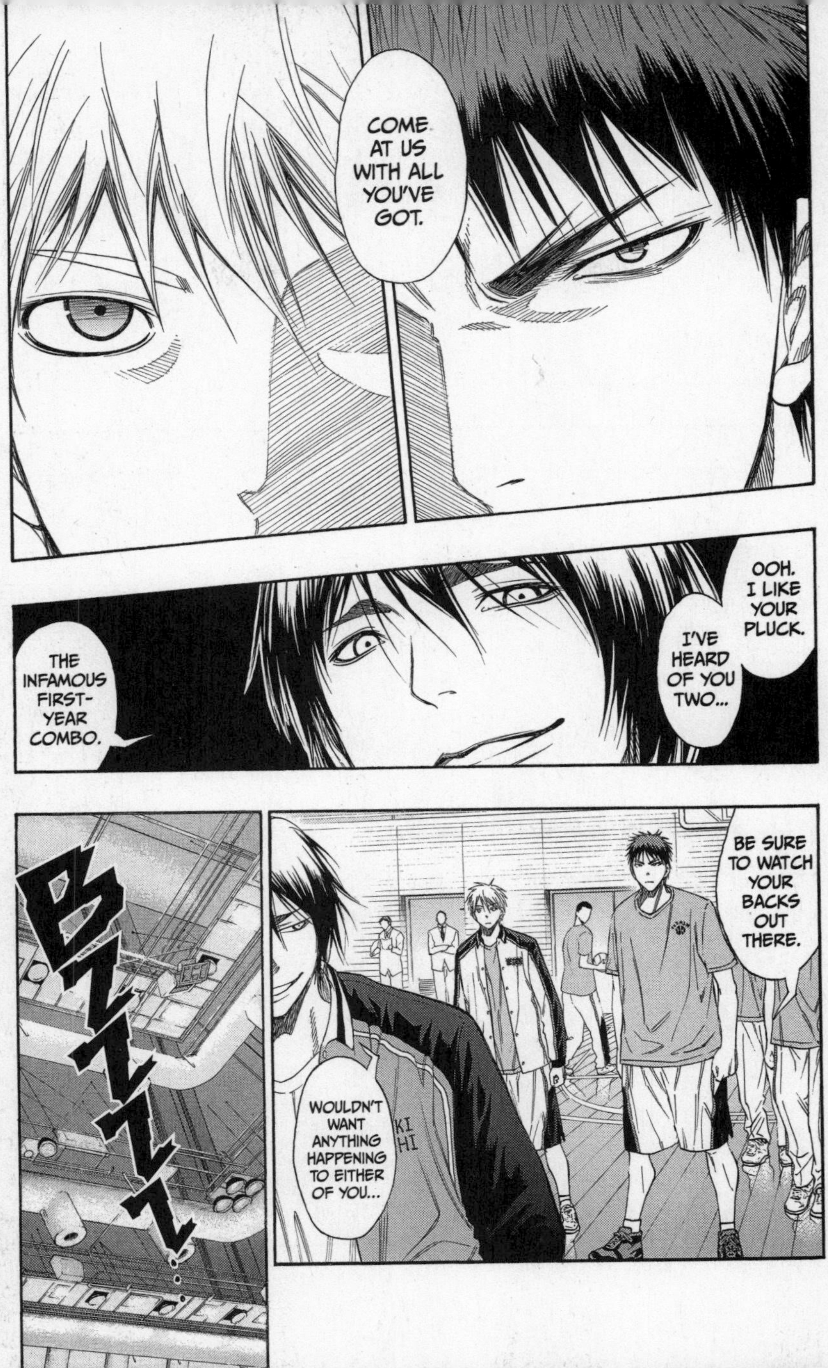
COME AT US WITH ALL YOU'VE GOT.
OOH. I LIKE YOUR PLUCK.
I'VE HEARD OF YOU TWO...
THE INFAMOUS FIRST-YEAR COMBO.
BE SURE TO WATCH YOUR BACKS OUT THERE.
WOULDN'T WANT ANYTHING HAPPENING TO EITHER OF YOU...
BZZZZZ...

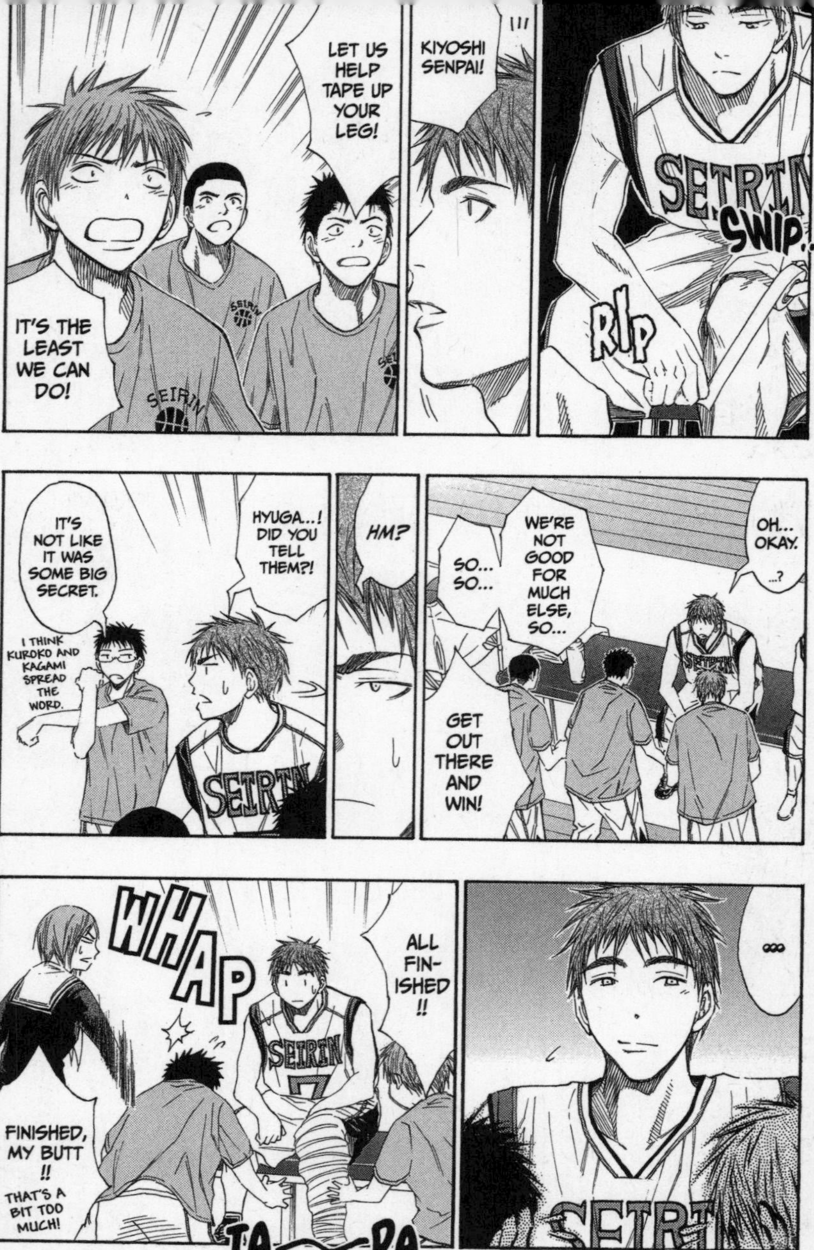
SWIP...
RIP
!!
KIYOSHI SENPAI!
LET US HELP TAPE UP YOUR LEG!
IT'S THE LEAST WE CAN DO!
OH... OKAY.
...?
WE'RE NOT GOOD FOR MUCH ELSE, SO...
SO... SO...
GET OUT THERE AND WIN!
HM?
HYUGA...! DID YOU TELL THEM?!
IT'S NOT LIKE IT WAS SOME BIG SECRET.
I THINK KUROKO AND KAGAMI SPREAD THE WORD.
...
ALL FIN-ISHED !!
WHAP
FINISHED, MY BUTT !!
THAT'S A BIT TOO MUCH!
TA—DA

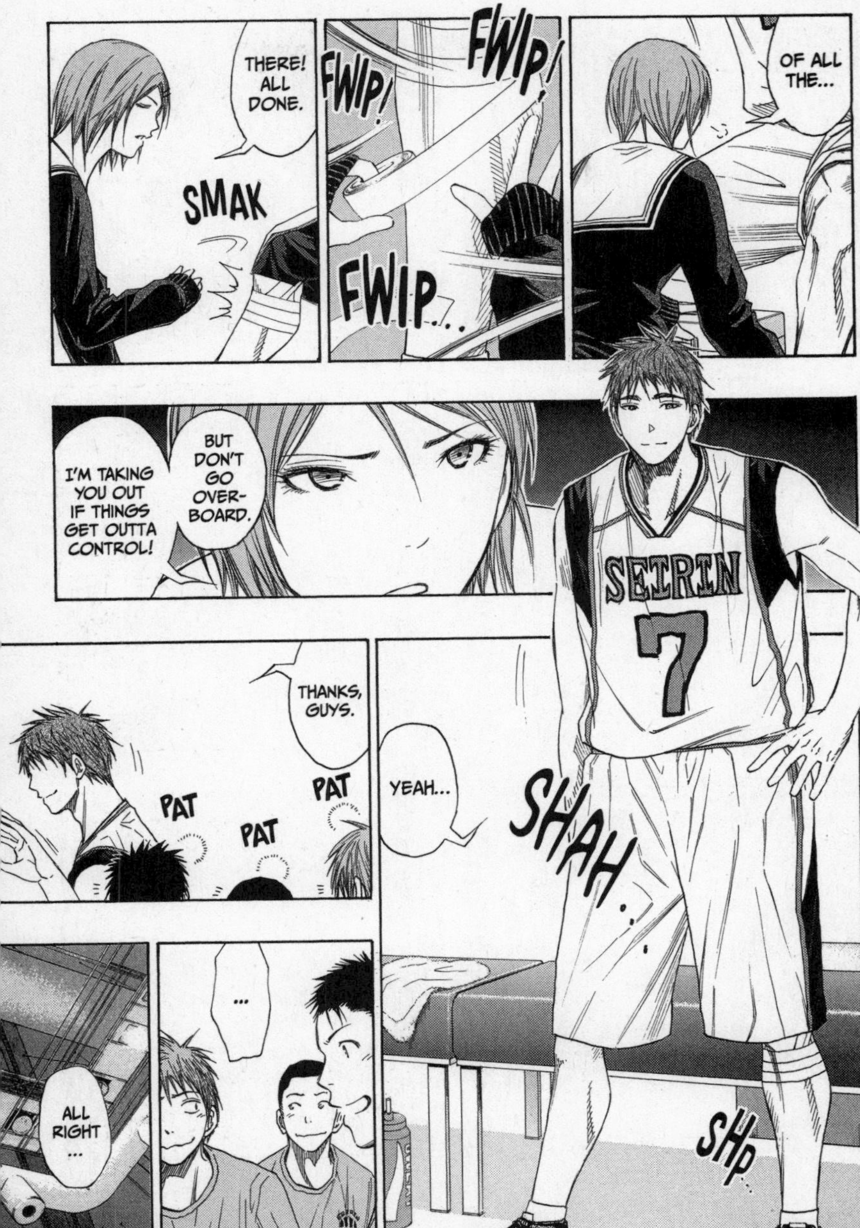
OF ALL THE...
FWIP!
FWIP!
FWIP...
THERE! ALL DONE.
SMAK
SHAH...
SHP...
BUT DON'T GO OVER-BOARD.
I'M TAKING YOU OUT IF THINGS GET OUTTA CONTROL!
YEAH...
THANKS, GUYS.
PAT
PAT
PAT
...
ALL RIGHT ...

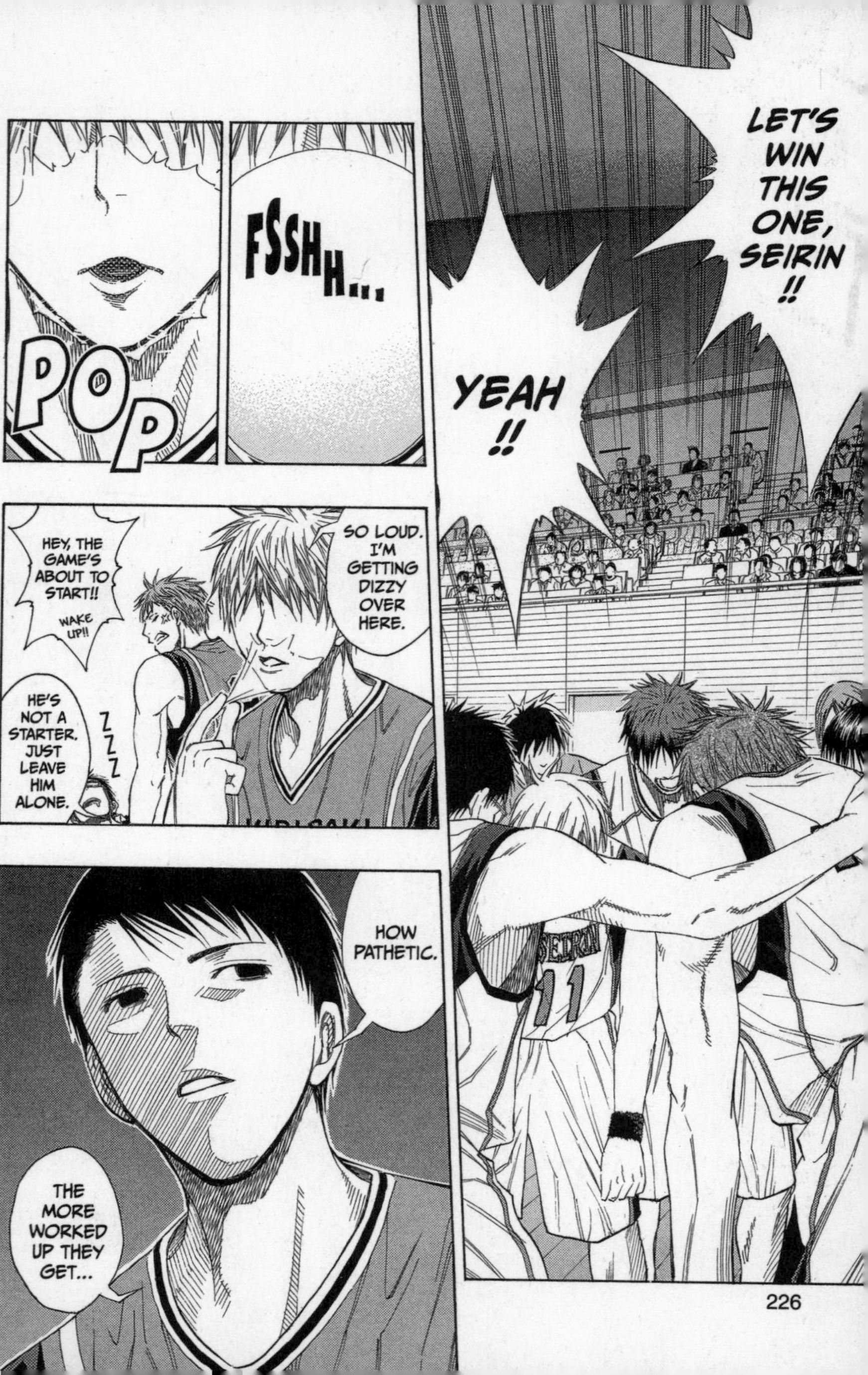
LET'S WIN THIS ONE, SEIRIN!!
YEAH!!
FSSHH...
POP
SO LOUD. I'M GETTING DIZZY OVER HERE.
HEY, THE GAME'S ABOUT TO START!!
WAKE UP!!
HE'S NOT A STARTER. JUST LEAVE HIM ALONE.
ZZZ
KIRISAKI
SEIRIN
HOW PATHETIC.
THE MORE WORKED UP THEY GET...

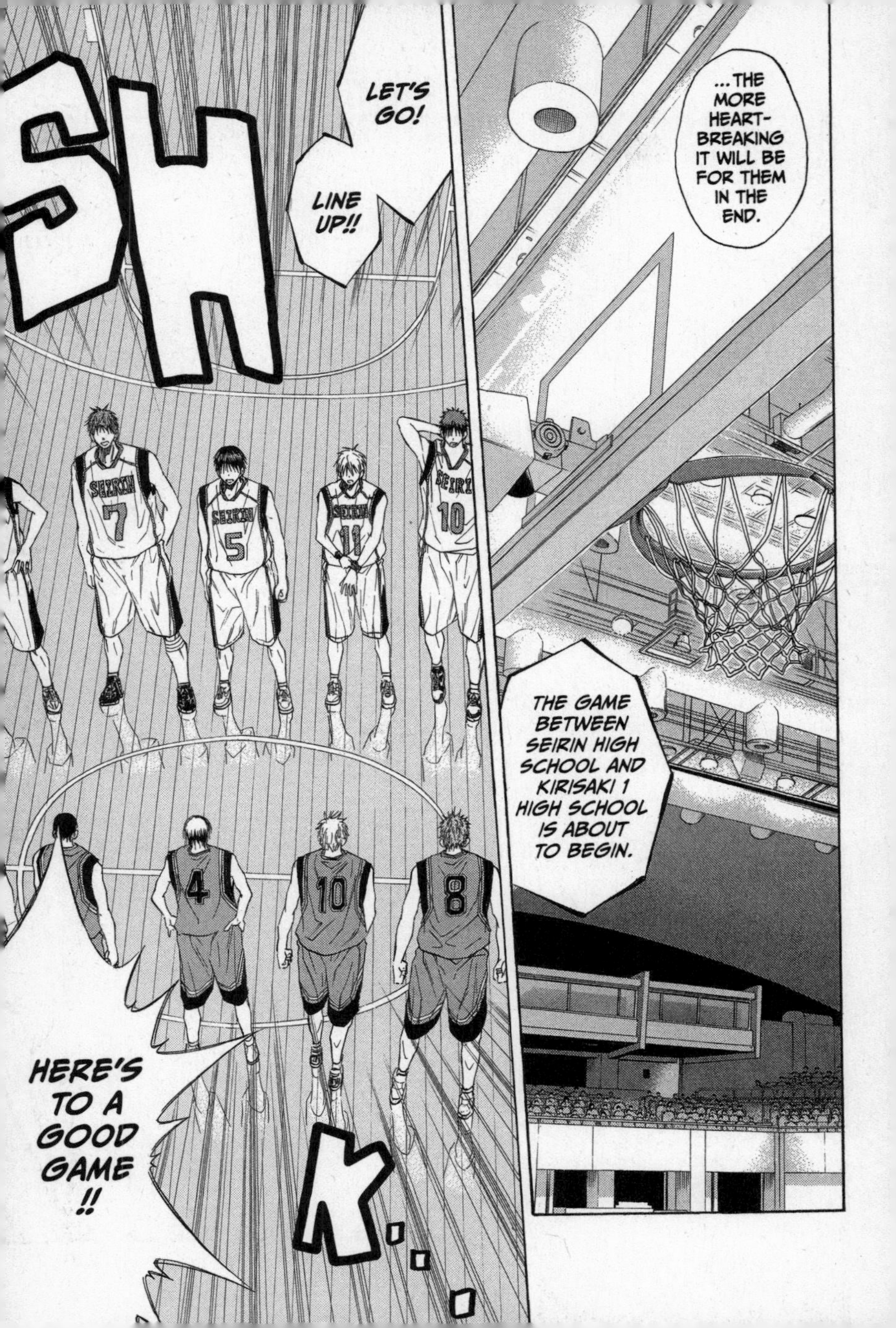
...THE MORE HEARTBREAKING IT WILL BE FOR THEM IN THE END.
THE GAME BETWEEN SEIRIN HIGH SCHOOL AND KIRISAKI 1 HIGH SCHOOL IS ABOUT TO BEGIN.
SH
LET'S GO!
LINE UP!!
HERE'S TO A GOOD GAME!!
K...

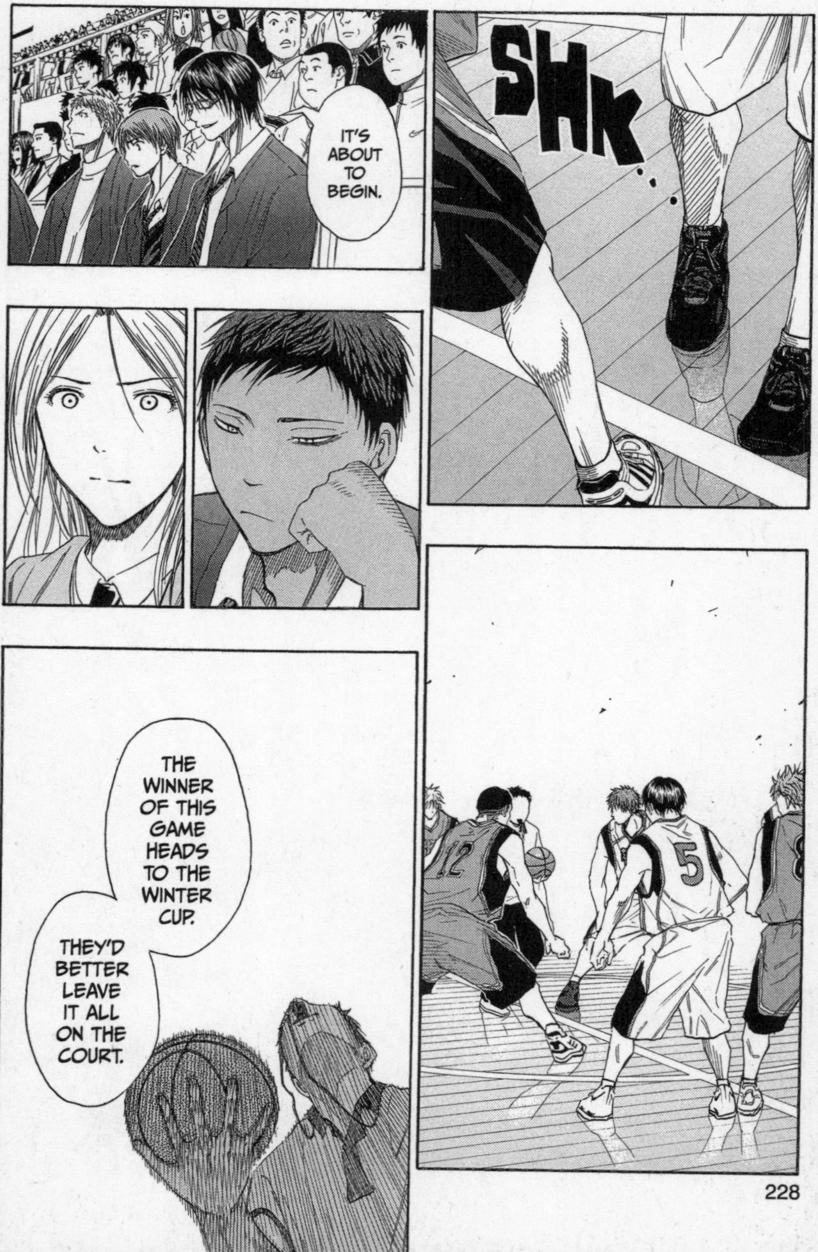
SHK...
IT'S ABOUT TO BEGIN.
THE WINNER OF THIS GAME HEADS TO THE WINTER CUP.
THEY'D BETTER LEAVE IT ALL ON THE COURT.

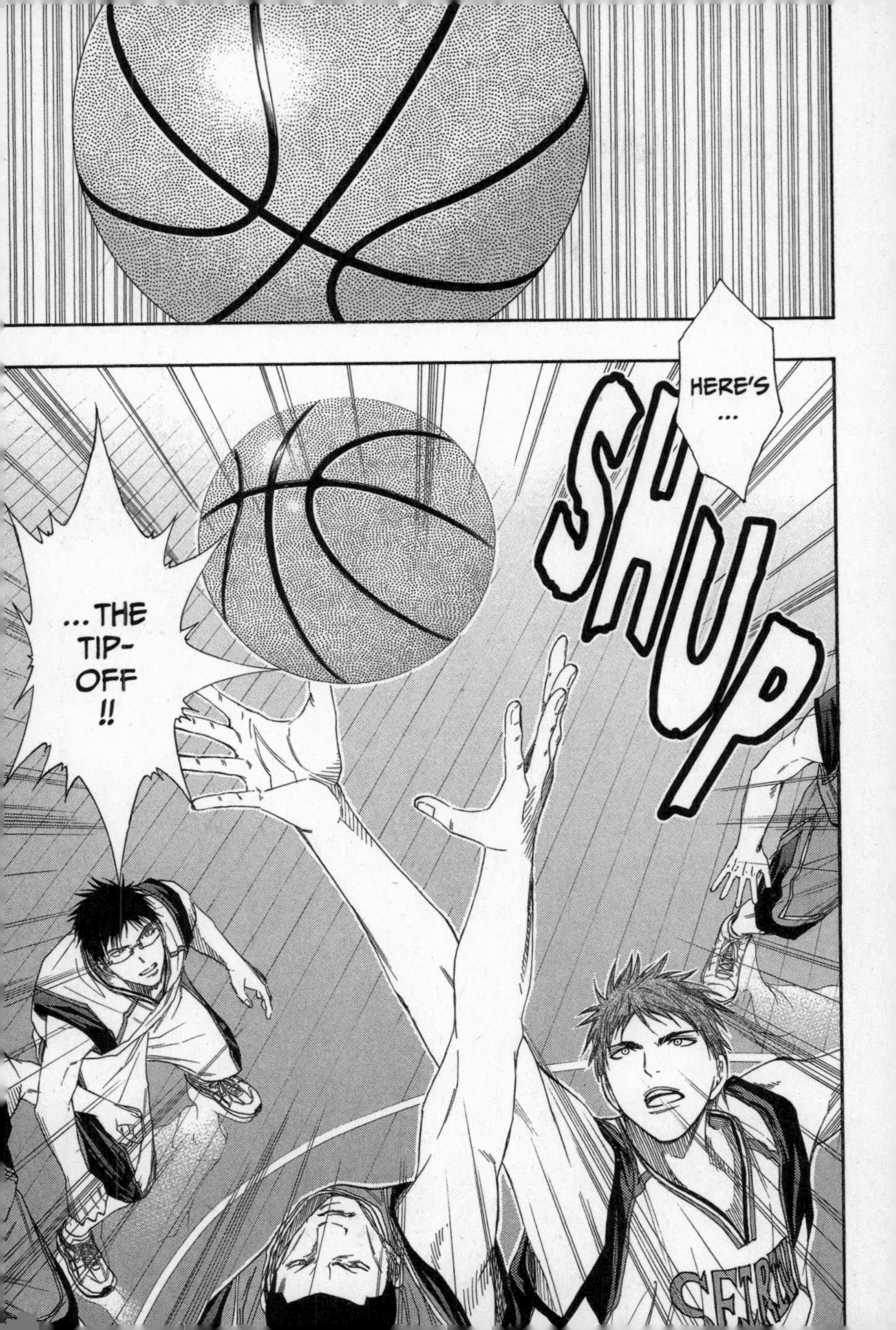
HERE'S ...
SHUP
... THE TIP-OFF !!

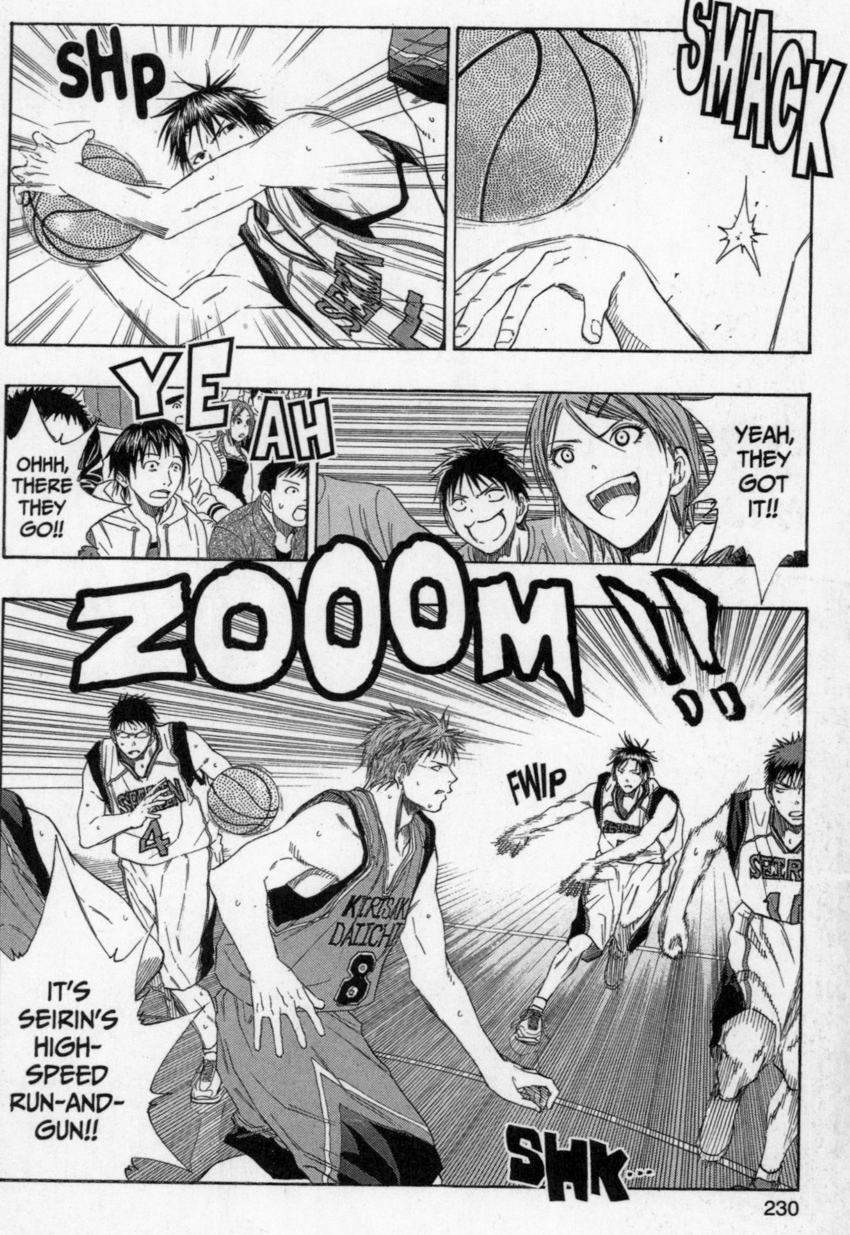

SMACK
SHP
YEAH, THEY GOT IT!!
YEAH
OHHH, THERE THEY GO!!
ZOOOM!!
FWIP
IT'S SEIRIN'S HIGH-SPEED RUN-AND-GUN!!
SHK...

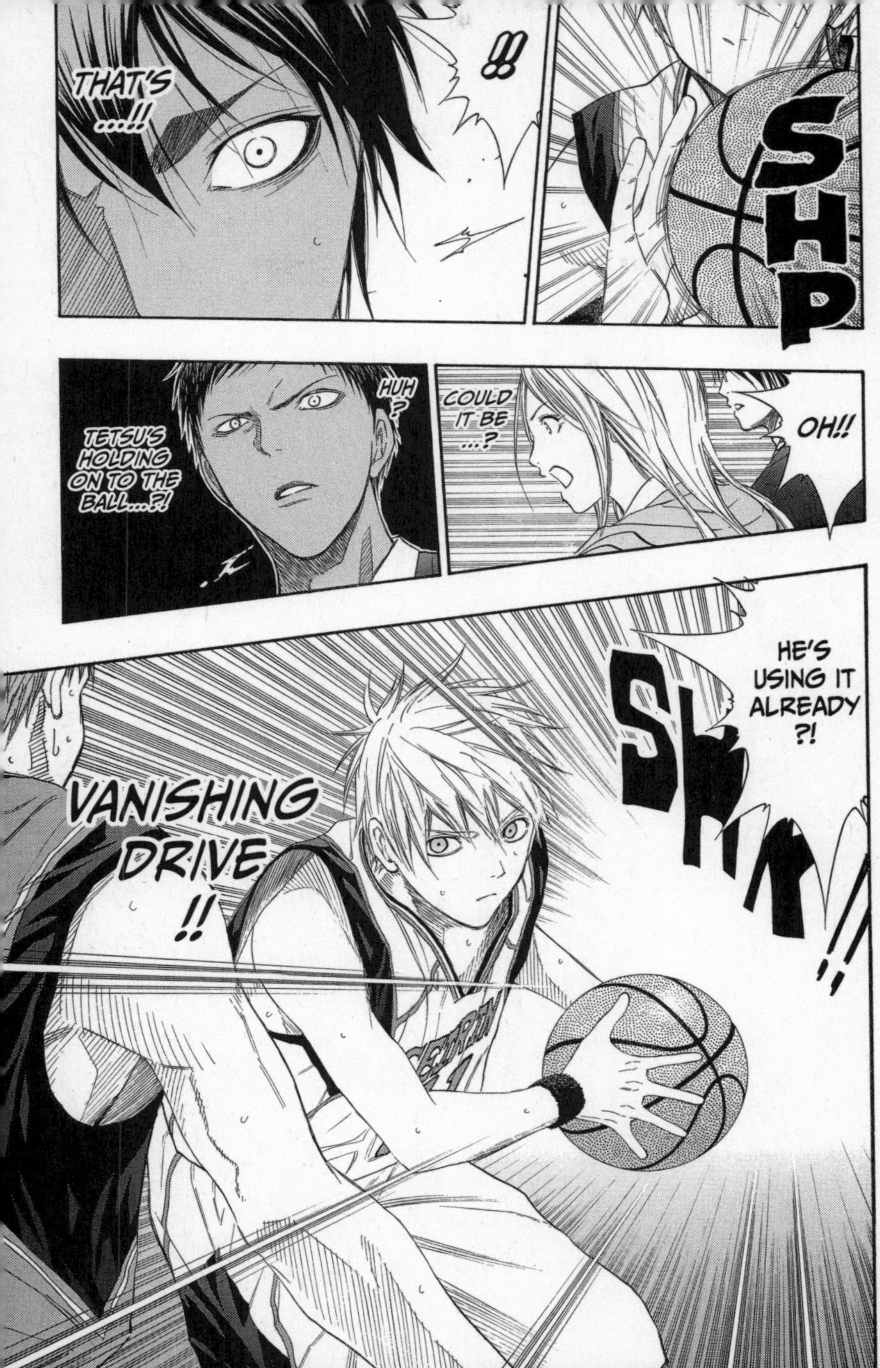
SHP
!!
THAT'S ...!!
OH!!
COULD IT BE ...?
HUH?
TETSU'S HOLDING ON TO THE BALL...?!
HE'S USING IT ALREADY ?!
SHIN!!
VANISHING DRIVE !!

KUROKO'S BASKETBALL BLOOPERS TAKE 2

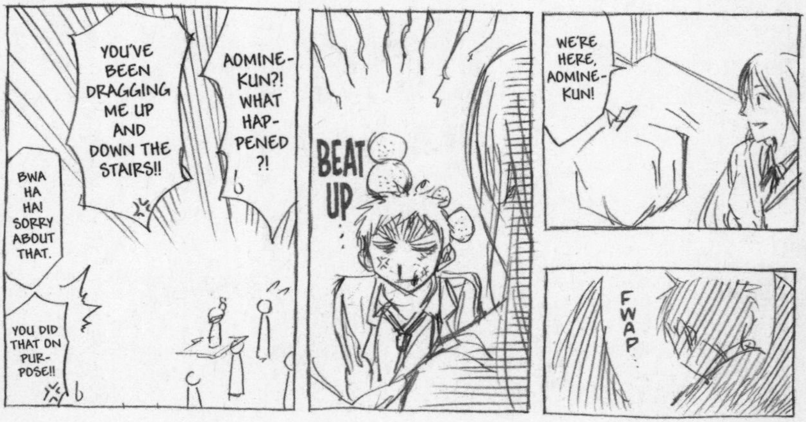
WE'RE HERE, AOMINE-KUN!
FWAP...
BEAT UP...
AOMINE-KUN?! WHAT HAPPENED?!
YOU'VE BEEN DRAGGING ME UP AND DOWN THE STAIRS!!
BWA HA HA! SORRY ABOUT THAT.
YOU DID THAT ON PURPOSE!!
DIE!!

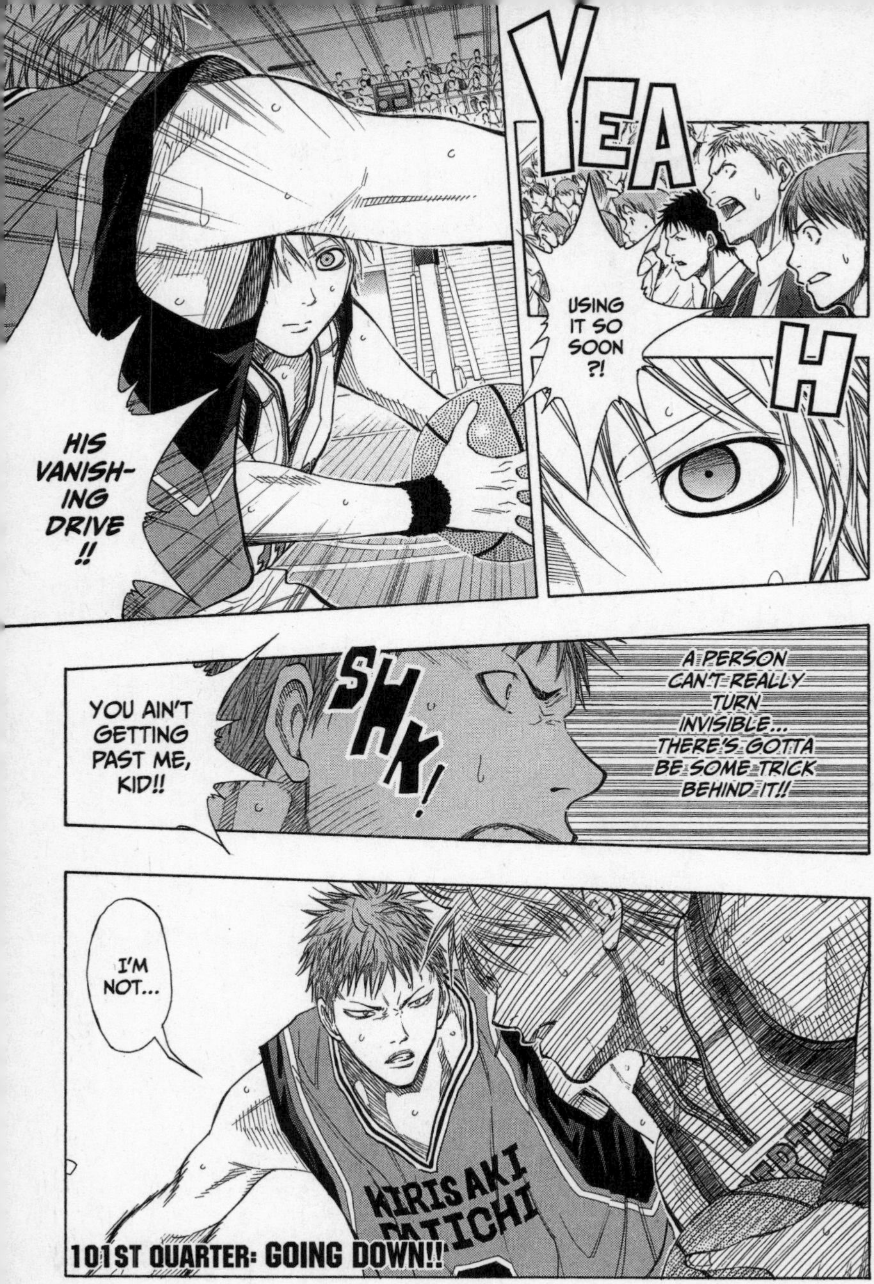
YEA
USING IT SO SOON?!
H
HIS VANISHING-ING DRIVE!!
A PERSON CAN'T REALLY TURN INVISIBLE... THERE'S GOTTA BE SOME TRICK BEHIND IT!!
SHK!
YOU AIN'T GETTING PAST ME, KID!!
I'M NOT...
KIRISAKI DAIICHI
101ST QUARTER: GOING DOWN!!

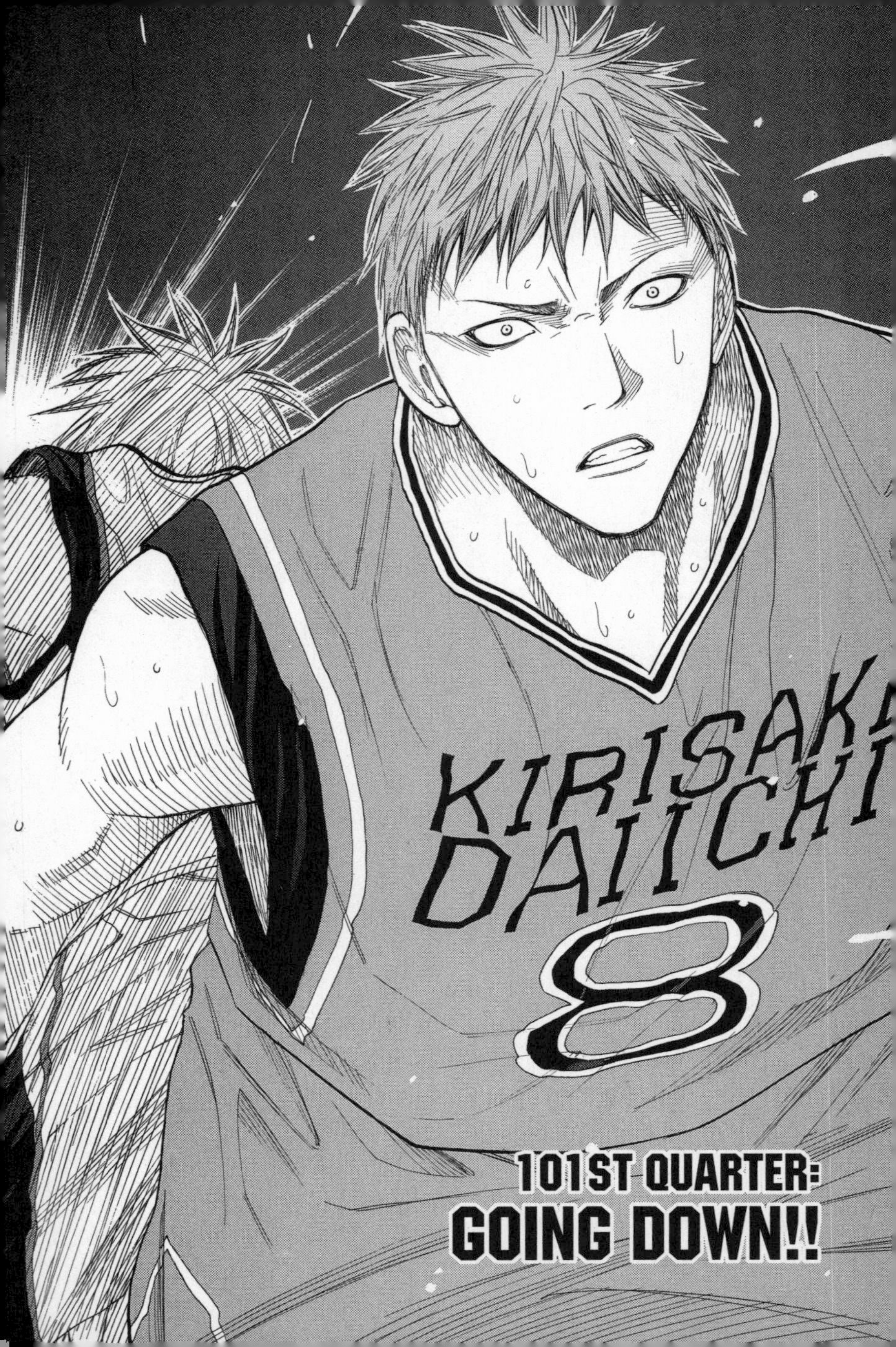
KIRISAKI DAIICHI
8
101ST QUARTER:
GOING DOWN!!

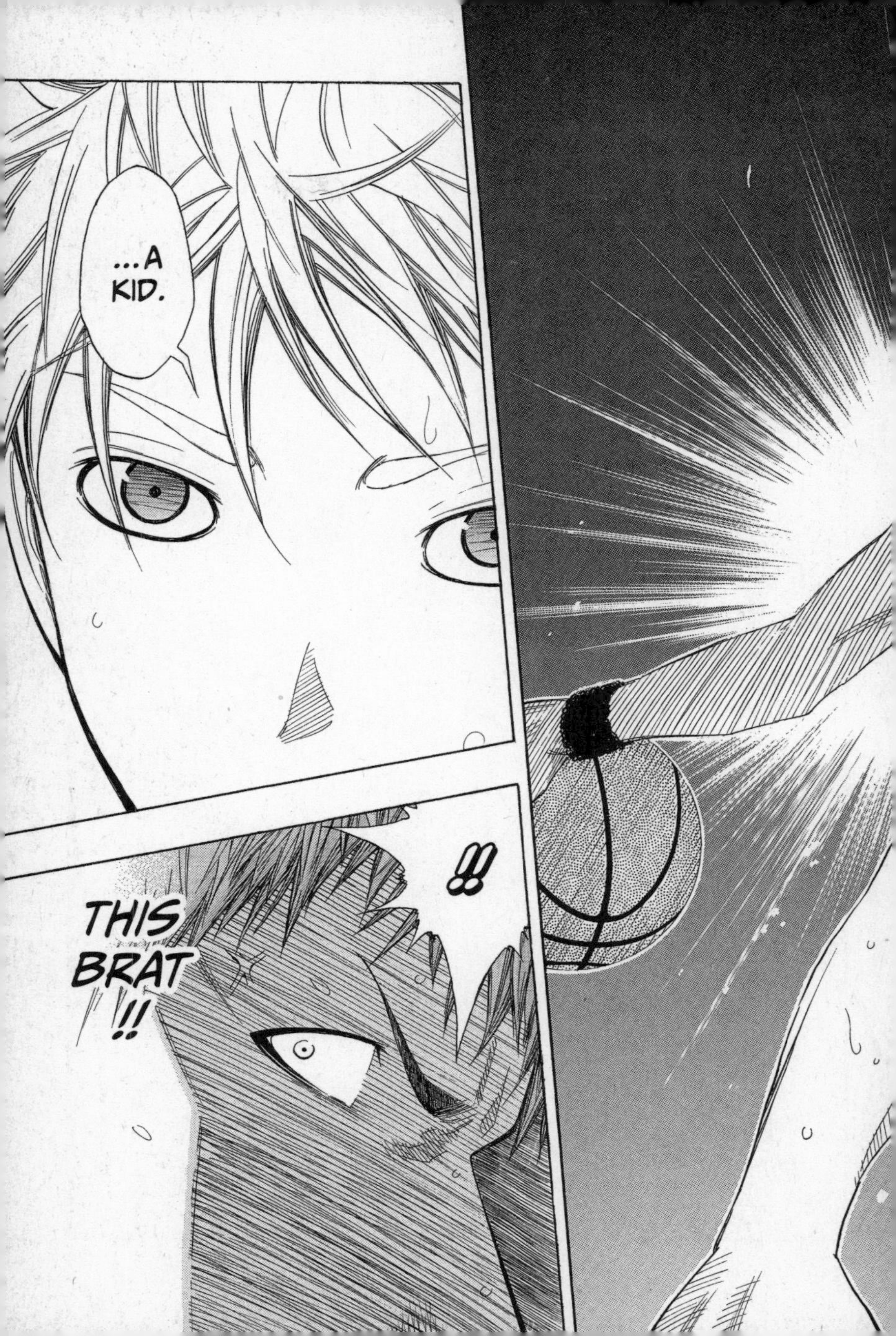
...A KID.
!!
THIS BRAT !!

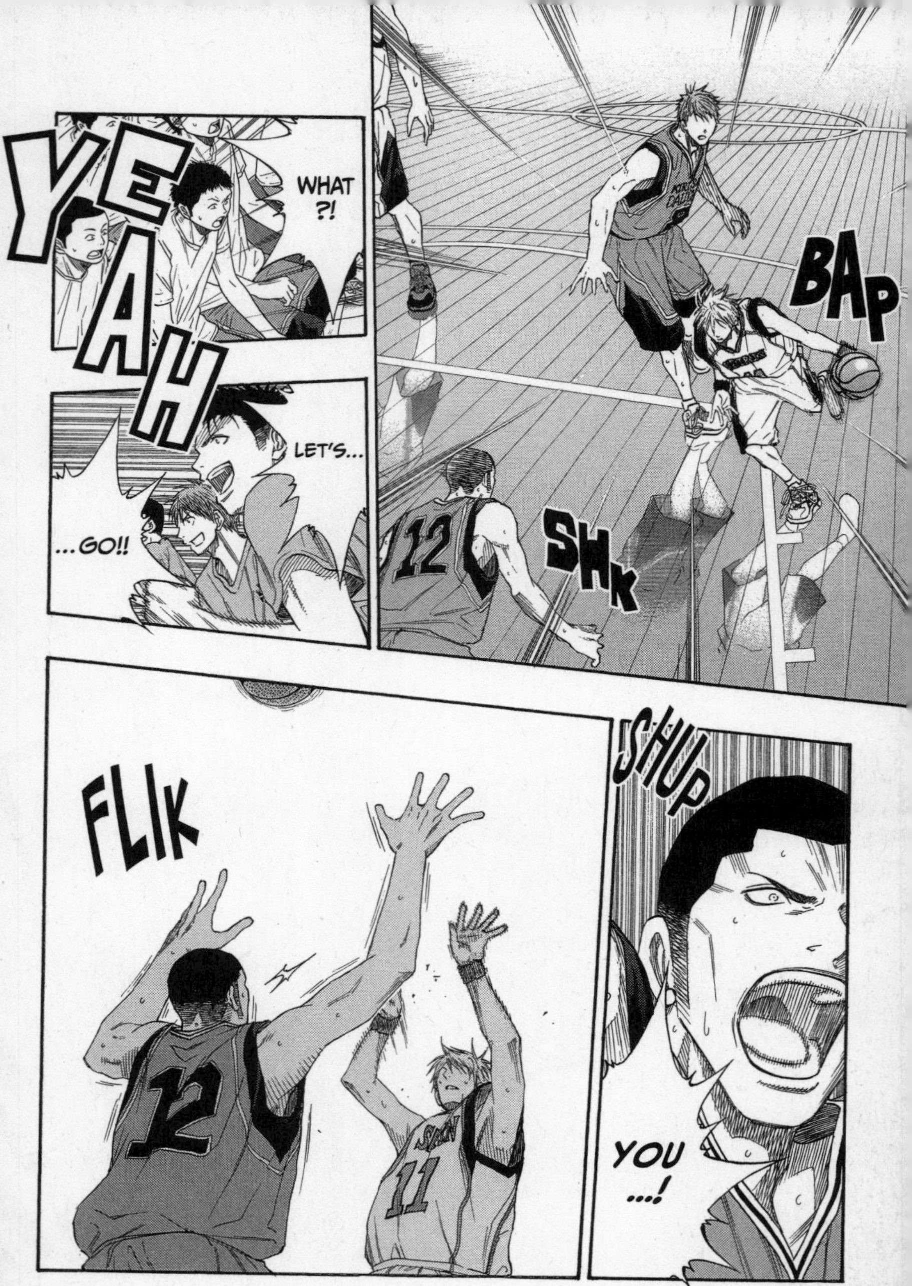
BAP
SHK
YEAH
WHAT ?!
LET'S...
...GO!!
SHUP
YOU ...!
FLIK

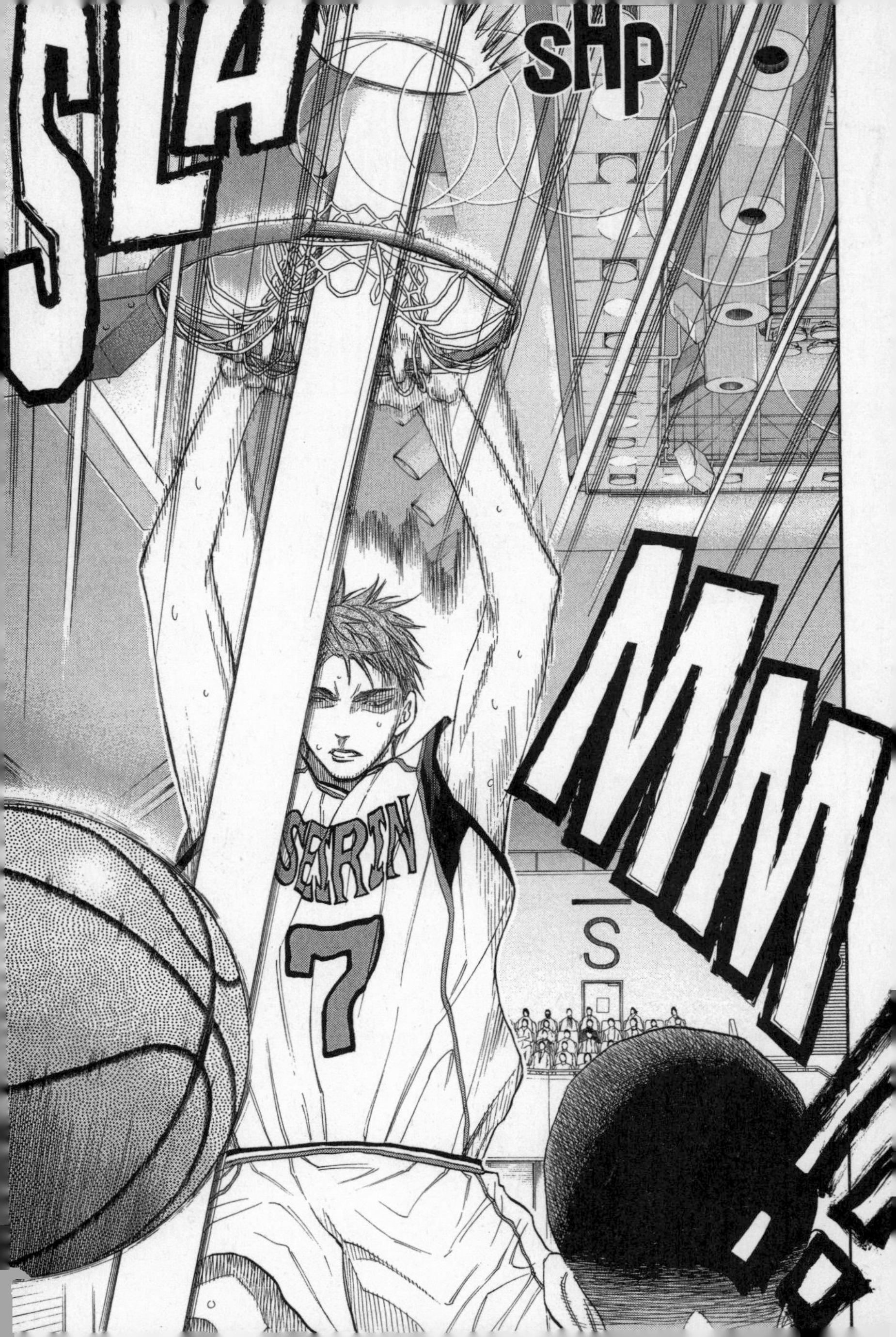
SLA
SHP
MM
SEIRIN
7

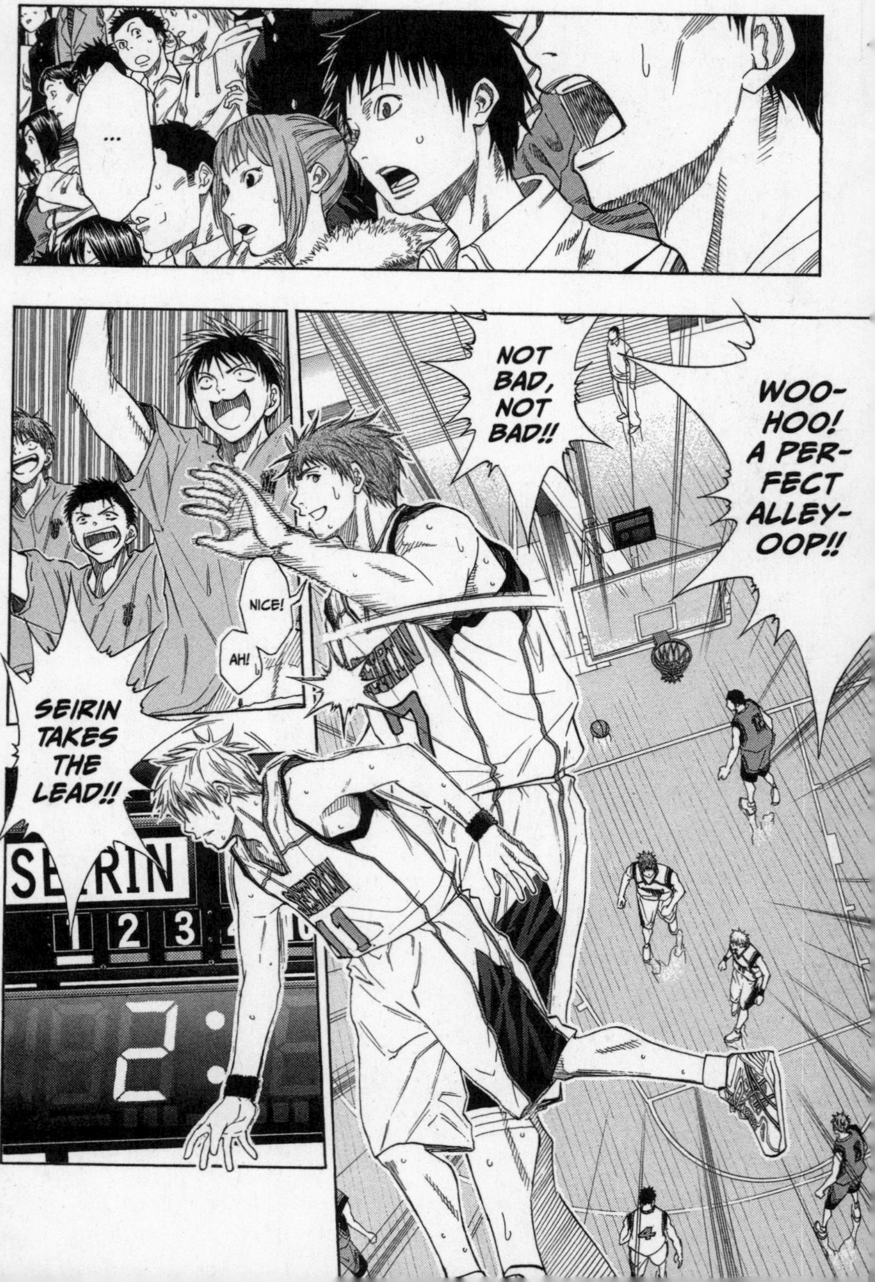
...
WOO-HOO! A PERFECT ALLEY-OOP!!
NOT BAD, NOT BAD!!
NICE!
AH!
SEIRIN TAKES THE LEAD!!
SEIRIN
1 2 3

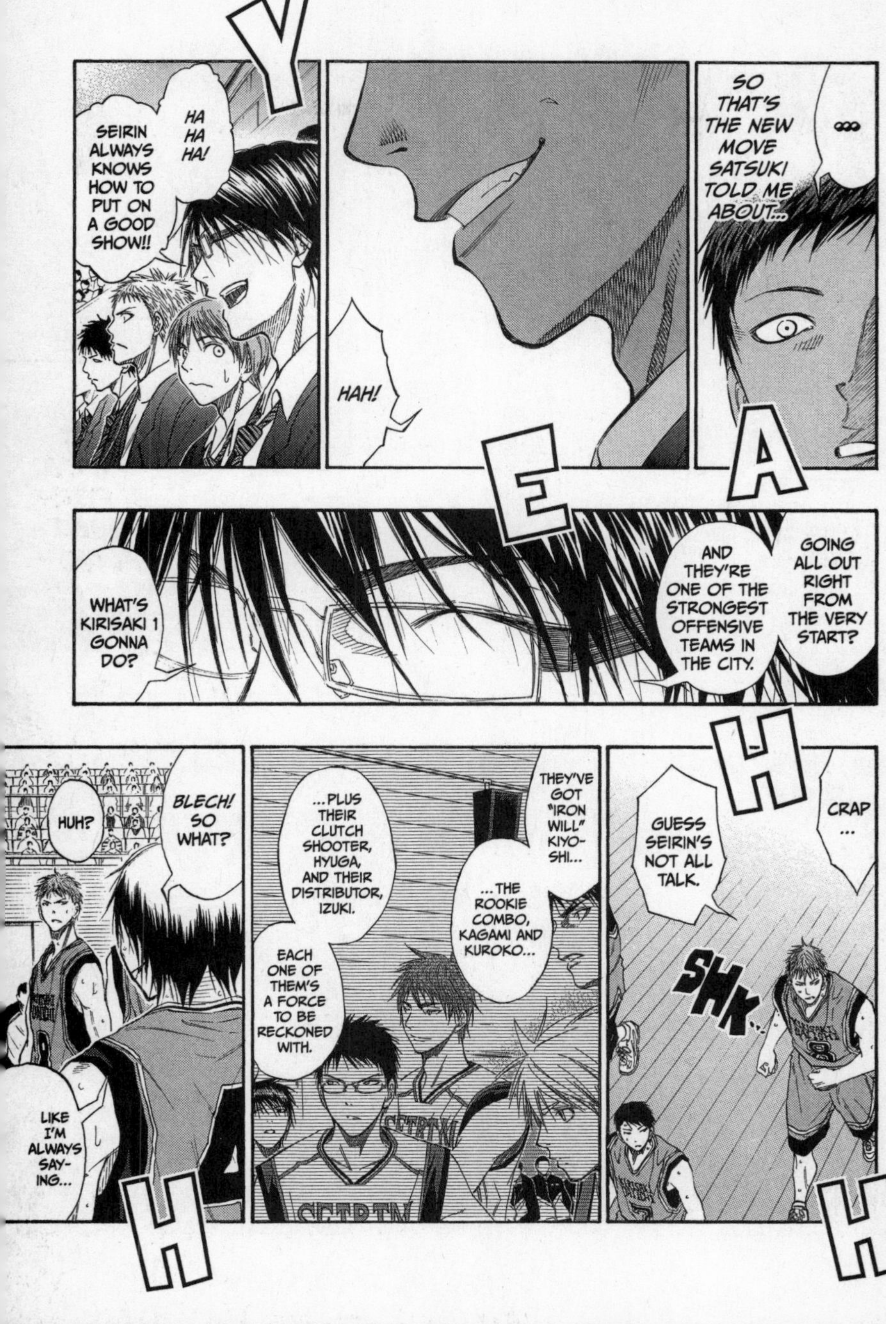
Y
...
SO THAT'S THE NEW MOVE SATSUKI TOLD ME ABOUT...
HAH!
HA HA HA!
SEIRIN ALWAYS KNOWS HOW TO PUT ON A GOOD SHOW!!
E
A
GOING ALL OUT RIGHT FROM THE VERY START?
AND THEY'RE ONE OF THE STRONGEST OFFENSIVE TEAMS IN THE CITY.
WHAT'S KIRISAKI 1 GONNA DO?
H
CRAP...
GUESS SEIRIN'S NOT ALL TALK.
SHK...
H
THEY'VE GOT "IRON WILL" KIYOSHI...
...THE ROOKIE COMBO, KAGAMI AND KUROKO...
...PLUS THEIR CLUTCH SHOOTER, HYUGA, AND THEIR DISTRIBUTOR, IZUKI.
EACH ONE OF THEM'S A FORCE TO BE RECKONED WITH.
BLECH! SO WHAT?
HUH?
LIKE I'M ALWAYS SAYING...
H

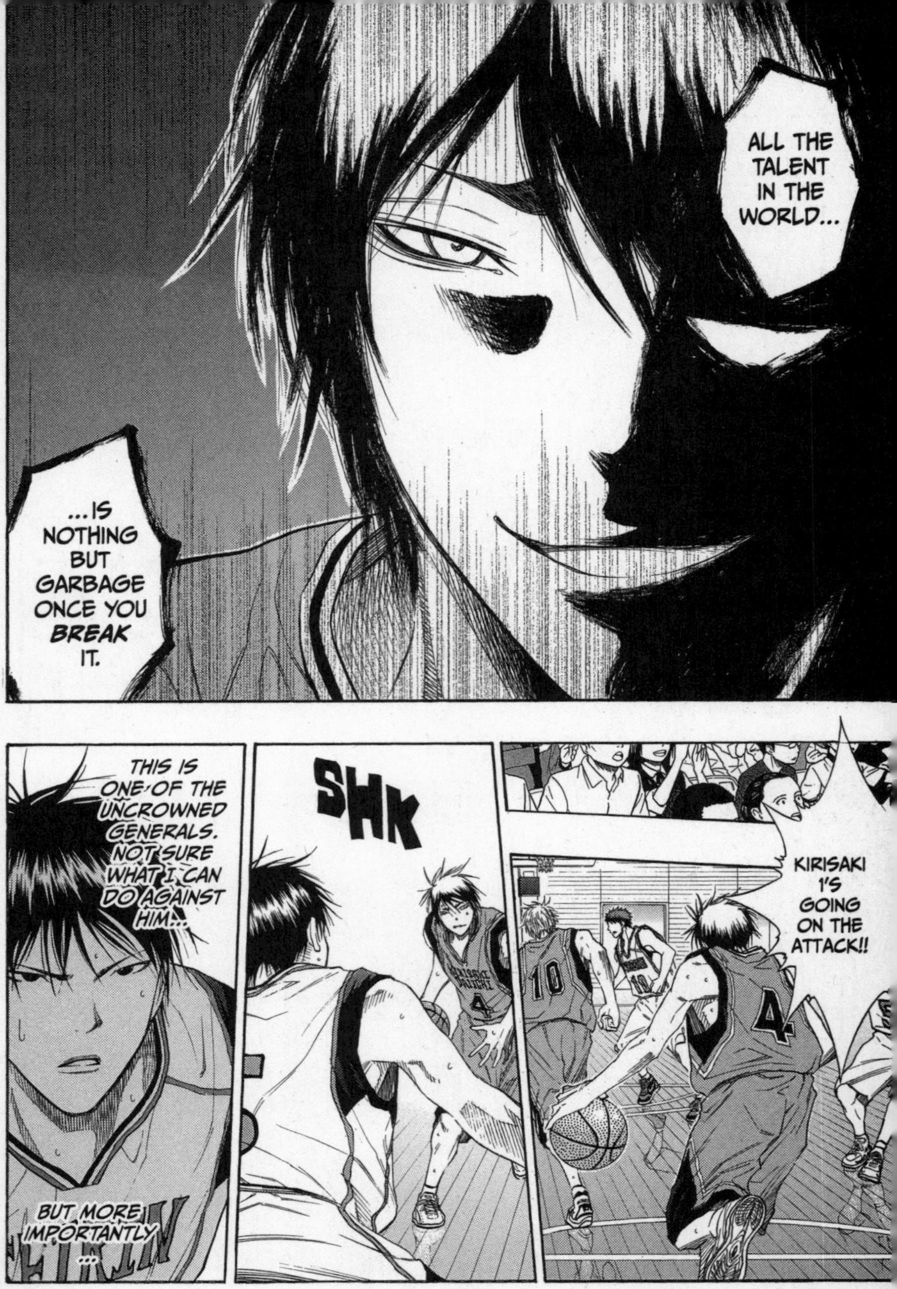
ALL THE TALENT IN THE WORLD...
...IS NOTHING BUT GARBAGE ONCE YOU ***BREAK*** IT.
KIRISAKI IS GOING ON THE ATTACK!!
SHK
THIS IS ONE OF THE UNCROWNED GENERALS. NOT SURE WHAT I CAN DO AGAINST HIM...
BUT MORE IMPORTANTLY...

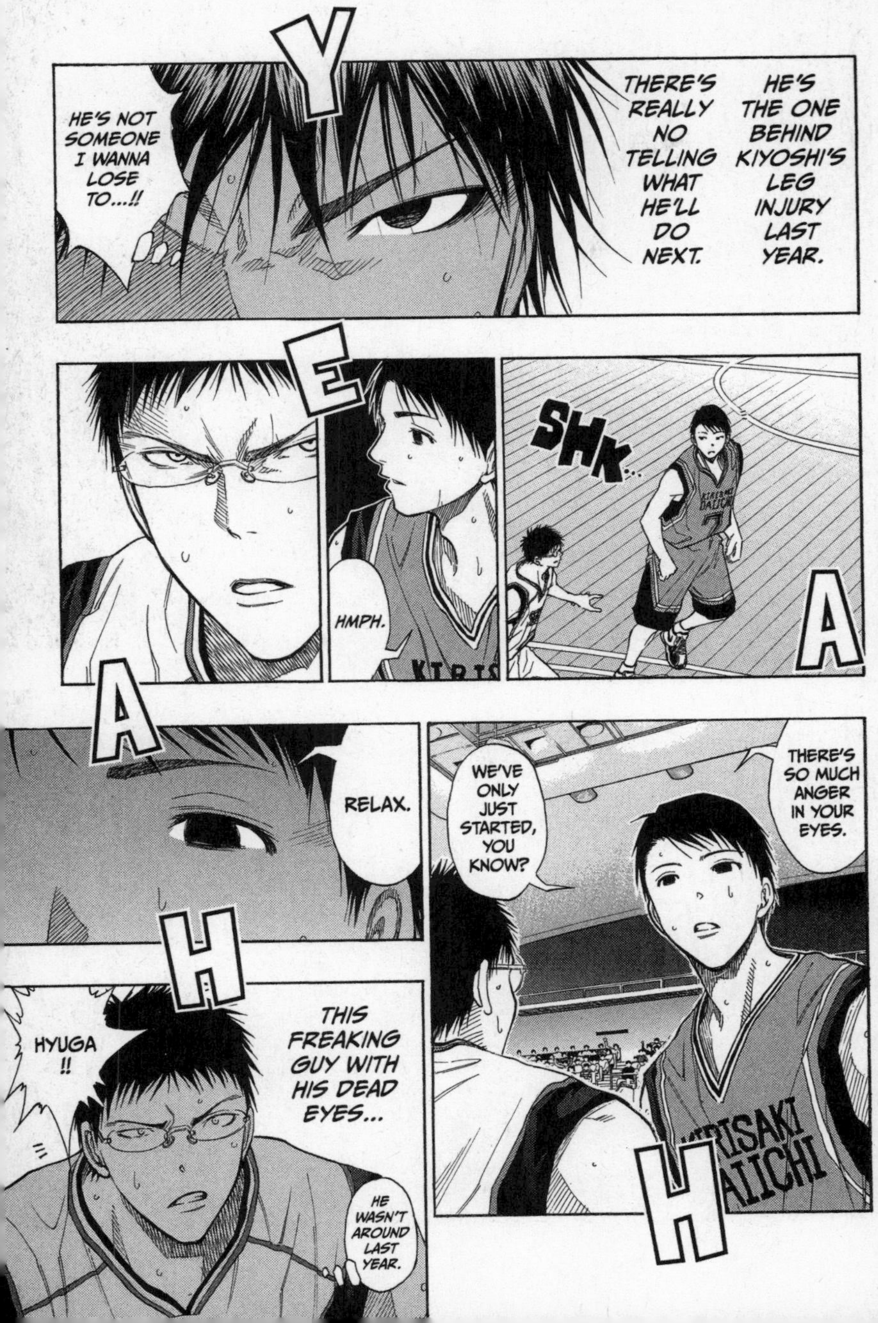
Y
HE'S THE ONE BEHIND KIYOSHI'S LEG INJURY LAST YEAR.
THERE'S REALLY NO TELLING WHAT HE'LL DO NEXT.
HE'S NOT SOMEONE I WANNA LOSE TO...!!
SHK...
A
HMPH.
E
THERE'S SO MUCH ANGER IN YOUR EYES.
WE'VE ONLY JUST STARTED, YOU KNOW?
H
A
RELAX.
H
THIS FREAKING GUY WITH HIS DEAD EYES...
HYUGA !!
HE WASN'T AROUND LAST YEAR.

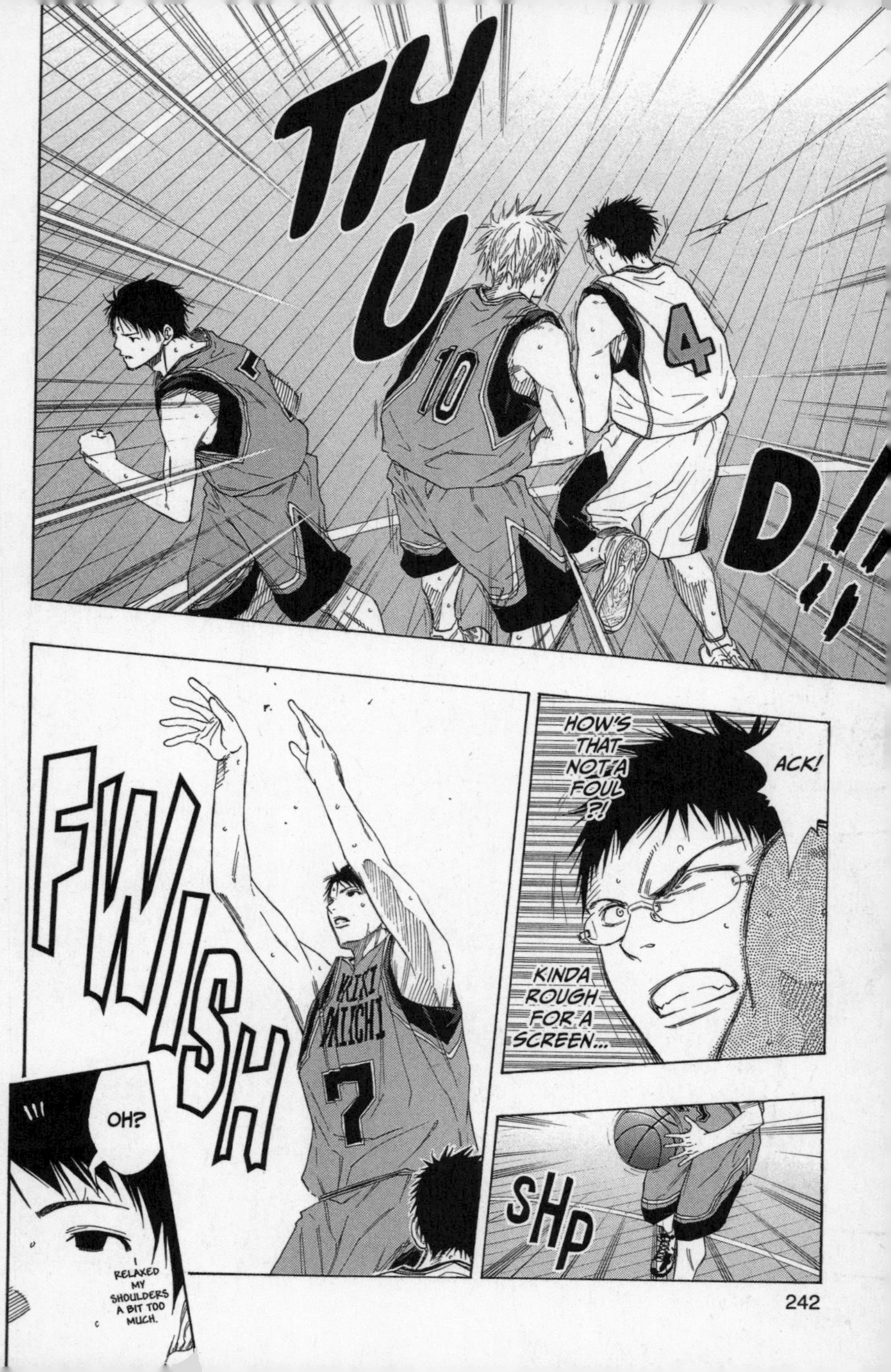
THUD!!
ACK!
HOW'S THAT NOT A FOUL?!
KINDA ROUGH FOR A SCREEN...
SHP
FWISH
OH?
I RELAXED MY SHOULDERS A BIT TOO MUCH.

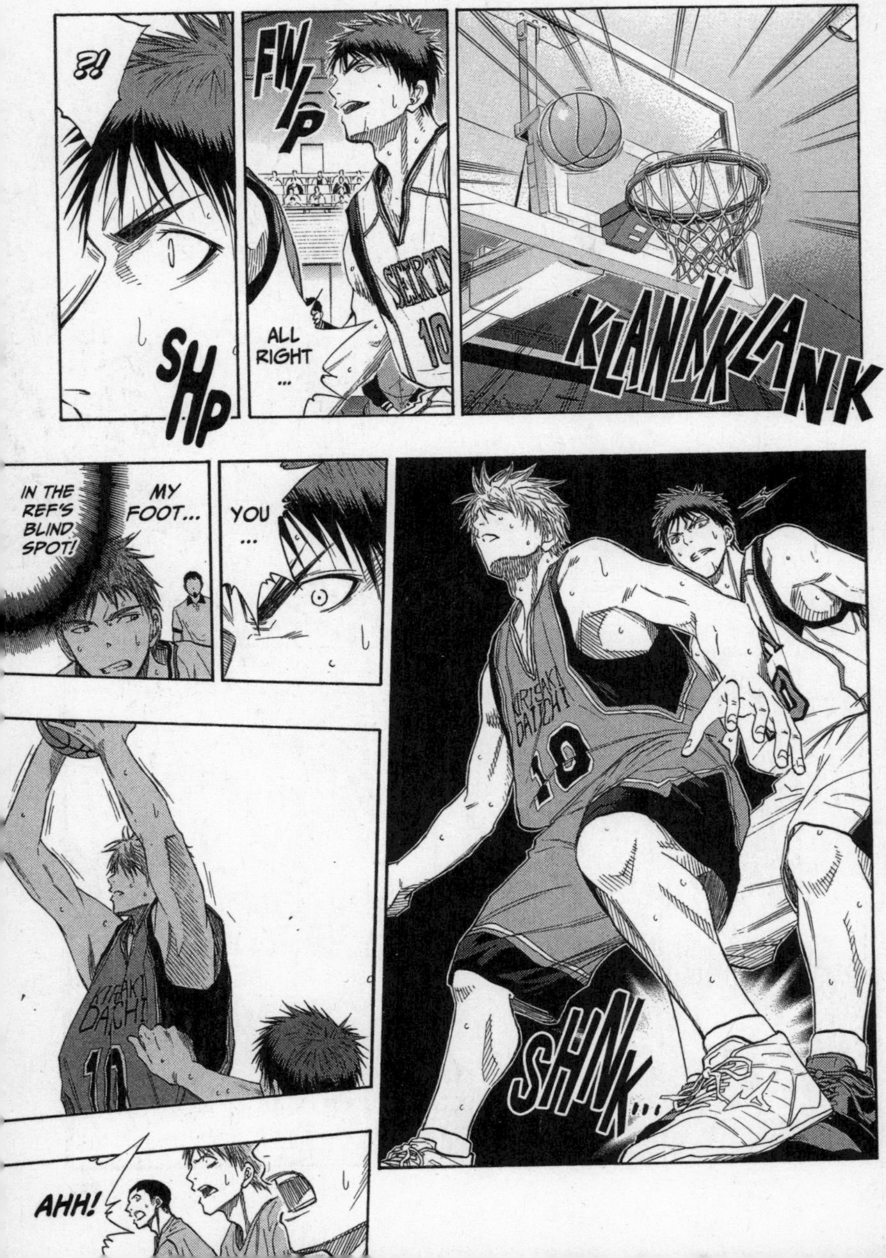
KLANK
KLANK
FWIP
ALL RIGHT ...
?!
SHP
SHNK...
YOU ...
MY FOOT...
IN THE REF'S BLIND SPOT!
AHH!

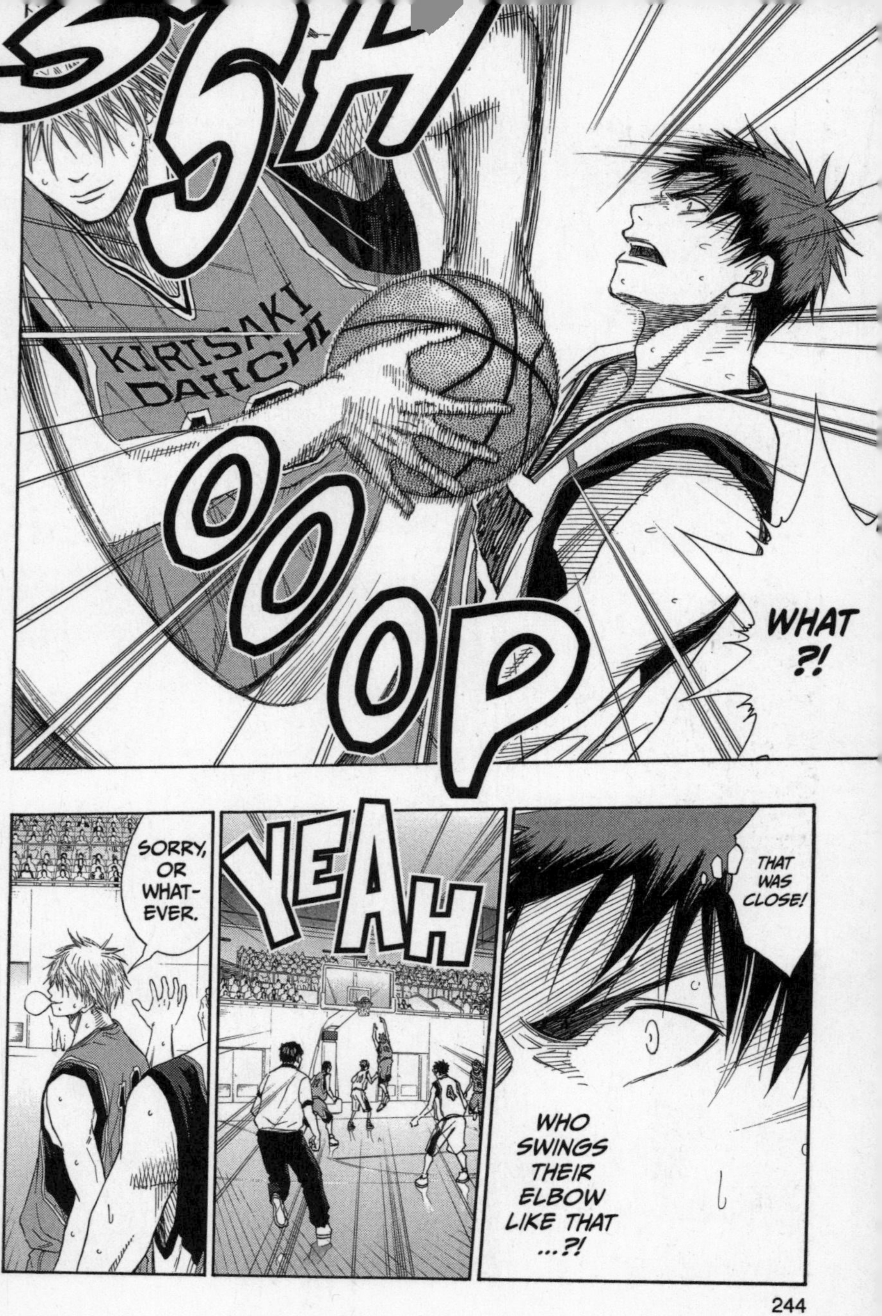
OOOOP
WHAT ?!
THAT WAS CLOSE!
WHO SWINGS THEIR ELBOW LIKE THAT ...?!
YEAH
SORRY, OR WHAT-EVER.

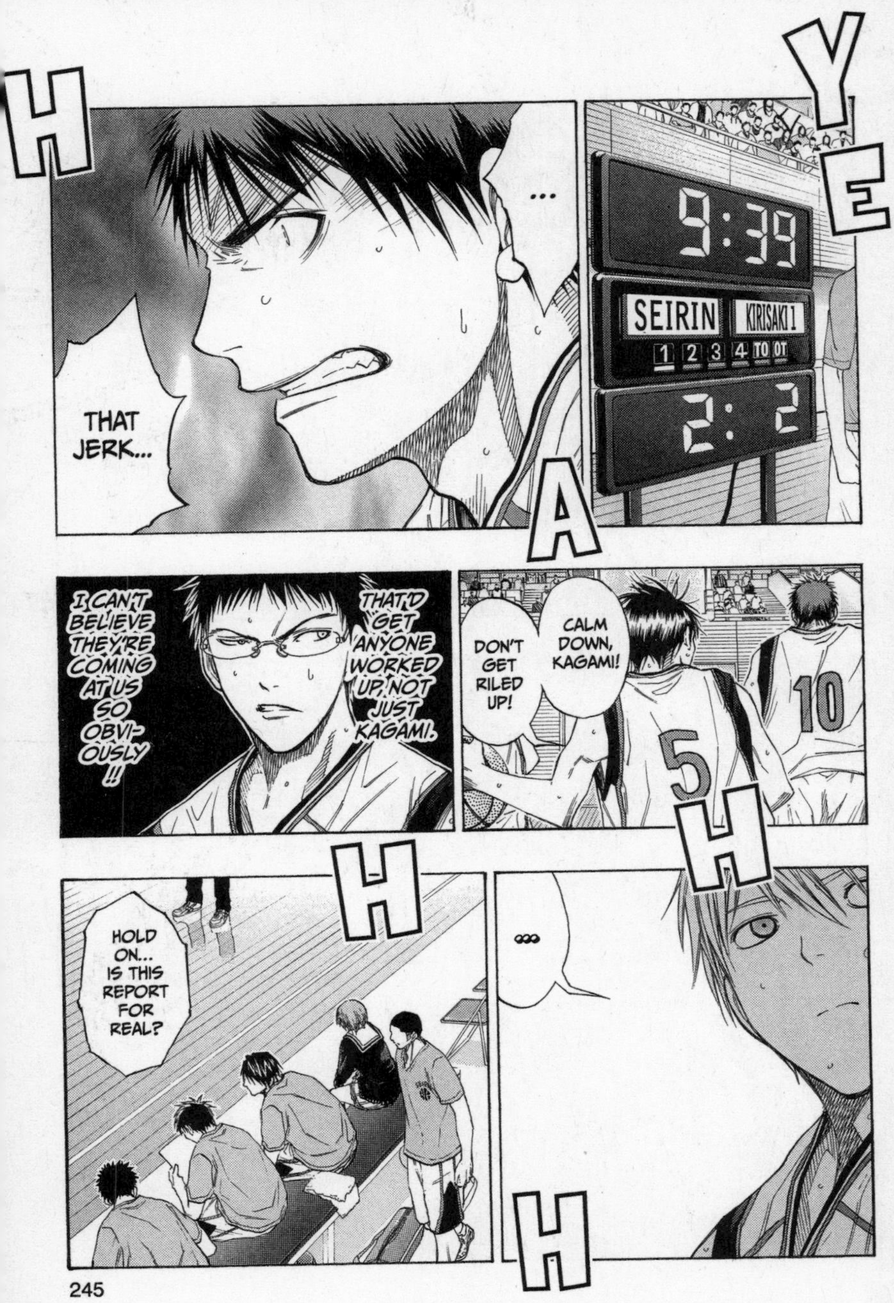
HYEAHHH
9:39
SEIRIN
KIRISAKI 1
1 2 3 4 TO OT
2: 2
...
THAT JERK...
CALM DOWN, KAGAMI!
DON'T GET RILED UP!
THAT'D GET ANYONE WORKED UP, NOT JUST KAGAMI.
I CAN'T BELIEVE THEY'RE COMING AT US SO OBVIOUSLY!!
...
HOLD ON... IS THIS REPORT FOR REAL?

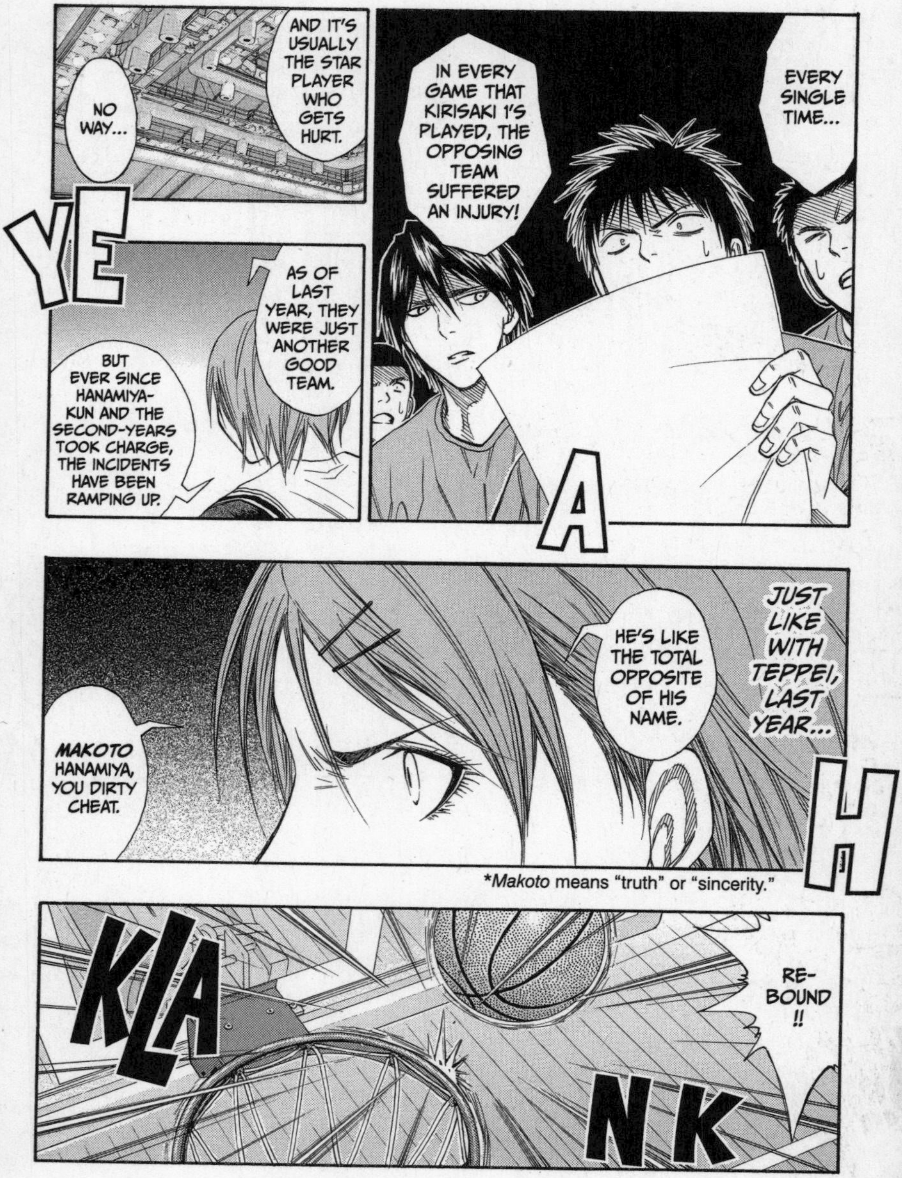
EVERY SINGLE TIME...
IN EVERY GAME THAT KIRISAKI 1'S PLAYED, THE OPPOSING TEAM SUFFERED AN INJURY!
AND IT'S USUALLY THE STAR PLAYER WHO GETS HURT.
NO WAY...
AS OF LAST YEAR, THEY WERE JUST ANOTHER GOOD TEAM.
BUT EVER SINCE HANAMIYA-KUN AND THE SECOND-YEARS TOOK CHARGE, THE INCIDENTS HAVE BEEN RAMPING UP.
YE
A
H
JUST LIKE WITH TEPPEI, LAST YEAR...
HE'S LIKE THE TOTAL OPPOSITE OF HIS NAME.
MAKOTO HANAMIYA, YOU DIRTY CHEAT.
REBOUND !!
KLA
NK

*Makoto means "truth" or "sincerity."

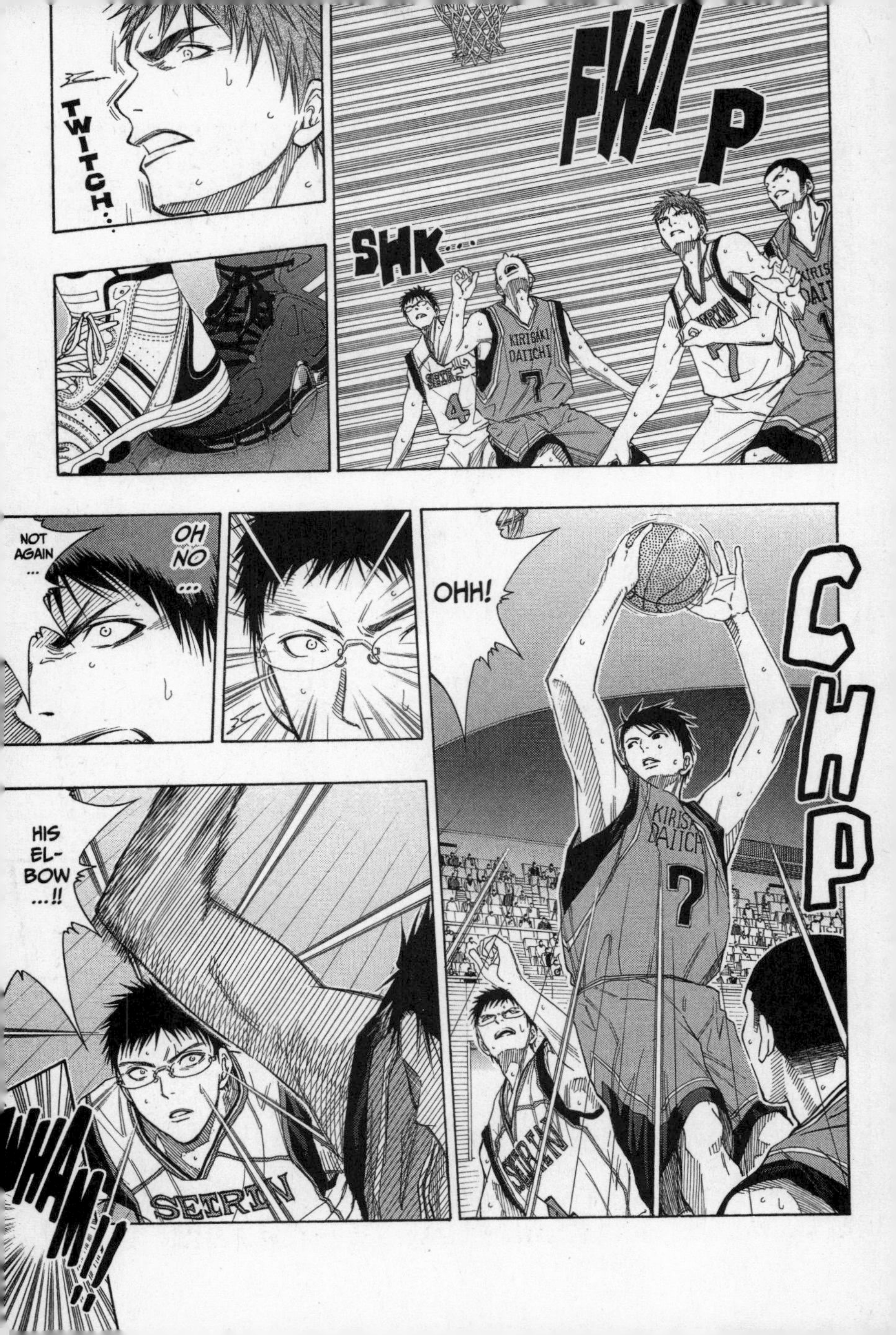

FWIP
SHK...
TWITCH...
CHP
OHH!
OH NO...
NOT AGAIN...
HIS EL-BOW...!!
WHAM!!

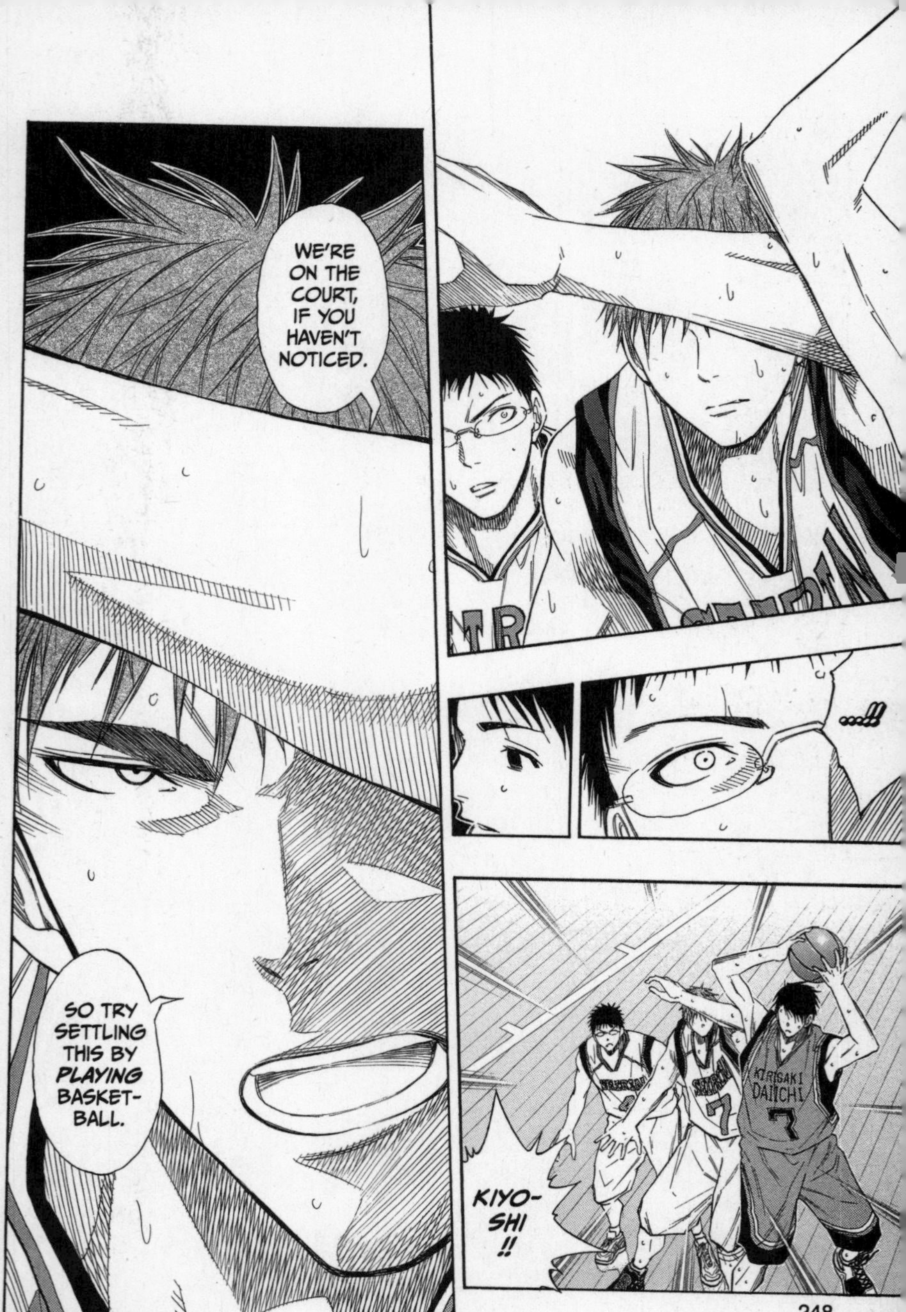

...!!
KIYO-SHI!!
WE'RE ON THE COURT, IF YOU HAVEN'T NOTICED.
SO TRY SETTLING THIS BY *PLAYING* BASKET-BALL.

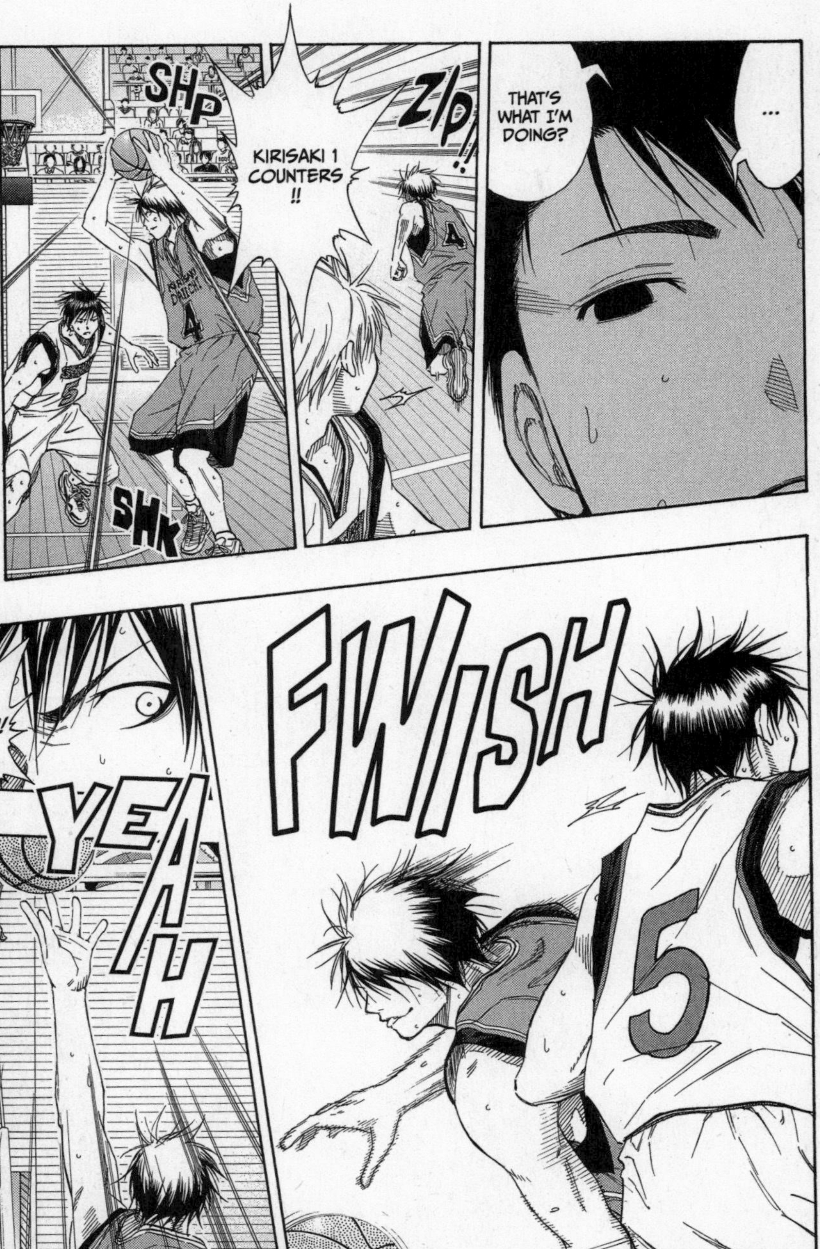
...
THAT'S WHAT I'M DOING?
ZIP!!
KIRISAKI 1 COUNTERS!!
SHP
SHK
FWISH
TCH!
YEAH

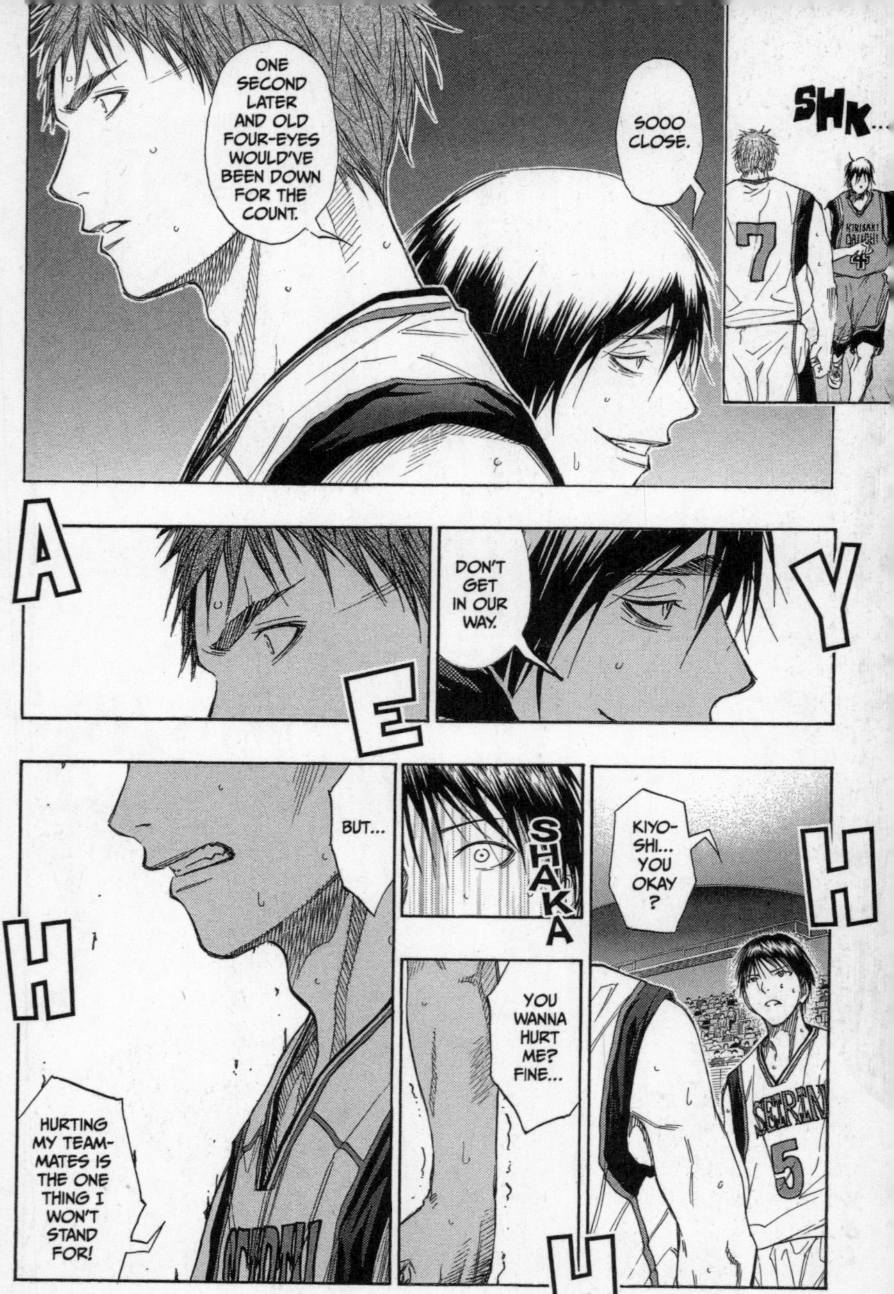
SHK...
ONE SECOND LATER AND OLD FOUR-EYES WOULD'VE BEEN DOWN FOR THE COUNT.
SOOO CLOSE.
DON'T GET IN OUR WAY.
YEAHHH
KIYO-SHI... YOU OKAY?
SHAKA
YOU WANNA HURT ME? FINE...
BUT...
HURTING MY TEAM-MATES IS THE ONE THING I WON'T STAND FOR!

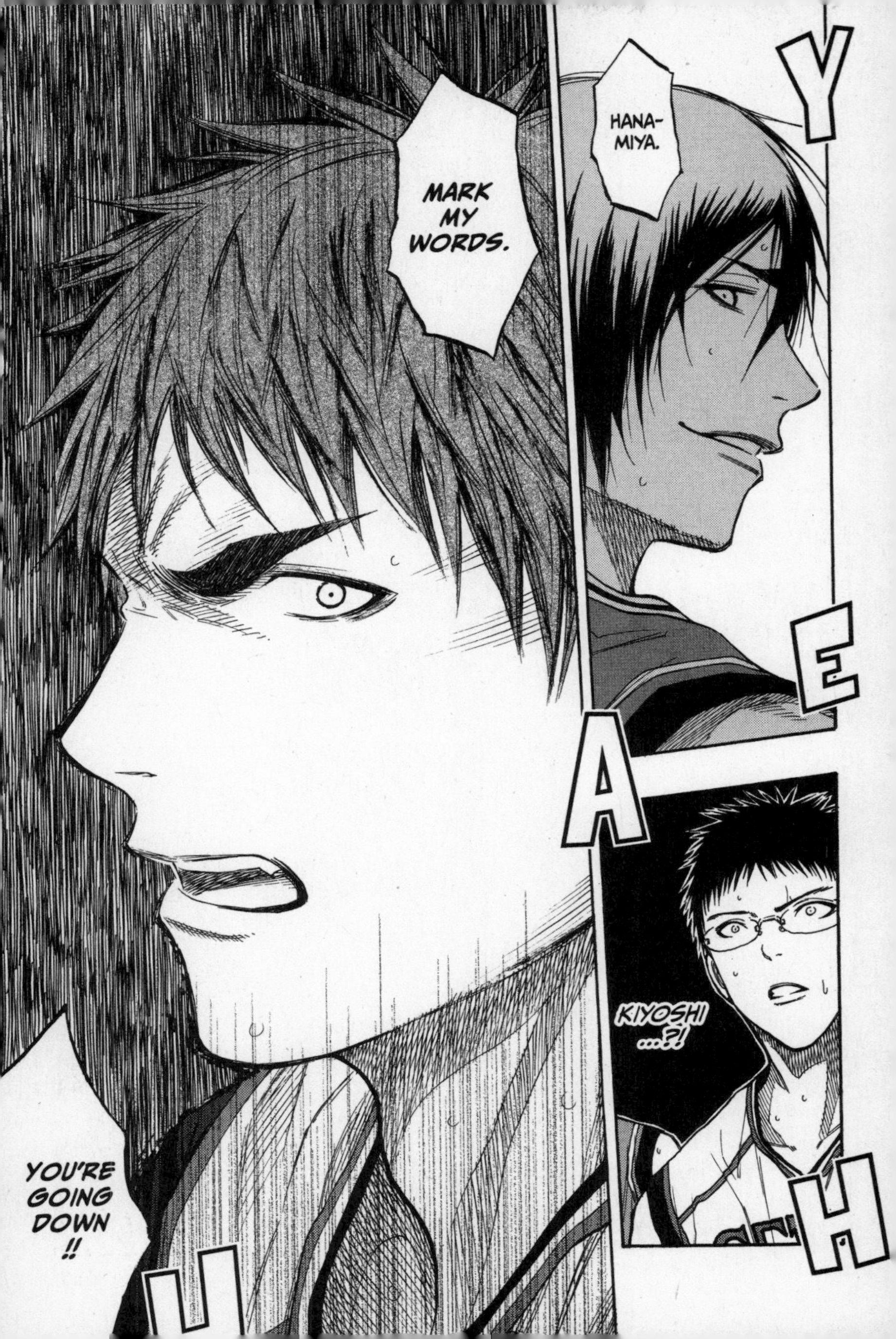
HANA-MIYA.
YEAH
KIYOSHI ...?!
MARK MY WORDS.
YOU'RE GOING DOWN !!

KUROKO'S BASKETBALL BLOOPERS
TAKE 1

WOO-HOO! A PERFECT ALLEY-OOP!!
YEAHHHH
NICE!
HM?
WHAP
HE TOTALLY SHUT ME DOWN. LOOKED JUST LIKE THE TIME I PROTECTED HYUGA...
GLOOM
IT'S NOT PERSONAL. HE'S ALWAYS GETTING KO'D IN THESE BLOOPERS, SO HE'S A LITTLE SENSITIVE.
WHYYY?!
STOP CRYING.

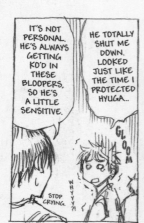

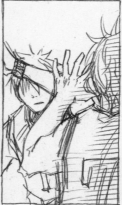

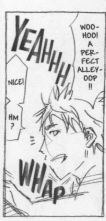

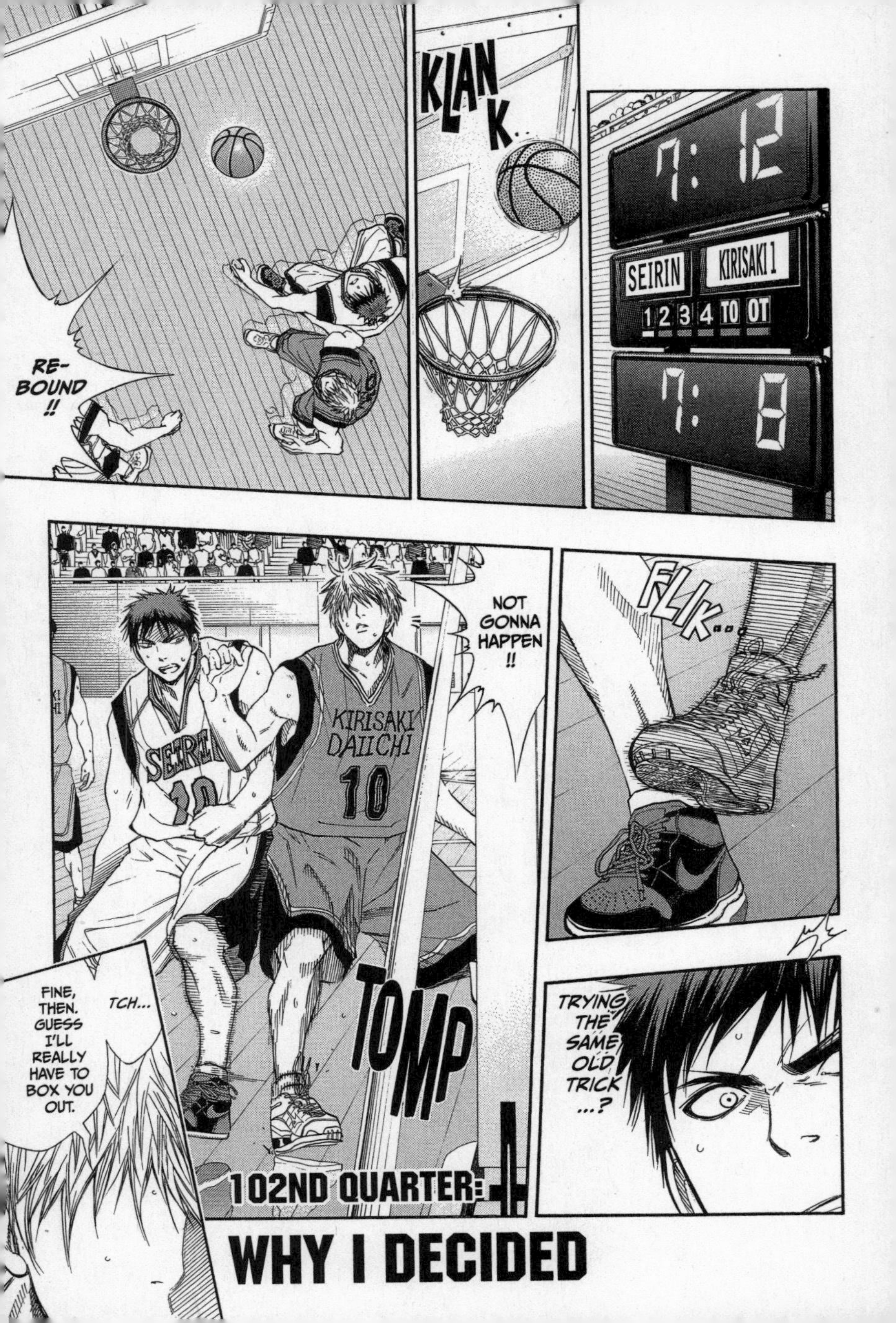
7:12
SEIRIN
KIRISAKI 1
1 2 3 4 TO OT
7:8
KLANK...
REBOUND!!
FLIK...
NOT GONNA HAPPEN!!
TOMP
TRYING THE SAME OLD TRICK...?
TCH...
FINE, THEN. GUESS I'LL REALLY HAVE TO BOX YOU OUT.
102ND QUARTER: WHY I DECIDED

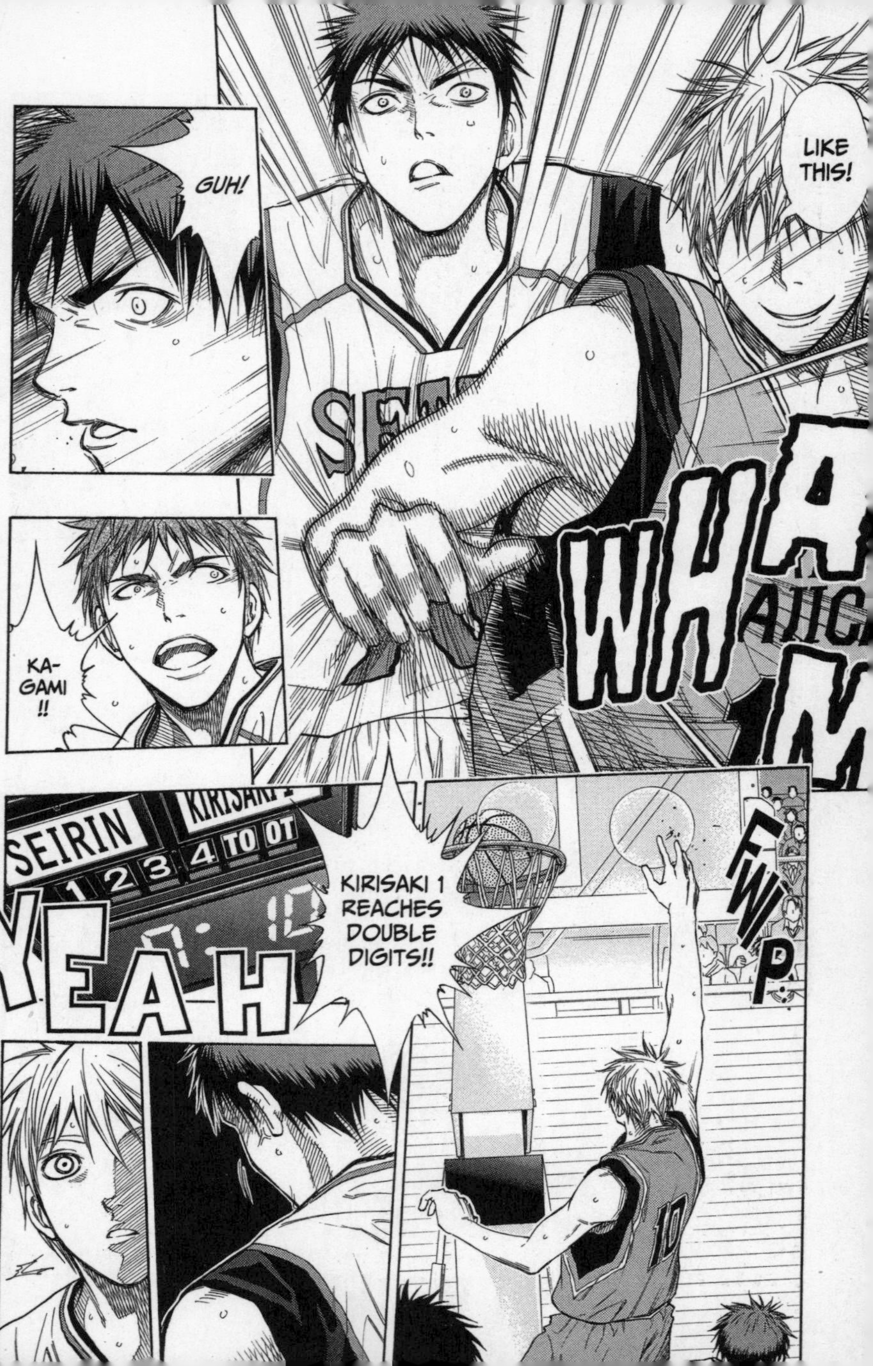
LIKE THIS!
GUH!
KA-GAMI!!
FWIP
KIRISAKI 1 REACHES DOUBLE DIGITS!!
SEIRIN
1 2 3 4 TO OT
YEAH

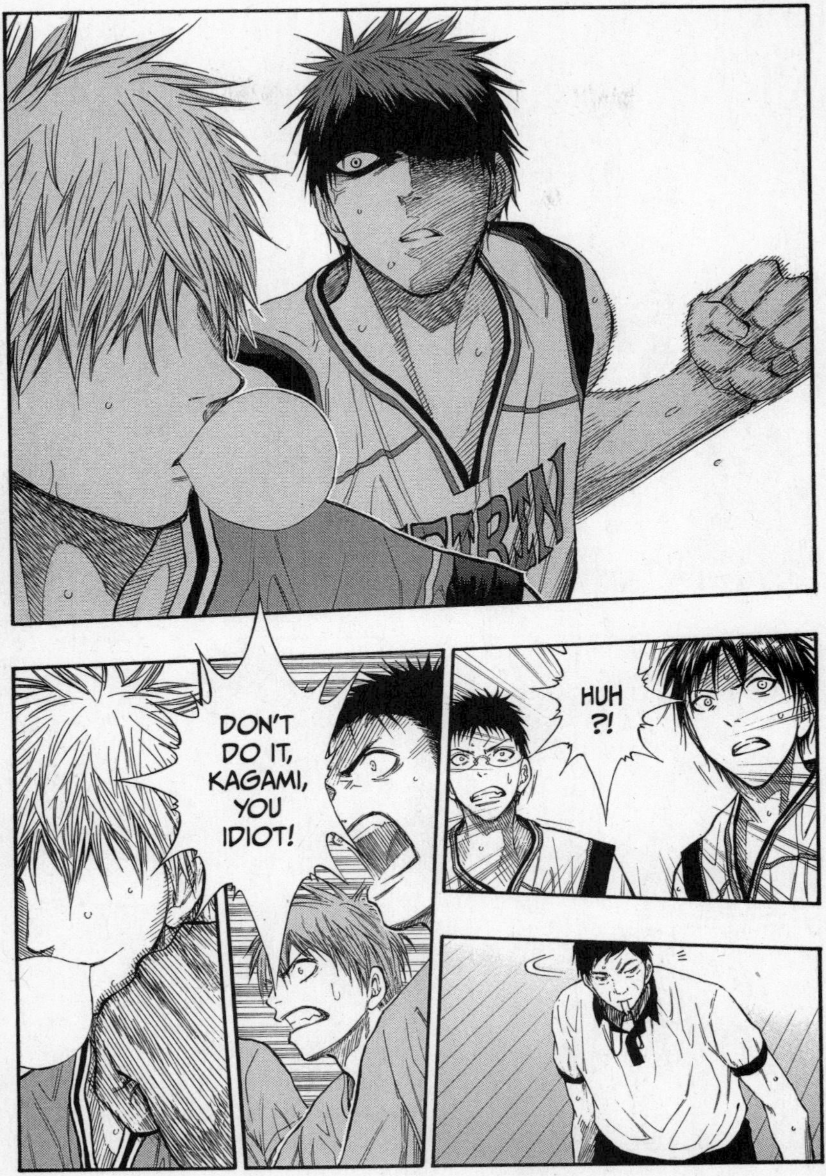
HUH ?!
DON'T DO IT, KAGAMI, YOU IDIOT!

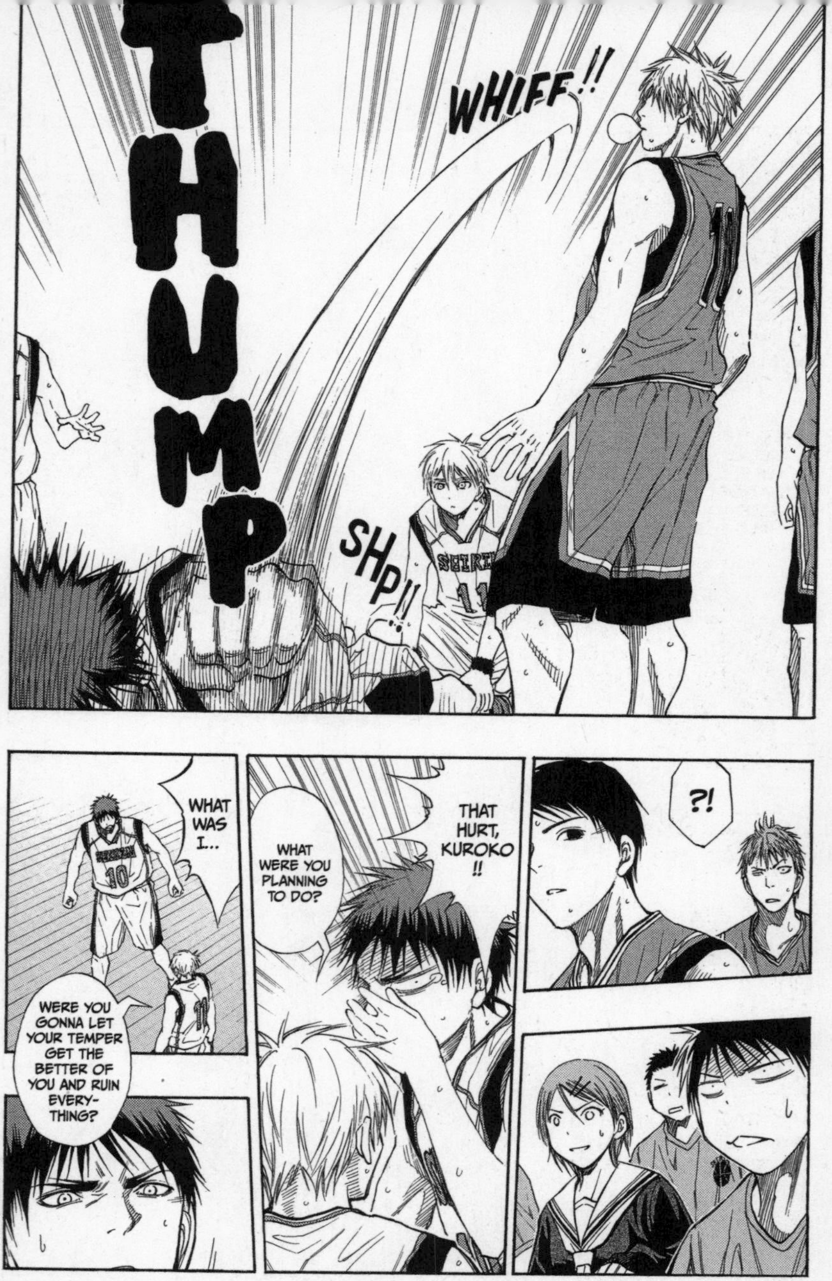
WHIFF!!
THUMP
SHP!!
?!
THAT HURT, KUROKO!!
WHAT WERE YOU PLANNING TO DO?
WHAT WAS I...
WERE YOU GONNA LET YOUR TEMPER GET THE BETTER OF YOU AND RUIN EVERY-THING?

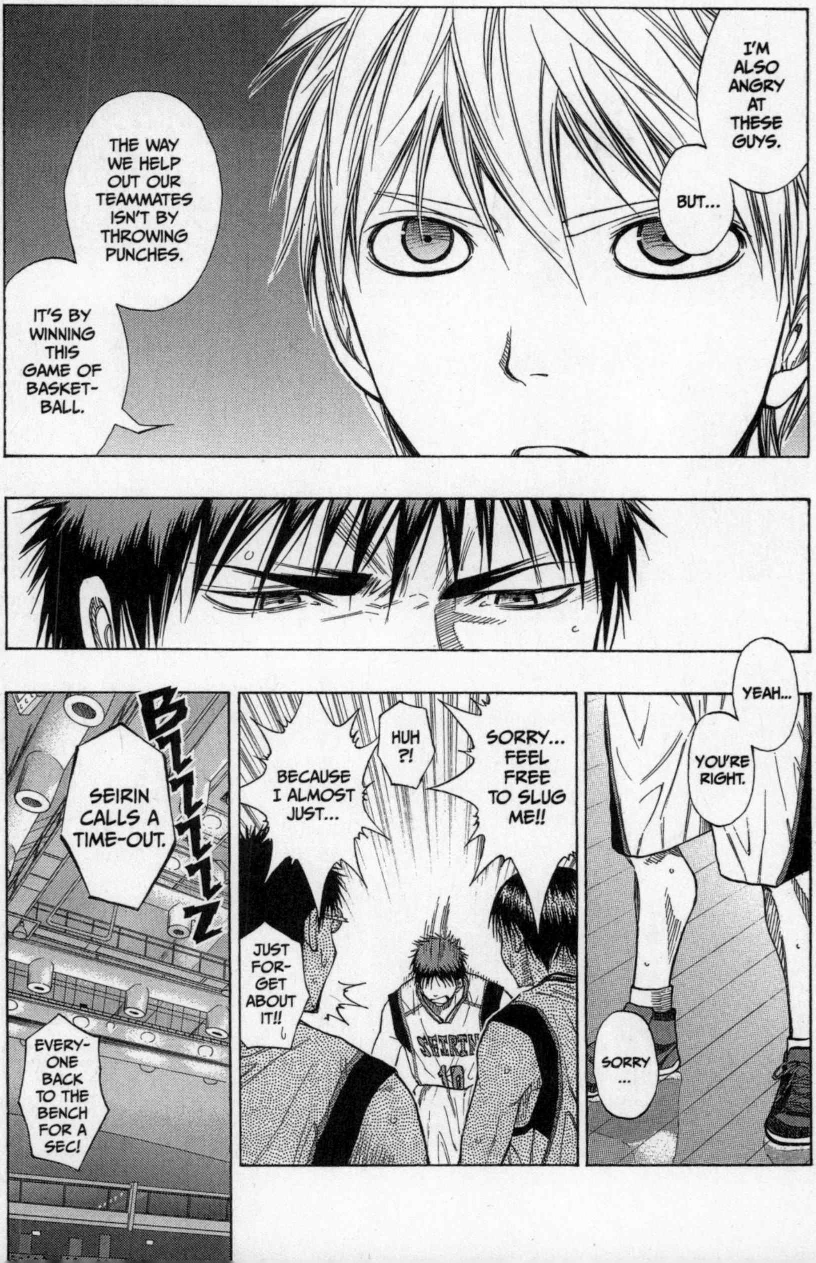
I'M ALSO ANGRY AT THESE GUYS.
BUT...
THE WAY WE HELP OUT OUR TEAMMATES ISN'T BY THROWING PUNCHES.
IT'S BY WINNING THIS GAME OF BASKET-BALL.
YEAH...
YOU'RE RIGHT.
SORRY ...
SORRY... FEEL FREE TO SLUG ME!!
HUH ?!
BECAUSE I ALMOST JUST...
JUST FOR-GET ABOUT IT!!
BZZZZZ
SEIRIN CALLS A TIME-OUT.
EVERY-ONE BACK TO THE BENCH FOR A SEC!

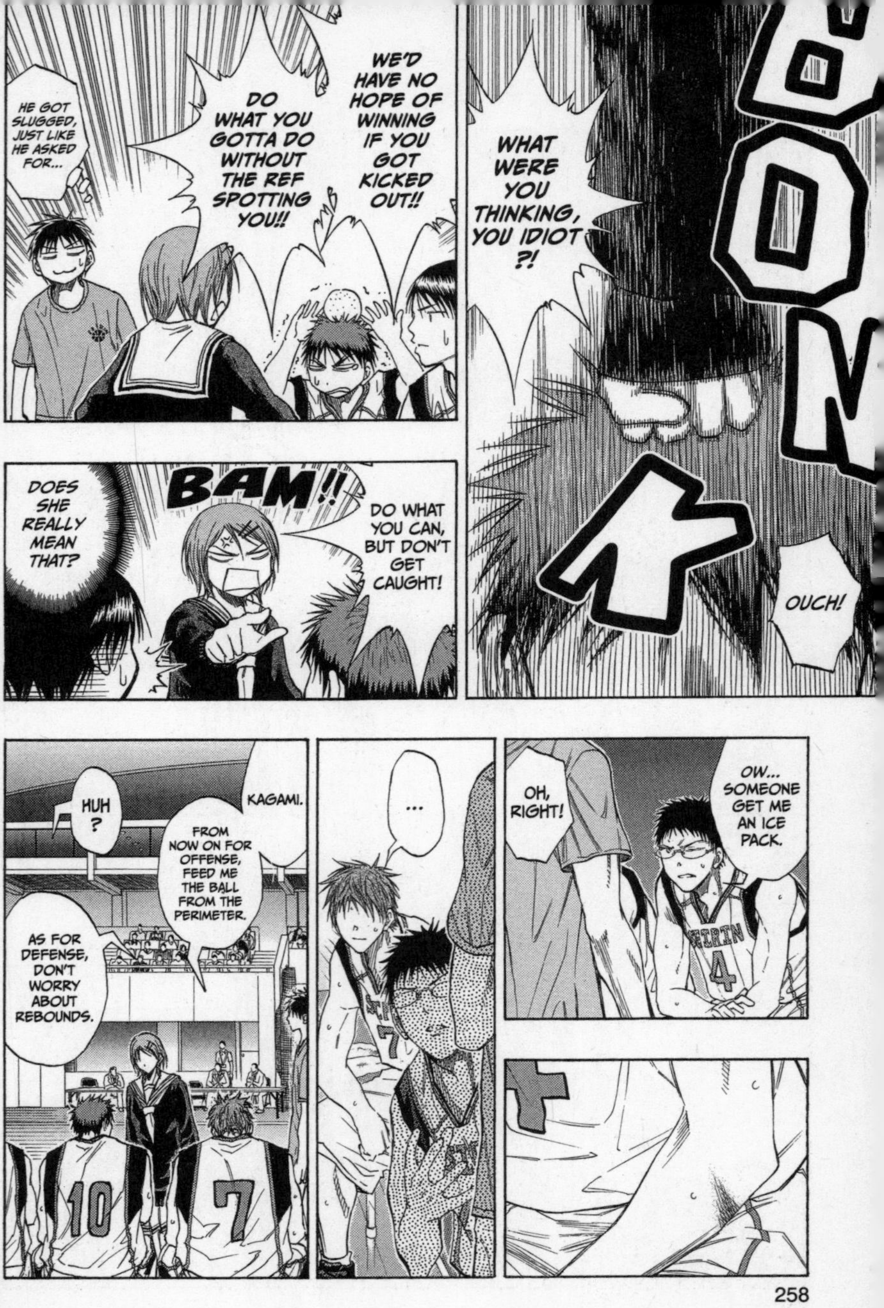
WHAT WERE YOU THINKING, YOU IDIOT?!
DON
OUCH!
WE'D HAVE NO HOPE OF WINNING IF YOU GOT KICKED OUT!!
DO WHAT YOU GOTTA DO WITHOUT THE REF SPOTTING YOU!!
HE GOT SLUGGED, JUST LIKE HE ASKED FOR...
DO WHAT YOU CAN, BUT DON'T GET CAUGHT!
BAM!!
DOES SHE REALLY MEAN THAT?
OW... SOMEONE GET ME AN ICE PACK.
OH, RIGHT!
SEIRIN 4
...
KAGAMI.
FROM NOW ON FOR OFFENSE, FEED ME THE BALL FROM THE PERIMETER.
HUH?
AS FOR DEFENSE, DON'T WORRY ABOUT REBOUNDS.

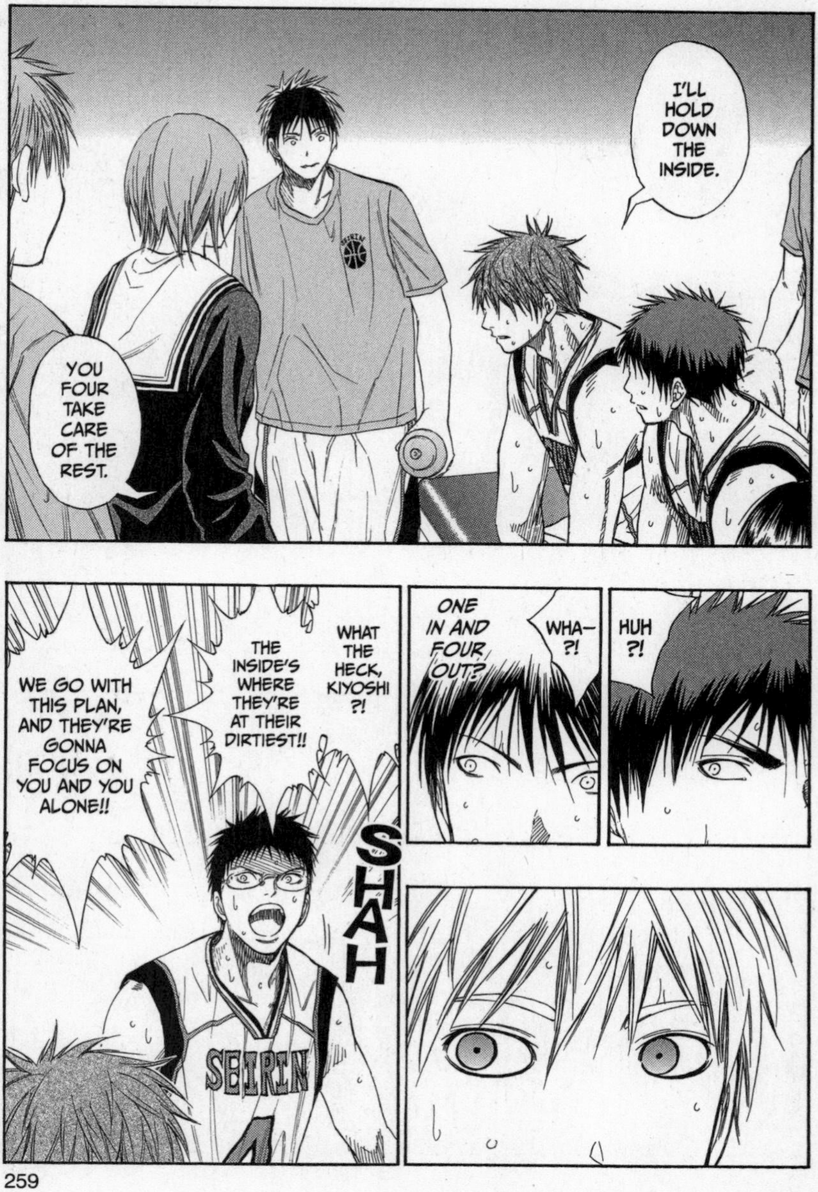
I'LL HOLD DOWN THE INSIDE.
YOU FOUR TAKE CARE OF THE REST.
HUH ?!
WHA— ?!
ONE IN AND FOUR OUT?
WHAT THE HECK, KIYOSHI ?!
THE INSIDE'S WHERE THEY'RE AT THEIR DIRTIEST!!
WE GO WITH THIS PLAN, AND THEY'RE GONNA FOCUS ON YOU AND YOU ALONE!!
SHAH
SEIRIN

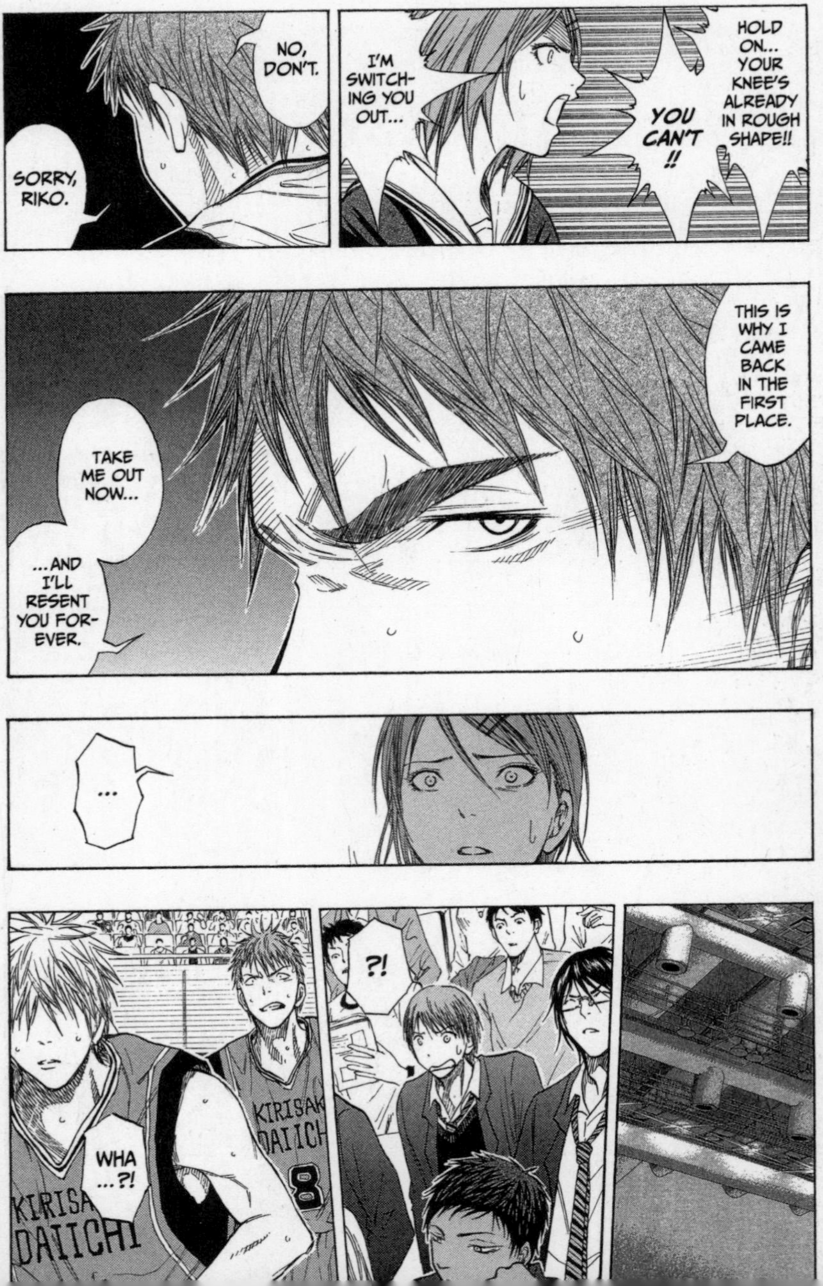
HOLD ON... YOUR KNEE'S ALREADY IN ROUGH SHAPE!!
YOU CAN'T !!
I'M SWITCHING YOU OUT...
NO, DON'T.
SORRY, RIKO.
THIS IS WHY I CAME BACK IN THE FIRST PLACE.
TAKE ME OUT NOW...
...AND I'LL RESENT YOU FOREVER.
...
?!
KIRISAKI DAIICHI
WHA ...?!

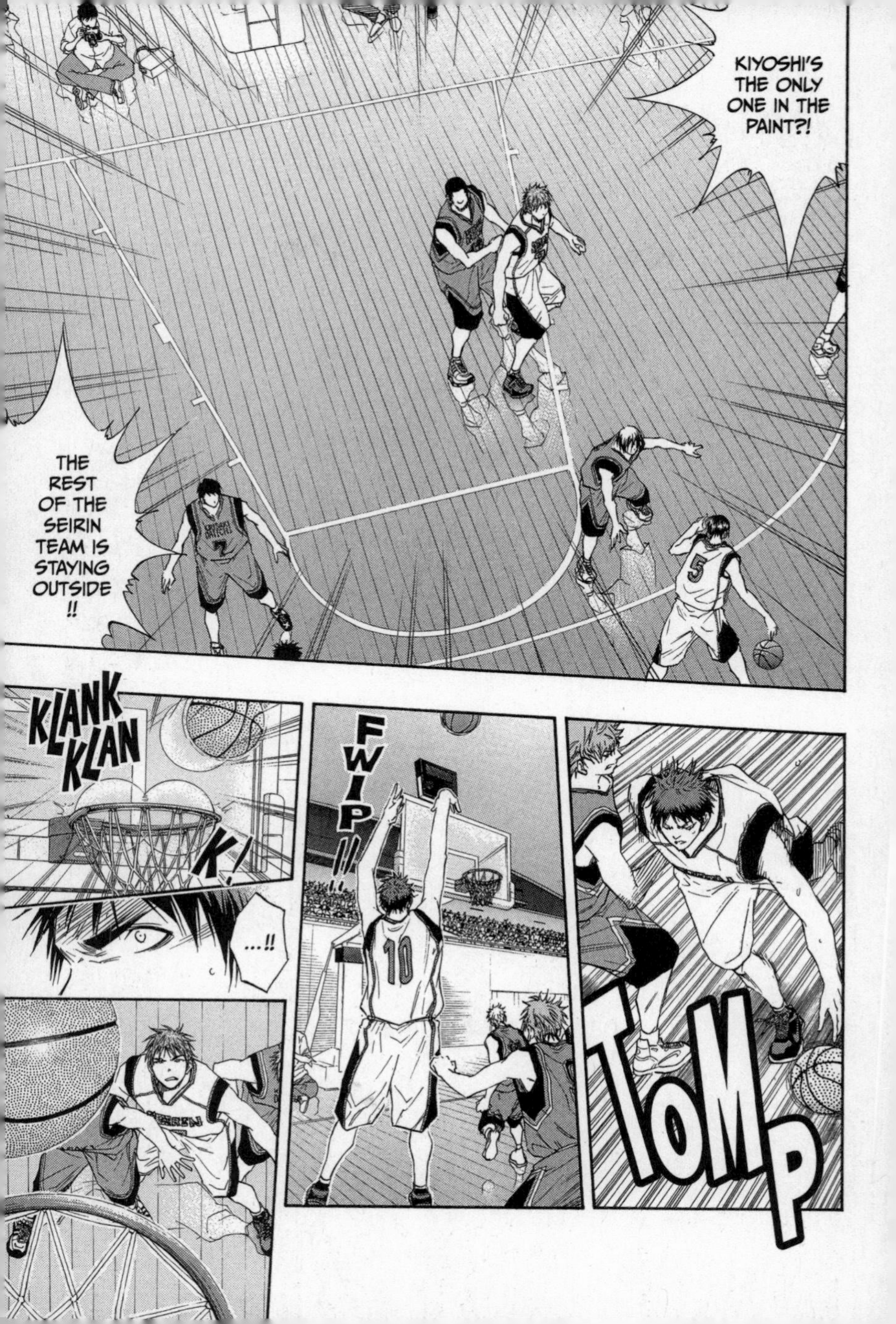
KIYOSHI'S THE ONLY ONE IN THE PAINT?!
THE REST OF THE SEIRIN TEAM IS STAYING OUTSIDE !!
TOMP
FWIP!!
KLANK KLANK!
...!!

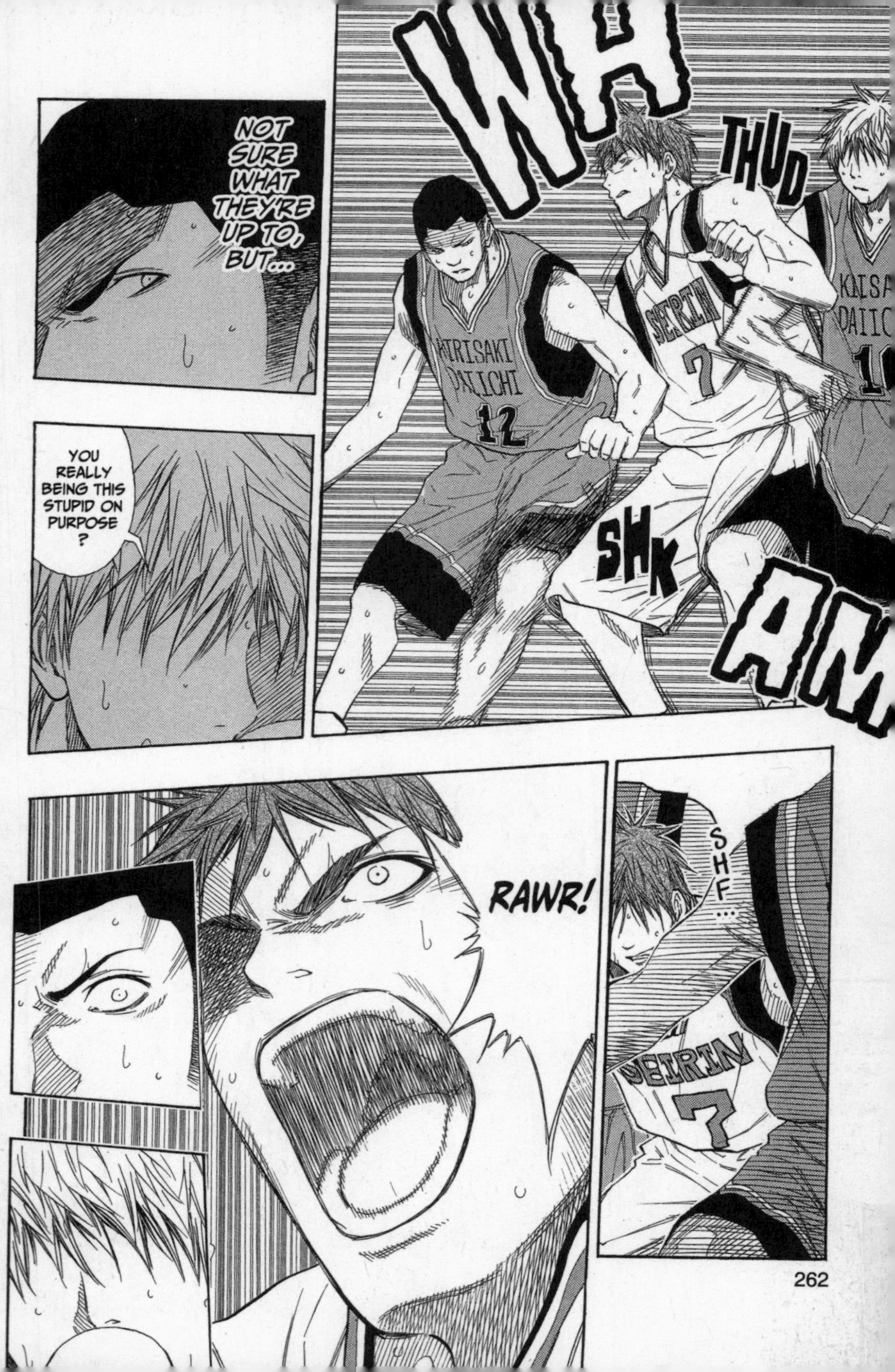
WHA
THUD
SHK
AM
NOT SURE WHAT THEY'RE UP TO, BUT...
YOU REALLY BEING THIS STUPID ON PURPOSE?
SHF...
RAWR!

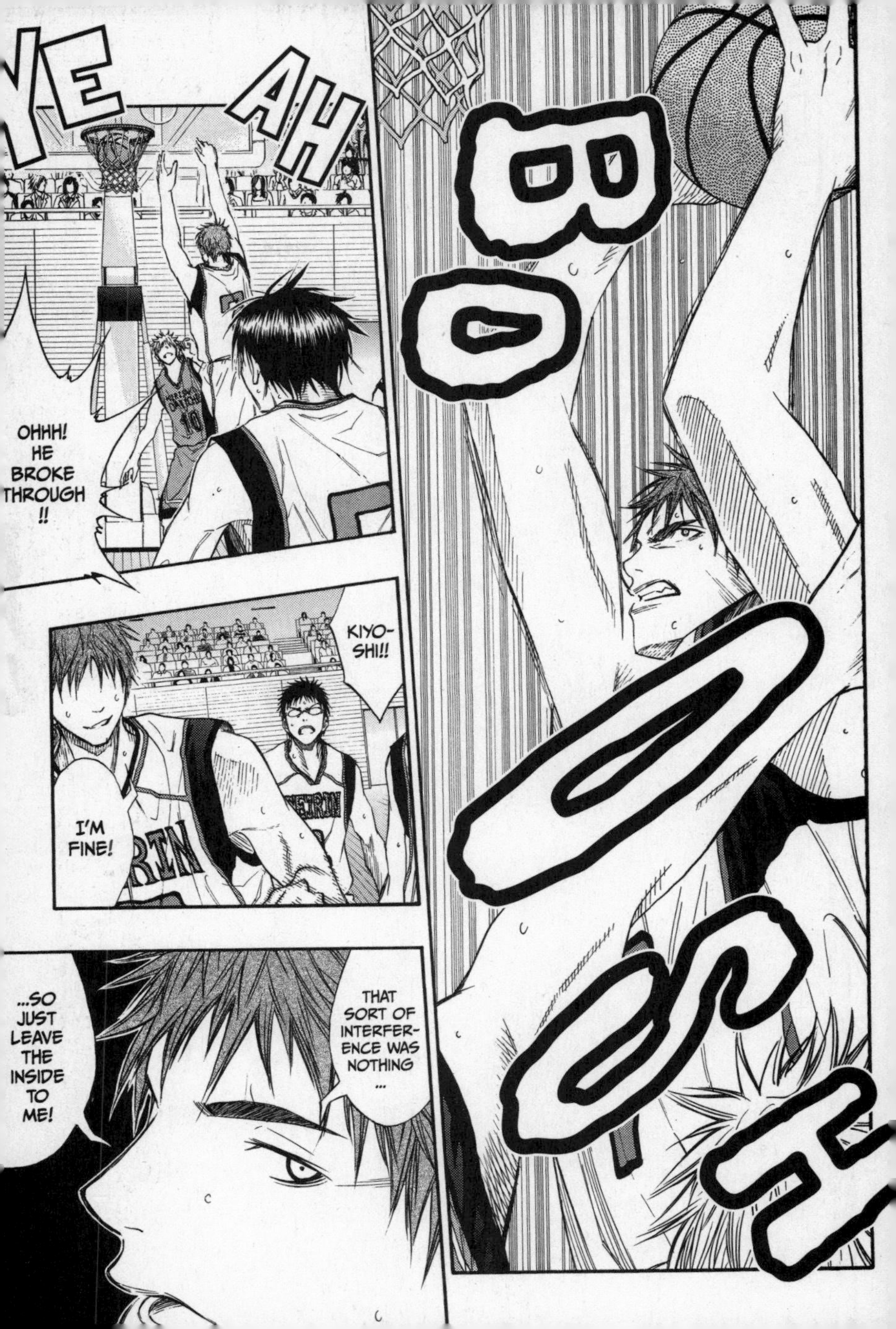
BOOSH
YEAH
OHHH! HE BROKE THROUGH!!
KIYOSHI!!
I'M FINE!
THAT SORT OF INTERFERENCE WAS NOTHING...
...SO JUST LEAVE THE INSIDE TO ME!

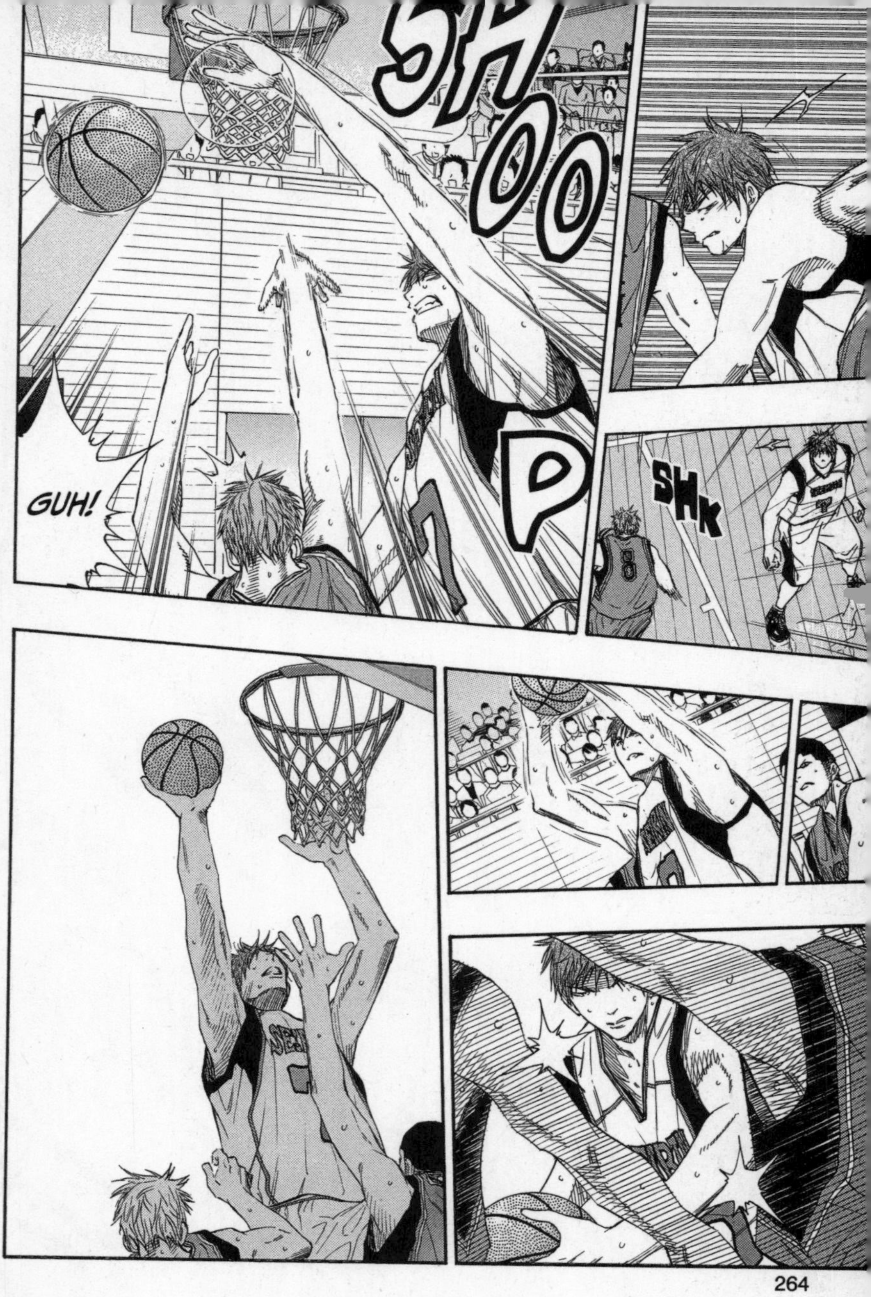

SHK
SHOOP
GUH!

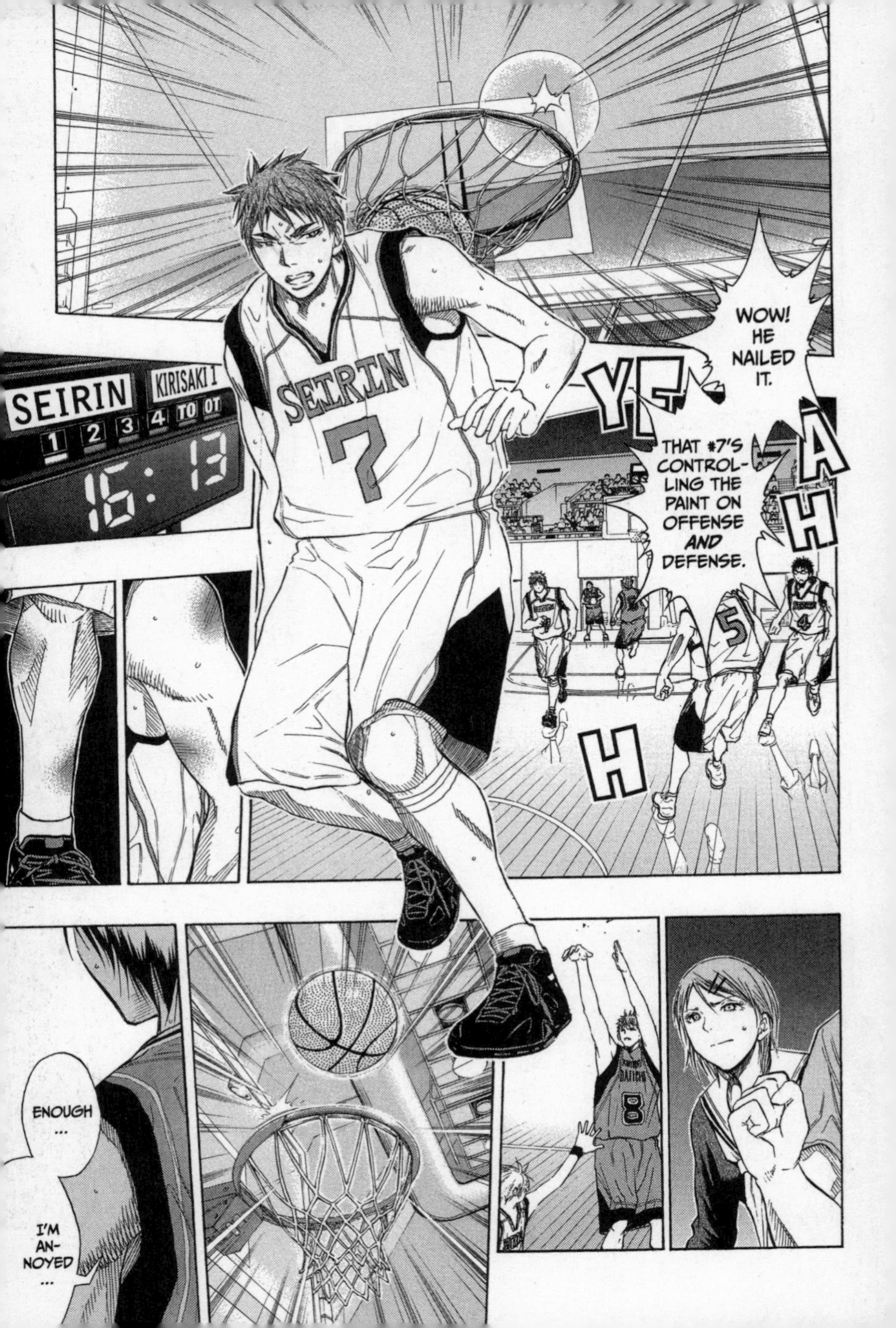

WOW! HE NAILED IT.
YEAHH
THAT #7'S CONTROL-LING THE PAINT ON OFFENSE *AND* DEFENSE.
SEIRIN
7
SEIRIN
KIRISAKI 1
1 2 3 4 TO OT
16: 13
ENOUGH ...
I'M AN-NOYED ...

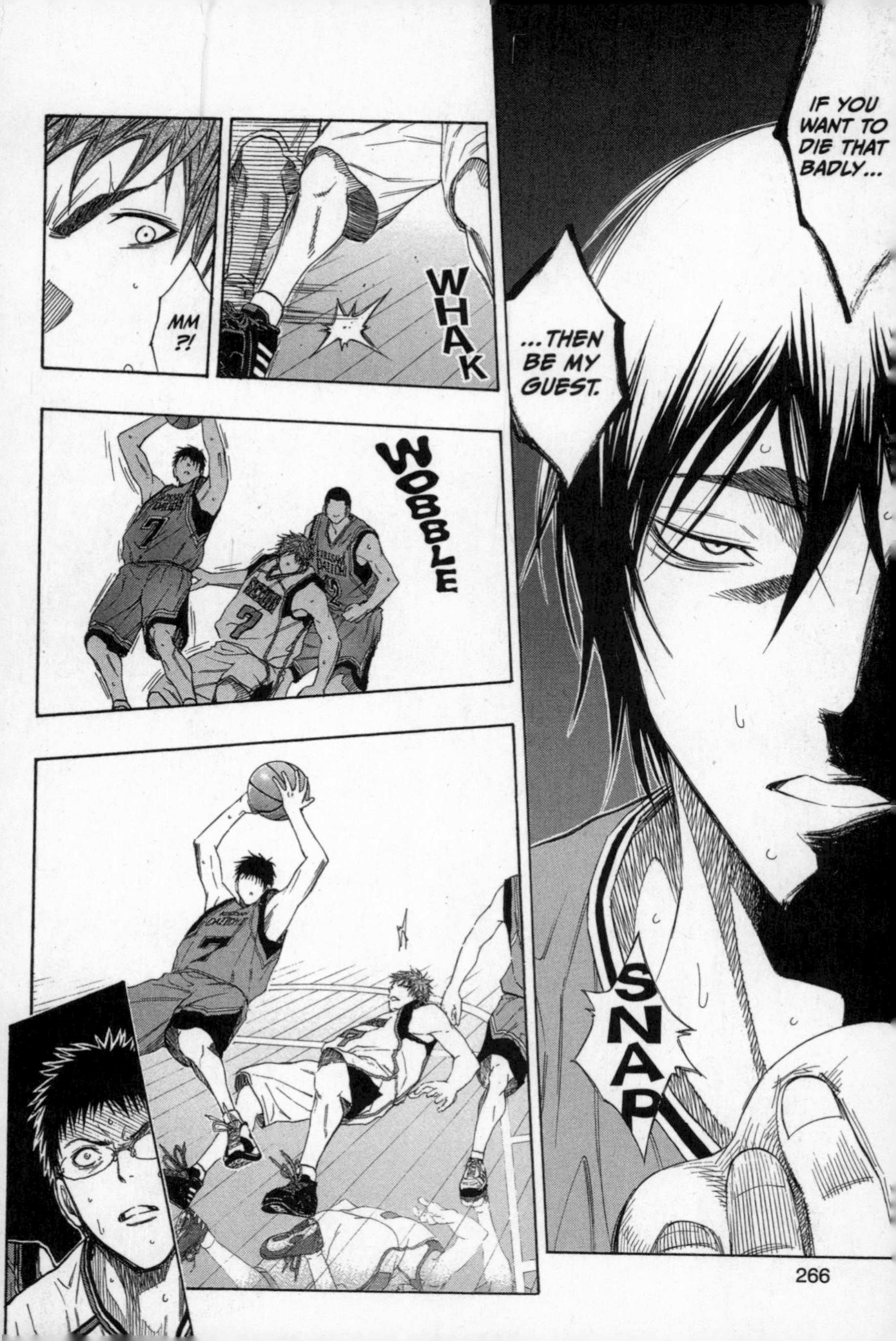
IF YOU WANT TO DIE THAT BADLY...
...THEN BE MY GUEST.
SNAP
WHAK
MM ?!
WOBBLE

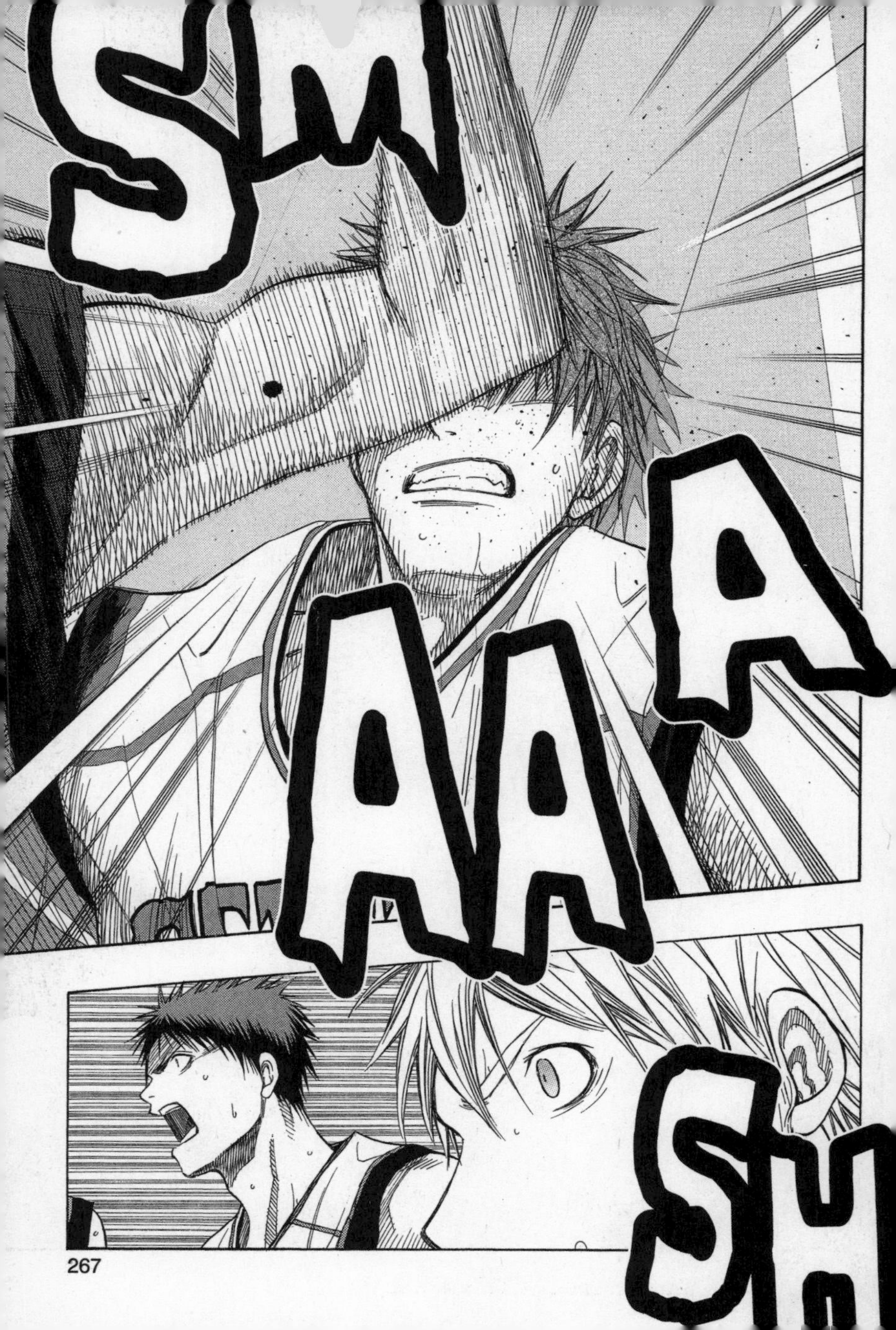
SWAAA
SH

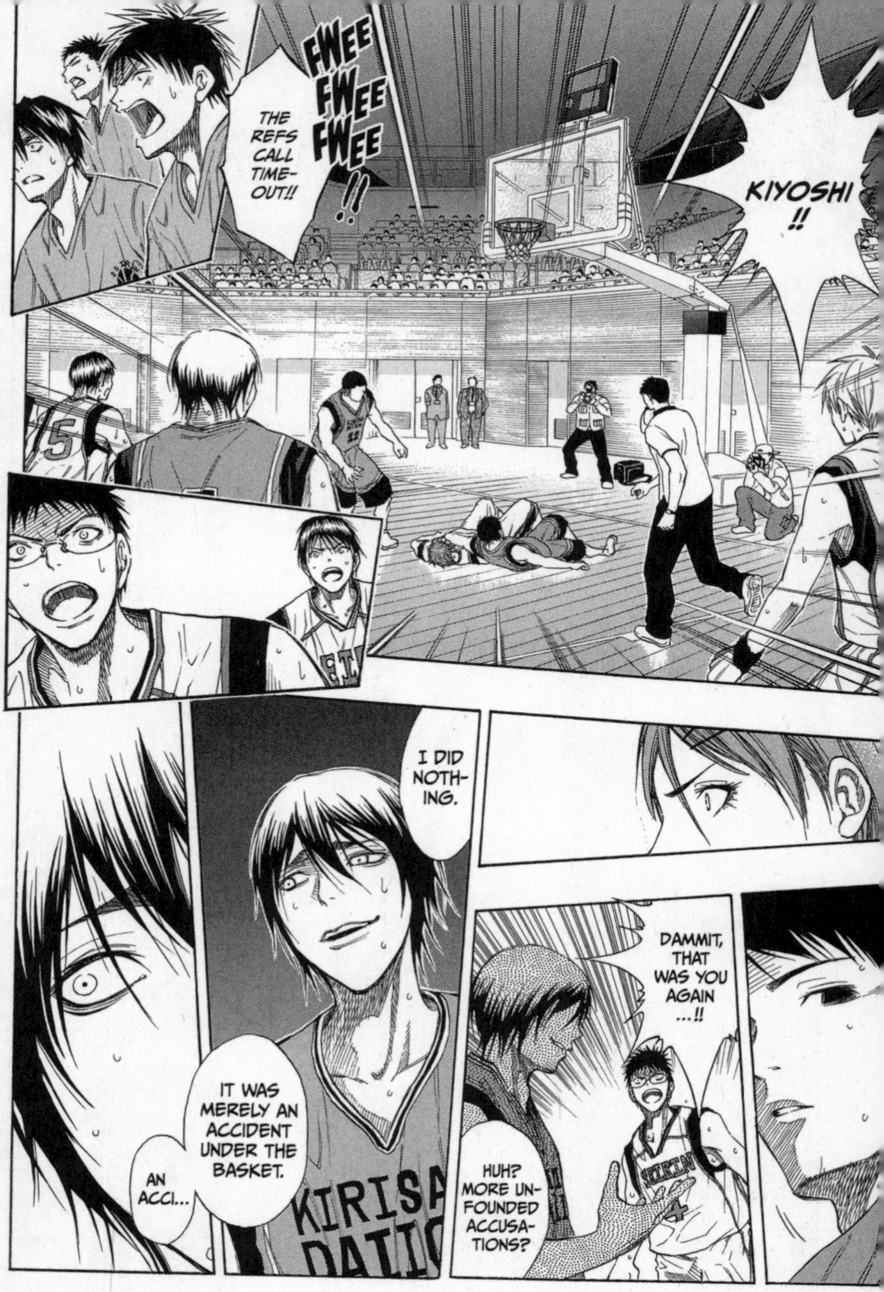
KIYOSHI !!
FWEE FWEE FWEE !!
THE REFS CALL TIME-OUT!!
DAMMIT, THAT WAS YOU AGAIN ...!!
HUH? MORE UN-FOUNDED ACCUSA-TIONS?
I DID NOTH-ING.
IT WAS MERELY AN ACCIDENT UNDER THE BASKET.
KIRISA DAIIC
AN ACCI...

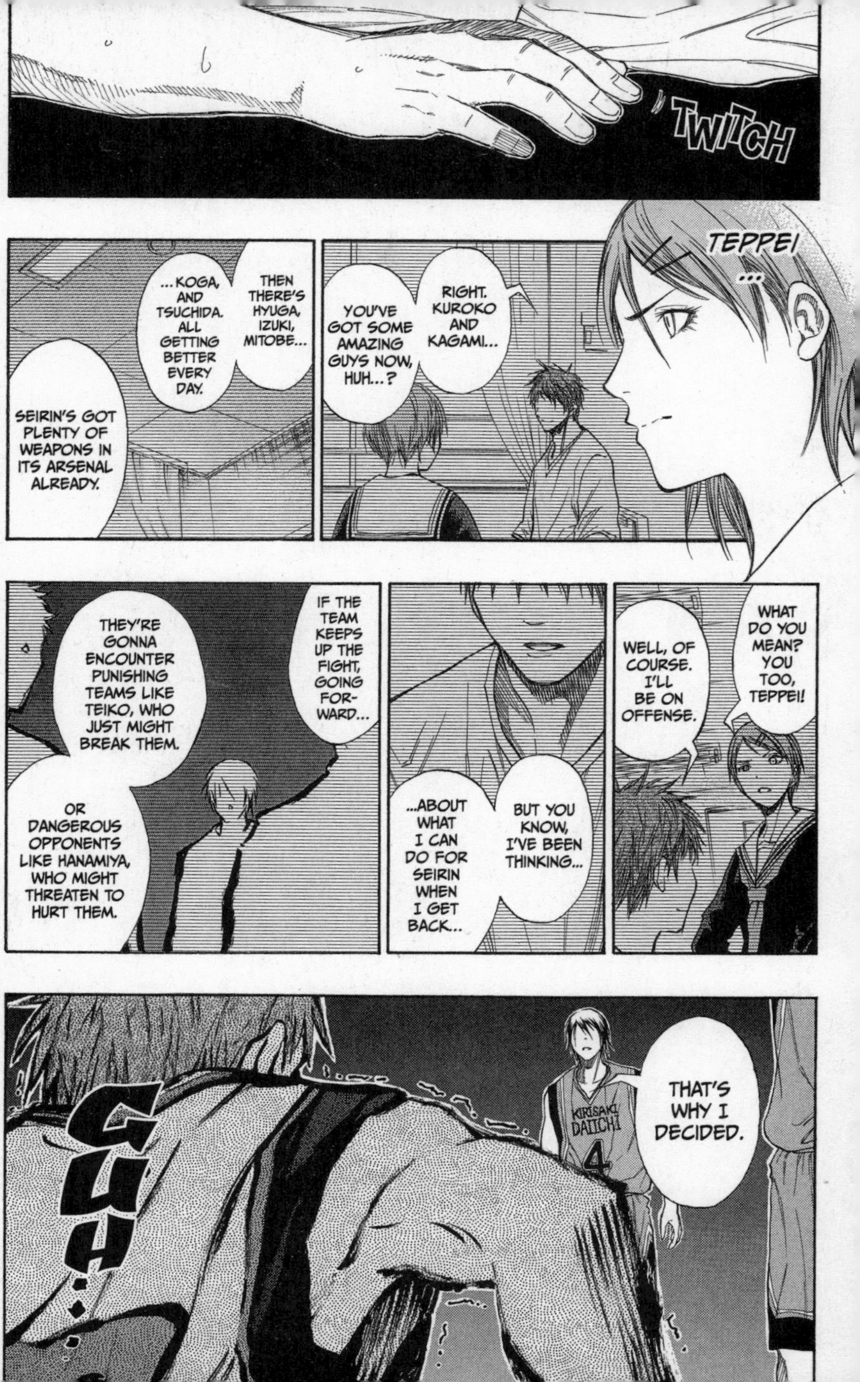
TWITCH
TEPPEI ...
RIGHT. KUROKO AND KAGAMI...
YOU'VE GOT SOME AMAZING GUYS NOW, HUH...?
THEN THERE'S HYUGA, IZUKI, MITOBE...
...KOGA, AND TSUCHIDA. ALL GETTING BETTER EVERY DAY.
SEIRIN'S GOT PLENTY OF WEAPONS IN ITS ARSENAL ALREADY.
WHAT DO YOU MEAN? YOU TOO, TEPPEI!
WELL, OF COURSE. I'LL BE ON OFFENSE.
BUT YOU KNOW, I'VE BEEN THINKING...
...ABOUT WHAT I CAN DO FOR SEIRIN WHEN I GET BACK...
IF THE TEAM KEEPS UP THE FIGHT, GOING FOR-WARD...
THEY'RE GONNA ENCOUNTER PUNISHING TEAMS LIKE TEIKO, WHO JUST MIGHT BREAK THEM.
OR DANGEROUS OPPONENTS LIKE HANAMIYA, WHO MIGHT THREATEN TO HURT THEM.
THAT'S WHY I DECIDED.
KIRISAKI DAIICHI 4
GUH...

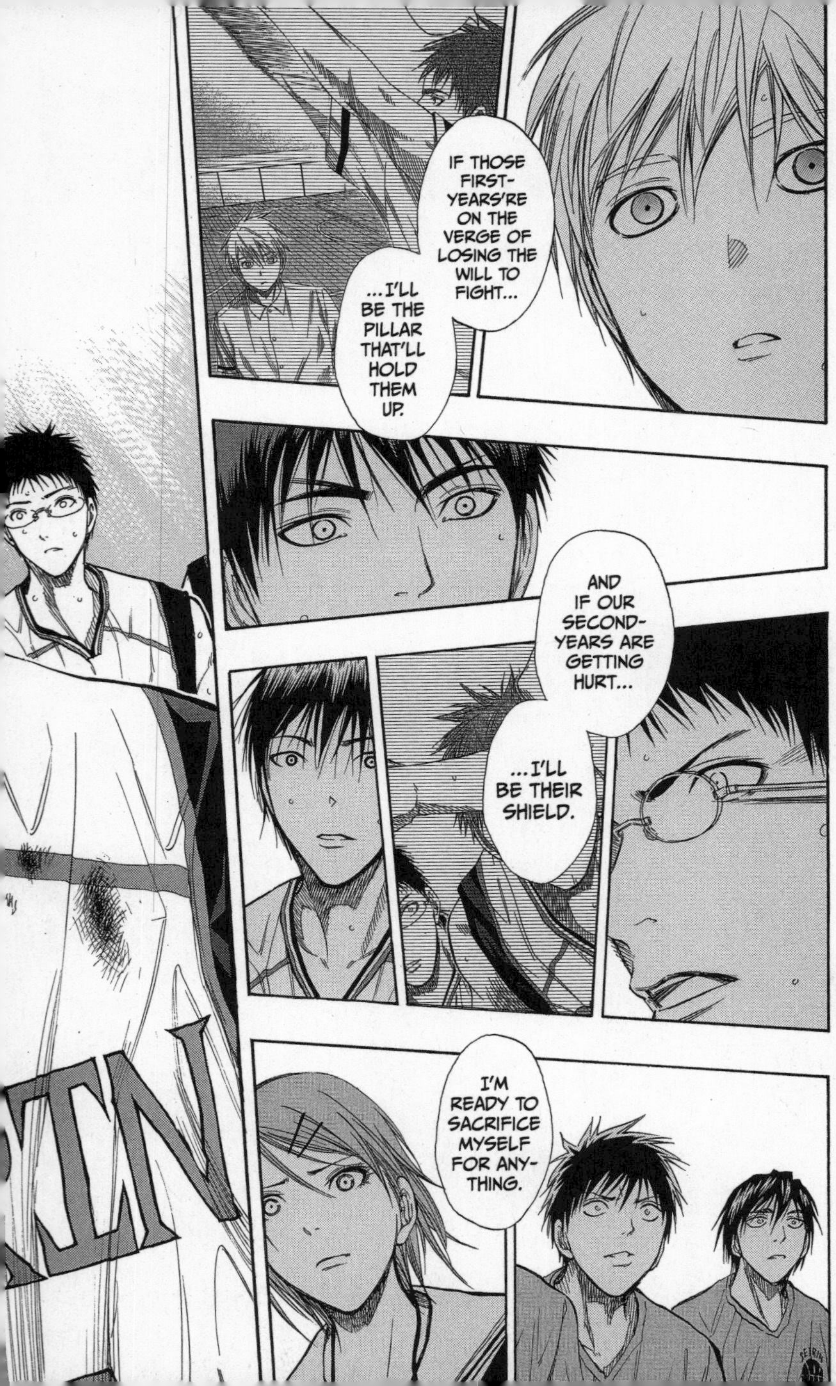
IF THOSE FIRST-YEARS'RE ON THE VERGE OF LOSING THE WILL TO FIGHT...
...I'LL BE THE PILLAR THAT'LL HOLD THEM UP.
AND IF OUR SECOND-YEARS ARE GETTING HURT...
...I'LL BE THEIR SHIELD.
I'M READY TO SACRIFICE MYSELF FOR ANY-THING.

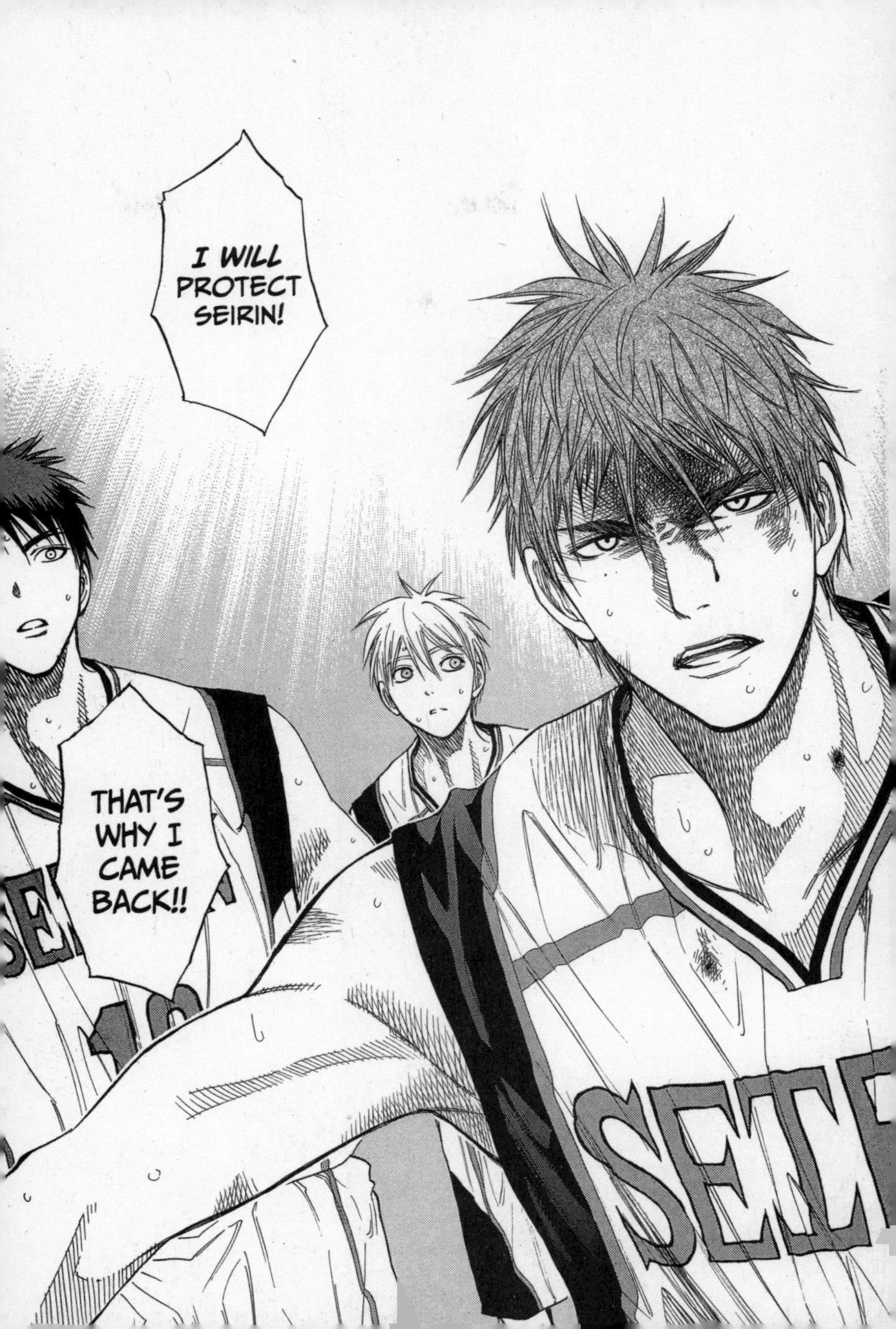
I WILL PROTECT SEIRIN!
THAT'S WHY I CAME BACK!!

KUROKO'S BASKETBALL BLOOPERS
TAKE 3

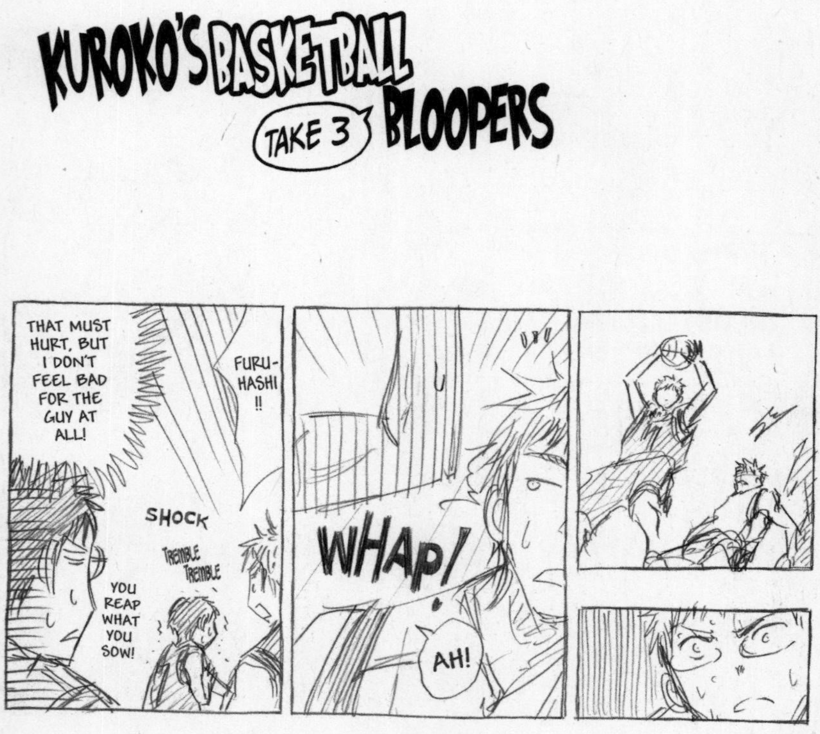
WHAP!
AH!
FURU-HASHI!!
THAT MUST HURT, BUT I DON'T FEEL BAD FOR THE GUY AT ALL!
SHOCK
TREMBLE TREMBLE
YOU REAP WHAT YOU SOW!

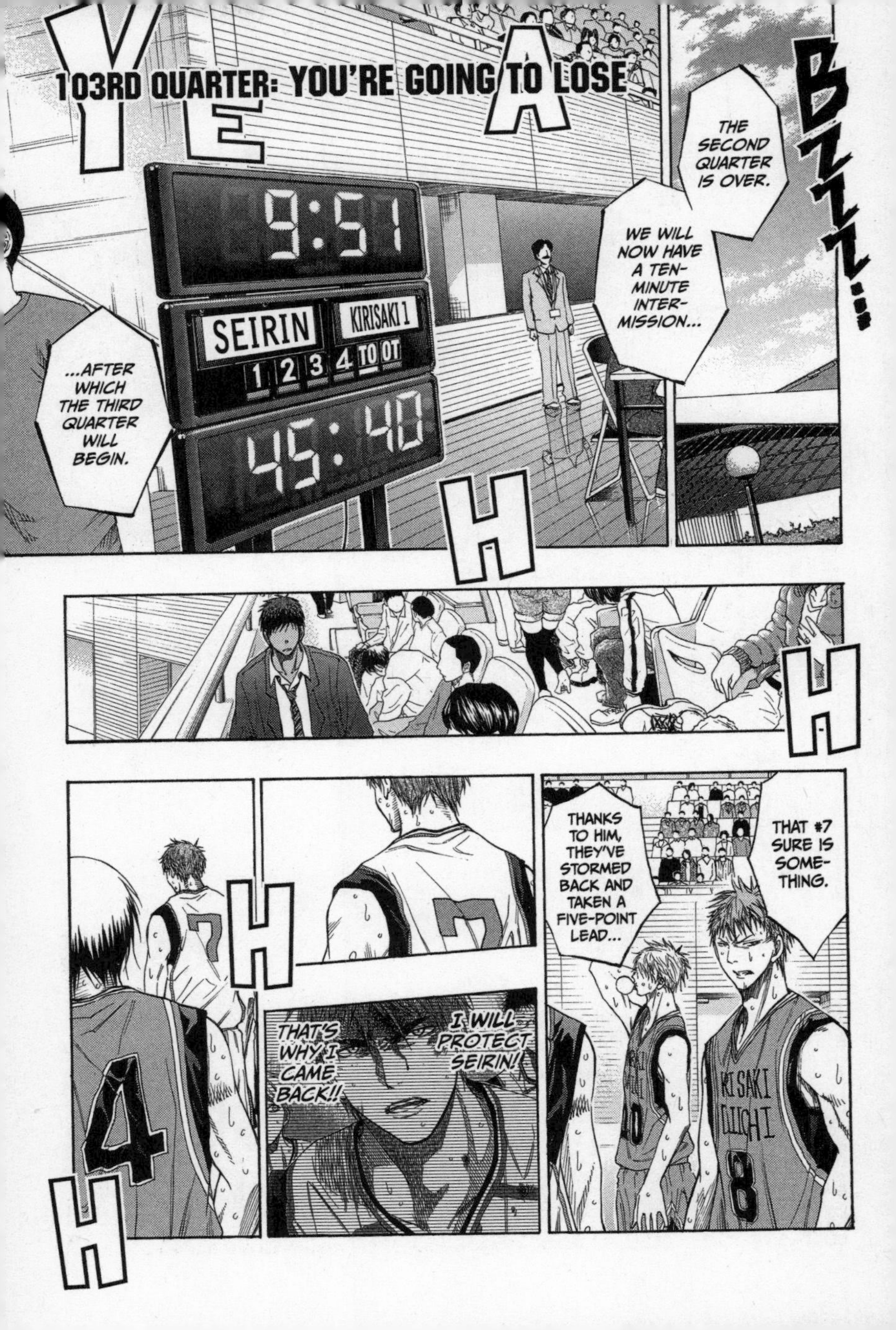
103RD QUARTER: YOU'RE GOING TO LOSE
YEAH
BZZZZ...
THE SECOND QUARTER IS OVER.
WE WILL NOW HAVE A TEN-MINUTE INTERMISSION...
...AFTER WHICH THE THIRD QUARTER WILL BEGIN.
9:51
SEIRIN
KIRISAKI 1
1 2 3 4 TO OT
45:40
HH
THAT #7 SURE IS SOMETHING.
THANKS TO HIM, THEY'VE STORMED BACK AND TAKEN A FIVE-POINT LEAD...
I WILL PROTECT SEIRIN!
THAT'S WHY I CAME BACK!!
HH

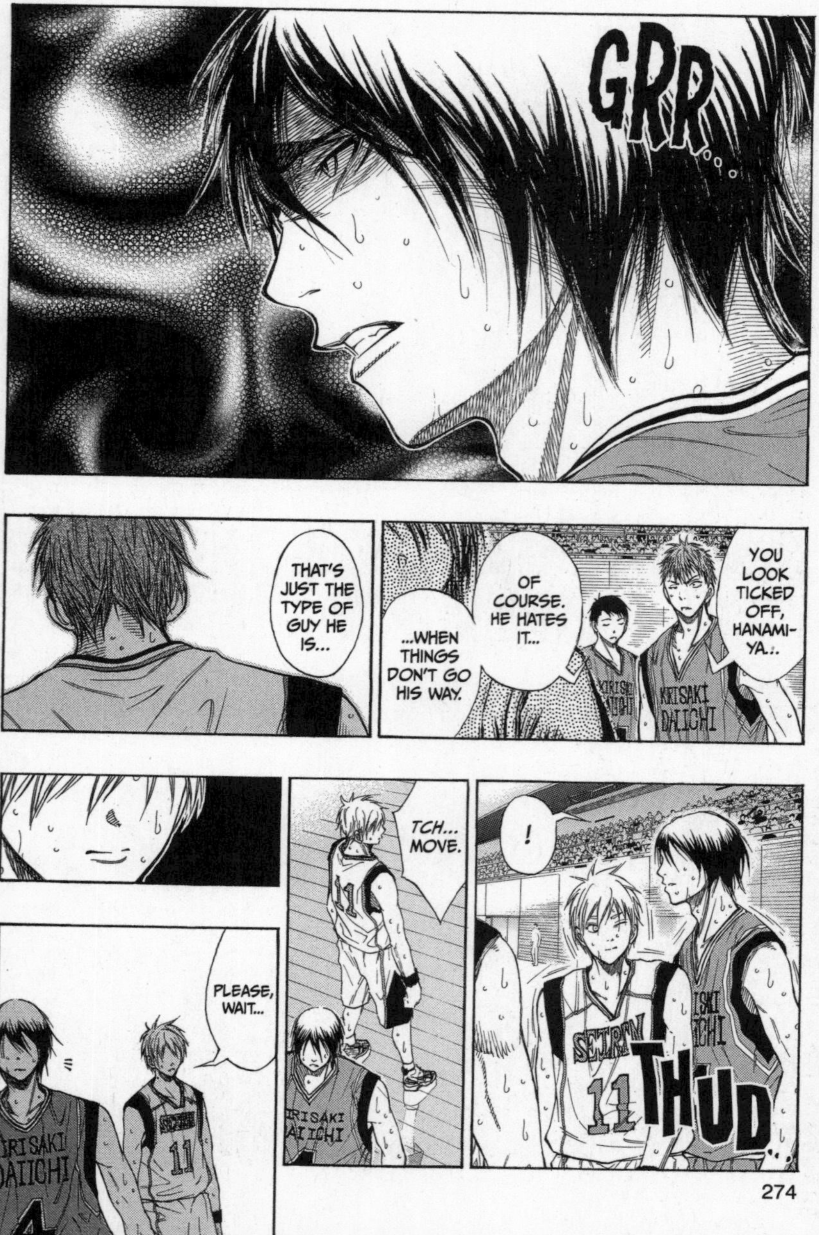
GRR...
YOU LOOK TICKED OFF, HANAMIYA...
OF COURSE. HE HATES IT...
...WHEN THINGS DON'T GO HIS WAY.
THAT'S JUST THE TYPE OF GUY HE IS...
!
THUD...
TCH... MOVE.
PLEASE, WAIT...

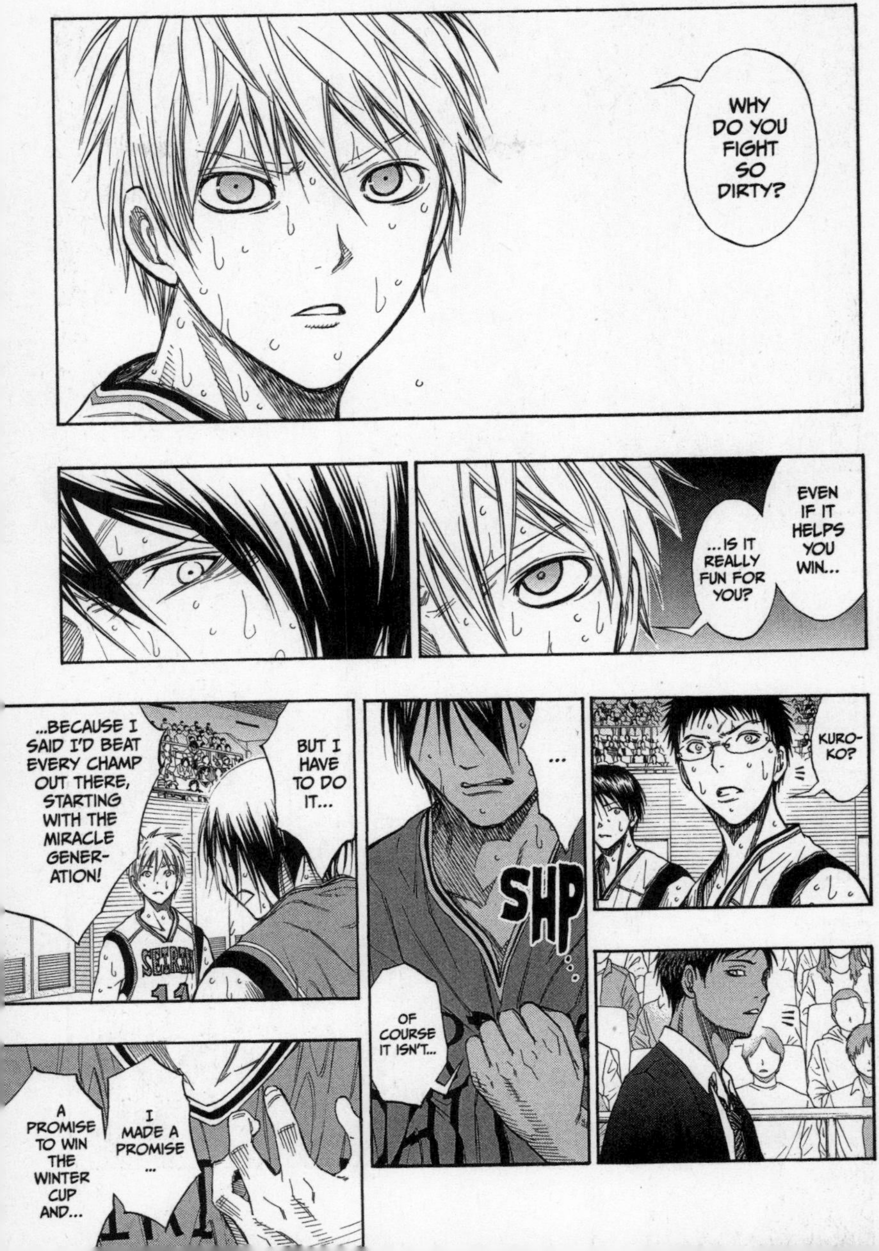
WHY DO YOU FIGHT SO DIRTY?
EVEN IF IT HELPS YOU WIN...
...IS IT REALLY FUN FOR YOU?
KURO-KO?
...
SHP
OF COURSE IT ISN'T...
BUT I HAVE TO DO IT...
...BECAUSE I SAID I'D BEAT EVERY CHAMP OUT THERE, STARTING WITH THE MIRACLE GENER-ATION!
I MADE A PROMISE...
A PROMISE TO WIN THE WINTER CUP AND...

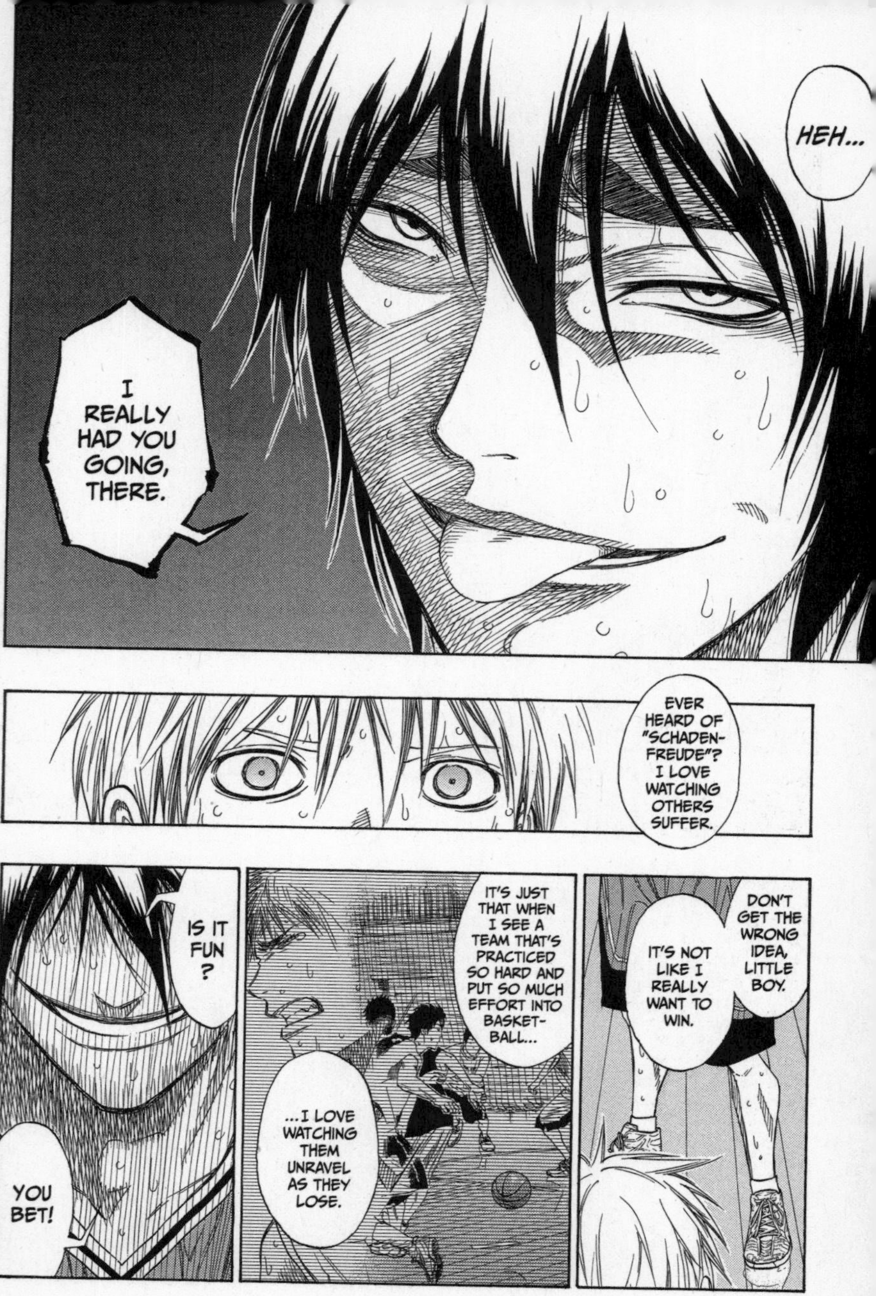
HEH...
I REALLY HAD YOU GOING, THERE.
EVER HEARD OF "SCHADEN-FREUDE"? I LOVE WATCHING OTHERS SUFFER.
DON'T GET THE WRONG IDEA, LITTLE BOY.
IT'S NOT LIKE I REALLY WANT TO WIN.
IT'S JUST THAT WHEN I SEE A TEAM THAT'S PRACTICED SO HARD AND PUT SO MUCH EFFORT INTO BASKET-BALL...
...I LOVE WATCHING THEM UNRAVEL AS THEY LOSE.
IS IT FUN?
YOU BET!

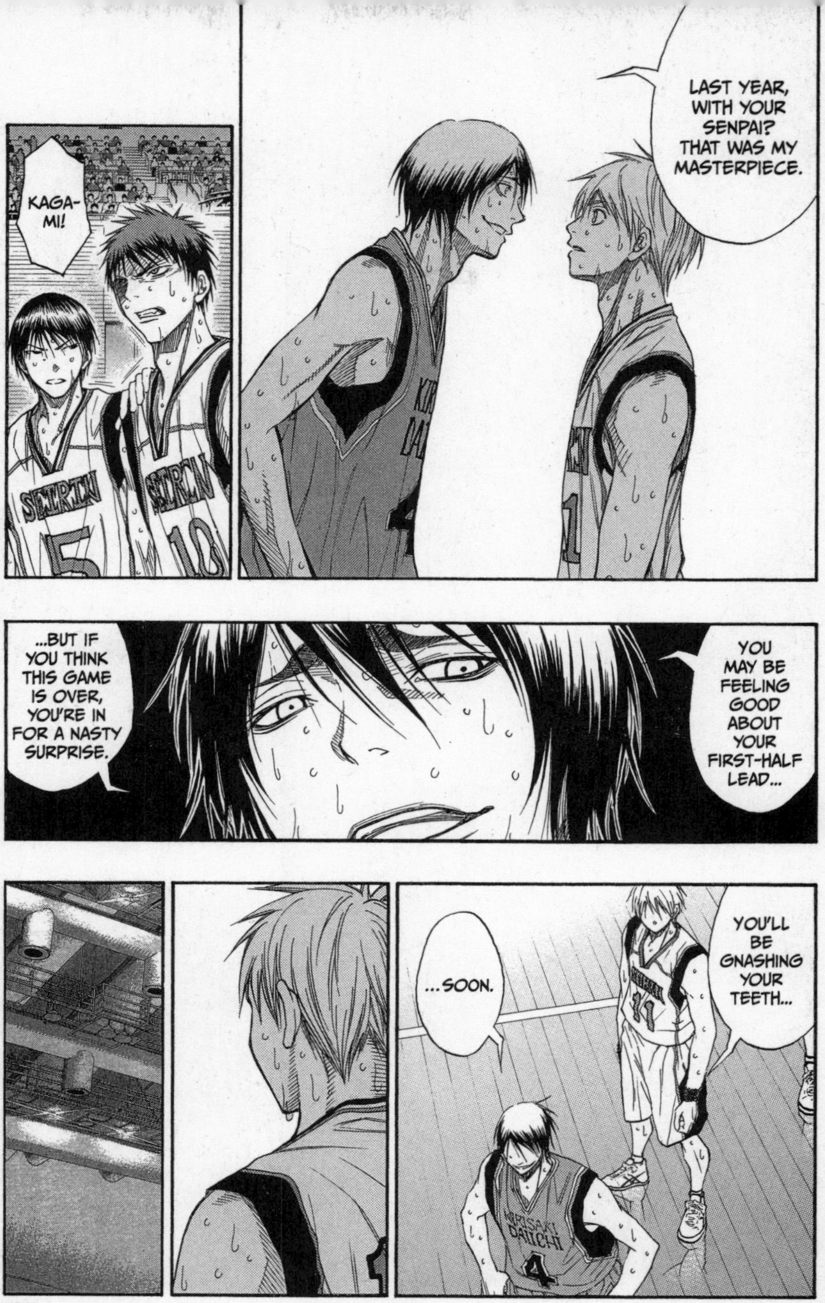
LAST YEAR, WITH YOUR SENPAI? THAT WAS MY MASTERPIECE.
KAGA-MI!
YOU MAY BE FEELING GOOD ABOUT YOUR FIRST-HALF LEAD...
...BUT IF YOU THINK THIS GAME IS OVER, YOU'RE IN FOR A NASTY SURPRISE.
YOU'LL BE GNASHING YOUR TEETH...
...SOON.

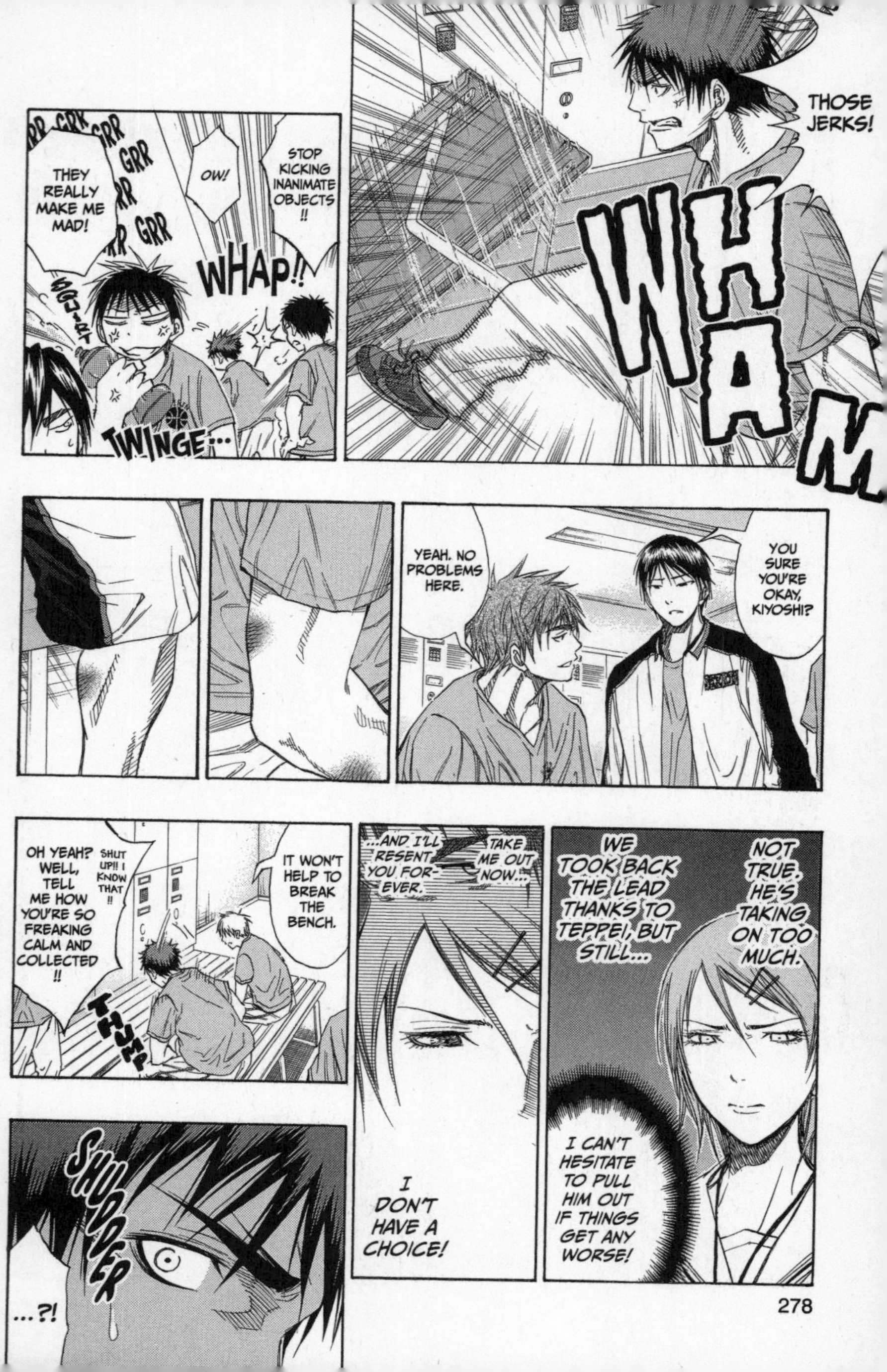
THOSE JERKS!
WHAM
STOP KICKING INANIMATE OBJECTS!!
OW!
THEY REALLY MAKE ME MAD!
GRR GRR GRR GRR GRR GRR
WHAP!!
SQUIRT
TWINGE...
YOU SURE YOU'RE OKAY, KIYOSHI?
YEAH. NO PROBLEMS HERE.
NOT TRUE. HE'S TAKING ON TOO MUCH.
WE TOOK BACK THE LEAD THANKS TO TEPPEI, BUT STILL...
I CAN'T HESITATE TO PULL HIM OUT IF THINGS GET ANY WORSE!
TAKE ME OUT NOW...
...AND I'LL RESENT YOU FOREVER.
I DON'T HAVE A CHOICE!
IT WON'T HELP TO BREAK THE BENCH.
SHUT UP!! I KNOW THAT!!
OH YEAH? WELL, TELL ME HOW YOU'RE SO FREAKING CALM AND COLLECTED!!
THUMP
SHUDDER
...?!

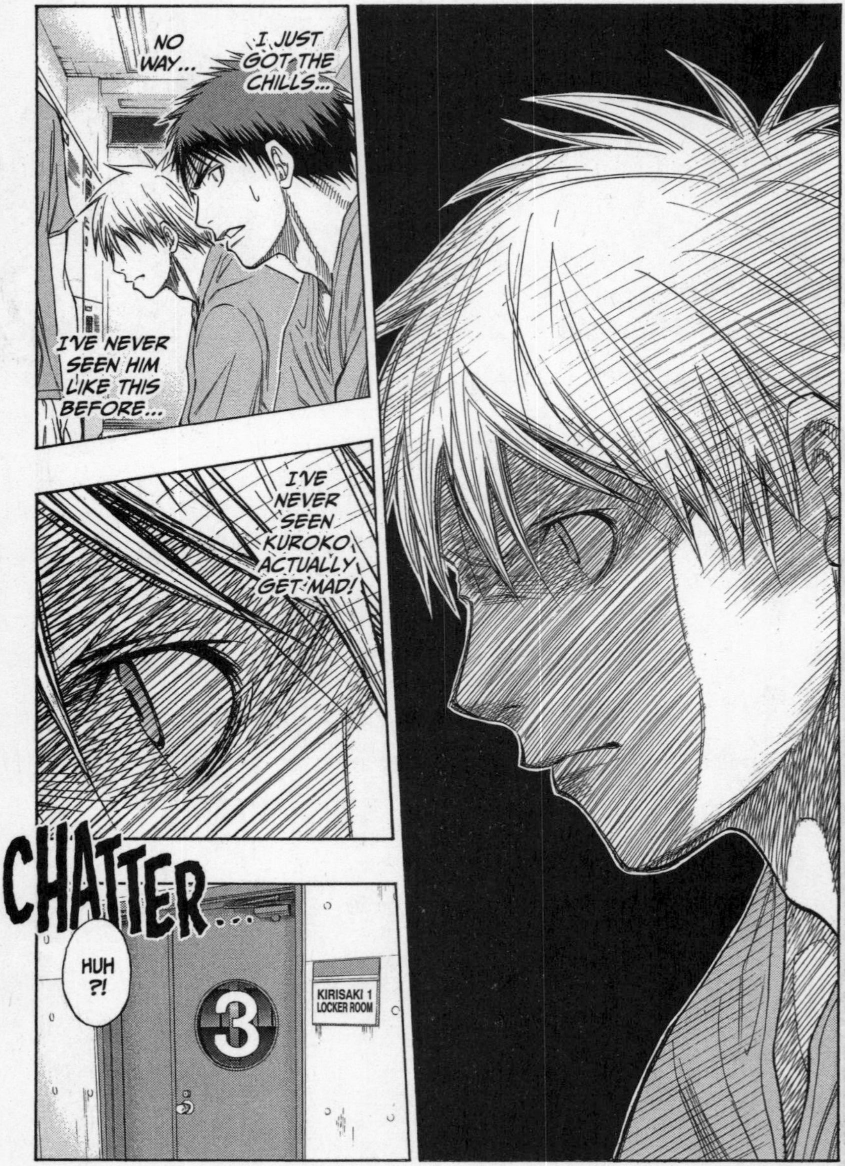
I JUST GOT THE CHILLS...
NO WAY...
I'VE NEVER SEEN HIM LIKE THIS BEFORE...
I'VE NEVER SEEN KUROKO ACTUALLY GET MAD!
CHATTER...
HUH ?!
3
KIRISAKI 1 LOCKER ROOM

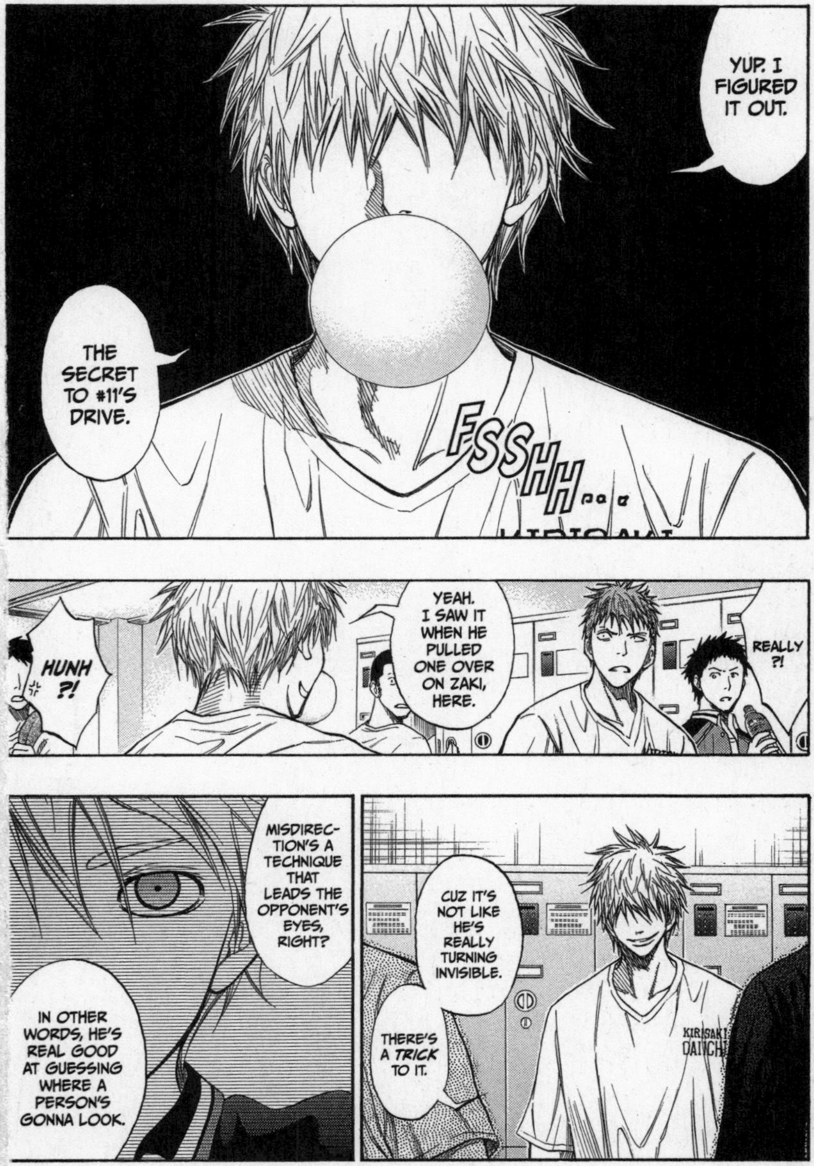
YUP. I FIGURED IT OUT.
THE SECRET TO #11'S DRIVE.
FSSHH
REALLY ?!
YEAH. I SAW IT WHEN HE PULLED ONE OVER ON ZAKI, HERE.
HUNH ?!
CUZ IT'S NOT LIKE HE'S REALLY TURNING INVISIBLE.
THERE'S A *TRICK* TO IT.
MISDIREC-TION'S A TECHNIQUE THAT LEADS THE OPPONENT'S EYES, RIGHT?
IN OTHER WORDS, HE'S REAL GOOD AT GUESSING WHERE A PERSON'S GONNA LOOK.

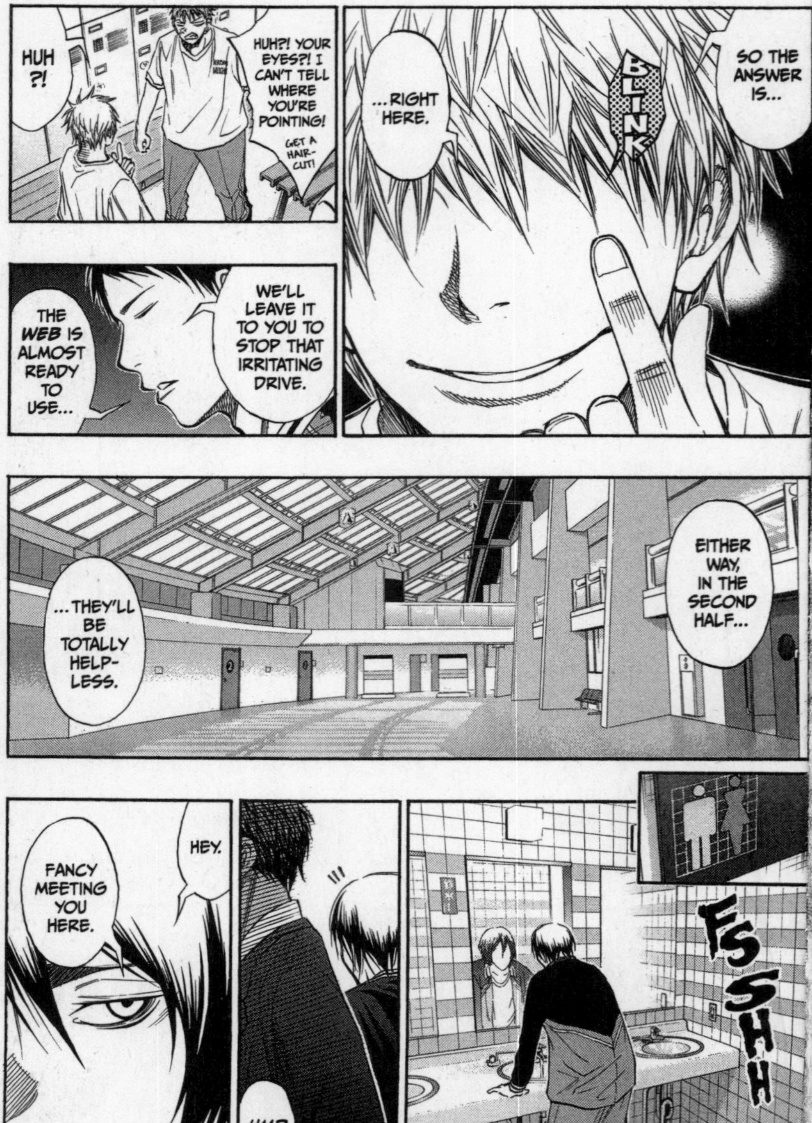

SO THE ANSWER IS...
BLINK
...RIGHT HERE.
HUH?! YOUR EYES?! I CAN'T TELL WHERE YOU'RE POINTING!
GET A HAIR-CUT!
HUH ?!
WE'LL LEAVE IT TO YOU TO STOP THAT IRRITATING DRIVE.
THE WEB IS ALMOST READY TO USE...
EITHER WAY, IN THE SECOND HALF...
...THEY'LL BE TOTALLY HELPLESS.
FSSHH
!!
HM?
HEY.
FANCY MEETING YOU HERE.

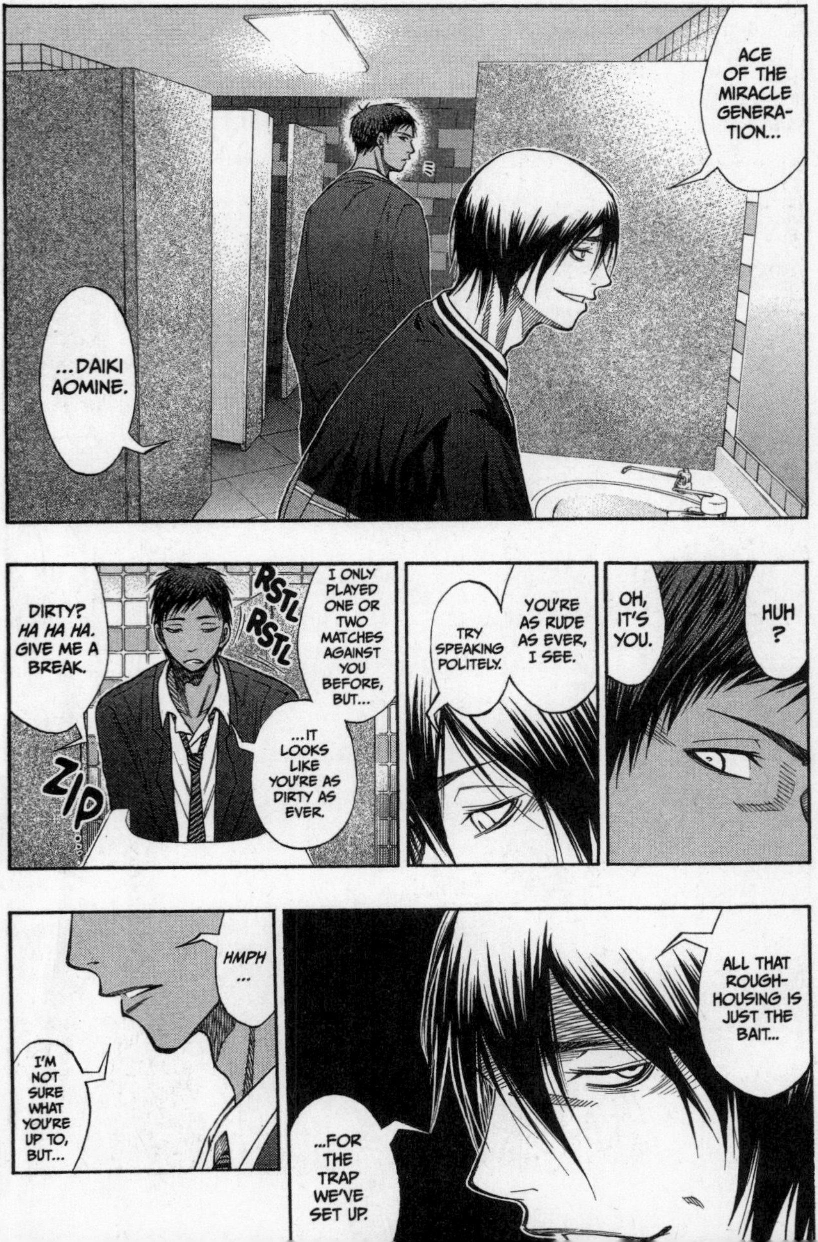
ACE OF THE MIRACLE GENERATION...
...DAIKI AOMINE.
HUH?
OH, IT'S YOU.
YOU'RE AS RUDE AS EVER, I SEE.
TRY SPEAKING POLITELY.
I ONLY PLAYED ONE OR TWO MATCHES AGAINST YOU BEFORE, BUT...
RSTL RSTL
...IT LOOKS LIKE YOU'RE AS DIRTY AS EVER.
DIRTY? *HA HA HA.* GIVE ME A BREAK.
ZIP
ALL THAT ROUGH-HOUSING IS JUST THE BAIT...
...FOR THE TRAP WE'VE SET UP.
HMPH...
I'M NOT SURE WHAT YOU'RE UP TO, BUT...

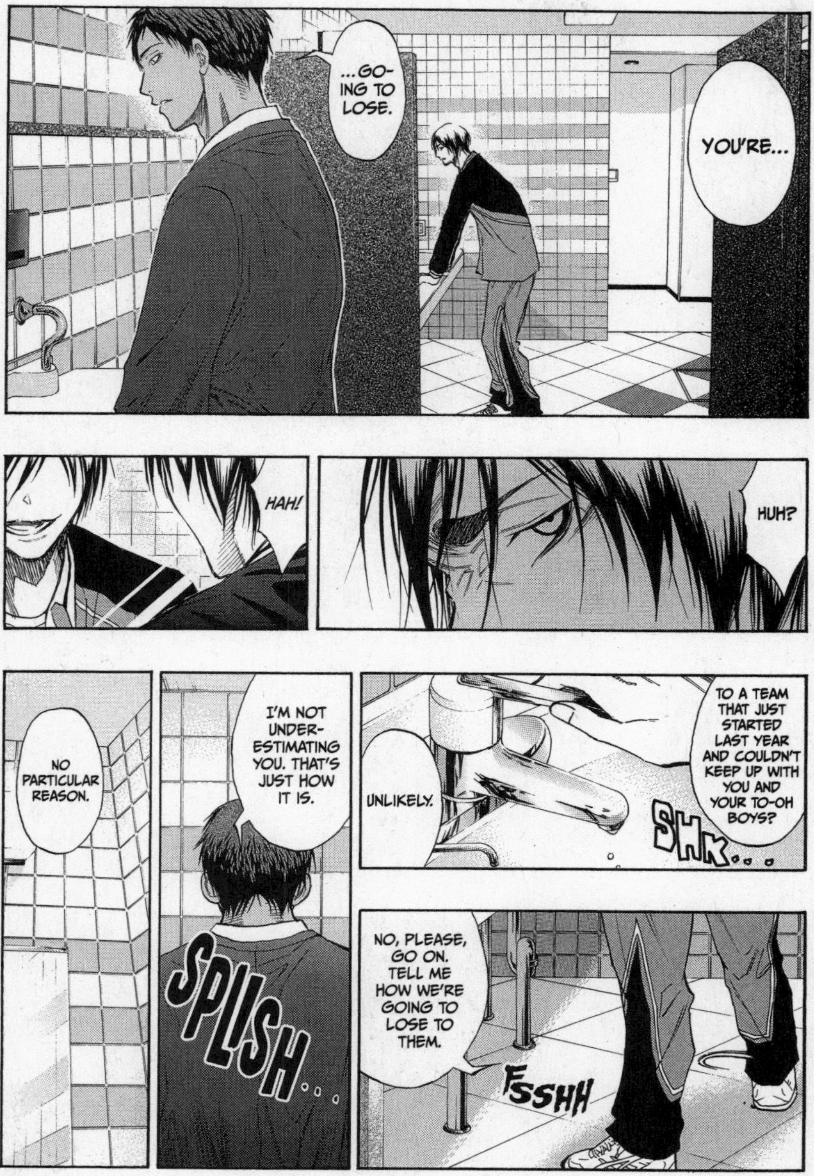
YOU'RE...
...GO-ING TO LOSE.
HUH?
HAH!
TO A TEAM THAT JUST STARTED LAST YEAR AND COULDN'T KEEP UP WITH YOU AND YOUR TO-OH BOYS?
SHK...
UNLIKELY.
NO, PLEASE, GO ON. TELL ME HOW WE'RE GOING TO LOSE TO THEM.
FSSHH
I'M NOT UNDER-ESTIMATING YOU. THAT'S JUST HOW IT IS.
SPLISH...
NO PARTICULAR REASON.

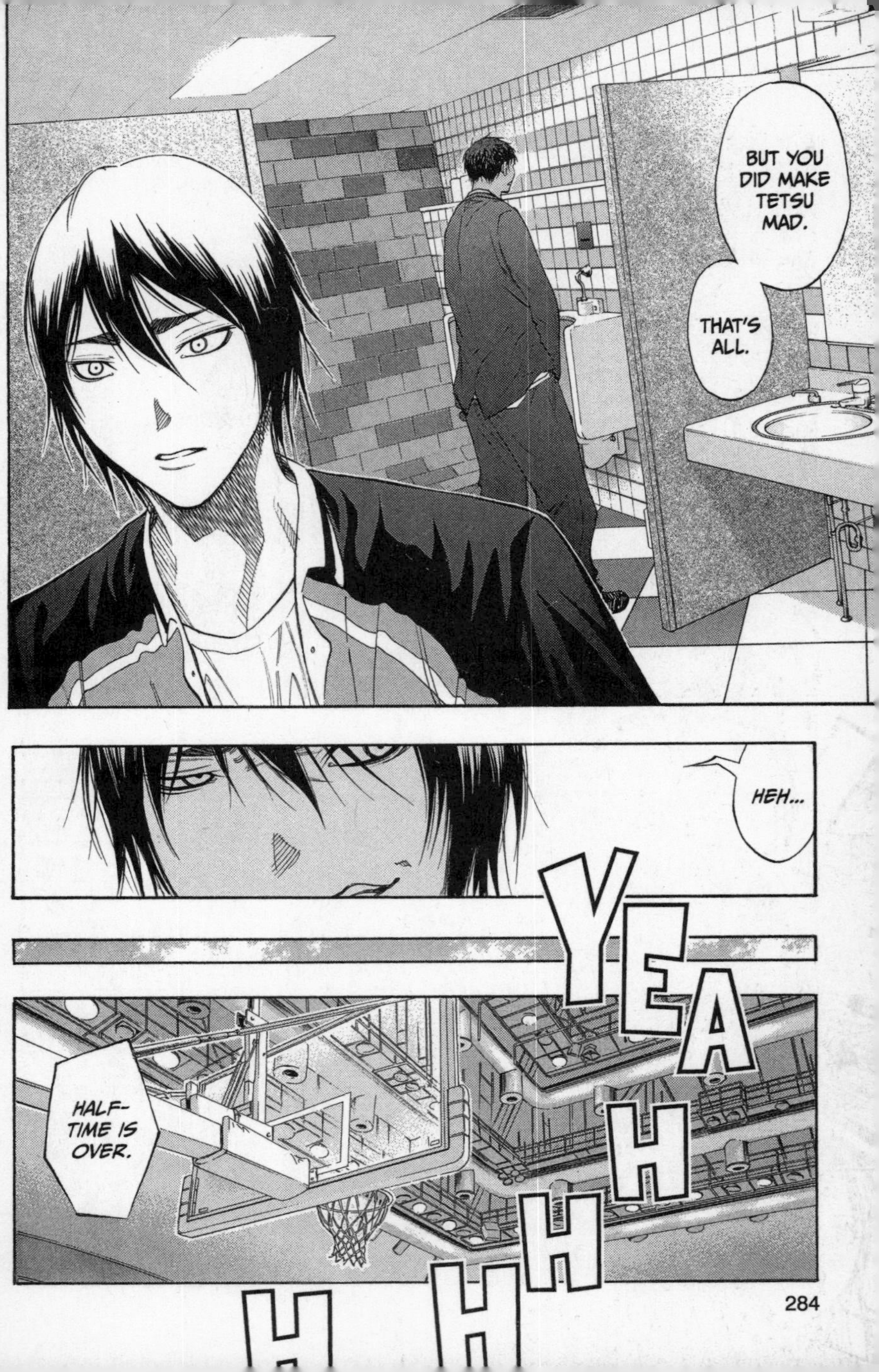

BUT YOU DID MAKE TETSU MAD.
THAT'S ALL.
HEH...
YEAHHHHH
HALF-TIME IS OVER.

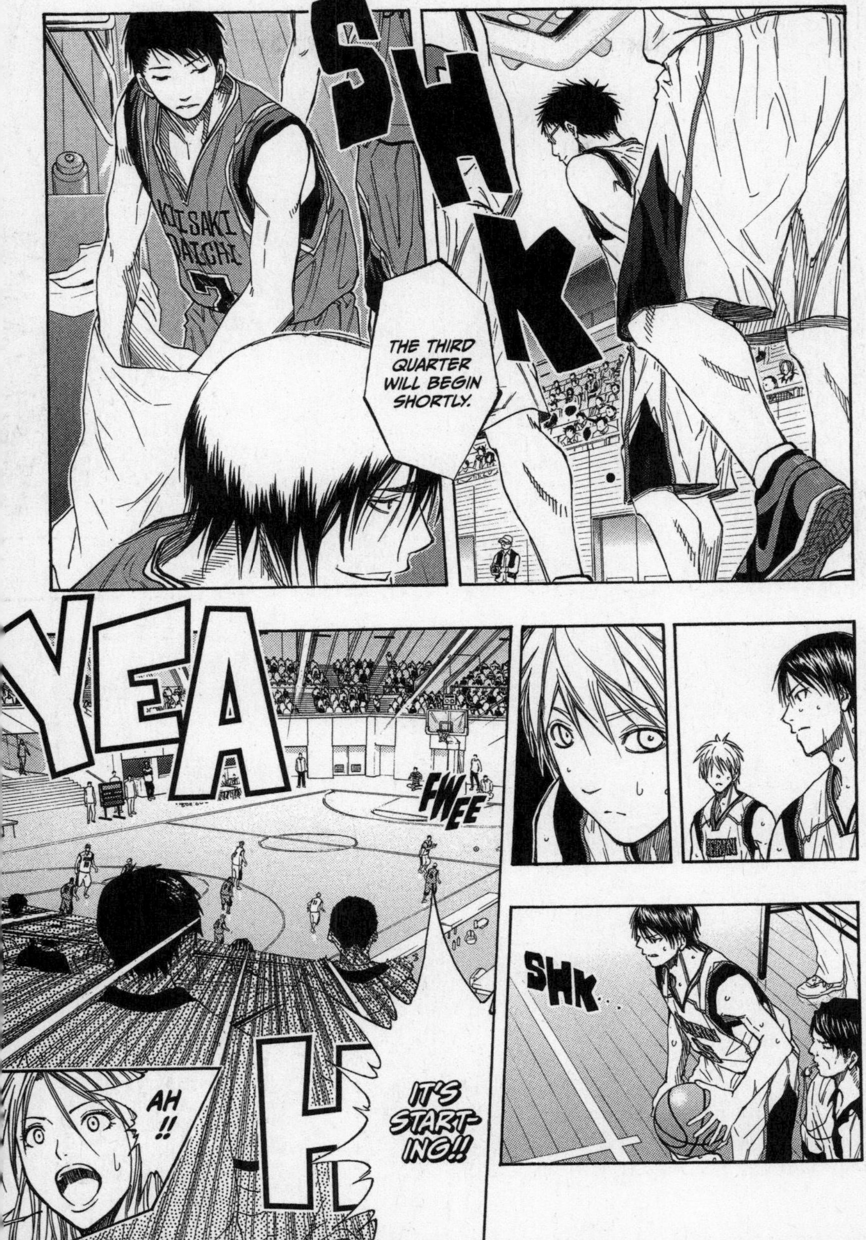
SHK
THE THIRD QUARTER WILL BEGIN SHORTLY.
SHK...
YEAH
FWEE
IT'S STARTING!!
AH!!

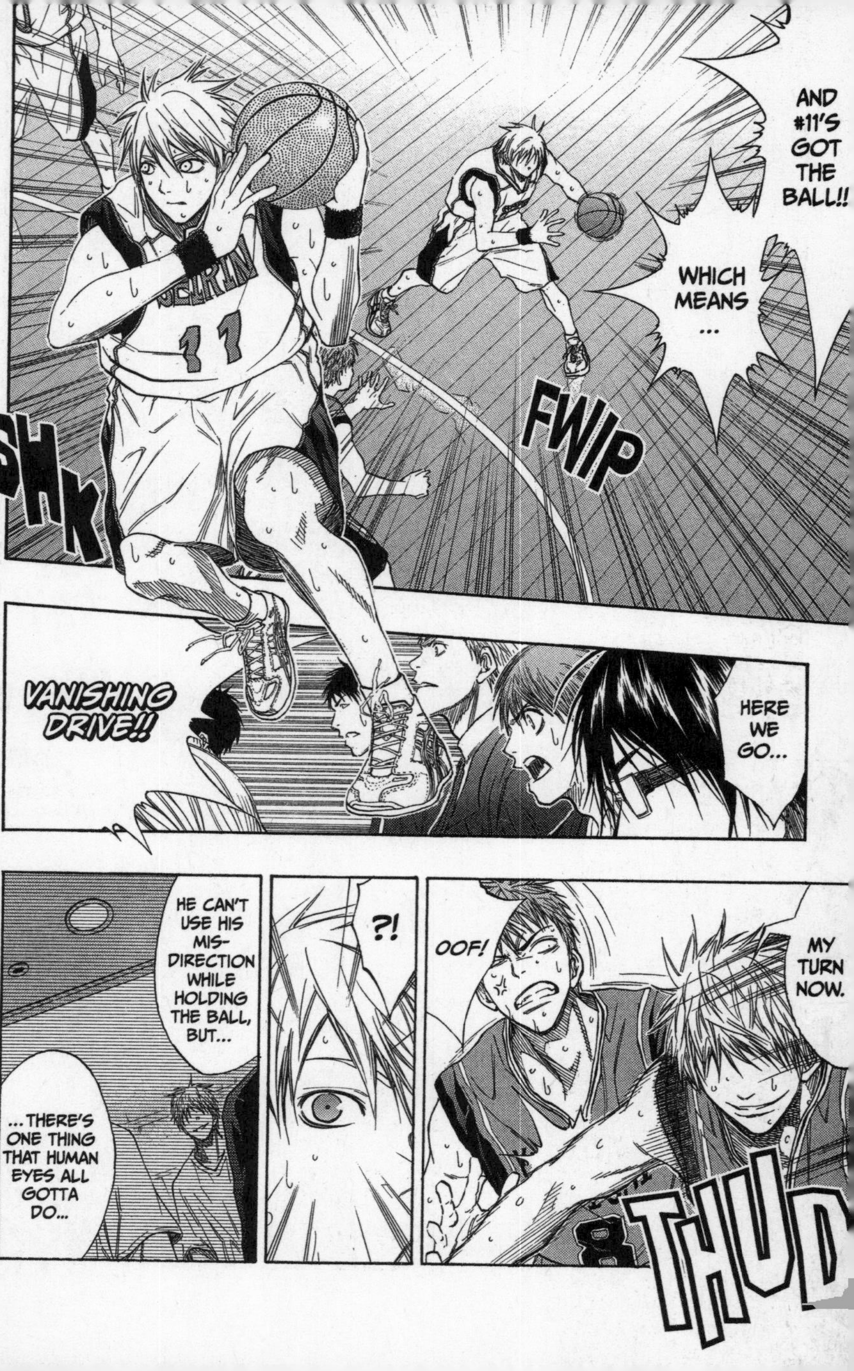
AND #11'S GOT THE BALL!!
WHICH MEANS ...
FWIP
SHK
HERE WE GO...
VANISHING DRIVE!!
MY TURN NOW.
OOF!
THUD
?!
HE CAN'T USE HIS MIS-DIRECTION WHILE HOLDING THE BALL, BUT...
...THERE'S ONE THING THAT HUMAN EYES ALL GOTTA DO...

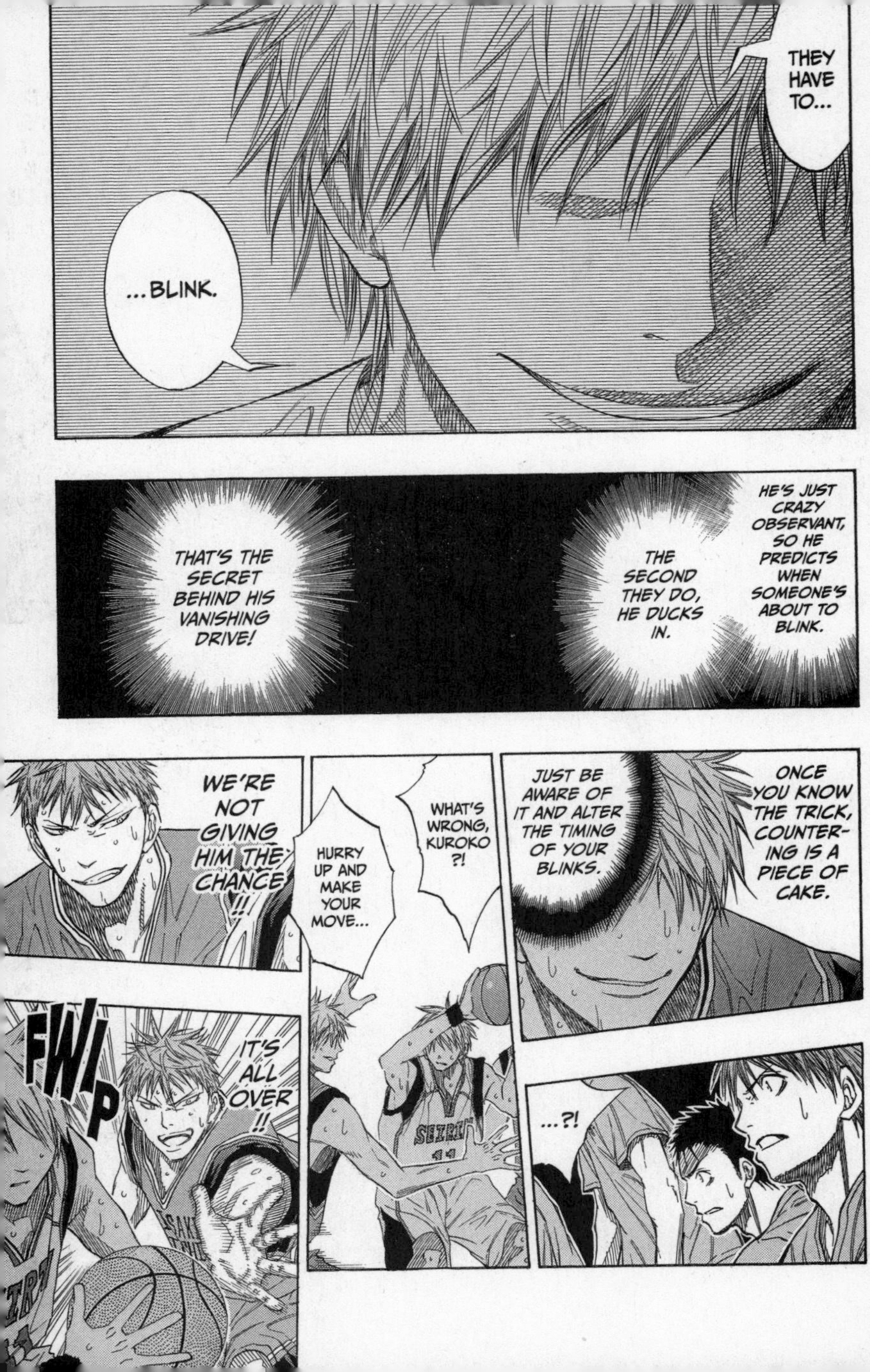
THEY HAVE TO...
...BLINK.
HE'S JUST CRAZY OBSERVANT, SO HE PREDICTS WHEN SOMEONE'S ABOUT TO BLINK.
THE SECOND THEY DO, HE DUCKS IN.
THAT'S THE SECRET BEHIND HIS VANISHING DRIVE!
ONCE YOU KNOW THE TRICK, COUNTER-ING IS A PIECE OF CAKE.
JUST BE AWARE OF IT AND ALTER THE TIMING OF YOUR BLINKS.
...?!
WHAT'S WRONG, KUROKO ?!
HURRY UP AND MAKE YOUR MOVE...
WE'RE NOT GIVING HIM THE CHANCE !!
FWIP
IT'S ALL OVER !!

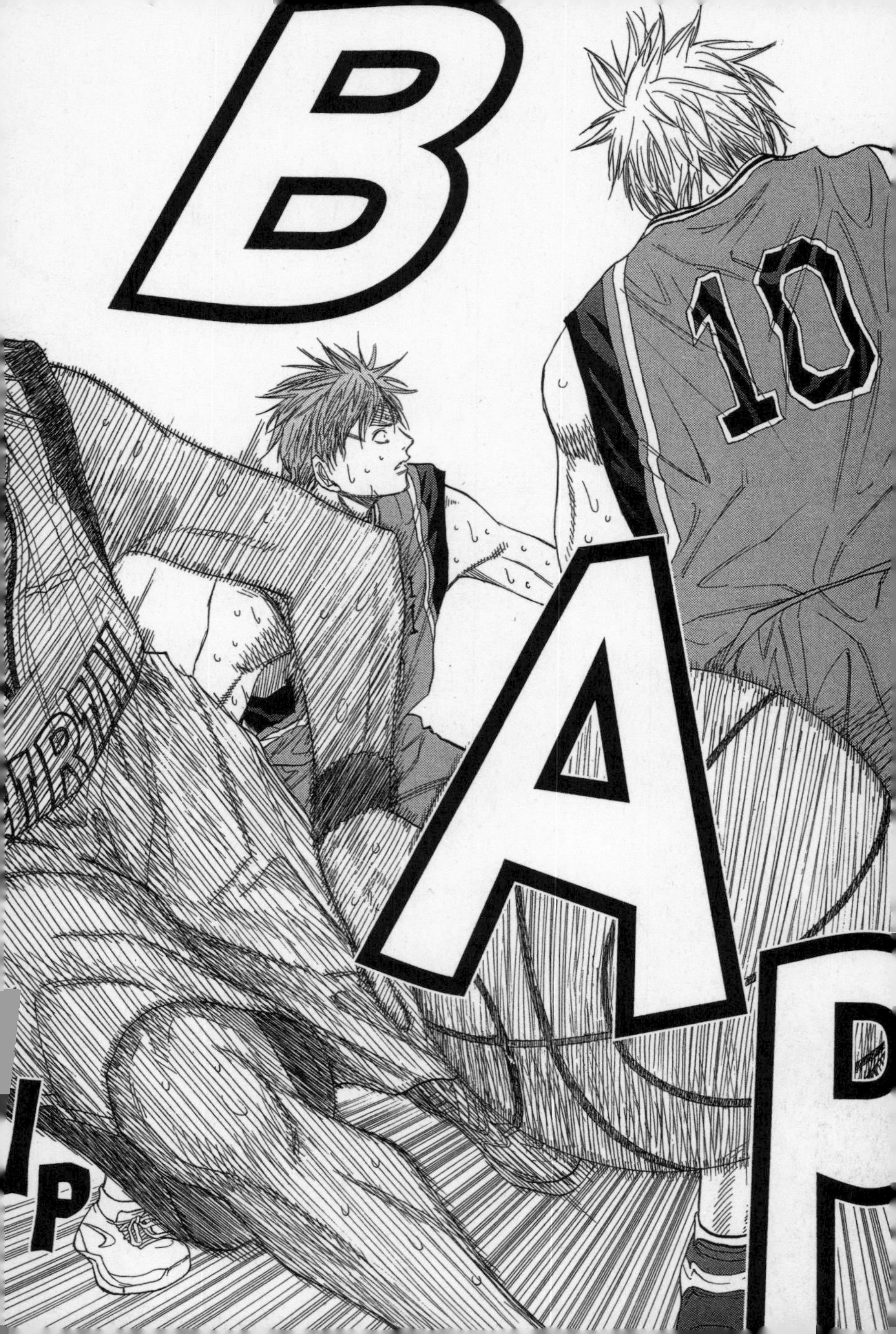
BAP

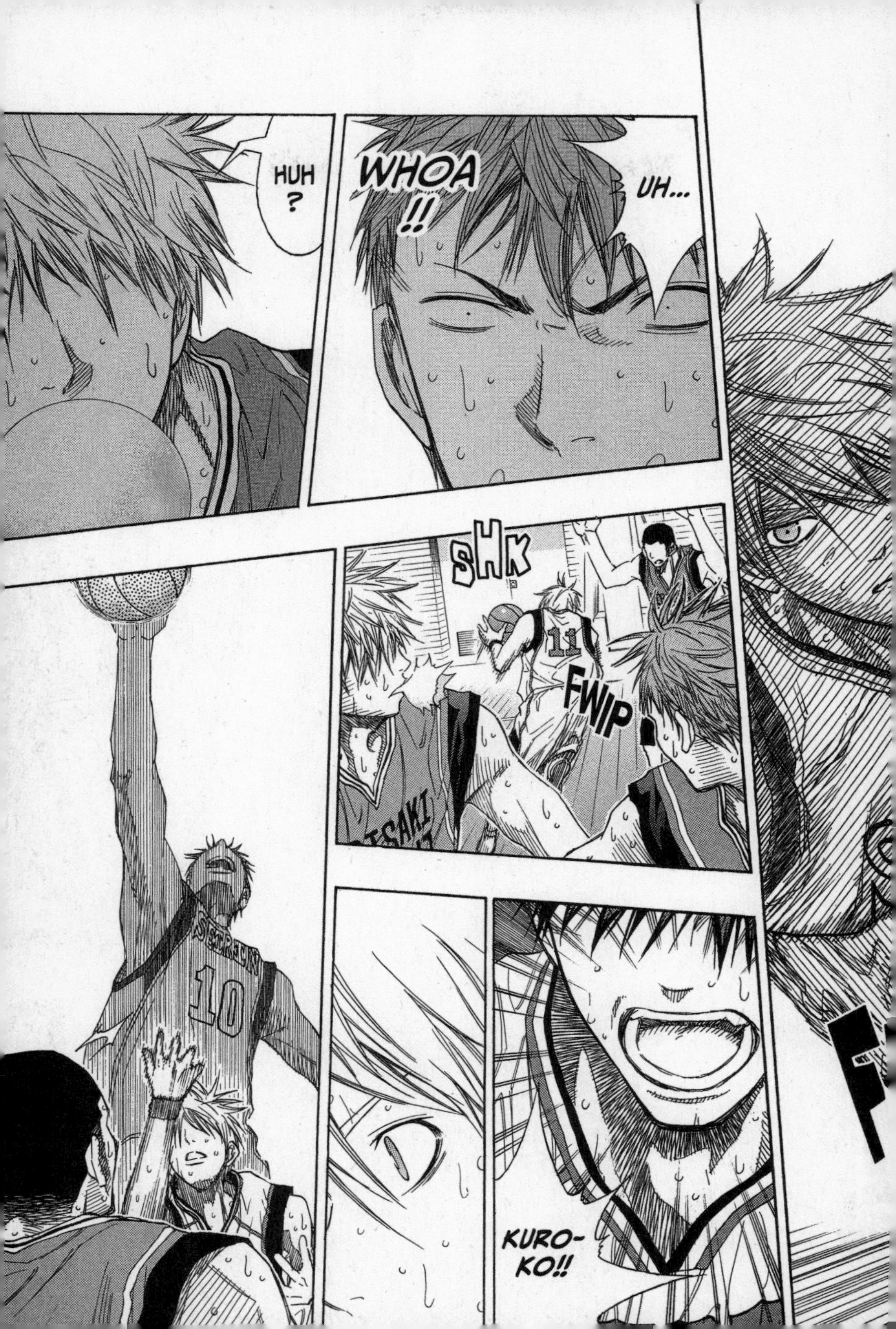
UH...
WHOA !!
HUH ?
SHK
FWIP
KURO-KO!!

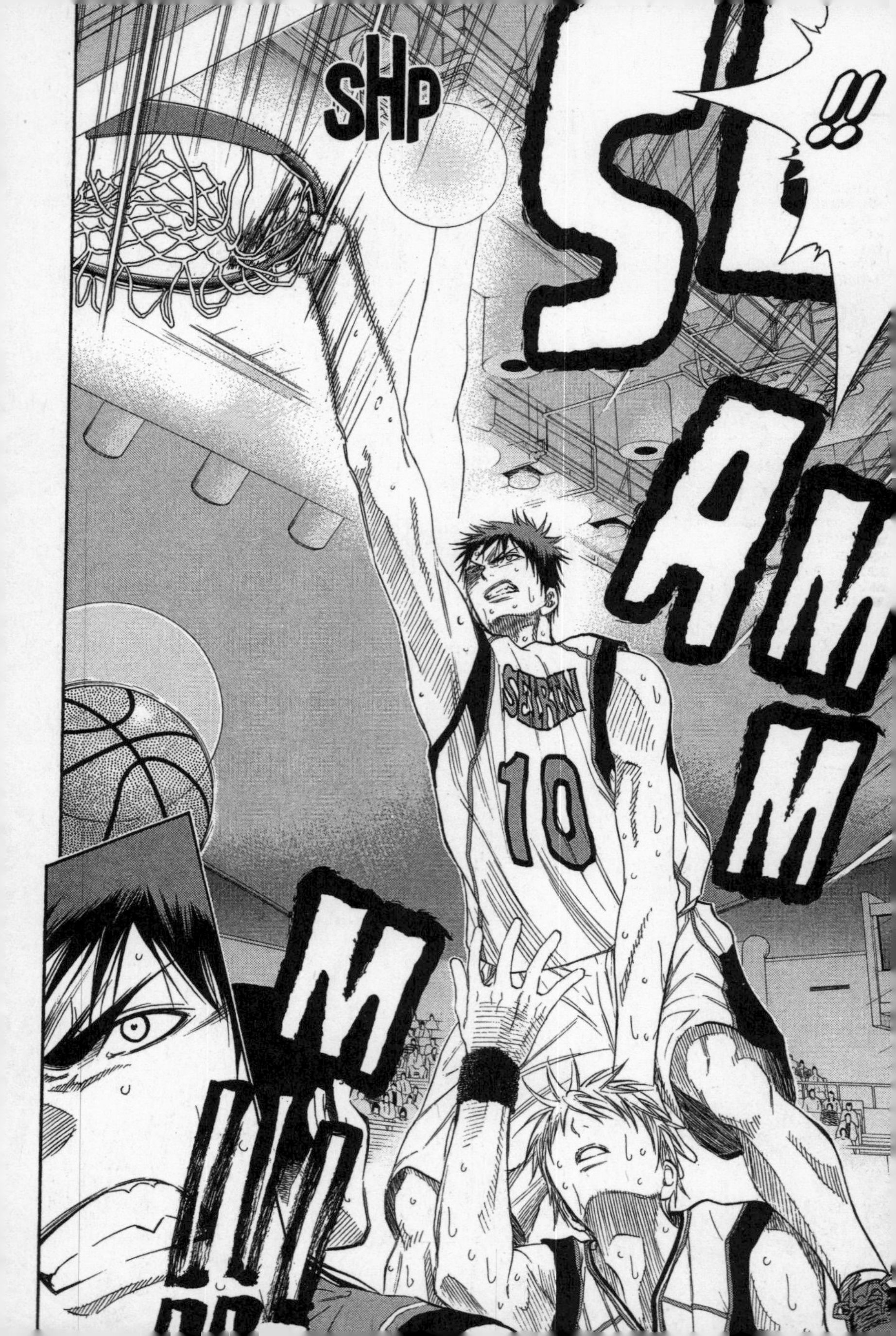
SLAMMMM!!
SHP
SEIRIN
10

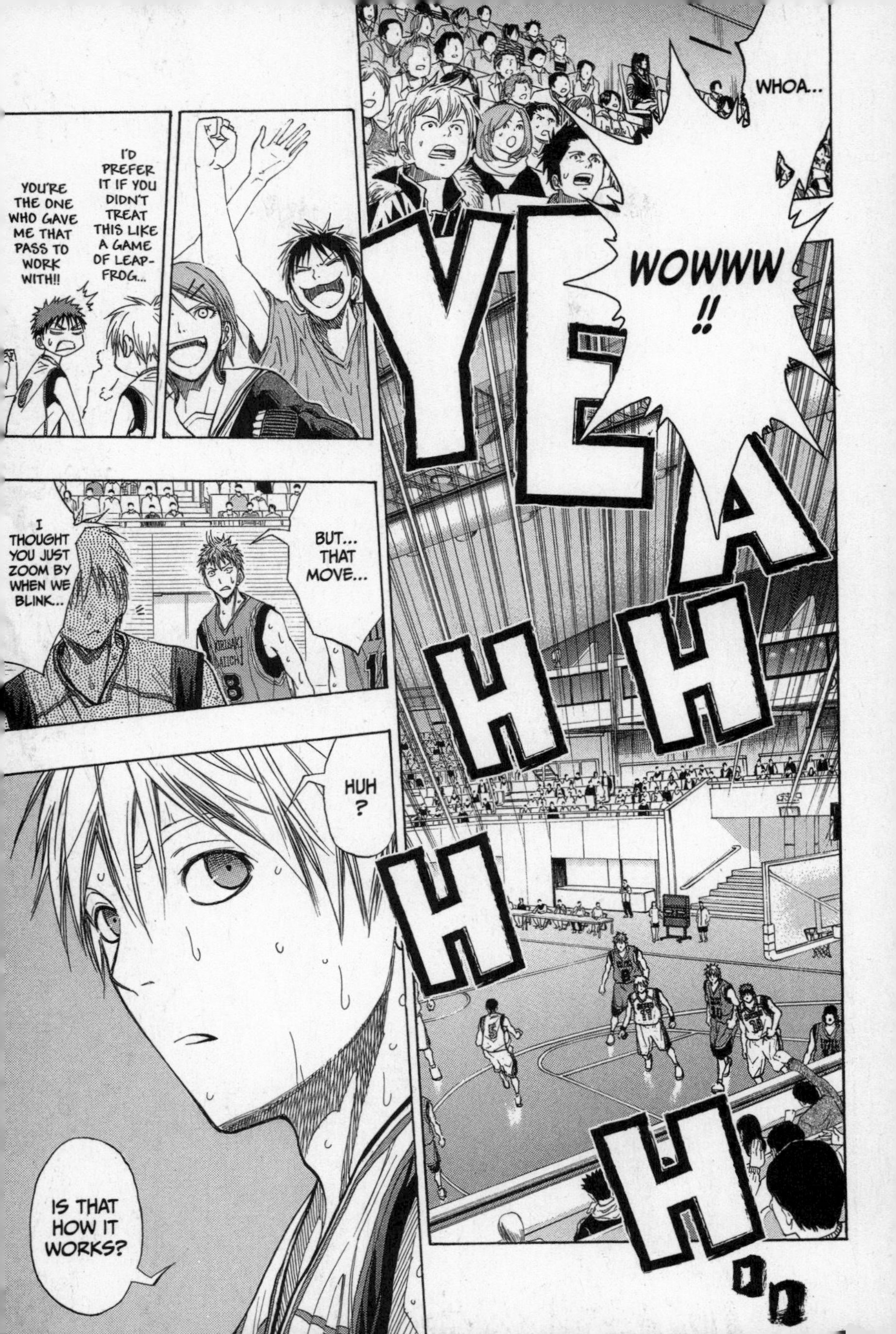
WHOA...
WOWWW!!
YEAHHHH...
I'D PREFER IT IF YOU DIDN'T TREAT THIS LIKE A GAME OF LEAP-FROG...
YOU'RE THE ONE WHO GAVE ME THAT PASS TO WORK WITH!!
BUT... THAT MOVE...
I THOUGHT YOU JUST ZOOM BY WHEN WE BLINK...
HUH?
IS THAT HOW IT WORKS?

KUROKO'S BASKETBALL BLOOPERS

TAKE 1

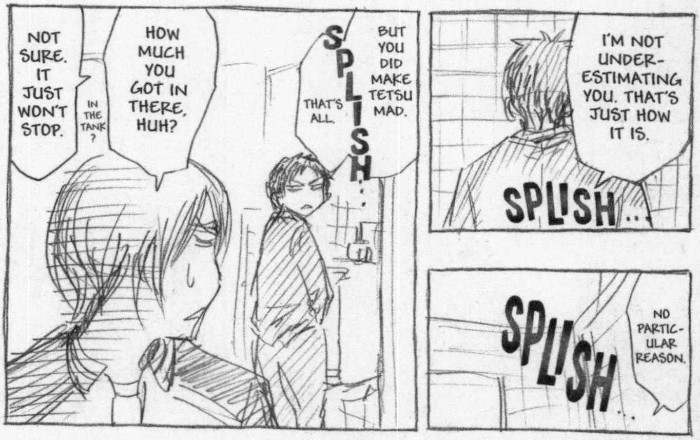
I'M NOT UNDER-ESTIMATING YOU. THAT'S JUST HOW IT IS.
SPLISH...
SPLISH
NO PARTIC-ULAR REASON.
BUT YOU DID MAKE TETSU MAD.
SPLISH...
THAT'S ALL.
HOW MUCH YOU GOT IN THERE, HUH?
IN THE TANK?
NOT SURE. IT JUST WON'T STOP.

104TH QUARTER: IT'S A TRAP

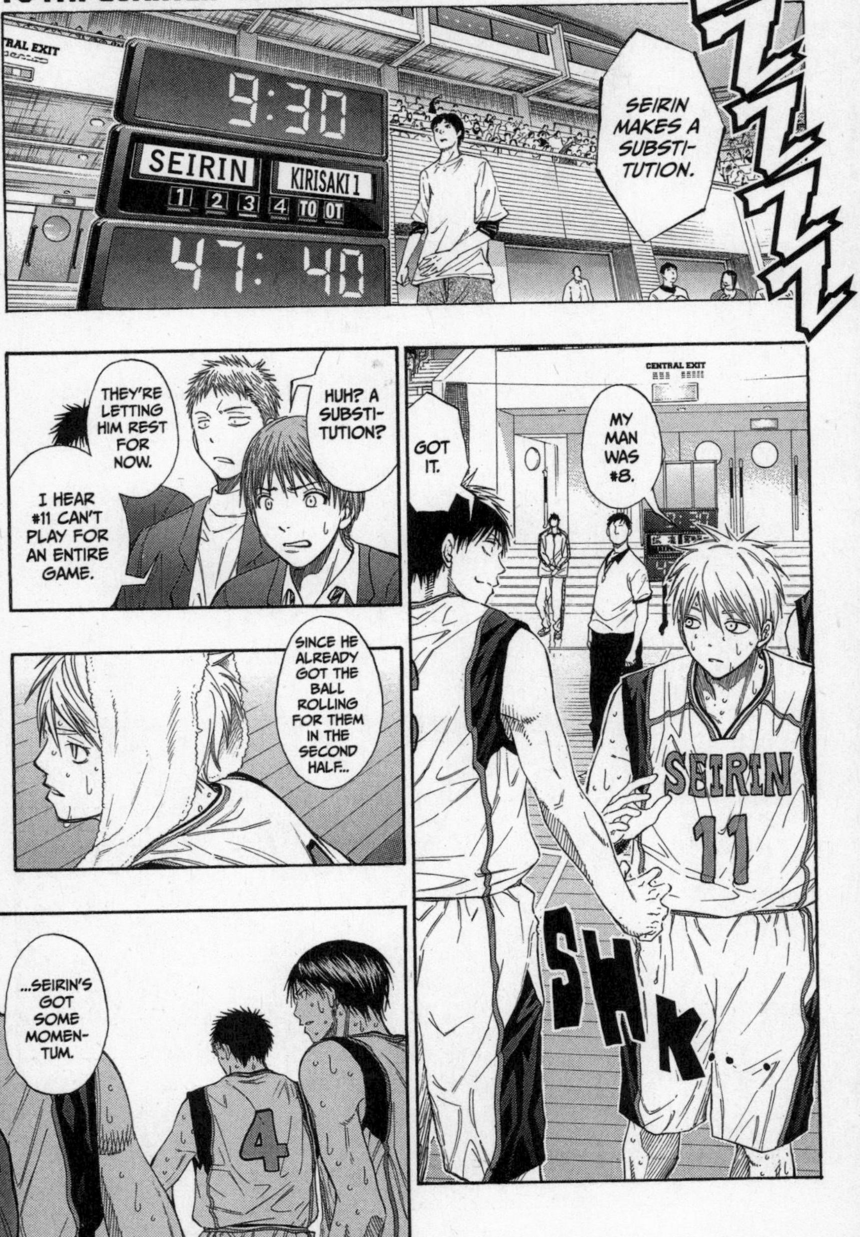
BZZZ
SEIRIN MAKES A SUBSTI-TUTION.
TRAL EXIT
9:30
SEIRIN
KIRISAKI 1
1 2 3 4 TO OT
47: 40
CENTRAL EXIT
MY MAN WAS #8.
GOT IT.
SHK
HUH? A SUBSTI-TUTION?
THEY'RE LETTING HIM REST FOR NOW.
I HEAR #11 CAN'T PLAY FOR AN ENTIRE GAME.
SINCE HE ALREADY GOT THE BALL ROLLING FOR THEM IN THE SECOND HALF...
...SEIRIN'S GOT SOME MOMEN-TUM.

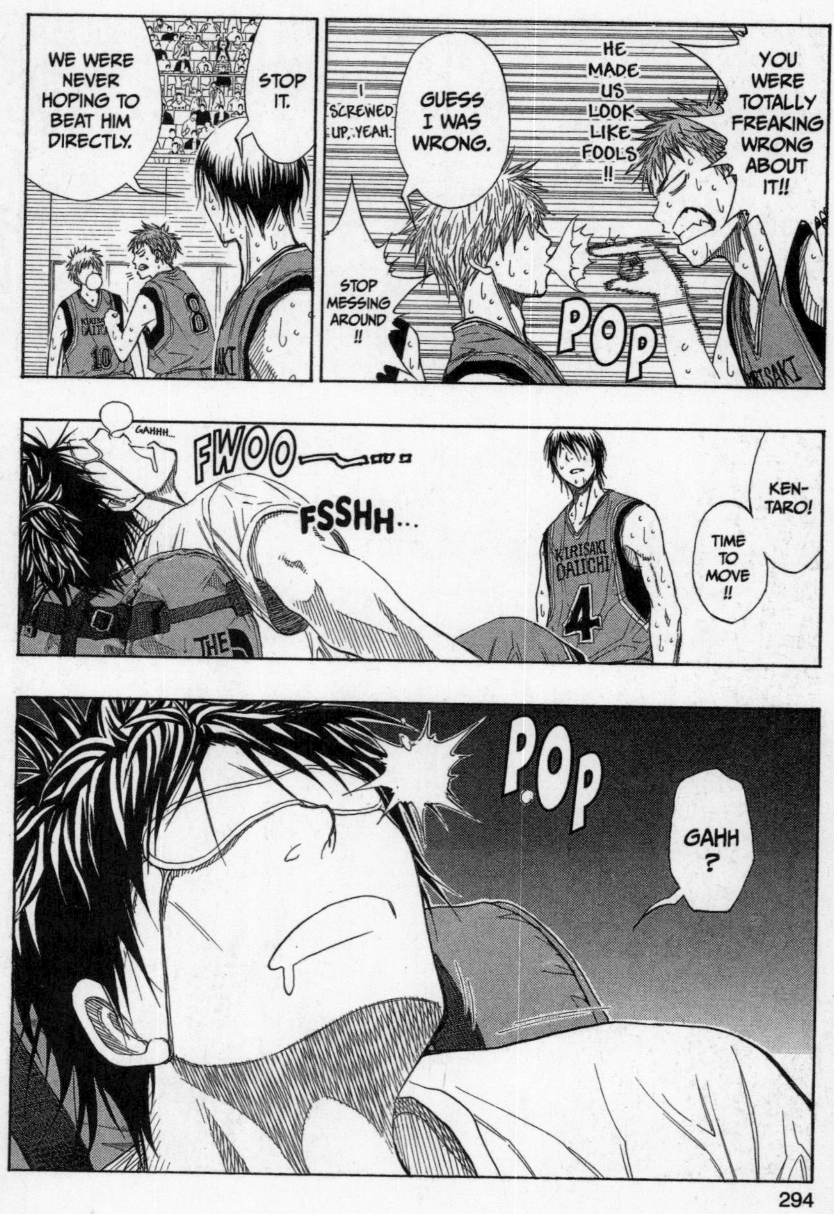
YOU WERE TOTALLY FREAKING WRONG ABOUT IT!!
HE MADE US LOOK LIKE FOOLS!!
GUESS I WAS WRONG.
I SCREWED UP, YEAH.
STOP MESSING AROUND!!
POP
STOP IT.
WE WERE NEVER HOPING TO BEAT HIM DIRECTLY.
KEN-TARO!
TIME TO MOVE!!
FSSHH...
FWOO—
GAHHH...
POP
GAHH?

104TH QUARTER:
IT'S A TRAP

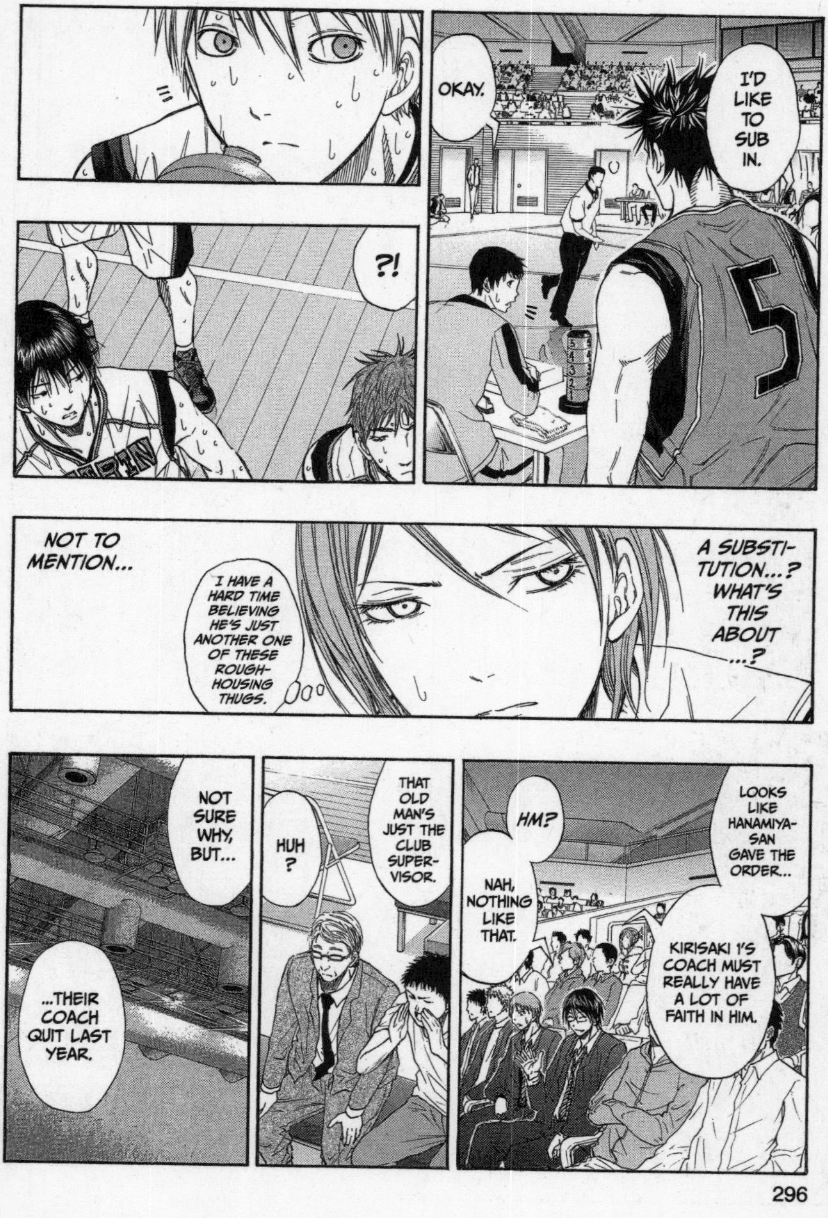
I'D LIKE TO SUB IN.
OKAY.
?!
A SUBSTI- TUTION...? WHAT'S THIS ABOUT ...?
NOT TO MENTION...
I HAVE A HARD TIME BELIEVING HE'S JUST ANOTHER ONE OF THESE ROUGH- HOUSING THUGS.
LOOKS LIKE HANAMIYA-SAN GAVE THE ORDER...
KIRISAKI 1'S COACH MUST REALLY HAVE A LOT OF FAITH IN HIM.
HM?
NAH, NOTHING LIKE THAT.
THAT OLD MAN'S JUST THE CLUB SUPER- VISOR.
HUH ?
NOT SURE WHY, BUT...
...THEIR COACH QUIT LAST YEAR.

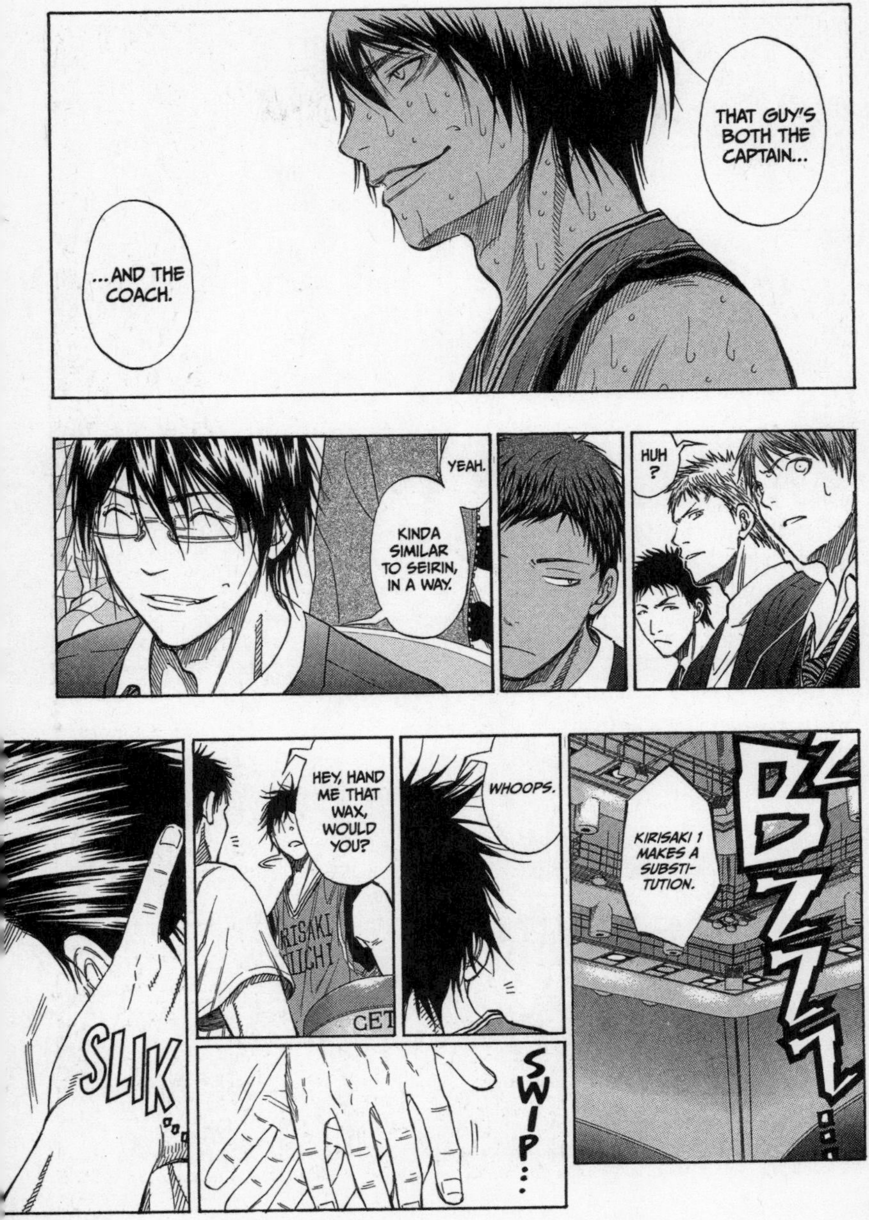
THAT GUY'S BOTH THE CAPTAIN...
...AND THE COACH.
HUH ?
YEAH.
KINDA SIMILAR TO SEIRIN, IN A WAY.
BZZZT...
KIRISAKI 1 MAKES A SUBSTITUTION.
WHOOPS.
HEY, HAND ME THAT WAX, WOULD YOU?
SWIP...
SLIK...

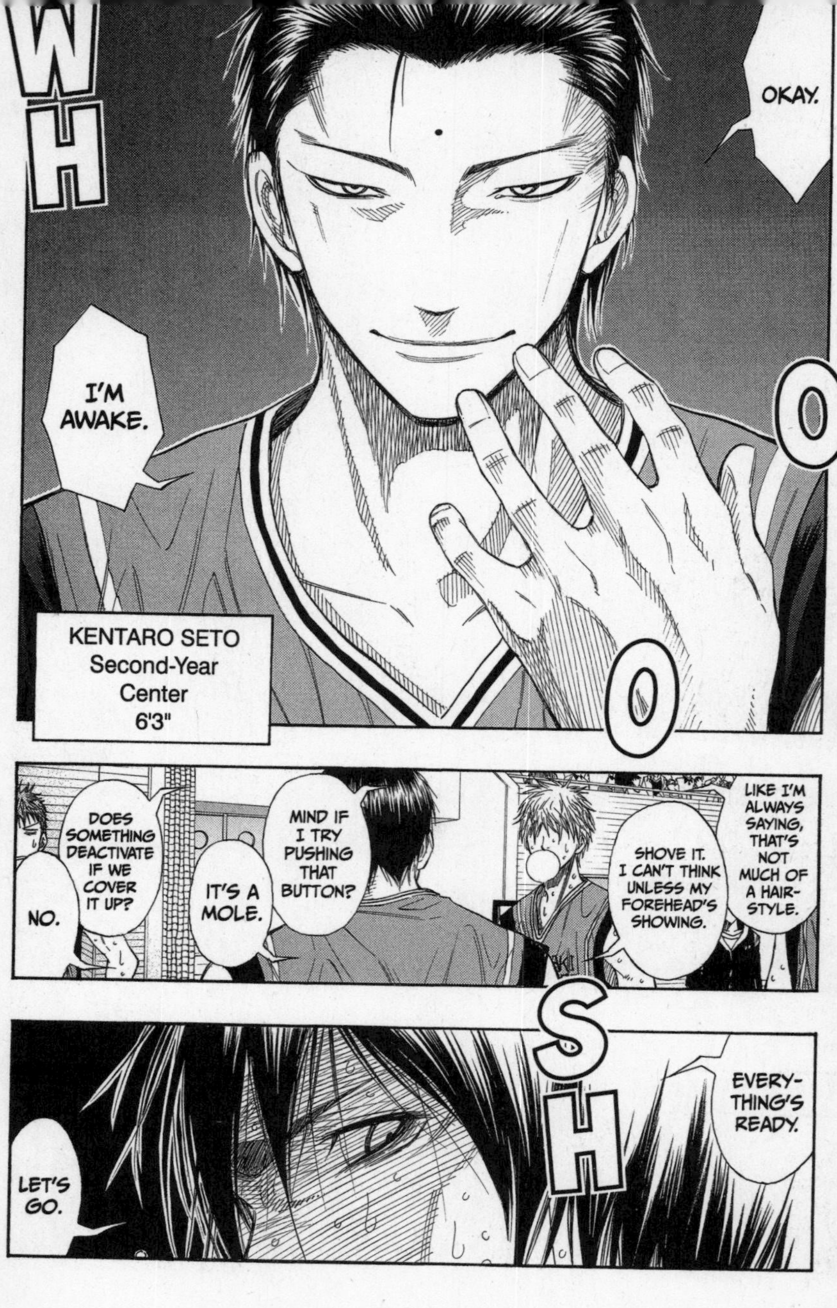
OKAY.
I'M AWAKE.
WHOO
KENTARO SETO
Second-Year
Center
6'3"
LIKE I'M ALWAYS SAYING, THAT'S NOT MUCH OF A HAIR-STYLE.
SHOVE IT. I CAN'T THINK UNLESS MY FOREHEAD'S SHOWING.
MIND IF I TRY PUSHING THAT BUTTON?
IT'S A MOLE.
DOES SOMETHING DEACTIVATE IF WE COVER IT UP?
NO.
SH
EVERY-THING'S READY.
LET'S GO.

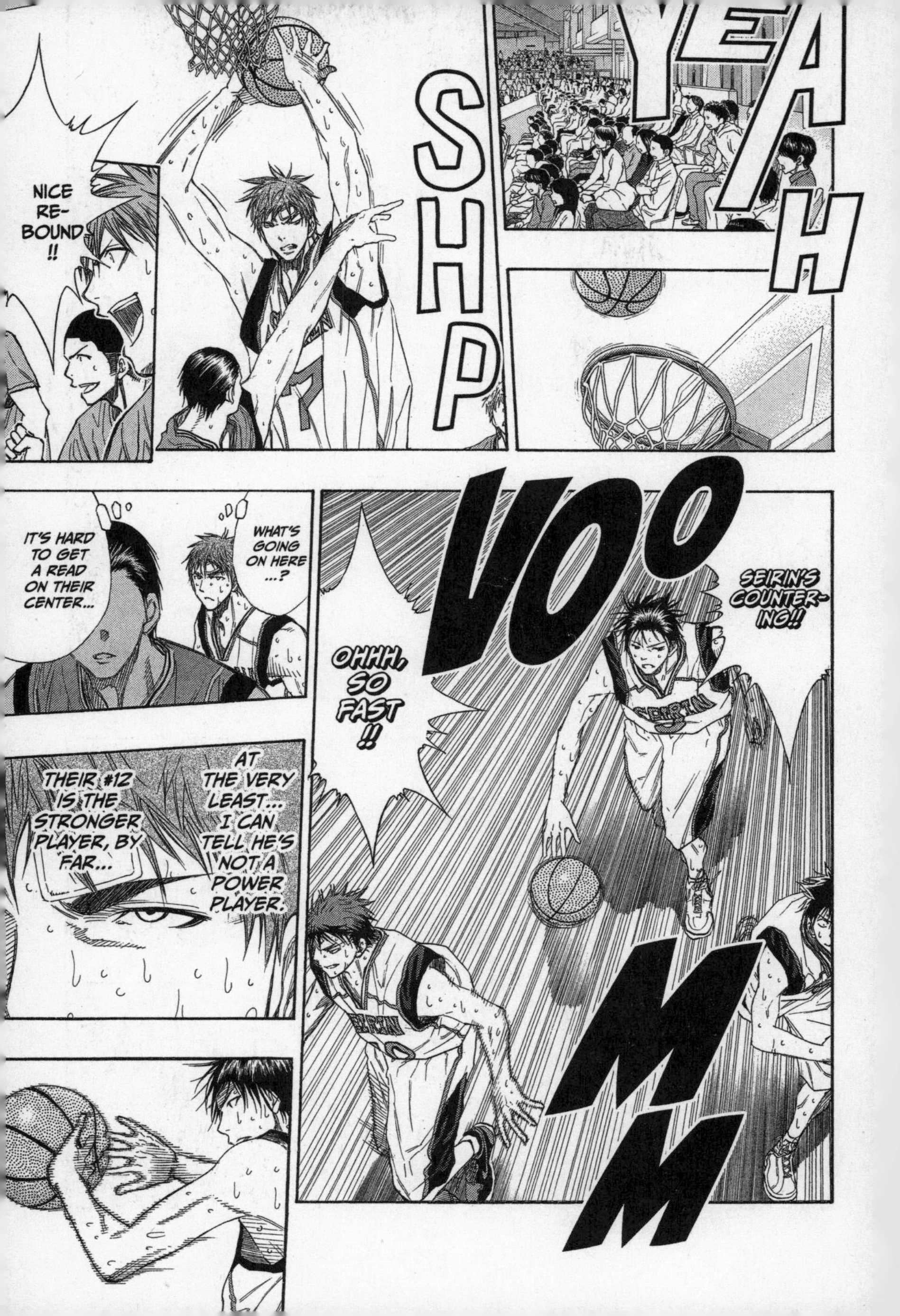
YEAH
SHP
NICE RE-BOUND!!
VOOMM
SEIRIN'S COUNTER-ING!!
OHHH, SO FAST!!
WHAT'S GOING ON HERE...?
IT'S HARD TO GET A READ ON THEIR CENTER...
AT THE VERY LEAST... I CAN TELL HE'S NOT A POWER PLAYER.
THEIR #12 IS THE STRONGER PLAYER, BY FAR...

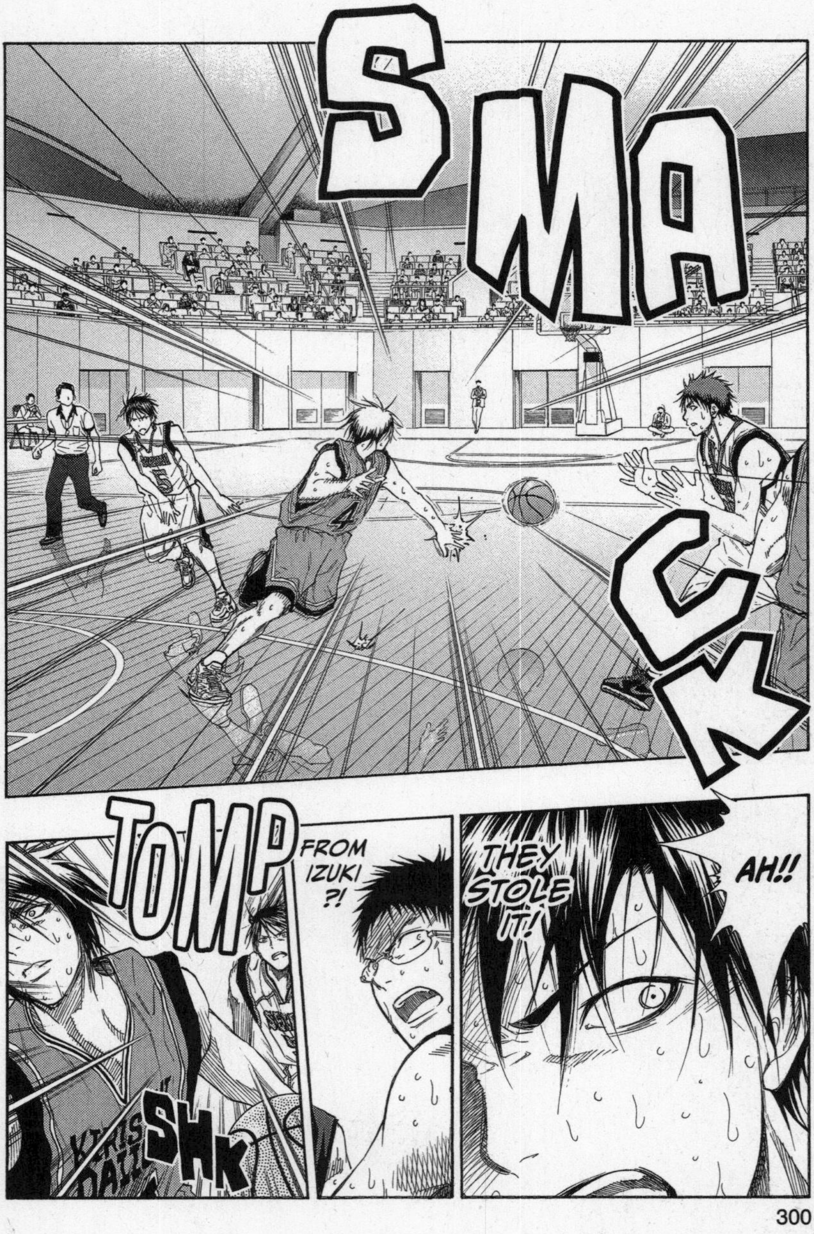
SMACK
AH!!
THEY STOLE IT!
FROM IZUKI ?!
TOMP
SHK

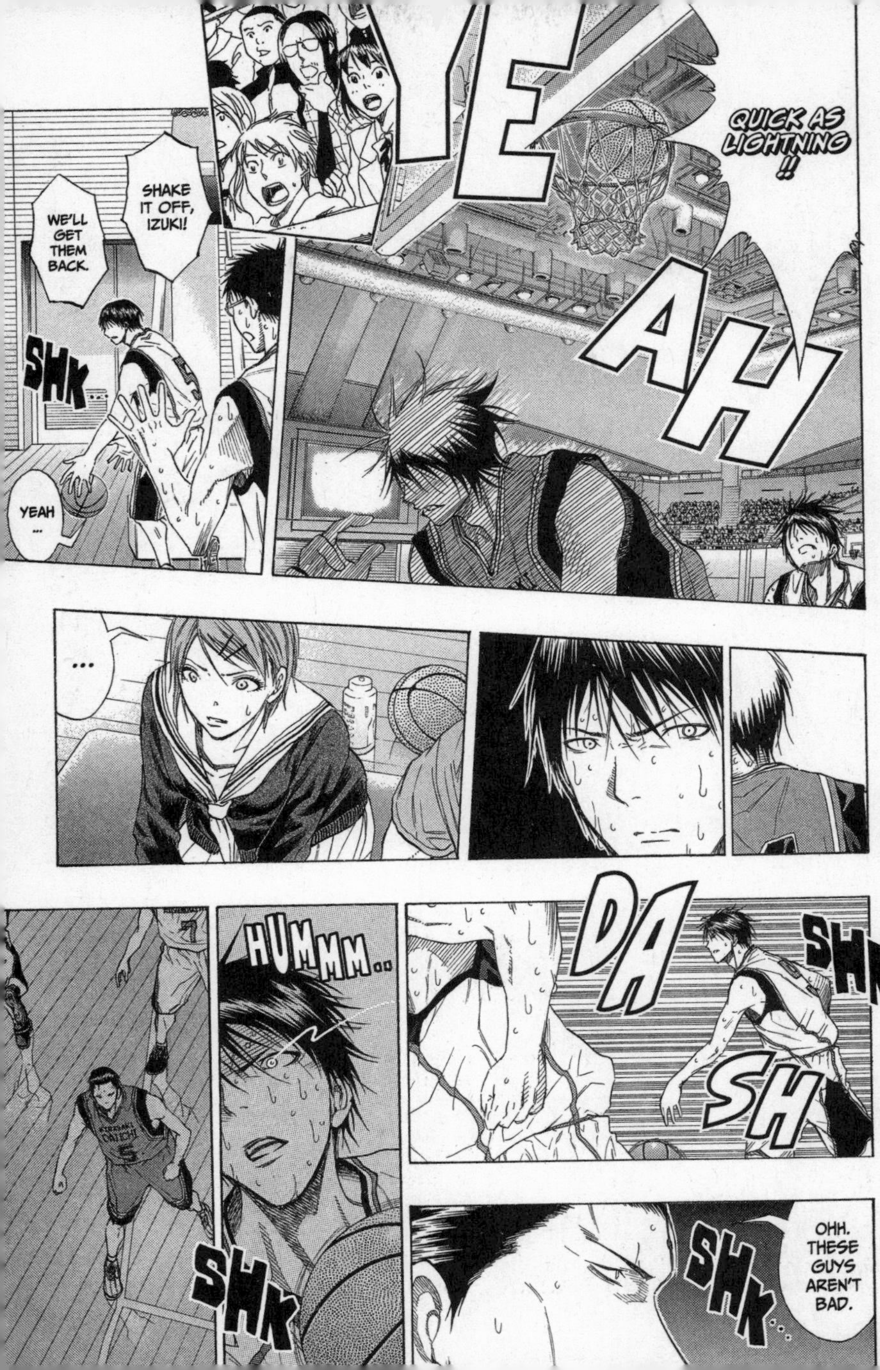

QUICK AS LIGHTNING !!
AH
SHAKE IT OFF, IZUKI!
WE'LL GET THEM BACK.
SHK
YEAH ...
...
DASH
SHK
HUMMM..
SHK
SHK...
OHH. THESE GUYS AREN'T BAD.

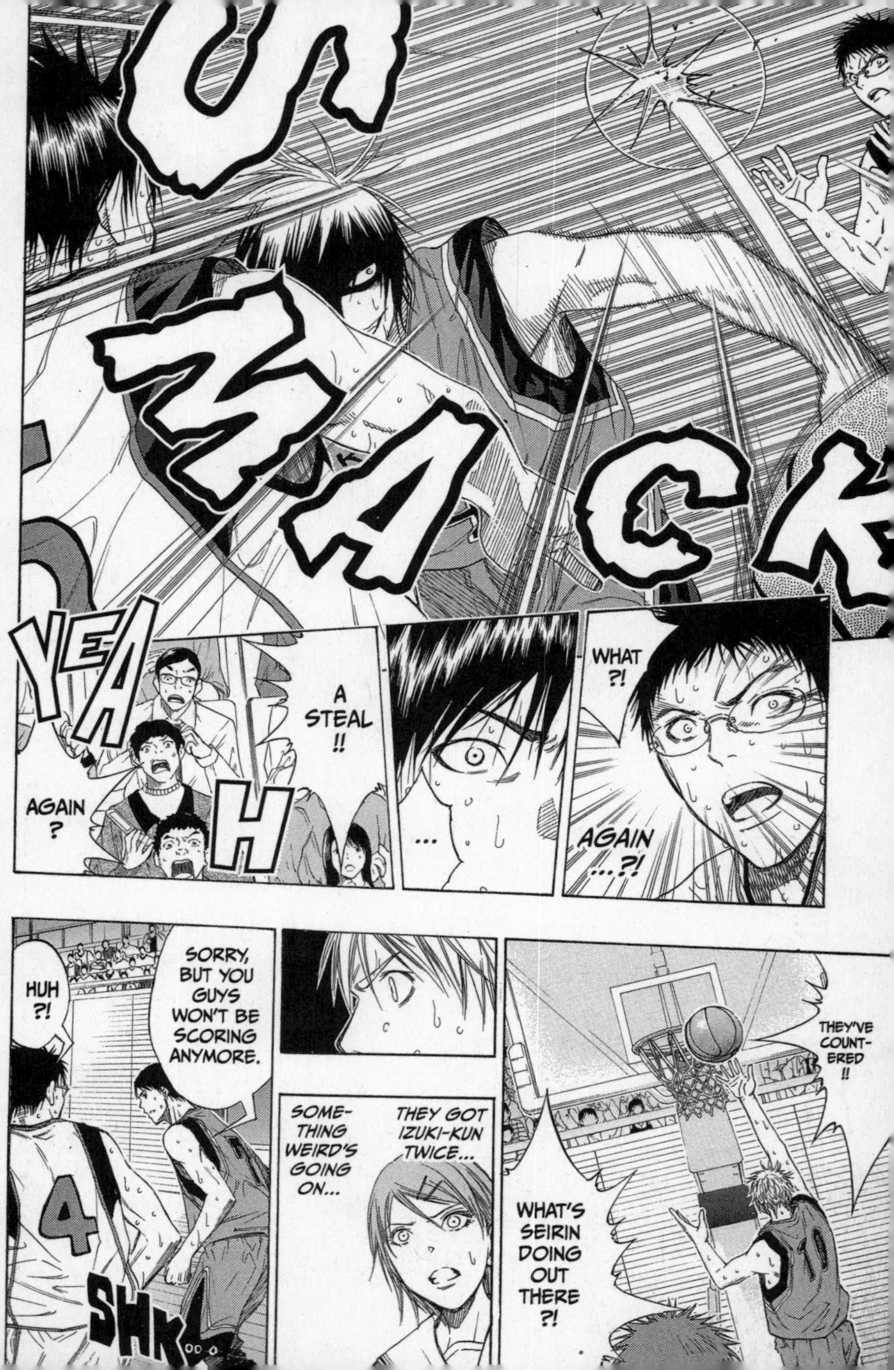
WHAT ?!
AGAIN ...?!
...
A STEAL !!
AGAIN ?
YEAH
THEY'VE COUNTERED !!
WHAT'S SEIRIN DOING OUT THERE ?!
THEY GOT IZUKI-KUN TWICE...
SOMETHING WEIRD'S GOING ON...
SORRY, BUT YOU GUYS WON'T BE SCORING ANYMORE.
HUH ?!
SHK...

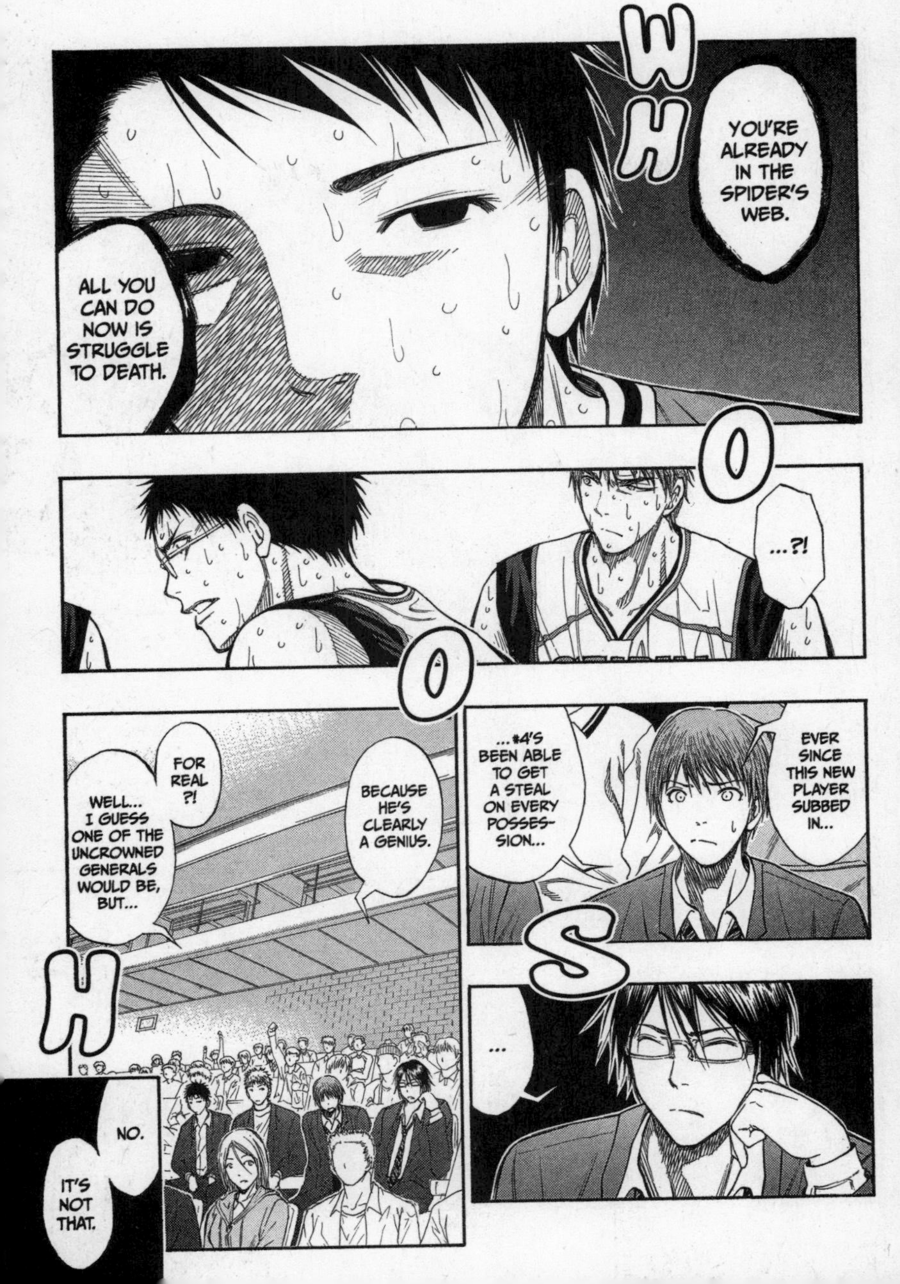
WHOOSH
YOU'RE ALREADY IN THE SPIDER'S WEB.
ALL YOU CAN DO NOW IS STRUGGLE TO DEATH.
...?!
EVER SINCE THIS NEW PLAYER SUBBED IN...
...#4'S BEEN ABLE TO GET A STEAL ON EVERY POSSES-SION...
BECAUSE HE'S CLEARLY A GENIUS.
FOR REAL ?!
WELL... I GUESS ONE OF THE UNCROWNED GENERALS WOULD BE, BUT...
...
NO.
IT'S NOT THAT.

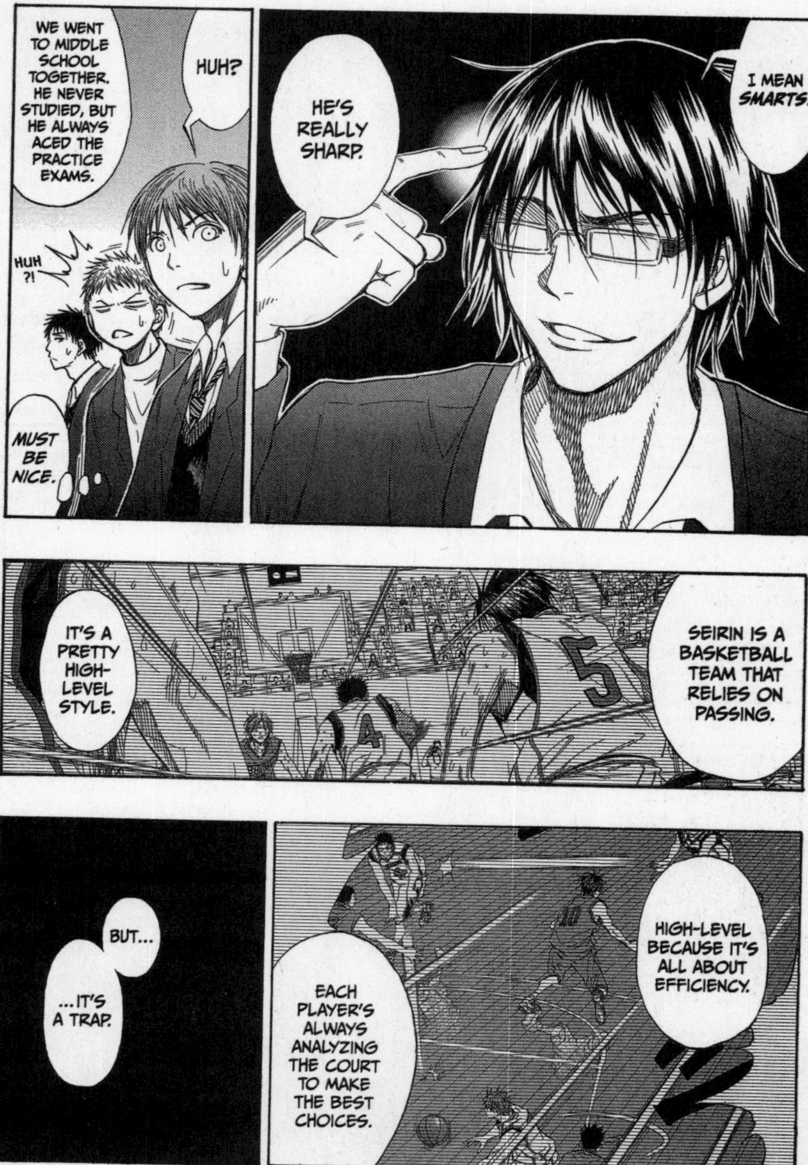
I MEAN SMARTS.
HE'S REALLY SHARP.
HUH?
WE WENT TO MIDDLE SCHOOL TOGETHER. HE NEVER STUDIED, BUT HE ALWAYS ACED THE PRACTICE EXAMS.
HUH ?!
MUST BE NICE.
SEIRIN IS A BASKETBALL TEAM THAT RELIES ON PASSING.
IT'S A PRETTY HIGH-LEVEL STYLE.
HIGH-LEVEL BECAUSE IT'S ALL ABOUT EFFICIENCY.
EACH PLAYER'S ALWAYS ANALYZING THE COURT TO MAKE THE BEST CHOICES.
BUT...
...IT'S A TRAP.

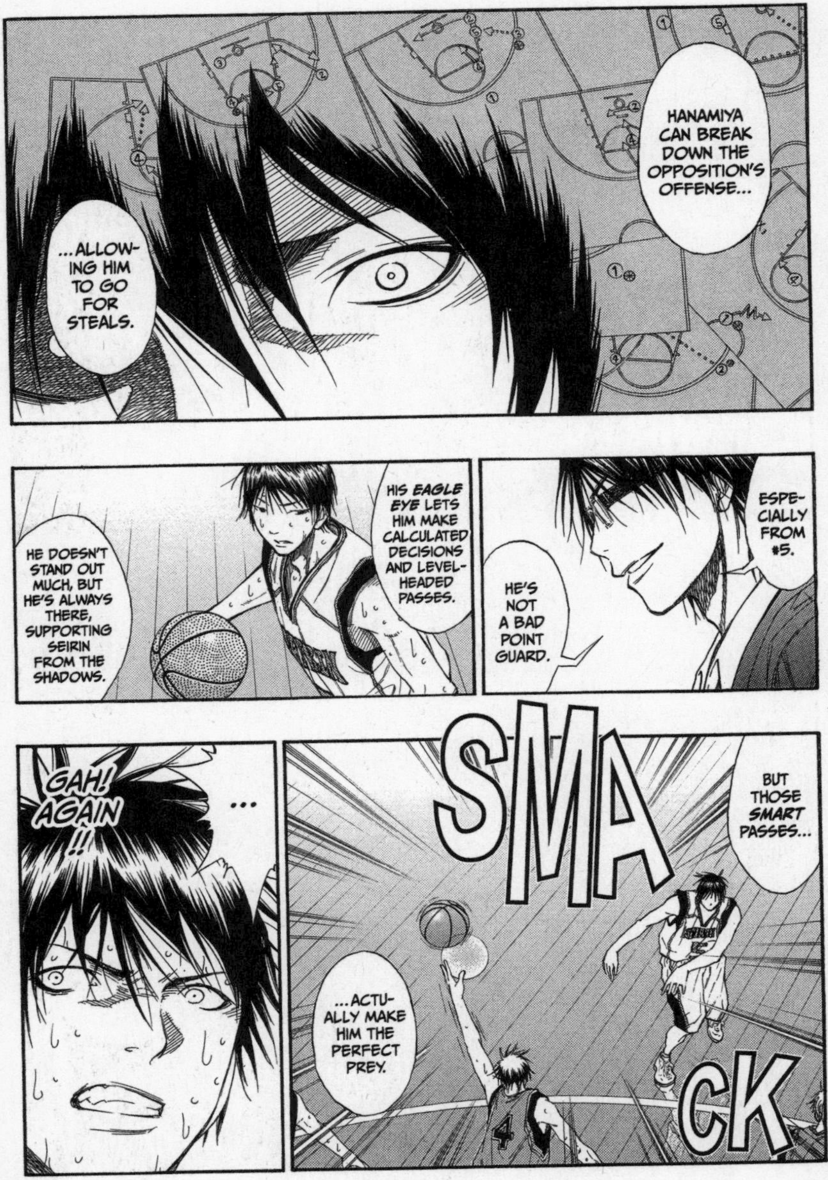
HANAMIYA CAN BREAK DOWN THE OPPOSITION'S OFFENSE...
...ALLOWING HIM TO GO FOR STEALS.
ESPECIALLY FROM #5.
HE'S NOT A BAD POINT GUARD.
HIS *EAGLE EYE* LETS HIM MAKE CALCULATED DECISIONS AND LEVEL-HEADED PASSES.
HE DOESN'T STAND OUT MUCH, BUT HE'S ALWAYS THERE, SUPPORTING SEIRIN FROM THE SHADOWS.
BUT THOSE *SMART* PASSES...
SMACK
...ACTUALLY MAKE HIM THE PERFECT PREY.
...
GAH! AGAIN!!

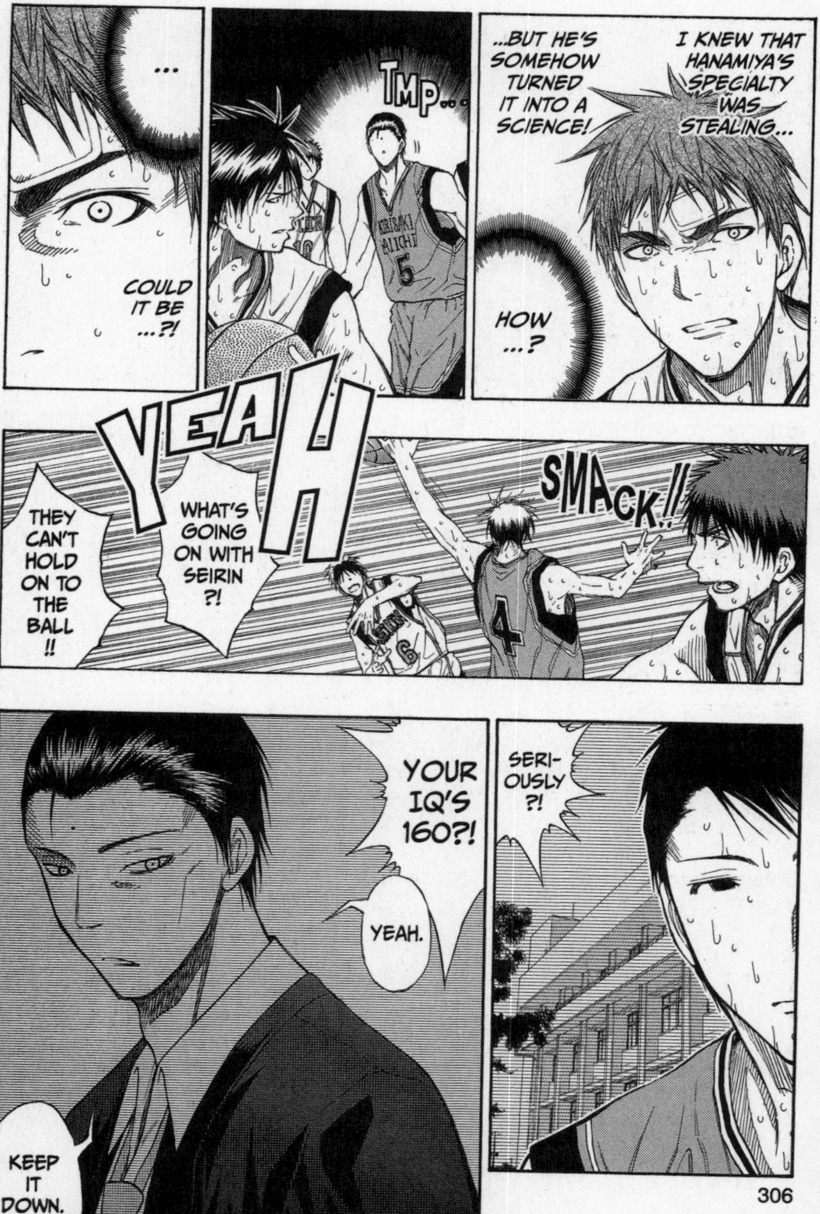
I KNEW THAT HANAMIYA'S SPECIALTY WAS STEALING...
...BUT HE'S SOMEHOW TURNED IT INTO A SCIENCE!
HOW ...?
TMP...
...
COULD IT BE ...?!
SMACK!!
YEAH
WHAT'S GOING ON WITH SEIRIN ?!
THEY CAN'T HOLD ON TO THE BALL !!
SERI-OUSLY ?!
YOUR IQ'S 160?!
YEAH.
KEEP IT DOWN.

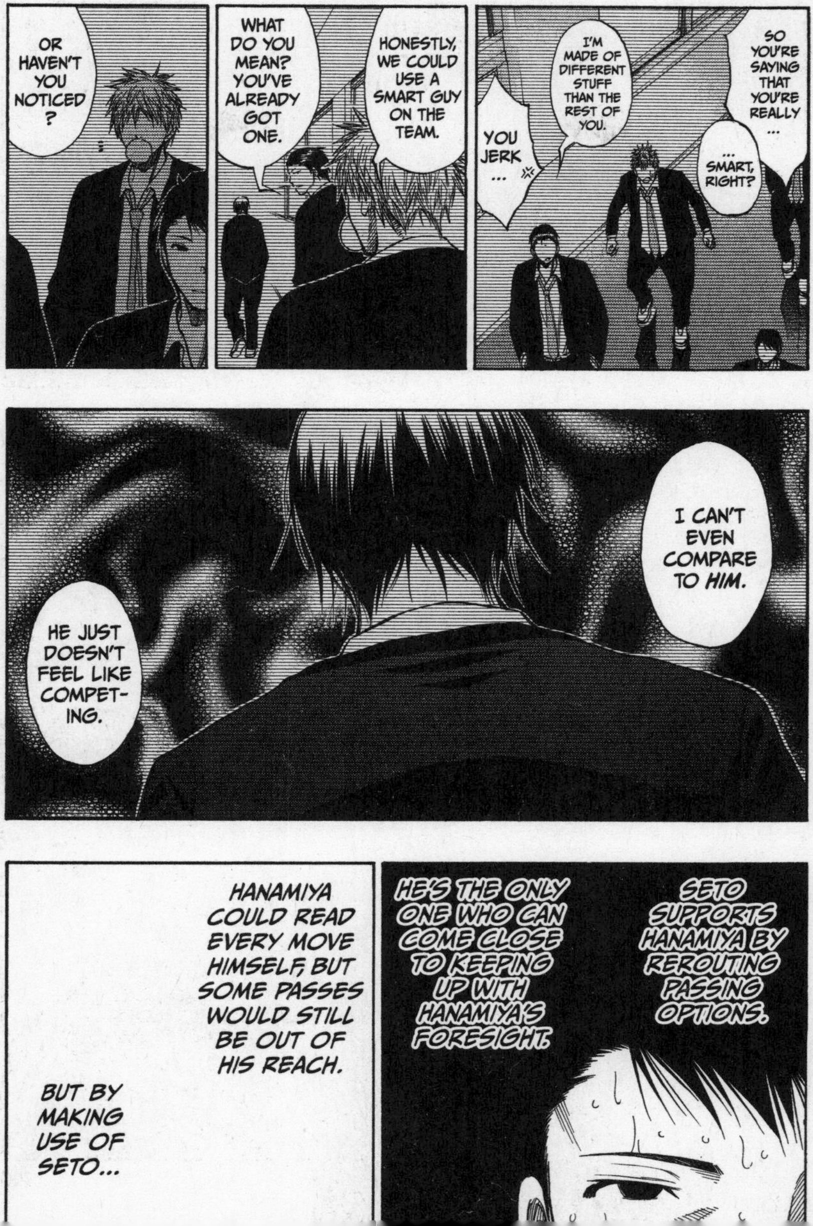
SO YOU'RE SAYING THAT YOU'RE REALLY ...
... SMART, RIGHT?
I'M MADE OF DIFFERENT STUFF THAN THE REST OF YOU.
YOU JERK ...
HONESTLY, WE COULD USE A SMART GUY ON THE TEAM.
WHAT DO YOU MEAN? YOU'VE ALREADY GOT ONE.
OR HAVEN'T YOU NOTICED?
I CAN'T EVEN COMPARE TO *HIM*.
HE JUST DOESN'T FEEL LIKE COMPETING.
SETO SUPPORTS HANAMIYA BY REROUTING PASSING OPTIONS.
HE'S THE ONLY ONE WHO CAN COME CLOSE TO KEEPING UP WITH HANAMIYA'S FORESIGHT.
HANAMIYA COULD READ EVERY MOVE HIMSELF, BUT SOME PASSES WOULD STILL BE OUT OF HIS REACH.
BUT BY MAKING USE OF SETO...

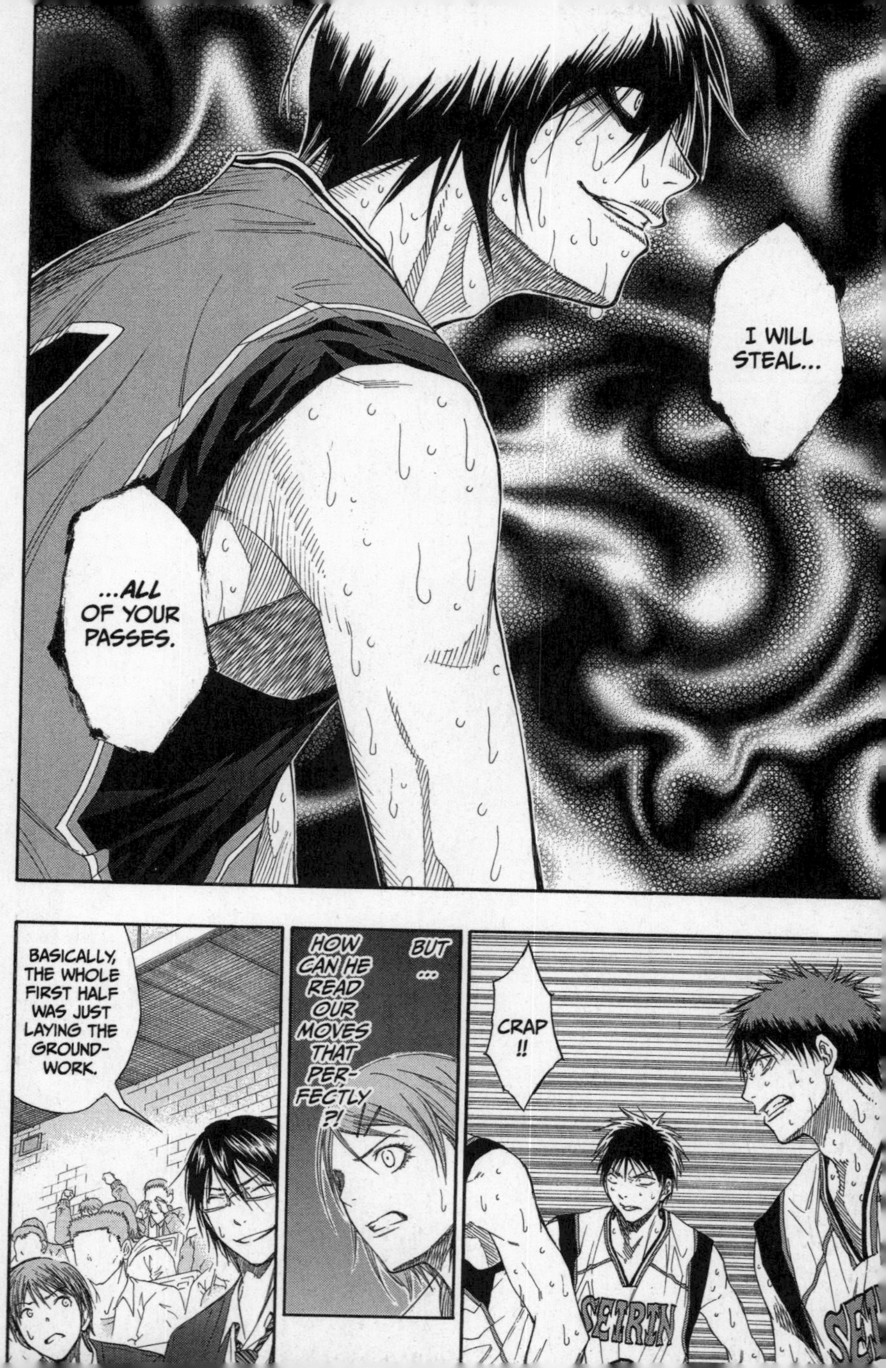
I WILL STEAL...
...ALL OF YOUR PASSES.
CRAP !!
BUT ...
HOW CAN HE READ OUR MOVES THAT PER- FECTLY ?!
BASICALLY, THE WHOLE FIRST HALF WAS JUST LAYING THE GROUND- WORK.

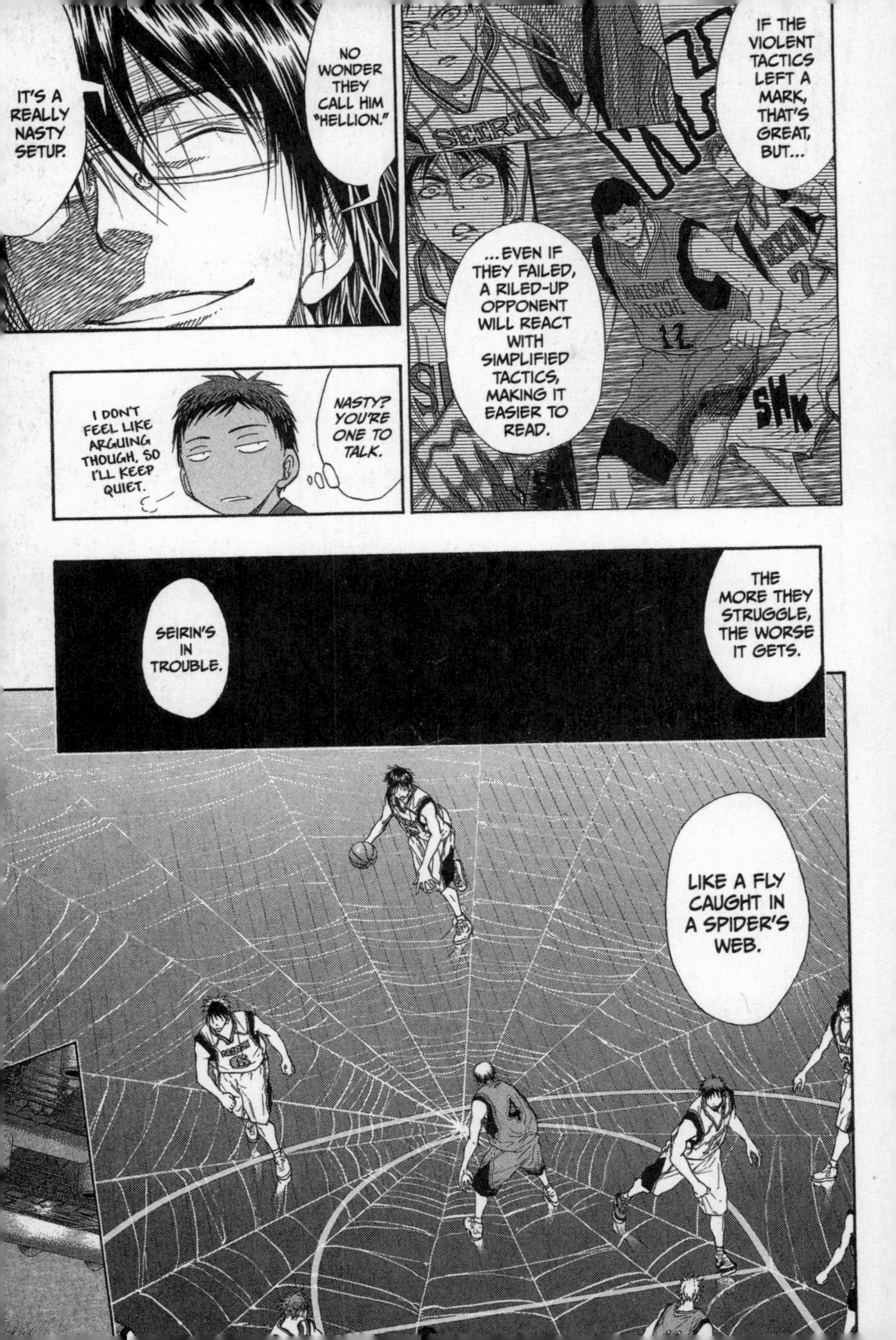
IF THE VIOLENT TACTICS LEFT A MARK, THAT'S GREAT, BUT...
...EVEN IF THEY FAILED, A RILED-UP OPPONENT WILL REACT WITH SIMPLIFIED TACTICS, MAKING IT EASIER TO READ.
SHK
NO WONDER THEY CALL HIM "HELLION."
IT'S A REALLY NASTY SETUP.
NASTY? YOU'RE ONE TO TALK.
I DON'T FEEL LIKE ARGUING THOUGH, SO I'LL KEEP QUIET.
THE MORE THEY STRUGGLE, THE WORSE IT GETS.
SEIRIN'S IN TROUBLE.
LIKE A FLY CAUGHT IN A SPIDER'S WEB.

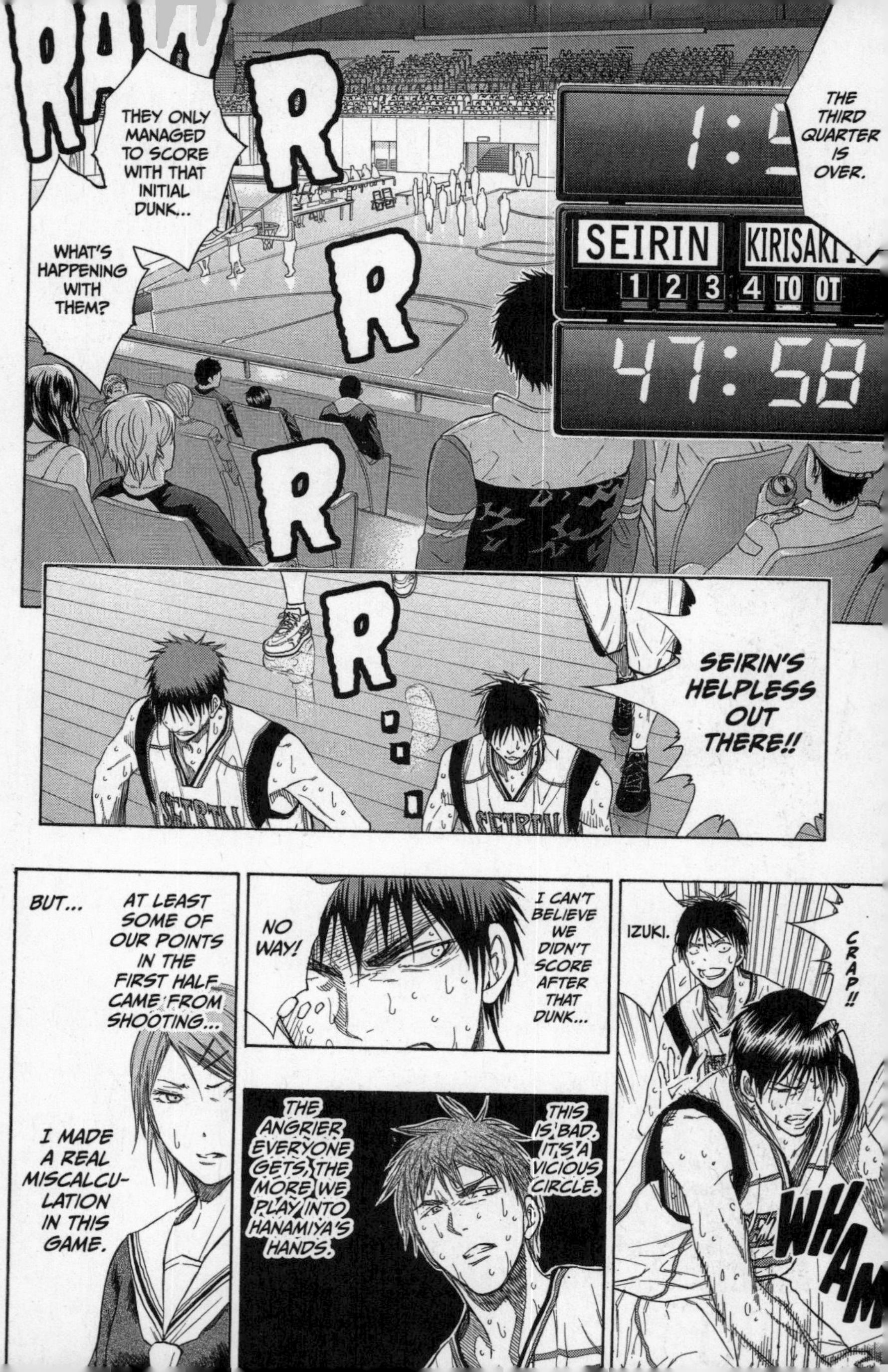
THE THIRD QUARTER IS OVER.
SEIRIN
KIRISAKI
1 2 3 4 TO OT
47 : 58
THEY ONLY MANAGED TO SCORE WITH THAT INITIAL DUNK...
WHAT'S HAPPENING WITH THEM?
RAW R R R R...
SEIRIN'S HELPLESS OUT THERE!!
CRAP!!
IZUKI.
WHAM
I CAN'T BELIEVE WE DIDN'T SCORE AFTER THAT DUNK...
NO WAY!
THIS IS BAD. IT'S A VICIOUS CIRCLE.
THE ANGRIER EVERYONE GETS, THE MORE WE PLAY INTO HANAMIYA'S HANDS.
AT LEAST SOME OF OUR POINTS IN THE FIRST HALF CAME FROM SHOOTING...
BUT...
I MADE A REAL MISCALCULATION IN THIS GAME.

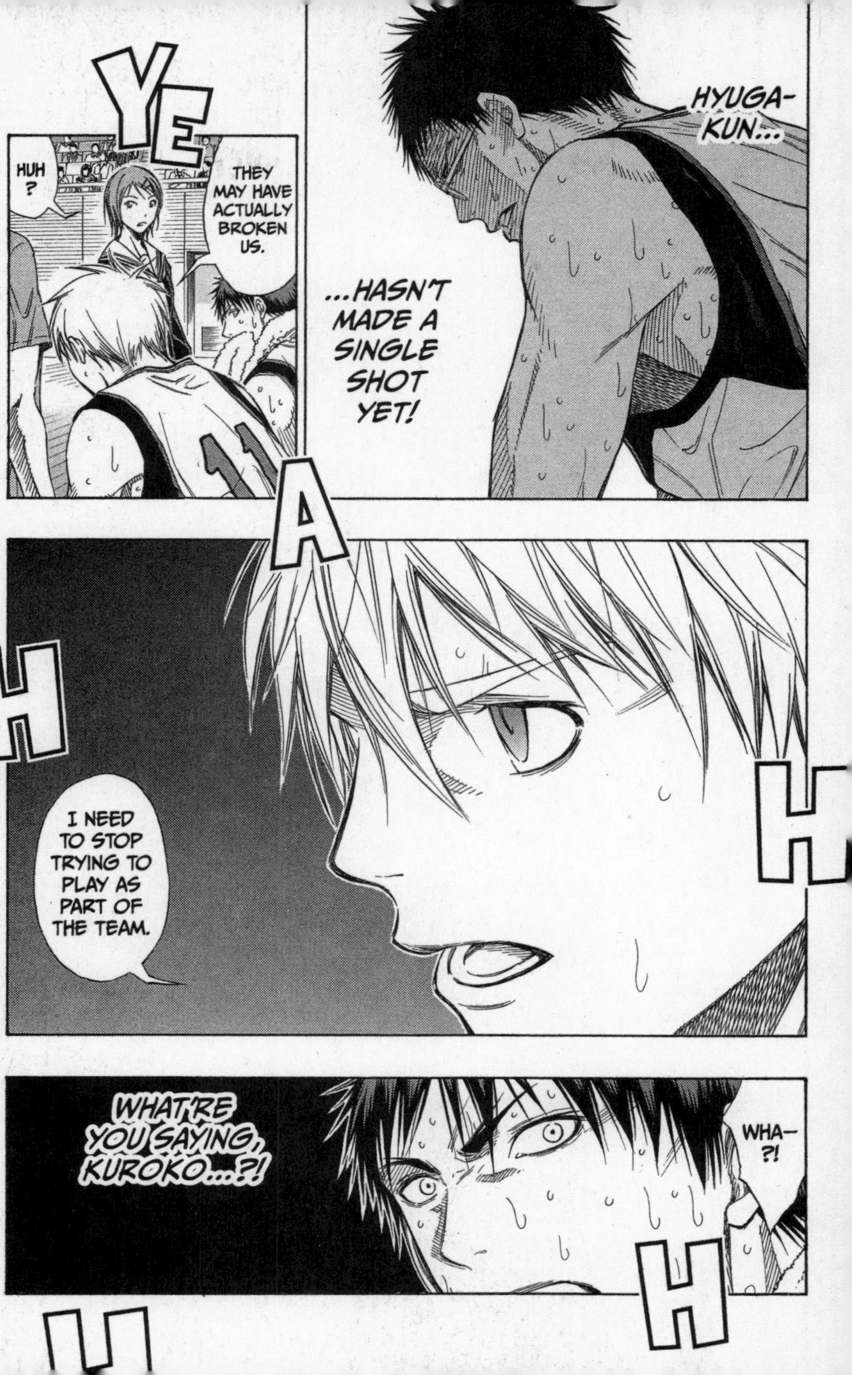
HYUGA-KUN...
...HASN'T MADE A SINGLE SHOT YET!
THEY MAY HAVE ACTUALLY BROKEN US.
HUH ?
YEAHHHH
I NEED TO STOP TRYING TO PLAY AS PART OF THE TEAM.
WHA-?!
WHAT'RE YOU SAYING, KUROKO...?!

KUROKO'S BASKETBALL BLOOPERS TAKE 4

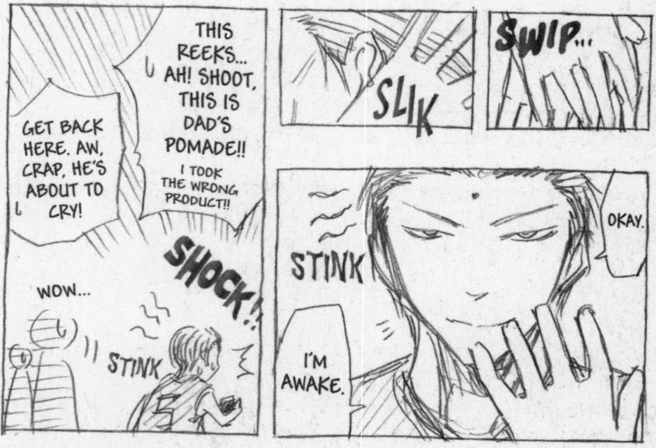
SWIP...
SLIK
OKAY.
STINK
I'M AWAKE.
THIS REEKS... AH! SHOOT, THIS IS DAD'S POMADE!!
I TOOK THE WRONG PRODUCT!!
GET BACK HERE. AW, CRAP, HE'S ABOUT TO CRY!
SHOCK!!
WOW...
STINK

105TH QUARTER: TRUST

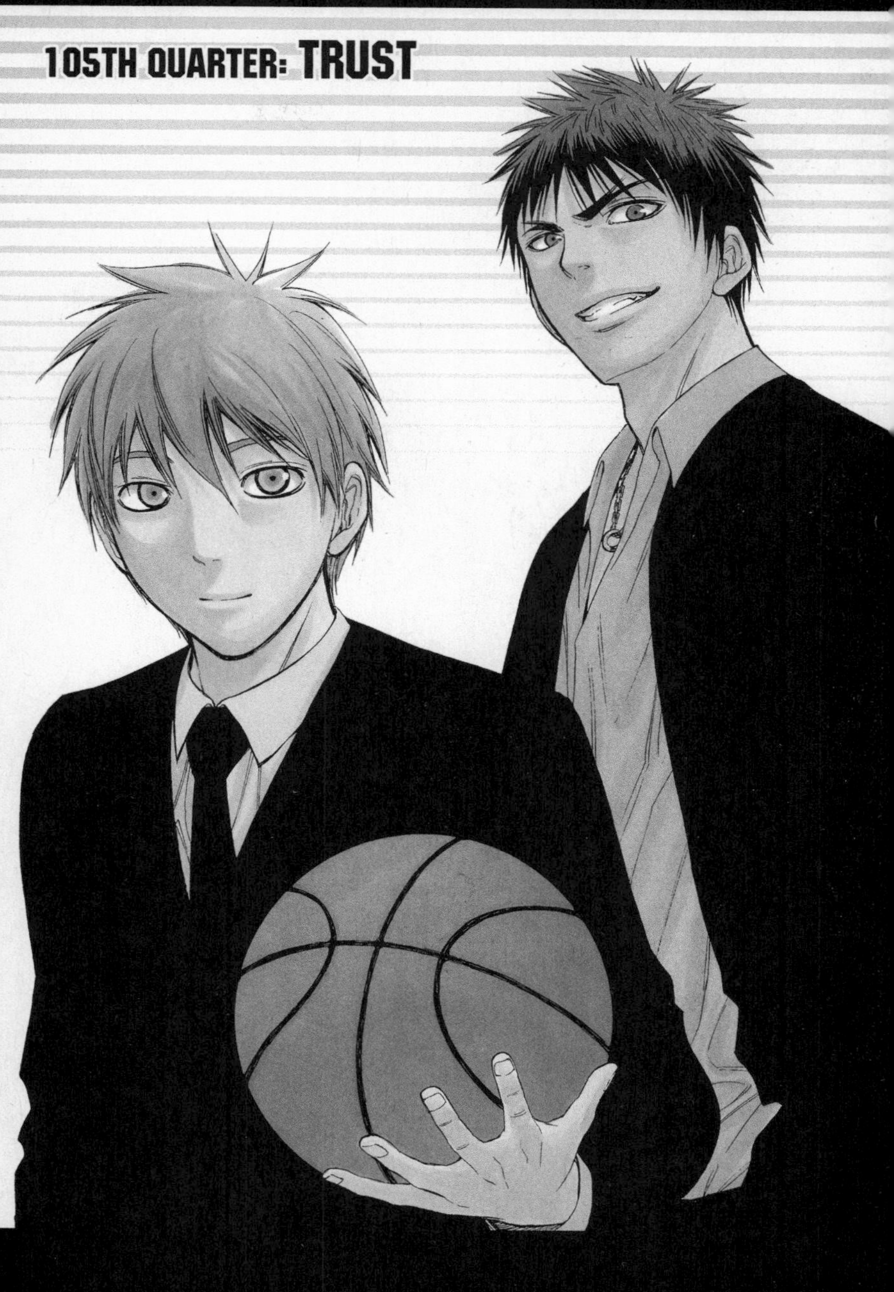

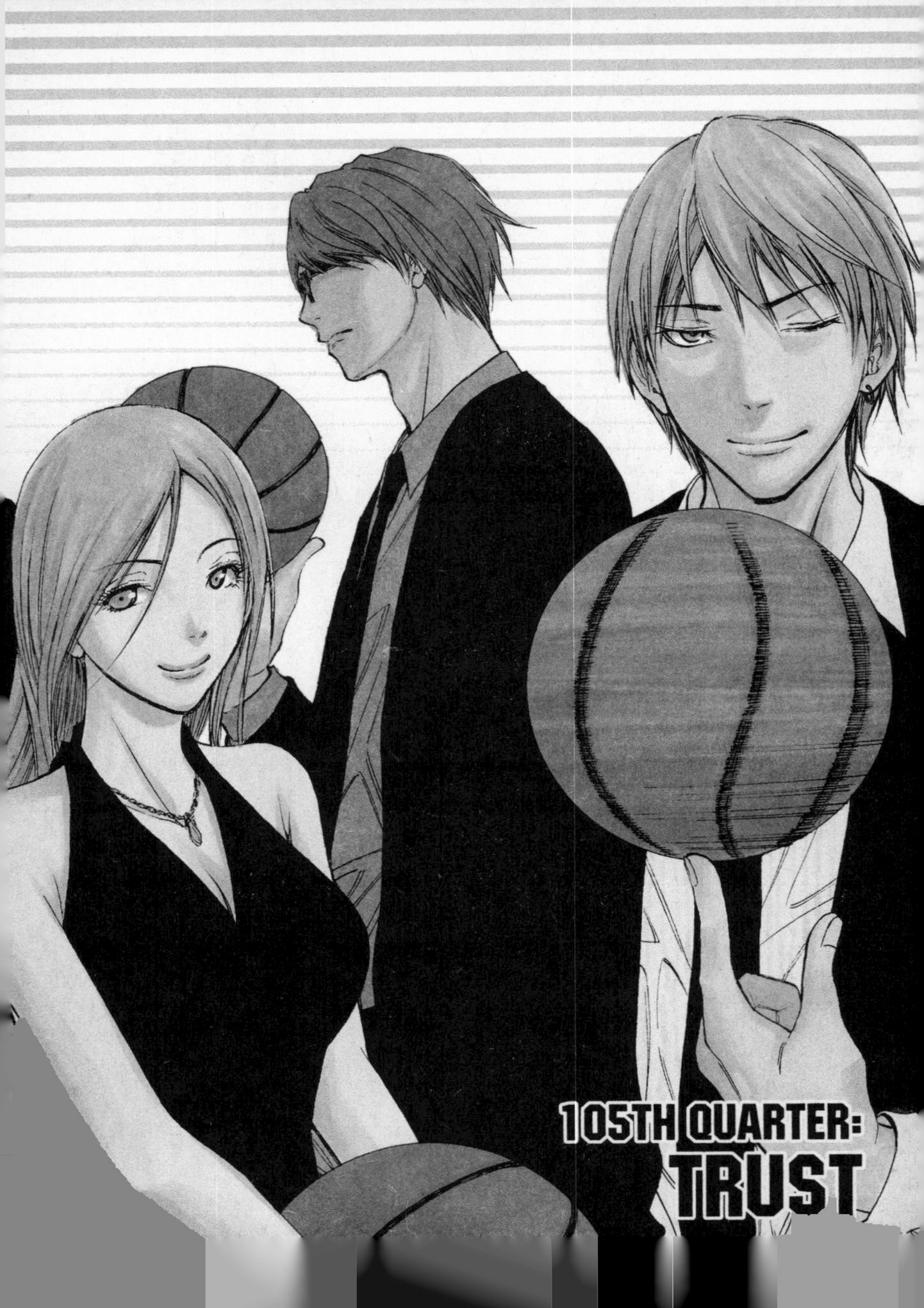
105TH QUARTER:
TRUST

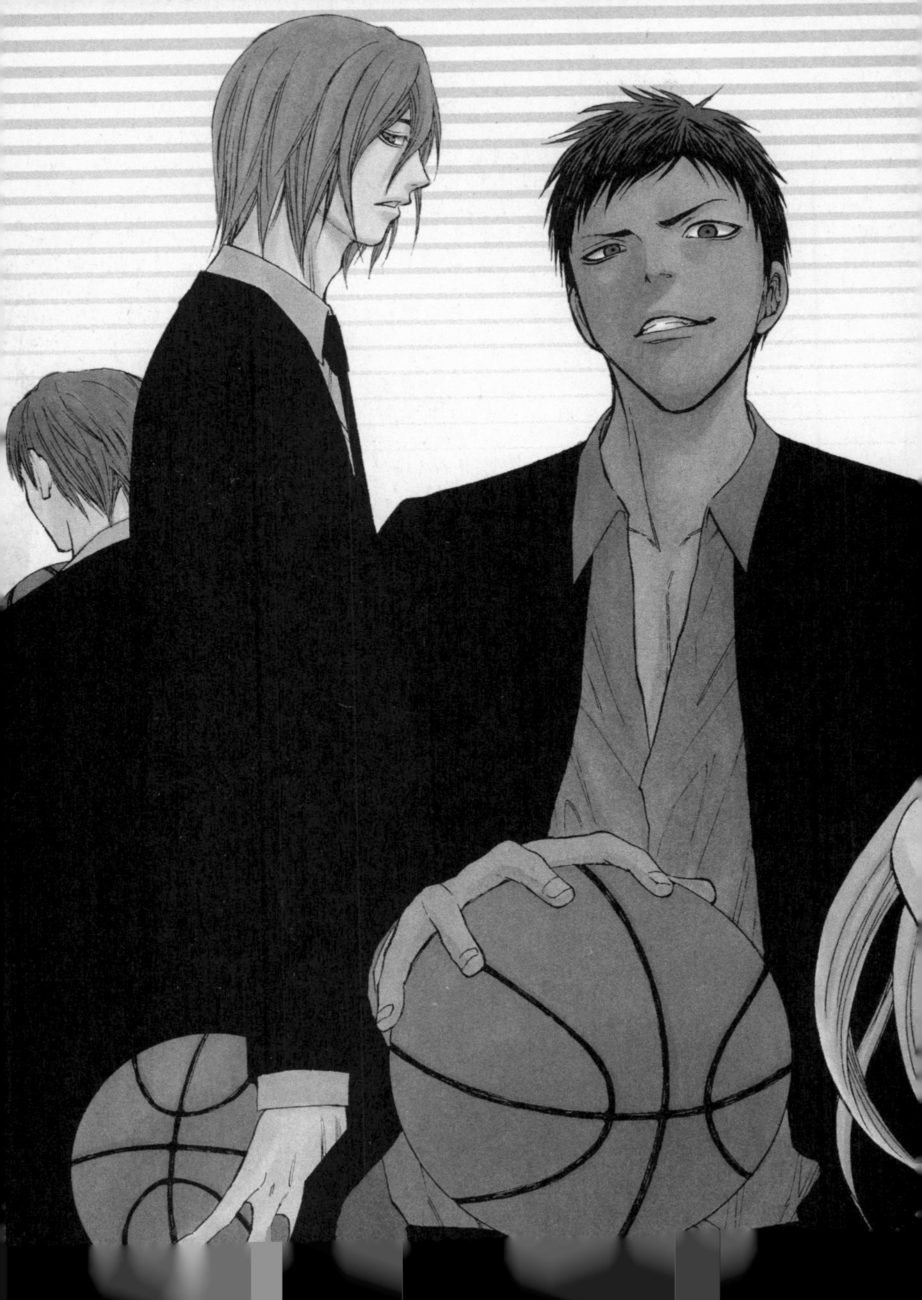

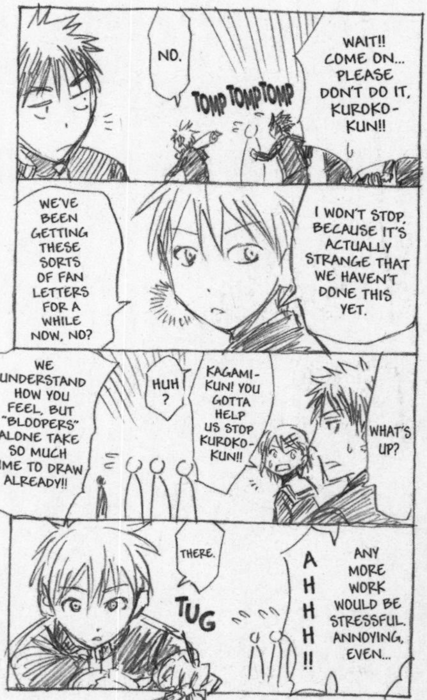
WAIT!! COME ON... PLEASE DON'T DO IT, KUROKO-KUN!!
TOMP TOMP TOMP
NO.
I WON'T STOP, BECAUSE IT'S ACTUALLY STRANGE THAT WE HAVEN'T DONE THIS YET.
WE'VE BEEN GETTING THESE SORTS OF FAN LETTERS FOR A WHILE NOW, NO?
WHAT'S UP?
KAGAMI-KUN! YOU GOTTA HELP US STOP KUROKO-KUN!!
HUH?
WE UNDERSTAND HOW YOU FEEL, BUT "BLOOPERS" ALONE TAKE SO MUCH TIME TO DRAW ALREADY!!
ANY MORE WORK WOULD BE STRESSFUL. ANNOYING, EVEN...
AHHHH!!
TUG
THERE.

KUROKO'S BASKETBALL
"WE WANT FAN ART" CORNER!!

Now collecting fan art!!
Submit your fan art entries to:
viz.com/fanart-cosplay

We want to showcase your amazing *Kuroko's Basketball* fan art on our site! Submit yours today!

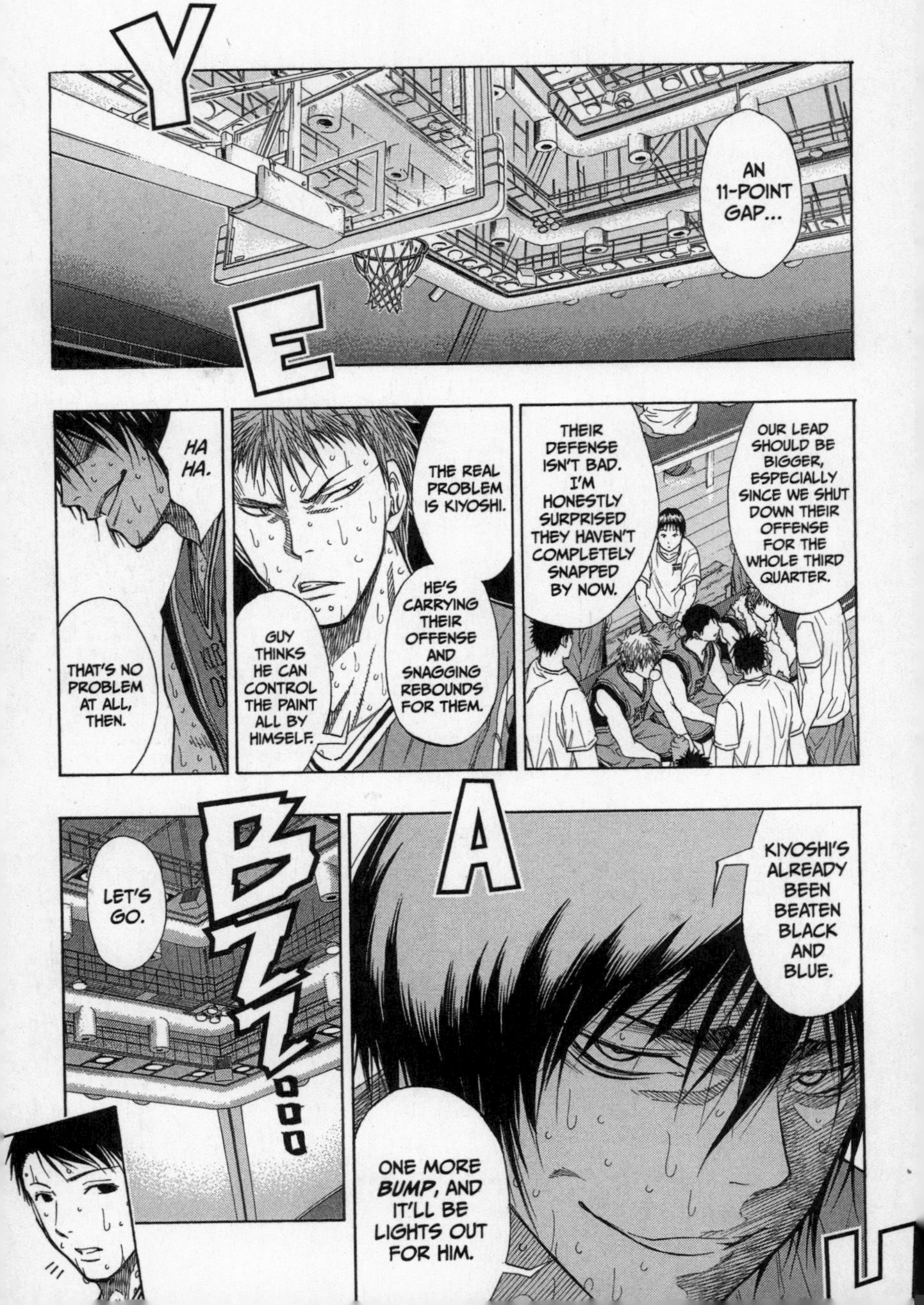
YEAH
AN 11-POINT GAP...
OUR LEAD SHOULD BE BIGGER, ESPECIALLY SINCE WE SHUT DOWN THEIR OFFENSE FOR THE WHOLE THIRD QUARTER.
THEIR DEFENSE ISN'T BAD. I'M HONESTLY SURPRISED THEY HAVEN'T COMPLETELY SNAPPED BY NOW.
THE REAL PROBLEM IS KIYOSHI.
HE'S CARRYING THEIR OFFENSE AND SNAGGING REBOUNDS FOR THEM.
GUY THINKS HE CAN CONTROL THE PAINT ALL BY HIMSELF.
HA HA.
THAT'S NO PROBLEM AT ALL, THEN.
KIYOSHI'S ALREADY BEEN BEATEN BLACK AND BLUE.
ONE MORE *BUMP*, AND IT'LL BE LIGHTS OUT FOR HIM.
BZZ
LET'S GO.

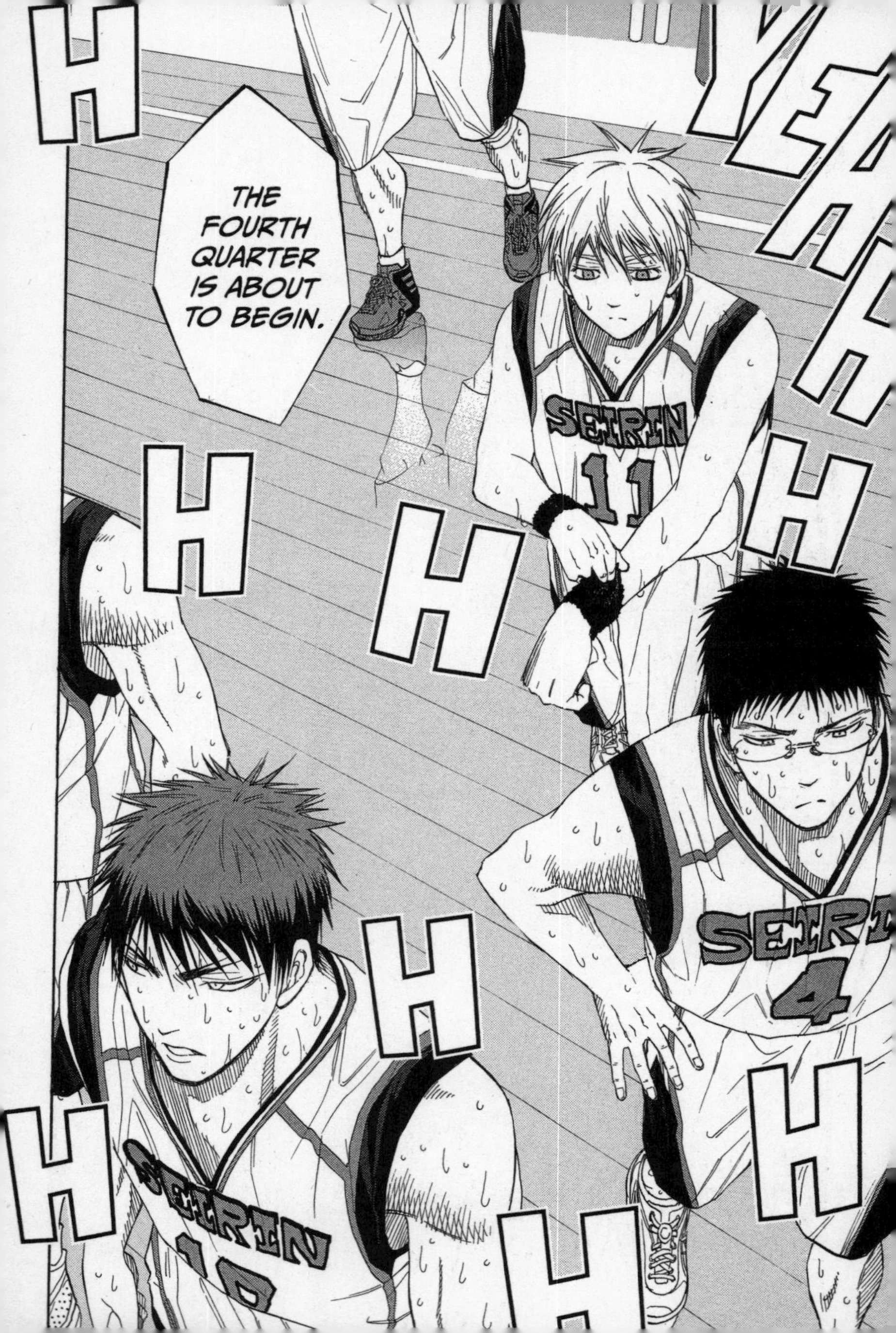
THE FOURTH QUARTER IS ABOUT TO BEGIN.
H H H H H H H H

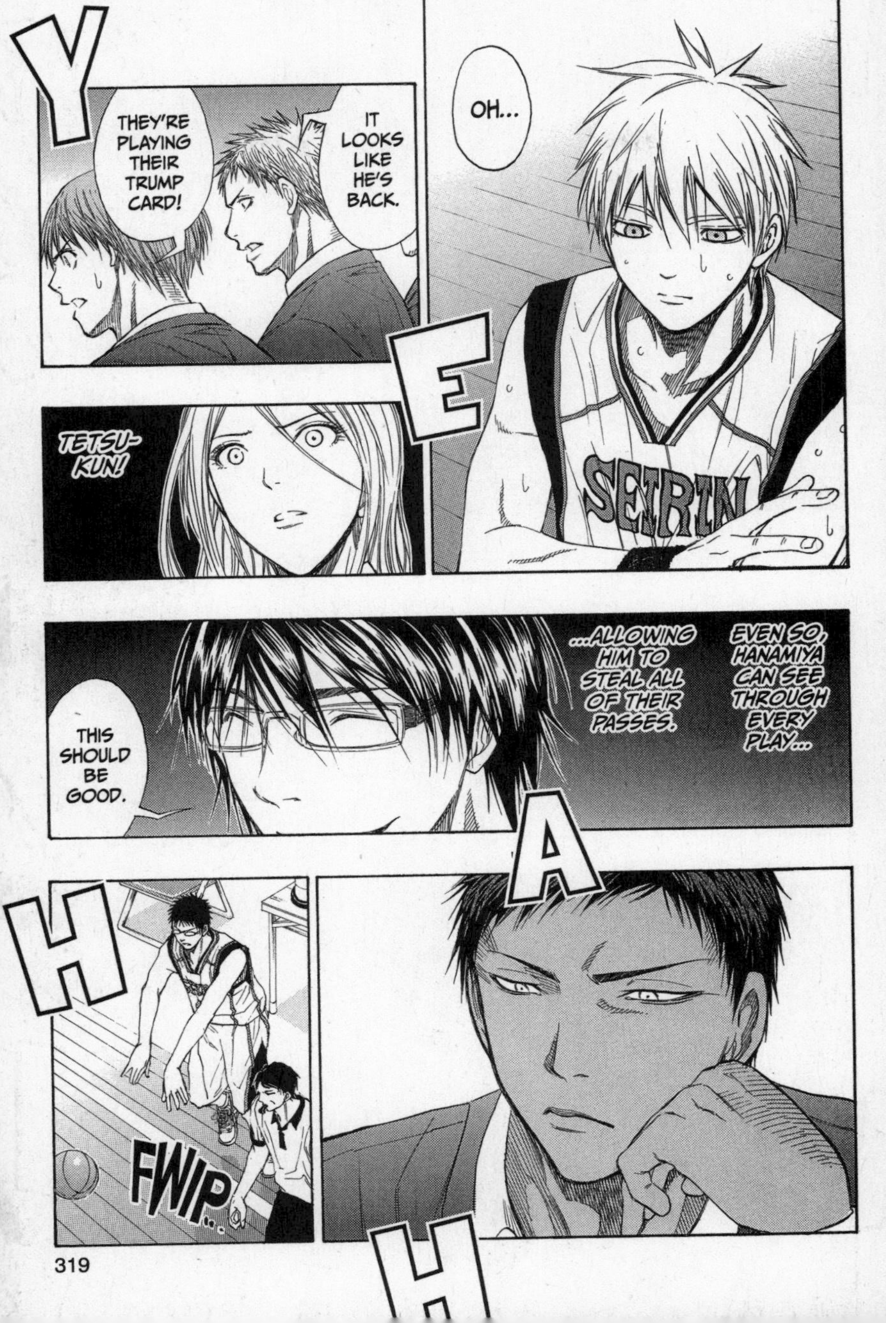
YEAHH
OH...
IT LOOKS LIKE HE'S BACK.
THEY'RE PLAYING THEIR TRUMP CARD!
TETSU-KUN!
EVEN SO, HANAMIYA CAN SEE THROUGH EVERY PLAY...
...ALLOWING HIM TO STEAL ALL OF THEIR PASSES.
THIS SHOULD BE GOOD.
FWIP..

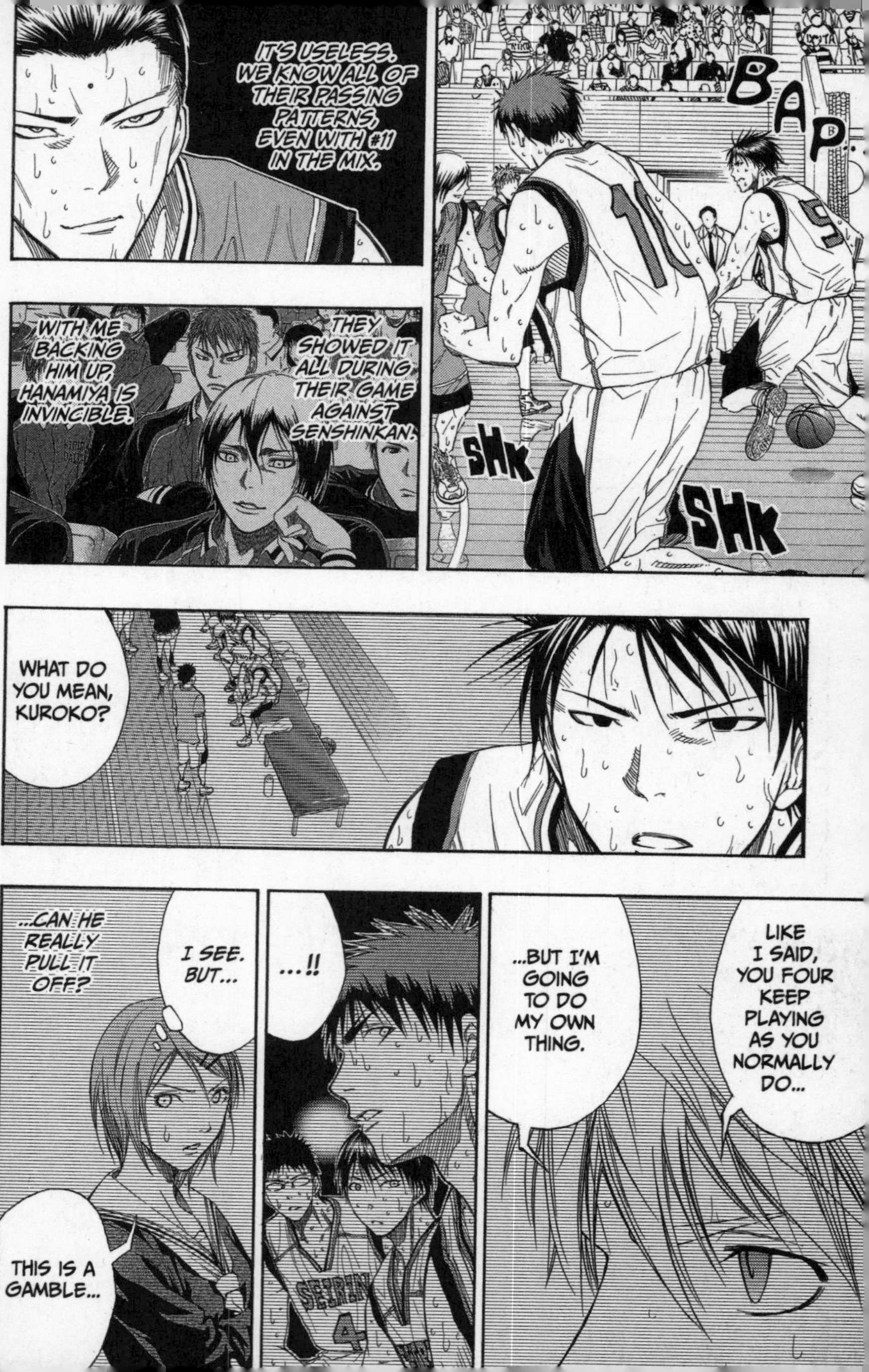
BAP...
SHK
SHK
IT'S USELESS. WE KNOW ALL OF THEIR PASSING PATTERNS, EVEN WITH #11 IN THE MIX.
THEY SHOWED IT ALL DURING THEIR GAME AGAINST SENSHINKAN.
WITH ME BACKING HIM UP, HANAMIYA IS INVINCIBLE.
WHAT DO YOU MEAN, KUROKO?
LIKE I SAID, YOU FOUR KEEP PLAYING AS YOU NORMALLY DO...
...BUT I'M GOING TO DO MY OWN THING.
...!!
I SEE. BUT...
...CAN HE REALLY PULL IT OFF?
THIS IS A GAMBLE...
SEIRIN
4

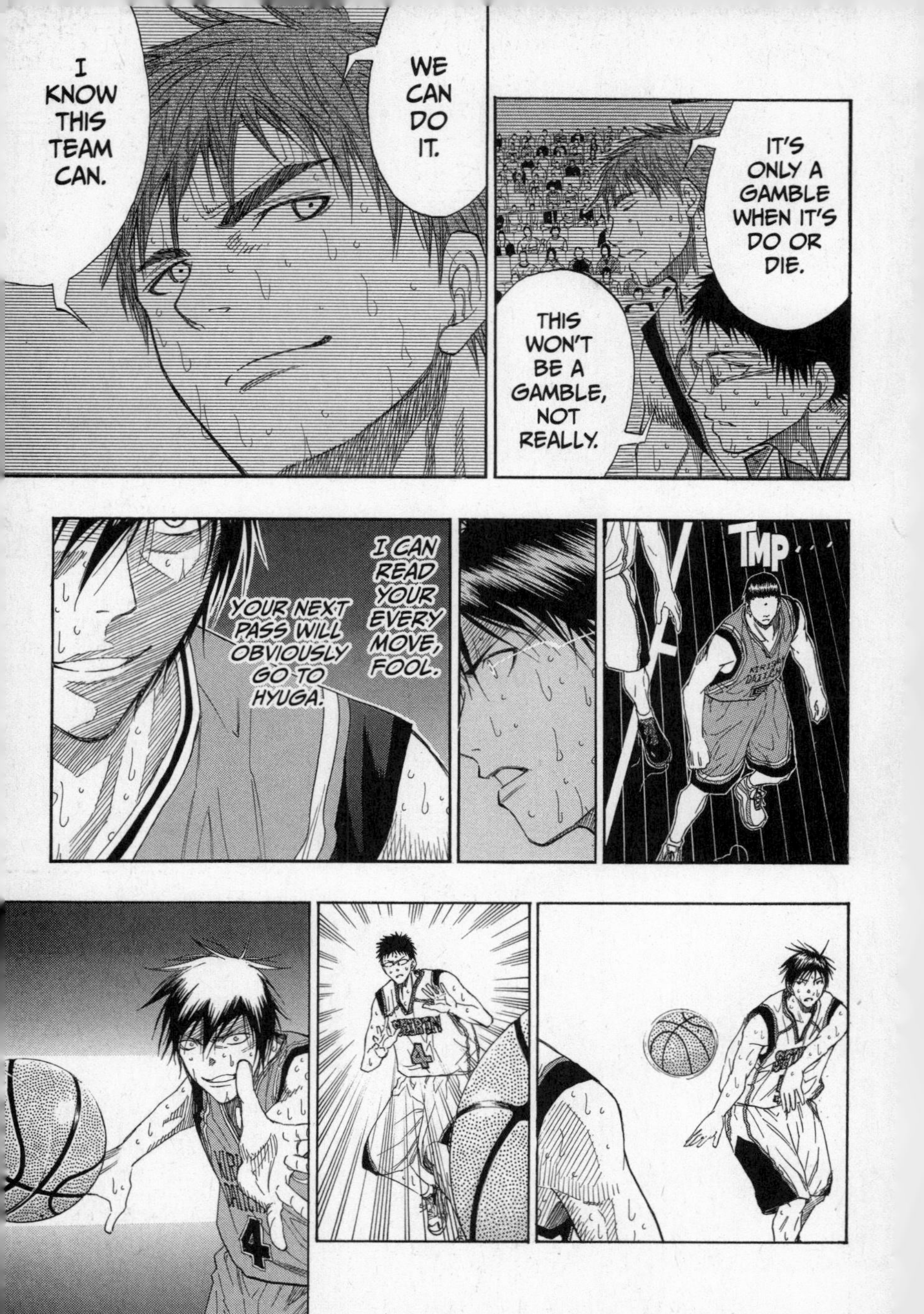
IT'S ONLY A GAMBLE WHEN IT'S DO OR DIE.
THIS WON'T BE A GAMBLE, NOT REALLY.
WE CAN DO IT.
I KNOW THIS TEAM CAN.
TMP...
I CAN READ YOUR EVERY MOVE, FOOL.
YOUR NEXT PASS WILL OBVIOUSLY GO TO HYUGA.

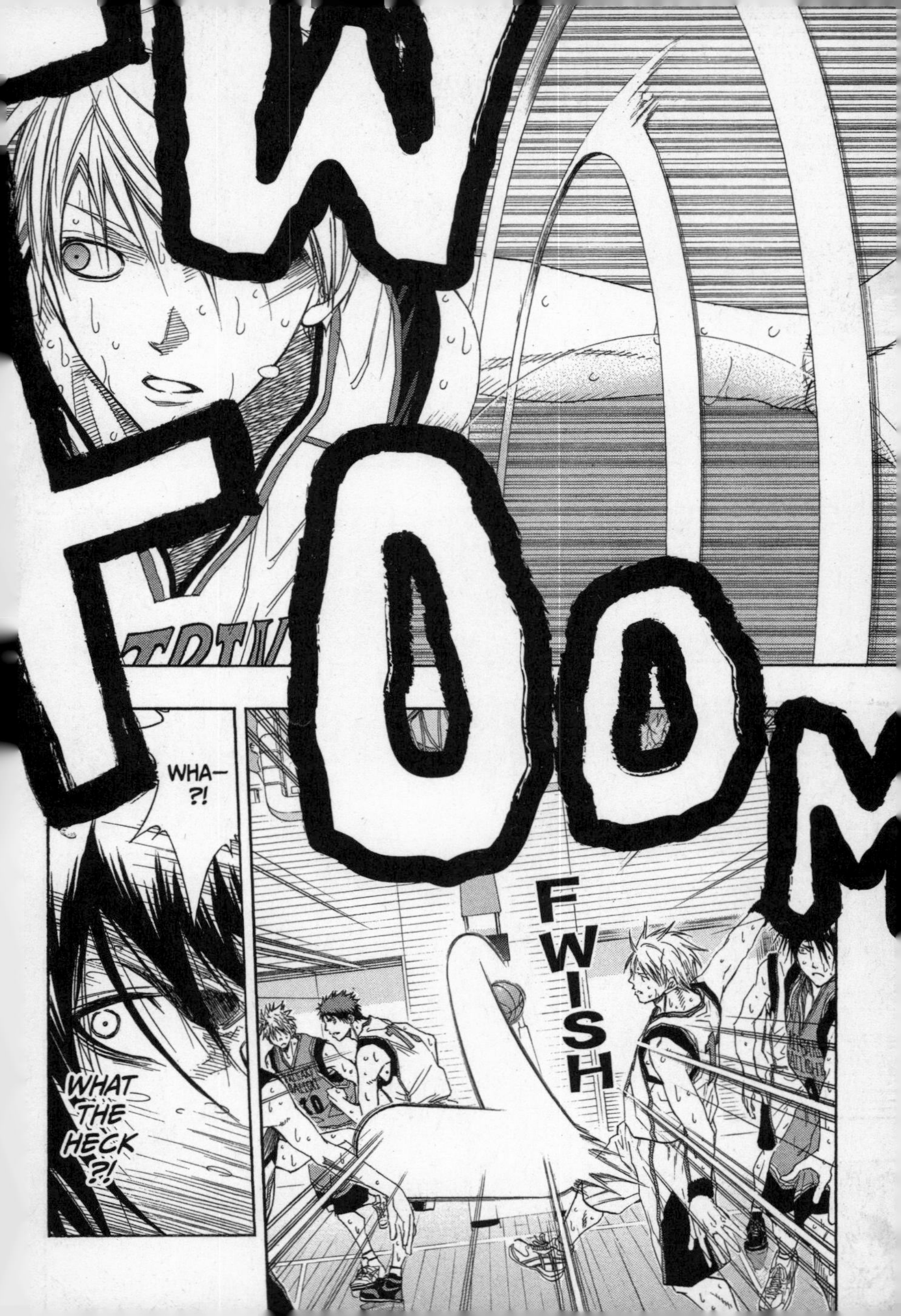
WHOOM
FWISH
WHA—?!
WHAT THE HECK?!

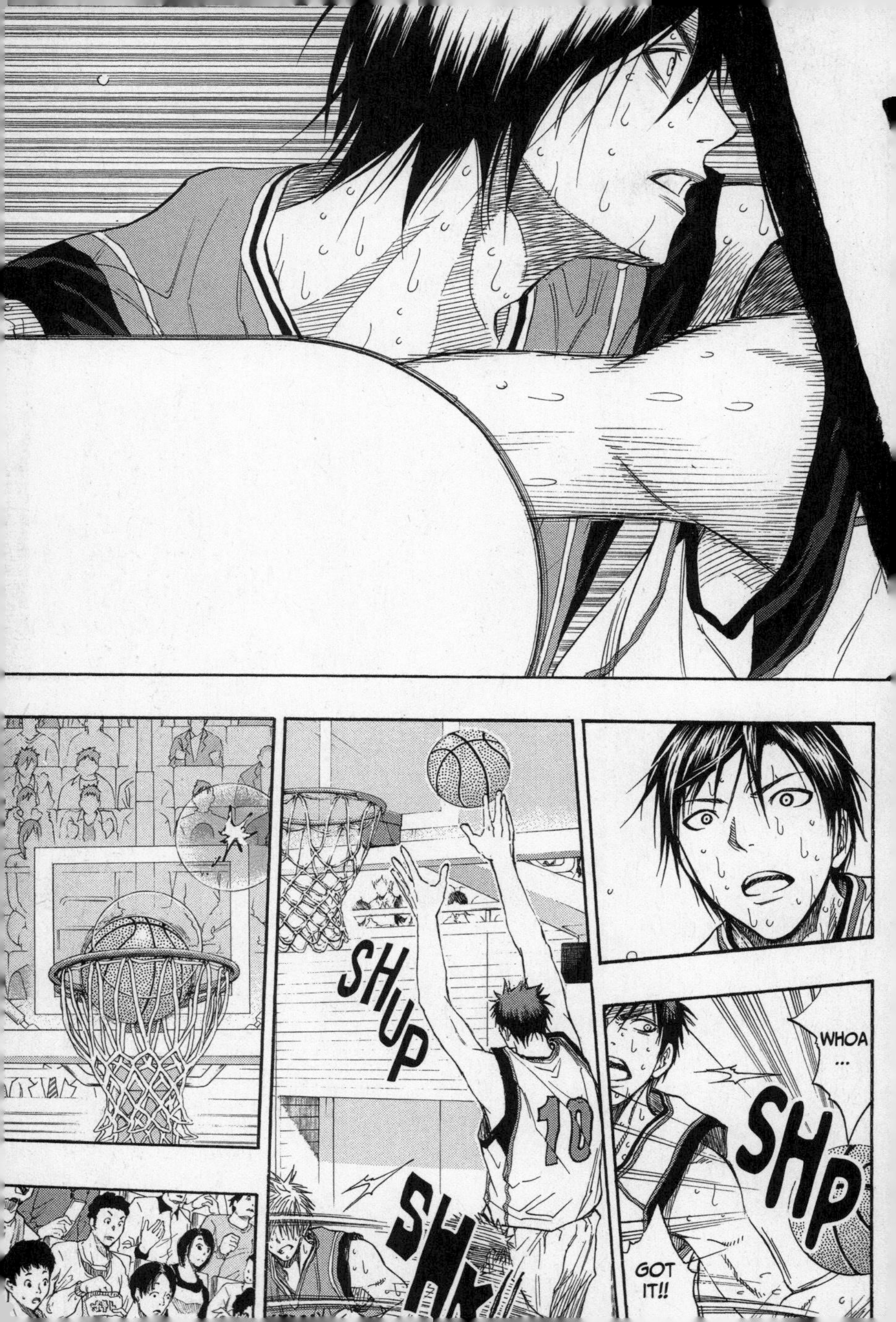
WHOA ...
SHP
GOT IT!!
SHUP
SHK

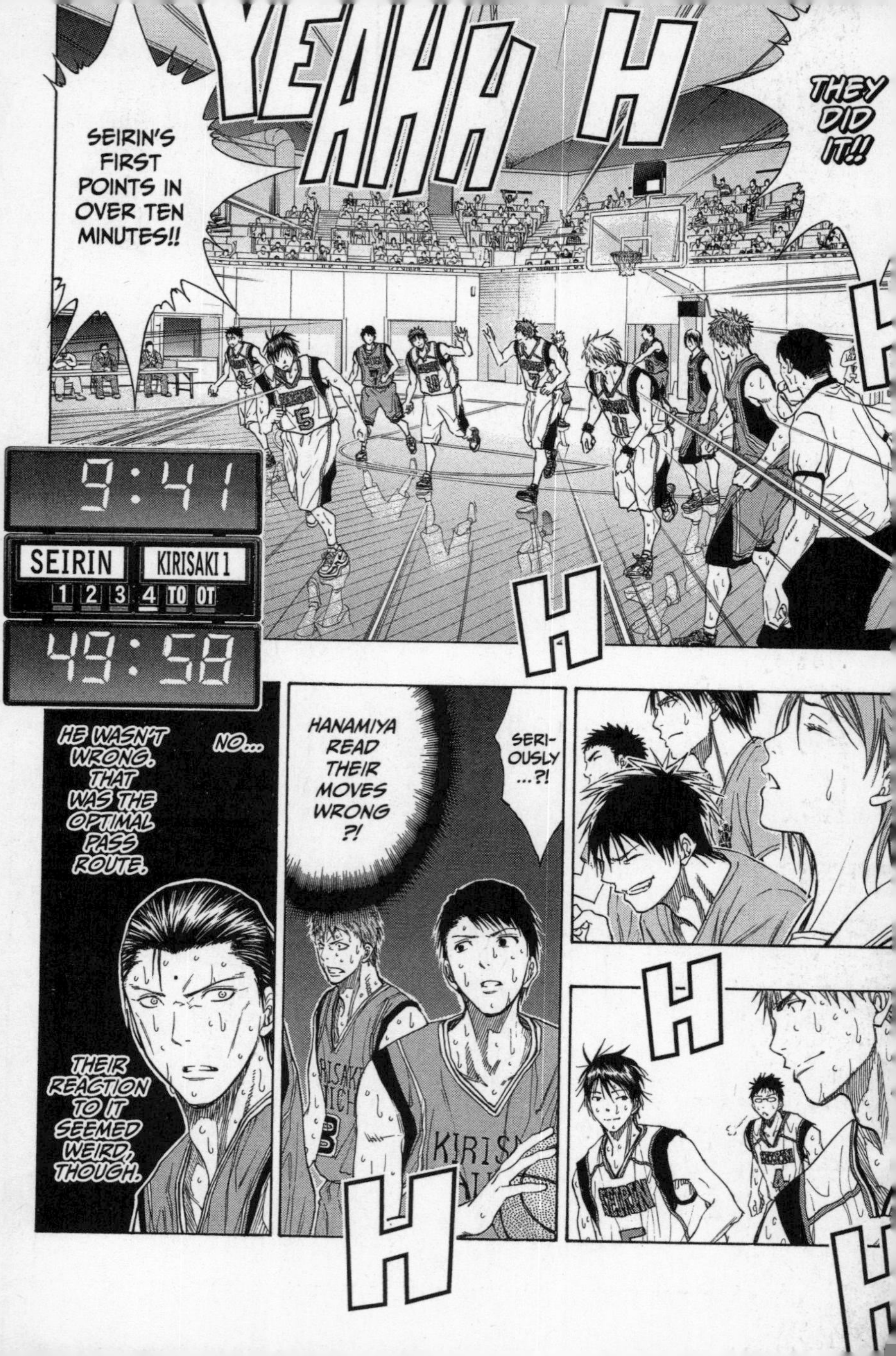
THEY DID IT!!
YEAHHH H
SEIRIN'S FIRST POINTS IN OVER TEN MINUTES!!
9:41
SEIRIN
KIRISAKI 1
1 2 3 4 TO OT
49:58
H
SERI-OUSLY ...?!
H
HANAMIYA READ THEIR MOVES WRONG ?!
H
NO...
HE WASN'T WRONG. THAT WAS THE OPTIMAL PASS ROUTE.
THEIR REACTION TO IT SEEMED WEIRD, THOUGH.

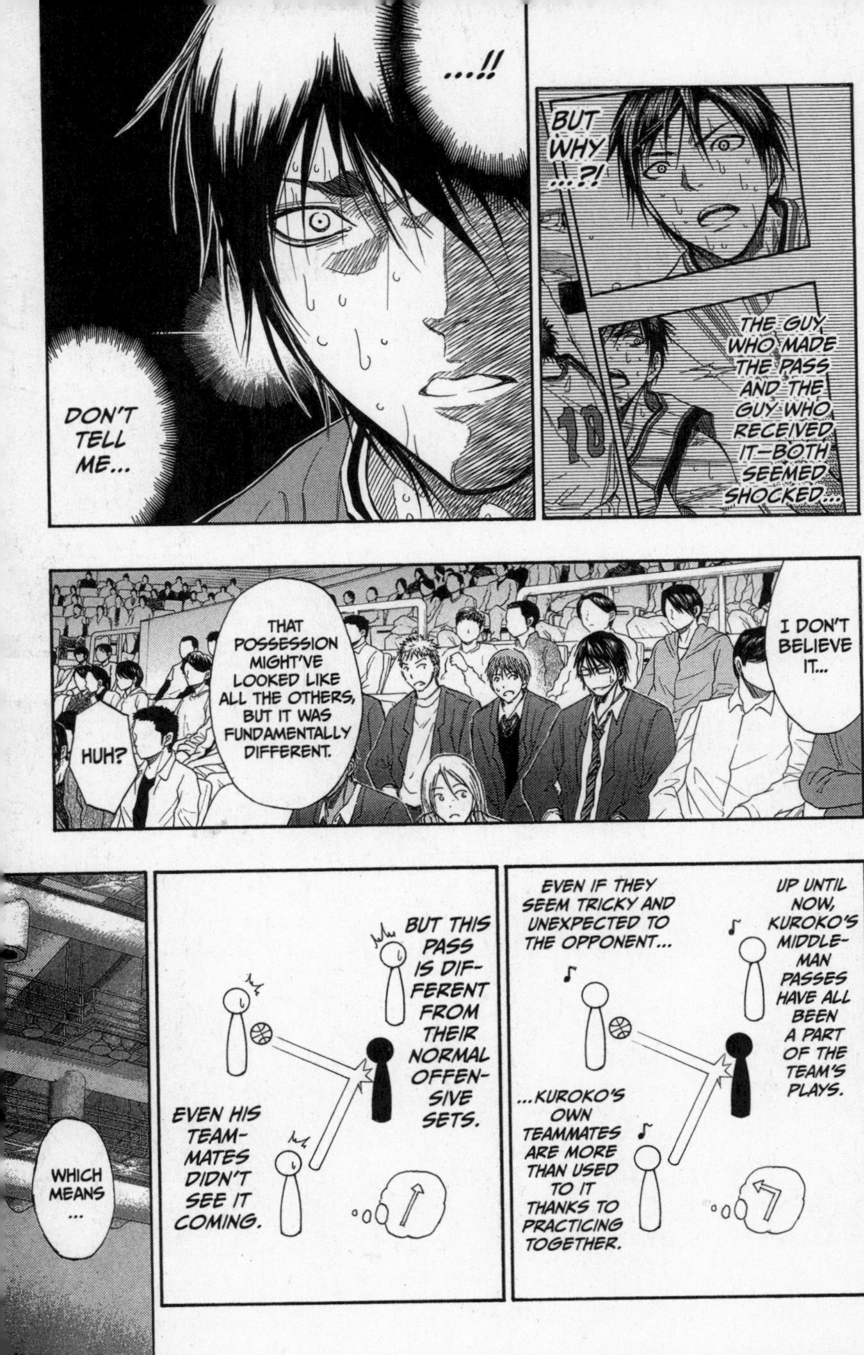
BUT WHY...?!
THE GUY WHO MADE THE PASS AND THE GUY WHO RECEIVED IT—BOTH SEEMED SHOCKED...
...!!
DON'T TELL ME...
I DON'T BELIEVE IT...
THAT POSSESSION MIGHT'VE LOOKED LIKE ALL THE OTHERS, BUT IT WAS FUNDAMENTALLY DIFFERENT.
HUH?
UP UNTIL NOW, KUROKO'S MIDDLEMAN PASSES HAVE ALL BEEN A PART OF THE TEAM'S PLAYS.
EVEN IF THEY SEEM TRICKY AND UNEXPECTED TO THE OPPONENT...
...KUROKO'S OWN TEAMMATES ARE MORE THAN USED TO IT THANKS TO PRACTICING TOGETHER.
BUT THIS PASS IS DIFFERENT FROM THEIR NORMAL OFFENSIVE SETS.
EVEN HIS TEAMMATES DIDN'T SEE IT COMING.
WHICH MEANS...

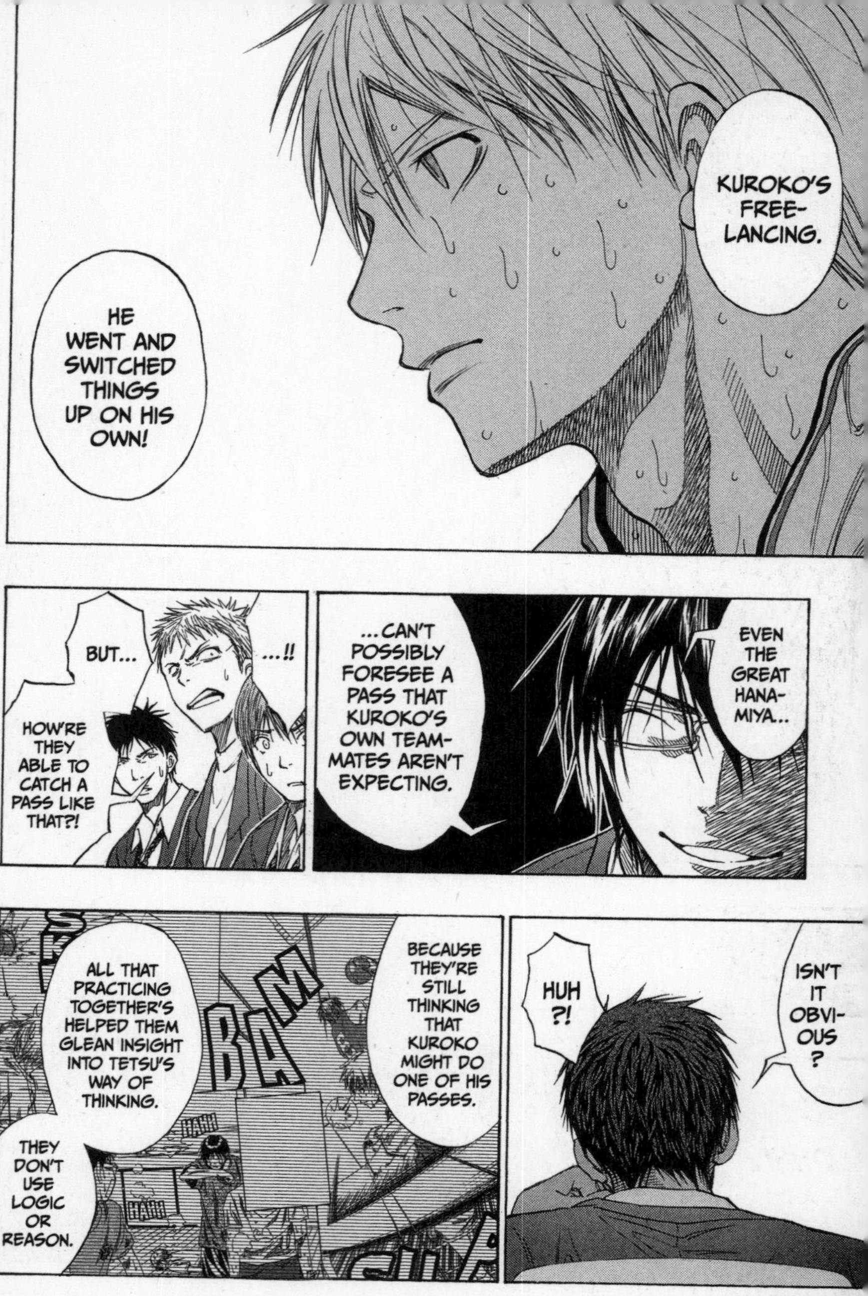
KUROKO'S FREE-LANCING.
HE WENT AND SWITCHED THINGS UP ON HIS OWN!
EVEN THE GREAT HANA-MIYA...
...CAN'T POSSIBLY FORESEE A PASS THAT KUROKO'S OWN TEAM-MATES AREN'T EXPECTING.
...!!
BUT...
HOW'RE THEY ABLE TO CATCH A PASS LIKE THAT?!
ISN'T IT OBVI-OUS?
HUH?!
BECAUSE THEY'RE STILL THINKING THAT KUROKO MIGHT DO ONE OF HIS PASSES.
BAM
ALL THAT PRACTICING TOGETHER'S HELPED THEM GLEAN INSIGHT INTO TETSU'S WAY OF THINKING.
THEY DON'T USE LOGIC OR REASON.

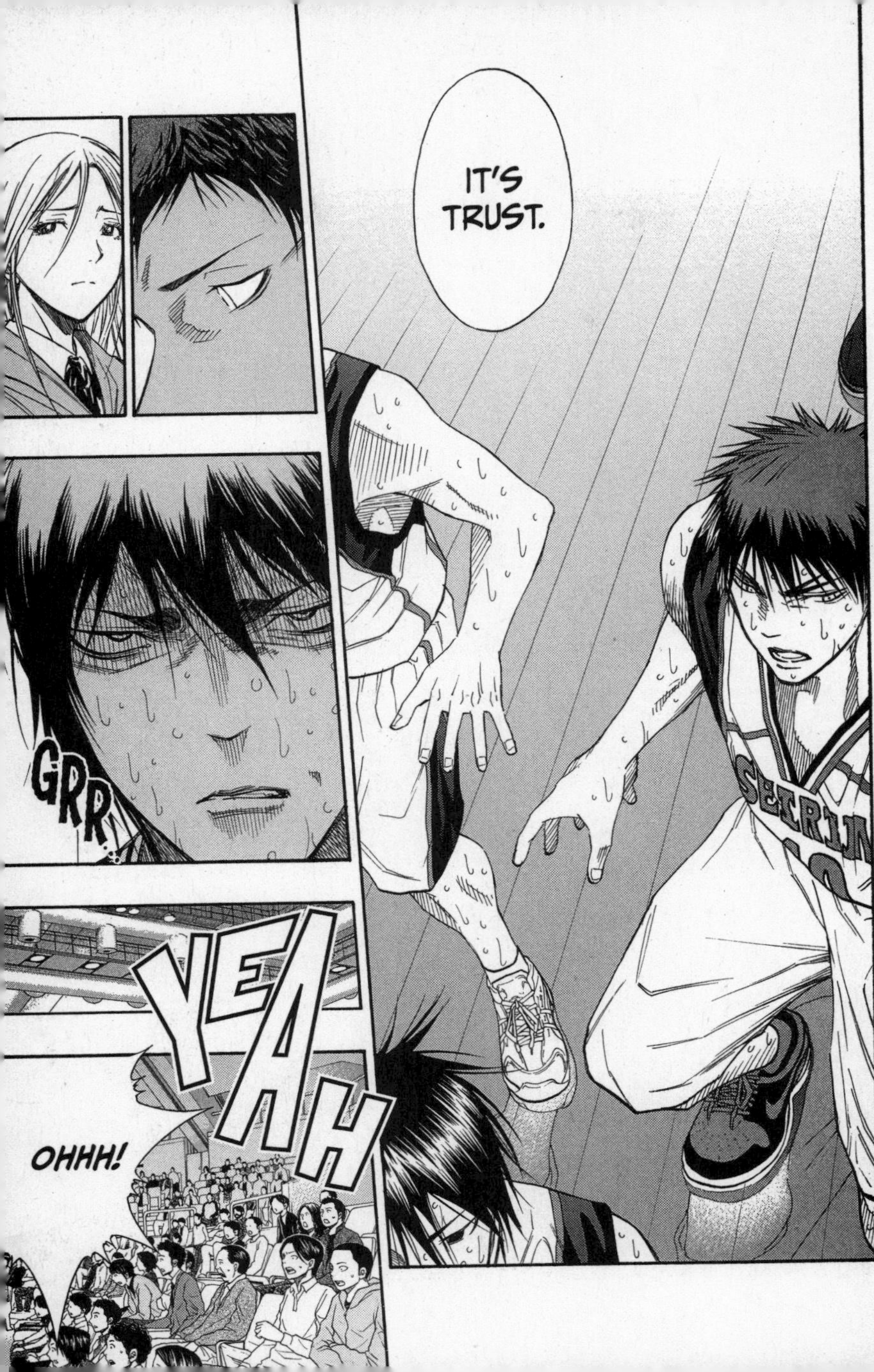
IT'S TRUST.
GRR
YEAH
OHHH!

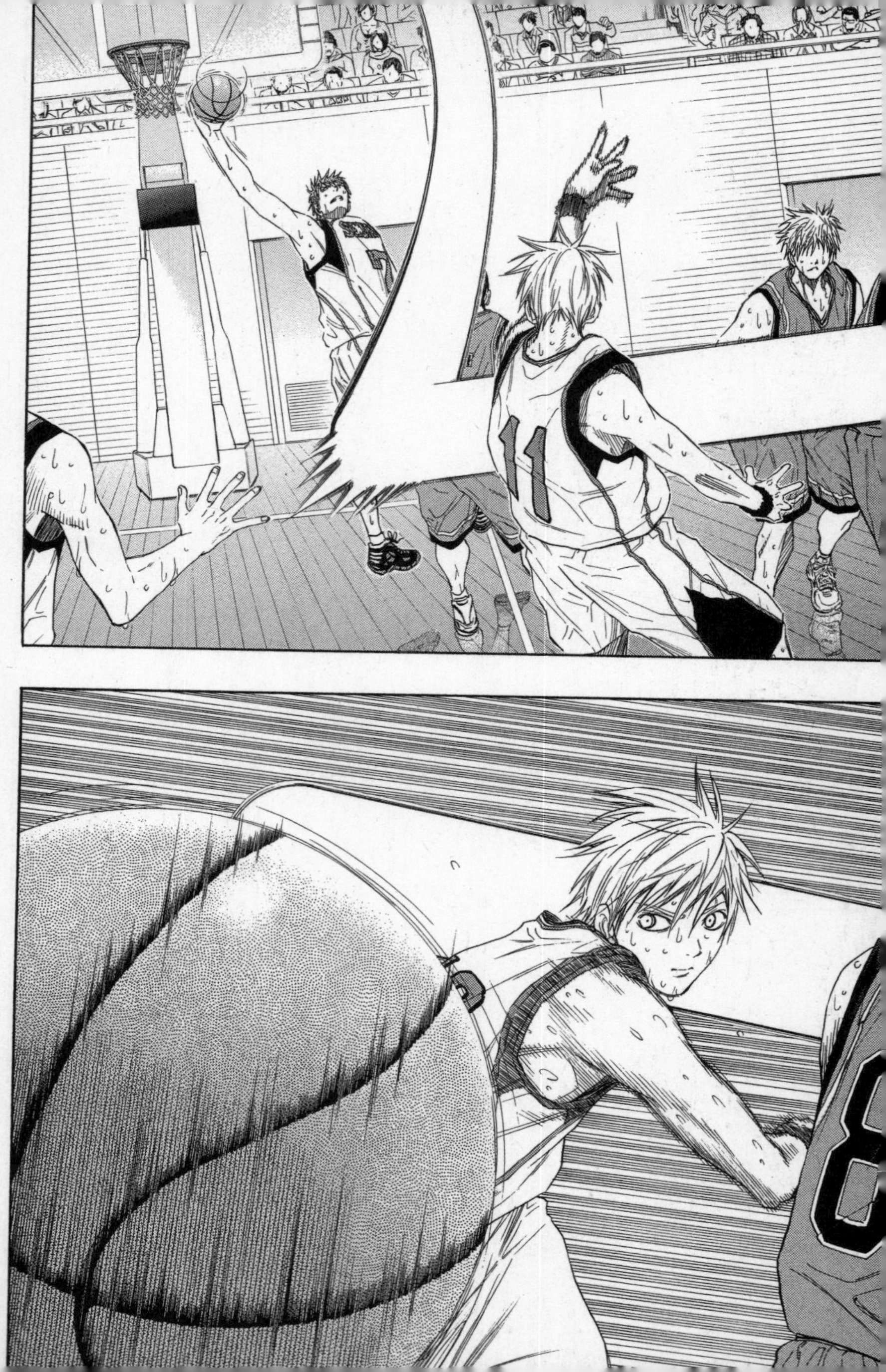

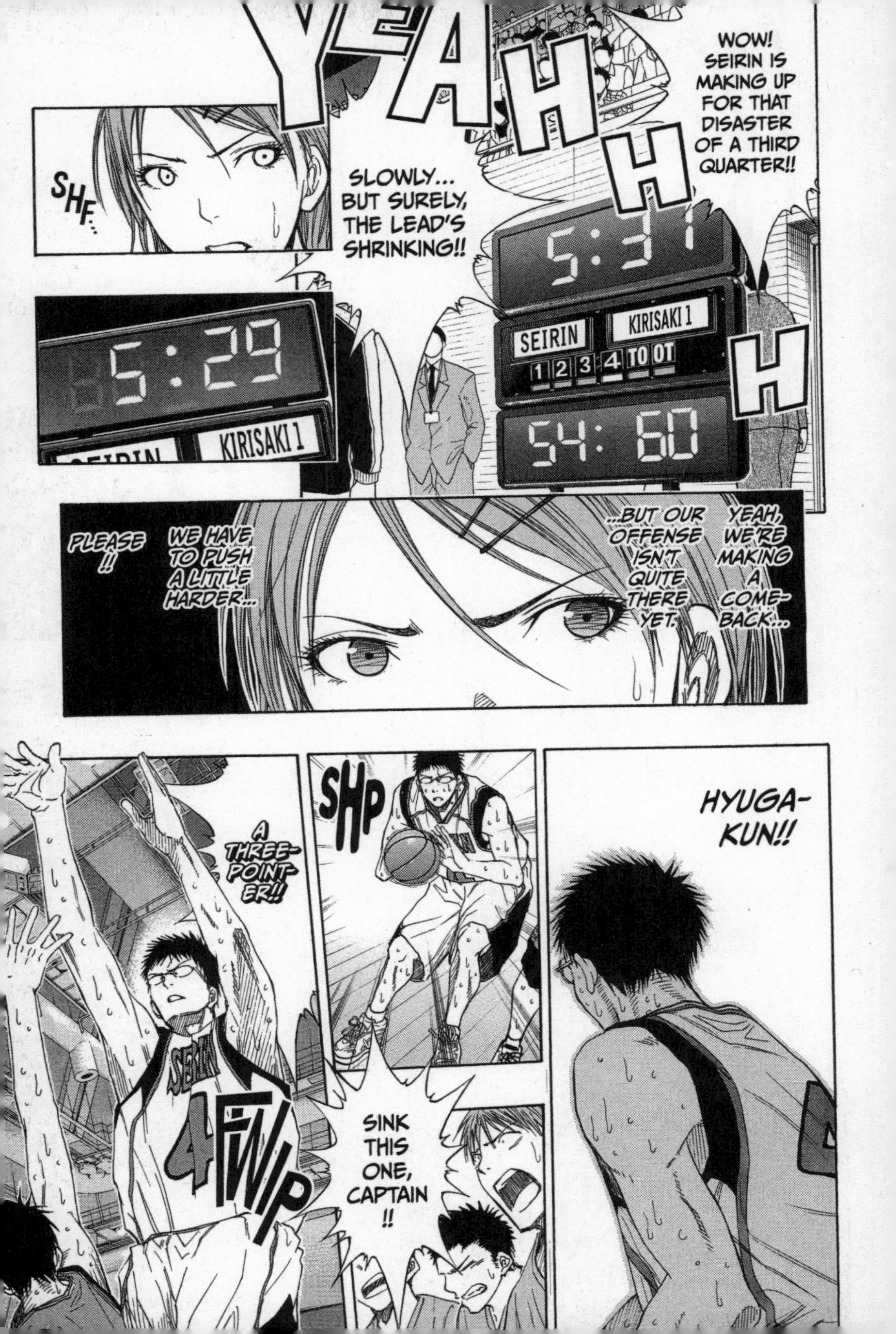
YEAHHHH
WOW! SEIRIN IS MAKING UP FOR THAT DISASTER OF A THIRD QUARTER!!
5:31
SEIRIN
KIRISAKI 1
1 2 3 4 TO OT
54: 60
SLOWLY... BUT SURELY, THE LEAD'S SHRINKING!!
SHF...
5:29
KIRISAKI 1
YEAH, WE'RE MAKING A COME-BACK...
...BUT OUR OFFENSE ISN'T QUITE THERE YET.
WE HAVE TO PUSH A LITTLE HARDER...
PLEASE!!
HYUGA-KUN!!
SHP
SINK THIS ONE, CAPTAIN!!
A THREE-POINTER!!
FWIP

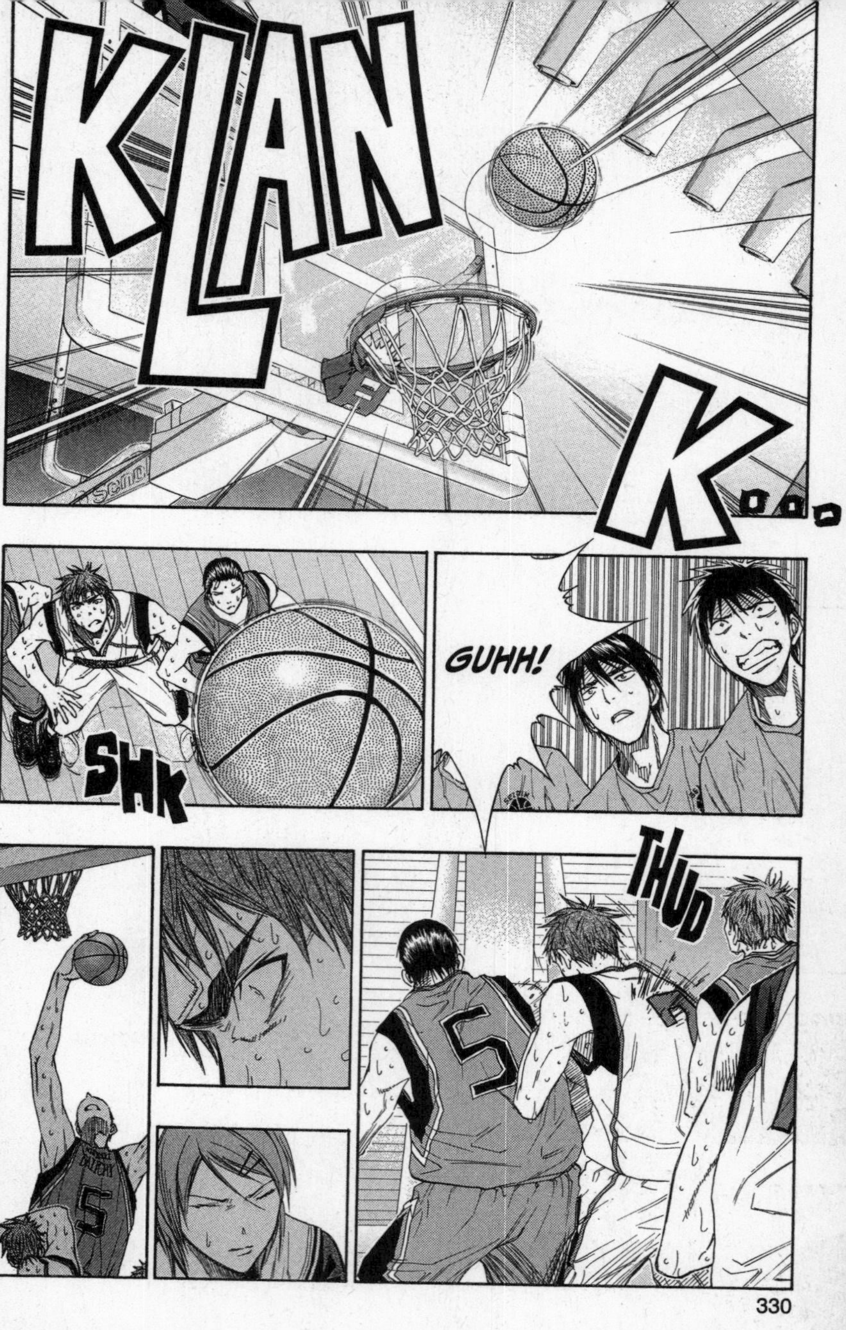
KLAN
K...
GUHH!
SHK
THUD

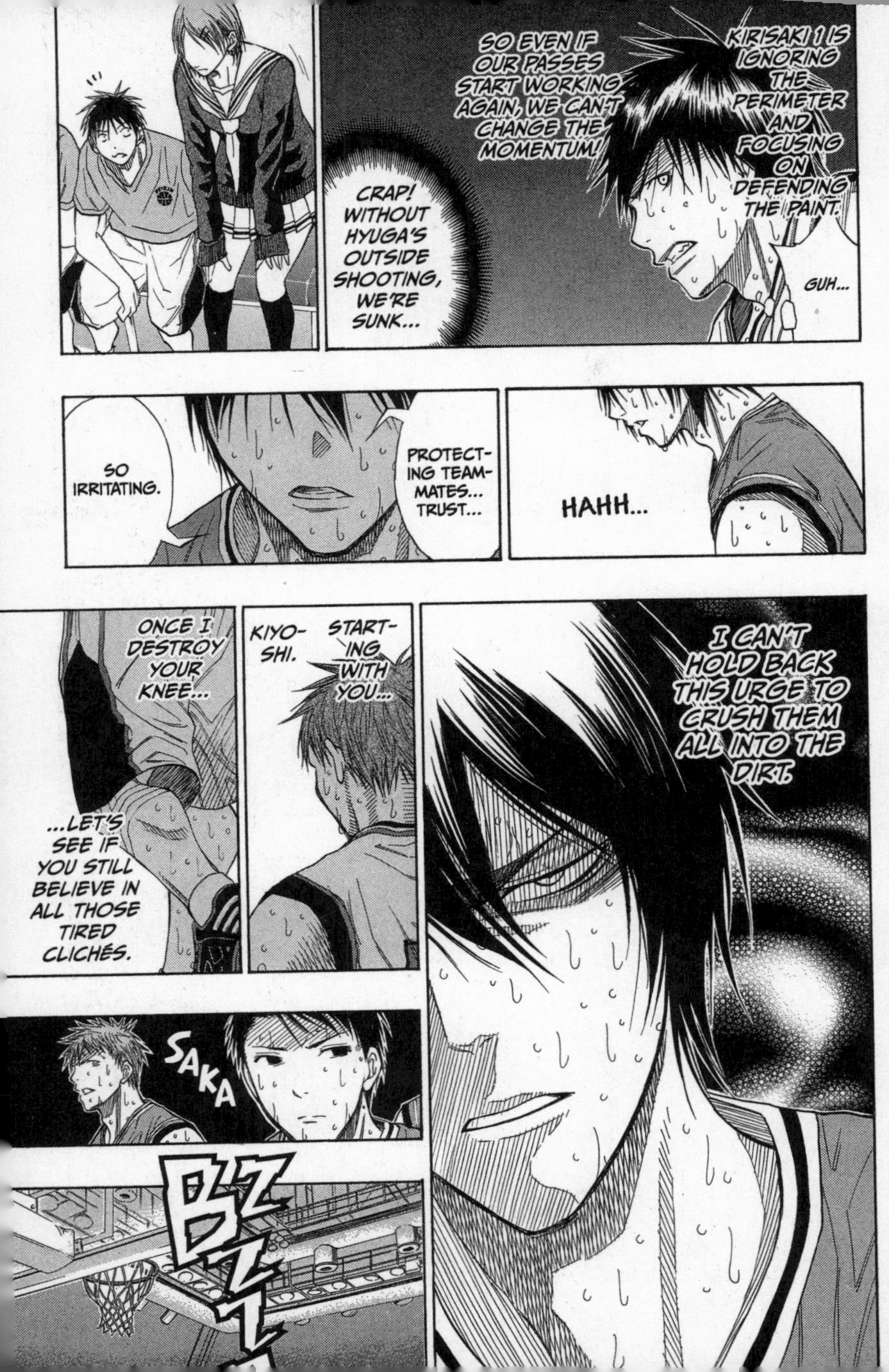
KIRISAKI 1 IS IGNORING THE PERIMETER AND FOCUSING ON DEFENDING THE PAINT.
SO EVEN IF OUR PASSES START WORKING AGAIN, WE CAN'T CHANGE THE MOMENTUM!
GUH...
CRAP! WITHOUT HYUGA'S OUTSIDE SHOOTING, WE'RE SUNK...
HAHH...
PROTECT-ING TEAM-MATES... TRUST...
SO IRRITATING.
I CAN'T HOLD BACK THIS URGE TO CRUSH THEM ALL INTO THE DIRT.
START-ING WITH YOU...
KIYO-SHI.
ONCE I DESTROY YOUR KNEE...
...LET'S SEE IF YOU STILL BELIEVE IN ALL THOSE TIRED CLICHÉS.
SAKA
BZZT

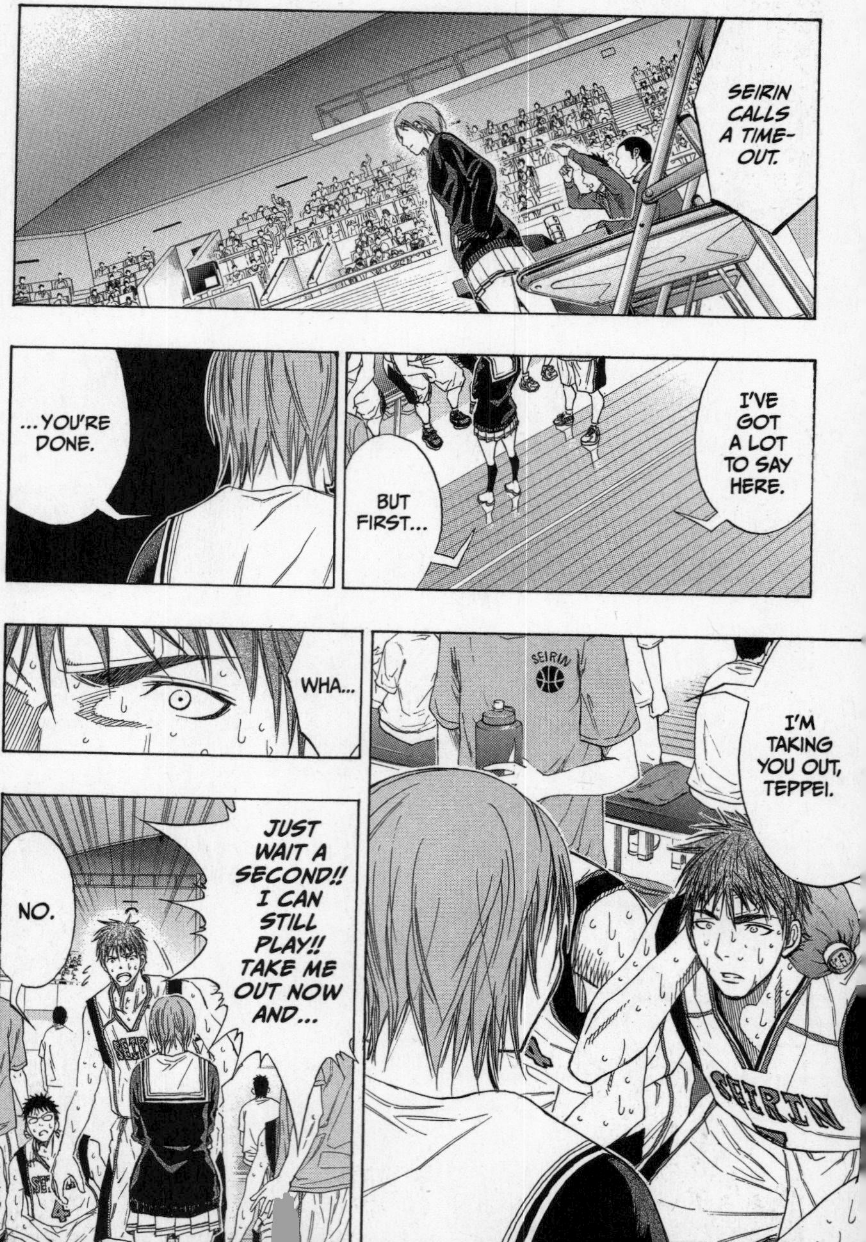
SEIRIN CALLS A TIME-OUT.
I'VE GOT A LOT TO SAY HERE.
BUT FIRST...
...YOU'RE DONE.
I'M TAKING YOU OUT, TEPPEI.
WHA...
JUST WAIT A SECOND!! I CAN STILL PLAY!! TAKE ME OUT NOW AND...
NO.

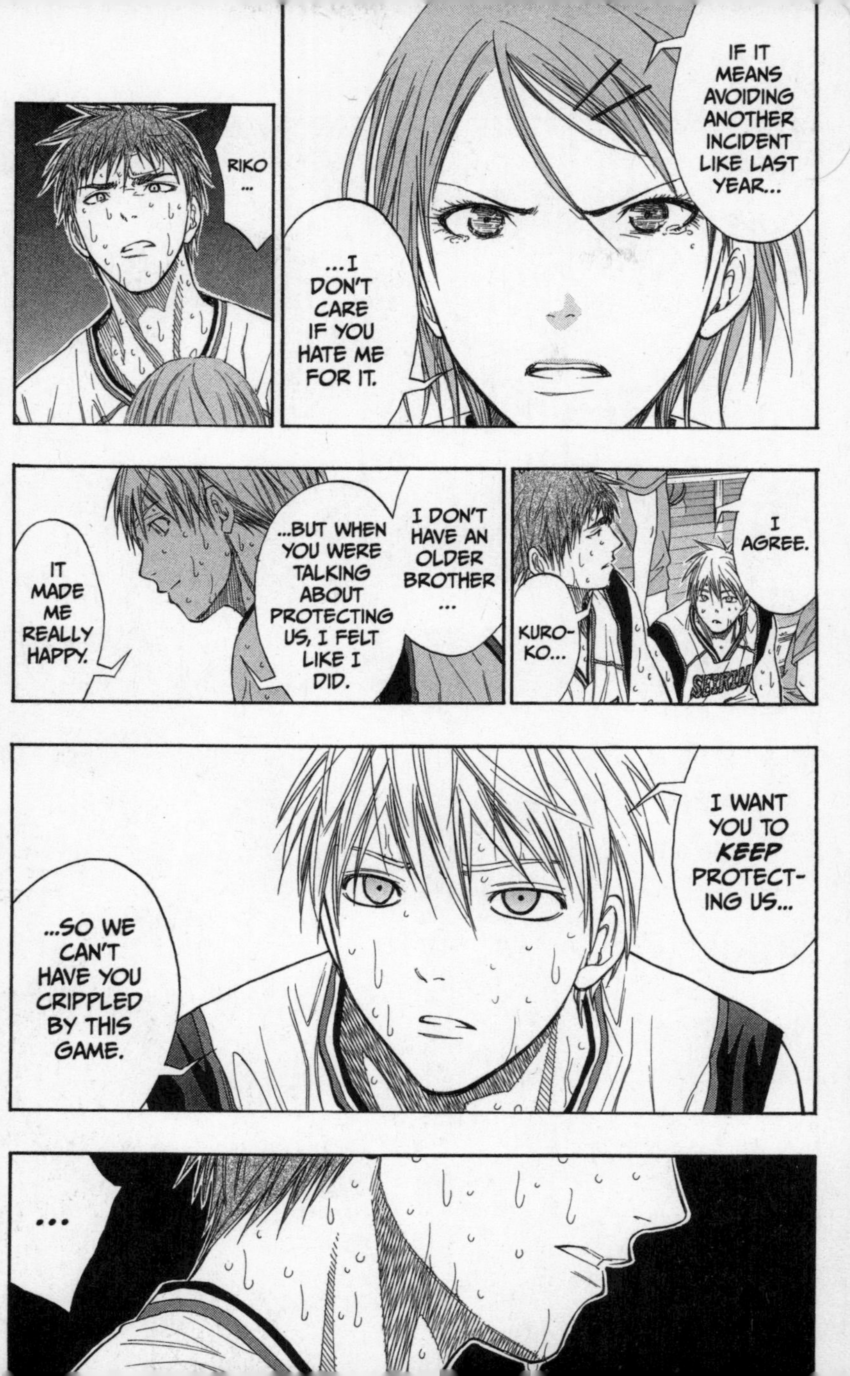
IF IT MEANS AVOIDING ANOTHER INCIDENT LIKE LAST YEAR...
...I DON'T CARE IF YOU HATE ME FOR IT.
RIKO ...
I AGREE.
KURO-KO...
I DON'T HAVE AN OLDER BROTHER ...
...BUT WHEN YOU WERE TALKING ABOUT PROTECTING US, I FELT LIKE I DID.
IT MADE ME REALLY HAPPY.
I WANT YOU TO *KEEP* PROTECT-ING US...
...SO WE CAN'T HAVE YOU CRIPPLED BY THIS GAME.
...

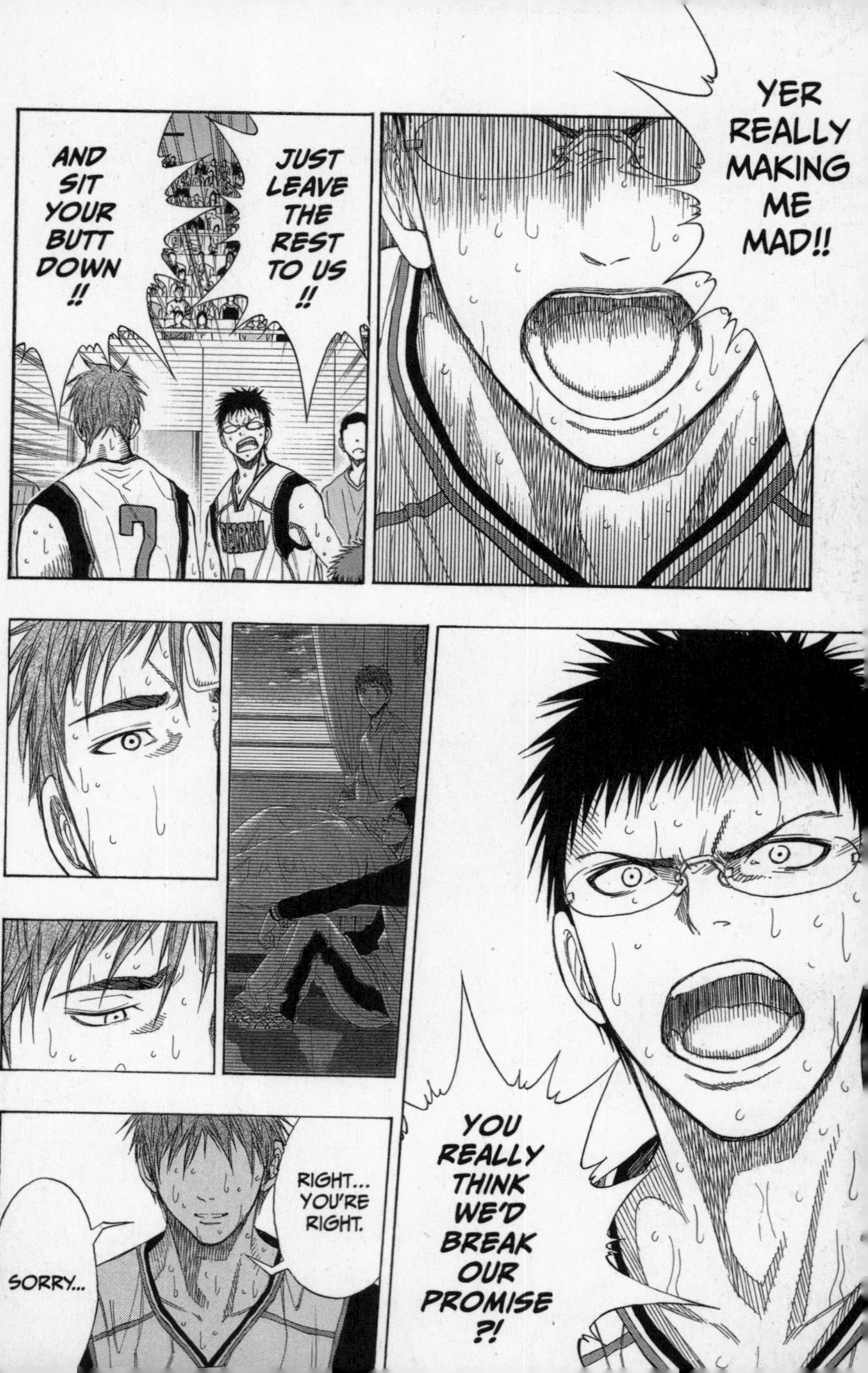
YER REALLY MAKING ME MAD!!
JUST LEAVE THE REST TO US!!
AND SIT YOUR BUTT DOWN!!
YOU REALLY THINK WE'D BREAK OUR PROMISE?!
RIGHT... YOU'RE RIGHT.
SORRY...

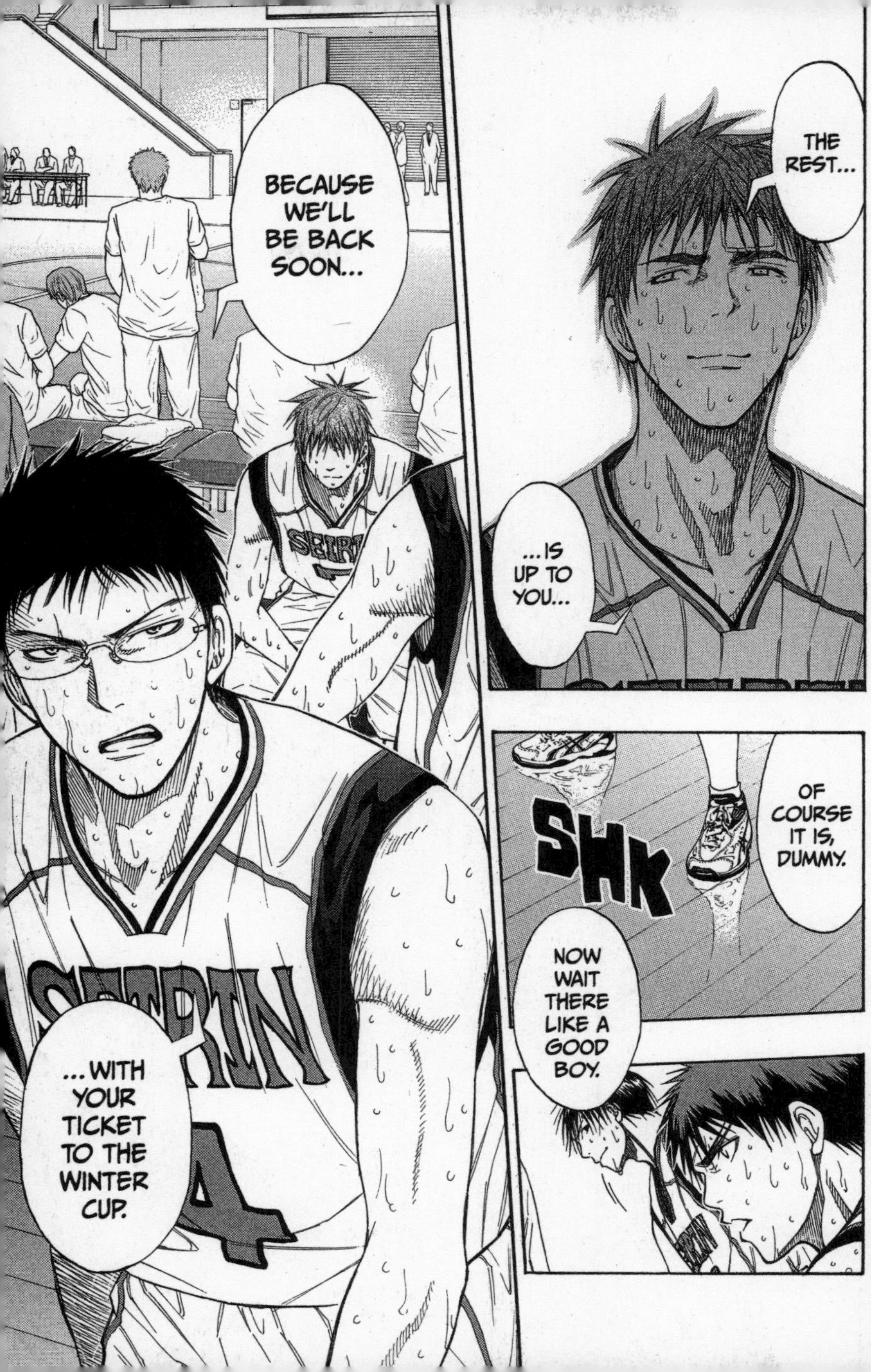
THE REST...
...IS UP TO YOU...
SHK
OF COURSE IT IS, DUMMY.
NOW WAIT THERE LIKE A GOOD BOY.
BECAUSE WE'LL BE BACK SOON...
...WITH YOUR TICKET TO THE WINTER CUP.

KUROKO'S BASKETBALL BLOOPERS

TAKE 5

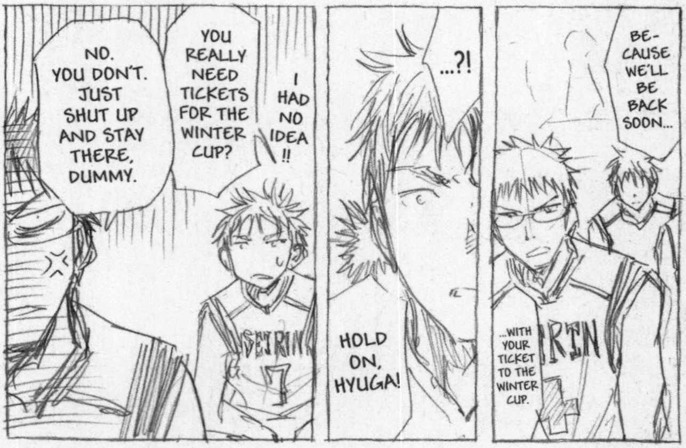
BE-CAUSE WE'LL BE BACK SOON...
...WITH YOUR TICKET TO THE WINTER CUP.
...?!
HOLD ON, HYUGA!
I HAD NO IDEA!!
YOU REALLY NEED TICKETS FOR THE WINTER CUP?
NO. YOU DON'T. JUST SHUT UP AND STAY THERE, DUMMY.

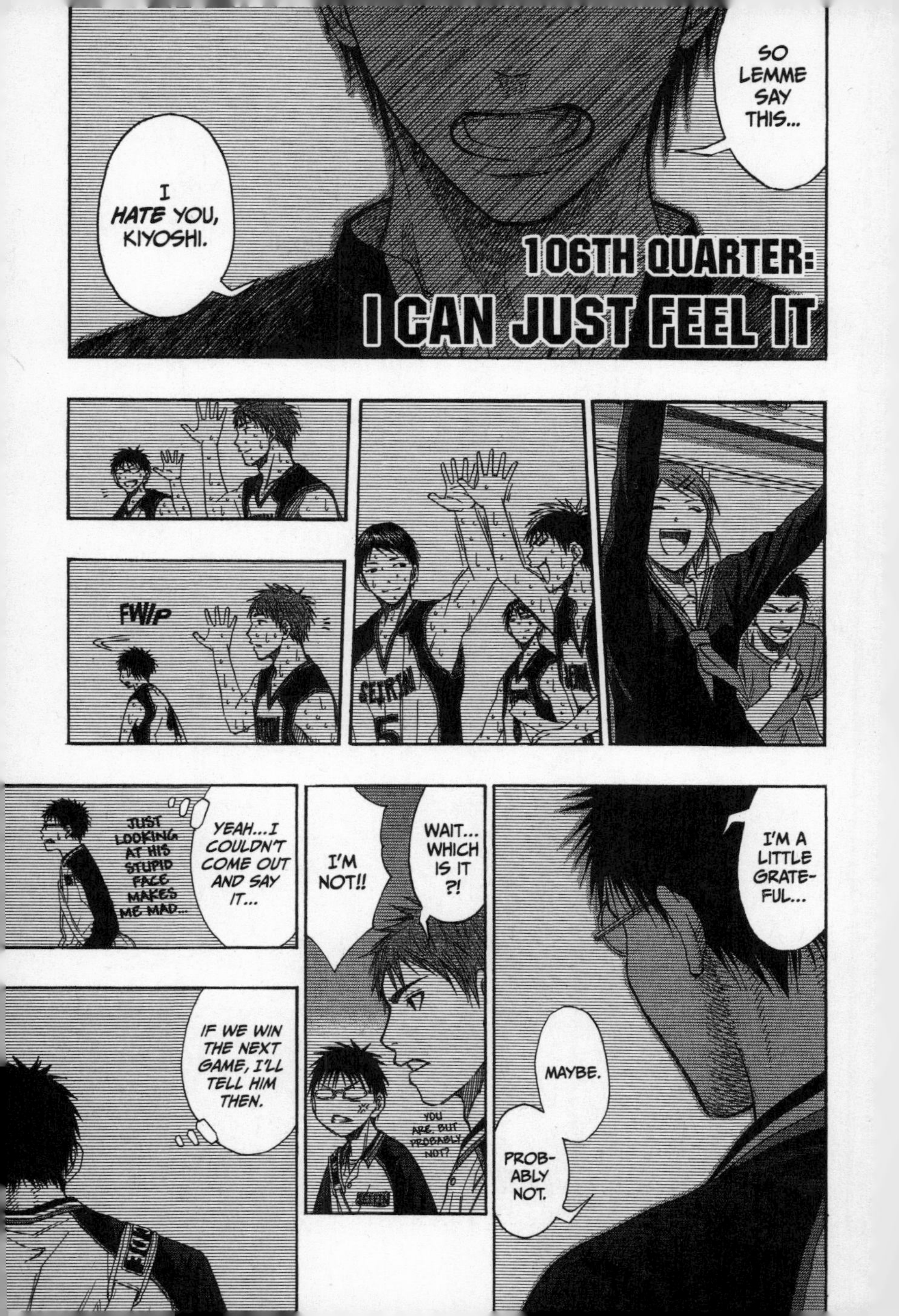
SO LEMME SAY THIS...
I HATE YOU, KIYOSHI.
106TH QUARTER:
I CAN JUST FEEL IT
FWIP
I'M A LITTLE GRATE-FUL...
MAYBE.
PROBABLY NOT.
WAIT... WHICH IS IT ?!
I'M NOT!!
YOU ARE BUT PROBABLY NOT?
YEAH...I COULDN'T COME OUT AND SAY IT...
JUST LOOKING AT HIS STUPID FACE MAKES ME MAD...
IF WE WIN THE NEXT GAME, I'LL TELL HIM THEN.

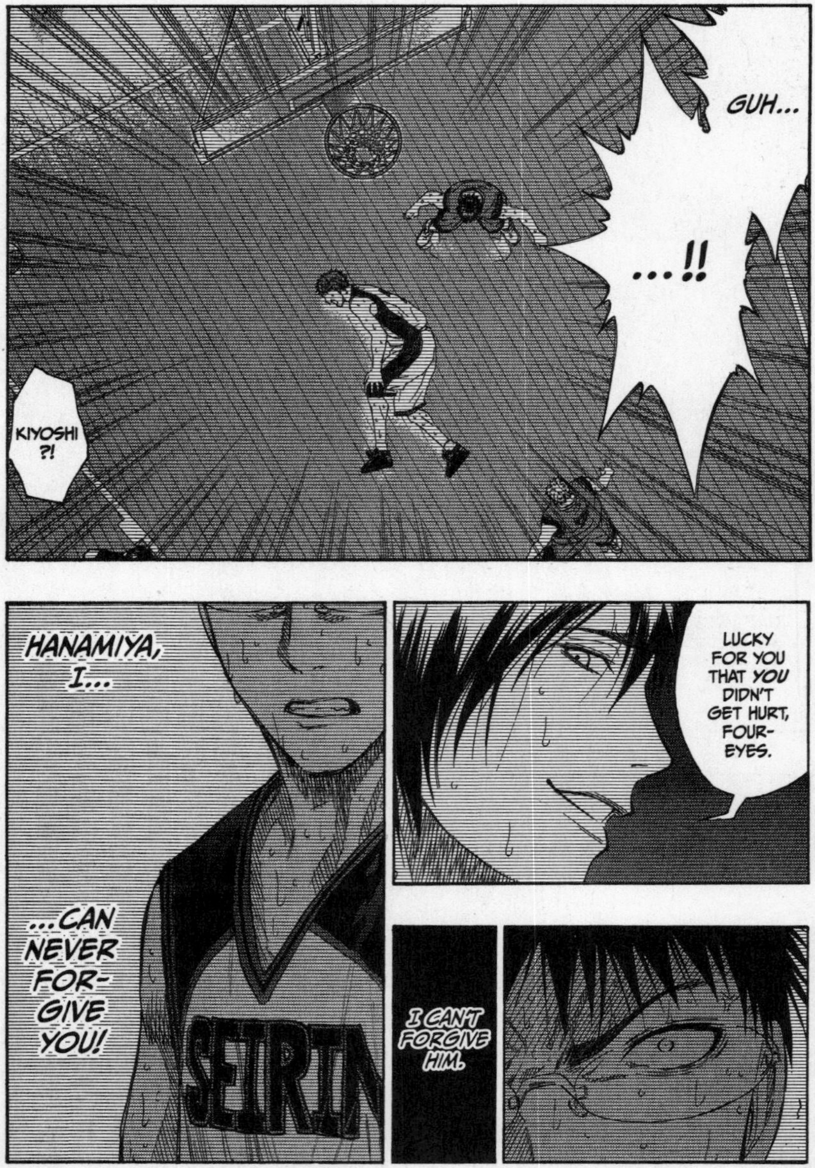
GUH...
...!!
KIYOSHI?!
LUCKY FOR YOU THAT YOU DIDN'T GET HURT, FOUR-EYES.
I CAN'T FORGIVE HIM.
HANAMIYA, I...
...CAN NEVER FOR-GIVE YOU!

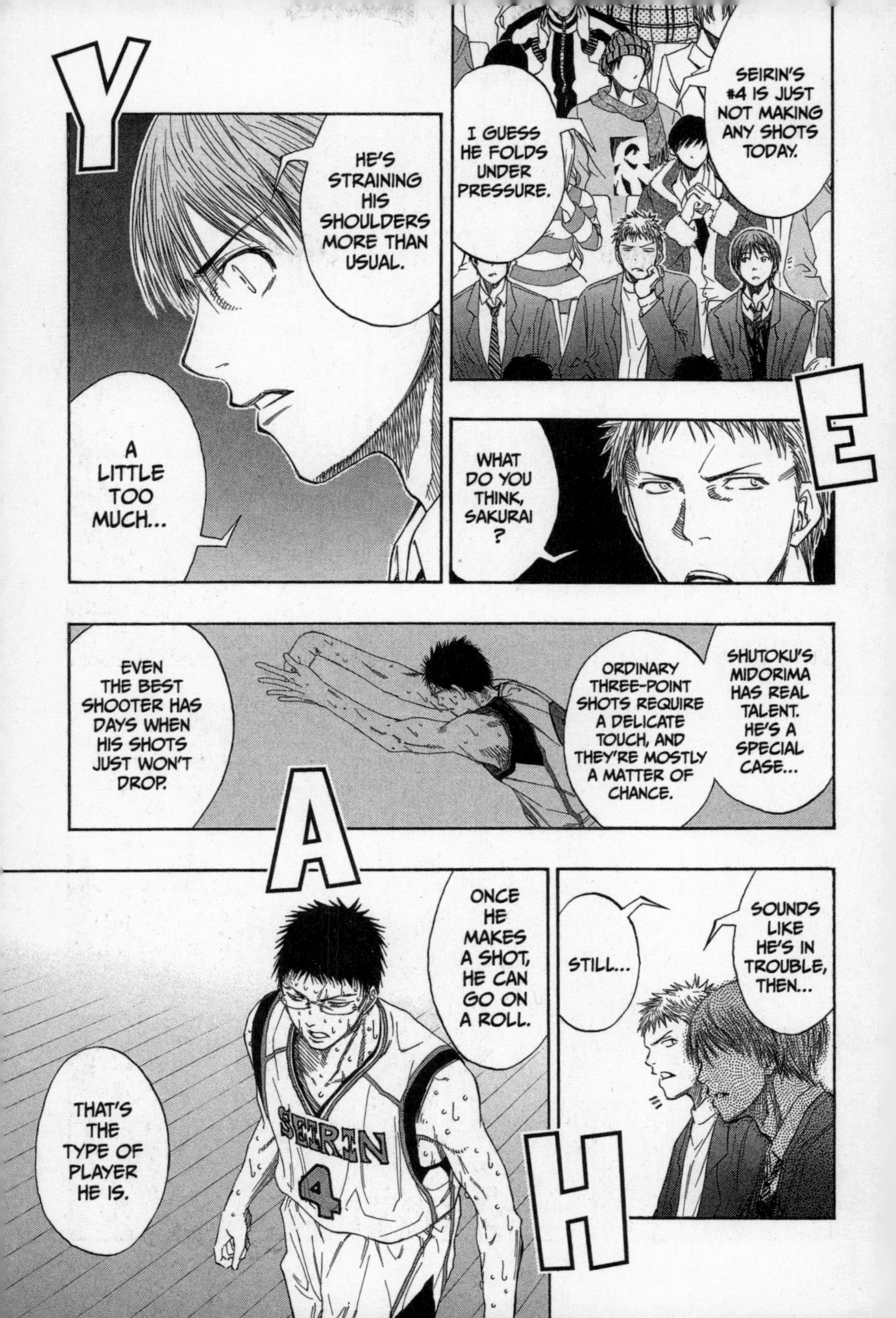
Y
SEIRIN'S #4 IS JUST NOT MAKING ANY SHOTS TODAY.
I GUESS HE FOLDS UNDER PRESSURE.
E
WHAT DO YOU THINK, SAKURAI?
HE'S STRAINING HIS SHOULDERS MORE THAN USUAL.
A LITTLE TOO MUCH...
SHUTOKU'S MIDORIMA HAS REAL TALENT. HE'S A SPECIAL CASE...
ORDINARY THREE-POINT SHOTS REQUIRE A DELICATE TOUCH, AND THEY'RE MOSTLY A MATTER OF CHANCE.
EVEN THE BEST SHOOTER HAS DAYS WHEN HIS SHOTS JUST WON'T DROP.
A
SOUNDS LIKE HE'S IN TROUBLE, THEN...
STILL...
ONCE HE MAKES A SHOT, HE CAN GO ON A ROLL.
THAT'S THE TYPE OF PLAYER HE IS.
H

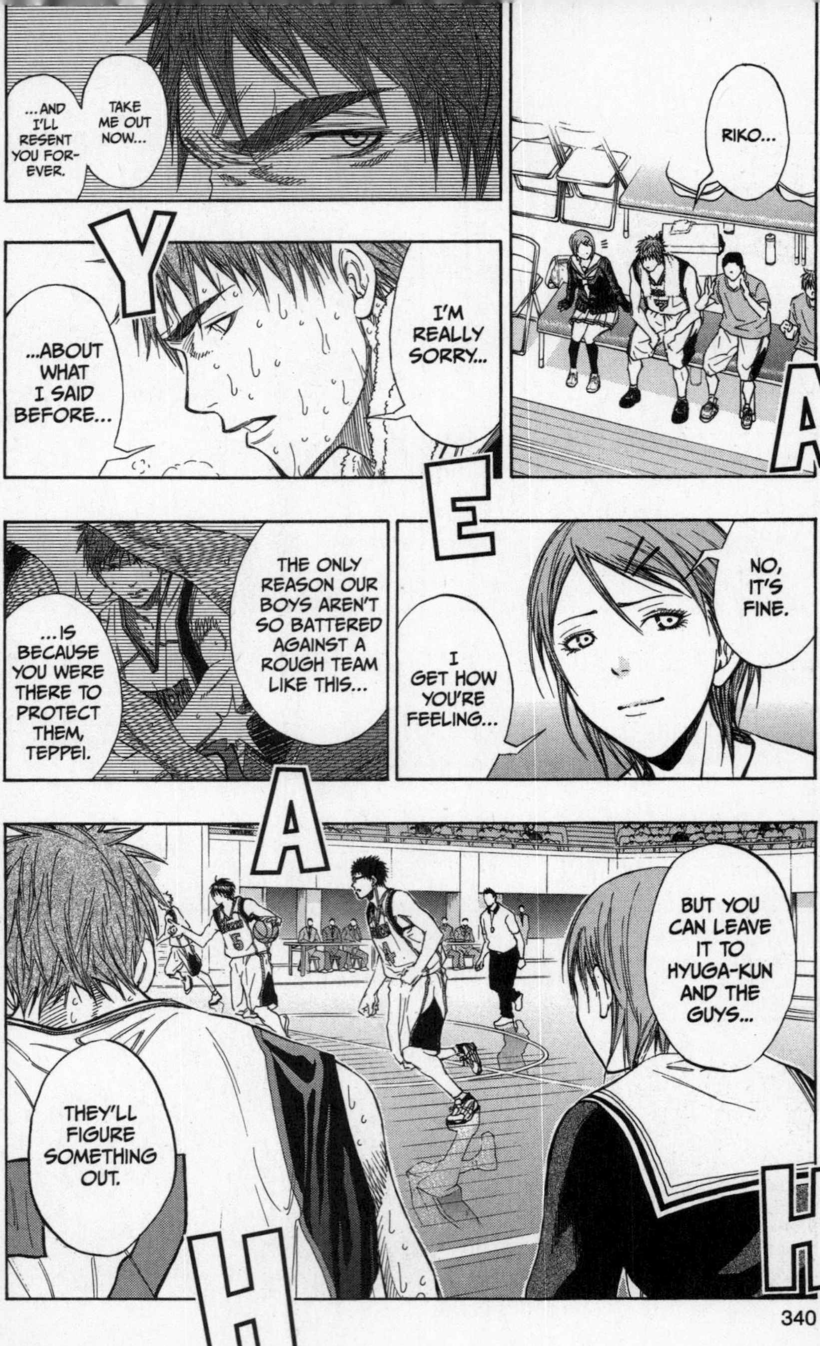
RIKO...
TAKE ME OUT NOW...
...AND I'LL RESENT YOU FOREVER.
I'M REALLY SORRY...
...ABOUT WHAT I SAID BEFORE...
YEAAHHH
NO, IT'S FINE.
I GET HOW YOU'RE FEELING...
THE ONLY REASON OUR BOYS AREN'T SO BATTERED AGAINST A ROUGH TEAM LIKE THIS...
...IS BECAUSE YOU WERE THERE TO PROTECT THEM, TEPPEI.
BUT YOU CAN LEAVE IT TO HYUGA-KUN AND THE GUYS...
THEY'LL FIGURE SOMETHING OUT.

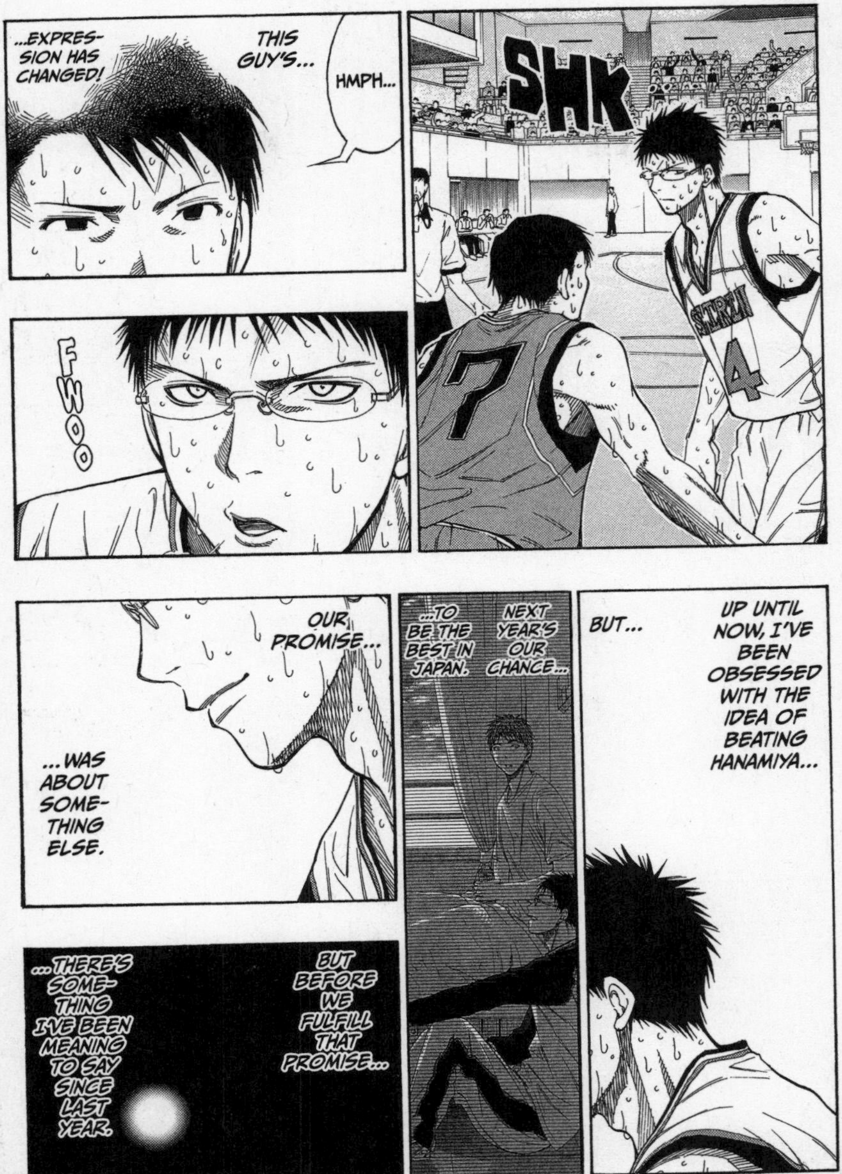
SHK
HMPH...
THIS GUY'S...
...EXPRESSION HAS CHANGED!
FWOO
UP UNTIL NOW, I'VE BEEN OBSESSED WITH THE IDEA OF BEATING HANAMIYA...
BUT...
NEXT YEAR'S OUR CHANCE...
...TO BE THE BEST IN JAPAN.
OUR PROMISE...
...WAS ABOUT SOMETHING ELSE.
BUT BEFORE WE FULFILL THAT PROMISE...
...THERE'S SOMETHING I'VE BEEN MEANING TO SAY SINCE LAST YEAR.

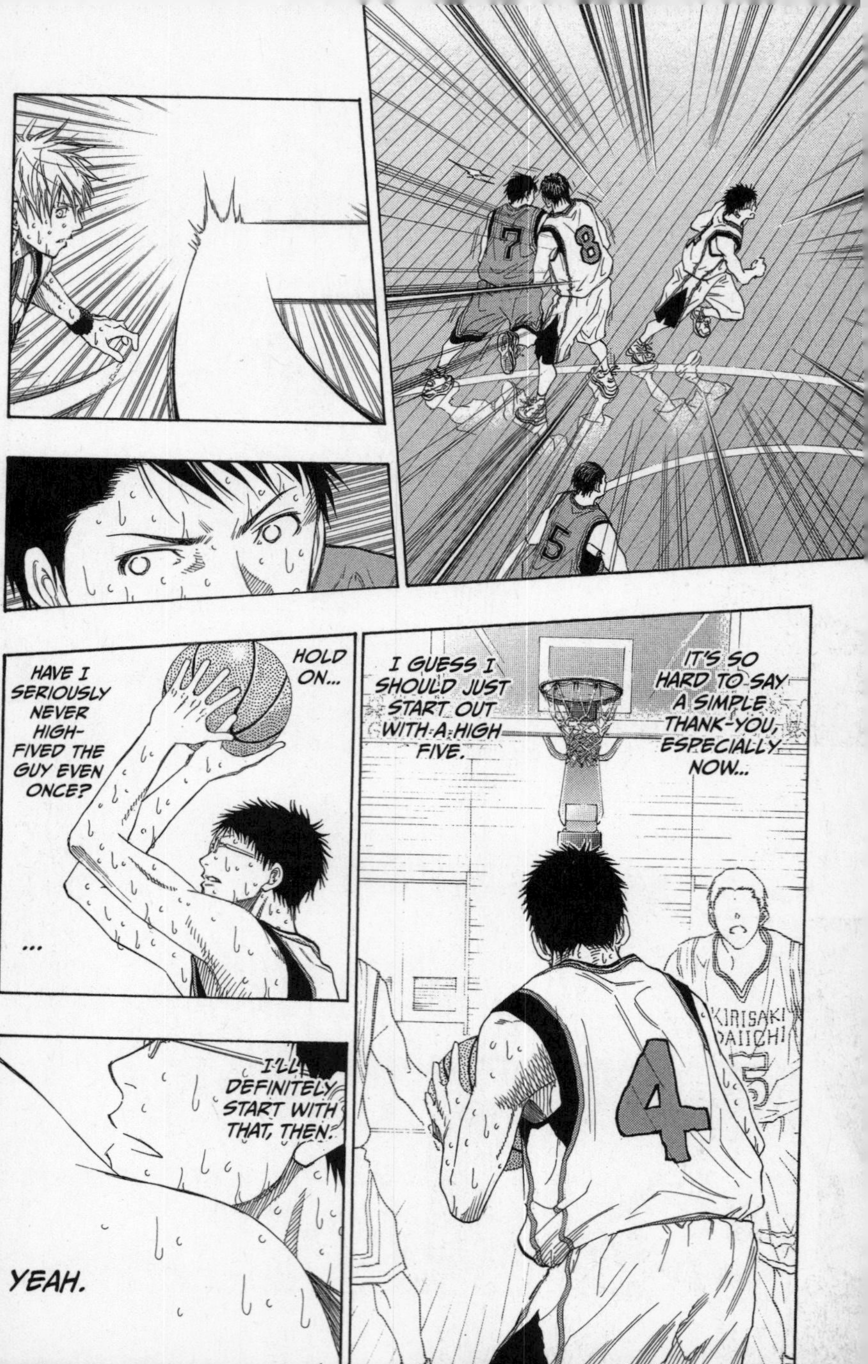
IT'S SO HARD TO SAY A SIMPLE THANK-YOU, ESPECIALLY NOW...
I GUESS I SHOULD JUST START OUT WITH A HIGH FIVE.
KIRISAKI DAIICHI
HOLD ON...
HAVE I SERIOUSLY NEVER HIGH-FIVED THE GUY EVEN ONCE?
...
I'LL DEFINITELY START WITH THAT, THEN.
YEAH.

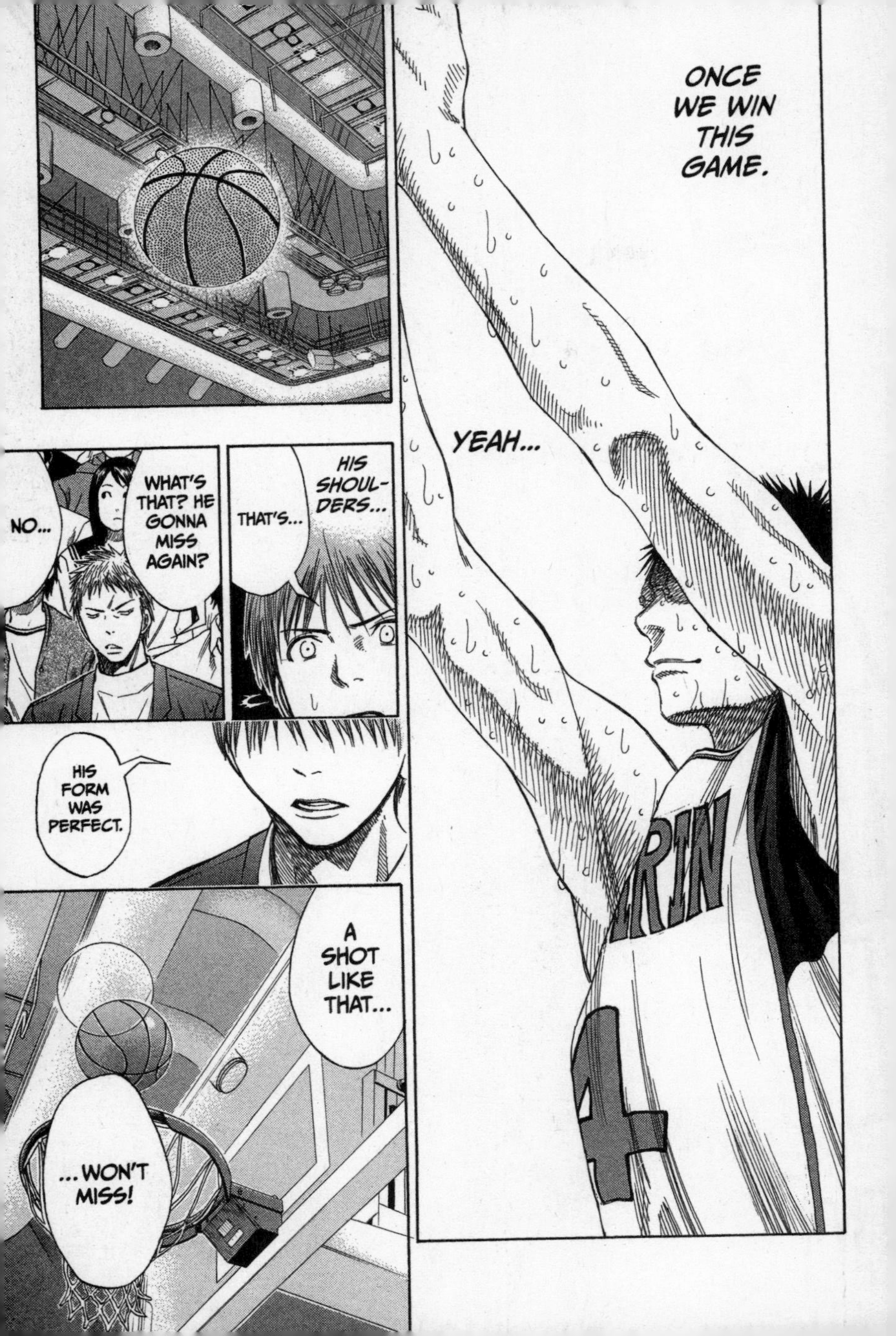
ONCE WE WIN THIS GAME.
YEAH...
HIS SHOULDERS...
THAT'S...
WHAT'S THAT? HE GONNA MISS AGAIN?
NO...
HIS FORM WAS PERFECT.
A SHOT LIKE THAT...
...WON'T MISS!

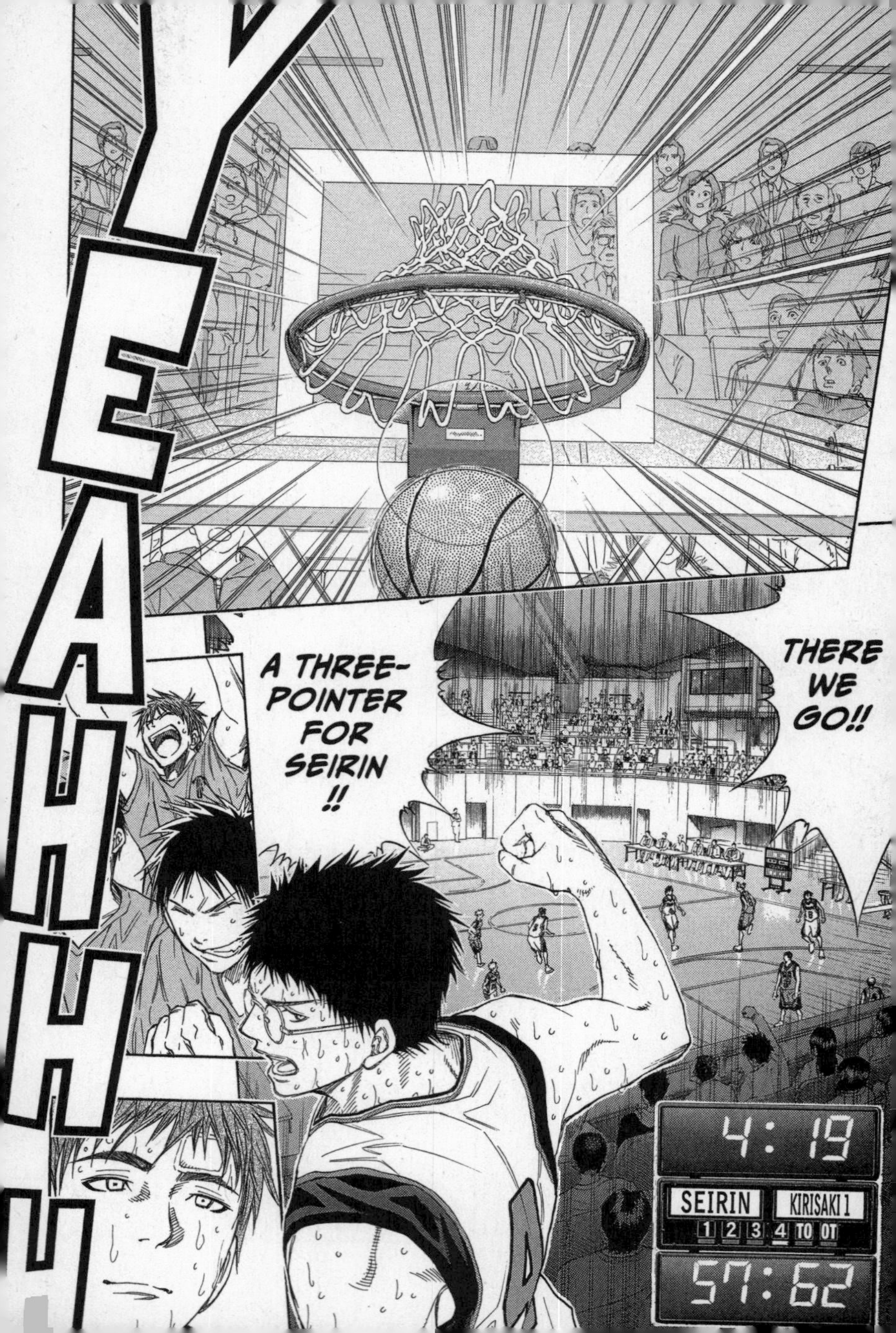
YEAHHHH
THERE WE GO!!
A THREE-POINTER FOR SEIRIN!!
4:19
SEIRIN
KIRISAKI 1
1 2 3 4 TO OT
57:62

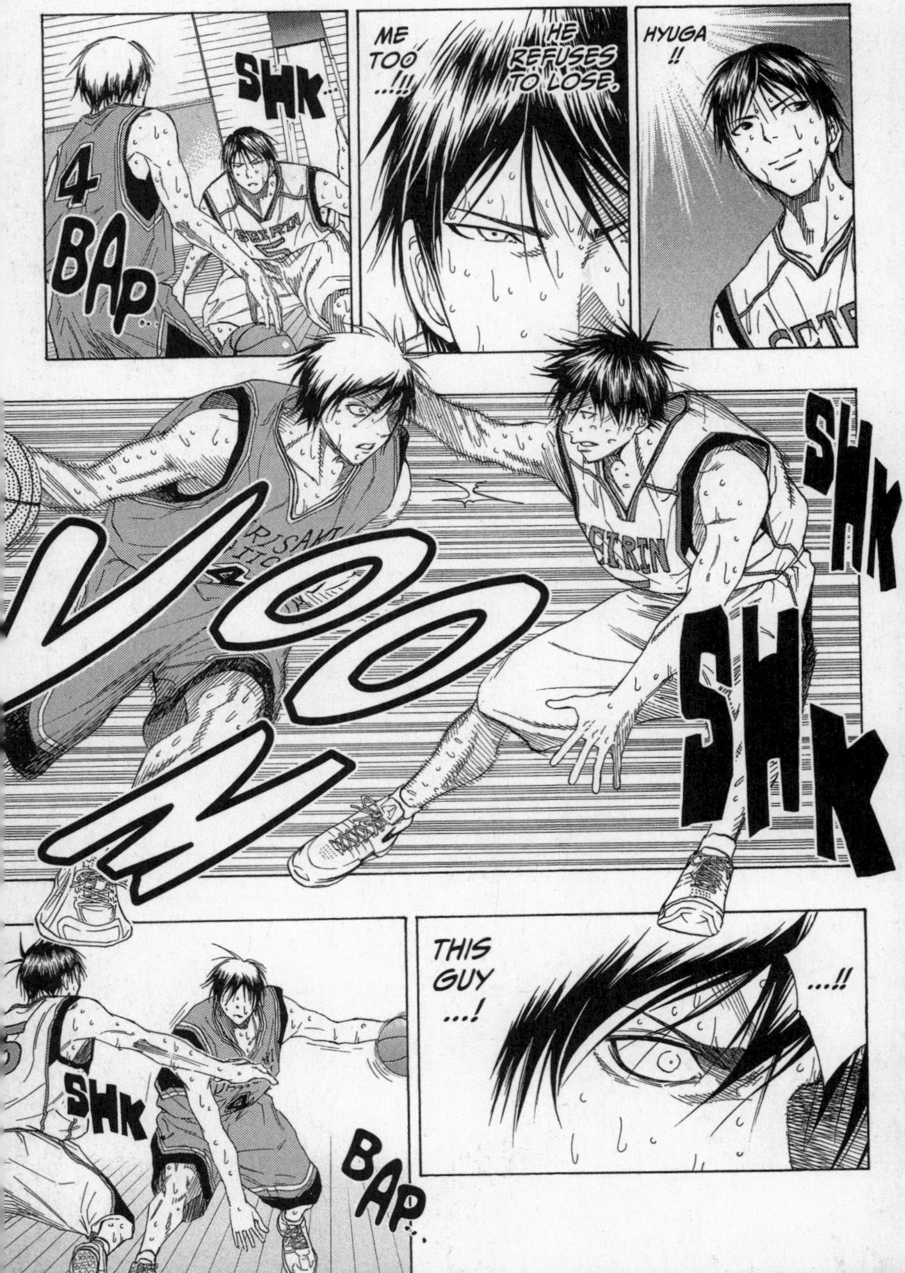
HYUGA !!
HE REFUSES TO LOSE.
ME TOO ...!!!
SHK...
BAP...
SHK
SHK
VOOM
...!!
THIS GUY ...!
SHK
BAP...

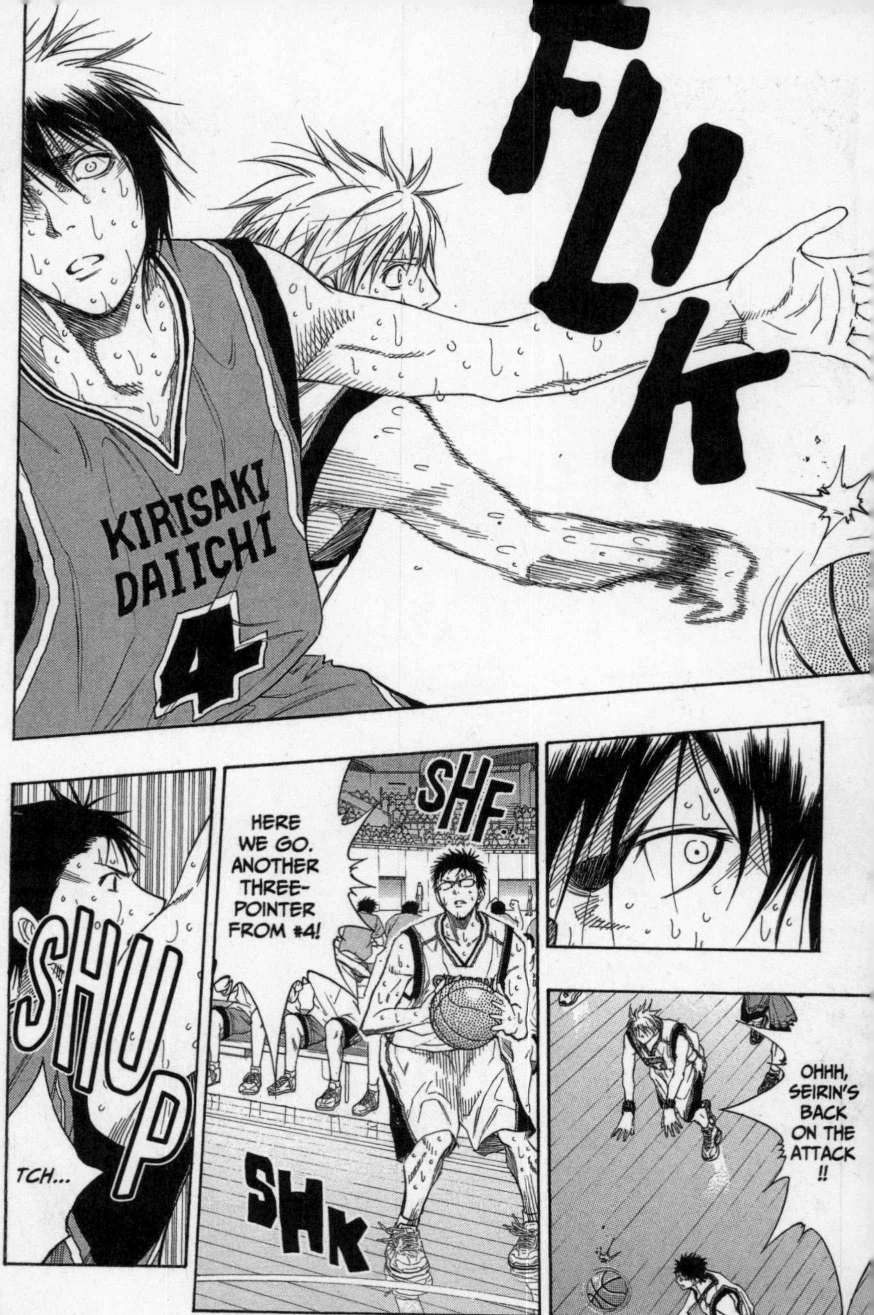
FLIK
KIRISAKI DAIICHI
4
OHHH, SEIRIN'S BACK ON THE ATTACK!!
SHF
HERE WE GO. ANOTHER THREE-POINTER FROM #4!
SHK
SHUP
TCH...

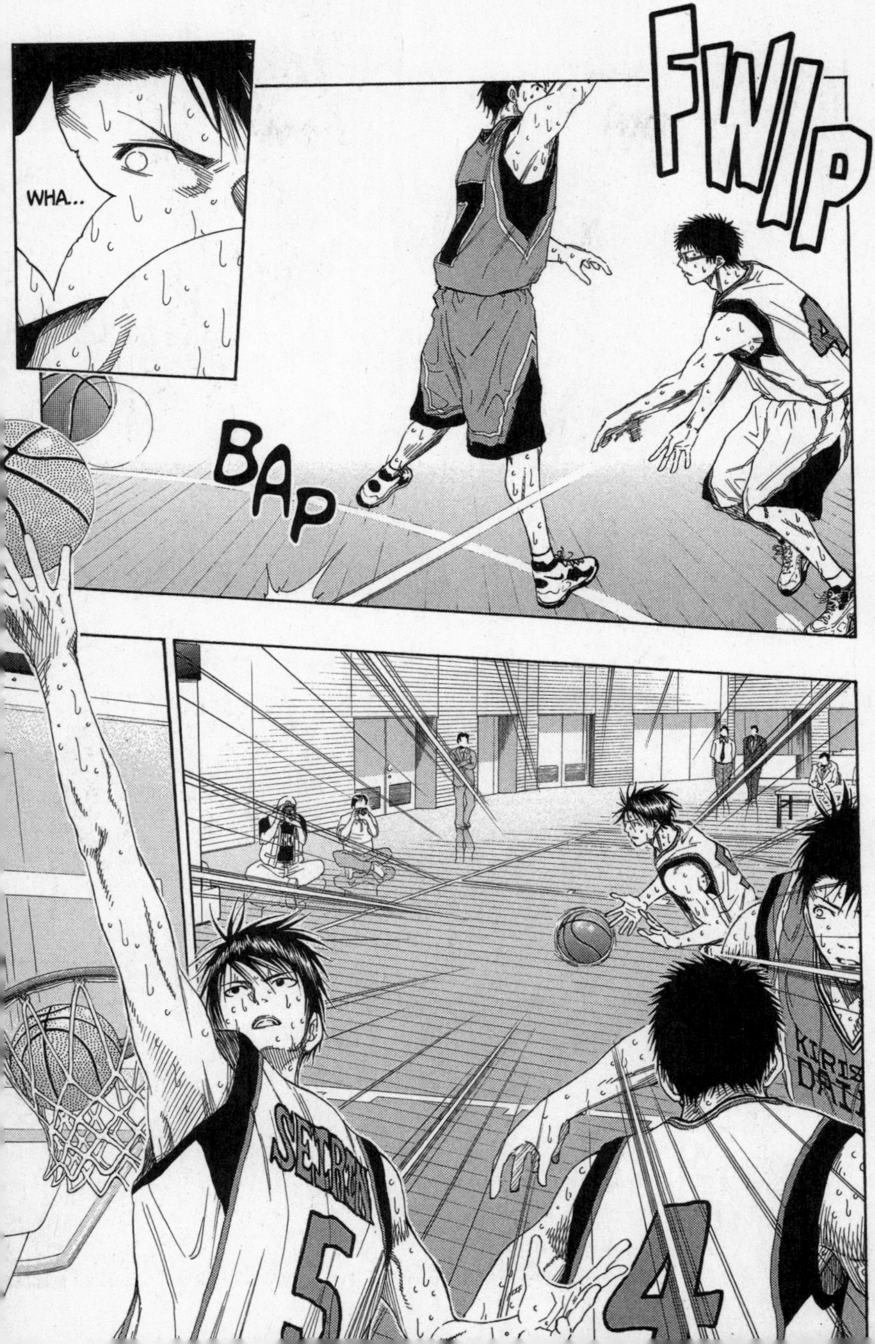
FWIP
BAP
WHA...
SEIRIN

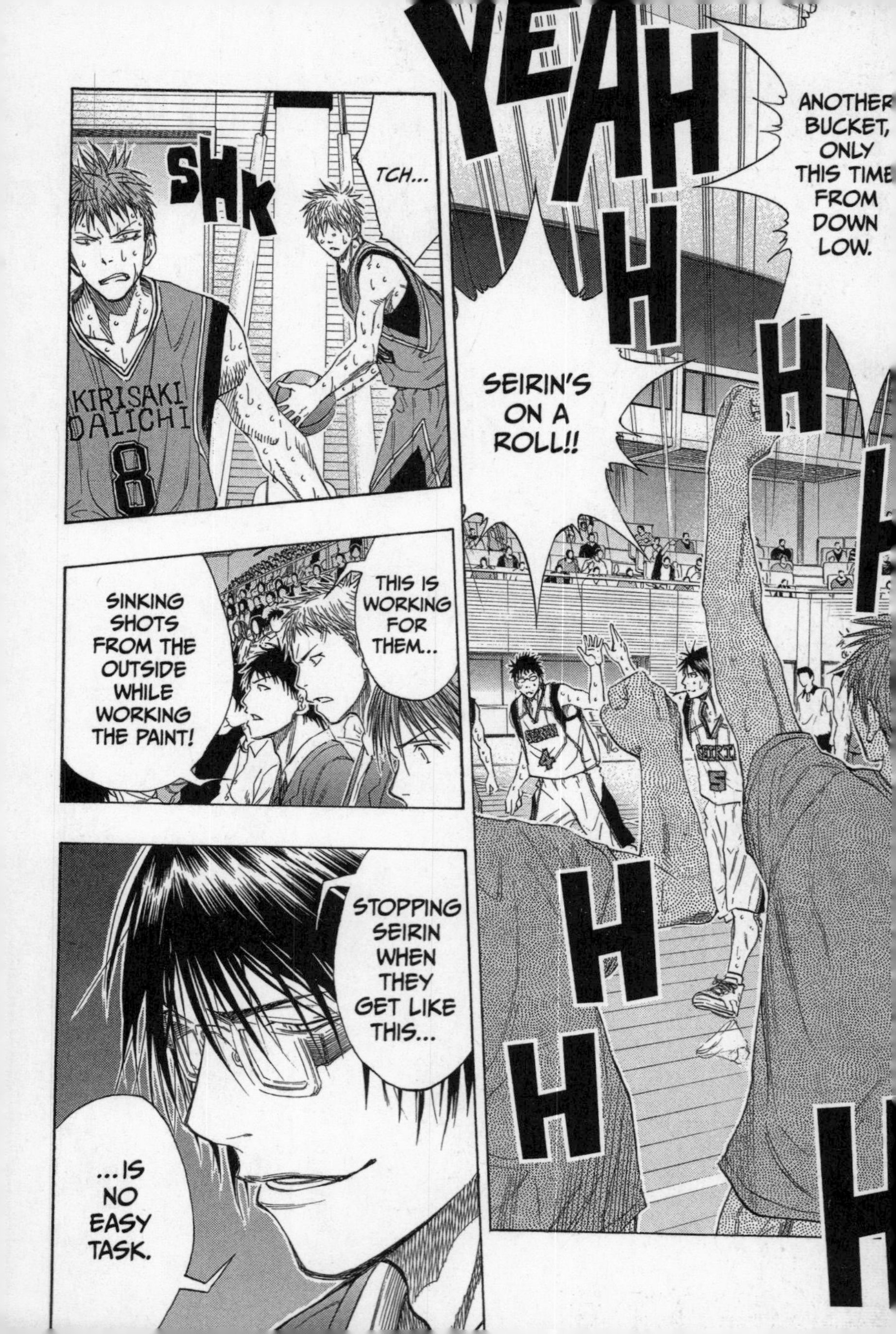
YEAHHHHHHH
ANOTHER BUCKET, ONLY THIS TIME FROM DOWN LOW.
SEIRIN'S ON A ROLL!!
SHK
TCH...
KIRISAKI DAIICHI
THIS IS WORKING FOR THEM...
SINKING SHOTS FROM THE OUTSIDE WHILE WORKING THE PAINT!
STOPPING SEIRIN WHEN THEY GET LIKE THIS...
...IS NO EASY TASK.

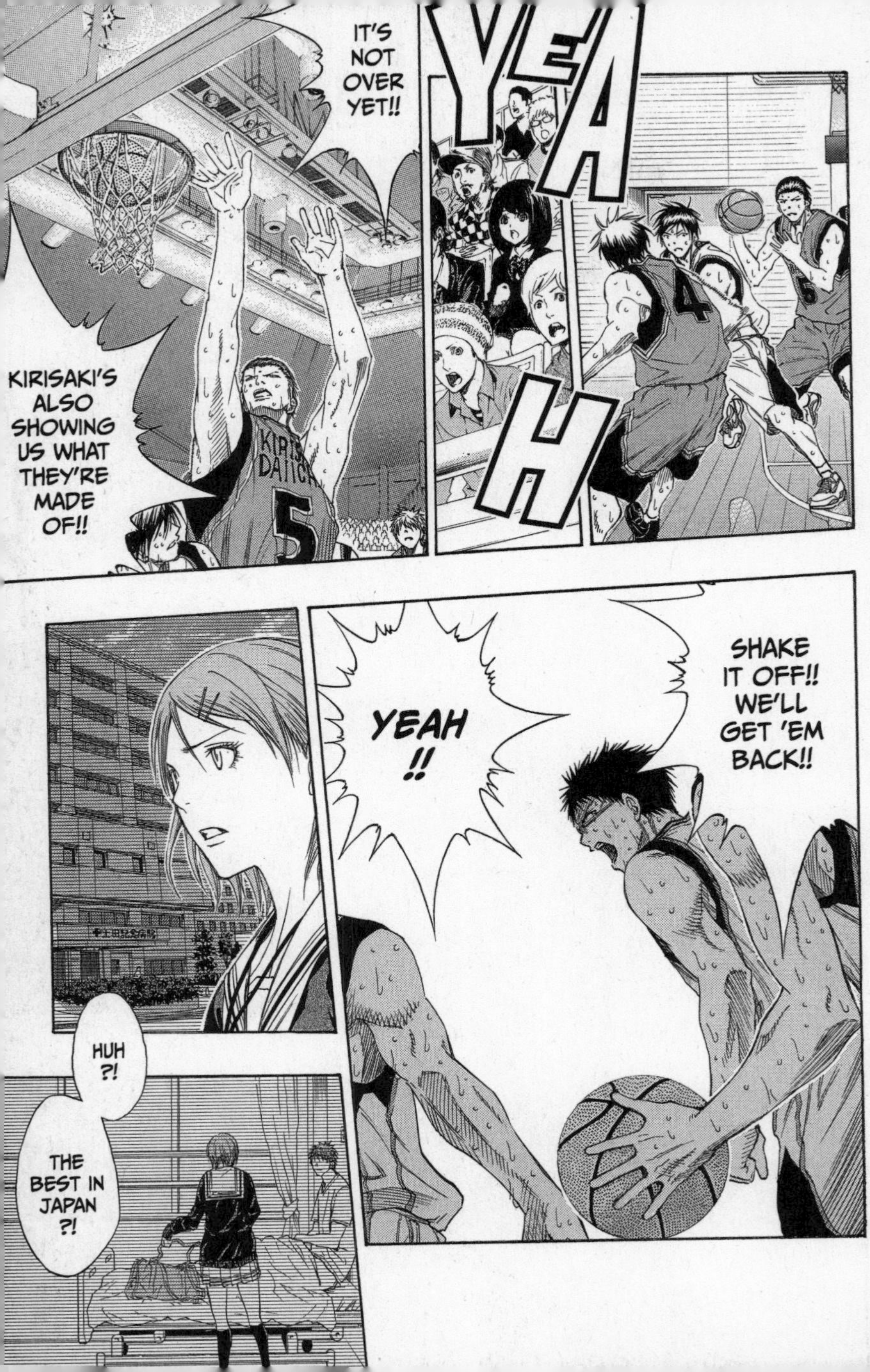

YEAH
IT'S NOT OVER YET!!
KIRISAKI'S ALSO SHOWING US WHAT THEY'RE MADE OF!!
KIRISAKI DAIICHI
5
4
SHAKE IT OFF!! WE'LL GET 'EM BACK!!
YEAH !!
HUH ?!
THE BEST IN JAPAN ?!

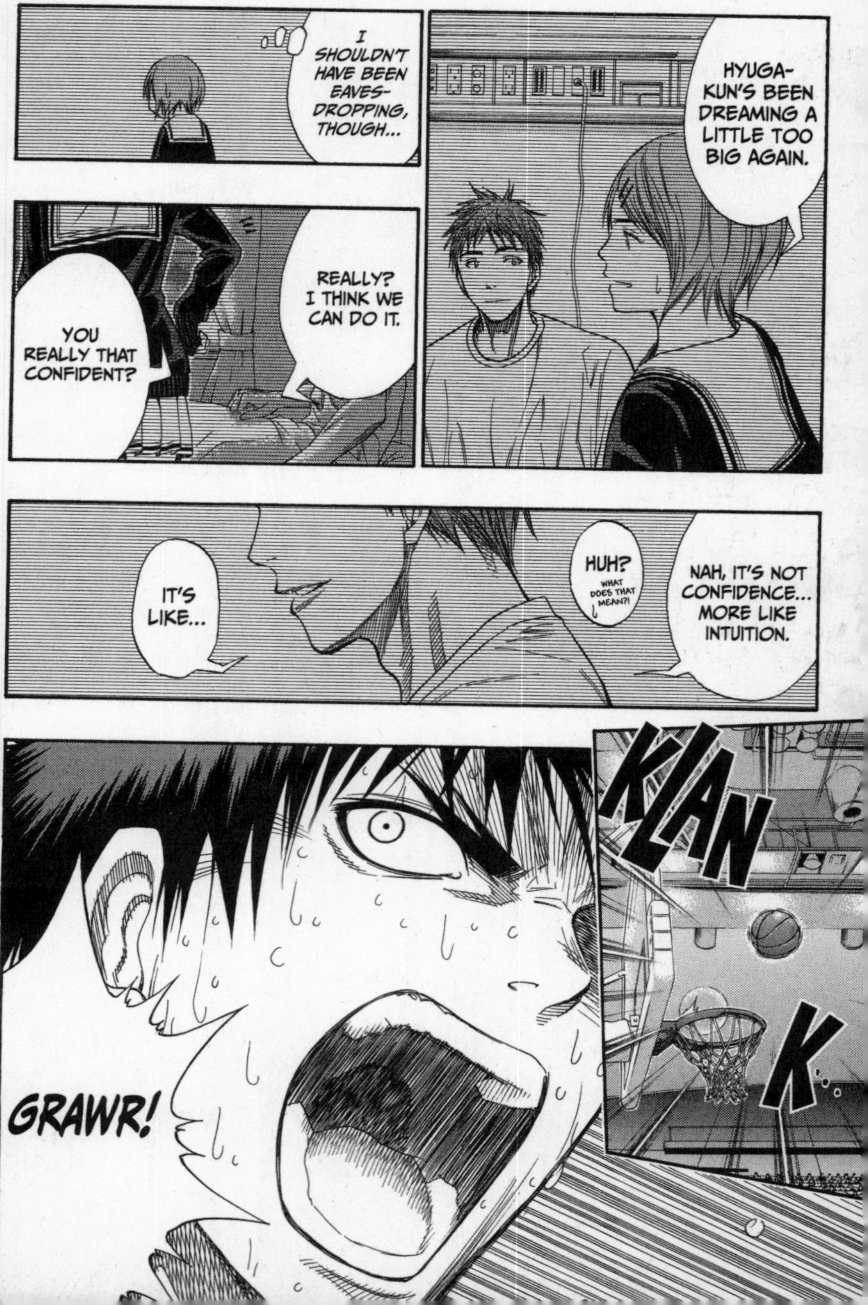
HYUGA-KUN'S BEEN DREAMING A LITTLE TOO BIG AGAIN.
I SHOULDN'T HAVE BEEN EAVES-DROPPING, THOUGH...
REALLY? I THINK WE CAN DO IT.
YOU REALLY THAT CONFIDENT?
NAH, IT'S NOT CONFIDENCE... MORE LIKE INTUITION.
HUH?
WHAT DOES THAT MEAN?!
IT'S LIKE...
KLANK
GRAWR!

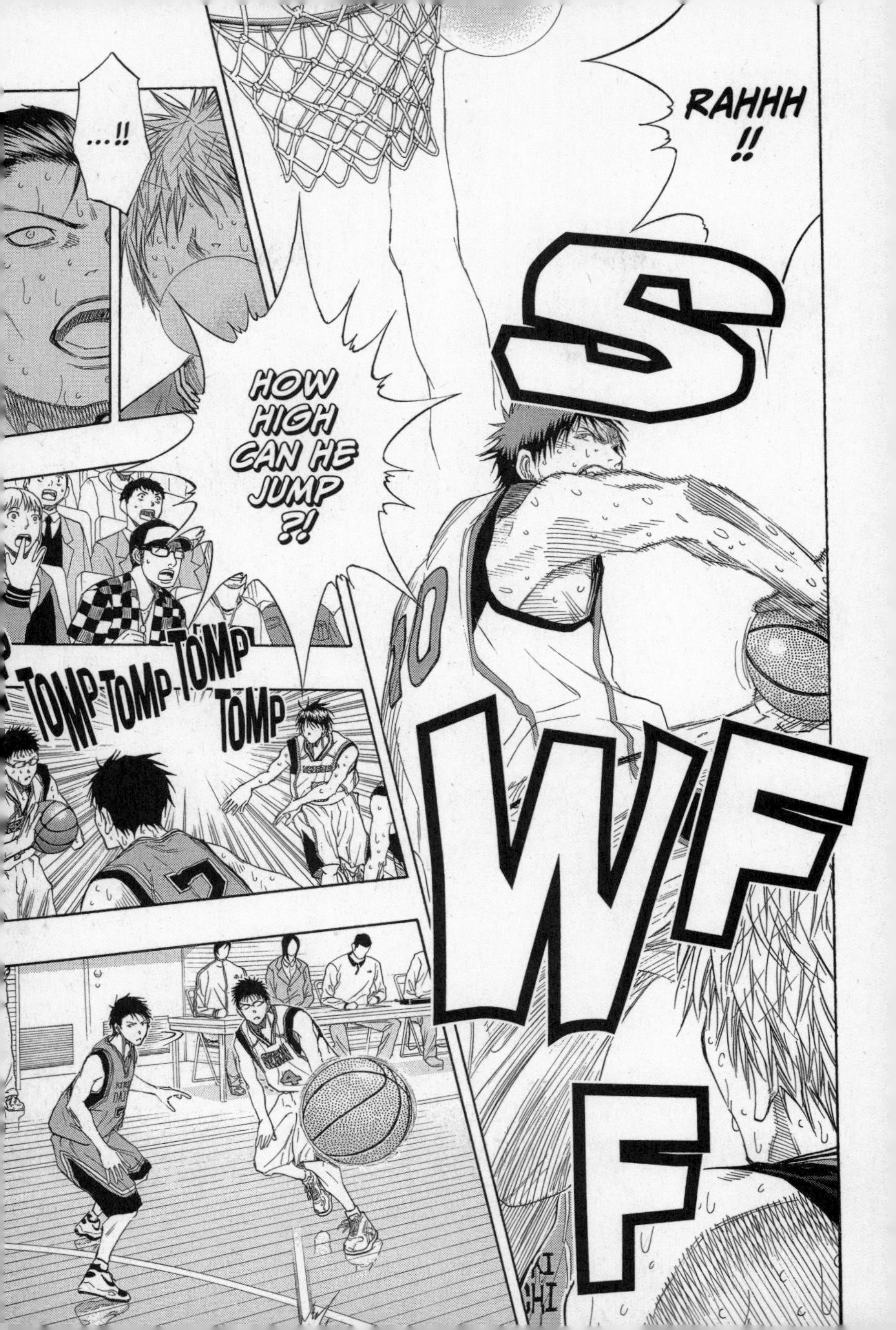
RAHHH !!
SWFF
...!!
HOW HIGH CAN HE JUMP ?!
TOMP TOMP TOMP TOMP

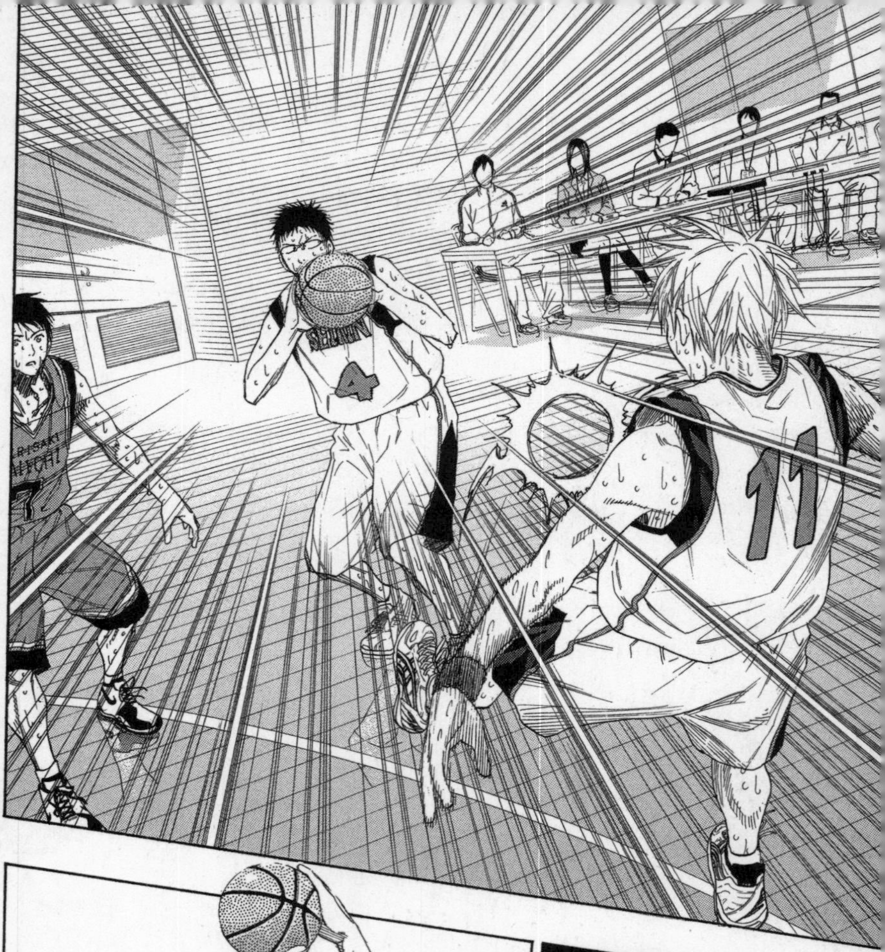
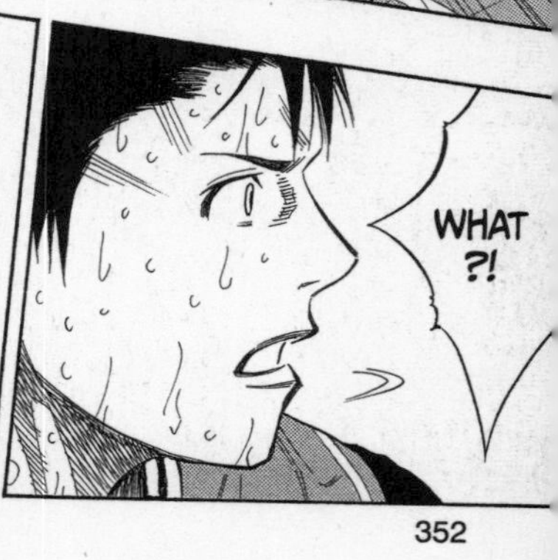
WHAT
?!
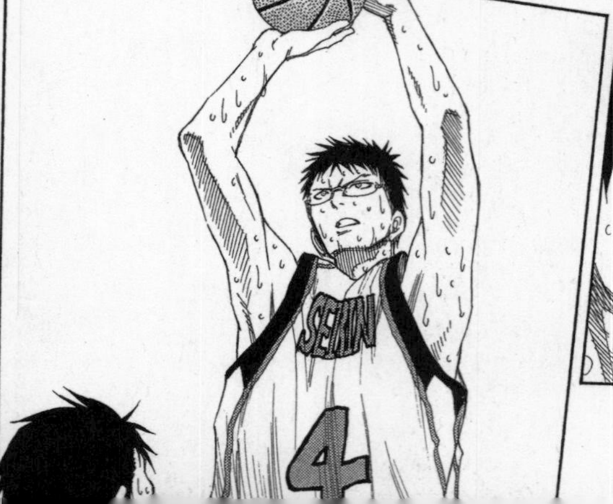

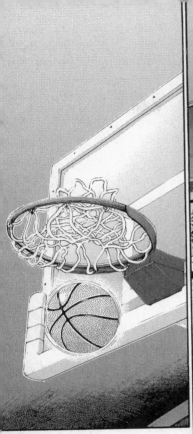

IT'S
LIKE...

353

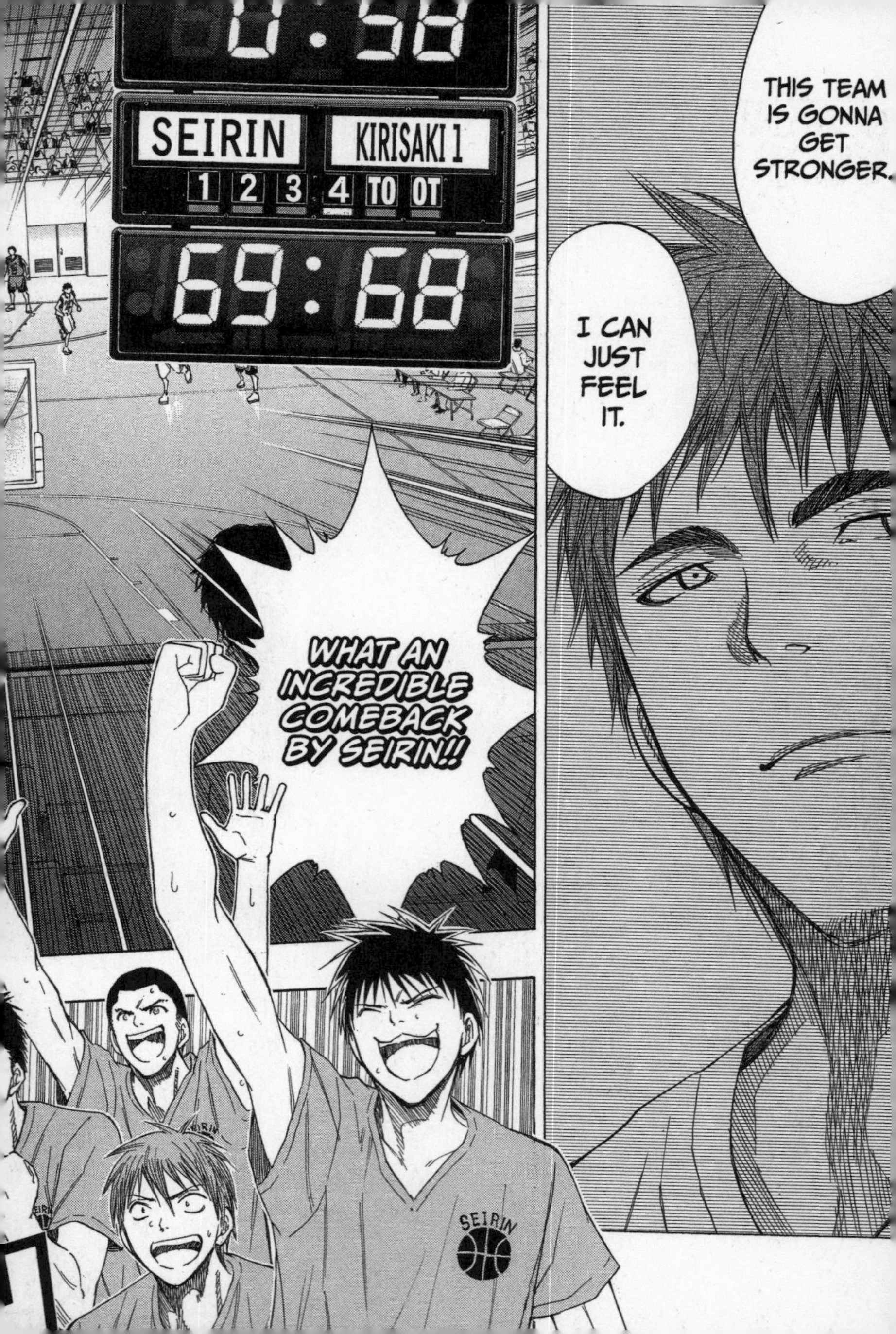
THIS TEAM IS GONNA GET STRONGER.
I CAN JUST FEEL IT.
SEIRIN
KIRISAKI 1
1 2 3 4 TO OT
69 : 68
WHAT AN INCREDIBLE COMEBACK BY SEIRIN!!
SEIRIN

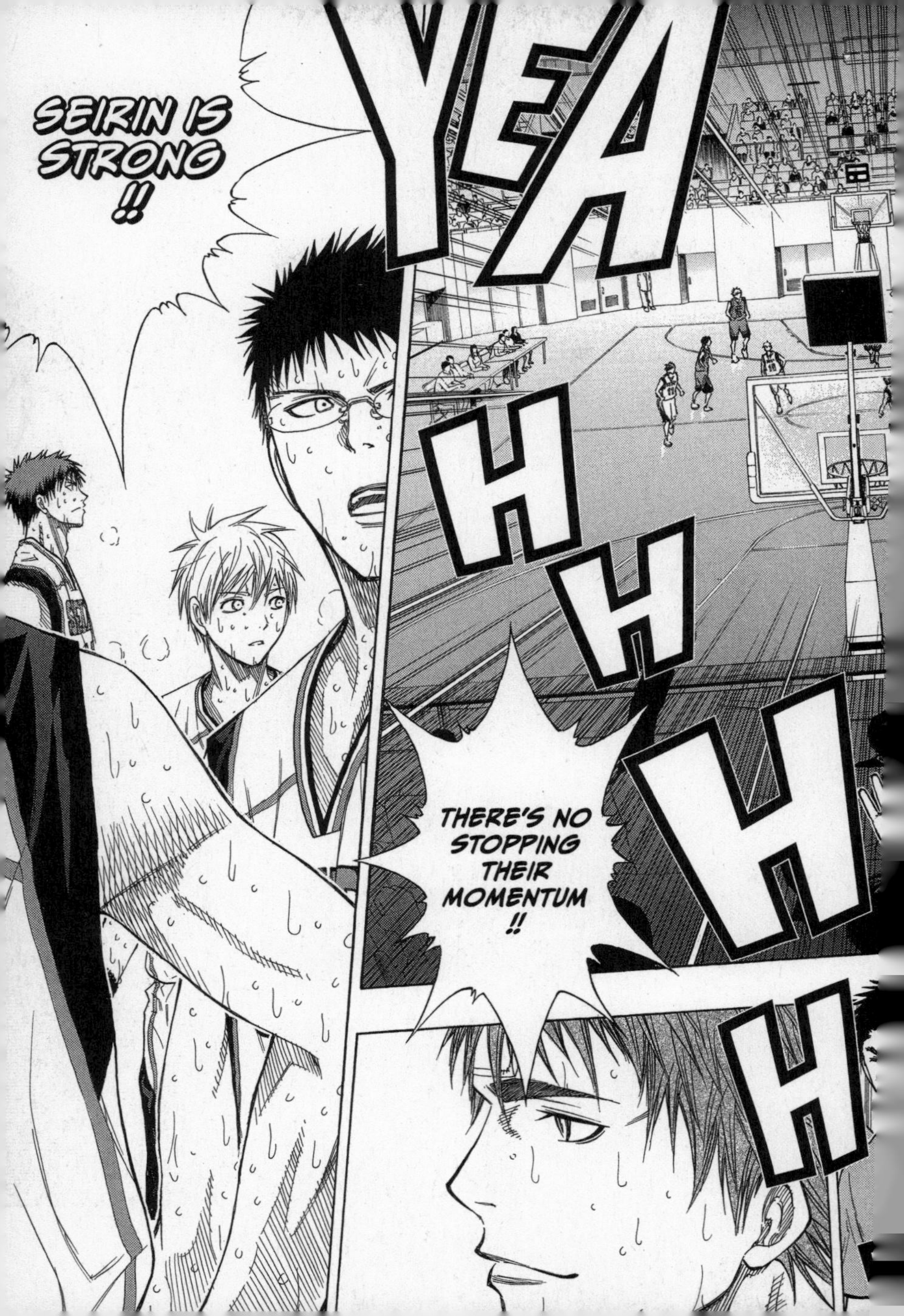
YEAHHHHH
THERE'S NO STOPPING THEIR MOMENTUM!!
SEIRIN IS STRONG!!

KUROKO'S BASKETBALL BLOOPERS

TAKE 8

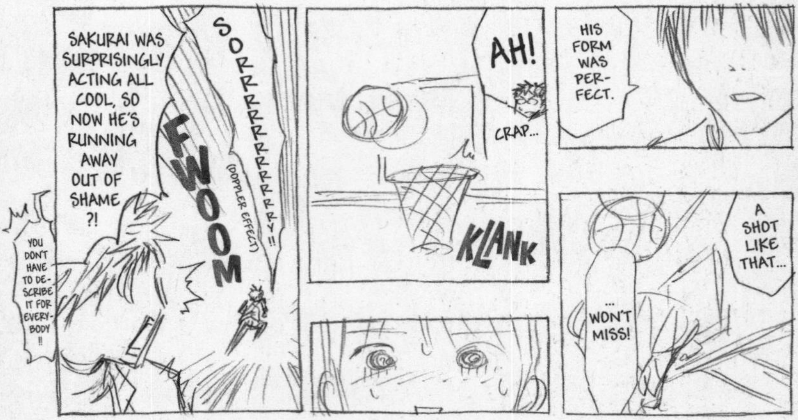
HIS FORM WAS PERFECT.
A SHOT LIKE THAT...
... WON'T MISS!
AH!
CRAP...
KLANK
SAKURAI WAS SURPRISINGLY ACTING ALL COOL, SO NOW HE'S RUNNING AWAY OUT OF SHAME?!
YOU DON'T HAVE TO DESCRIBE IT FOR EVERYBODY!!
SORRRRRRRRRRRY!!
(DOPPLER EFFECT)
FWOOM

107TH QUARTER: NOT A CHANCE

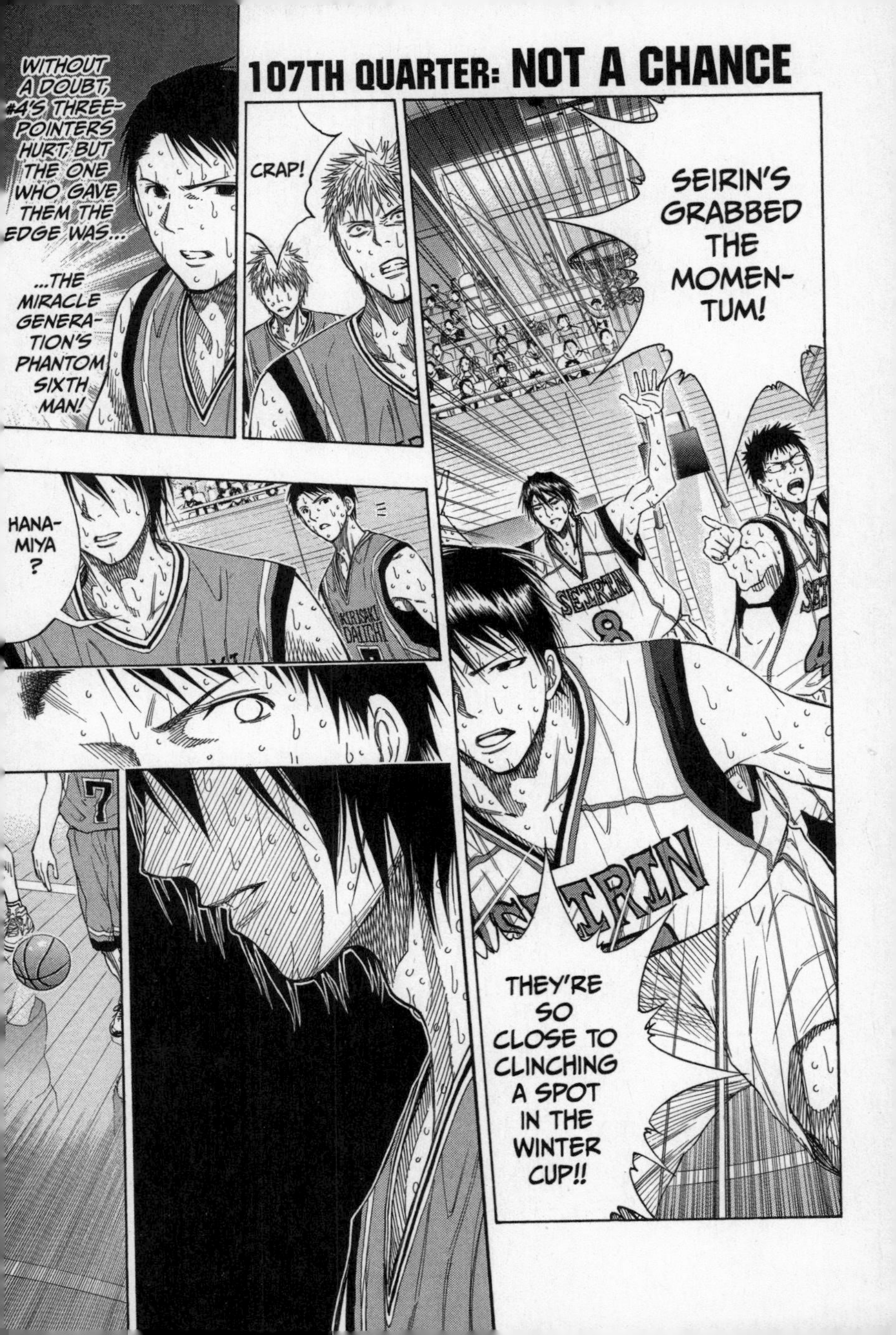
SEIRIN'S GRABBED THE MOMEN-TUM!
THEY'RE SO CLOSE TO CLINCHING A SPOT IN THE WINTER CUP!!
CRAP!
WITHOUT A DOUBT, #4'S THREE-POINTERS HURT, BUT THE ONE WHO GAVE THEM THE EDGE WAS...
...THE MIRACLE GENERA-TION'S PHANTOM SIXTH MAN!
HANA-MIYA?
SEIRIN
KIRISAKI DAIICHI

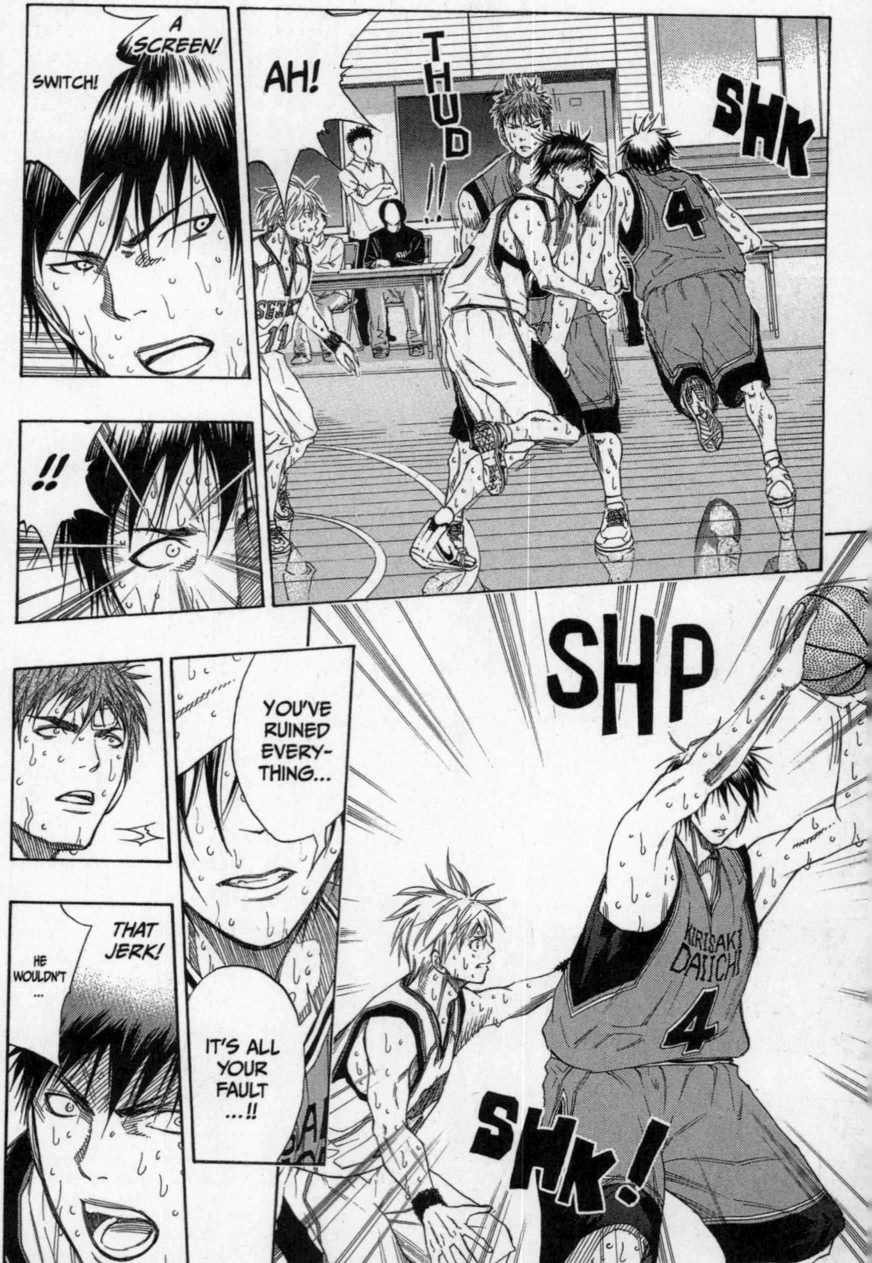

AH!
THUD!!
SHK
A SCREEN!
SWITCH!
!!
SHP
SHK!
YOU'VE RUINED EVERYTHING...
IT'S ALL YOUR FAULT...!!
THAT JERK!
HE WOULDN'T ...

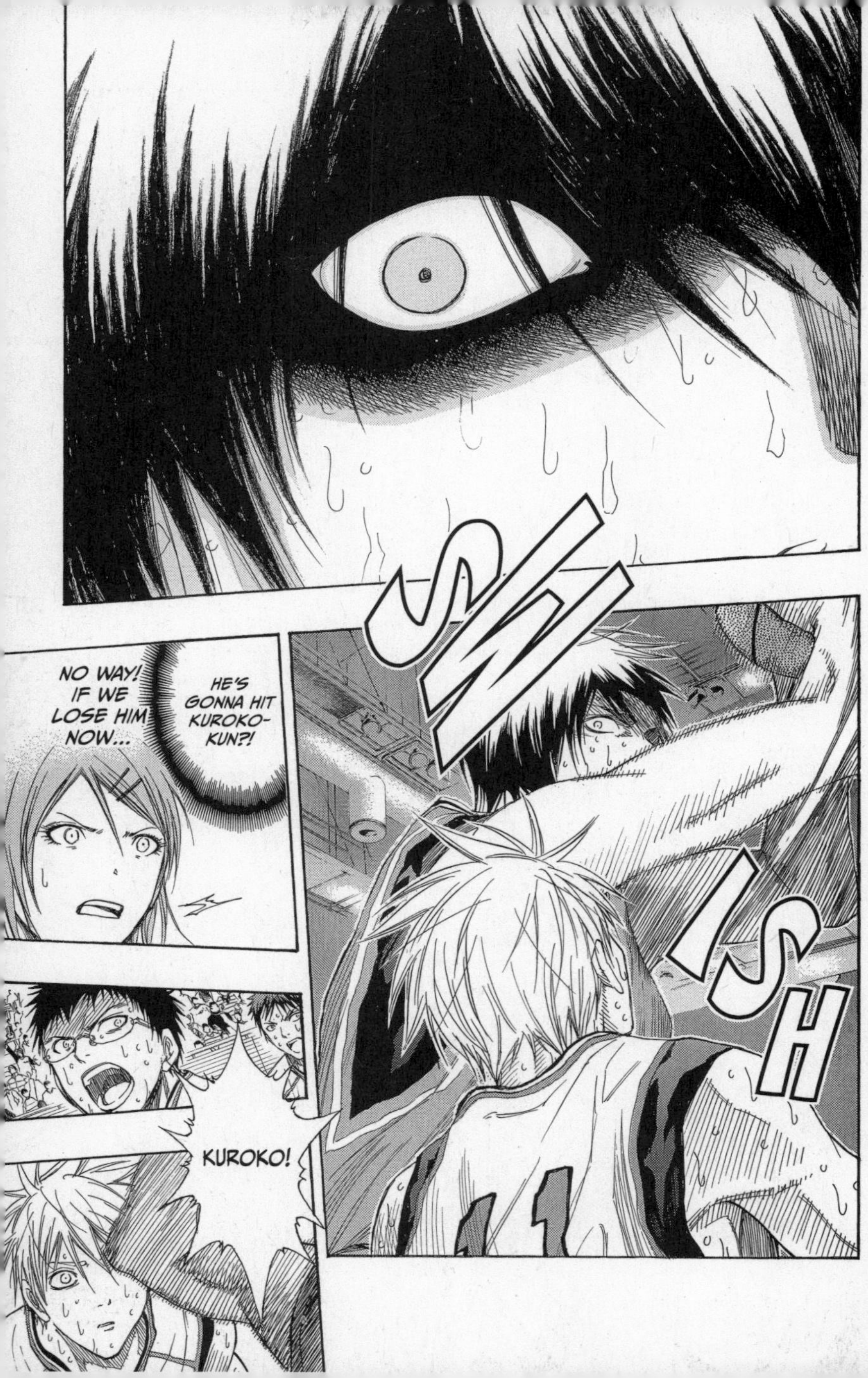
SWISH
HE'S GONNA HIT KUROKO-KUN?!
NO WAY! IF WE LOSE HIM NOW...
KUROKO!

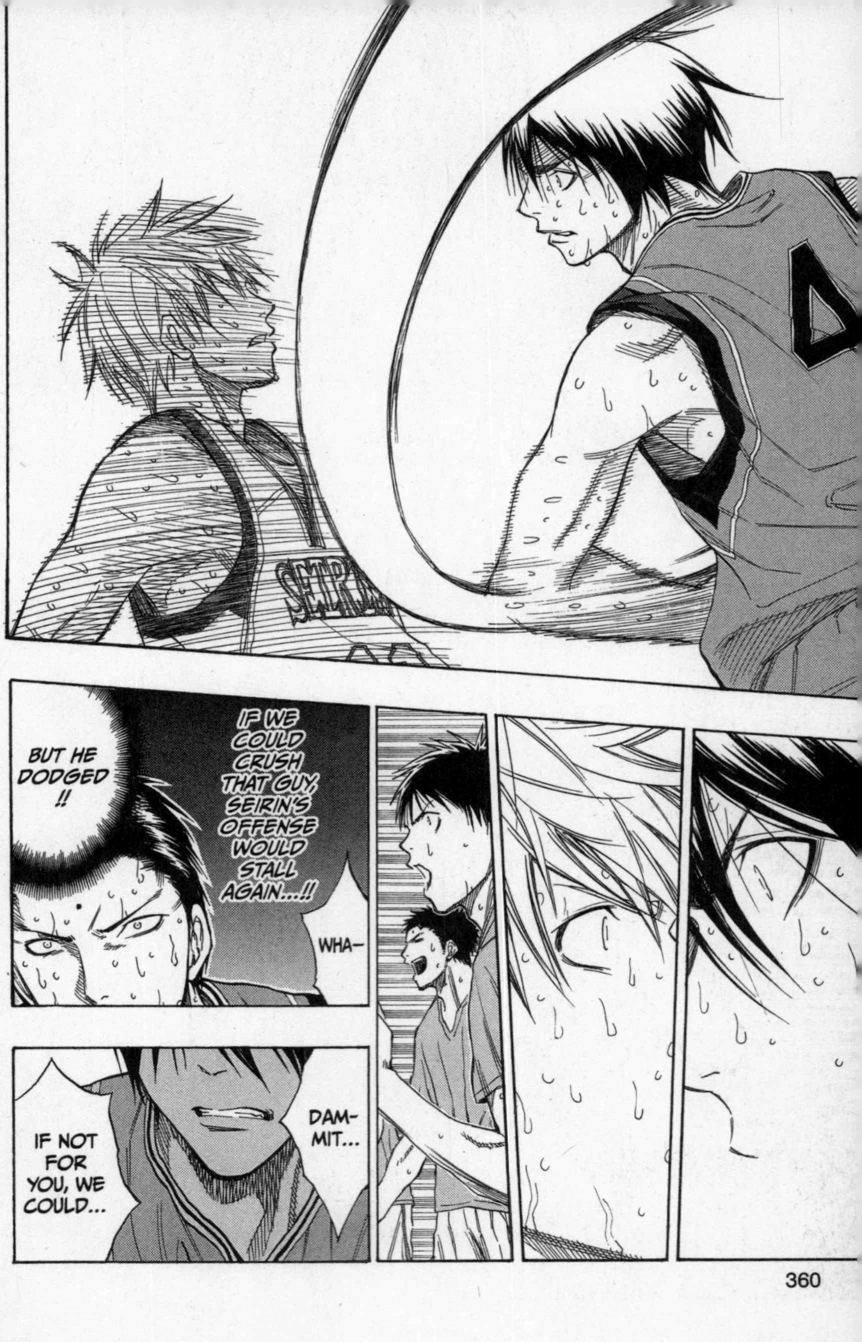
IF WE COULD CRUSH THAT GUY, SEIRIN'S OFFENSE WOULD STALL AGAIN...!!
BUT HE DODGED!!
WHA-
DAM-MIT...
IF NOT FOR YOU, WE COULD...

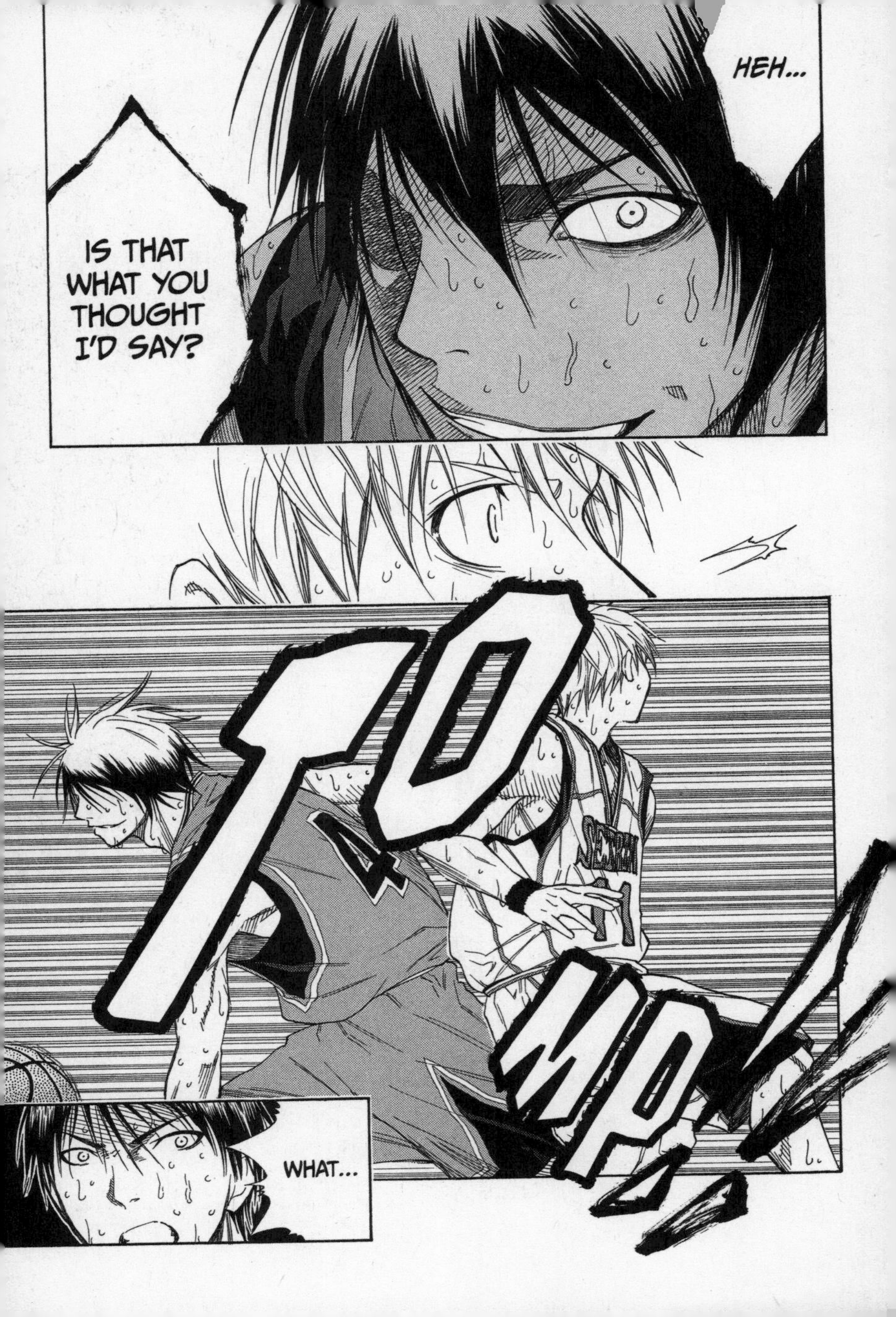
HEH...
IS THAT WHAT YOU THOUGHT I'D SAY?
TOMP!!
WHAT...

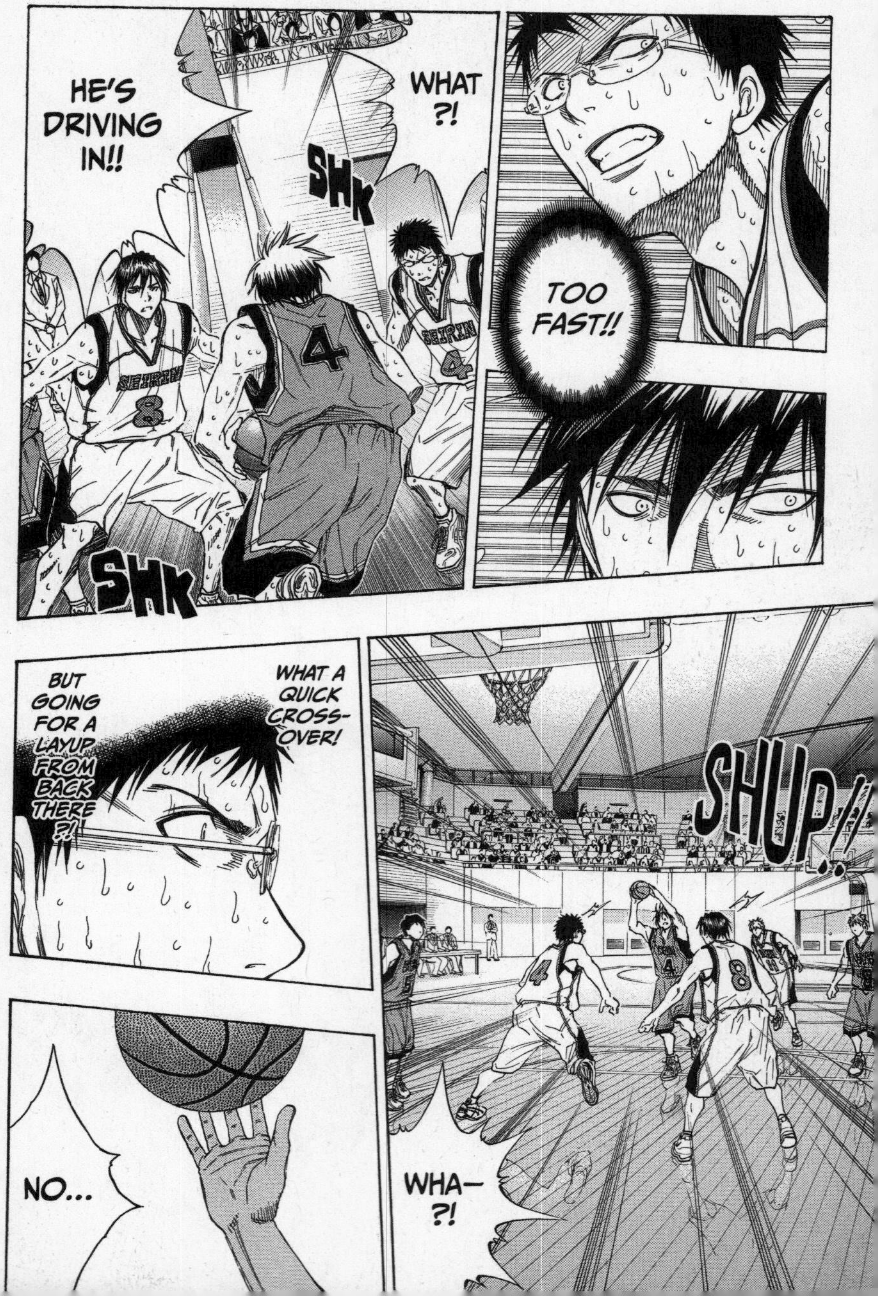
TOO FAST!!
WHAT ?!
HE'S DRIVING IN!!
SHK
SHK
SHUP!!
WHA— ?!
WHAT A QUICK CROSS-OVER!
BUT GOING FOR A LAYUP FROM BACK THERE ?!
NO...

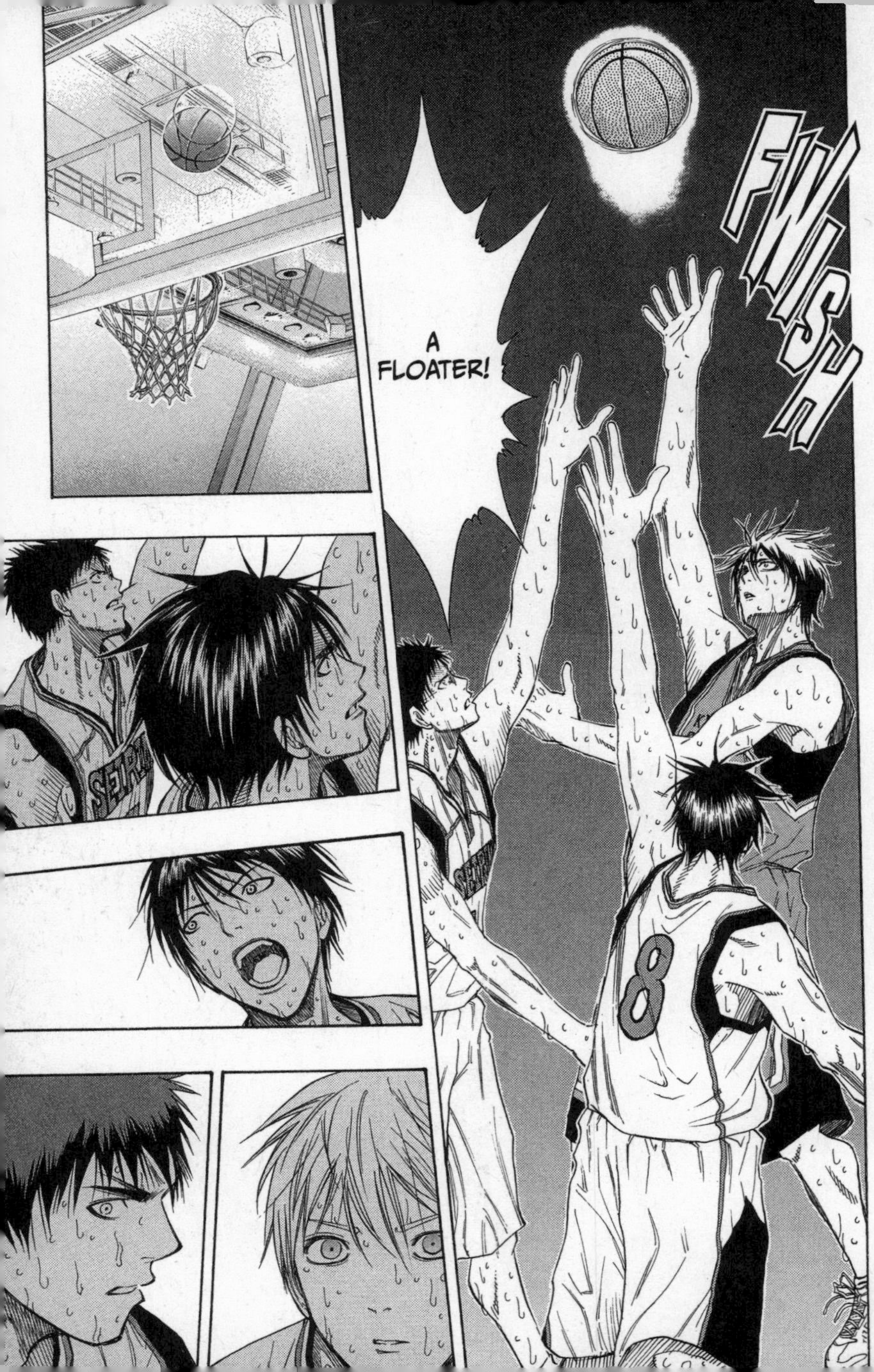
FWISH
A FLOATER!

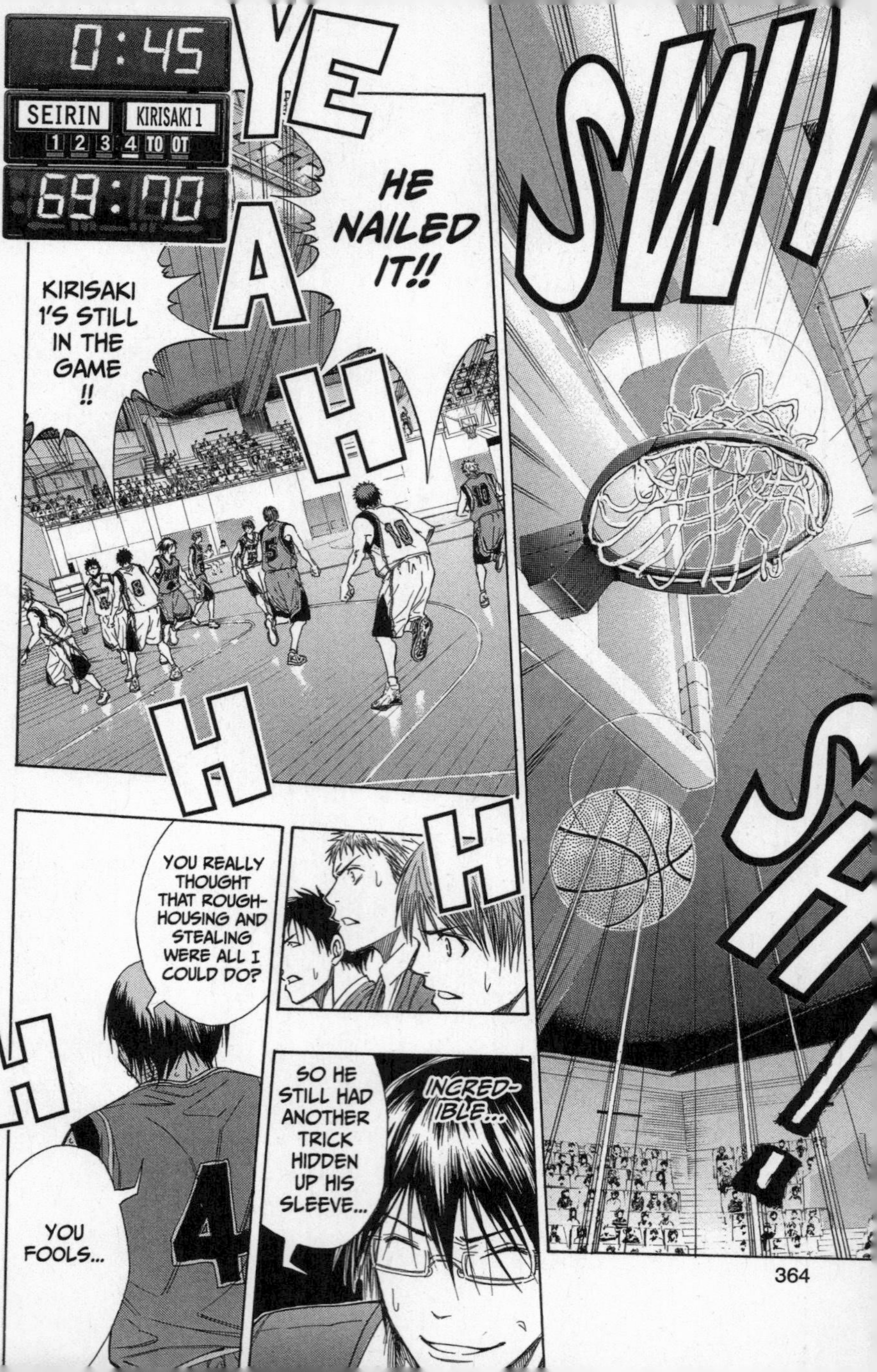
SWISH
0:45
SEIRIN
KIRISAKI 1
1 2 3 4 TO OT
69:70
YEAHHHH
HE NAILED IT!!
KIRISAKI 1'S STILL IN THE GAME!!
H
SO HE STILL HAD ANOTHER TRICK HIDDEN UP HIS SLEEVE...
INCREDIBLE...
YOU REALLY THOUGHT THAT ROUGH-HOUSING AND STEALING WERE ALL I COULD DO?
H
YOU FOOLS...

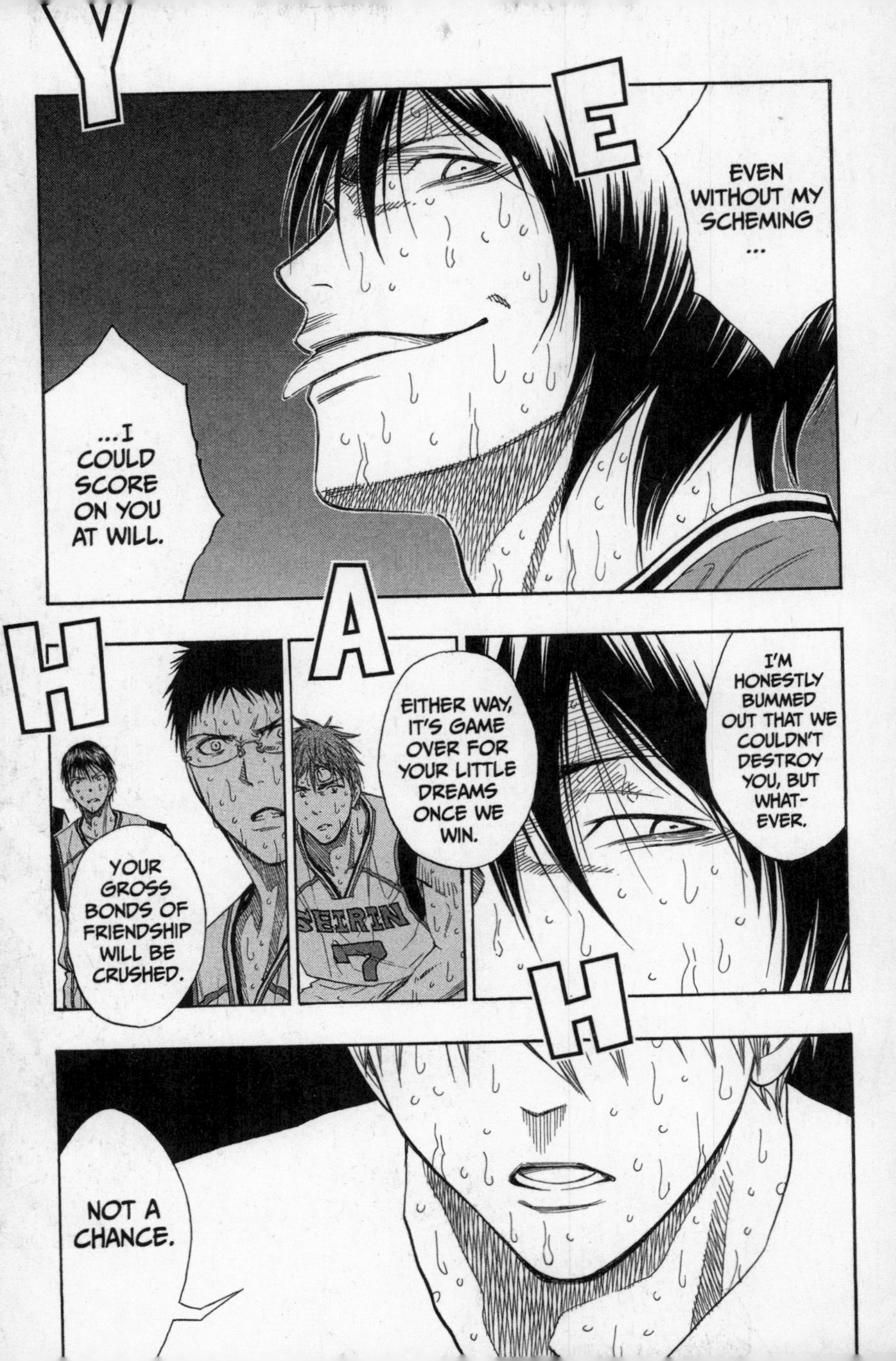
Y
E
EVEN WITHOUT MY SCHEMING ...
...I COULD SCORE ON YOU AT WILL.
H
A
I'M HONESTLY BUMMED OUT THAT WE COULDN'T DESTROY YOU, BUT WHAT-EVER.
EITHER WAY, IT'S GAME OVER FOR YOUR LITTLE DREAMS ONCE WE WIN.
YOUR GROSS BONDS OF FRIENDSHIP WILL BE CRUSHED.
SEIRIN 7
H
NOT A CHANCE.

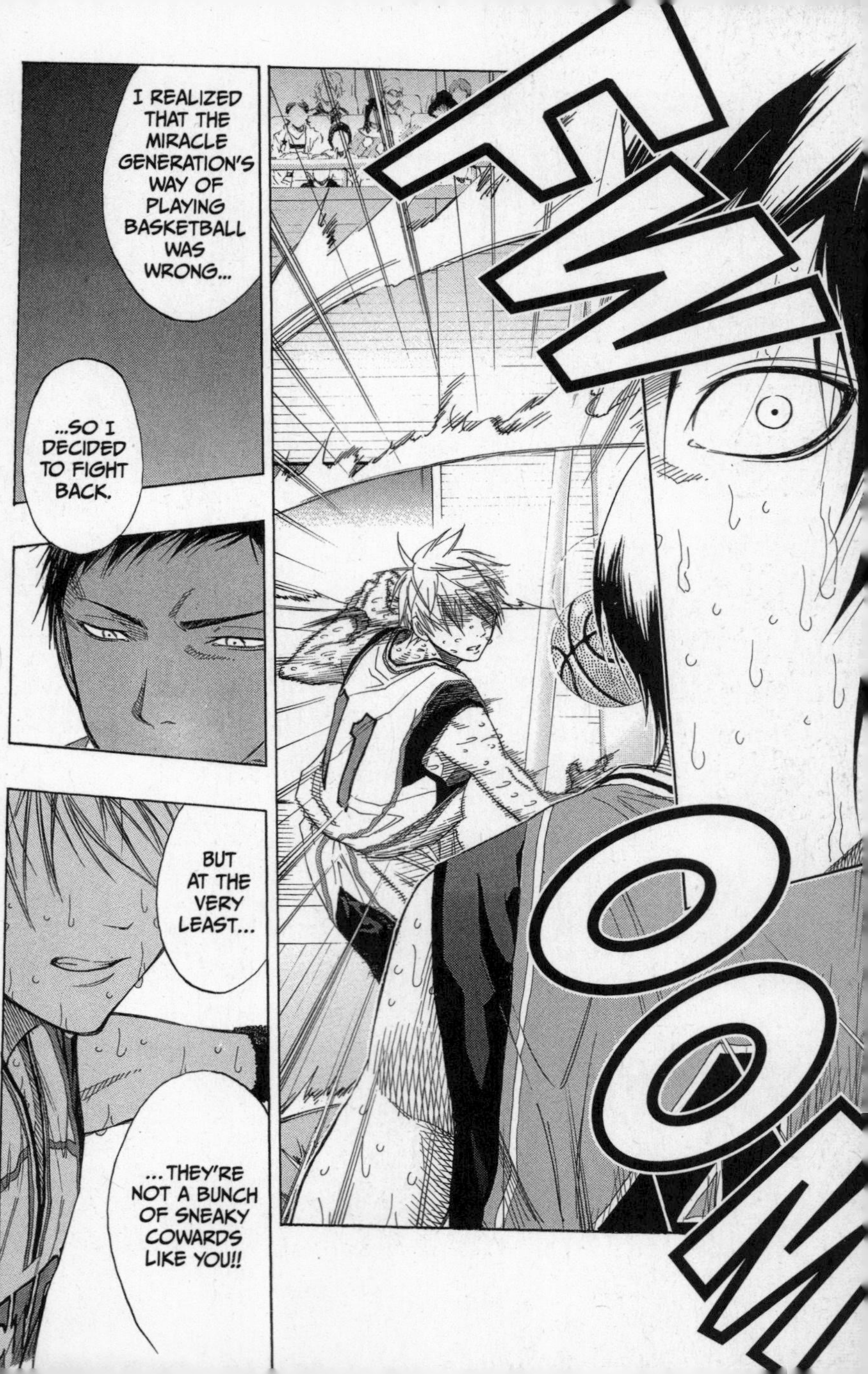
FWOOM
I REALIZED THAT THE MIRACLE GENERATION'S WAY OF PLAYING BASKETBALL WAS WRONG...
...SO I DECIDED TO FIGHT BACK.
BUT AT THE VERY LEAST...
...THEY'RE NOT A BUNCH OF SNEAKY COWARDS LIKE YOU!!

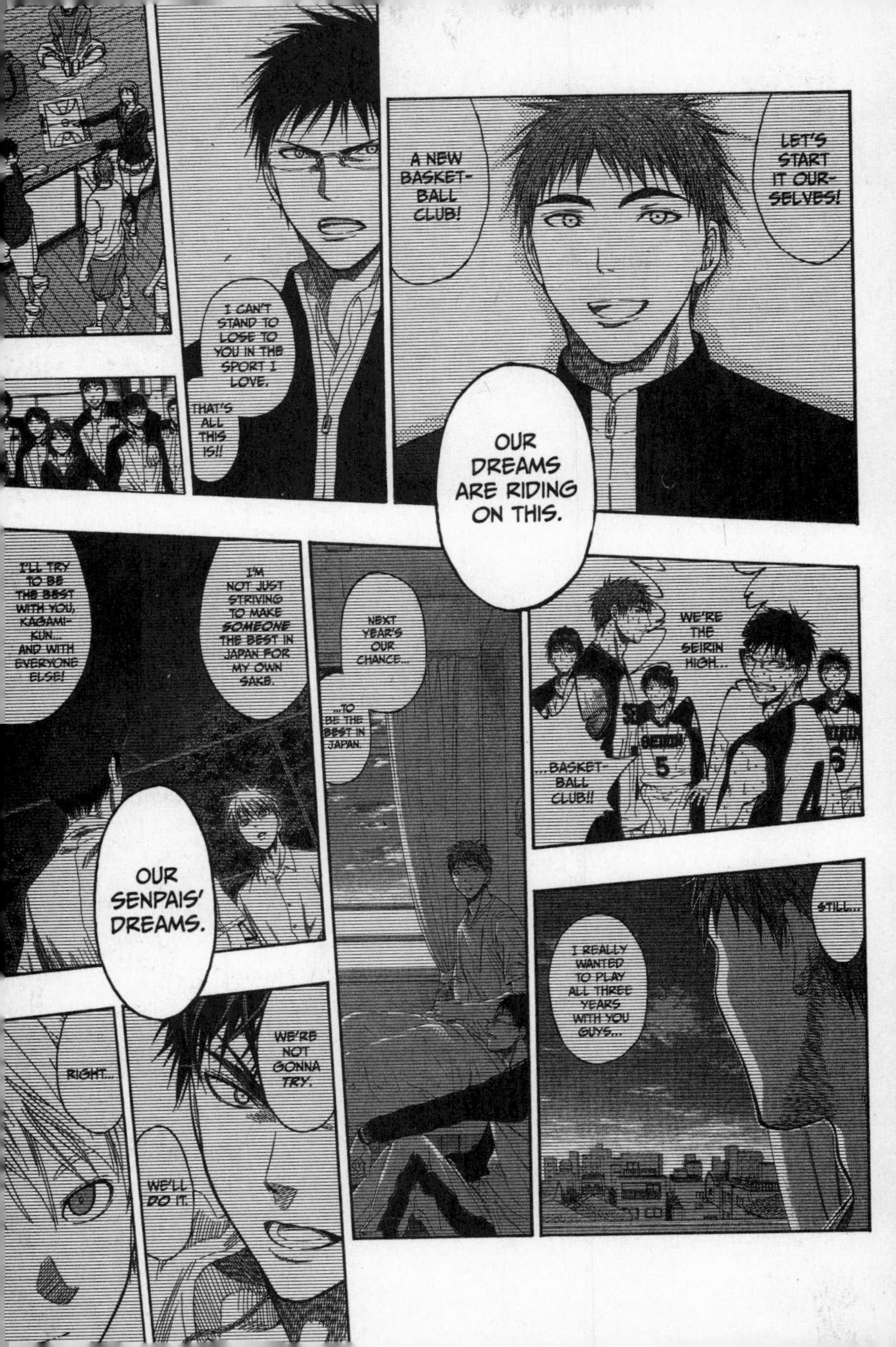
LET'S START IT OURSELVES!
A NEW BASKETBALL CLUB!
OUR DREAMS ARE RIDING ON THIS.
I CAN'T STAND TO LOSE TO YOU IN THE SPORT I LOVE.
THAT'S ALL THIS IS!!
WE'RE THE SEIRIN HIGH...
...BASKETBALL CLUB!!
NEXT YEAR'S OUR CHANCE...
...TO BE THE BEST IN JAPAN.
I'M NOT JUST STRIVING TO MAKE *SOMEONE* THE BEST IN JAPAN FOR MY OWN SAKE.
I'LL TRY TO BE THE BEST WITH YOU, KAGAMI-KUN... AND WITH EVERYONE ELSE!
OUR SENPAIS' DREAMS.
STILL...
I REALLY WANTED TO PLAY ALL THREE YEARS WITH YOU GUYS...
WE'RE NOT GONNA *TRY*.
WE'LL *DO* IT.
RIGHT...

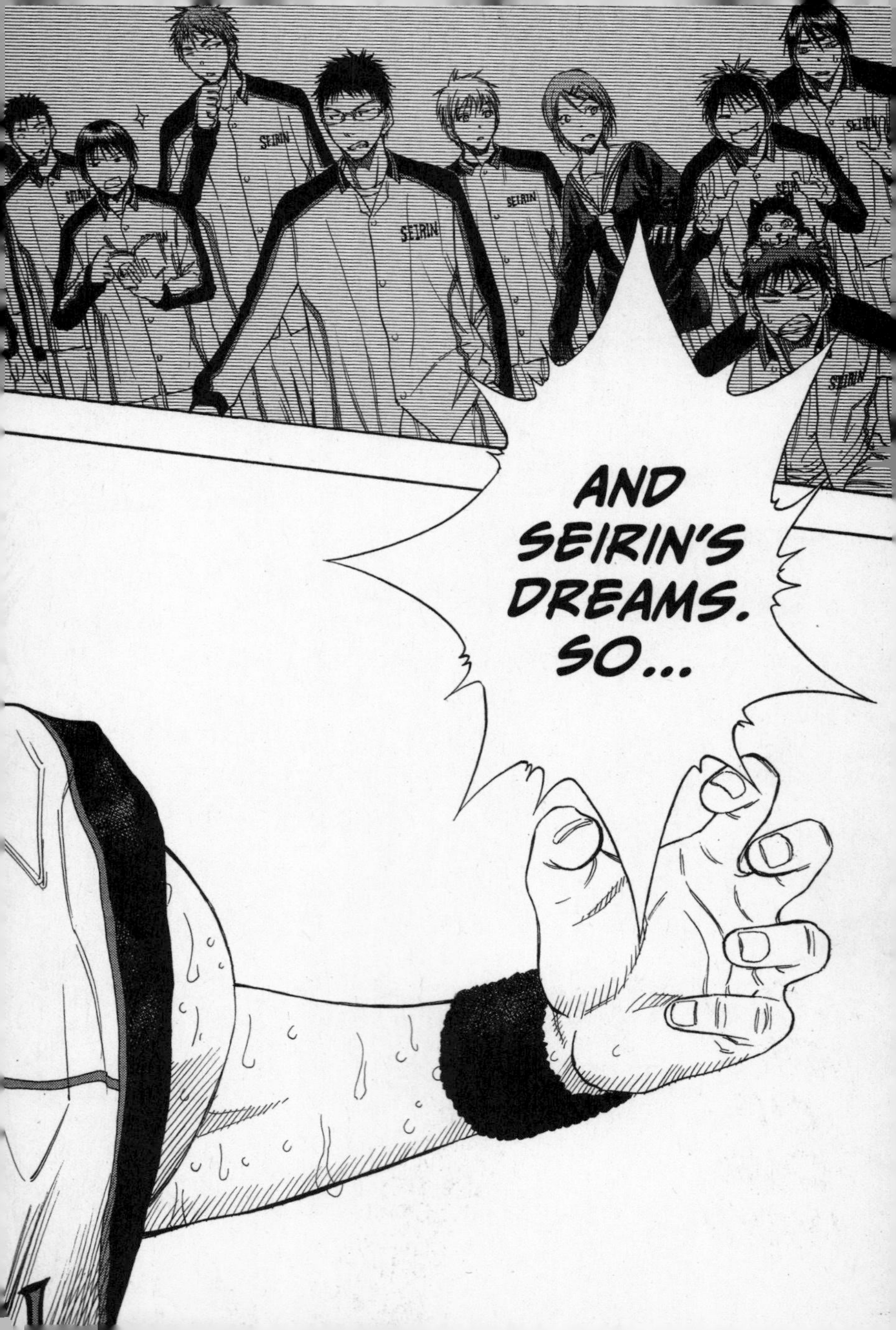
AND SEIRIN'S DREAMS. SO...

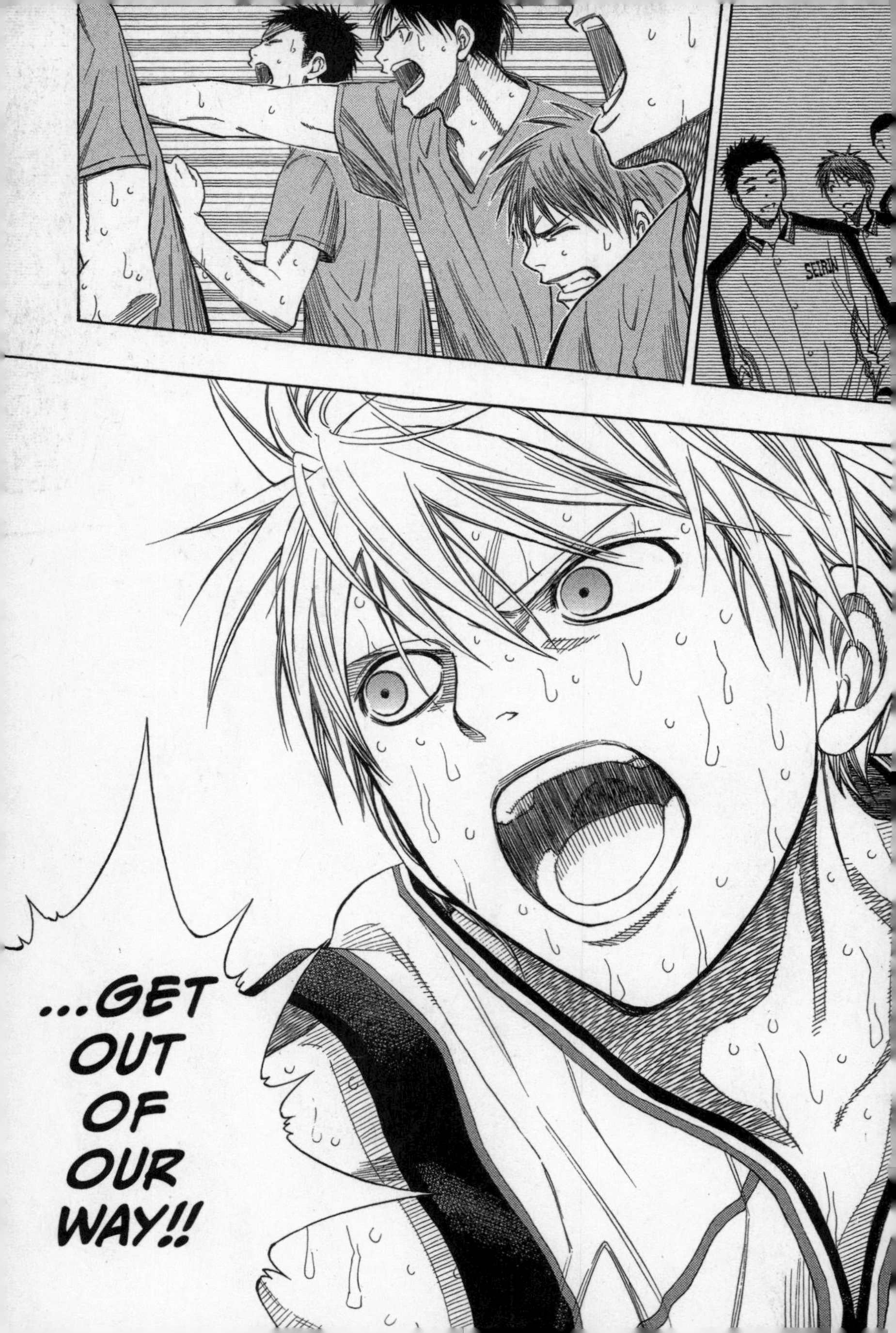
SEIRIN
...GET OUT OF OUR WAY!!

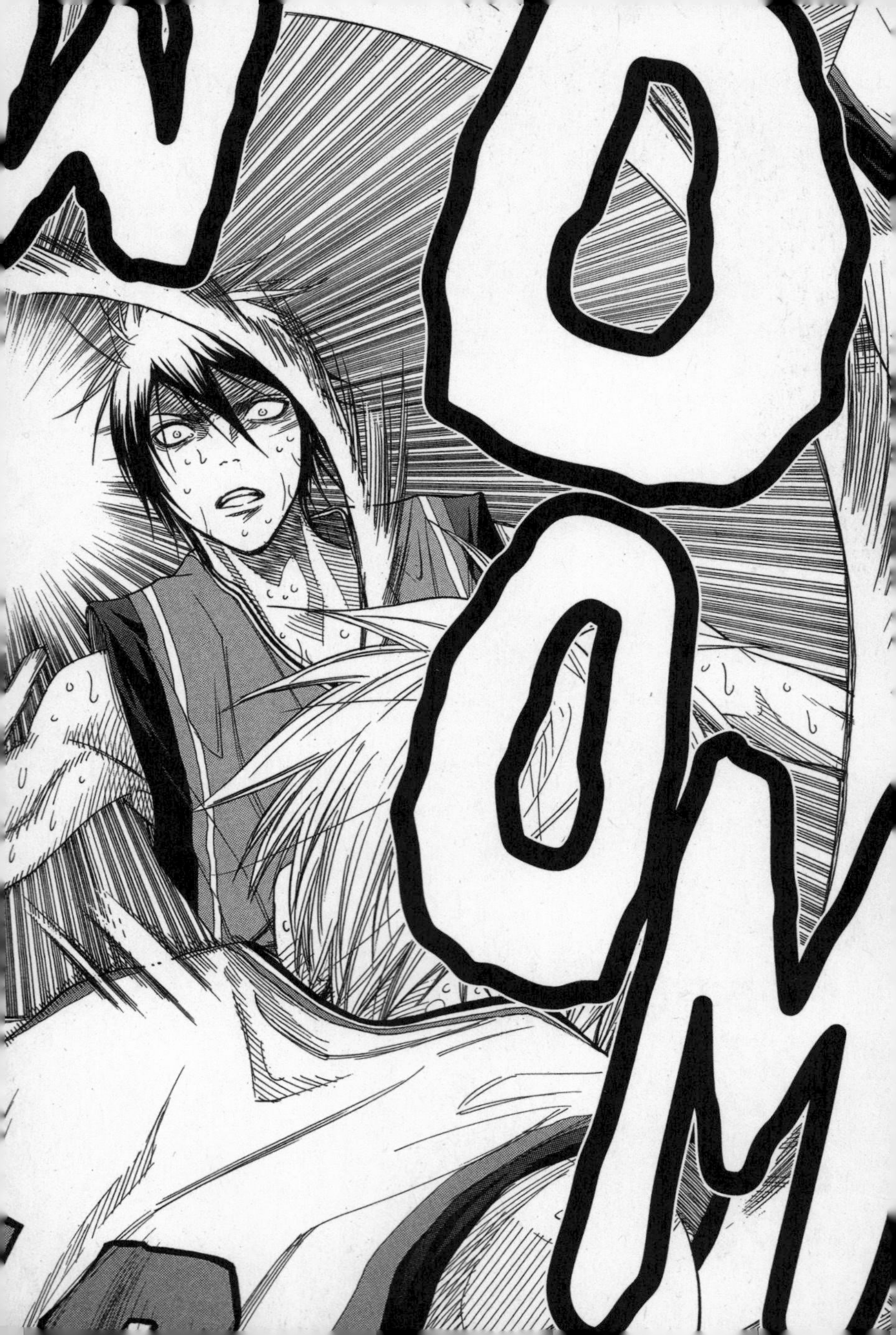

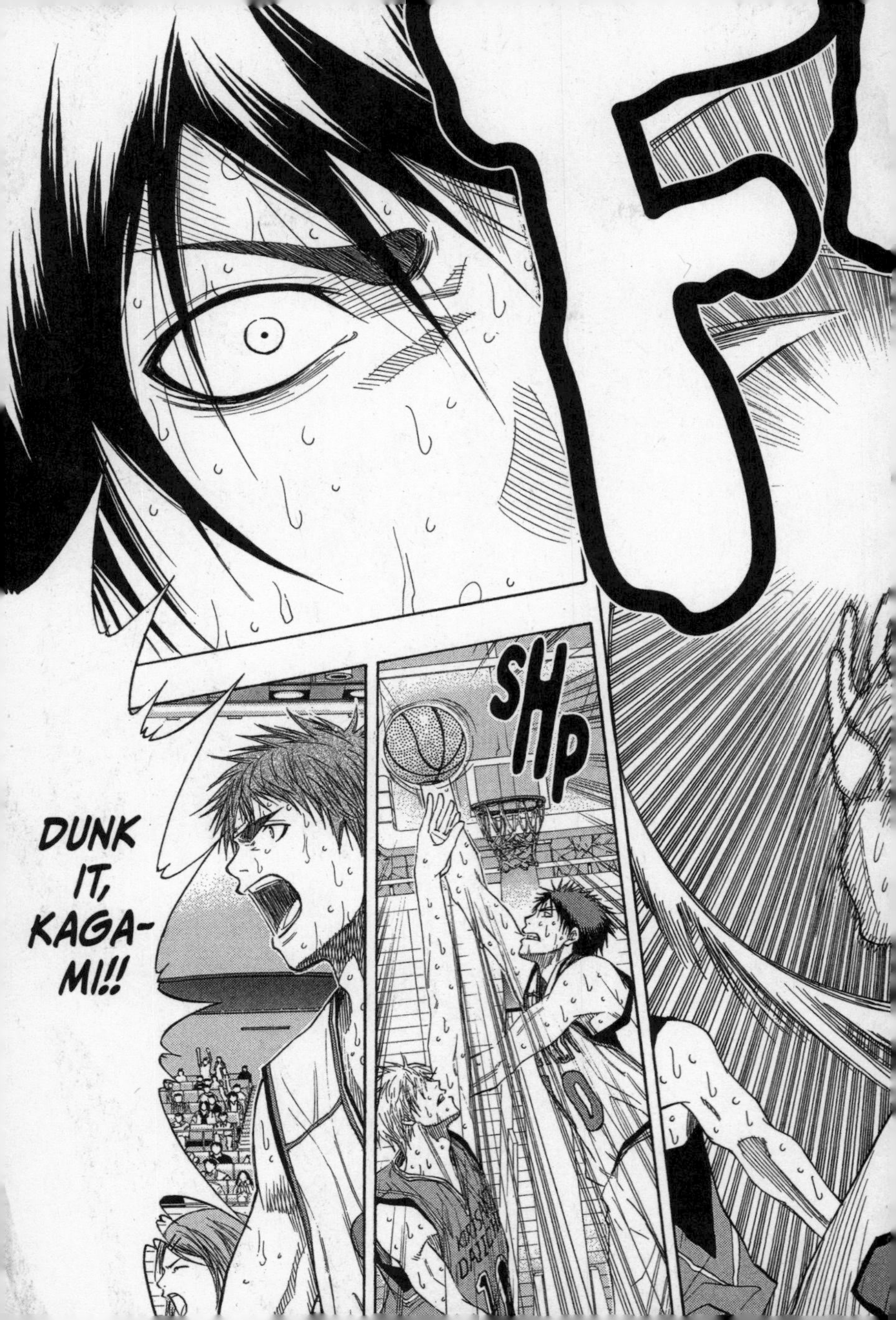
SHP
DUNK IT, KAGA-MI!!

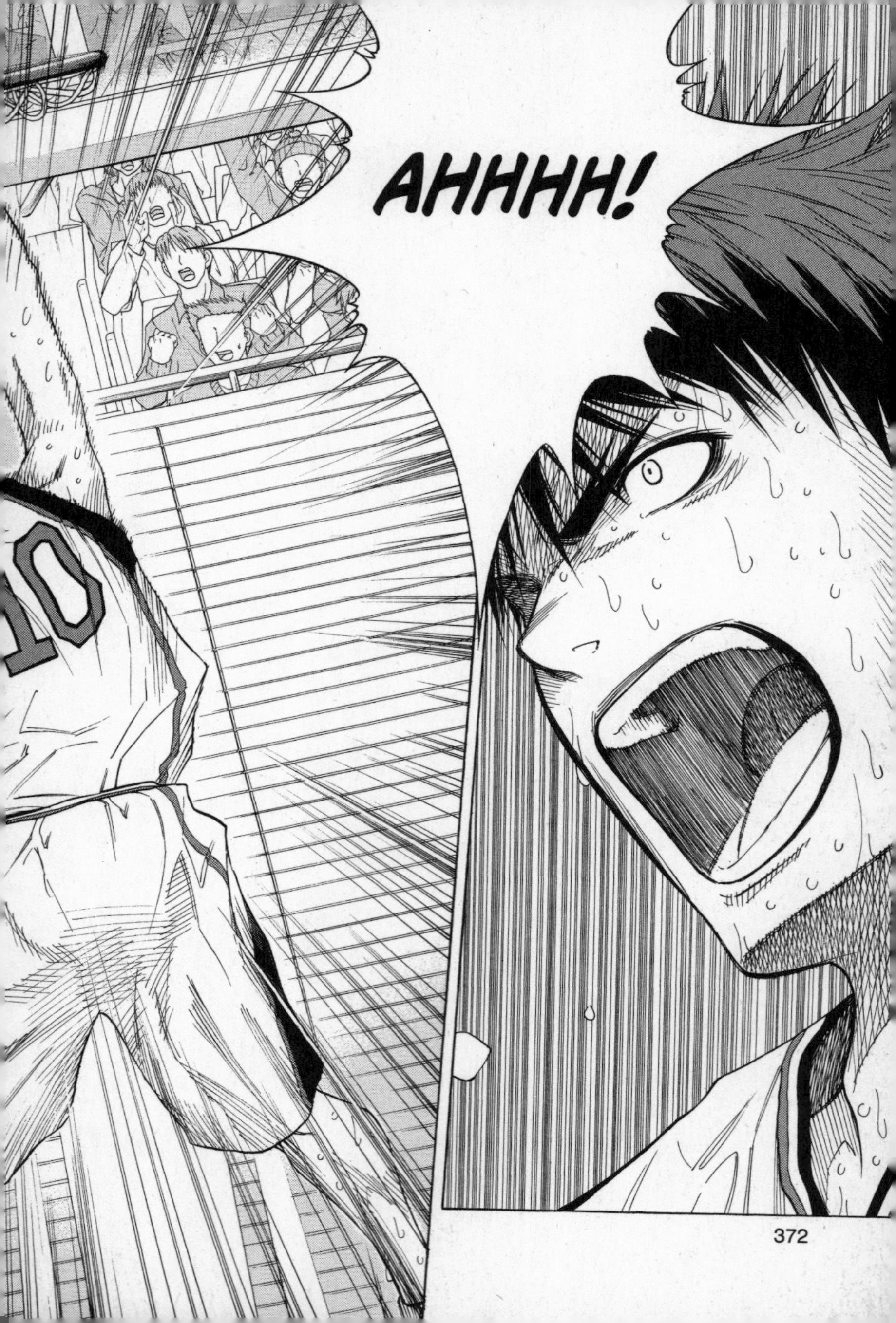
AHHHH!

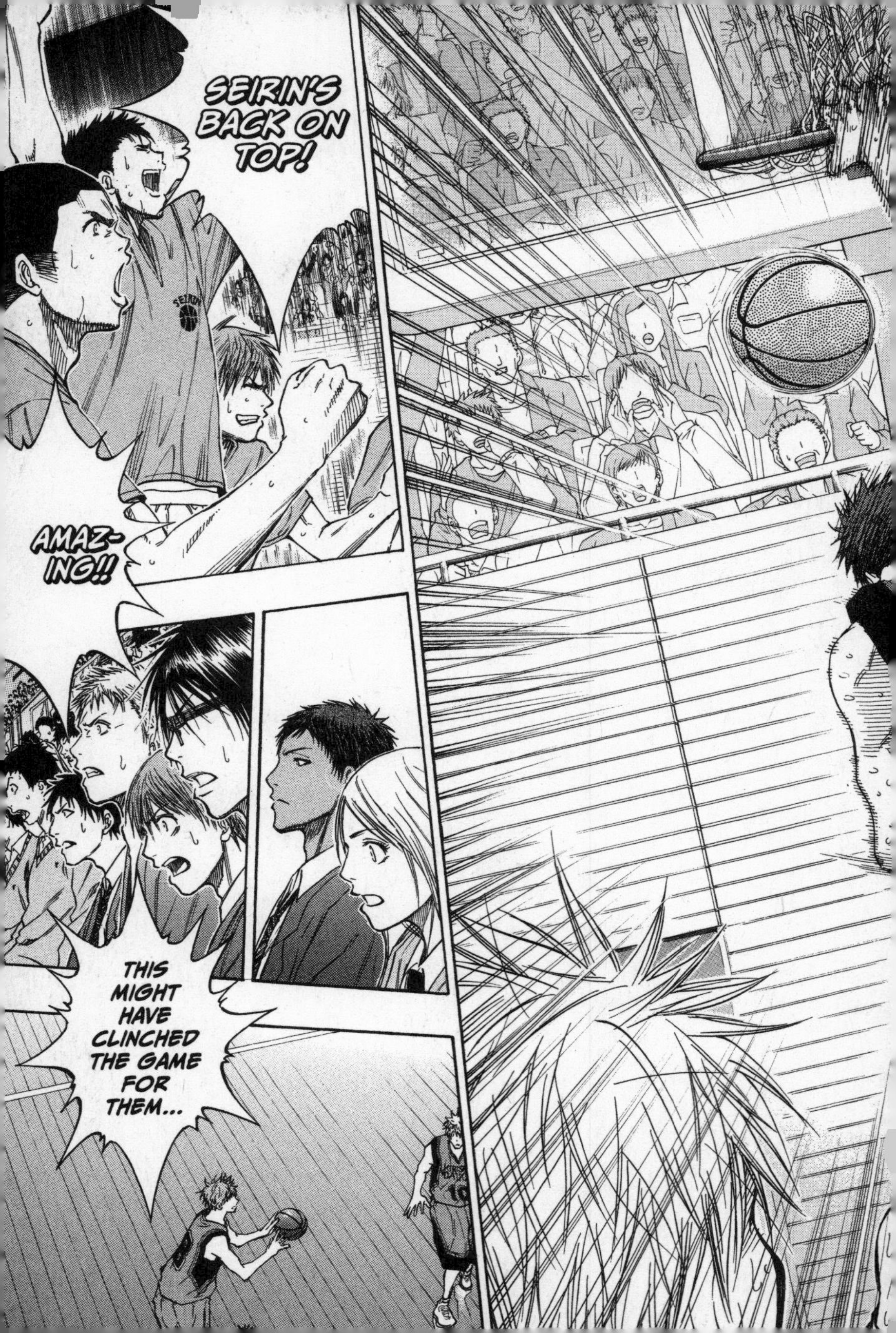
SEIRIN'S BACK ON TOP!
AMAZ-ING!!
THIS MIGHT HAVE CLINCHED THE GAME FOR THEM...

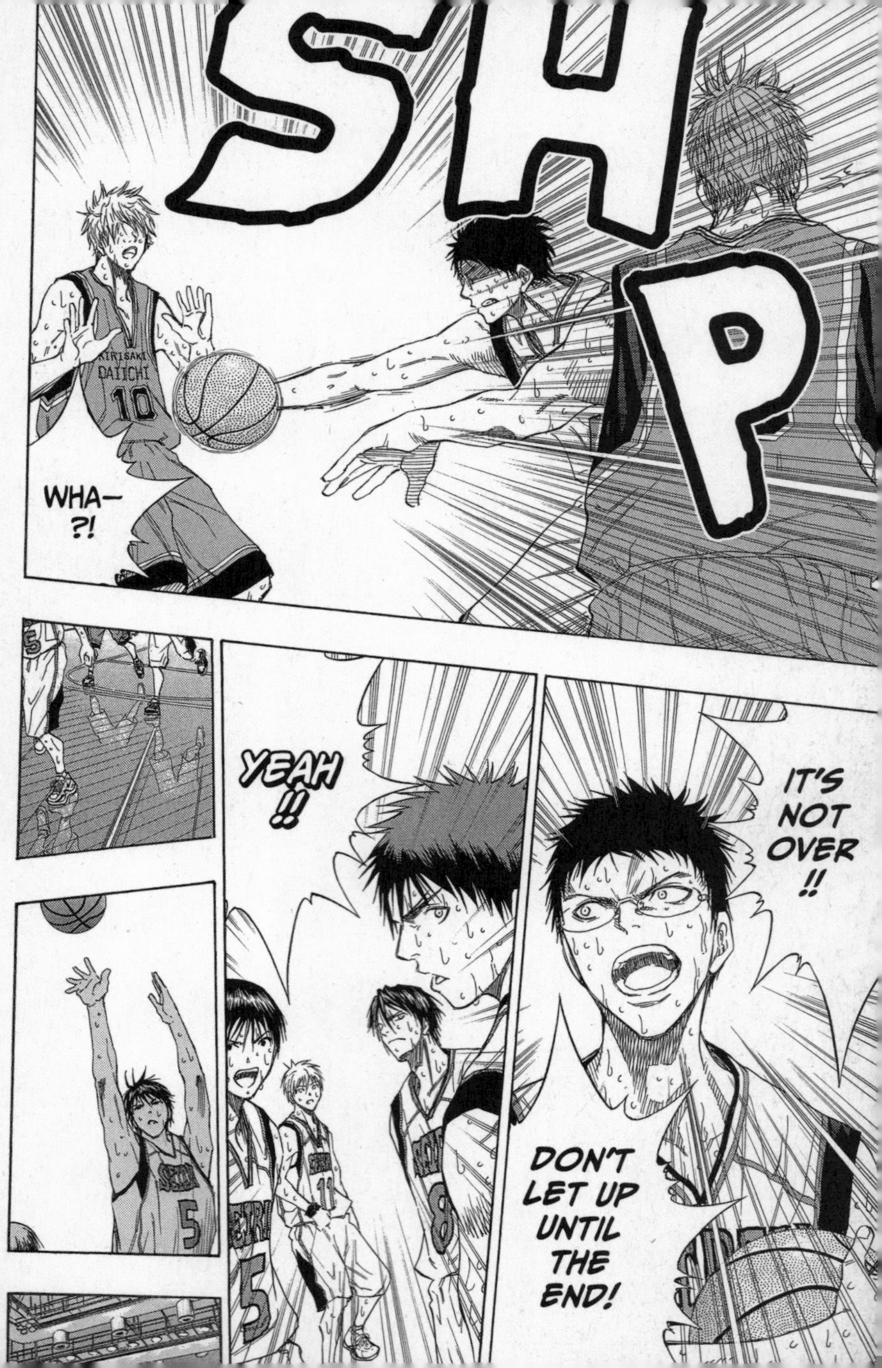
SHP
KIRISAKI DAIICHI 10
WHA—?!
IT'S NOT OVER!!
DON'T LET UP UNTIL THE END!
YEAH!!

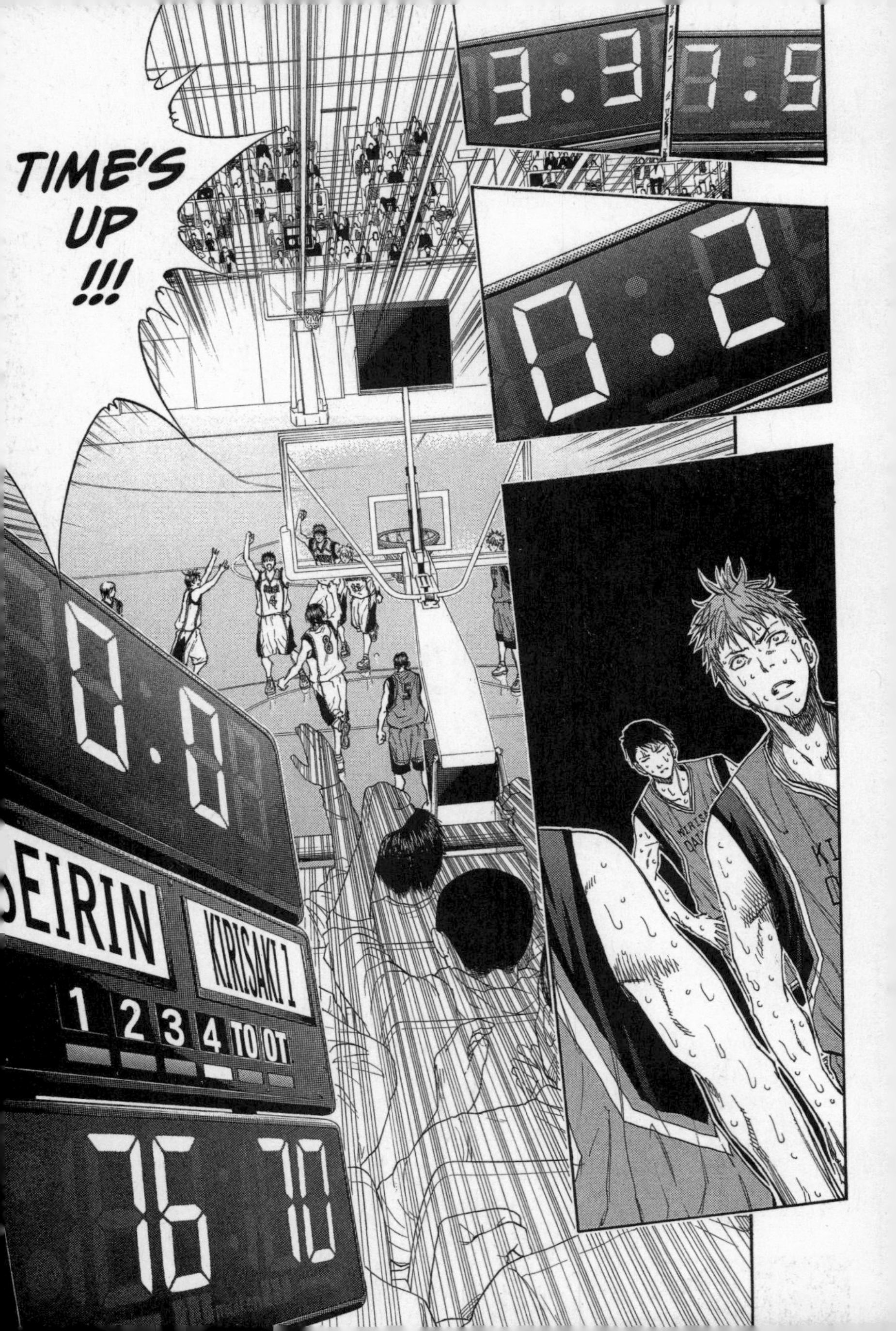
3.9
1.5
0.2
TIME'S UP !!!
0.0
SEIRIN
KIRISAKI 1
1 2 3 4 TO OT
76 70
KIRISAKI DAIICHI

KUROKO'S BASKETBALL BLOOPERS
TAKE 31

FWOOM
I REALIZED THAT THE MIRACLE GENERATION'S WAY OF PLAYING BASKETBALL WAS WRONG, SO I DECIDED TO FIGHT BACK. OUR DREAMS ARE RIDING ON THIS. AND SEIRIN'S DREAMS. SO...
WHOOSH
...GET OUT OF OUR WAY!
AH!
KAGA-MI
KUROKO, YOU FORGOT "OUR SENPAIS' DREAMS."
OH!
WHOA... HOW WAS THAT EVEN POSSI-BLE?!
WHIFF
BAP
KIYO-SHI
SAYING THAT WHOLE SPEECH BEFORE THE BALL FELL?!

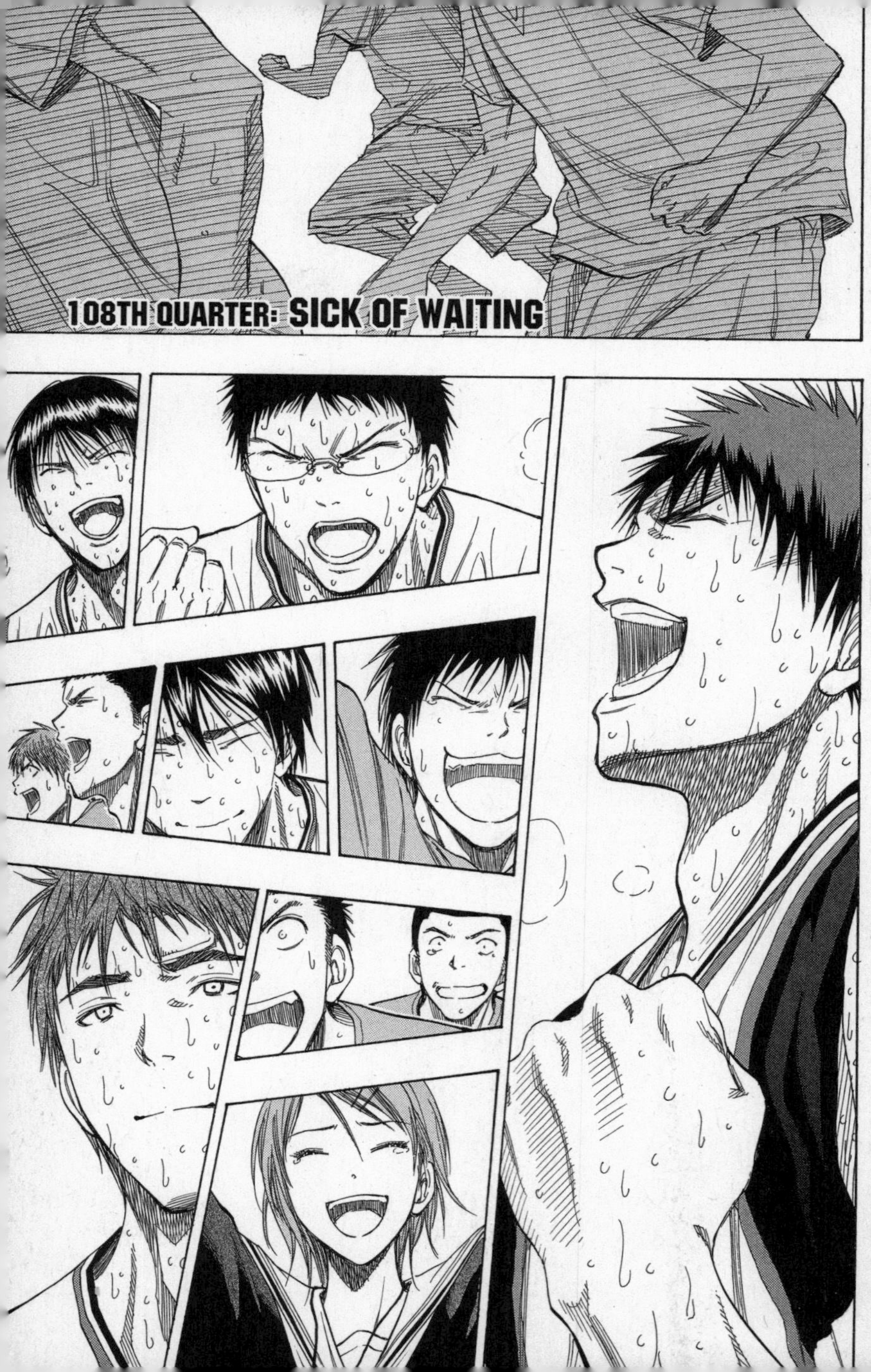
108TH QUARTER: SICK OF WAITING

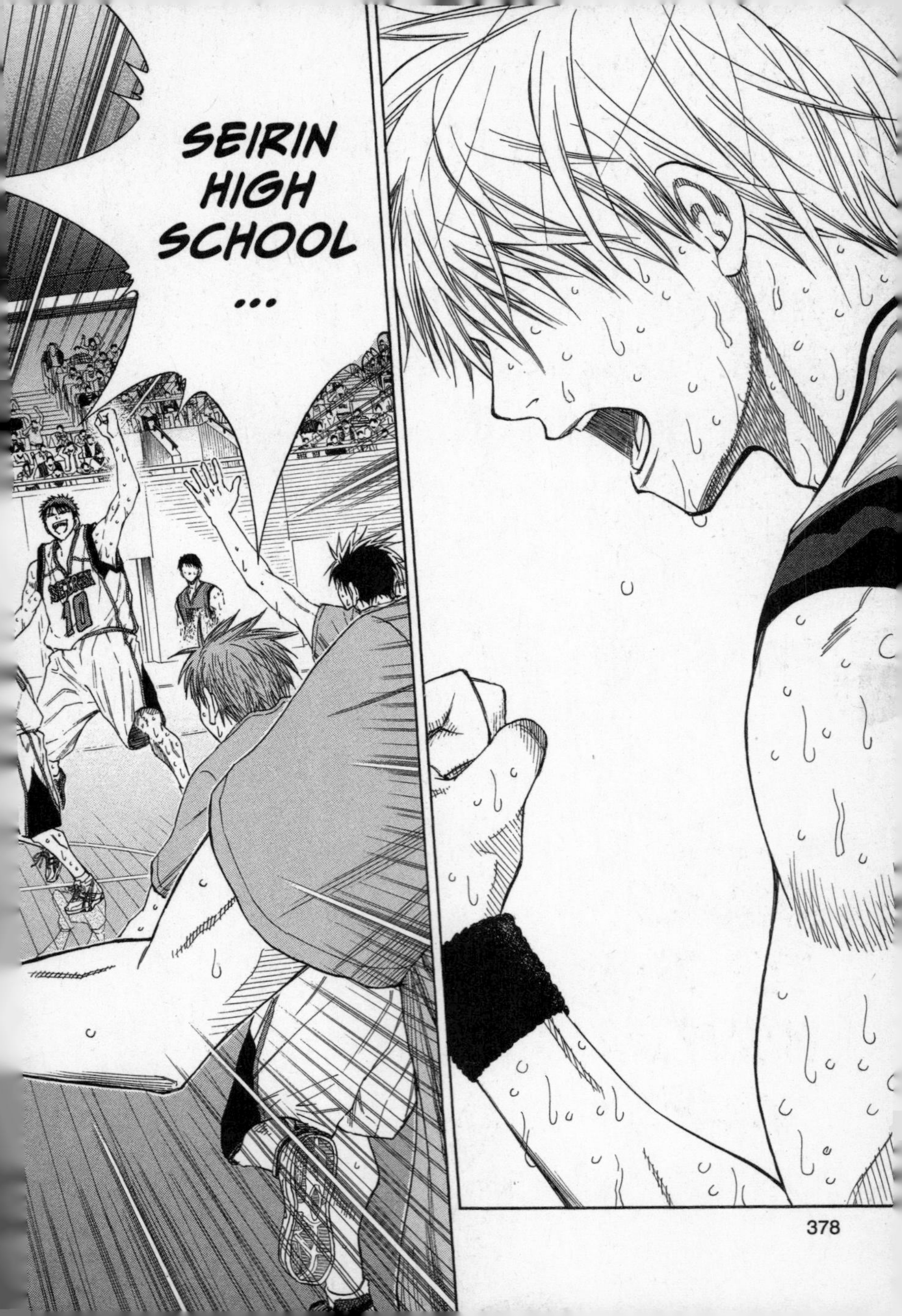
SEIRIN HIGH SCHOOL...

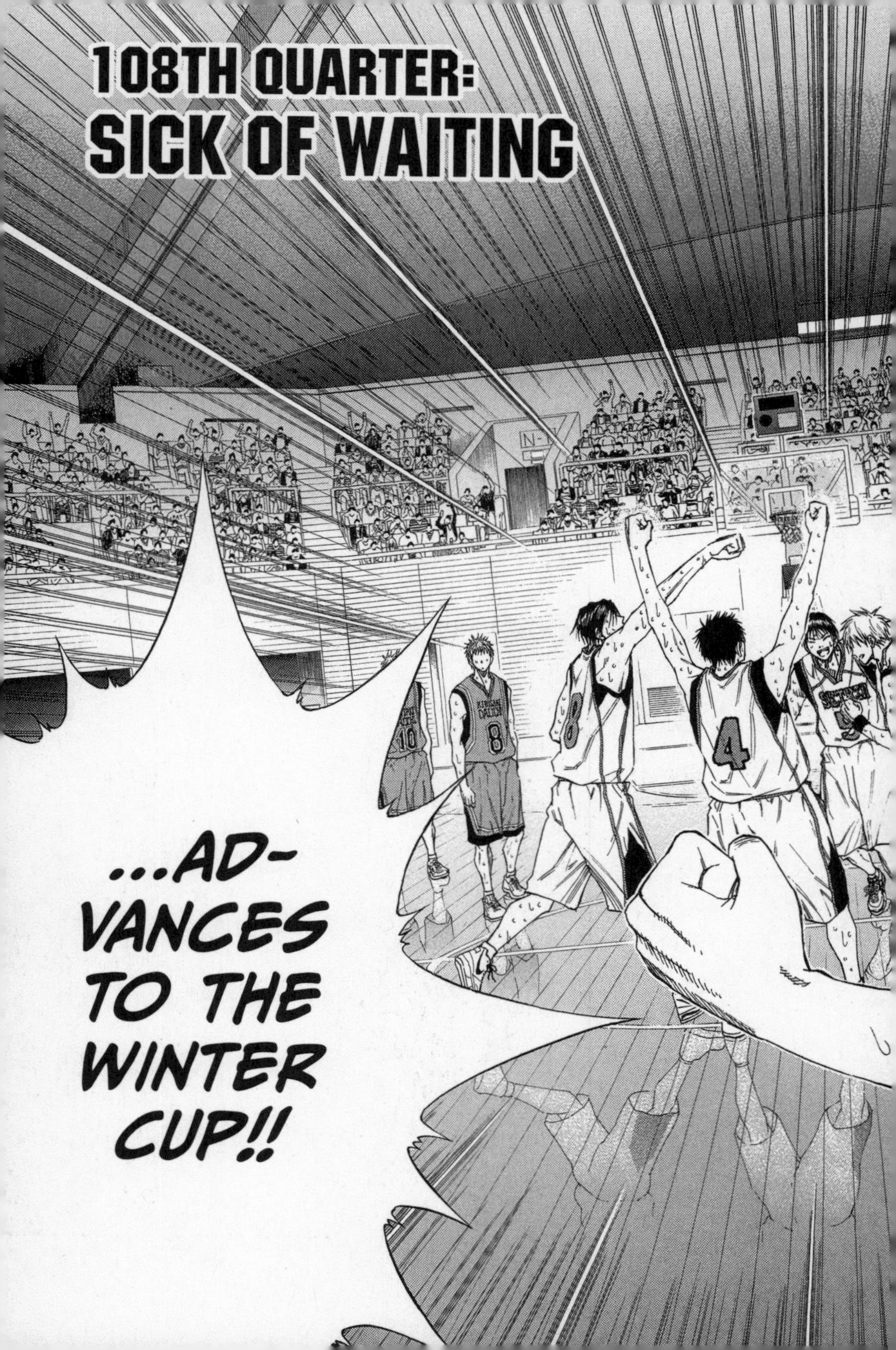
108TH QUARTER: SICK OF WAITING
...AD-VANCES TO THE WINTER CUP!!

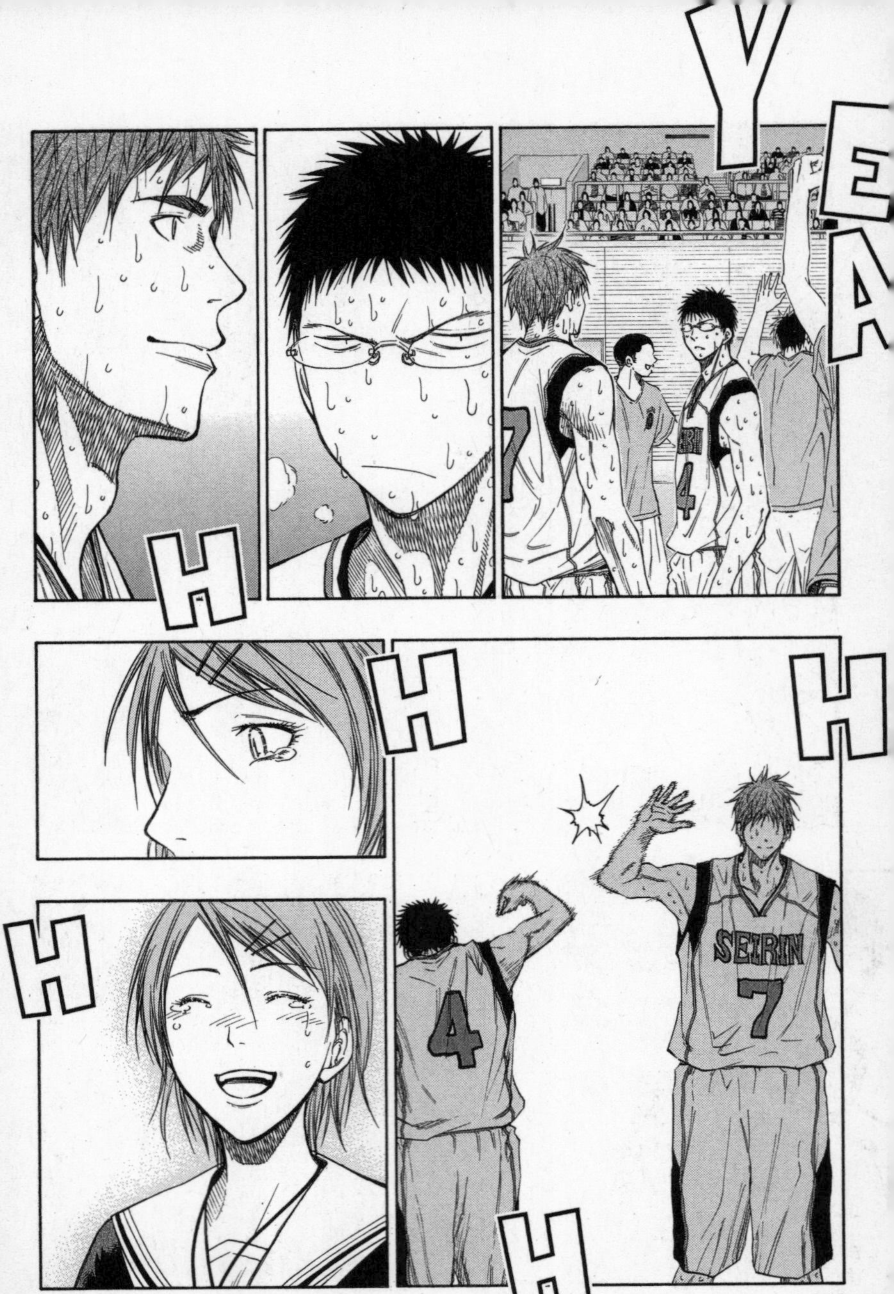
YEAHHHHH
SEIRIN

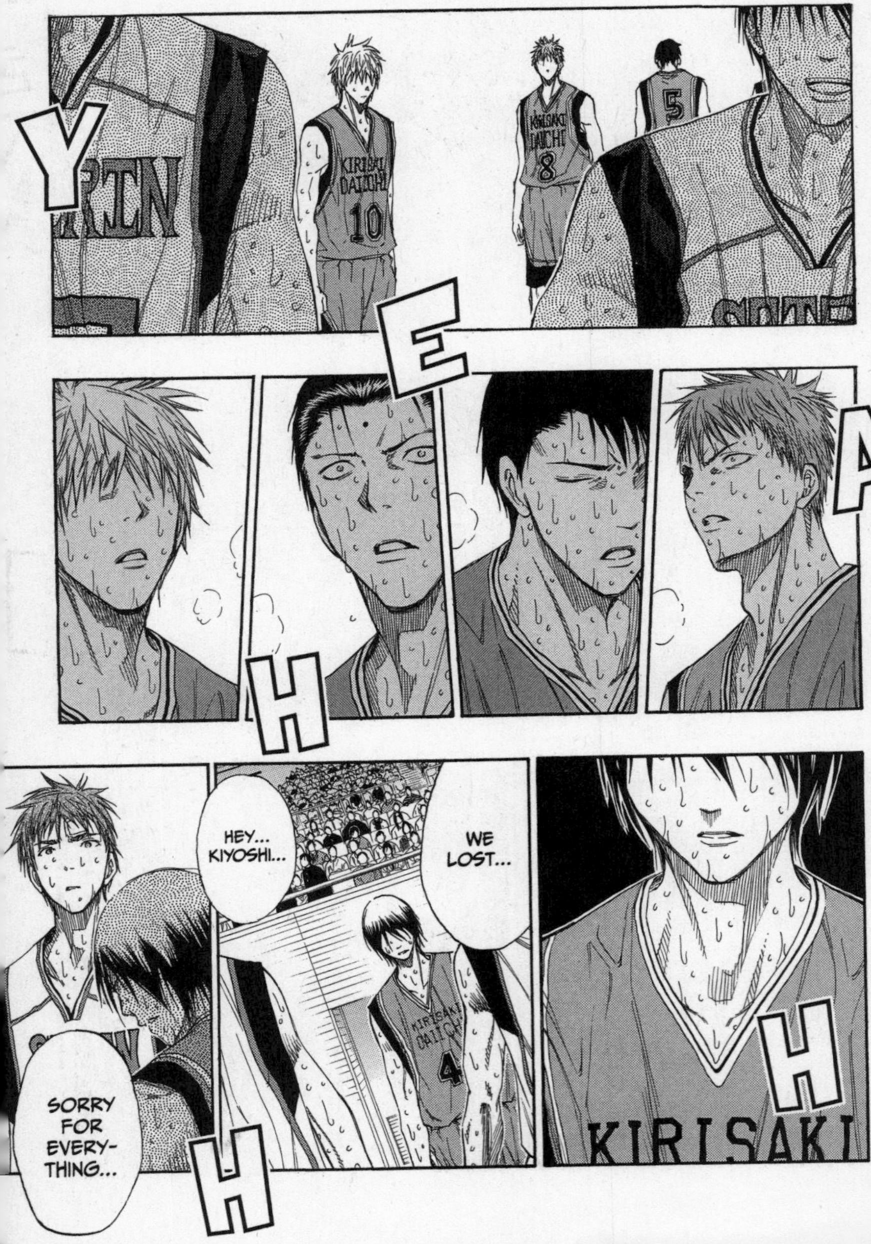
Y
E
A
H
H
WE LOST...
HEY... KIYOSHI...
SORRY FOR EVERY-THING...
H

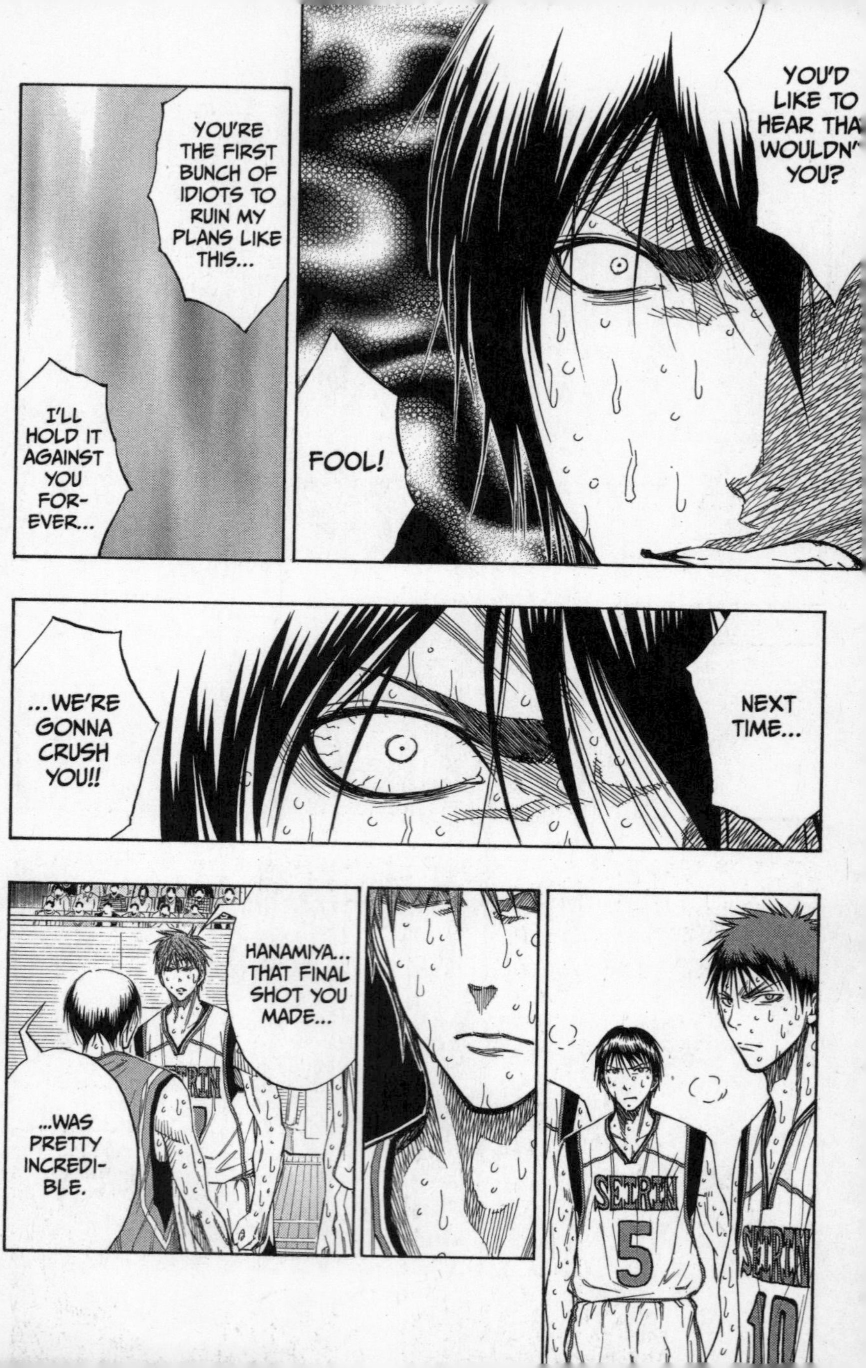
YOU'D LIKE TO HEAR THA WOULDN' YOU?
FOOL!
YOU'RE THE FIRST BUNCH OF IDIOTS TO RUIN MY PLANS LIKE THIS...
I'LL HOLD IT AGAINST YOU FOR-EVER...
NEXT TIME...
...WE'RE GONNA CRUSH YOU!!
HANAMIYA... THAT FINAL SHOT YOU MADE...
...WAS PRETTY INCREDI-BLE.
SEIRIN
5
SEIRIN
10

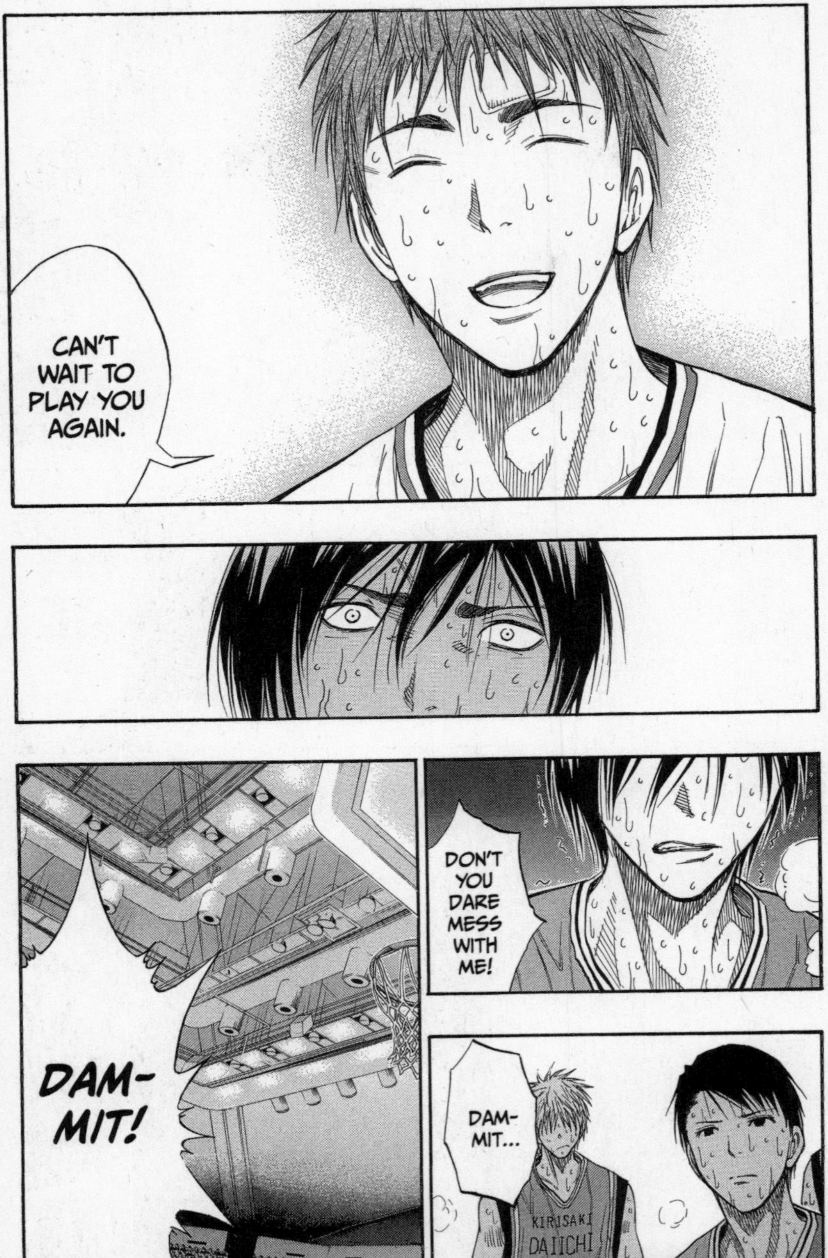
CAN'T WAIT TO PLAY YOU AGAIN.
DON'T YOU DARE MESS WITH ME!
DAM-MIT...
KIRISAKI DAIICHI
DAM-MIT!

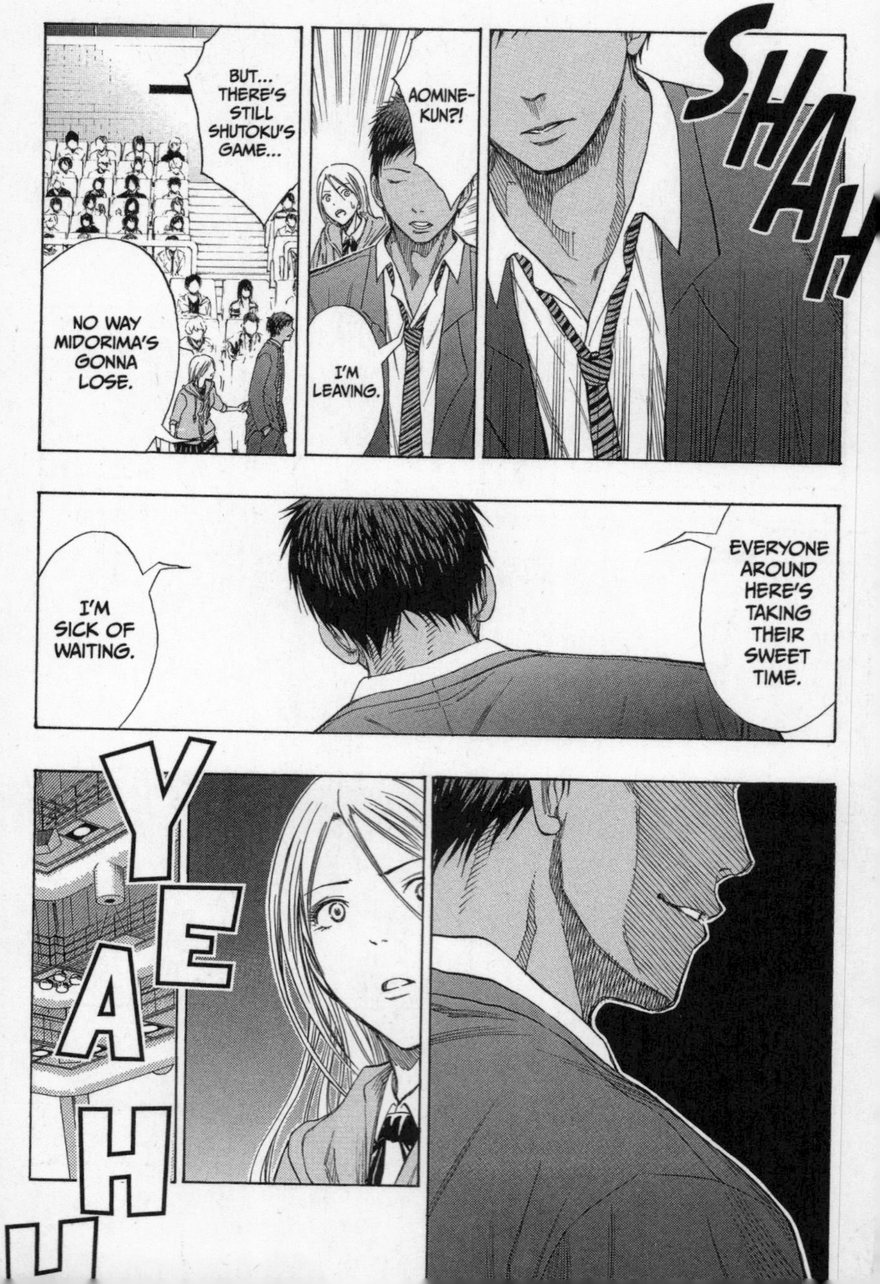
SHAH
AOMINE-KUN?!
I'M LEAVING.
BUT... THERE'S STILL SHUTOKU'S GAME...
NO WAY MIDORIMA'S GONNA LOSE.
EVERYONE AROUND HERE'S TAKING THEIR SWEET TIME.
I'M SICK OF WAITING.
YEAHH

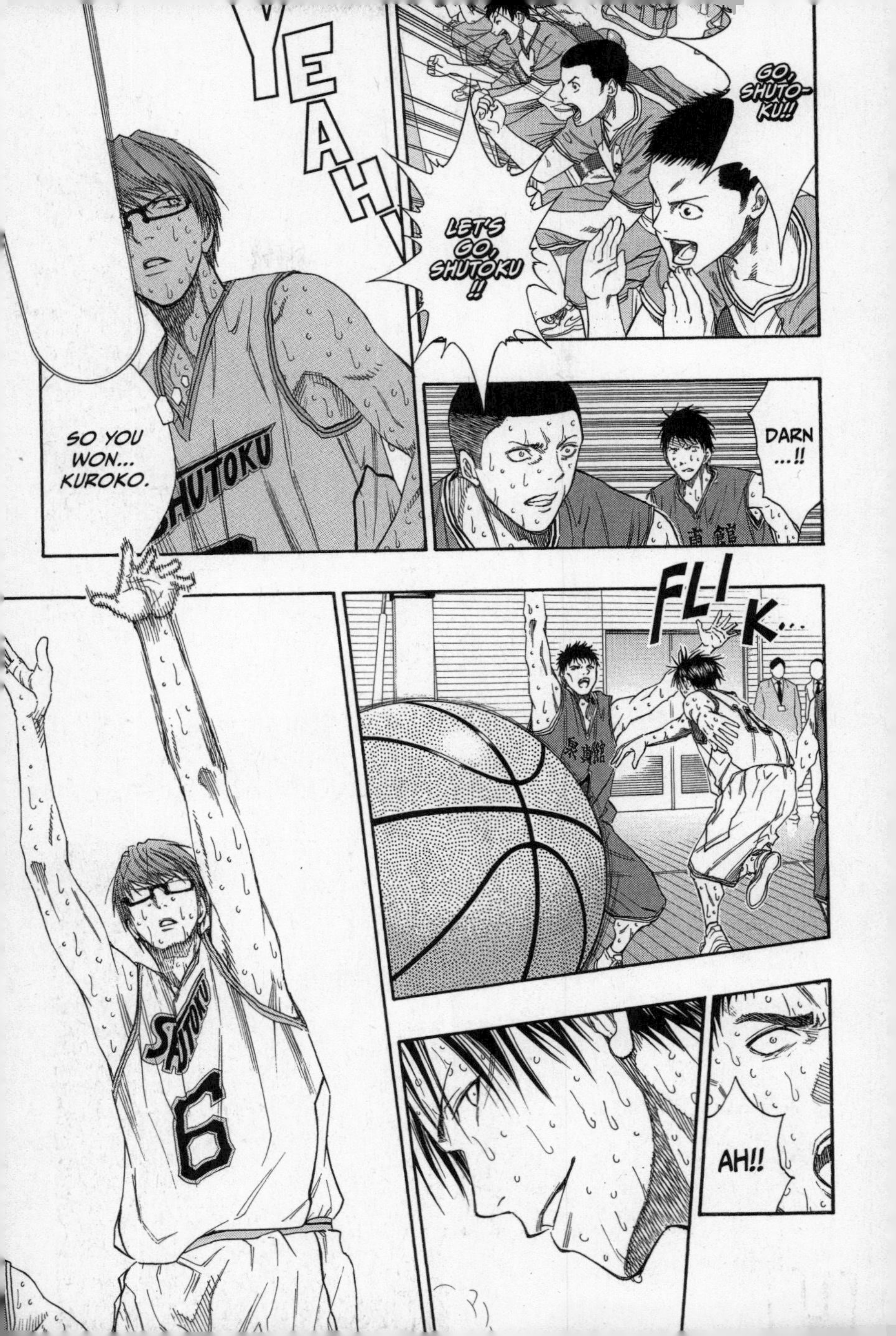
GO, SHUTOKU!!
LET'S GO, SHUTOKU!!
DARN...!!
YEAH
SO YOU WON... KUROKO.
FLIK...
AH!!

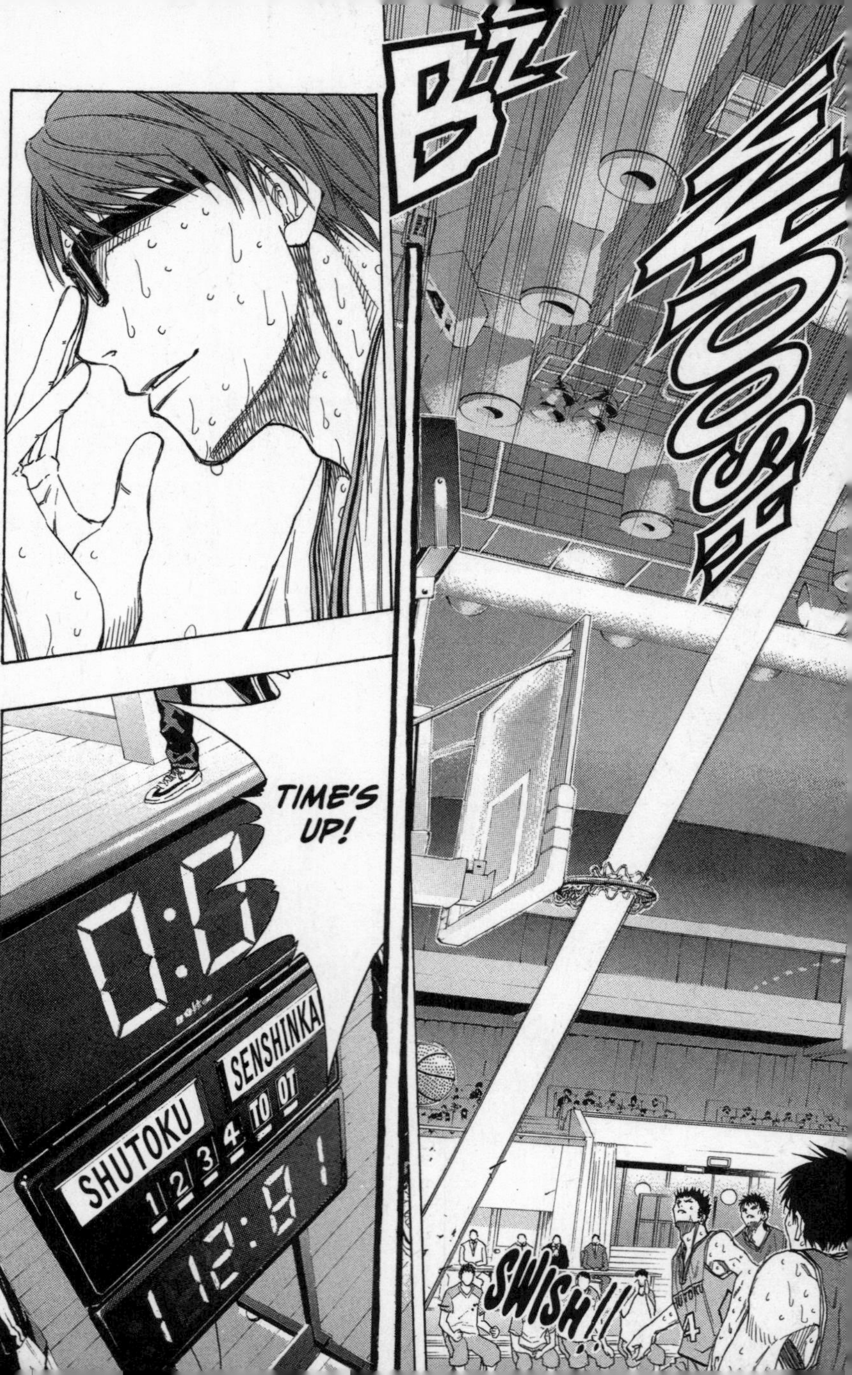
BZZ
WHOOSH
SWISH!!
TIME'S UP!
SENSHINKA
SHUTOKU
1 2 3 4 TO OT

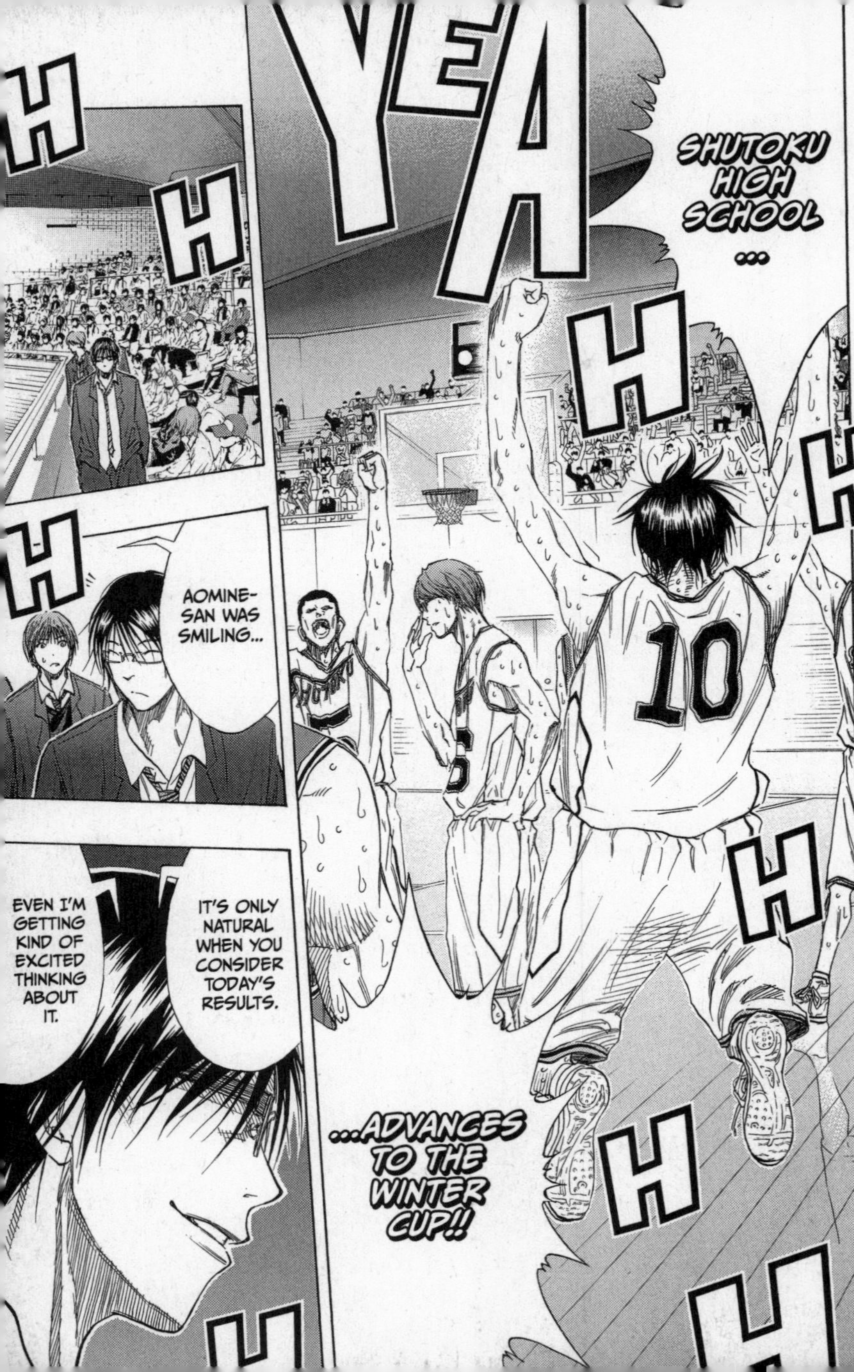
YEAHHHH
SHUTOKU HIGH SCHOOL...
...ADVANCES TO THE WINTER CUP!!
HHH
AOMINE-SAN WAS SMILING...
IT'S ONLY NATURAL WHEN YOU CONSIDER TODAY'S RESULTS.
EVEN I'M GETTING KIND OF EXCITED THINKING ABOUT IT.
H

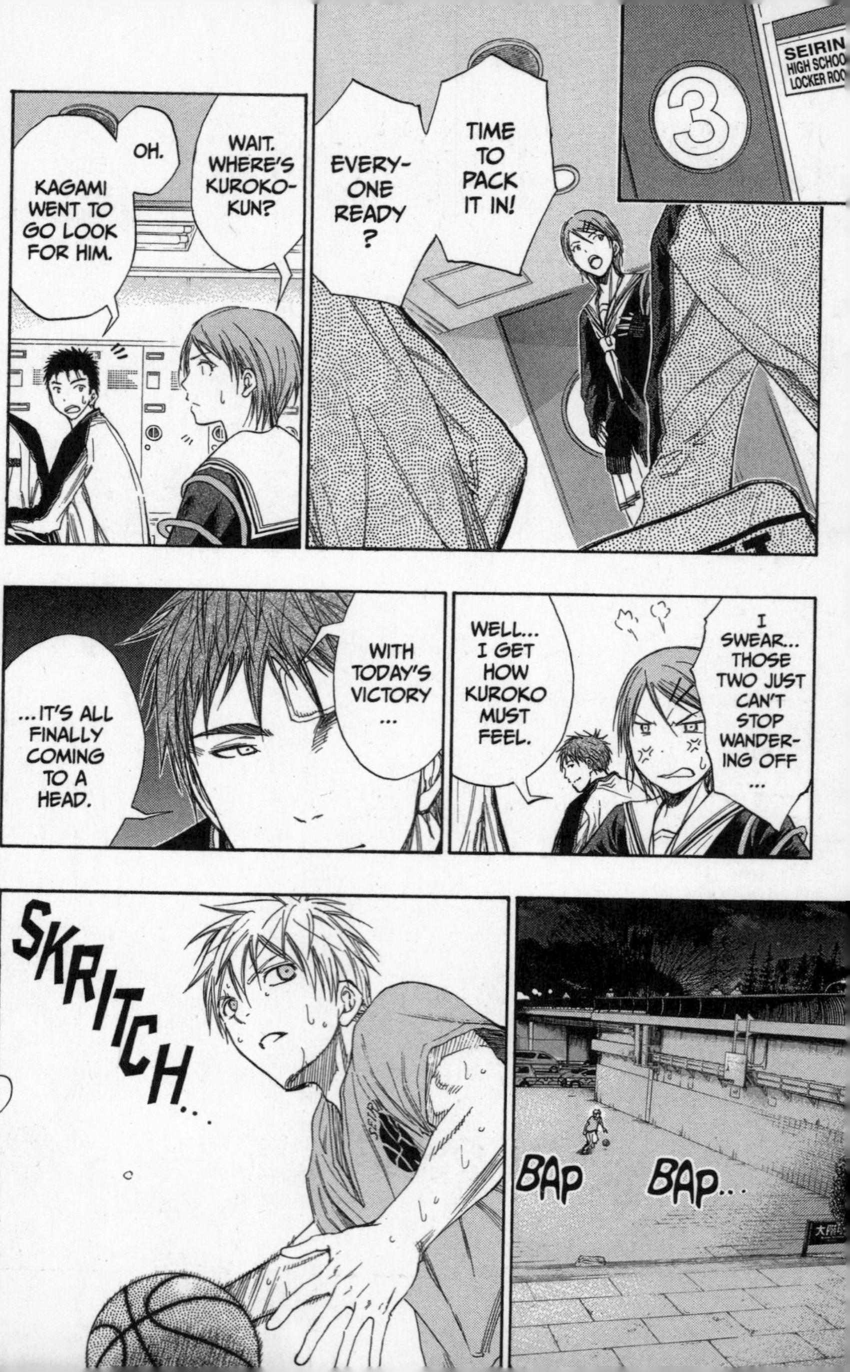
SEIRIN
HIGH SCHOO
LOCKER ROO
3
TIME TO PACK IT IN!
EVERY-ONE READY?
WAIT. WHERE'S KUROKO-KUN?
OH.
KAGAMI WENT TO GO LOOK FOR HIM.
I SWEAR... THOSE TWO JUST CAN'T STOP WANDER-ING OFF...
WELL... I GET HOW KUROKO MUST FEEL.
WITH TODAY'S VICTORY...
...IT'S ALL FINALLY COMING TO A HEAD.
BAP BAP...
SKRITCH...

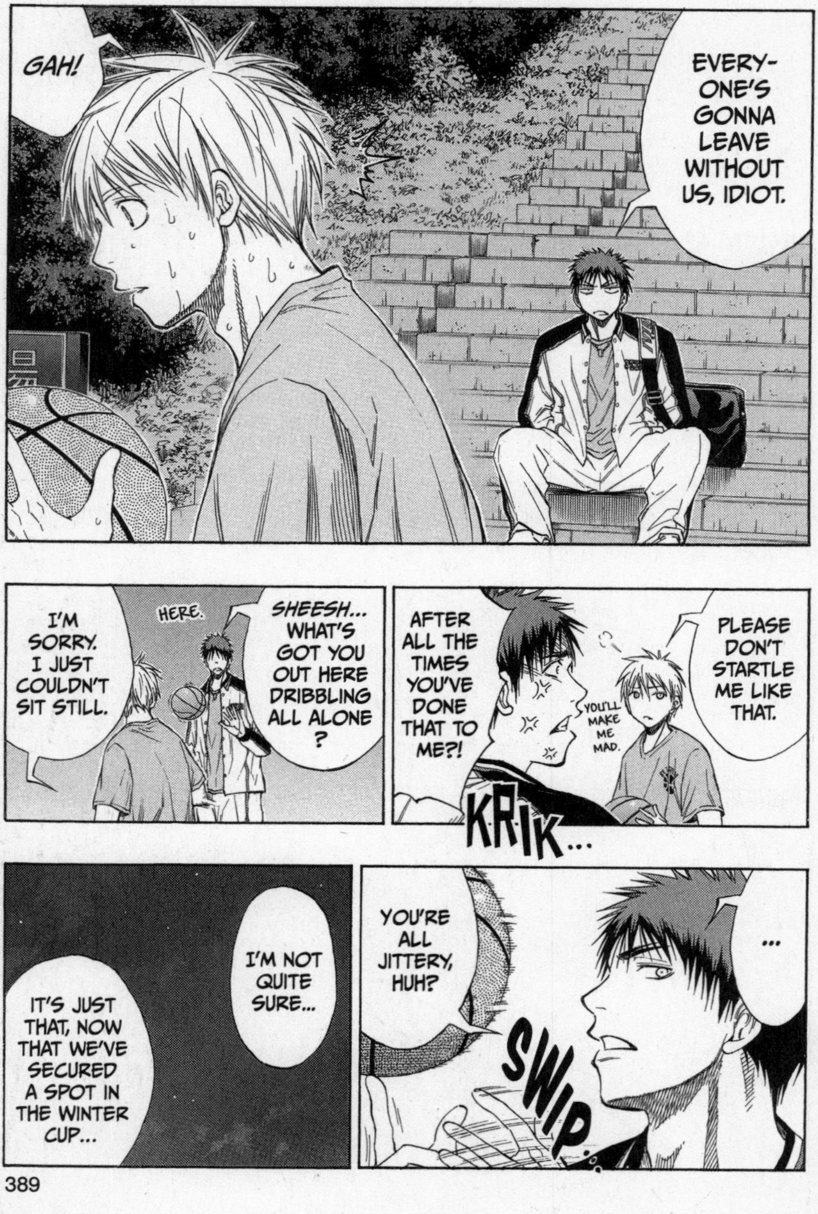
EVERY-ONE'S GONNA LEAVE WITHOUT US, IDIOT.
GAH!
PLEASE DON'T STARTLE ME LIKE THAT.
YOU'LL MAKE ME MAD.
AFTER ALL THE TIMES YOU'VE DONE THAT TO ME?!
KRIK...
SHEESH... WHAT'S GOT YOU OUT HERE DRIBBLING ALL ALONE?
HERE.
I'M SORRY. I JUST COULDN'T SIT STILL.
...
YOU'RE ALL JITTERY, HUH?
SWIP.
I'M NOT QUITE SURE...
IT'S JUST THAT, NOW THAT WE'VE SECURED A SPOT IN THE WINTER CUP...

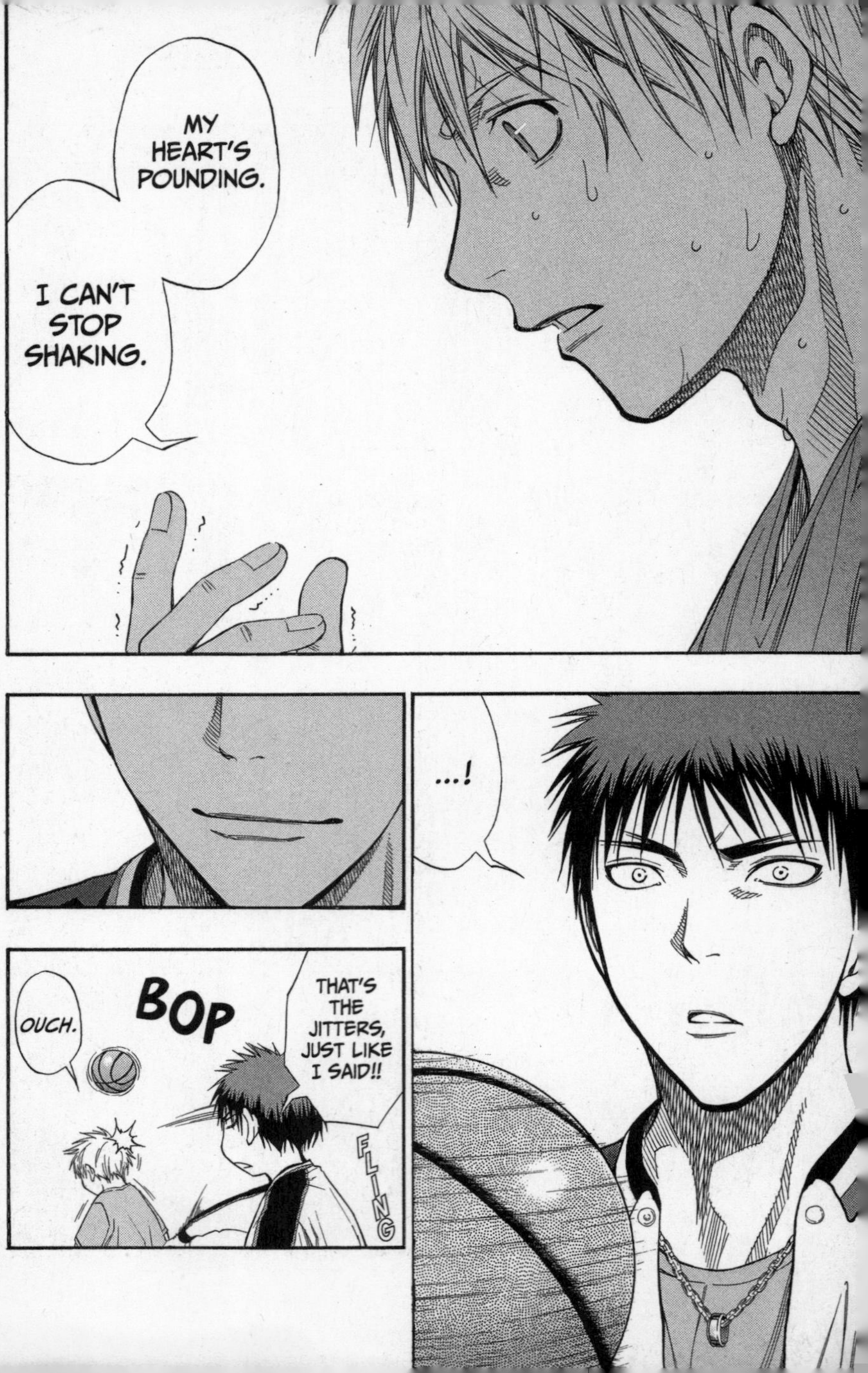
MY HEART'S POUNDING.
I CAN'T STOP SHAKING.
...!
THAT'S THE JITTERS, JUST LIKE I SAID!!
BOP
OUCH.
FLING

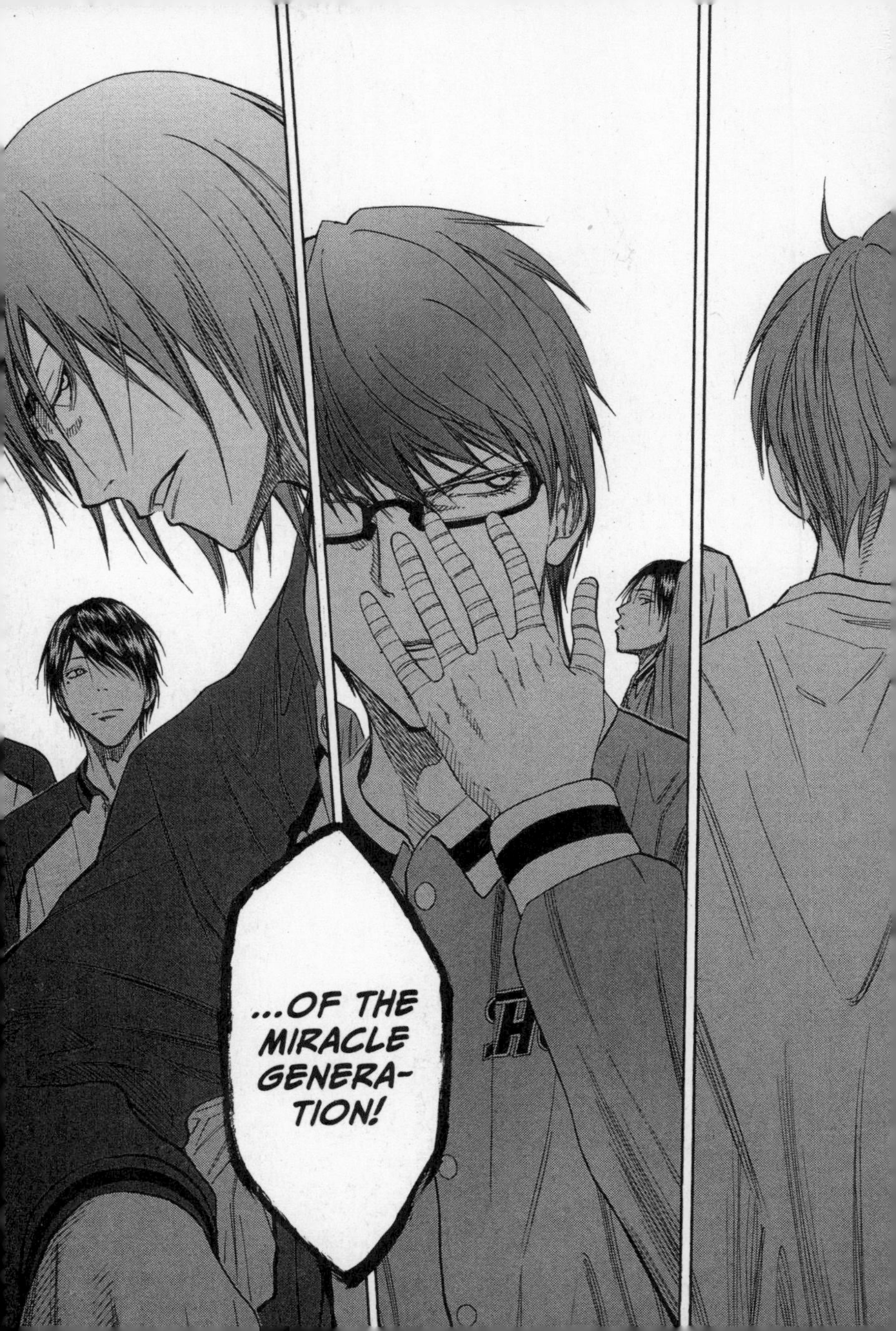
...OF THE MIRACLE GENERA- TION!

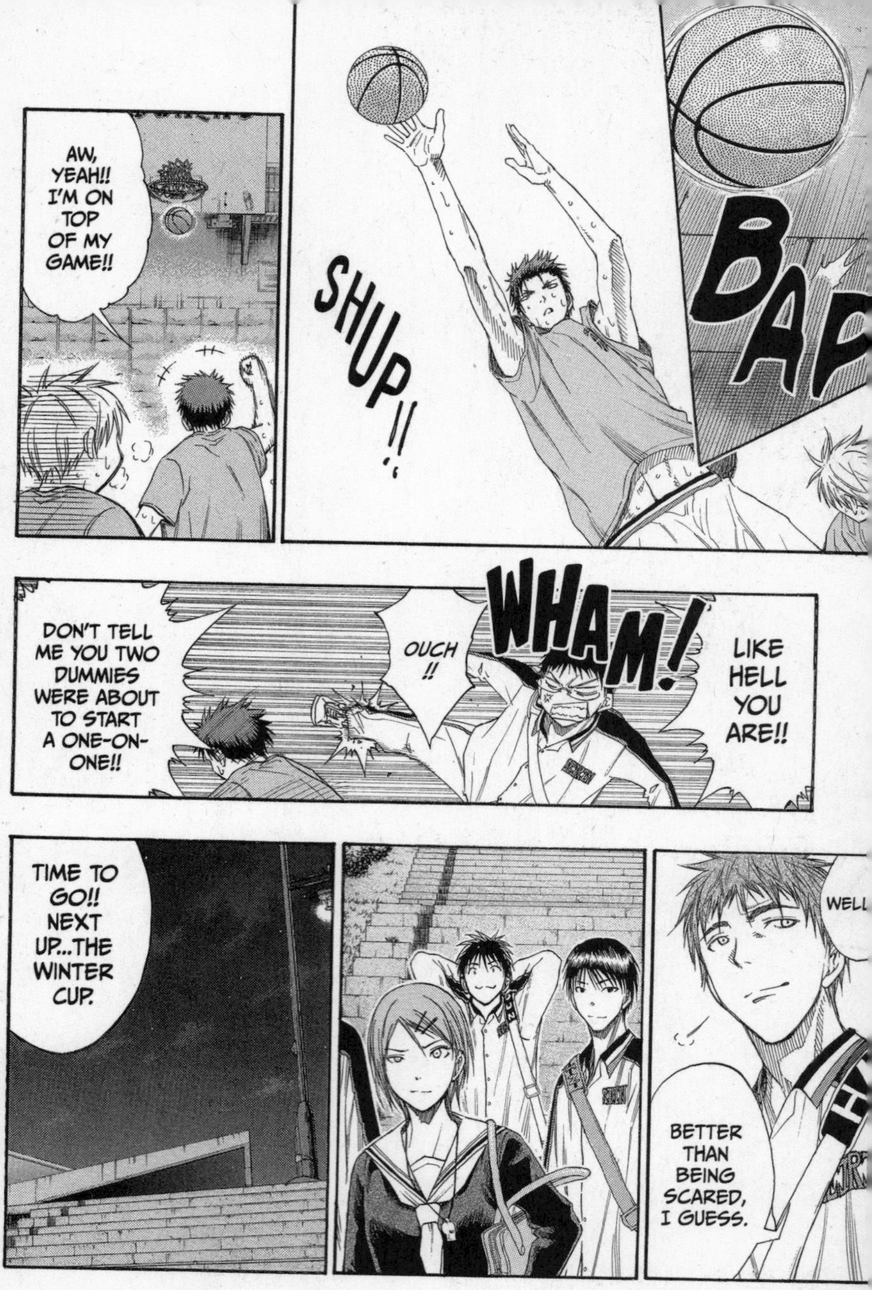
BA
SHUP!!
AW, YEAH!! I'M ON TOP OF MY GAME!!
WHAM!
LIKE HELL YOU ARE!!
OUCH!!
DON'T TELL ME YOU TWO DUMMIES WERE ABOUT TO START A ONE-ON-ONE!!
WELL
BETTER THAN BEING SCARED, I GUESS.
TIME TO GO!! NEXT UP...THE WINTER CUP.

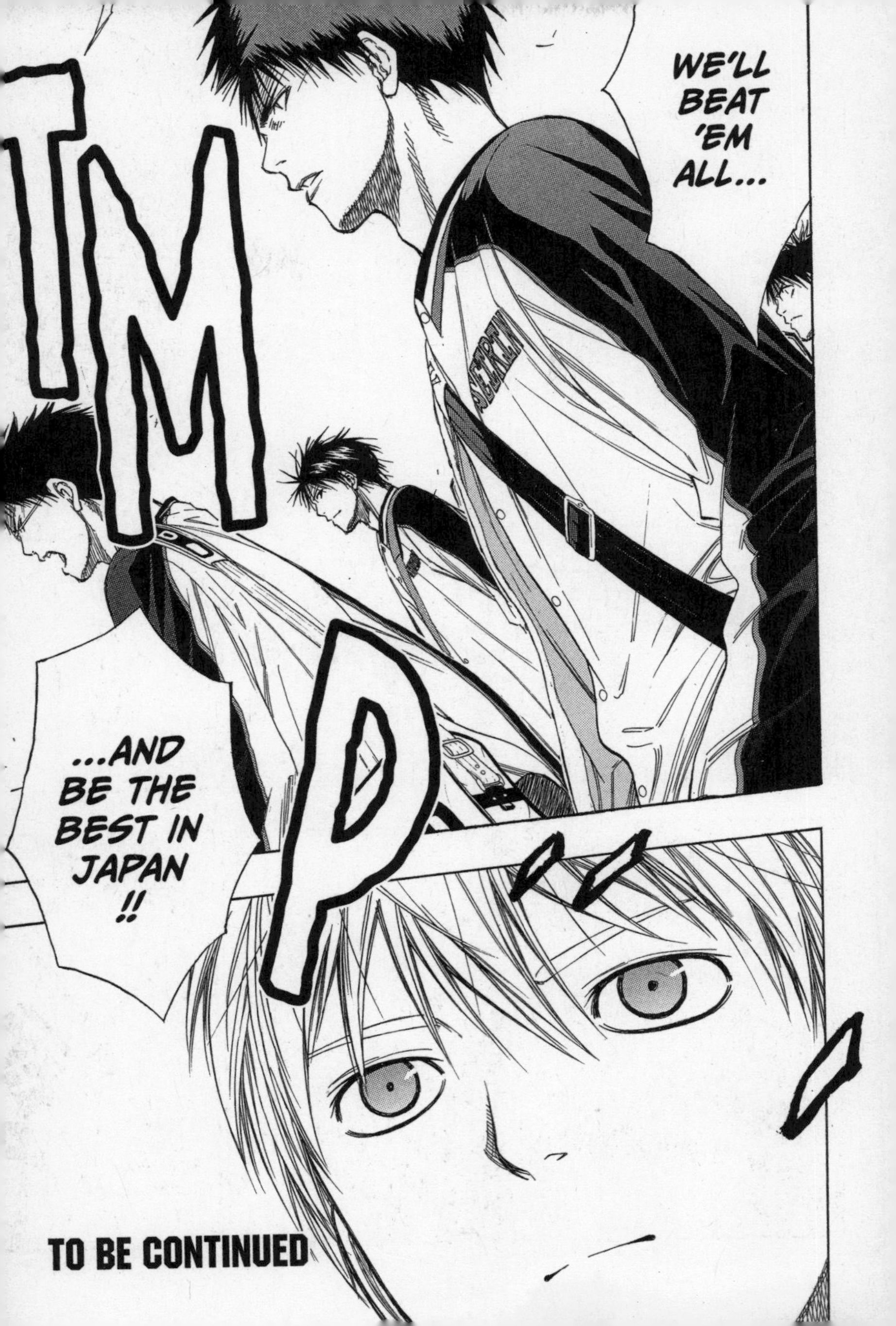
WE'LL BEAT 'EM ALL...
TMP
...AND BE THE BEST IN JAPAN!!
TO BE CONTINUED

KUROKO'S BASKETBALL

TAKE 9 BLOOPERS

BEAT UP

WE HAD A FIGHT.

HUHH ?!

...

BUH ?!

THAT HURT.

WHAP

OUCH.

BOP!

THAT'S THE JITTERS, JUST LIKE I SAID!!

...

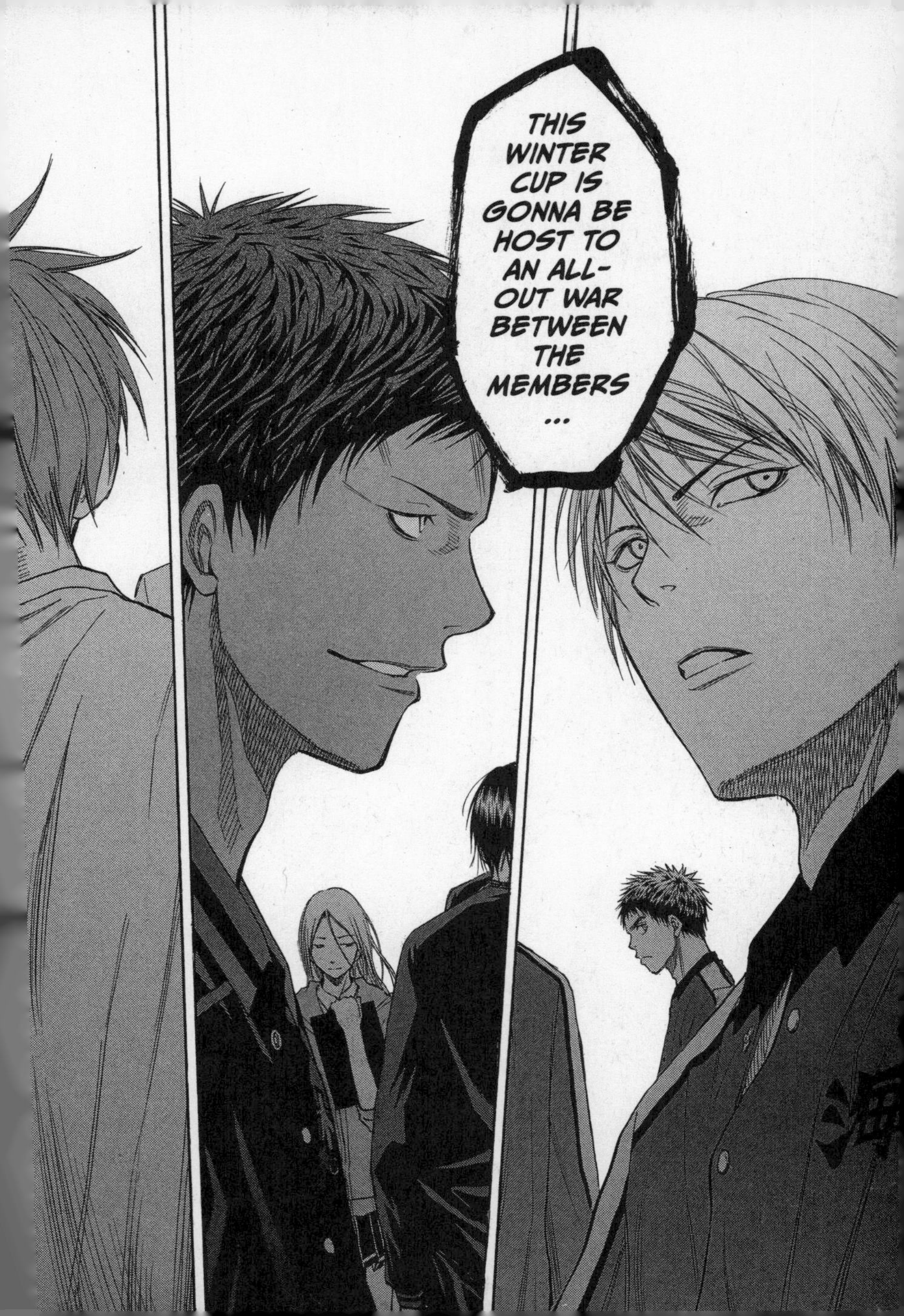
THIS WINTER CUP IS GONNA BE HOST TO AN ALL-OUT WAR BETWEEN THE MEMBERS...

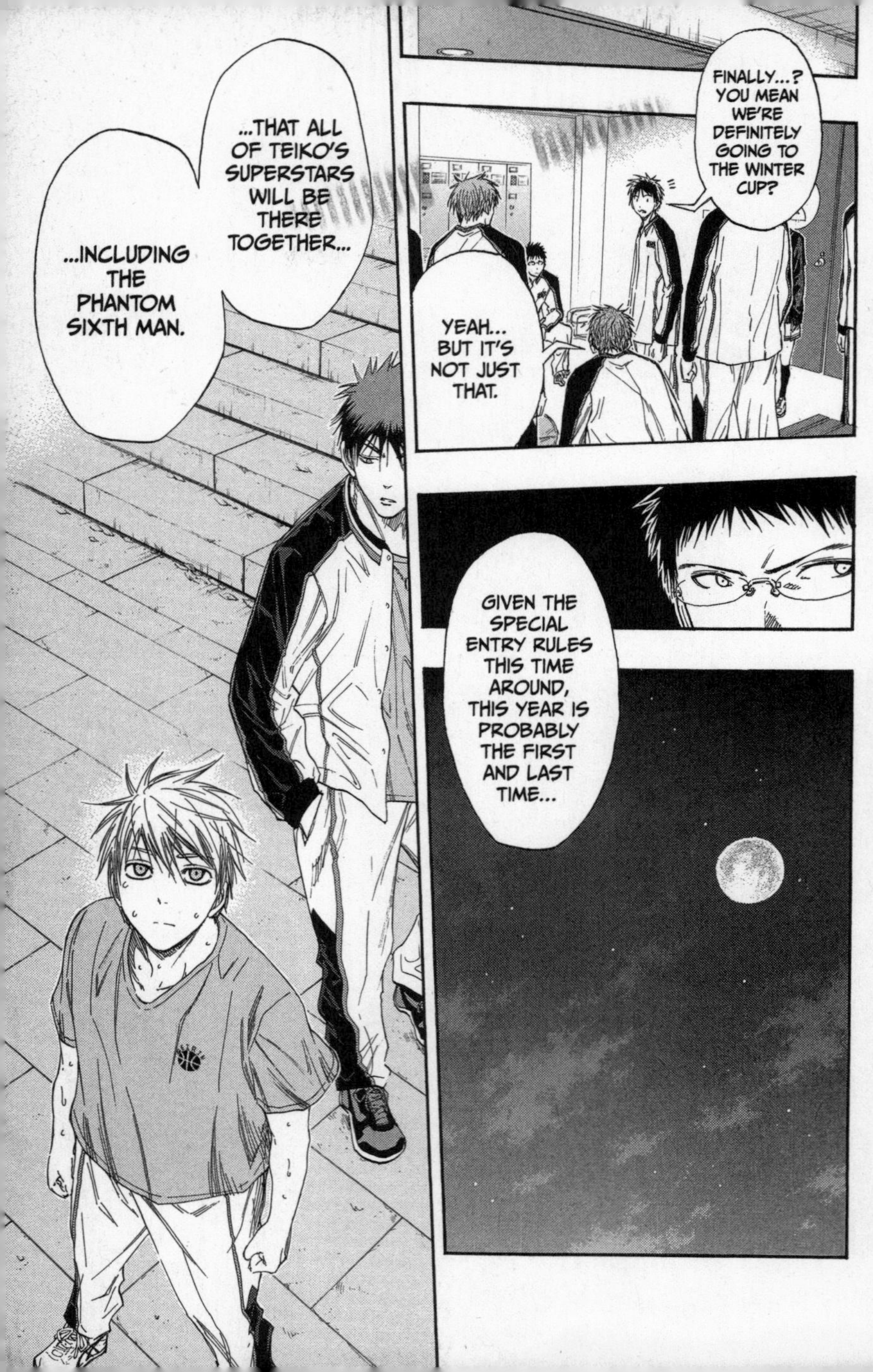
FINALLY...? YOU MEAN WE'RE DEFINITELY GOING TO THE WINTER CUP?
YEAH... BUT IT'S NOT JUST THAT.
GIVEN THE SPECIAL ENTRY RULES THIS TIME AROUND, THIS YEAR IS PROBABLY THE FIRST AND LAST TIME...
...THAT ALL OF TEIKO'S SUPERSTARS WILL BE THERE TOGETHER...
...INCLUDING THE PHANTOM SIXTH MAN.

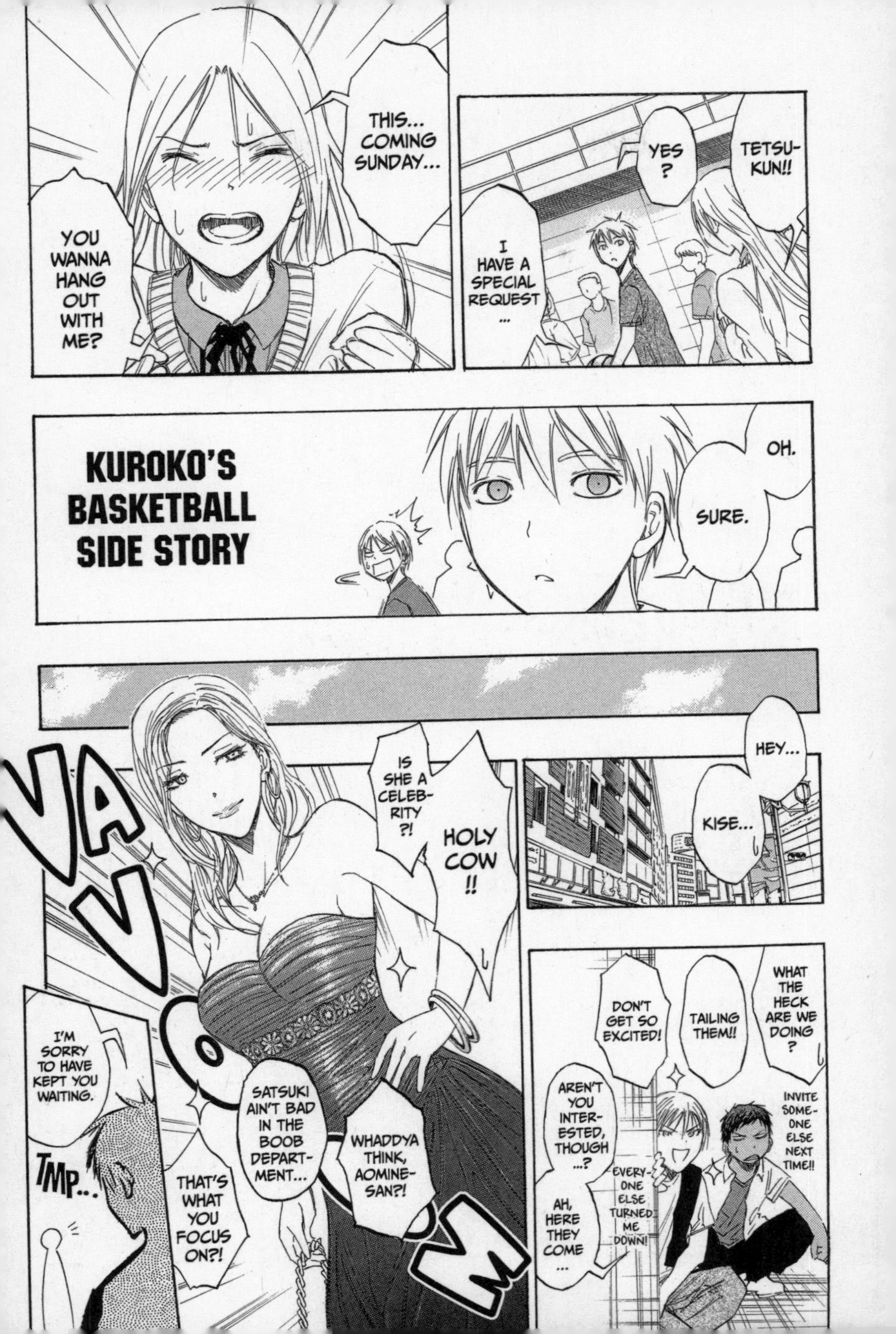
TETSU-KUN!!
YES?
I HAVE A SPECIAL REQUEST...
THIS... COMING SUNDAY...
YOU WANNA HANG OUT WITH ME?
OH.
SURE.
KUROKO'S BASKETBALL SIDE STORY
HEY...
KISE...
WHAT THE HECK ARE WE DOING?
TAILING THEM!!
DON'T GET SO EXCITED!
AREN'T YOU INTERESTED, THOUGH...?
INVITE SOMEONE ELSE NEXT TIME!!
EVERYONE ELSE TURNED ME DOWN!
AH, HERE THEY COME...
I'M SORRY TO HAVE KEPT YOU WAITING.
VAVOOM
HOLY COW!!
IS SHE A CELEBRITY?!
WHADDYA THINK, AOMINE-SAN?!
SATSUKI AIN'T BAD IN THE BOOB DEPARTMENT...
THAT'S WHAT YOU FOCUS ON?!
TMP...

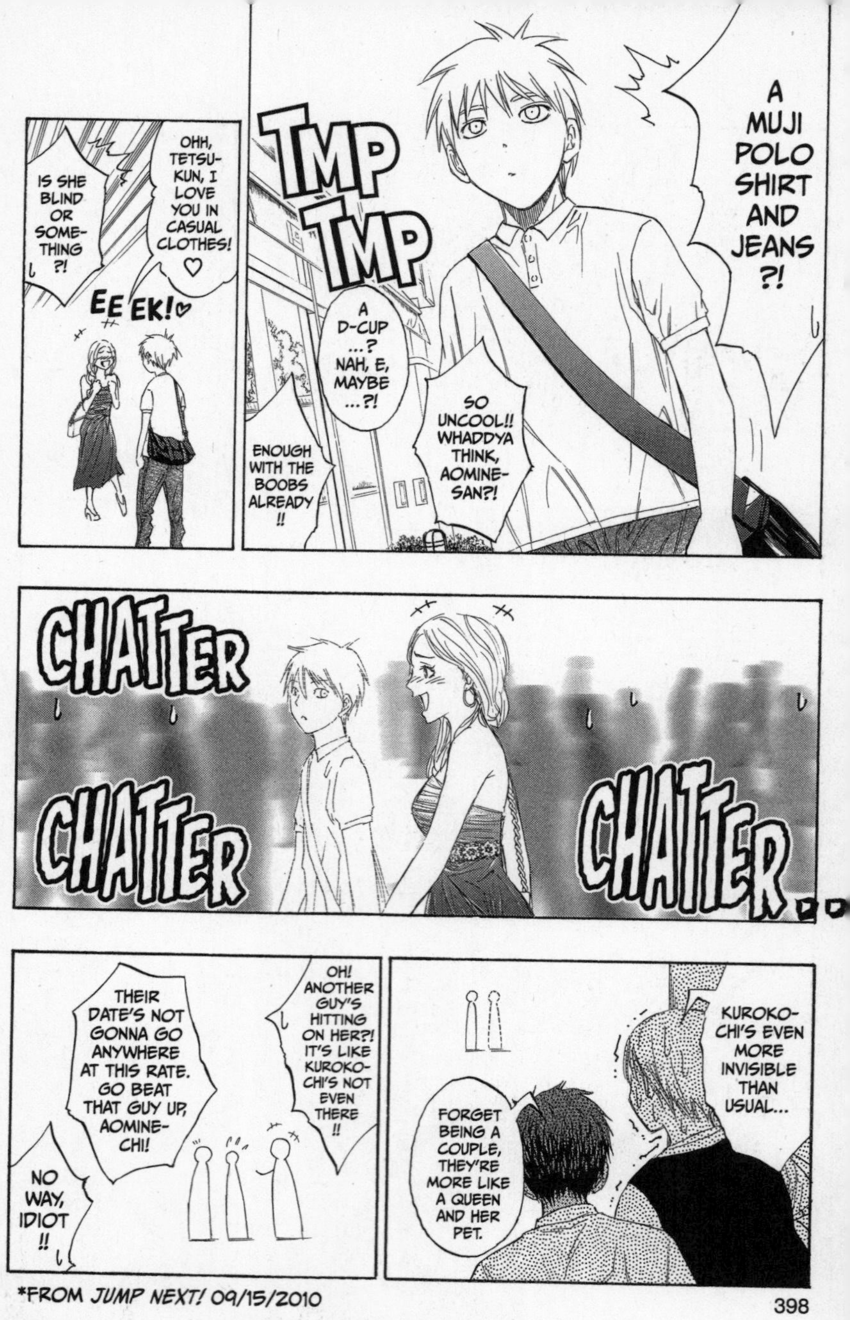
A MUJI POLO SHIRT AND JEANS ?!
TMP TMP
SO UNCOOL!! WHADDYA THINK, AOMINE-SAN?!
A D-CUP ...? NAH, E, MAYBE ...?!
ENOUGH WITH THE BOOBS ALREADY !!
OHH, TETSU-KUN, I LOVE YOU IN CASUAL CLOTHES! ♡
IS SHE BLIND OR SOME-THING ?!
EE EK!♡
CHATTER
CHATTER
CHATTER
KUROKO-CHI'S EVEN MORE INVISIBLE THAN USUAL...
FORGET BEING A COUPLE, THEY'RE MORE LIKE A QUEEN AND HER PET.
OH! ANOTHER GUY'S HITTING ON HER?! IT'S LIKE KUROKO-CHI'S NOT EVEN THERE !!
THEIR DATE'S NOT GONNA GO ANYWHERE AT THIS RATE. GO BEAT THAT GUY UP, AOMINE-CHI!
NO WAY, IDIOT !!

*FROM *JUMP NEXT!* 09/15/2010

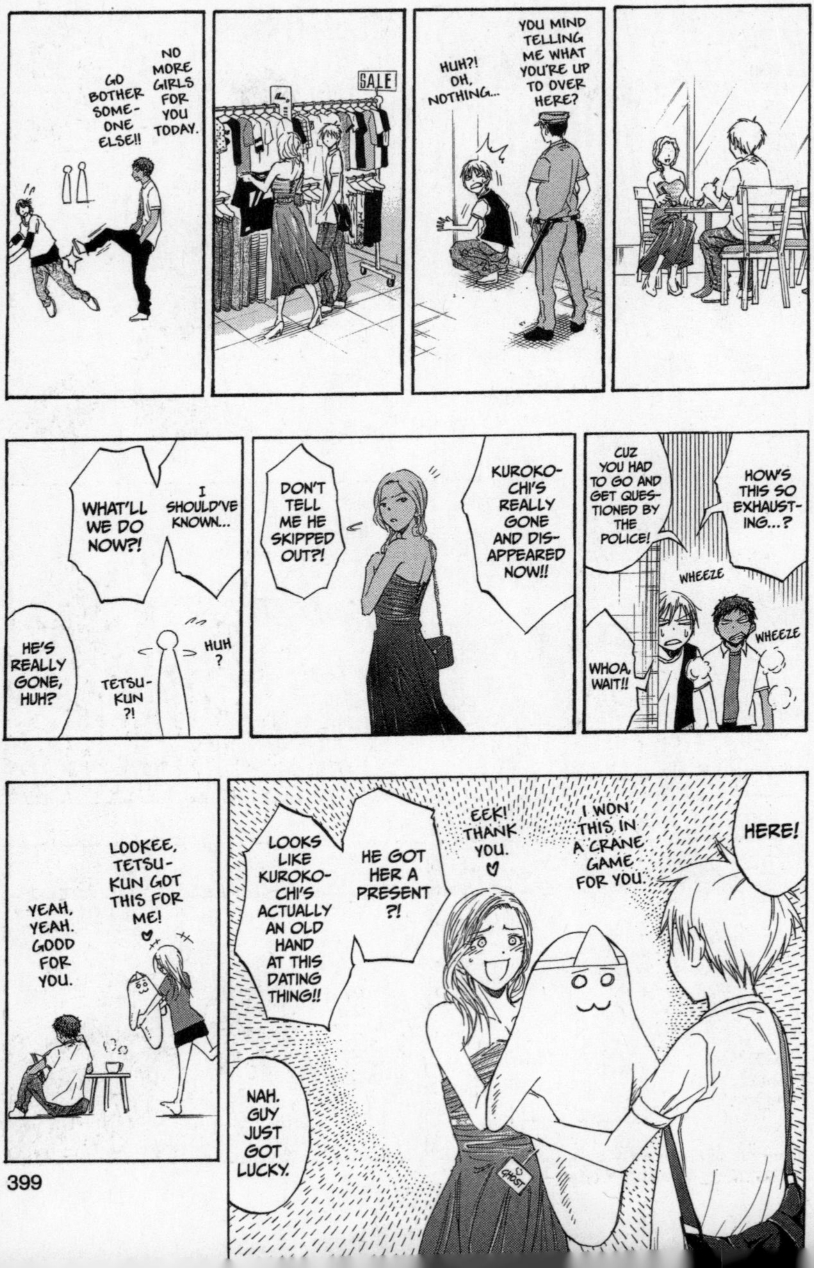
YOU MIND TELLING ME WHAT YOU'RE UP TO OVER HERE?
HUH?! OH, NOTHING...
SALE
NO MORE GIRLS FOR YOU TODAY.
GO BOTHER SOME-ONE ELSE!!
HOW'S THIS SO EXHAUST-ING...?
CUZ YOU HAD TO GO AND GET QUES-TIONED BY THE POLICE!
WHEEZE
WHEEZE
WHOA, WAIT!!
KUROKO-CHI'S REALLY GONE AND DIS-APPEARED NOW!!
DON'T TELL ME HE SKIPPED OUT?!
I SHOULD'VE KNOWN...
WHAT'LL WE DO NOW?!
HUH?
TETSU-KUN?!
HE'S REALLY GONE, HUH?
HERE!
I WON THIS IN A CRANE GAME FOR YOU.
EEK! THANK YOU. ♥
HE GOT HER A PRESENT?!
LOOKS LIKE KUROKO-CHI'S ACTUALLY AN OLD HAND AT THIS DATING THING!!
NAH. GUY JUST GOT LUCKY.
GHOST
LOOKEE, TETSU-KUN GOT THIS FOR ME! ♥
YEAH, YEAH. GOOD FOR YOU.

I CAN DO IT

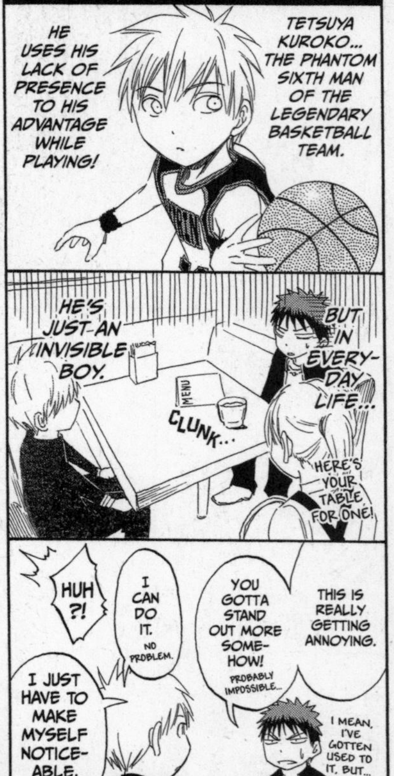
TETSUYA KUROKO... THE PHANTOM SIXTH MAN OF THE LEGENDARY BASKETBALL TEAM.
HE USES HIS LACK OF PRESENCE TO HIS ADVANTAGE WHILE PLAYING!
BUT IN EVERY-DAY LIFE...
HE'S JUST AN INVISIBLE BOY.
MENU
CLUNK...
HERE'S YOUR TABLE FOR ONE!
THIS IS REALLY GETTING ANNOYING.
YOU GOTTA STAND OUT MORE SOME-HOW!
PROBABLY IMPOSSIBLE...
I CAN DO IT.
NO PROBLEM.
HUH ?!
I MEAN, I'VE GOTTEN USED TO IT, BUT...
I JUST HAVE TO MAKE MYSELF NOTICE-ABLE, RIGHT?
WHAT'S THAT KID DOING?
HUH...
NOT LIKE THAT!!
ARE YOU JAMILA FROM ULTRA-MAN?

LIVE LONGER

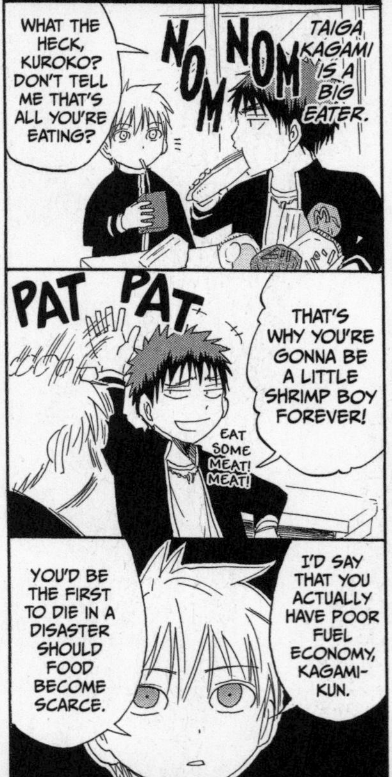
TAIGA KAGAMI IS A BIG EATER.
NOM NOM
WHAT THE HECK, KUROKO? DON'T TELL ME THAT'S ALL YOU'RE EATING?
THAT'S WHY YOU'RE GONNA BE A LITTLE SHRIMP BOY FOREVER!
EAT SOME MEAT! MEAT!
PAT PAT
I'D SAY THAT YOU ACTUALLY HAVE POOR FUEL ECONOMY, KAGAMI-KUN.
YOU'D BE THE FIRST TO DIE IN A DISASTER SHOULD FOOD BECOME SCARCE.
WHAT'S WITH YOUR WEIRD LOGIC ?!
I CAN SUBSIST ON SMALL AMOUNTS OF FOOD, SO I'LL LIVE LONGER THAN YOU.
I'M ALSO HELPING THE ENVIRONMENT THIS WAY.
WHAT'S FOOD GOT TO DO WITH BEING GREEN ?!
THEY'RE ALWAYS FIGHT-ING.

IMPOSSIBLE

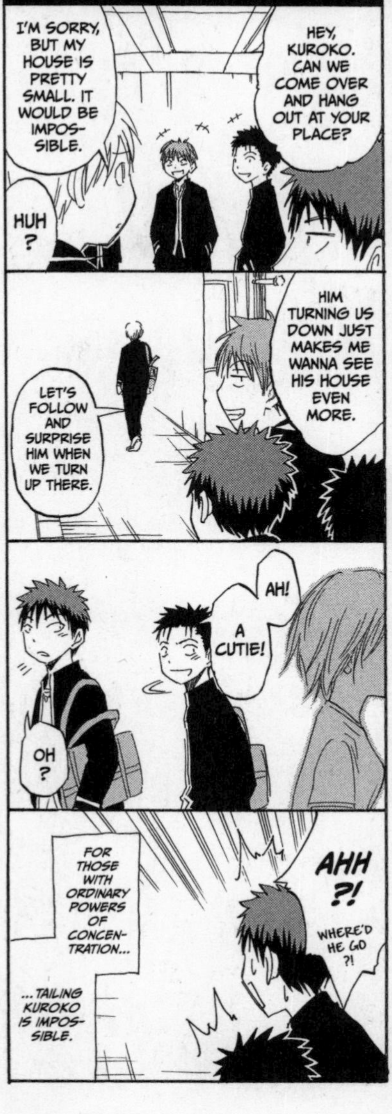
HEY, KUROKO. CAN WE COME OVER AND HANG OUT AT YOUR PLACE?
I'M SORRY, BUT MY HOUSE IS PRETTY SMALL. IT WOULD BE IMPOSSIBLE.
HUH?
HIM TURNING US DOWN JUST MAKES ME WANNA SEE HIS HOUSE EVEN MORE.
LET'S FOLLOW AND SURPRISE HIM WHEN WE TURN UP THERE.
AH!
A CUTIE!
OH?
AHH?!
WHERE'D HE GO?!
FOR THOSE WITH ORDINARY POWERS OF CONCENTRATION...
...TAILING KUROKO IS IMPOSSIBLE.

POWERING UP

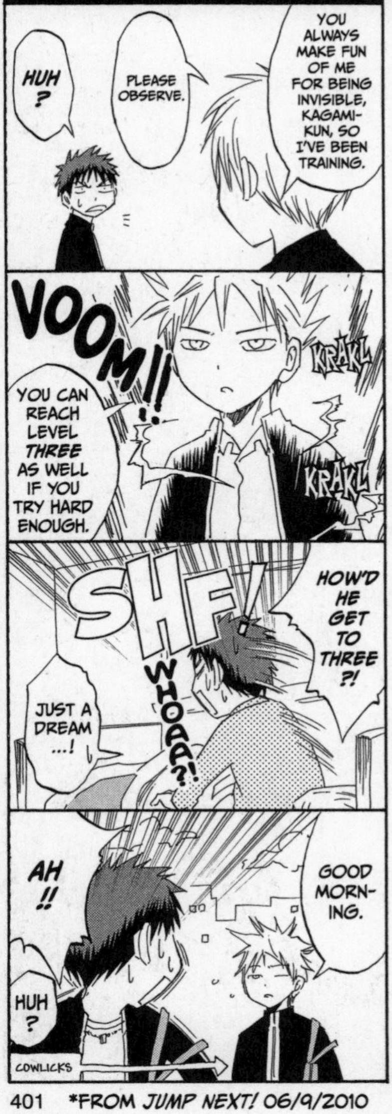
YOU ALWAYS MAKE FUN OF ME FOR BEING INVISIBLE, KAGAMI-KUN, SO I'VE BEEN TRAINING.
PLEASE OBSERVE.
HUH?
KRAKL
KRAKL
VOOM!!
YOU CAN REACH LEVEL THREE AS WELL IF YOU TRY HARD ENOUGH.
HOW'D HE GET TO THREE?!
SHF!
WHOAAA?!
JUST A DREAM ...!
GOOD MORNING.
AH!!
HUH?
COWLICKS

 *FROM *JUMP NEXT!* 06/9/2010

COMING NEXT VOLUME

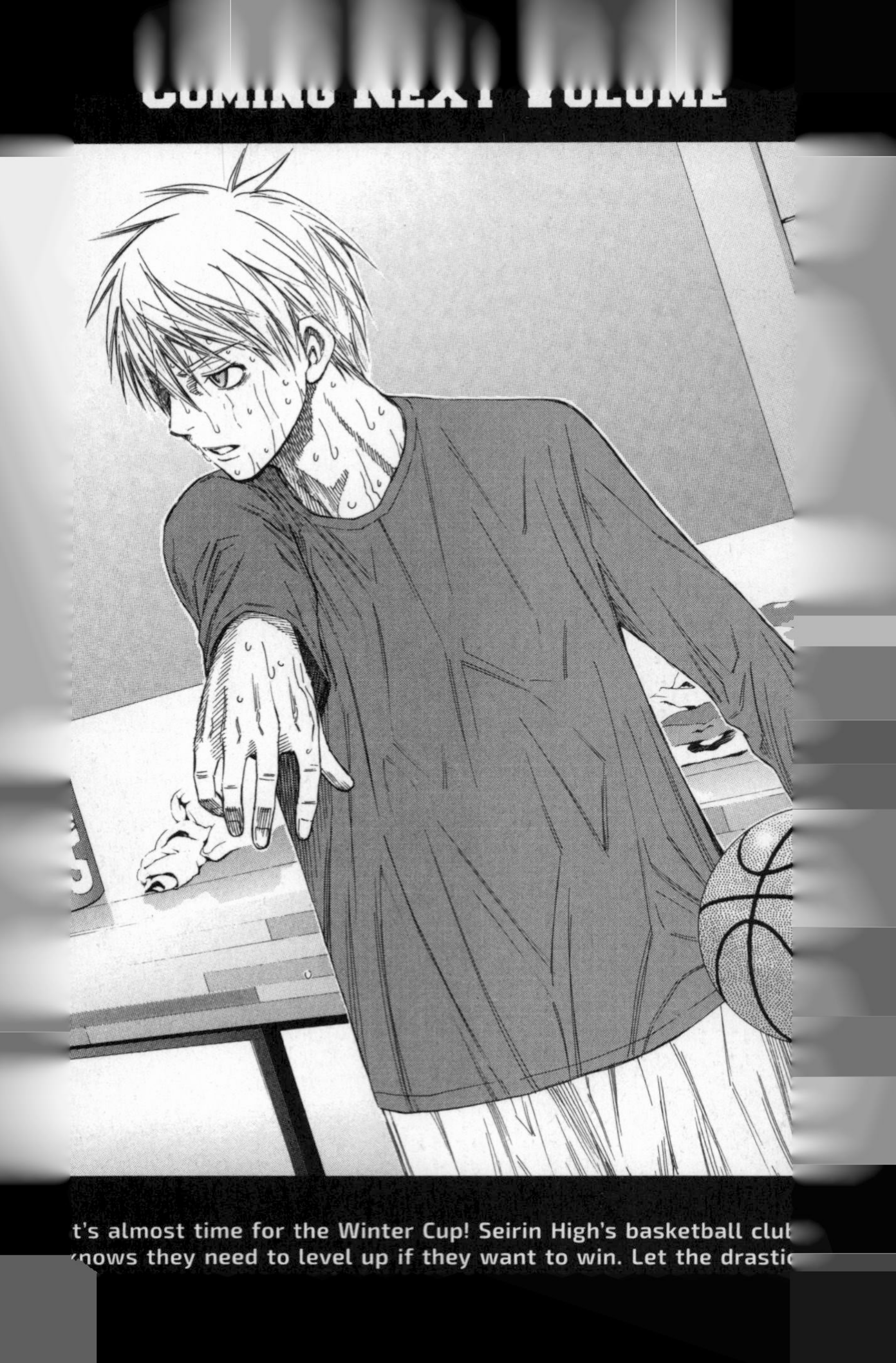

t's almost time for the Winter Cup! Seirin High's basketball club
knows they need to level up if they want to win. Let the drastic

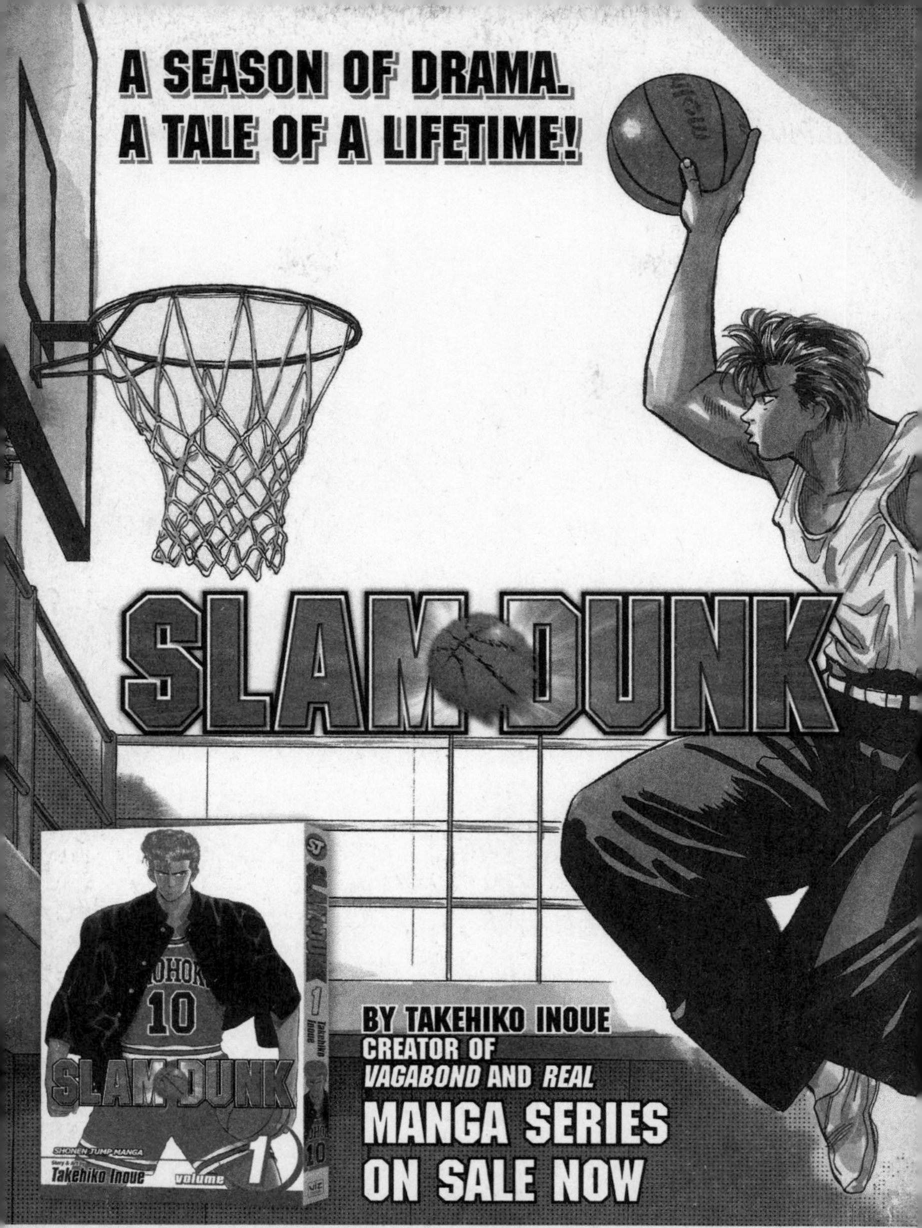
A SEASON OF DRAMA.
A TALE OF A LIFETIME!
SLAM DUNK
SHOHOKU
10
SLAM DUNK
SHONEN JUMP MANGA
Takehiko Inoue
volume 1
BY TAKEHIKO INOUE
CREATOR OF
VAGABOND AND REAL
MANGA SERIES
ON SALE NOW

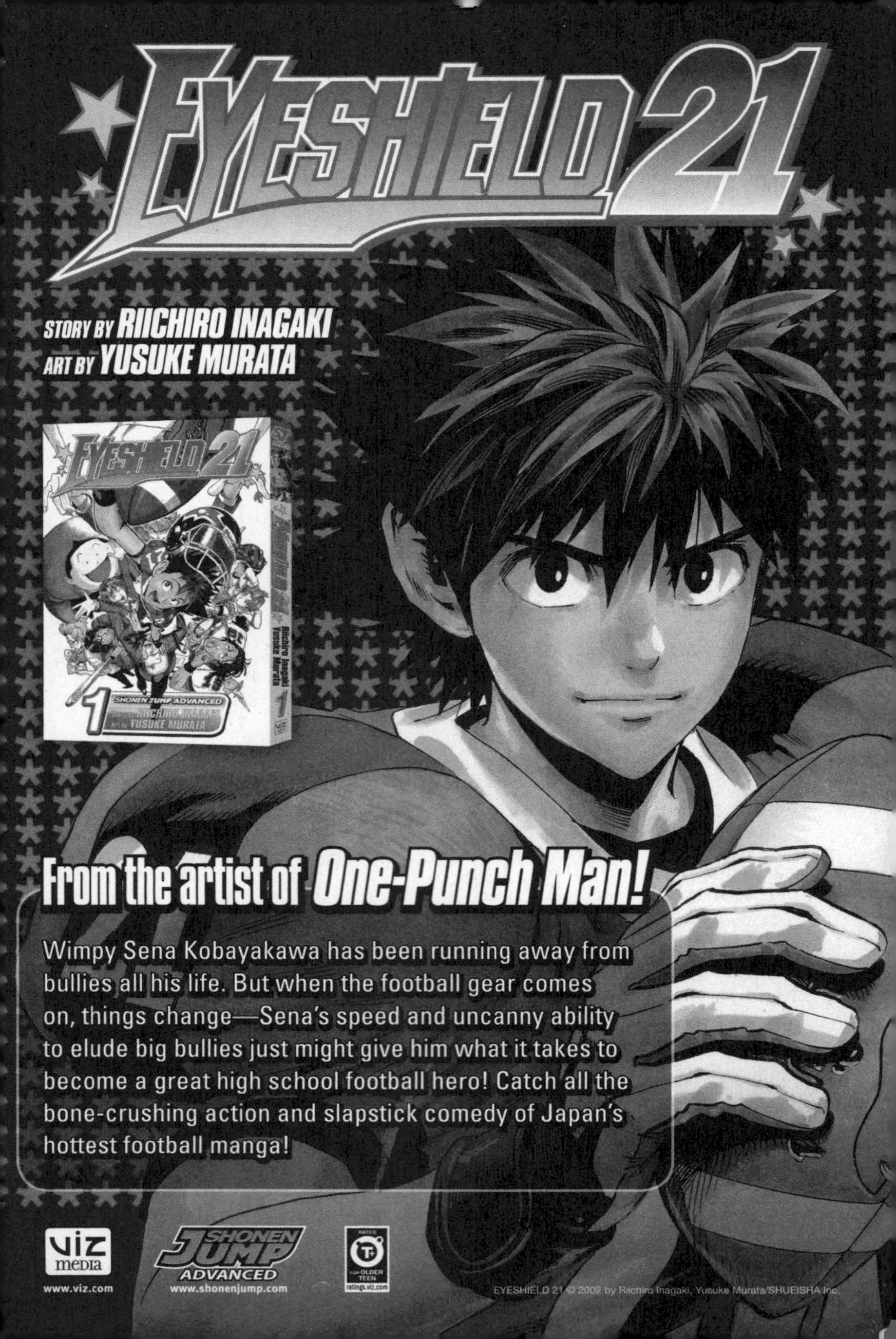
EYESHIELD 21
STORY BY RIICHIRO INAGAKI
ART BY YUSUKE MURATA
EYESHIELD 21
1 SHONEN JUMP ADVANCED
Art by YUSUKE MURATA
Riichiro Inagaki Yusuke Murata
From the artist of One-Punch Man!
Wimpy Sena Kobayakawa has been running away from bullies all his life. But when the football gear comes on, things change—Sena's speed and uncanny ability to elude big bullies just might give him what it takes to become a great high school football hero! Catch all the bone-crushing action and slapstick comedy of Japan's hottest football manga!
viz media
www.viz.com
SHONEN JUMP ADVANCED
www.shonenjump.com
RATED T+ FOR OLDER TEEN
ratings.viz.com
EYESHIELD 21 © 2002 by Riichiro Inagaki, Yusuke Murata/SHUEISHA Inc.

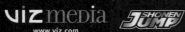

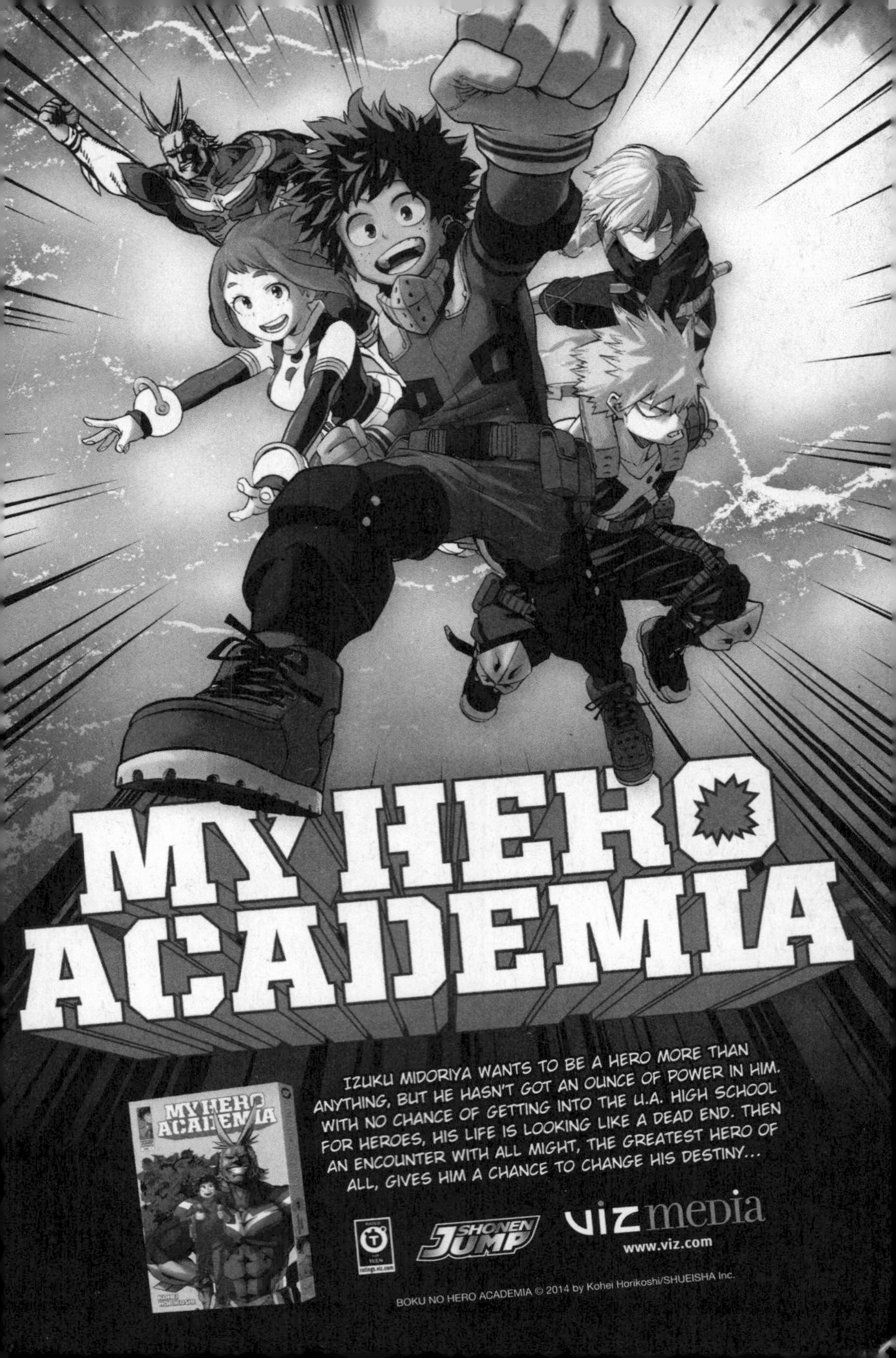
MY HERO ACADEMIA
IZUKU MIDORIYA WANTS TO BE A HERO MORE THAN ANYTHING, BUT HE HASN'T GOT AN OUNCE OF POWER IN HIM. WITH NO CHANCE OF GETTING INTO THE U.A. HIGH SCHOOL FOR HEROES, HIS LIFE IS LOOKING LIKE A DEAD END. THEN AN ENCOUNTER WITH ALL MIGHT, THE GREATEST HERO OF ALL, GIVES HIM A CHANCE TO CHANGE HIS DESTINY...
MY HERO ACADEMIA
KOHEI HORIKOSHI
TEEN
ratings.viz.com
SHONEN JUMP
viz media
www.viz.com
BOKU NO HERO ACADEMIA © 2014 by Kohei Horikoshi/SHUEISHA Inc.

Black ✳ Clover

STORY & ART BY YŪKI TABATA

Asta is a young boy who dreams of becoming the greatest mage in the kingdom. Only one problem—he can't use any magic! Luckily for Asta, he receives the incredibly rare five-leaf clover grimoire that gives him the power of anti-magic. Can someone who can't use magic really become the Wizard King? One thing's for sure—Asta will never give up!

You're Reading the Wrong Way!

KUROKO'S BASKETBALL reads from right to left, starting in the upper-right corner. Japanese is read from right to left, meaning that action, sound effects and word-balloon order are completely reversed from English order.

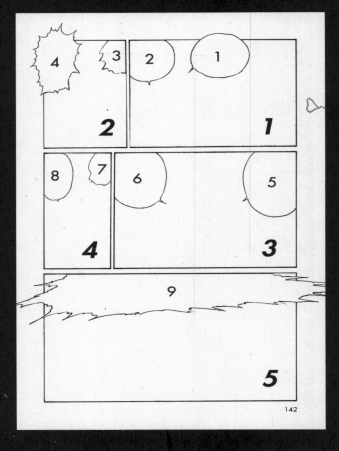

FLIP IT OVER TO GET STARTED!